Promoting Community Change

Making It Happen in the Real World

SECOND EDITION

Promoting Community Change

Making It Happen in the Real World

SECOND EDITION

Mark S. Homan

Brooks/Cole Publishing Company

I**T**P® An International Thomson Publishing Company

Pacific Grove • Albany • Belmont • Bonn • Boston • Cincinnati • Detroit • Johannesburg • London • Madrid
Melbourne • Mexico City • New York • Paris • Singapore • Tokyo • Toronto • Washington

Sponsoring Editor: *Lisa I. Gebo*
Marketing Team: *Steve Catalano, Aaron Eden, Jean Thompson*
Editorial Assistant: *Susan Wilson*
Production Editor: *Nancy L. Shammas*
Manuscript Editor: *Kay Mikel*
Permissions Editor: *May Clark*
Senior Design Editor: *E. Kelly Shoemaker*

Interior Illustration: *Graphic World Illustration Services*
Interior and Cover Design: *F. tani Hasegawa*
Cover Photo: *Adobe Image Library*
Art Editor: *Jennifer Mackres*
Indexer: *John Brotzman*
Typesetting: *Graphic World, Inc.*
Printing and Binding: *Webcom*

For more information, contact:

BROOKS/COLE PUBLISHING COMPANY
511 Forest Lodge Road
Pacific Grove, CA 93950
USA

International Thomson Publishing Europe
Berkshire House 168-173
High Holborn
London WC1V 7AA
England

Thomas Nelson Australia
102 Dodds Street
South Melbourne, 3205
Victoria, Australia

Nelson Canada
1120 Birchmount Road
Scarborough, Ontario
Canada M1K 5G4

International Thomson Editores
Seneca 53
Col. Polanco
11560 México, D. F., México

International Thomson Publishing GmbH
Königswinterer Strasse 418
53227 Bonn
Germany

International Thomson Publishing Asia
60 Albert Street
#15-01 Albert Complex
Singapore 189969

International Thomson Publishing Japan
Hirakawacho Kyowa Building, 3F
2-2-1 Hirakawacho
Chiyoda-ku, Tokyo 102
Japan

Printed in Canada

10   9   8   7   6   5   4   3   2   1

Library of Congress Cataloging-in-Publication Data

Homan, Mark S., [date]
   Promoting community change : making it happen in the real world /
Mark S. Homan. — 2nd ed.
      p.   cm.
   Includes bibliographical references and index.
   ISBN   0-534-35682-6
   1. Community development—United States.   2. Community
organization—United States.   I. Title.
HN90.C6H66   1998
307.1′4—dc21   98-24344
                                                                        CIP

To Stephanie, Jeff, and Kurt

who continue to strengthen our first community.

———————

About the Author

Mark S. Homan has been a full-time faculty member in the Social Services Department of Pima Community College since 1978; he has been the chairman of the department for the past several years. In addition to his duties at Pima, Mark has served as an adjunct faculty member in the Department of Sociology and Social Work at Northern Arizona University and in the Graduate School of Social Work at Arizona State University. He received his M.S.W. from Arizona State University in 1975 and is a certified independent social worker in the state of Arizona.

A strong advocate of community empowerment, Mark continues to use his very active involvement in the community to contribute to its improvement and to enhance his own learning. For 25 years he has worked with diverse populations in urban, rural, and reservation communities on a broad range of issues, including neighborhood stabilization and empowerment, hunger, reproductive rights, children with special health needs, family planning, capital punishment, public schools and community development, political campaign organizing, foster care, and adoption. In addition to his roles as organizer, lobbyist, consultant, and teacher, Mark has developed and directed several human services programs. He has also been a founding member of many community organizations and agencies and has served on numerous community boards and councils.

Mark is the author of *Rules of the Game: Lessons from the Field of Community Change,* a concise handbook that offers practical wisdom and 135 guidelines that demystify the community change process. He has conducted many workshops and delivered numerous presentations dealing with various aspects of community building and community power. He is frequently asked by public and private organizations to assist them in increasing effectiveness.

Mark serves on the editorial board of the journal *Human Service Education.* He is the recipient of the President's Award from the National Organization for Human Service Education,

At this stage in his career Mark has finally come to recognize that he will not be playing shortstop for the San Francisco Giants.

Contents

Preface

They had been listening intently for over two hours, occasionally asking questions, devotedly taking notes. No one had even brought up the subject of taking a break. All professionals in the fields of health and human services, they were excited to be getting some understanding of how they could work more effectively to strengthen the communities in which they were working. How do we involve parents? How do we keep people motivated? How do we do advocacy? How can we work with the legislature? So many different concerns, but the same general theme: How do we deal more effectively with the conditions that affect the people we serve?

I was first impressed with the fact that these people really wanted to learn this. I was pleased, and maybe even a little flattered. It can be a little heady when people seem to value the things you have to say. Then I was struck with the realization that they had never heard this before. I had to ask why. How, in all their education, did this information get missed? Doubtless they had had many sessions on developing interviewing skills. Why had they apparently had few, if any, on developing communities? How could they know so much about techniques for dealing with individuals and so little about techniques for improving the communities in which these individuals live?

The answers are probably many. Perhaps the profession rewards work to fix individual situations but not situations that affect a host of individuals. Perhaps our professional culture is informed by a larger culture that prefers to keep people in need unorganized and dependent, their combined strengths unrecognized and underutilized. Perhaps as workers we see more clearly the individual faces of anguish and want so much to do what we can to bring relief quickly. No doubt some combination of these and several other factors explains why many professionals who work with people have not been expected to know much about communities before they graduate. The skills related to community change may have been taken for granted, as if it were sufficient that they be learned on the fly—if they needed to be learned at all.

This is changing. There is renewed recognition of the role strengthened communities can play in preventing problems and producing solutions to problems that individuals and families experience. We see that healthy communities nurture the health of their members. In the professional fields of social work, human services, and health care, we are taking steps to provide students with intentional training in how to organize people to deal constructively and powerfully with the conditions they face. Equally important, students are expecting to learn, and, in some cases, they are urging us forward. I am particularly pleased to bring this new edition into this developing conversation.

In preparing the new edition I have benefited from extensive feedback from reviewers and readers alike. My own experience in using the book, both in the classroom and in the field, has given me further direction. I have made a number of significant changes to strengthen the text. A new chapter has been added to provide a unifying set of principles, offering a framework for understanding the specific chapter topics. These fundamental concepts can guide your decisions and actions as you go about the work of community change. This new chapter establishes a solid foundation for understanding the underlying themes of community change.

Another new chapter has been included in this edition to help you recognize and use advances in information technology. Community change agents have a new set of powerful tools to gain a better grasp of issues and to communicate more effectively with members, colleagues, and the broader public. Moreover, emerging technology allows you to manage the work of the change effort in a more efficient and timely manner. Ways to use information technologies to boost your efforts have been included in several other chapters as well.

Numerous other refinements have been incorporated into this new edition. Expanded attention has been given to the value of cultural awareness, statistics have been updated and additional data introduced, new fund-raising information has been provided, and the importance of recognizing and utilizing community assets has been more clearly emphasized. In addition, new techniques for promoting effectiveness have been introduced.

I have retained the features readers and reviewers have found useful in the original version. I have drawn extensively from my experiences, and I have benefited from the work and writing of other change agents and scholars. While writing this book, I frequently asked myself: "What do I wish I had known when I was starting out?" The answer to this question has guided my selection of topics and the depth of my descriptions.

Certainly, a number of students will work at the community level. The information in the following pages provides these students with a strong foundation for understanding the elements of community change and offers practical approaches for taking action. However, many other students envision primary professional roles that lead them to work more at the individual and family level. A book on community change needs to speak directly to these students as well. They too will be faced with conditions that require organized action. Although the nature of their involvement with promoting community change may be different, they need an understanding of change principles and techniques that can apply to conditions they commonly face. Thus, the material is oriented to the real-world experiences these workers encounter.

Promoting community change is not something students should only study and discuss in theory. It is something they should learn how to do. The topics covered here and the way they are presented are designed with this in mind. Part 1 looks at the need for community change and considers how community change activities relate to the change agent's professional and personal life. The new chapter addressing fundamental principles provides a framework for understanding the nature of this work. Part 2 gives clear, practical direction on how to go about the business of promoting change. Each of these chapters concentrates on a specific issue with which a successful change agent needs to be familiar. Part 3 offers more detailed insights into three common arenas of change. These chapters help the reader understand typical settings where change can occur. Building on principles and techniques described in earlier chapters, the reader is introduced to particular knowledge and skills that apply to these circumstances.

I approach the reader as a potential change agent and a partner in discovery. Several features of the book support this approach. I speak directly to the reader in a down-to-earth, jargon-free language, using examples and anecdotes to aid understanding. The opening story for each chapter connects the content to the real world. From time to time I ask readers to "Take a Moment to Discover." In these sections I invite the reader to consider how the material relates to his or her personal experiences, or I suggest some simple activity that can help the reader solidify understanding of the topic. "Change Agent Tips" offer specific tricks of the trade to help the reader deal with typical situations or problems. "Chapter Highlights" orient the reader to key theoretical principles and other important points contained in the chapter. Cartoons are used to lighten the discussion and illustrate concepts. Fundamental ideas are clarified or defined in brief "Capturing Concepts" sections.

Community change is an interesting, exciting and, at times, humorous activity. I hope that you get a flavor of this in my description of the subject.

This book is written for all those students and professionals who truly want to make a difference. I hope you find inspiration, direction, and confidence in the following pages. You will certainly find challenges in the real world. With your sense of purpose and the knowledge you gain from this book, you will be better prepared to face those challenges.

Acknowledgments

Much like a community change effort, a project of this sort cannot be completed by one individual acting alone. It requires the successful collaboration of many partners and the application of a wide range of knowledge and talents. Dr. Ann Nichols of Arizona State University has continued to be a source of inspiration and thoughtful critique. I will always value the guidance of my early mentor, Jack Cotter. The imagination and humor of cartoonist David Fitzsimmons enlivened our work sessions that even managed to produce a few cartoons. Barry Corey provided valuable direction with his review of material relating to the law. Robert Johnson's extensive knowledge of media relations strengthened my understanding of that subject. Jan Lesher's expertise in the legislative process contributed important refinements of the material related to lobbying. I am grateful to Mary Huerstel for pointing me in the right direction as I wandered through the labyrinth of the tax code. Mort Smith provided valuable answers to numerous questions about the use of computers. Jean Lewis, Tucson-Pima Public Library reference librarian, helped me to discover the treasures of the Foundation Center Collection and a host of other resources related to fundraising. Kaye Godbey, of Pro-Neighborhoods, offered numerous insights on neighborhood development. The ongoing support of my colleagues at Pima Community College, especially Richard Fridena, Tommie Miller, Alvin Lewis, Luba Chliwniak, Rosaisela Valenzuela, Diana Montano, Beth Doyle, Sheila Hughes, and Mike Curry has proved especially helpful.

Two people who offered me a tremendous amount of their time, patience, and professional skills deserve particular attention. Jo Namsick, Pima Community College reference librarian, worked miracles in helping me secure needed resource materials in a timely way. Mark Coppola, Director of the Academic Computing Center at Pima Community College, helped broaden my understanding of information technology and markedly increase my skills. Both of these individuals have made themselves readily available to answer questions and offer friendly guidance. I recognize that the excellent assistance I have received is nothing out of their routine way contributing to our College community.

I also received assistance from national organizations, particularly the Independent Sector and the National Society of Fund Raising Executives.

I want to give special recognition to the reviewers whose insightful comments led to significant improvements in this edition: Karen

Bojar, Community College of Philadelphia; William Buffum, University of Houston; Mary Davidson, Columbia Greene Community College; Leona Phillips, Springfield College; Peggy Quinn, University of Texas, Arlington; Terry Tirrito, University of South Carolina; and Mary E. Zwaanstra, Calvin College.

Many members of the Brooks/Cole team had a hand in strengthening this text. I am sure there are some unknown to me. I do want to particularly thank Lisa Gebo, Nancy Shammas, and Susan Wilson. I want to convey my fondness and utmost respect for Kay Mikel, copy editor extraordinaire.

I find myself unable to appropriately thank the many students who have taught me so much over the years. Their dedication, intelligence, and challenges continue to be an inspiration to me.

Finally, whatever I have accomplished here could not have occurred without the encouragement, tolerance and love of my family. May you know that you are my treasure. I continue to realize what an important fact that is.

Mark S. Homan

PART I

Responding to the Need for Community Change

Norman Karpenfussen didn't know how much longer he could put up with this insubordination. He could remember, word for word, the warnings issued to staff in his last two memos. If anyone were to question his memory, he could pull the memos from the file and show them. Every memo, in fact everything that issued forth from his office, was copied and placed in a file. Norman liked everything in its place. Norman liked order and orders. The sounds coming from the agency conference room (right next door to his office) flaunted these very notions, and Norman could feel the anger rising up in him.

He allowed himself a shrewd little smile as he recalled the words of his last memo: "No member of the Health Clinic staff, including volunteers, is authorized to speak to private citizens regarding the alleged matter of contamination of groundwater in the vicinity. Such action is not under the purview [he particularly liked that word] of this agency and is an unwarranted exacerbation [he liked that one too] of an increasingly volatile situation. Any staff member ignoring this admonition will be dealt with in accordance with the full measure of the administrator's authority [he *loved* that one]."

His smile quickly faded as the scraping of chairs in the adjoining room brought him once again to the realization that preparations for a community meeting were under way—a meeting organized by the clinic's staff. How could this have happened? The staff used to be so docile, so afraid of his authority, of him, that they almost apologized to suggest any new direction for the agency. He knew that the people in the surrounding community were poor, uneducated immigrants, if, indeed, they were legal at all, and they needed to be treated like children lest their fears get the better of them. His staff seemed to think so too. Now this! His staff, stirring up trouble, organizing the community to protest the city's supposed cover-up of groundwater contamination, raising fears of dangers to community health. This was not their job. Didn't they know that? The Neighborhood Health Clinic's purpose was to treat sick people, refer people to other programs in the community, and maybe do a little counseling. They were certainly not supposed to be agitators. Norman realized he would have to go next door and put a stop to all this nonsense.

As he opened the door, he was greeted by Grace Marquez,

the director of volunteers, who seemed to be running the show. "Welcome, Mr. Karpenfussen," she said with a smile. "Ladies and gentlemen," she continued, "this is Mr. Karpenfussen, our Executive Director, who has come to join us. He will explain the clinic's role in helping you get your groundwater cleaned up." And then Mrs. Gaxiola, a longtime Clinic volunteer, chimed in . . . "Señoras y señores, bienvenidos a Señor Karpenfussen . . . "

Now what am I going to do? Norman wondered.

Part 1 introduces you to the idea of promoting community change—the idea that you do not have to contribute to the presence of problems by inattention and inaction. You are encouraged to consider the concepts central to an understanding of community change. I believe you should look at, not look away from, problems that go beyond the individual. You must be willing to confront some of those problems with the knowledge and skills at your disposal. You cannot take sole responsibility for the problems you see, nor can you tackle them all. You do, however, need to make a conscious decision to help change policies and improve conditions whose limitations contribute to problems people in your community experience. It is important that you acknowledge this as a legitimate, if not fundamental, part of your role as a social worker or human services professional.

As in any significant aspect of your life, being a community change agent requires a sense of conviction and balance. This is not to be confused with being devoid of passion. Far from it. Your strong feelings that the rights of the people you serve be acknowledged and fully granted provide a necessary fuel to your involvement. A spirit of principle should infuse your actions, but your passion should not substitute for purpose.

Four chapters make up Part 1. In Chapter 1, Understanding the Challenge to Change, I provide an overview of the enterprise of community change. You will glimpse the range of community problems you may confront as a professional working in the human services field. Further, I explore some of the fundamental issues involved in working to promote change, including the critical importance of recognizing the diversity of cultures. This discussion will help you see the community itself, not just its individual members, as a client, and I will describe a number of ways your work can help improve your community. Finally, in this chapter I recognize the value of idealism as a source of strength and clarity.

In Chapter 2, A Framework for Action, I present the basic premise for promoting community change, along with the theoretical principles that provide a structure for understanding how you can promote action to change conditions that affect people. I examine the elements that contribute to a healthy community and the circumstances that must be present for change to occur. Several models of community change are described, which will acquaint you with a variety of different approaches. I will introduce the factors necessary for you to achieve success, including the orientation toward this work that will strengthen and guide your efforts. As an agent of community change your ability to recognize and develop the assets available in the community and your belief that the members of the community are the most important contributors to actions and decisions will influence everything you do.

In Chapter 3, Relating Community Change to Professional Practice, I describe the role community change plays in the provision of service. Perhaps you aren't sure how community change fits with your picture of what people in the human services professions do. This is a common and legitimate reservation. Many workers aren't striving very visibly for community change, so it is hard to recognize its function. To help explore this issue, I examine the basic purposes of social welfare, surveying traditional approaches used by human services professionals and relating community change activities to professional values. I question professional tolerance for conditions that not only harm clients but restrict the extent and quality of professional services themselves. The material in the chapter encourages you to recognize and confront these conditions, but I caution you to exercise some selection in the causes you commit yourself to. Your professional preparation gives you the theoretical framework and practical skills you can put to use in the context of community change. You start off well equipped for this kind of work.

In Chapter 4, Putting Yourself in the Picture, I focus on you as a change agent. Much

of the writing in the field of community change talks about community change agents, almost as if we were talking about a group of people it would be nice to know about . . . but not become. I take a different approach, speaking directly to you as an individual who will be involved in the business of promoting community change. Everyday matters with which you must contend as a worker engaged in community change are examined. Questions such as How do you get your boss to go along with your change efforts? How do you fit activism in with other aspects of your job? and How do you avoid becoming burned out? are explored. Finally, I provide some simple down-to-earth tips on increasing your effectiveness.

Working to promote community change is an exciting endeavor that will energize you and make your decision to become a professional in the field of human services more meaningful. Many of the changes you make may seem small or relatively minor, but they represent a new direction that over time will account for meaningful improvement of a situation. Some of your efforts may start small, but you will see them grow to secure significant changes. Perhaps you will even initiate actions that substantially alter the balance of power in your community, producing significant, permanent change. All these opportunities are open to you as a human services worker. All of them result in a situation that is better for your having acted. All give you the chance to help eliminate problems rather than contribute to their maintenance.

I invite you to consider these opportunities more fully in the following pages.

CHAPTER 1

Understanding the Challenge to Change

Chapter Highlights	
✥ Acknowledge systemic problems	✥ Empowerment
✥ All human service professionals are confronted by the challenge to promote change	✥ Resistance to change
	✥ Superficial versus fundamental change
✥ Recognize human concern and helpful action	✥ Cultural awareness and respect
✥ You can have an impact regardless of your professional role	✥ The community as client
	✥ Community change opportunities
✥ You cannot and should not do everything by yourself	✥ Value idealism
✥ Understand the terms *community, community problems,* and *community* (system) *change* or *improvement*	

Melanie Woodard has worked at San Ignacio Family Services Agency for the past 3 years. An important part of her job involves work with adolescents and young families. Most of her clients feel the weight of poverty as an added burden to their struggles. She has begun to notice that quite a number of the children are in poor health, particularly the babies born to teenage moms. Sure, babies are tiny at birth, but too many of these babies are too tiny. Many of them do not leave the hospital for a long time after they are born. Some never leave.

Between appointments Melanie thinks about these things. She wonders why this is happening. What are the problems? What should she be doing about them? What can she do?

Down the hall Ben Redondo hangs up the phone. More bad news. Ben, a "veteran" of 4 years at San Ignacio, fancies himself somewhat the agency Court Jester. He likes to joke around and have fun, helping to keep the atmosphere around the place from getting too dull or deadly serious. He could use a good joke now. It seems that the county budget woes may result in even fur-

ther reduction in their support for social services, and this follows the news that the state has received far fewer federal health care dollars than it was expecting. How will San Ignacio pick up the slack? Is it even their responsibility? Can these cutbacks be prevented?

"Maybe," Ben thinks, "I should talk with Melanie about this. We've got to be able to do more than just sit back and wait."

The phone rings in Melanie's office. Her next appointment has arrived. At the same time Ben is answering his phone. It's someone from the State Health Department.

What Is Going On Out There?

Some time back Saul Alinsky made these observations on social workers:

> They come to the people of the slums not to help them rebel and fight their way out of the muck . . . most social work does not even reach the submerged masses. Social work is largely a middle class activity and guided by a middle class psychology. In the rare instances where it reaches the slum dwellers it seeks to get them adjusted to their environment so they will live in hell and like it. A higher form of social treason would be difficult to conceive. (as cited in Meyer, 1945)

Strong words aren't they? How do they apply to the way you will provide human services? Will you address only the singular problems of individuals, or will you stand back from time to time and bring into focus the larger picture these individual images combine to form? Will you look beyond the immediate situation to understand the fundamental barriers your clients face? Will you shake your head and wring your hands, or will you do something about it? What kind of a human services worker do you intend to be?

As Melanie and Ben are coming to realize, a variety of forces outside the office contribute to the problems people bring to their office. Paying attention to those outside forces may improve the lives of the people we see every day in our agencies more than the individual service we offer there. Maybe some of these people wouldn't have to come to us at all if we addressed these outside forces directly.

What You Will See If You Look

A report by the Center for Budget and Policy Priorities concludes that the poorest one fifth in our nation receive 4% of the nation's income per year, whereas the richest one fifth garner a whopping 49%. This income gap has continued to widen since 1990. From 1977 to 1994 the very poor lost almost 16% of their income, whereas the very rich gained 25% (Shapiro & Greenstein, 1997). Is this a condition you find acceptable?

The Children's Defense Fund (1997) reports that "*every day* in America" 3 children die from abuse or neglect; 87 infants die; 1,788 children are born without health insurance; 2,556 children are born into poverty; 3,356 children drop out of high school; 5,702 children are arrested; 8,523 children are reported abused or neglected; 100,000 children are homeless. These are our children. The portrait of our nation's future is being painted by these numbers *every day*. Is this a condition you find acceptable?

The *Washington Post* reported that the United States Department of Agriculture altered a study to downplay the beneficial effects of a federal food program for low-income pregnant women. This, even though it is clearly understood that women who do not eat well during pregnancy have 30 to 40% more low birth weight infants, which leads to permanent physical and mental impairment (Hollyday, 1990). Is this a condition you find acceptable?

That same Department of Agriculture tells us that Americans *waste* 27% of their food—365 pounds for every child, woman, and man per year. This is much more than was wasted 20 years ago. If only 5% of that 96 billion pounds of edible food were saved, it could feed 4 million people a day for a year. Still, almost 12% of households below the poverty line—a little more than 4 million people—do not have enough to eat (Castaneda, 1997). Is this condition acceptable?

Maybe the state will authorize only a few days of treatment for a young client of yours who needs much more than that to cope with her years of being the victim of molestation. You might wonder how the administrators of the school district you work for go jetting from this conference to the next, yet deny the use of a school bus for the fifth-graders to go on an educational outing because of a "lack of funding for travel." How frustrated will you be when you realize that the young man sitting across from you, disheveled and insolent, has had four different doctors in the last year "directing" his treatment, and that his case is not a whole lot different from others you have seen this week? These are actual situations workers face. Are these conditions you find acceptable?

Other problems are less sweeping or poignant; you will see some evidence of them almost daily as you work in human services. Taken together, they imply that your clients have little dignity. Clients have to wait too long for an appointment, wait too long to be seen on the day of their appointment, and have too little time with you or other professionals when they are finally seen. Forms clients must fill out are lengthy and confusing. Some agency staff are insensitive, unhelpful, or downright rude. Are these conditions you find acceptable?

Will you grow to accept a system that employs denial and defensiveness as primary responses? Will you care if workers and agencies are isolated from the day-to-day lives of their clients? Will you too ignore the needs of chronically underserved or unreached populations? Will you tolerate mediocrity as the standard of your profession and keep silent about a "service" system that lives in fear of being found out?

Many of us don't like to be confronted with these questions. We get fidgety and hope they will just go away . . . but they don't. Can't somebody *else* just do something?

These challenges are yours. These are situations you will face. "Oh great," you may be thinking, "here I am planning to help make the lives of individuals or families happier and more fulfilling, and now I'm expected to save the whole world."

Relax. Unless your presence here on earth is some fantastic historical event, you are not going to save the world (though some of you may well have a pretty significant impact on it). Most of you are not going to work for community change as your primary professional role. Most of you will be case managers, therapists, or generalist human services practitioners. But all of you will be confronted from time to time with the challenge to promote change. All of you will face barriers to your practice. All of you will have your professional ethics tested—will you respond or look away?

Beyond a Consideration of Problems

An honest reflection on the many national, community, and personal problems that exist can be intimidating, even discouraging. You may look at our provision of human services in the face of so many needs and conclude that people just don't care about each other. Plain and simple, we—including you—just don't care. That could be, but, frankly, I don't think so. Take another look.

People are burdened by their fears; held back by their prejudices; confused by their myths. This is undeniable. These factors exist, and they play a part in shaping the availability of services. But just as these limitations are facts of life, so too is the genuine concern we feel for those in distress. People are moved by suffering; emboldened in the face of injustice; and strengthened by their desire to contribute. People are touched by the recognition of their common humanity.

If you believe people have an interest in and the capacity for good, you will act to capitalize on it. If you don't, you will quickly be burned out in your cynicism. Surely, your belief in good will be tested, sometimes to the point where you fail to see its signs right around you, but you will pass these tests. You will find strength and energy when you convert the power of caring and common decency into an active force to counter those influences that flaw the system in which you work as a professional.

You care enough to think about your own involvement in human services. Don't you think it highly unlikely that you are the only one who feels this way?

Can You Really Do Anything About All Those Problems?

Perhaps a better question is: Can you do anything about *any* of the problems you are likely to encounter? You will have to leave many problems for other people, but you can tackle a

CAPTURING CONCEPTS

Community, Community Problems, and Community Change

Throughout this book you will be encouraged to consider concerns that affect a community of people and that can be addressed through the actions of a community of people working together. Therefore, it is a good idea for you to understand the concept of community. For our purposes, a **community** consists of a number of people who have something in common with one another that connects them in some way and that distinguishes them from others. This common connection could be a place where members live—a city or a neighborhood. It may be an activity, like a job, or perhaps something like ethnic identification could provide the connection. When I use the term *community,* I do not presuppose any particular size or number of people.

Some communities are more fully developed than others, recognizing certain common interests and working to provide mutual benefits. Members of other communities may barely even notice any common bond or characteristic among themselves. Further, communities are usually made up of sets of smaller communities. For example, cities have different neighborhoods, universities have different colleges and departments, softball leagues have different teams, and so on.

So, when I refer to "your" community, I mean any of those sets of people with whom you are connected in some way and whose interests or actions are important enough for you to be concerned about.

Communities have needs. These can include things such as the health of members, economic vitality, or effective policy making. When these needs are not

adequately met and discomfort to members results, **community problems** exist. If things stay the same, the problems and the discomfort will persist. The only way to get rid of the problems or to reduce them is for people to do things differently. This means **community change** must occur. Because communities function as systems, community change can be seen as system change. Community change is the process of producing modification or innovation in attitudes, policies, or practices in the community for the purpose of reducing (or eliminating) problems or providing for general improvement in the way needs are met. This process enhances the quality of life of individual members and the relationships among members. Community change means community improvement. The terms can be used interchangeably. In Chapter 6 you will learn more about communities.

---

fair share of your own quite well. Some thought, some planning, some common sense, some interest, a sense of purpose, and, yes, a touch of luck are the basic ingredients. You can do quite a lot with just these. Add some understanding of human behavior, some skill in determining tactics, and creativity and you have a potent combination that will definitely produce results.

All these components are available to any human services worker.

You can provide significant leadership in bringing people together to make needed changes, although you may not be the only leader or even the most "important" one. You can make a difference in your community, even if you have other primary professional responsibilities. But you must remember one fundamental principle: any problem that involves more than one person requires the involvement of more people than just you to resolve. In other words, don't try to do everything by yourself. In fact, I will often use the word *you,* but generally I mean not only you as an individual but also those with whom you are working as well.

Community problems, like personal problems, provide opportunities for growth or decline. Persistent patterns of denial or withdrawal harm the community or service agency just as they harm the individual. Halfhearted or poorly managed attempts at solving problems can prove discouraging. However, purposeful, organized efforts—even less than perfect ones—yield results that can improve present conditions and set the stage for effectively confronting future challenges. Recognizing and confronting problems creates the possibility that things will be different, most likely better. When problems are accepted as permanent, these opportunities for change are missed.

Some Basic Issues That Deserve Your Attention

As you begin to think about confronting some of the problems you will routinely encounter as a human services worker, consider the following themes: empowerment, resistance to working for change, and fundamental or superficial responses to hardship.

Empowerment

Working with others to promote change means more than you being a leader with a bunch of followers. To be successful, you will be working with others who are acting powerfully and in concert. People can come to feel more capable through the skills they acquire, but it is through their connections with others that they become more powerful. You will assist your partners in developing stronger beliefs in their own personal power and in the power of your organized

Take a Moment to Discover . . . .

Why don't people, especially human services professionals, take up the banner for change more readily and more often? The best answer is probably found by asking yourself: "When I see something that needs to be changed or fixed, why don't I act?" How do any of these responses fit your reactions?

- I'm afraid of what might happen.
- I really don't know enough about the situation.
- I'm afraid that people won't like me, especially my friends or colleagues or people I think are more important than I am.
- I don't think anyone really sees the situation in the same way that I do.
- I really don't have the right to make changes.
- I really don't deserve for things to be better.
- I really don't know what to do.
- I'm too busy . . . with more important matters.
- It's too big, and I'm only one person.
- It's not my job.

Choose any one of these responses and think about it for a minute. What ways could you devise to challenge the statement?

• •

group. When people feel a greater sense of worth and personal control, they recognize that they can participate with others to influence conditions that affect them. This process and its outcome are known as empowerment. (Bishop, 1994; DuBois & Krogsrud-Miley, 1996; Gutierrez, 1995; Mancoske & Hunzeker, 1994). You cannot make people feel and act more powerful, but you can increase the likelihood that they will act with power.

Empowerment of those participating in a change effort depends on five factors:

- Personal interest or investment in the project—a feeling of being an important part of things
- Belief in the possibility of a successful outcome
- Development and recognition of individual and group resources
- Opportunity to take action and to make meaningful contributions
- Recognition of common interests and common risk taking

By keeping four simple points in mind you can further the process of empowerment considerably. First, provide members with opportunities for making decisions and for performing tasks. Group leaders need to spread these opportunities around. Second, offer encouragement to one another. This should be done in a way that communicates a belief in each member's capabilities. Third, recognize members' contributions and their results, as well as the overall progress that is taking place. This will keep the focus on productivity and accomplishment. It will also build members' beliefs in their capabilities. Finally, act as a group whenever possible. This will give members an experience of united power and reinforce an awareness of common commitment and shared risk taking.

There are other specific techniques for helping members to discover their own power; some of these are discussed in Chapter 7. However, if you remember only these basic elements of empowerment and the strategies promoting it, you will find that you are not doing things all by yourself.

Resistance to Working for Change

A good insight into resistance is provided by Filley, House, and Kerr (1976), who describe the phenomenon of "sunk costs" to explain a source of opposition to change. Many people, or at least enough people in a position to make a difference, have made a significant investment in

either shaping the current situation or learning how to function within it. Change suggests that the time, energy, skill, or experience these people have invested is no longer relevant or needed. Change implies that these investments were either poorly spent or are no longer of value. Considered from this standpoint, the introduction of a new invention or a new procedure may threaten individuals' investments in their own experiences and may even jeopardize their careers. Further, people who have invested an extraordinary amount of time and effort to master the game as it is presently played may well be unreceptive to playing it differently.

Perhaps the most profound source of resistance to change is simply what we tell ourselves. People who hold onto problems frequently send themselves messages that rob them of their power by stating and confirming current limitations—both real and imagined—in a way that implies that constraints are forever fixed. People who act to improve problem conditions acknowledge current limitations but acknowledge current assets as well. They are willing to use assets to test limitations and to break them down.

If you take assertive action, you will receive some direct benefits. You will feel better about yourself and be more highly regarded by others who have taken part in the experience, including opponents.

Change can cause discomfort and provoke fear. Even little changes, like gaining or losing weight, can cause discomfort. Your clothes don't feel right, and people look at you differently. Major changes are often accompanied by more significant discomforts. Parents must let go of their accustomed control over their children as they grow; children chafe at parental direction that no longer seems reasonable. These are times of anxiety and anger. The mayor and the city council don't want to share their power with those who used to be so docile, so apathetic. Those who have always been favored in community decisions don't like others receiving attention. Those who want change don't even act until their discomfort with present conditions provokes them to act. Someone will feel uncomfortable in some way when change is under way. Attempts to prevent or quiet this discomfort are powerful sources of resistance.

Change means things aren't predictable anymore. This can be scary. Uncertainty produces tension. A child caught alone in a candy store when the lights suddenly go out knows there are goodies all around, but the darkness may hide monsters as well. Danger may lurk behind what we do not see or do not know.

There is nothing wrong with feeling some trepidation about promoting change. It is fairly natural. Here are some steps you can take to overcome your hesitancy.

- *Confront the source of your concerns.* If time is a concern, see how you can better organize the things you have to do. If uncertainty about the outcome or the success of the effort bothers you, take stock of your assets, including the things you know how to do, the support you currently have, and other factors working in your favor. Knowing that you can improve the odds in your favor may help you accept a lack of certainty as a condition of working for change.
- *Develop support.* Act in concert with others so you can share the work, receive encouragement, and benefit from group problem-solving efforts. Purposefully cultivate support and increase communication with others who have promoted change. This will go a long way toward building your confidence and overcoming resistance.
- *Remind yourself of why the change is important.* If you keep in touch with the feelings that provoked your interest in the first place, you will have a strong source of motivation. Consider what the consequences of inattention will be.
- *Take advantage of training opportunities.* Participate in workshops, classes, or in-service training programs to increase your knowledge and skills in program development or community change. This will strengthen your sense of personal capability.
- *Identify a simple starting point.* Feelings

of being overwhelmed can undermine your willingness to take action. Look for easy ways to get started.
- *Decide to act.* "Sort of" doing things will lead to mediocre results and discontent. Make a clear decision to act.

Weeds and Roots, Bandages and Balms

I remember mowing the lawn when I was a kid. (I remember mowing the lawn last week too, but that's a different story.) One section of the yard produced a fair number of weeds. As is the nature and duty of weeds, they grew faster than the grass. I was supposed to pull them, but pulling weeds was not how I envisioned spending a summer's day, not when there was baseball to be played. To save time, I just mowed the whole yard—grass and weeds and all. Heck, the weeds were green; who would know? It worked too, for a week.

I won't go into the details, but the subsequent conversation on the matter with my mother (Supervisor of Grounds) went something like this: "You didn't do an adequate job. Forget baseball today. I want *all* the weeds pulled out. Now!"

"Shucks, Mom, what's the big deal? Nobody can tell the difference anyway. . . . Well, OK" (the last sentence having been offered in response to a look that conveyed that further argument would not benefit my cause).

The yard did look better when I was done. Yes, the grass did eventually replace the weeds, which, by the way, needed more than one afternoon's attention. But looking around, it's pretty easy to see that I'm not the only one who tries to skip grabbing a problem by its roots.

Operation and Regeneration

Not every change requires a change in national priorities. Something as simple as involving clients in program planning, developing a food buying club, or replacing dollars for massive

Take a Moment to Discover. . . . .

Why do we put so much energy into developing shelters for the homeless instead of getting rid of homelessness? Why do we feel so good about food banks providing emergency food instead of taking steps to eliminate hunger and the widespread need for emergency food? Are these problems too big for a nation like ours to solve? Hardly, though we can con ourselves into thinking so.

There are probably a hundred reasons why we mow over the weeds rather than pull them out by the roots. Let's look at some of the reasons community problems remain despite the fact that we are well aware of them.

- We believe that we don't have the time to do the job right.
- The problems are hopelessly complex. Where do you start?
- It is too much work.
- It is better to smooth things over than to cause disruption.
- The people who would be disturbed by changing things are more important than the people who are hurting now.
- The people who are feeling the problem aren't worth the trouble.
- Significant intervention costs too much.
- Major surgery might kill the patient.
- We would rather cover up things we don't want to look at.
- We fear the possibility that things are out of control, or will be.
- It is just a bad habit.
- It is easier to shut up those who feel the problem than it is to challenge those in authority because those in need are less threatening and are appreciative of any help we can give them.
- We need to feel that we are at least doing something.
- When we are up to our behinds in alligators, we forget that our original intention was to drain the swamp.

Consider this list. Is this the way a nation or a community responds? How might this guide your actions as an agent of community change?

new road projects with dollars for bike paths may constitute a significant new direction. By tugging at the "weeds" that detract from the beauty of your community, you make room for new, more positive growth.

As you might guess, not all weeds are easy to pull. So, too, some of the problems you face will have long histories and deeply entrenched interests. Getting rid of them requires sustained and powerful action. If your work is not primarily in the area of community change, playing a prominent organizing or leadership role in these cases may not be possible. However, even in these cases you have ample opportunity to play a supporting role.

Finally, weeds never disappear altogether. Maybe signs of racial discrimination have disappeared from your school. Perhaps procedures that undermine client dignity have been removed from your agency. Even in areas that look pretty clear, weeds will crop up from time to time. Just keep an eye out to prevent them from taking over again.

Take a Moment to Discover . . . .

Imagine yourself walking into a room filled with people who are similar to one another but very different from you.

- What are you feeling?
- Can you identify the source of your feelings?
- What feelings would you like to have in this situation?
- How will you act on this intention?
- What do these people look like?
- What does this picture of whom you select as "different" tell you?

The Need for Cultural Awareness and Respect

"Nobody is showing up at the meetings," I said. "Oh, yes they are," came the response. "We just meet a little differently than you do. We all get together at Marta's house and talk. By the time we leave everyone has had a chance to say what they want." One lesson.

"We can't seem to get anyone interested in getting something going around here. What's the matter?" His smile told me that he had taken for granted that I knew some things that I didn't. "Well, for one thing, everybody has a family member who just maybe hasn't completed all the legal paperwork to be here. Maybe even the whole family. Staying a little less visible might strike them as a good idea." Another lesson.

"I have never had such a hard time trying to figure out where we should hold a first meeting," I said, probably with a little exasperation. "These things have to be done carefully," my guide reminded me. "It's a big reservation. Just where we meet for the first time matters. We can't look like we are making one leader or one family seem more important." Yet one more lesson.

The first step in working with any group of people is to assume that you have much to learn about them and they about you. Further, you need to learn about factors that influence your relationship. This is always true, but special attention and reflection is especially important in situations in which you are working with people whose culture and life experiences are different from your own.

To successfully work with anyone or any community, you must have some idea about how people see and relate to the world. You can only approach people within their frame of reference—their ability to recognize, pay attention to, and make sense of what is happening. Fundamental to this notion is the understanding that other people perceive the world in a different way than you do and that sometimes their perceptions are quite different. Respect those differences, particularly as they are shaped by people's culture. In doing so you show that you value that other person.

By increasing your ability to comprehend events and situations from the perspective of another, you improve your ability to communicate and your mutual expectations are more appropriately related to each other's attitudes and patterns of behavior. You increase the relevance of your actions and reduce the possibilities of unwanted surprises. Conversely, remaining culturally insensitive or ignorant increases the risk that you will act in a way that is irrelevant or even offensive. This is hardly a promising style. Awareness of and respect for cultural differences recognizes the legitimacy of another's experience and its significance to your common enterprise (Gutierrez, 1995; Lum, 1996).

A few training workshops won't be enough. We all know that, but we don't seem to put that knowledge into practice very well. Delivering culturally appropriate direct services is more rare than common (Fong & Gibbs, 1995). It requires an honest commitment. The challenge to appreciate another's perspective, shaped by different experiences and cultural standards, has always been upon us. But today in the United States this challenge grows stronger.

The faces of this nation are changing. The Hispanic population (Mexicans, Puerto Ricans,

Cubans, and other Spanish-speaking peoples) is growing rapidly, constituting 9% of the total U.S. population in 1990. This is an increase of 53% over 1980 (Montiel & Gasca, 1995). By 2015 the Hispanic population will likely almost double, growing to about 40 million people (Turner, 1995). By 2010 the African American population, now about 12% of the U.S. population, is expected to increase by 10 million over 1980 figures (Marger, 1997; Turner, 1995). The Asian population more than doubled between 1980 and 1990, and the growth rate for Asian and Pacific Islanders was expected to be 48.2 per 1,000 between 1991 and 1995 (Lum, 1996, p. 7). This is almost seven times the growth rate of the White population (7.1 per 1,000), the slowest growing population group in the United States (Turner, 1995, p. 8; Lum, 1996, p. 6). In fact, the White population as a percentage of the total U.S. population dropped 3% between 1980 and 1990 and more than 8% between 1960 and 1990, with continued declines anticipated (Marger,

1997; Turner, 1995). These population shifts bring into sharp focus the need for people to learn more about one another and more about cultural diversity itself. This is particularly true for members of the currently dominant culture—who can less and less afford the privilege of ignorance.

Respect for cultural diversity requires that you confront the fact of racism. Rooted in ignorance and fear, racism pits different groups of people against each other by viewing those who are different as a threat that must be contained, if not defeated. Differences between groups are identified, seen as evidence of some sort of defect in the other group, and exaggerated. The other group then comes to be explained or even defined in terms of these exaggerated imperfections. These demeaning attitudes are directed at different ethnic groups as well as at different so-called racial groups.

The entire notion of race itself is ambiguous. Marger (1997) calls it "one of the most misunderstood, misused, and often dangerous concepts in the modern world" (p. 18). Racism has categorized people of different skin color, different religions, or different nationalities. Although the concept of race itself is of dubious scientific validity, the ideas of "different from" and "less than" can be very powerful.

Racism allows the fear and consequent dislike of others simply because they are members of different groups to have more potency than the belief in the potential for gain that could occur by working together. It breaks down the ability of members of one group to work effectively with members of another. This is further aggravated by the perception that there is a limited set of resources, rather than an expanding (or potentially expanding) set, over which groups must fight. One group's gain must therefore be seen as another's loss. Any attempt by one group to better its position must be done at the expense of the other. The group in the most advantaged position must protect the system that grants them their edge. These built-in advantages are so commonly accepted as normal by the privileged group that they don't even notice they are there. When those well-entrenched arrangements are challenged—when equal accommodations are sought by a less advantaged group or when one group seems to be thwarted in its efforts to improve its lot—conflict heightens the fears and divisions.

What is good or bad about a system in our society is measured against how it is seen as helping one group at the expense of another. That fear, recognized or not, acknowledged or not, colors almost all our perceptions. Competing groups hold one another responsible for what is going wrong (Marger, 1997; Shepard, 1991).

The expected way for members of diverse ethnic or racial groups to be successful is to deny their own culture in favor of adopting attributes of the dominant group. The dominant group, in many overt or subtle ways, demands allegiance to its own culture in exchange for social and economic benefits. By eroding the strength of diverse groups, the dominant group reduces their potential to threaten the status quo. Some members of diverse groups may try to resist this control by undermining or attacking the interests of the dominant group. Others, succumbing to hopelessness and despair, may exploit one another or simply refuse to participate at all. Still others may sacrifice their cultural identity to make economic gains, while harboring a deep-seated resentment for the exchange they have made. Actions such as these result in a loss for all groups (Devore & Schlesinger, 1996).

Even the informal racism rooted in our institutions, norms, and traditions divides people and leads to differences in opportunity. These more subtle forms of racism perpetuate patterns of discrimination and their consequences. Many problems you will see as a worker are expressions of these fears and divisions. And as a worker your own relationship with the community you are trying to help may be colored by racism. Devaluing those who are different or the need to keep somebody different from getting ahead means that opportunities for mutual gain are squandered and a lot of people will be left behind. Further, efforts to help those suffering the effects from all this must be marginal, keeping the semblance of peace while preventing groups from stepping out of their place.

Racism has consequences for everyone involved in a community change effort. A group that has directly suffered from racism may need to confront not only the immediate issue at hand but the racist conditions that led to it and continue to support it. A group whose practices have limited another group's freedom and choice may need to examine whether or not their desired course of action in a particular circumstance perpetuates these practices. A multiethnic group may need to face the strain of a history of divisiveness.

Difficulties can arise when members of different cultural groups interact with one another. Some misunderstandings can be expected when groups have different cultural norms, rituals, and belief systems. However,

---

CAPTURING CONCEPTS

Ethnic Hierarchy in America Today

1. Top range: White Protestants of various national origins, for whom ethnicity has no real significance except to distinguish them from the remainder of the ethnic hierarchy.

2. Intermediate range: White Catholics of various national origins, Jews, and many Asians, for whom ethnicity continues to play a role in the distribution of society's rewards and continues to influence social life, but in both instances, decreasingly so.

3. Bottom range: racial-ethnic groups—Blacks, Hispanics, American Indians, and some Asians—for whom ethnicity today has the greatest consequences and for whom it continues to shape the basic aspects of social life.

This hierarchy has remained amazingly resilient for a century and a half, and though distance among groups has been reduced, their rank order hasn't. Further, the gap between the bottom group and the other two is much greater than between the top two. (Marger, 1997, pp. 150–151)

---

when one group historically has politically, economically, and culturally subjugated another, limiting that group's opportunities and expressions, the undercurrents of tension and anxiety are profound. The burden becomes even heavier when members of the offending group are ignorant of this history or deny it altogether.

Certainly a possibility of such tension exists when White workers attempt to organize people of color or when groups that are predominately White attempt to collaborate with other people of color. This tension has affected, for example, the collaboration of White feminists and feminists of color. Women of color have harbored and have expressed deep dissatisfaction with an agenda focused too exclusively on gender, not giving sufficient attention to matters of White racism in which White women have participated (Gutierrez & Lewis, 1995; Lum, 1996). The failure of White feminists to acknowledge the role that racism plays in the lives of women of color has been a hindrance to more powerful action.

Marger (1997) reminds us that "dominance of one group over another is an enduring fact of human life" (p. 547). In the United States this takes the form of Anglo conformity. Despite pluralistic rhetoric, "the preeminence of Anglo cultural values has consistently overlain public policies in education, language, law, welfare, even religion. From the beginning, the expectation held sway that entering groups—immigrant, conquered, or enslaved—would conform to this core culture" (p. 148).

As an agent of community change you cannot ignore the fact that these conditions affect you, the people with whom you work, and your relationships. Is it hopeless? Should we live only in fear and guilt? No, of course not. We should live in acknowledgment of this reality and in reflection on what our actions do to maintain or challenge disabling social conditions like racism. We should be challenged, not dispirited. Though these conditions are an aspect of our relationship, other aspects have meaning as well; among these is a belief in our abilities to contend with our impediments. People of goodwill can build on their common interests and employ their unique strengths to break down barriers. We can learn.

The term *culture* gets tossed around pretty freely and has been defined broadly. Rivera and

Erlich (1995) describe culture as "a collection of behaviors and beliefs that constitute 'standards' for deciding what is, standards for deciding what can be, standards for deciding how one feels about it, standards for deciding what to do about it, and standards for deciding how to go about doing it" (p. 8). Barker (1995) defines culture as "the customs, habits, skills, technology, arts, science, and religious and political behavior of a group of people in a specific time period" (p. 87). Notions of culture are not limited to identified ethnic groups. Many groups have developed standards or customs for interpreting the world and acting in it (Longres, 1995). Members of fraternities and sororities have their own culture. Employees of large public welfare agencies experience the culture of their organizations. Police officers have a special language and established codes of behavior that reflect their perception of their uniqueness.

Understanding differences between groups is central to an appreciation of human diversity. Johnson (1998) points out that "though there are common human needs, people fulfill those needs in different ways" (p. 8). In fact, behavior cannot be understood apart from the cultural context in which it occurs. For example, going out in public with one side of your face painted blue and the other side painted white, further adorned by pictures of the devil, could raise a few eyebrows. If you compound that by yelling and wildly waving your arms, you could get arrested—unless you happen to be in Cameron Indoor Stadium, the University of Duke's basketball arena, cheering for the Duke Blue Devils. In this situation, your behavior is not only perfectly understandable, it is encouraged. As Johnson explains, affirming human diversity means understanding that "normal" behavior is situational. Behavior is "functional or dysfunctional relative to the social situation in which a person is operating. What may be functional in one situation may be dysfunctional in another" (p. 8).

Although it is important to appreciate differences, it is a mistake to regard all individuals solely in terms of the general traits of their culture. Shulman (1991) warns of the dangers of "teaching culturally specific techniques that are then implemented without regard to within-group heterogeneity" (p. 227). This results in new stereotypes that reduce members of the group to simple categories of behavior and response. Cormier and Hackney (1993) caution that knowing something about a culture does not mean that you know its individual members. Shulman (1991) also emphasizes a crucial skill that involves "the use of cultural knowledge to prepare for and to understand clients' lives and helping encounters while avoiding the trap of using generalizations to substitute for the here and now" (p. 228). He further points out that not differentiating in the "application of culturally sensitive principles can itself be an inadvertent form of racism" (p. 228). Members of any group vary in the extent of their identification with specific cultural characteristics. Acknowledging the potential for differences allows you to avoid replacing one stereotype with another.

What should you know to work with culturally diverse client groups? A general understanding of the cultures involved is a necessary first step (Nelson-Jones, 1992). Important cultural factors include: values; ways of relating to other persons, the physical world, and the spiritual world; family structure and the nature of family relationships; history, including the meaning attached to change and development; communication patterns, including nonverbal aspects; community life and structure; and coping mechanisms (Johnson, 1998). It is also important to understand the experience of the minority group with the dominant culture (Corey & Corey, 1998; Gutierrez & Lewis, 1995; Johnson, 1998; Rivera & Erlich, 1995). For example, what is the history of this group? How much and what type of interaction has there been between the groups? What similarities and differences exist between the groups? How have group members reacted to efforts by the dominant group to control them? What impact have these experiences had on each group? By answering questions like these, you begin to develop an awareness of the sources of harmony and tension that are likely to affect the way members of different groups work together.

Rivera and Erlich (1995, pp. 13–18) list a number of important considerations when working with diverse communities of color:

- Become familiar with customs, traditions, social networks, and values
- Learn the language and subgroup slang
- Understand leadership styles and development
- Know who has power and recognize sources of mediating influences between ethnic communities and wider communities
- Review past organizing strategies and analyze their strengths and limitations
- Acquire skills in conscientization (developing a critical consciousness) and empowerment
- Acquire skills in assessing community psychology
- Be aware of your personal strengths and limitations

Rivera and Erlich wisely point out that these are a set of ideals, adding that "those few who have already attained the lofty heights described can probably also walk on water" (p. 13).

Of all the things to know, perhaps the most important is to know yourself. Question the biases you hold, your fears, assumptions, expectations, intentions, desire and capability to learn, and the limitations of your own experiences. An honest appraisal will increase your self-awareness and give you confidence in gaining a better awareness of others. You will never master it all, not because it is hopeless but because it is a lifelong process of learning. Accept the simple fact that you can never fully understand another's experience and perspective. You can, however, move to greater and greater levels of understanding.

If you don't know something you need to know, ask. An important aspect of working with any client is your ability to gather information to increase your understanding. This is true whether the client is an individual or a community. Here are a few more ideas that can increase your cultural competence:

- Find resource people, particularly from the community, who can help you understand the group with whom you will be working (Fong & Gibbs, 1995; Lum, 1996).
- Recognize that you are coming to the community not to do things *for* them but *with* them.
- Avoid romantically stereotyping any group. It's dishonest.
- Refuse to define any group solely in terms of its oppression. That is a demeaning and limiting view.
- Teach what you are learning. Do not support by your silence those words and behaviors that diminish members of other groups.
- Encourage other voices to speak and listen to them.
- Acknowledge that your life experiences influence your perceptions and that other people's life experiences shape their perceptions as well. Acknowledge that these can be very different.

I cannot provide the key factors for each different group with whom you might be working. You will have to find out these things for yourself. Do be skeptical about anyone who purports to tell you all about any group. There are over 500 Native American tribal groups; although there may be some common perspectives, there are some significant differences as well (Edwards & Edwards, 1995). Be wary of those who know what you should do when "working with Hispanics." Which Hispanics? Cubans? Salvadorans? Those living in the Southwest, or those living in New York? I think you get the point. Members of groups with a common identity share many cultural beliefs, but there are distinct and important differences

CULTURAL ETIQUETTE

Amoja Three Rivers has many tips for cultural etiquette. Here are just a few. What others would you add?

- All people are people. It is ethnocentric to use a generic term such as "people" to refer only to White people and then racially label everyone else. This creates and reinforces the assumption that Whites are the norm, the real people, and all others are aberrations.
- Within the cultures of many people, more value is placed on relationships, and on the maintenance of tradition and spirituality, than on development and acquisition of machinery.
- There is no up or down in outer space, therefore north as "up" and south as "down" are purely arbitrary designations. The familiar picture of Europe and North America being at the top of maps and globes then, is just a visual device to reinforce the idea that it is right and proper for White people to be on top,

to dominate the world. To reorient yourself, rotate maps and globes 180 degrees.
- All hair is "good" hair. Dreadlocks, locks, dreads, natty dreads, etc. is an ancient traditional way that African people sometimes wear their hair. It is not braided, it is "locked." Locking is a natural tendency of African hair to knit and bond to itself. It locks by itself; we don't have to do anything to make it lock. It is permanent; once locked, it cannot come undone. It gets washed as regularly as anyone else's hair. No, you may not touch it, don't ask.
- Slavery is not a condition unique to African people. In fact, the word *slave* comes from the Slav people of Eastern Europe. Because so many Slavs were enslaved by other people (including Africans), especially in the Middle Ages, their very name came to be synonymous with the condition. Virtually every

human group has been enslaved by some other human group at one time or another.
- Everyone speaks with an accent.
- Do not use a Jewish person or a person of color to hear your confession of past racist transgressions. Also don't assume that Jews and people of color necessarily want to hear about how prejudiced your Uncle Fred is.
- Words like "gestapo" and "Hitler" are only appropriate when used in reference to the Holocaust.
- Many non-Indians profess love and respect for our "nobleness." But almost worse than the insults is the insensitivity of those who care more about their fantasies of who they want Native Americans to be than they care about the real needs and wishes of living, breathing Native Americans.
- Racism is a disease that has killed more people than AIDS.

Source: Amoja Three Rivers (1991).

as well. Read, participate in community events, reflect on what does and does not work, talk to people, and, yes, do go to some of those workshops (Gutierrez & Lewis, 1995).

With all this emphasis on differences, do

not lose sight of the many similarities among people. By exaggerating differences or focusing on them to the exclusion of our similarities, we run the risk of emphasizing our separateness (Corey & Corey, 1998). This can make it very difficult for people of different cultures to acknowledge their ability to work together.

The Community as Client

When we hear the word *client,* most of us think of an individual who needs some assistance to solve a personal problem. But a community can be a client too (see Figure 1-1). Just like an individual or a family, a community has resources and limitations. Communities have established coping mechanisms to deal with problems. To promote change in a community, the community must believe in its own ability to change and must take responsibility for its actions or inactions.

Some problems are community problems. They directly or indirectly touch most if not every member of the community. Gang violence, AIDS, and inadequate health care will persist if we work on them only at the individual level. Community problems must also be addressed by the community that feels the problem. When you are able to see the community as a distinct

entity capable of taking action, you understand that you can treat the community as a client (Kettner, Daley, & Nichols, 1985).

Jim Jackson came into class Monday morning, late, and he is fuming. "Mr. Jackson," the professor comments, "it looks like your week is getting off to a bad start."

"Damn bookstore," Jim snaps.

Once again, the campus bookstore has unlocked its doors 10 minutes later than the posted 8:30 A.M. opening time. Even if they did open on time, many students almost certainly would be late because their classes begin at 8:40 A.M. Students often schedule classes back-to-back to dash off to jobs as soon as class is over. There just is not a lot of time to buy books once the semester starts. Class cancellations and other schedule changes over the first couple of weeks of the semester can also make for trying times for many students.

The professor and the rest of the class could offer a little group support by letting Jim blow off steam and by showing him that they understand it has been a frustrating morning for him. A couple of students might comment that

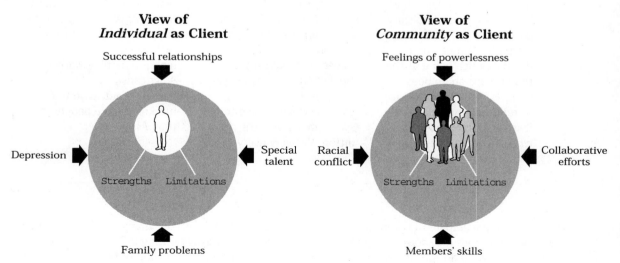

Figure 1-1
Conceptualizing the client

they too have experienced similar exasperation. Maybe group members will share books until Jim can get his own. It is also possible that someone can sit down with Jim to help him plan his schedule differently so he can get to the bookstore when it is open and still make it to class on time. All these approaches have some benefit, but the problem remains. They put a bandage on the situation, providing some attention to the discomfort and a little temporary relief while covering the real sore from view. The fact is that Jim is not the only person affected by the bookstore's insensitivity and poor planning. The entire class has been involved—some have had the same experience as Jim, others have had class disrupted by an angry latecomer. The bookstore's policies and practices affect the *student community,* not just Jim.

Once this is realized, the focus can shift from helping Jim to improving the community. It doesn't take long for the class to work out a strategy for involving other students in confronting the bookstore about its hours of operation, especially during the first month of the semester. By looking at the student community as the client in need of attention, the perception provides a strategy for change that does more than temporarily relieve one person's discomfort.

There are many examples of the community as client. Perhaps a major employer pulls out of town, throwing the whole community into crisis. Those who have lost their jobs are in a daze. So, too, are the shopkeepers whose businesses will suffer. So are the educators who see a major part of the tax base disappear. How will the community come together to deal with this disruption of so many lives? How will it attend to immediate needs as well as long-term ones? Or will this crisis further weaken an endangered community?

The suicide of a popular high school student shocks a small rural town. His parents and friends are distraught, and the entire student body is stunned. Is a community response to the tragedy possible?

Recognizing that people share common interests allows you to approach the community in a way that unifies individual concerns and capabilities. This is a much more powerful approach than separating each individual problem, one from the other. Certainly, individuals experience common problems in unique ways. Yet by acting on the commonness of experience rather than the uniqueness, you open the door to the possibility of shared action. This orientation allows for the combination of energy and resources to create fundamental community change.

Targets for Community Change

Where can you start? How can you begin to make an impact on your community? Your desire to improve conditions you and your clients face can take you into five basic arenas of action. In addition to being active in the community itself, you can have a considerable effect by making efforts to improve the service delivery system, directing attention to your own agency, working in the political field, or taking action through the courts.

Community Involvement

Of the many forms of community activities, five are fairly typical for change agents.

1. *Neighborhood empowerment* helps people within a particular geographic area develop their resources and lay claim to their right to control their own destinies. After the family, the neighborhood is the first building block of the community. Helping people in a neighborhood band together to determine their own living conditions is a primary strategy for improving the quality of a community.

2. *Community problem solving* is another approach for bringing people together. Using this method, you bring together various, even apparently competing interests within a community to creatively resolve a particular problem that affects them all. Crime, transportation, education, or environmental concerns could be the focus of such an effort. Though no permanent organization for redistributing community power is likely to be put in place, this approach is liable to stimulate a discovery of underlying community issues that may be the focus of future problem-solving efforts. Further, members of the community gain experience working with one another, which may have benefits beyond the resolution of the particular problem being tackled at the moment.

3. *Developing community support systems* is another way to promote community change efforts. This approach counters the painful aspect of living in a community of strangers. People who do not feel they are part of the community live in numbing isolation, struggling alone against problems that can overwhelm them. A community is a rich source of sustenance that can offer practical assistance and psychological support, but people need to find each other amid all the noise and confusion. Developing community support systems provides the means for community members to be in routine contact with one another in a climate of giving and receiving. Parents grappling with the challenges of caring for children with mental illnesses, teens struggling with the consequences of pregnancy, human services workers feeling separated from the ideals that originally brought them to their profession—all could gain strength from a system of mutual assistance and support.

4. *Community education* is a basic means for assisting the community by bringing matters to the community's attention and preparing it for knowledgeable action. Keeping the community from ignoring the needs of its citizens or from relying on myths to guide its direction is a steady challenge.

5. *Developing a broad-based community organization* that wields real power and works to redistribute community resources and access to community decision making is a meaningful approach for producing far-reaching change. The presence of such an organization establishes a new force within the community to recognize and take sustained action on issues that affect people other than the rich and powerful. These organizations activate many members of the community to press for a clearly articulated issue agenda. They often utilize the strength (including the financial support) of significant community institutions, such as religious congregations, as critical building blocks. In larger communities these organizations mobilize thousands of people. Unless you intend to specialize in the practice of community organization and development, you will probably not serve as the lead organizer of such a group. However, there will be many important leadership roles within this type of organization that you can fill.

Improving the Service Delivery System

At least five opportunities await you if you want to make improvements in the services clients receive:

- Change program regulations
- Improve program delivery
- Encourage cooperation between agencies
- Develop a new program
- Empower clients

Public program regulations, believe it or not, are not always developed with a keen eye for discerning the most effective manner of benefiting program participants. Sometimes those who establish the rules are looking out for other interests (Fabricant, 1985; Lipsky, 1984). You will face regulations that frustrate at least as much as they help. You can join the chorus of souls who would rather complain than act, or you can start your own choir giving voice to the need for change. Confronting regulations that hinder your work will make life easier for you and your clients. Many workers simply conclude that "those are the rules and we can't change them." They are wrong. Yes, regulations established by the federal government are more difficult to change than regulations generated by local authorities, but any and all are subject to scrutiny and modification. A well-organized group, perhaps working in alliance with other groups, can make great improvements in services simply by changing regulations, thereby helping a program work better.

Similarly, remaining attentive to opportunities for program improvement can lead you to helpful changes in the way services are provided. Experimenting with program design and service methods can result in significant benefits for both the sponsoring agency and the client. By capitalizing on a desire by both line staff and management to do a better job more easily, you can accomplish some significant gains. Old habits and other barriers to innovation exist, but forces for program improvement also exist in most situations.

Cooperation between human services agencies is not a common state of affairs in many communities. Not only do agencies not work with each other, they sometimes undermine one another's efforts. This can be baffling and discouraging to new human services workers, and it certainly can interfere with clients' opportunities to receive the best services. Helping agencies overcome their individualistic ways and their jealousies and fears of working together, even on a very limited project, can provide for the creative and efficient use of limited resources and set the stage for future collaborative efforts.

Developing a new human services program or agency to add to the community's arsenal of resources is an exciting and productive endeavor. This kind of activity sparks the creative interest of people who not only like the prospect of providing a needed service but who also enjoy the process of bringing an idea to life.

Organizing clients is an underused approach to upgrading community services. Actively assisting client populations to act powerfully to hold the service delivery system accountable is not a common human services activity. Neither do human services workers routinely and systematically involve clients in planning, developing, and refining services in a

way that vests the clients with real authority. Given what we profess about the right of the client to self-determination and the need for clients to recognize and assume responsibility for important aspects of their lives, client involvement would seem to be almost automatic. It is not. A counseling approach that so routinely denies clients' input and responsible decision making would be roundly criticized in professional circles. Yet paternalistic attitudes regarding what is best for the client remain fairly unchallenged in the arena of service delivery. This state of affairs offers a wonderful opportunity to human services workers who seek fundamental changes in the way services are provided. Certainly, such an approach must include an awareness of the risks. Altering the perception of clients as powerless and dependent is a challenge in itself. Regarding clients of public programs as relatively powerless and dependent sustains the interests of many individuals both inside and outside the human services system. You must understand that those interests will feel threatened when you work to increase client participation in decision making.

Making Improvements Within Your Own Agency

You will not often need to look beyond your own agency to recognize situations that call for change. Much of what you can do to improve the human services system in your community applies just as well to the organization for which you work. Needed changes in agency regulations, policies, or procedures may demand your attention. You will have the opportunity to create new programs or to improve existing ones to better serve people in need. Developing more cooperative working relationships among members of the staff and volunteers may well be a necessity. Finally, helping clients have a legitimate say over the services they receive will undoubtedly be both a challenge and an opportunity.

Few systems, in fact none that I can think of, are created perfectly. It is always possible to make things better. This is as true for your own agency as it is for any other system we humans have fashioned.

Political Involvement

Your participation in the political process occurs in two fundamental areas. The first and most obvious is electing people to office in the first place. In this instance you will be working in a political campaign. The second involves dealing with the people who have been elected, working to influence them as they perform the duties of their office. This work is generally referred to as lobbying. (Although lobbying is most often directed at elected officials, it is not limited to them. Other policy makers, such as regulators, can be the focus of lobbying activities.) Lobbying involves your use of argument and political power to help shape the development of public policy, usually by refining and promoting the passage of "good" policies, or by blocking the advancement of "bad" ones.

Working to elect or to influence government officials at local, state, or national levels is a powerful means of affecting policies that regulate behavior as well as those that shape how existing resources are distributed and who has access to those being developed. The efforts of an organized, dedicated group of people can have a tremendous impact here, even if these people do not have much money.

Using the Courts

Shaping laws through the political process may contribute to improving conditions in your community, but using those laws currently in place may have far-reaching consequences as well. The courts do not solve all our problems for us, but they can "mediate interpretations of our own indecisiveness" (Pollack, 1997, p. 1). Essentially, this is what you are doing when you work through the courts.

You may well find that the rights of the people you serve are being ignored and, in practice, denied. Litigation can secure the action your clients require. Getting powerful interests in the community to apply rights and protections equally to all its citizens may take more than good intentions. The courts may have to step in and hold individuals or even the public at large accountable.

Opportunities for taking part in the process of strengthening your community are plentiful. Through your participation, you may gain experience in a wide variety of change venues. Much like different games, each arena will hold its special appeal and unique challenges. You will come to appreciate the impact you can have regardless of where you perform.

A Modest Recognition of Idealism

Most real progress occurs when individuals take hold of the idea that there is a better, more humane, or more just way. They assert that our capacity for excellence, in ourselves and in our affairs with one another, matters and that acting on that capacity is as much a choice as is rejecting it. They are just not willing to settle for mediocrity or meanness. These people are idealists.

Idealism is the belief that things could be better, that they *should* be better, and that an individual can play a part in making them better. This is not easy. Idealism requires faith, commitment, and courage. There is certainly an imposing array of forces to push back against a belief in a higher purpose. Greed, corruption, selfishness, deceit, and their kin are real, and they easily discourage the faint of heart.

It requires no challenge to be seduced into cynicism. Cynicism is a cowardly condition. It is resignation, a retreat from the test of principle. It is easy. In an attempt to justify an unwillingness to contend, cynicism argues for impotence.

Cynicism turns away because it cannot face up to the demands of character.

Idealism is not to be confused with naiveté. Idealism is a purposeful, powerful belief. A real idealist is willing to take a hard, uncompromising look at the world and reckon with it, trusting in his or her own power, the strength of decency, and others who share those convictions. An idealist simply refuses to capitulate to a plodding dullness of spirit.

Francisco Sagasti (1990) said, "at least we have the capacity to imagine a better situation than the one we are in at present. . . . The basis of our optimism is being able to link imagination, visions of what can be better, what can work . . . to existing situations . . . and work out from them."

Someone may say to you, "You are an idealist." Take it as a compliment.

Conclusion

No matter what role you play in providing human services, you will recognize opportunities to determine a new direction in furthering human growth. Sometimes it will not be enough to tackle problems one at a time or to tolerate inefficiencies or abuses that are an affront to human dignity. You will not allow ignorance to keep problems alive, and you will no longer accept community problems as inevitable or unsolvable.

You will acknowledge that there are a number of sources of community problems, but there is also a huge reservoir of concern and resources to deal with them. You will recognize that others share your capacity to care and to act.

You will come to believe that you can make a contribution in a fundamental way. You will learn how to overcome your own and others' resistance to change. You will combine your talents and actions with others in ways that increase your belief in your abilities and your potential to make a difference.

You will come to see that problems are not isolated phenomena touching individuals only. You will see how they affect a community of people, and you will work with that community to solve them. You will recognize and respect the different cultural perspectives on the issues all of you face. You will learn how the unique strengths of different cultures add vitality to your overall effort.

You will learn different ways to express your interest in making things better. You may work to help a neighborhood develop or utilize its resources. You may start a new program in response to a community need. You may help elect an ally to office. Or, you may work to determine a greater role for clients in shaping the services that can improve the quality of their lives.

You will hold to your ideals, and you will act on them. You will have understood well the challenge to change.

CHAPTER 2

A Framework for Action

Chapter Highlights

- Healthy communities produce healthy people
- Systems theory
- Characteristics of healthy communities
- Social capital
- Close communities provide a context for action

- Organizing for community change
  - overview of approaches
- The community development model
- Conditions for community action
- Elements of successful action strategies

Key in hand, Ben walked through the parking garage looking for his car. "Gad, I've got too much on my mind. How can I lose a car in a building?" he mutters to the headlights and license plates that don't recognize him either. He's ready to go home, ready to take time to connect with his own private worries, or maybe even have a few laughs not connected at all to jokes about work. Like so many others, he just wants to close the door on a day of frustrations and a world of hurt. If he can retreat only a little further, close enough doors, maybe he can find a place where the order of things seems to make sense. Of course, he's not conscious of these thoughts that distract his search. He just wants to find the dang car.

"Garage hiking again, Ben?" Melanie's voice brings him back into focus.

"Yeah, I thought I'd get a little exercise." Her humor, even if it's a little sarcastic, feels good, and in spite of himself, Ben perks up.

"I know. It's been a long day for me too. I don't know if I am impatient with myself for sitting back or frustrated that I can't seem to get a clear picture of how I can make a difference."

"Think we can?"

"Yeah, I do. Good word 'we,' huh?"

"Thanks, Mel. What do you say we go get something to eat?"

Principles can direct action for change, but they are like so many puzzle pieces scattered over the kitchen table. To begin to make some sense out of the emerging picture, it is often helpful to find those pieces with a straight side—the frame that holds the picture together. Fundamental principles provide such a frame for understanding how you can promote action to change conditions that affect people. This framework does not reveal the whole picture, just its outlines, and maybe a few central ideas you can build around. Other concepts will be provided throughout this book. Fitting those concepts together will help you bring your own picture to life.

Ben and Melanie are on the verge of figuring out that by joining together, and with others, they won't get knocked back as readily as when they struggle alone. Through organized action, they can indeed make a difference. Understanding some basic notions about how all this works will make it a lot easier for them.

Deciding to try to do it the best they can is all that is required to start. A commitment to keep learning is a key for success. Making decisions like these doesn't guarantee success, but it certainly increases the chance of a successful outcome. After all, there are only so many doors we can lock behind us.

The framework for action presented in this chapter provides the key factors you will need to shape your efforts to promote change.

Healthy Communities Produce Healthy People

Healthy communities tend to produce healthy people. Distressed and depressed communities tend to produce distressed and depressed people. Fostering healthy communities is the fundamental purpose of community change. Human services workers are directly concerned with the well-being of people; strengthening communities promotes individual as well as group health. The consequences of health or distress are experienced by all members of the community; therefore, promoting healthy communities serves both our self-interest and our interest in others.

It is naive to assume that a person can be divorced from his or her surroundings (Lynch, 1996). Consistently significant for all but the tiniest handful of people is participation in the human community. We do not live apart from it, and the communities we create affect each and every one of us.

We derive physical, intellectual, emotional, and spiritual sustenance from our membership in the human community. We cannot pursue our interests or correct our maladies without regard to the presence and actions of others. Even acts of exploitation or withdrawal require a community to give them meaning.

A healthy community sustains healthy connections among its members, as well as with other sources of strength within the community, such as safe housing, natural resources, and social institutions like schools. A healthy com-

munity also maintains connections outside itself to access what the community needs: raw materials for manufacturing, capital for economic development, or new forms of art to engage the human spirit.

Faulty connections can weaken the community. Anything that restricts access to a needed resource represents a faulty connection. For example, inadequate public transportation systems can block members' access to employment. Racism or heterosexism (a largely unrecognized bias in favor of heterosexuals) can interfere with relationships among people (Berkman & Zinberg, 1997; DiAngelo, 1997). Connections to unsafe substances also weaken. A tainted water supply or the use of harmful drugs are examples of these types of faulty connections.

Communities are connected in ever-widening circles, but people draw their most important nourishment from their close communities. These close communities are small enough in size and complexity that members acting in concert with others around them can more noticeably influence change. Healthy communities can more readily fend off harmful forces from outside while finding and using productive forces that can benefit members. Unhealthy communities are vulnerable to external destructive influences and are unable to draw in adequate levels of vitalizing energy.

We thrive in a healthy environment; we wither in an unhealthy one.

Systems Theory and Communities

Each organism—a city, a neighborhood, an individual—is a system that requires ongoing input in the form of nutrients and other energy. The system takes in energy to grow, produce, and sustain life and to maintain its equilibrium. As the system processes the input it receives, this energy is converted to productive output, which is expressed in activity (such as work), in seeking new input, or in discarding used input as waste. Further, each system interprets the reactions it receives from the broader environment and makes adjustments, operating as a thermostat to regulate itself and maintain some sort of balance. The cycle of a system is to effectively take in energy, use that energy, and express its use in the form of productivity or waste. Anything that impairs its ability to do any of these things will harm the system. Anything that promotes its ability will strengthen the system.

A number of authors have helped inform my view of systems, among them are Cowan and Egan (1979); Brill (1998); Senge, Kleiner, Roberts, Ross, and Smith (1994); Dubois and Krogsrud-Miley (1996); Johnson and Schwartz (1997); Kirst-Ashman and Hull (1997); Lumsden and Lumsden (1997); and Schmolling, Youkeles, and Berger (1997).

Another important aspect of systems theory is the notion that a system operates in some degree of relationship to other systems. Further, each particular system is part of a larger set of systems and is itself made up of smaller sets of systems. For example, a neighborhood is part of a city, which is part of a county, which is part of a state, and so on. Within the neighborhood itself are several streets, and on each street live a number of households, and within each household are individuals. Even individuals are made up of various smaller systems, such as a respiratory system, a skeletal system, and so on. No matter which system you look at, it must be able to meet its needs and nourish its internal parts while at the same time managing its relationships with the series of larger systems within which it lives.

As a result of the interconnectedness of systems, what happens in any part of the system affects the entire system, and what occurs outside the system can also affect the system. To take a closer look at how this works, imagine that the system we are talking about is you. If you have too much harmful food or drink in your stomach, your well-being is affected. You feel pain in a part of your body, you don't feel like moving around or going to work, and even

your outlook on life suffers. One of your subsystems—your digestive system—has affected how your whole body functions today. Now let's say that you are feeling fine—until you learn that the plant where you work is being closed and you are going to be out of a job. In this case something that has occurred outside yourself affects your well-being.

Whether the system is an individual or a family or a community, transactions that occur within and between systems can affect a number of people. The closer you are to the transaction, the more strongly you will feel its effect. You feel your stomachache or your loss of job more keenly than other members of your household do, but they are likely to be affected as well. Your immediate neighbors, the places where you shop, and other people whom your life touches may also be affected, but the more distant their connection with you, the less likely they are to notice.

Systems theory helps us understand that the actions of a group of people within the community can positively or negatively affect the health of the community and its members, resulting in an opportunity or a risk. It can also help us to see that actions that occur outside the community itself also affect community health. Here, too, are conditions of opportunity or risk.

A healthy community takes care of its component parts while conducting transactions with larger systems so that it gets what it needs. A change agent can use this understanding to help a community take care of itself, perhaps by encouraging a group within the community to assert its rights to get the attention it needs or by helping a number of groups within the community work together for mutual benefit. A change agent might also assist a community by helping it relate more effectively to a wider community in which it sits. At an even broader level, a change agent can help provoke a response from the wider community (including government) to fulfill its responsibilities to smaller communities. This may take the form of providing direct resources (such as money), technical assistance, legal protection, or other support a smaller community needs so that it can flourish. (Systems theory is explained in more detail in Chapter 3.)

Characteristics of Healthy Communities

Healthy communities meet the needs of its members. Larger, more comprehensive communities can provide for a full range of members' physical, social, emotional, intellectual, and spiritual needs. Smaller or more narrowly defined communities may be organized around a particular set of needs; for example, faith communities primarily attend to spiritual needs. Whether the community is comprehensive or narrow, it can be considered healthy if the expectations of its members regarding what it should provide are met.

In healthy communities members are able to meet their needs sufficiently well that energy can be directed beyond matters of basic survival to those of personal and community development. Healthy communities provide ways for members not only to survive but to grow; not only to receive but to contribute. Three contributors to community health that change agents should acknowledge are: recognizing and valuing resources, inclusivity, and social capital.

Recognizing and Valuing Resources

A healthy community acknowledges its resources and uses them to foster growth of the community and its members. These resources include natural elements (such as rivers or minerals), elements shaped by human intervention (such as bridges and public libraries), and talents and skills available throughout the population (such as music and storytelling). A healthy community demonstrates an appreciation of the value of these resources, particularly valuing its members.

Unhealthy communities see only the limita-

Take a Moment to Discover . . . .

As you drive around, ride the bus, or walk through town today, notice the people who are more or less pushed to the fringes of the community, those people who certainly aren't invited into the life of the community. Who are they? The scruffy guy with the "Will Work for Food" sign? That teenager with the baggy pants or the one carrying her soon to be born baby? How about that woman who is cursing at the cars, the trees, and the street signs as she pushes the shopping cart crammed with her life's possessions? What do you think about these people? How do you invite them in? How do you help keep them away from the rest of us?

Do you have any gated or walled neighborhoods in your community? What's that all about?

Are there people in your workplace or where you go to school that you wish we could get rid of? You can probably justify your feelings, can't you? Inclusivity is not easy.

tions imposed by their problems and faulty connections. These define the community. Change efforts that promote a deficit orientation reinforce this belief.

Healthy communities believe in their abilities and assets. Change efforts that promote this notion accelerate the discovery and use of community strengths (Kretzman & McNight, 1993; Lofquist, 1996; McNight, 1995; Ronnby, 1995; Scheie, Williams, Mayer, Kroll, & Dewar, 1997; Suchman, 1994).

Inclusivity

Healthy communities are inclusive communities. They purposefully seek methods for including members in community benefits and community decision making. Flowing from the notion of recognizing resources, healthy communities accept the challenge of accepting all their members.

Unhealthy communities turn to exclusivity as a response to difficulties. They find formal and informal ways for excluding those whose behaviors or appearance are different. Different becomes bad. Children with developmental disabilities are excluded from schools, people of color are discouraged from home buying, and the encampments of "homeless" people are bulldozed. The rationalizations of exclusivity seek to protect the community from facing the very real challenges of inclusivity and power sharing.

Healthy communities provide mechanisms for affiliation, shared problem solving, and mutual growth. They appreciate and celebrate differences. They recognize diversity as a resource, a richness, and a benefit.

Social Capital

The concept of social capital has received increased attention in recent years, although not so much in social work and human services discussions. Robert Putnam is perhaps the leading voice in the discussion of social capital, and much of the following discussion is drawn from his writings (Putnam, 1993, 1995, 1996) and the work of James Coleman (1988, 1993).

Social capital refers to community wealth derived from active engagement of individuals with other members of the community and with what might be called "community life." These engagements provide opportunities for affiliation among members and benefits to the community. According to Putnam (1995), social capital "refers to the features of social organization such as networks, norms, and social trust that facilitate coordination and cooperation for mutual benefit" (p. 66). These features include

civic enterprises such as voter turnout, newspaper readership, and membership in groups such as the League of Women Voters, PTA, Elks Club, labor unions, or even choral societies (Putnam 1993, 1995, 1996). In other words, we create social capital whenever we become involved with the affairs of our community and with one another in routine, often organized ways.

Civic engagement and social connectedness are vitally important to the health of communities. High levels of social capital produce tremendous benefits in the form of increased trust, networks of coordination and communication, and resolution of common problems. It also discourages exploitive opportunism as members' sense of self expands from "I" to "we." Successes from civic engagement provide encouragement for shared efforts and models for future collaboration.

Communities with strong social bonding and that are rich in social capital experience lower school dropout rates, less juvenile delinquency, and less drug use (Case & Katz, 1991; Coleman, 1988; Zunz, 1997). Members pitch in to solve common problems (Herbert, 1996), increasing the moral quality of community life (Papworth, 1995). Governance structures and other social institutions function better. Life is simply easier (Putnam, 1995).

In contrast, communities in which the stock of social capital is low are trapped in mistrust and a belief that dealing with community affairs is somebody else's problem. People feel powerless and exploited, and even representative government works less well (Putnam, 1993).

Social capital is a source of fundamental strength for the community. Coleman's (1988) studies on school performance suggest that social capital available in the outside community can substitute for that missing from the family. It is a resource that actually grows as it is used and becomes depleted if *not* used.

The presence of social capital can help sustain a community's norms. Unfortunately, these norms may include intolerance and authoritarian rigidity (Coleman, 1993; Putnam,

1996). In a closed community, these attitudes are difficult to change. However, as healthy communities open up to new information and ideas, intolerance decreases.

The United States has experienced a remarkable decline in civic engagement and social capital since 1960 (Putnam, 1995). Nowadays, people vote less often, visit neighbors less often, attend fewer public meetings, are much less likely to be members of clubs and organizations, and so on. One striking piece of information is representative of the nation's movement toward individual pursuits: More Americans are bowling today than ever before, but participation in bowling leagues has plummeted, leading Putnam (1995) to capture the nation's declining social capital under the phrase, "bowling alone."

After reviewing and dismissing numerous possible causes—Americans are more busy, women have entered the workforce, and so on—Putnam (1996) has found his culprit right here in the living room: television. Heller (1996) and others have questioned this analysis, but Putnam has made at least an arguable case that the tube has planted us on the couch and away from conversations with our neighbors. Coleman (1993) sees social capital as belonging to a bygone social era. He argues that we should accept that fact and develop new structures to replace it. Others blame the helping professions for easing out citizenship and creating client communities (Kretzman & McNight, 1993; McNight, 1995). Of course the bogeyman "Big Government" also has been indicted (Olasky, 1996).

Are we doomed to conversations relegated to halftime or commercial breaks? Will we give up those fancy shirts with our names stitched above the pocket and go bowling alone? Maybe. Is this inevitable? I think not.

There are some signs of a reemergence of civic engagement and a civil society. Community groups are being formed to solve local problems and to shape community decisions (Bole, 1997; Herbert, 1996). Local governments are actively seeking community members to help set local budget priorities (Ibanez, 1997). Whether or not these developments represent a new direction is an open question.

Some trends do appear to be promising. Participation in *service learning,* an approach to education from kindergarten through graduate school that emphasizes civic responsibility and uses the community as the context for learning, has exploded in the last 10 years (National Campus Compact, 1997). In various parts of the country participation in neighborhood organizations has increased (Garth, 1997; Reid, 1997). The Pew Charitable Trust, the Stuart Mott Foundation, and others have redirected support to strengthening neighborhoods.

Communities marked by a lack of social connectedness fail to meet the needs of their members, who end up living in fear and pessimism. If we are to live in healthy communities, opportunities for increasing social capital need to be developed. But Putnam (1993) cautions: *"Social capital is not a substitute for effective public policy but rather a prerequisite for it and, in part, a consequence of it"* (p. 42). Agents of community change must be willing to use social capital to promote a synergy between private organizations and government.

Many questions still surround our understanding of this concept (Putnam, 1993). What kinds of civic involvement are most helpful? What other forms of civic engagement are developing? Is social capital created and destroyed, or does it just change form? How can we build (or rebuild) more? The answers to these questions will guide policy makers, professionals, and private citizens in strengthening their communities.

Close Communities Provide a Context for Action

Close communities are collections of people, larger than our family and immediate circle of friends, to whom we generally relate and from

Take a Moment to Discover . . . .

Most of us are less engaged in our communities than our parents were. Yet some of us are beginning to value a life more connected to a community of people outside our work.

What do you notice about your own contributions to social capital?

How many civic organizations do you participate in? When was the last time you went to a community meeting that wasn't required by your work? How often do you vote? Do you shop at stores that are locally owned or do you spend your time and dollars at one of those huge merchandise warehouses that are owned by a national chain?

Is public affairs somebody else's business, maybe the politicians?

whom we draw identity and meaning. The problems and benefits of these communities most noticeably affect us, and we and our immediate associates can have at least some degree of influence in regard to these factors. These communities are *close* to us, hence the term. This community may be our small town or the part of a large city in which we live. We all belong to several close communities—they include our place of work, the school we attend, our local professional association, or our faith community. Close communities provide the most likely arena for community change activities.

Using a systems orientation, each community is part of a larger community or a larger set of communities. At some point those communities become so large or so distant that it is difficult for us to readily feel a part of them (Papworth, 1995). Thus, it is difficult for us to feel compelled toward action on their behalf.

Close communities offer a context in which our actions are meaningful. Two benefits accrue from a focus on close communities. First, it is easier to mobilize for action. Precisely because we can have an impact on these communities we are more likely to engage in purposeful action to improve conditions there. We already have relationships with a number of other community members; action within this community close at hand is simply more relevant. Second, transforming our close communities holds the promise for transforming the society of which they are a part. The whole is benefited when people are encouraged to strengthen its parts. Papworth (1995) expresses this point well: "Realize that the future belongs not to the mass and the giant but to the small and the local, if only because no body can be healthier than the cells of which it is comprised" (p. 214).

The danger in all this is that we may divorce ourselves from the struggles and the hopes of other communities or fail to recognize that a number of issues cross community lines.

Capital punishment, air quality, or welfare reform transcend distinct communities. Addressing these issues requires an alliance of communities. Even though the focus of our action on broader issues may more effectively take place in the context of our close community, the power of our action increases when we ally our efforts with those of other communities.

For smaller local communities, such as neighborhoods, to assist one another, governing structures that promote a healthy interconnectedness among communities are necessary. Change agents must overcome attitudes that local communities can ignore one another without consequence or that local benefits only result from a competition of local interests. These attitudes are ultimately destructive, reducing the flow of resources and increasing the possibility of surrender of local control through manipulation.

The notion of community change may seem so big and intimidating that potential change agents do not consider its value or its possibility. However, by initiating community change in our close communities we begin to see its benefits.

Organizing for Community Change

Communities vary by culture, interest, geography, and a host of other factors, which render models for organizing community change somewhat imprecise. Furthermore, there is no one prototypical or standard "community" in which we can see various models in operation. Still, it is helpful to consider some different general approaches to the business of change (see Figure 2-1). So, given this understanding, what are some of the directions change efforts take?

Jack Rothman (1968) described three models of community change: locality development, social planning, and social action. Locality development involves "broad participation of a wide spectrum of people at the local community level in goal determination and action" (p. 23). This process emphasizes economic and social progress. It is intended that a "wide range of community people [are] involved in determining their 'felt' needs and solving their own problems" (p. 30). Thus, this model has a kind of self-help orientation to it.

The social planning approach "emphasizes a technical process of problem solving with regard to substantive social problems, such as delinquency, housing, and mental health" (p. 24). This model envisions that change occurring in a complex world calls for deliberate, rational steps. Such efforts require expert planners to guide changes through a maze of bureaucratic barriers with the intention of "establishing, arranging, and delivering goods and services to people who need them" (p. 24).

Social action methods seek more fundamental changes. They presuppose "a disadvantaged segment of the population that needs to be organized . . . to make adequate demands on the larger community . . . making basic changes in major institutions or community practices" (p. 24). The types of changes sought through social action are a redistribution of power, the reallocation of resources, or changes in community decision making.

Rothman and Tropman	Locality Development	Social Planning	Social Action	Policy Practice	Administrative Practice
	• Self-help • Emphasizes economic and social progress • Orientation to power structure: partners	• Rational, technical problem solving • Social problem focus • Orientation to power structure: sponsors	• Redistribution of power and resources • Deals with justice issues • Orientation to power structure: target/oppressors	• Management of policy process • Development or change of policies • Orientation to power structure: varies	• Improve functions of organization • Organizational goals, strategies, and program concerns • Orientation to power structure: varies

Kramer and Specht	Community Development		Social Planning		
	• Mobilizing "victims" of community conditions • Building new organizations • Action oriented		• Coordinates efforts of agencies • Changes in agency attitudes, structure, and so on • Workers tied to agencies		

Rubin and Rubin	Self-Help	Partnership	Coproduction	Pressure	Protest
Issue-based or Area-based	• Deal with internal problems • Service to community • Little outside help	• Community defined problems • Receive outside help	• Community takes over • Government functions • Some community decision making	• Community defined issues • Use conventional approaches • Government policy • Change concerns	• Economic and political change • Wide range of tactics • Force opponents to agree

Problem Focus, Power Focus, or Development Focus

Figure 2-1
Models for community change

In addition to these models for community organization practice, Rothman and Tropman (1987) suggest policy practice and administrative practice as additional approaches for enacting or managing change at the broad level.

Policy practice involves identifying, analyzing, refining or developing, and implementing policies that guide the operations of government and nongovernment organizations that have an impact on individuals, groups, and communities.

Administrative practice involves organizational development and manipulation, including some of the following abilities and activities: assessing community needs, designing programs, maintaining community relationships, and facilitating consensus among organizational constituencies. The administrator guides the processes by which service organizations order and arrange their activities and resources to accomplish their missions.

Kramer and Specht (1983) describe two basic approaches to community organizing they term community development and social planning. Community development methods work directly with the people who are feeling the problem to mobilize them to take action. Social action activities are included under community development in the model. Emphasizing participation of the previously unaffiliated or those who may be considered "victims," Kramer and Specht note that "a typical feature of such efforts is their concern with building new organizations among people who have not been previously organized to take social action on a problem" (pp. 15–16).

Their description of social planning activities is similar to Rothman's, characterized by actions designed to coordinate or change the practices of community agencies. Kramer and Specht further explain that "a major feature of this model is that the action system is composed of people who are legally and structurally tied to community agencies and organizations, and their behavior is regulated and guided by these commitments" (p. 16).

Rubin and Rubin (1986) describe five types of community organizations: self-help, partnership, coproduction, pressure, and protest organizations. Self-help organizations identify a problem, recruit members, and provide a service with minimal help from or interaction with outside agencies. Partnership organizations are developed by community members who themselves define which problems to work on. These organizations often rely on outside financial assistance. Coproduction means that community organizations undertake activities with government that in the past were carried out only by government agencies. Pressure organizations choose their own issues but try to work within the conventional rules of government to persuade politicians and bureaucrats to change their policies. Protest organizations usually

want to bring about a change in the economic or political system and often work outside conventional rules.

Rubin and Rubin also distinguish between issue-based and area-based organizations. "Issue-based organizations focus on a particular issue of concern to a number of people, regardless of where they live and work. An area-based organization focuses on a particular area, such as a neighborhood, dealing with a variety of problems that affect that particular area" (p. 9).

Each of these approaches organizes people in one of three ways. In the first case, people come together to solve a particular problem or make a particular improvement. Although the use of power is necessary for success, it is seen as the means for achieving the goal rather than being the goal itself. Most of the community change work you will be involved with as a human services worker will be problem focused. Even though these efforts may be short in duration and have a limited scope, it is important to leave the community in a more empowered condition upon completion of the change episode.

In the second case, people come together for the purpose of developing and asserting their own power or capacity. These groups generally have a broader agenda of issues, and they use the issues to build the group rather than using the group to tackle the issue. This approach seeks to establish a permanent organization able to take on a variety of issues, some not even recognized by early participants. If working for community change becomes the focus of your professional work, you may devote a lot of your time to operations like these.

The third case involves the development approach described in the next section.

Communities can benefit from any method that addresses community issues in a way that recognizes the capabilities and rights of its members. So there is no one "best" approach for all circumstances. Having said that, I would like to advance the idea that strategies that draw from community development philosophy and practices generally hold a greater likelihood of promoting the health of communities.

The Community Development Model

Community development promotes the acquisition, maturation, and connection of community assets to benefit the whole. Fundamental to this approach is the belief that members of the community itself have the primary responsibility for decision making and action. Community development produces self-reliant, self-sustaining communities that mobilize resources for the benefit of their members.

Elements of Community Development

Let's take a closer look at the elements of community development. Some of these elements of community development can be found in the work of Burkey (1993); McKnight and Kretzman (1993); McKnight (1995); and Ronnby (1995, 1996).

- *Build on community assets.* Resources are what a community has going for itself. Problems or unmet needs can be springboards to action, but action occurs through the use of resources. The simple act of recognizing assets gives a community a sense of confidence and a willingness and some energy to take action. When the community believes that assets exist, it finds them and uses them. This principle affects the entire way you as a change agent look at a community and decide what to do.
- *Increase skills of individuals.* Purposefully teach media relations skills, fund-raising skills, group meeting skills, computer skills, and a host of other important skills to increase the confidence of the community in addressing future situations with competence. Potency and competency are related concepts. Also important is the members' belief in their ability to teach new skills to other community members.
- *Connect people with one another.* Build relationships and share talents, information, work, and energy—everything happens through relationships. Connecting people with one another in a purposeful manner produces clear, intended benefits. However, unintended, serendipitous benefits can also be most intriguing. The fundamental question for building an organization is "Whom else should we be talking to?" Once this question becomes a habit, members will expect to build new relationships and will look forward to doing so.

In the early stages of organization, community members tend to funnel communication through the person who has initiated the organizing action or through a few other visible leaders. This is natural and understandable. These individuals are common points of contact, and they generally convey some degree of confidence. It is easy to reinforce this process in many subtle ways. It is also very limiting to the organization if this pattern persists. Patterns that promote less hierarchical or centralizing relationships increase strength.

- *Connect existing resources.* Any project requires the assembly of resources, and it is rare to find them all in one place. Yet the notion that "we can't do because we don't have . . ." commonly stalls development of good ideas. Assume two things. One, the group attempting to bring something to life does not have everything it needs. Two, most of what is needed can be found in the community. Any enterprise in your community, public or private, profit or volunteer, is a resource. Special interests or hobbies are resources. So are trees or water or a parcel of land.

Whenever you connect resources you create investors. You extend ownership and participation in the project, broadening its base of support. By connecting resources you get the things you need, but perhaps more important, you connect more people to what you are doing and why.

- *Create or increase community resources.* Community development adds to the community's stock of routinely available assets. Look beyond solving an immediate problem with an eye to bringing something new into existence that will continue to benefit the community. A child care cooperative, a water well, a basketball court, a social club, an art class, a choir, a new business, a tree-lined street—all enrich the community.

• *Allow the community to assume ownership of direction, action, and resources.* Community members do not just approve plans, they create them. Community members do not just provide input, they make decisions. The community decides what to do and how to do it. What they produce is theirs.

• *Promote the expectation that community members will do all work possible.* We more fully value the things we create, and we learn much better the things we do for ourselves. Here is an example from very basic community development to illustrate this point.

Imagine a community that needs a well dug. "Dig us a well," they say. "Nope," I say, "but I will help you dig a well." The community needs some technical guidance to figure out all the things that need to be done to dig a well. Next the community must decide what they can do right now. And, if they want that well, community members must do the work. (If the size of the project outstrips the available resources, community members may choose to work alongside others who can provide help.) Next the community must look at things they can't do now but that they can learn how to do in a reasonable amount of time. Teaching is a nurturing process and must address issues of confidence and belief in ability. Just because you know somebody can learn something doesn't mean that they know it too. Finally, only those things that still remain on the list will be done by people outside the community. The community has its well, more skilled members, and a sense of its ability.

Too often we train people for dependency, helplessness, and hopelessness. We train them to believe that they can't do things themselves. We usually do this in unthinking kindness—in the name of helping. Ask yourself: Whose well do we want it to be?

• *Create beneficial external relationships.* Each community has a tremendous amount of yet undiscovered assets, but it is likely that it will still need to draw in more resources from outside its boundaries. It may need to ally with other communities to increase power. It may

need to draw support from public sources. It may need to create economic enterprises that attract new dollars into its economy. Some specialized talents or particular materials may need to be imported.

Constructive relationships help promote an exchange of resources between the community and others, and it provides for collaborative partnerships among different communities for mutual benefit. Maintaining wider relationships also creates opportunities to influence external forces that affect the community.

• *Foster community self-reliance and confidence.* All these actions help a community to believe in itself and its abilities. It forgets how to back down and back away. When confronted with a challenge, members of the community assume that they can figure out what to do and do it. Also, they believe that they will be able to meet other challenges that come their way.

• *Build self-sustaining organizations.* For a community to continue to grow in strength, a mechanism for community decision making and action must be maintained. A community must continue to develop new leadership, extend connections to new members, and maintain existing ones. It is more likely to do this by remaining active, taking on new challenges from time to time. The organization takes care of itself as it takes care of community issues.

• *Enhance the quality of life.* Community development strives to move past problems to believe that better is possible, it is even likely, it is certainly deserved, and it can be expected.

Social Action and Community Development

Development activities enable a community to move forward on community building activities. Yet, on some occasions community groups need to first secure rights or opportunities that are being denied to them. Groups frequently need to go through a period of social action to assert or protect their interests and to engage the attention of community members. This is likely to be

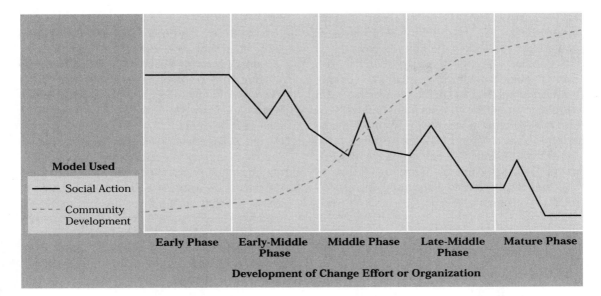

Figure 2-2
Progression from social action to community development

the case for communities whose members have been exploited or ignored by powerful interests from outside the immediate community. In these situations the conflict-oriented strategies typical of social action may be needed to initiate a new order in the wider community that recognizes and responds to the rights of the close community. In fact, a community group may need to engage in an extended period of social action before it can direct significant attention to development efforts. The conflict period can be followed by transition stages during which the group moves into more collaborative or developmental approaches. (See Figure 2-2.)

Social action can bring issues to light and an organization to life, but the danger is that the community may become stuck there—developing its conflict skills but little else. To become truly empowered, a community must move beyond reaction and assert its own agenda, cultivating the internal assets that can provide its members with a high quality of life. It needs to become self-directed, self-evaluating, and self-renewing. Some aspect of community

development work must take place very early in the organization's life for three reasons. First, many members of the community will shy away from a conflict agenda. However, these individuals still care about the community and want to contribute in some way. Development activities provide an opportunity to help. Second, development activities provide visible signs that the community intends to thrive and is doing so. These indicators become sources of encouragement and pride. Third, development activities create new resources and promote investment. These solidify the community's foundation and strengthen its ability to engage in conflict, while discouraging the opposition.

Even though a community may move from confrontation to development, it may need to invoke conflict strategies from time to time to prevent exploitation, to gain access to resources to which it has a rightful claim, or to bring a sense of drama to boost interest. The more a community is developed, the stronger it becomes and the less vulnerable it is to external threats. Well-organized neighborhoods that have constructively developed their internal assets usually get their fair share of resources and are rarely targeted as dumping grounds.

Conflict may be necessary because you cannot pursue opportunities if you cannot exercise your rights. Being concerned with people's rights is the starting point, but we must also pay attention to people's abilities and responsibilities. Many change advocates—often those from outside the community—miss this point. Treating people as needy rather than as able and responsible is demeaning, disrespectful, and patronizing.

Conditions for Community Action

Community change only occurs through action. Much as certain conditions are required before a thunderstorm can crack the heavens and drench the earth, a number of factors need to exist before community action will take place.

- *Tension between current discomfort with the present situation and attraction to a new situation.* If you are really hot and sweaty and you are standing beside a nice cool swimming pool, you may very well jump in. However, if you are a little warm, and you think the water in the pool might be freezing cold, you will probably stay dry. Communities act in much the same way. People will act for change if they are uncomfortable enough with the current circumstances or excited enough by a new possibility. Otherwise, they will maintain the status quo—even if they spend a lot of time complaining.

Over time a community can grow accustomed to its discomfort, even growing to tolerate incrementally increasing levels of frustration. A change agent may well act to stoke irritations so that members can break out of their passive acceptance of harmful circumstances.

- *Belief in the possibility that action will produce a successful outcome.* Only in extreme circumstances of duress will people act with little hope that they can be successful. More commonly we only do things if we think we have some chance of accomplishing what we intend. Whether it's giving up smoking, learning to use a computer, or fighting city hall, we won't choose to do anything we really don't think will work out. There has to be some reasonable chance for success.

- *Recognition of a course of action.* People may be prepared to act, and willing to act, but not know how to act. One of the most frustrating experiences is wanting to do something, but not knowing what to do. Even in an emergency situation people can feel helpless although they are highly motivated to act. For an action to occur, it has to exist in the awareness of the people who must act. Unless you can see what to do, you can't do it.

- *Sufficient credibility of the organizers of the effort, validity of the issue, and sustainability of the organization.* People only commit to and respond to things they believe are real. A sufficient degree of credibility will always be a precursor to the next level of action. The organization must continually meet spoken and unspoken tests of credibility prior to any action being taken.

- *Sufficient degree of emotion.* Intellectual understanding is insufficient for action. There has to be some level of feeling—joy, anger, excitement, frustration. A change agent must do more than provide information. He or she must arouse feelings, particularly an enthusiasm for action.

Elements of Successful Action Strategies

Action does not presuppose success. Successful organizations have some amount of luck along with a significant amount of thought and purpose. The following ingredients are essential for success. (These elements are examined in detail in Part 2.)

Knowledge of the community.   A community is somewhat like a musical instrument. To produce music, you must learn something about that instrument. You need to know what sounds it can produce and have some idea of how this occurs. You cannot expect a snare drum to sound like a violin nor expect a tuba to produce the tinkling notes of a piano. All instruments produce music, but each offers its own special beauty and each responds differently to the musician's urgings. Likewise, each community is unique. It is similar in some ways to other communities but has its own culture, capacities, and concerns. The community provides the obstacles and the opportunities for success. The change agent cannot operate in ignorance of these and hope to be successful. If you want to make beautiful music, you must first understand your instrument.

A base of power larger than the issue.   Lack of confidence and the subsequent lack of motivation come from attempting to take on too large an issue with too little power. Success only occurs when the ability to make the change is greater than the change that needs to be made. Power is not dominance, although power can be used to dominate. Power can also be used to create—this includes creating more power. The notion of power *with* is at least as important as the notion of power *over.* People must have enough power to control their own destiny. In fact, it is the very lack of such power that is at the root of many community problems.

Community issues are affected by many forces. Some of these are arguably international in scope. Changing the world is a pretty daunting proposition. So what is an activist, particularly a weekend activist, supposed to do? You and your organization are probably best served by selecting a level of intervention where the power you have or can assemble can make the most difference.

A compelling issue and sufficient information regarding it.   The issue addressed must be important enough and attractive enough to provoke and sustain involvement and action. By knowing the issue well, the organization—particularly its leadership—gains confidence,

credibility, and strategic direction. An organization without an action issue will flounder. An organization that is not well grounded in the issue it is working on is vulnerable to manipulation and to dismissal.

A vision of a better future and a clear plan of action.   Purposeful action requires a sense of what your intended outcomes are and which actions are needed to achieve them. Without clarity, your actions may well become purposeless, and you run the risk of spending a lot of time going sideways rather than forward. Aimless action can lead to a sense that the group is not accomplishing much, which contributes to loss of membership and burnout.

Plans must remain adaptable to changing conditions, and be based on what people actually will do, not just what they should do.

A sufficient number of people.   Enough people need to be involved to cause the external environment to take necessary notice and to respond as well as to provide support and empowerment to the members of the community taking action. Sufficient numbers provide the diversity of talent and other important resources, such as time. Two of the most critical factors of success are active leadership and people willing to take on work responsibilities.

An effective organization will acknowledge and legitimize different levels of participation and provide members with opportunities to increase their level of participation and involvement in leadership actions.

A sufficient amount of tangible resources or expertise.   Tangible resources include money to purchase what you cannot get for free. These resources fall into seven categories: expertise, communication, equipment, supplies, space, transportation, and the ever-popular miscellaneous category. If you have enough money—a rare condition for a community organization—you can buy what you need. However, getting contributions of the item itself rather than the money to buy it can create a closer connection between the contributor and the organization. All contributors are investors and become part owners of the change effort.

Good communication. Ongoing communication maintains the reality of effort among the organization's constituents as well as the wider public. Further, communication among constituents links people to a common identity and provides encouragement.

Good communication is necessary for the organization to contend with three powerful obstacles to success: uncertainty, particularly related to prospects for success; distraction from competing interests and priorities; and ignorance. For either constituents or the general public to make their commitment of support, they have to believe that action is going somewhere. To confirm that actions are being taken and that progress is occurring, people need to hear about it. They may well need to hear it several times and from different sources.

A matter must be on a community agenda for that community to take action on it. Numerous groups and interests compete for community attention, and those that do not receive some attention are quickly forgotten. Placing an item on a community agenda and keeping it there requires frequent and effective communication with the keepers of the agenda.

What is true about communities is also true about individual constituents. Even though you belong to the organization, it is only one of many things that demand your attention. Things can easily drift out of your attention or get shoved out by immediate demands such as paying the rent, preparing for an exam, or watching the dance portion of the national hula hoop finals. Things that are outside your attention are not acted on. Progress requires action, which requires people who know what to do. Communication is necessary for letting people know what needs to be done.

Organization. Activities that are not organized become sporadic and dissipate the power of action. Organization concentrates the power of action, gives meaning to action, and provides ways to simplify contributions of support. Some degree of structure is necessary to facilitate the actions of the group pursuing change. Structure provides methods for handling predictable or routine activities and tasks. The degree of structure necessary should emerge from the needs of the organization rather than being imposed on it.

Recognition of commonly shared intent and development of even the rudiments of structure brings an organism—the organization—to life. The more clearly members recognize this phenomenon, the more able they will be to act in ways that sustain it.

The organization creates an identity to which members can relate beyond their relating to one another. Further, the organization accepts contributions of energy from its members. Contributions of energy come in various forms. Work done to promote the organization's agenda is certainly a contribution. So too are investments in solving internal problems. Even general references to the organization in the wider community offer a form of energy. The organization stores this shared energy in reserve, much like a battery, and dispenses it back to the effort to keep it alive.

Development of leadership. Central to development of the organization is development of leadership. Leadership is an action that influences others to do something that benefits the group. More specifically, leadership occurs when direction is provided on critical matters facing the group. The direction needs to be appropriate to the situation and sufficiently compelling that a requisite number of individuals respond to change current circumstances. These changed circumstances produce progress. Leaders are those people on whom the group can routinely rely to provide needed direction. Leaders also represent the group's interests to those outside the group.

Success requires a number of different types of leadership actions. The ability to draw differing perspectives and opinions into agreement is a form of leadership. The ability to develop a coherent, cogent strategy with purposeful and creative tactics is a form of leadership. The ability to provide motivation, critical analysis, or to manage tasks are other necessary forms of leadership. No one person can provide all the forms of leadership required for the group to sustain itself and to move forward toward its goals. Therefore, an effective organization will always be in the process of grooming new leadership.

Leaders are the magnets that draw forward the powers of the group. They also provide the cutting edge that chisels openings in the barriers that hold back change. Without sufficient leadership a group will flounder.

Strategically determined actions appropriate to the situation. No degree of concern matters unless it is attached to action, and actions that are directed by a purposeful strategy and related tactics reinforce one another to accelerate effect. Strategies and tactics must relate both to the demands of the situation and the abilities of the people who have to implement them. If either of these conditions is not met, the selected strategy or tactic becomes at best irrelevant and more likely harmful.

A sufficiently receptive environment. For an actual change to take place, the environment in which it occurs must be willing to accept it. This does not necessarily mean that the environment is openly favorable to the change, just that it be willing to incorporate it. In fact, in many circumstances most people will not have strong feelings one way or the other. Under these conditions, as long as the demonstrated support for the change is greater than the expressed opposition, change can take place. If the environment is excessively hostile or resistant, key decision makers will reject the proposal and the change will not be allowed. In such circumstances, efforts may need to be directed toward decreasing hostility or overcoming resistance.

Change can occur in environments that are

Take a Moment to Discover . . . .

Take a closer look at your community, either one of your close communities or the wider community. What do you see? What resources can you name that might be underutilized? What treasures might be hidden from view?

See if today you can identify something of value that you didn't really recognize before.

. . . .

not outwardly encouraging, as long as those promoting the change can concentrate enough support at the critical points of acceptance or rejection to protect decision makers and provide the opportunity for the change to take root. Although the appearance of change can occur in a hostile environment, if the environment is truly inhospitable, ultimately the change will wither from a lack of sufficient support.

Conclusion

A change agent must be able to recognize and build on the resources available in the community. This requires both a belief in the presence of resources and an ability to note opportunities for their use. A change agent who sees only threats and weaknesses will invite the community to stay stuck in the belief of dependency and powerlessness.

One significant set of resources can be found in the people themselves. Believing in these resources means that you believe in the ability of the people to define their own issues and to rely on themselves to make their own decisions.

Look for signs of strength whenever you can, and draw attention to them. People, as individuals or as a community, move forward only through the use of their abilities. Perhaps the most important contributor to a community's success is a belief in its abilities rather than a belief in its problems. Help foster that belief.

You will recognize elements described in this framework for action in the pages that follow—sometimes in the forefront, sometimes singing harmony in the chorus. Other basic concepts of change will be woven into this understanding of how you can act to increase the health of your community. Understanding these concepts is important, but understanding is demonstrated and becomes meaningful only through action. Change comes by acting. Learn to apply these principles in practical ways that encourage community action.

CHAPTER 3

Relating Community Change to Professional Practice

Chapter Highlights		
	❖ Acknowledge arbitrary limitations on professional practice	❖ Principal practice methods
	❖ Learn to shape policy	❖ Examine person-environment transactions
	❖ Basic purposes of social welfare	❖ Apply professional values
	❖ Residual, institutional, and developmental views of social welfare	❖ Basic value orientations
	❖ Workers are change agents	❖ Superficial caring and its consequences
	❖ Understand the term *client*	❖ Pick your fights
	❖ Challenges faced by all workers	❖ Systems theory and how to apply it
		❖ Identify and use common skills

Melanie hangs up the phone, conscious now that she has been rubbing her forehead. She lets her hand drop to the desk. On the way down it forms a fist, meeting the desk rudely.

"What's the problem, Mel?" asks Ben, standing at the door to her office. "I don't mean to be nosy, but I couldn't help noticing that you don't seem too pleased about something."

"Monica. I finally got her to realize she needs to be seeing a doctor, and she actually got up the courage to go. Not too easy when you're 16, pregnant, and your parents won't talk to you."

"Yeah?"

"Well, she called from St. Joan's. She said they told her $800 would take care of everything: the prenatal care visits, the hospital stay, and anything else. Good deal, but she has to have the $800 first. They won't see her. She says she'll just show up at the hospital when it's time, and then they'll have to take her."

"Tough, Mel. Sorry."

"Tough, hell. Try criminal, or stupid, or any other word they wouldn't like hearing at any placed called 'Saint.' Do you know how hard it is for young women in this town to get prenatal care if they finally decide it's important?"

"Sounds like it's not too easy."

"You've got that right."

"So, what are you going to do about it?"

"Me? I'm just one social worker with a ton of work to do because of stupid things like this. What am I supposed to do?"

"Sorry, you're right. I guess you should just keep pounding your desk."

In this chapter we will take a closer look at how change activities fit with human services work. As you work to alleviate human distress, how can you respond to conditions that directly confront the profession itself? For example, Child Protective Services workers often labor under unreasonable demands that hamper their effectiveness. This is unfair to the children served by the worker, it is unfair to the worker, and it is unfair to the profession as a whole. All workers bear the criticism of a skeptical public all too willing to see the profession as the culprit in a situation in which meager resources produce meager results.

As a worker you will want to respond to these conditions, but can you really do this as a professional? Let us hope that private citizens take action on these issues, but let us also hope that actions to shape our communities and our public policies are well informed by professional social work and human services leadership. If not us, whom do we expect to do this work?

Do you think situations like the one causing Melanie to pound on her desk can be resolved by practitioners in human services fields? Is this a professional responsibility? I think you can guess my answer. What is yours? On what do you base your answer?

You may have questions regarding the relationship of community and policy change to professional practice. Many students studying social work and human services as well as many practitioners envision a very limited role for themselves in community change, yet we have a rich body of knowledge, powerful values, and a variety of skills to contribute. Dinitto and McNeece (1989) point out that social work's multilevel perspective makes the profession particularly well equipped to develop social welfare policies. Schmolling, Youkeles, and Burger (1997) emphasize the importance of social policy development for human services workers. They believe that "human services workers can be, and often are, instrumental in determining unmet needs and in influencing policy" (pp. 283–284).

I believe that community change efforts clearly relate to professional practice. We need to see this as part of our job. This is something we should do within our professional role, not outside of it. Here's why. First, taking action on problems at the community level responds to the basic purposes of social welfare. Second, it is one of the principal methods of traditional practice. Third, it is consistent with our ethics and our values. Fourth, it is needed to assert and protect our sanction for effective professional practice. Fifth, we have a strong theoretical base that aids our analysis of the need and provides the direction for action. Finally, our training clearly provides us with a base of skills to be effective in this endeavor. Let's take a close look at each of these points.

Basic Purposes of Social Welfare

The *Encyclopedia of Social Work* defines social welfare as "the full range of organized activities of voluntary and governmental agencies that seek to prevent, alleviate, or contribute to the solution to recognized social problems, or to improve the well-being of individuals, groups, or communities" (Pumphrey, 1971, p. 1446). To provide for the welfare of both the individual and the society, social welfare addresses the following issues:

- Ability of individuals and groups to function effectively together
- Availability of opportunities for individuals to meet basic physical and emotional needs
- Ability of individuals to recognize and take advantage of opportunities to meet their basic needs, to enhance their lives, and to contribute to the positive development of their society
- Ability of society to recognize and meet the needs of its individual members

Whenever these needs are not met, social problems occur.

Our social welfare institutions act to *prevent* social problems; *treat* or *resolve* social problems; *educate* ourselves, our clients, and our communities about the existence of problems and what can be done to address them; *enhance* the quality of people's lives; and (though we are sometimes reluctant to acknowledge this) *enforce* measures of social control to preserve social stability. To an important degree, each of these ends depends on community change efforts for its accomplishment.

We cannot prevent high school students from dropping out unless we are willing to make changes in our schools. We cannot assist a cocaine-abusing father of three kids if no treatment programs are available when he is willing to confront his condition. We cannot expect a community to be well informed about child abuse if we do not speak out to the people who most need to know. We cannot help people reach their full potential if the best we can offer is support for their labor to survive the daily struggle of their lives. We cannot promote social stability if we fragment our nation's social problems into 10 million isolated sorrows. Clearly, we are called to go beyond the routine if we intend to meet social welfare goals. And we are called to do this with skill and purpose.

Three Views of Social Welfare

There are three approaches to the purpose and delivery of social welfare. Community and institutional change figure prominently in two of them.

The *residual approach* (Wilensky & Lebeaux, 1965) characterizes much of the social welfare system in the United States. This approach assumes that the family and the market economy are the proper sources for meeting people's needs. Social welfare provides a safety net of supplementary services to catch those individuals who fall through the cracks (Burt & Pittman, 1985). Of course, they must fall first.

Certain basic assumptions go hand in hand with the residual approach. Individuals and families receive the main attention of residual efforts. The problems confronted are seen as being caused by those being helped rather than by the structural ineffectiveness of the systems in which these people participate. For example, families need help because they don't work hard enough, not because the prevailing wage rates are too low to feed a family. The first order of business is to encourage the recipient to change, to become more adequate. Services are provided on a temporary basis to get the recipient back in the game. The game itself is not much changed.

Often individuals must prove that they need the assistance and that they are worthy of it. Because individuals are seen as inadequate, there is usually some stigma attached to

receiving services and a dependency relationship is likely to develop. Typical residual programs include Temporary Assistance to Needy Families (TANF), counseling programs, and job training programs.

The *institutional approach* (Wilensky & Lebeaux, 1965) is based on a different set of assumptions. This approach sees welfare efforts as responses to shared social problems. These problems affect a large number of people in common, not one at a time. Services are the right of the client, regardless of the degree of the problem. There is no requirement to prove need or worthiness; that is assumed.

Institutional programs are routinely available and accessible, and those using them are not expected to undergo changes themselves because there is no assumption that something is wrong with them in the first place. Institutional programs are seen as appropriate primary sources for meeting needs, and there is little or no stigma attached to participation (Moroney, 1991).

Our public education system is an example of an institutional response to a common problem—ignorance. Students do not need to prove that they are ignorant before being admitted to first grade, nor that they have failed in learning sufficiently at home. Other examples include social insurance programs such as retirement benefits under Social Security, a full national health insurance program, or even public parks and recreation programs.

Change efforts are directed at our societal institutions, improving the availability as well as the appropriateness of services rather than improving the person receiving them. Here the emphasis is on narrowing the cracks in the system, not catching the people who fall through them. The key to solving social problems is developing the power to change conditions or to improve societal responses to them.

This story about a young woman who was walking along the banks of a river will help you see the difference between residual and institutional approaches to social welfare. It was a lovely spring day, and as is required on such days, butterflies flitted about and birds sang in the trees. Suddenly the young woman's pleasant daydreaming was broken by cries from the river: "Help me! Save me!" She dashed to the river and, seeing a person in desperate need of help, jumped in and pulled the struggling soul from the water.

Barely had she caught her breath when once again she heard cries of: "Help me! Save me!" In a flash she was in the river again, rescuing another victim from peril.

By this time a small crowd had gathered. When she jumped in yet a third time (a little slower now, she was not in *that* great of shape) to save another drowning individual, they all marveled at her courage and ability. But as she sat gasping for breath at the river's edge, more cries could be heard from the water. Instead of plunging back into the river, she struggled to her feet and began walking—away, up the river.

The crowd couldn't believe it, and they shouted, "You can't leave. Don't you see that people need your help here?"

"Yes," she sighed, "I can see that."

"Where are you going?" they demanded.

"I'm going up the river to see who's kicking all these people into the water to begin with, and I'm going to put a stop to it!"

The residual approach is the downstream form of helping. The institutional approach is the upstream form.

A third major view of social welfare is the *developmental approach* (Dolgoff, Feldstein, & Skolnik, 1997; Lofquist, 1996). Using this approach, delivery of services moves beyond a problem orientation. According to this view, "it is possible for society to set up a social welfare institution simply to make living better and to fulfill human development, not necessarily to solve a problem" (Dolgoff et al., 1997, p. 139). Community parks or recreation departments, for example, offer a variety of courses. When they do so simply to expand human potential or add to the quality of life rather than to correct a problem or overcome a deficiency, they are following a developmental approach to the provision of services.

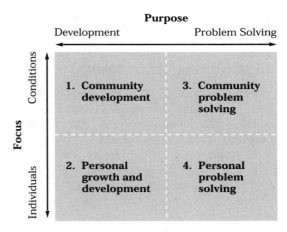

Development is an active process of creating conditions and fostering personal attributes that promote the well-being of people.

Problem solving is a reactive, corrective effort to bring about change where there is a recognized problem.

Figure 3-1
The arenas of action
Source: Lofquist, 1996.

Developmental approaches build on strengths, identifying resources within the individual or the community that can be more fully cultivated and utilized. The emphasis is on potential, not problem. The model of community development described in Chapter 2 resonates with this approach to the delivery of social welfare services. Figure 3-1 shows a number of approaches that can produce results. Instead of correcting one individual problem after another and another, community development can prevent problems by improving conditions that affect people.

Traditional Approaches

Does community change really have a place in the delivery of human services? Aren't most human services workers busy working directly with people in need? And, frankly, are there any jobs out there for change agents? Whew! Such a set of questions. The answer to them all is "yes."

But maybe you want more than a simple "yes." Here is the "why" to the "yes."

Working as a Change Agent

Working backward, let's look more closely at these questions. First of all, human services workers *are* change agents, at least the good ones are. True, too many end up being little more than problem processors rather than problem solvers. You know the type. They are the plague of all professions or occupations. They lose sleep wondering where or to whom they can pass problems along. The client is shifted from one person, department, agency, and, if possible, state to the next until they and their problems get lost. This is called making problems go away. Of course the real problem in the eyes of workers such as these is that they may be forced to actually grapple with things, some of which may be out of the ordinary.

To provide human services requires a willingness to take part in changing a condition. If that only means helping someone qualify for a public assistance program, rest assured that this is a pretty significant "only" in the life of the client. Because of the nature of their work or perhaps because of the depth of their commitment, many workers go beyond making these minimal but very real changes. Some assist clients in changing how they respond emotionally and behaviorally to their circumstances. Others assist in making changes in those circumstances. The differences are really only in scope, focus, and intensity. All workers must accept the simple fact that improvement means that something has to change—and they will play a part in promoting that change.

All jobs in human services require skill in changing conditions, but most workers are not full-time community change agents. *However, all workers will be confronted by the challenge to seek changes in the way things are—all workers.* Although few individuals are hired specifically for their ability to promote community change, most workers are expected not only to provide services but also to improve delivery of those services. The ability to take an active part in

---

CAPTURING CONCEPTS

The Client

I will use the word *client* to refer to people who utilize human services. There is no one good term to describe this relationship. Some writers prefer the term *consumer,* but this implies a greater sense of choice than many people really have. It also implies that people are only users, not contributors. The term *recipient* conveys a rather passive role. *Patient* implies an illness. Some have suggested that the term *citi-* *zen* conveys a sense of dignity and equality. This is useful, although it falls short of the implication of a professional relationship, and others have questioned whether noncitizens would consider themselves included. Though still somewhat insufficient, I have settled on *client* as the term of choice until something better comes along because it comes as close as any to connoting a relationship characterized by respect and professionalism. It is my intention that you understand this term in a sense of partnership, not dependency. Throughout this text you will see that I substitute the term *member* or *participant* to refer to those individuals with whom you will be working to promote community change. *Client* is reserved for individuals, groups, or communities who utilize the services of the worker to contend with problems they are facing or to enhance the current quality of their lives.

CAPTURING CONCEPTS

Five Stages of Partnership Development

The notion of partnership is central to working with clients to promote community change. Five levels of development characterize establishing a partnership relationship between professionals and clients in the community.

At the first level, by far the most predominant, professionals talk *to professionals* about clients and the problems they are having. In some instances things go a little further—to the second level. Here professionals talk *to clients.* This is usually one-way communication directed "downward" from those with more power to those with less power.

At the third level, clients begin talking with other clients about common concerns. And at level four organized groups of clients talk to professionals. Here it is the clients who initiate conversation, and the professionals are expected to respond. This level is rarely reached.

The fifth and most developed level of partnership is characterized by organized clients and professionals working together. They don't just talk to each other; they use their respective resources to collaborate on issues of common concern—concerns selected by the clients.

As an agent of change, at what level do you think your relationship with clients has "gone far enough"?

---

community leadership is a definite asset, especially for positions requiring more professional responsibility. The jobs that are out there—the ones that mean anything—require more than just filling out forms.

Direct Work with Individuals

Most human services workers work directly with people; unfortunately we are not short of clients. A worker who is too busy to assist a client in learning how to contend more powerfully with the situations causing discomfort is much like a teacher who insists that students passively receive information and ask no questions because there is so much material to cover. Perhaps the worker will not play a major role in changing the conditions for the client, but he or she certainly can do three specific things to help the client:

1. Assist the client to understand the forces in the environment that are causing distress and help the client develop skills to confront these forces

2. Identify those who can play a major role in fostering change, which could include bringing similarly affected clients together or referring clients to other programs or other professionals

3. Bring the existence of harmful conditions to the attention of those who are in a position to act on that awareness

These steps don't require mastering difficult new skills; they simply require that you adopt an attitude that these activities are a necessary consideration in the delivery of effective service.

One perspective holds that the role of social work is to provide enough services to the less powerful so they will not make larger demands that would threaten the prevailing balance of power (Richan & Mendelsohn, 1973). Although the idea of a gap between the politically powerful and those with little political power isn't much of a surprise, perhaps applying it to social work is. According to this notion, social work collaborates with the powerful, acting as a buffer to keep the gap in place. By focusing on individuals and promoting the belief that individual inadequacy or failure are at the root of individual and societal problems, social work provides some modest help while diverting attention from fundamental injustices. Thus, nothing fundamental changes. In fact, it is only when the flaws in social institutions threaten the interests of the powerful that broader changes are tolerated.

Perhaps you think this is so. Perhaps you think it is not. I hope you are at least thinking about it.

A Place for Community Change in Service Delivery

Let's examine how this business of community change fits into the basic methods professionals providing human services utilize. Imagine you are looking at a five-pointed star (see Figure 3-2). At each tip is one of the five basic activities or methods:

Casework/counseling, which involves face-to-face contact with individuals and families to help them resolve problems

Figure 3-3
Person-environment transaction model

Group work, which uses the resources and support available among members of a group to assist the members in achieving individual or shared goals

Community organization and development, which brings people together to get, maintain, and utilize power to improve the conditions they face

Research and education, which involves developing and testing theories, discovering information, and communicating theories and information to people who can put them to use

Administration, which involves managing or operating social welfare programs or agencies

Each tip of the star indicates a valid approach to human services. In the middle of the star is the problem or opportunity faced by the client. Solving a problem or a set of problems may involve using one approach or several sequential approaches to intervention.

Another way you can look at community change is through the *configural approach* Bloom (1990) describes (see Figure 3-3). Individuals operate in different milieus such as family, job, culture, and the physical environment, and each "interacts with the others, influencing and being influenced by them" (p. 6). Sometimes these transactions between the individual and the environment go well, and sometimes they don't. If exchanges are routinely unsatisfactory in a particular area, something needs to change, but what? Should efforts be

Figure 3-2
Basic methods

made to change the person, or should efforts be made to make changes in that person's environment? An analysis of these interactions can focus the worker's interventions and guide the choice of methods to be used.

As a worker in the human services field, you will function mainly as a caseworker or counselor; a group worker or group therapist; a community organizer, developer, or planner; an educator or researcher; or an administrator. However, rarely will you function exclusively in your primary role. At each level of practice, you will come face to face with problems that call out for action to improve conditions faced by a group of people.

For a caseworker who routinely assists pregnant teens, it may not be enough that clients understand the importance of prenatal care if such care is unavailable to them. A group worker running men's groups may find that many divorced men long for a closer relationship with their children but that certain forms of

legal bias consistently interfere with that desire. Of course, workers with neighborhood or other community groups can easily identify common problems shared by the people whom they serve. Educators cannot be oblivious to the institutional shortcomings that can block students' abilities to learn effectively. All of us working in social service agencies benefit when the community is informed about what we are doing and why. Administrators can acknowledge program limitations imposed by policies and regulations and can develop new program responses to community needs.

Implications of Professional Values

Social work's strong value base fosters an expectation for action and provides the rationale for these efforts. The *National Association of Social Workers Code of Ethics* (NASW, 1997)

clearly calls for workers to acknowledge their ethical responsibility to promote the general welfare of society through action and advocacy. This is not a casual recommendation to be pursued as a matter of convenience—it is a fundamental ethical responsibility equal to any other matter contained in the code.

Using categories established by Levy (1973) and drawing on the work of a number of other authors, Morales and Sheafor (1986) describe critical values that should direct professional practice:

- *Values as preferred conceptions of people.* This orientation focuses on people and their relationship to the environment. Five key statements characterize this category. First, professional human services workers believe in the inherent worth and dignity of all people (Klein, 1972). Second, each person has an inherent capacity and drive toward change that provides him or her with the potential for development throughout a lifetime (Gordon, 1965). Third, people have responsibility for themselves as individuals and for their fellow human beings, including society. Fourth, people need to belong. Fifth, although people have needs in common, each person is unique and different from all others (Bartlett, 1958).
- *Values as preferred outcomes for people.* This orientation focuses on quality of life issues and the way society should be organized so people can achieve fulfillment. Three value statements appear in this category. First, society must provide opportunities for growth and development that allow each person to realize his or her fullest potential (Smalley, 1967). Second, society must provide resources and services to help people meet their needs and to avoid such problems as hunger, inadequate education, discrimination, illness without care, and inadequate housing. Third, people must have equal opportunity to participate in molding society (Pumphrey, 1959).
- *Values as preferred instruments for dealing with people.* This orientation focuses on how people should be treated. Morales and Sheafor

(1986) describe this as a belief that "all people should be treated with respect and dignity, should have maximum opportunity to determine the direction of their lives, should be urged and helped to interact with other people to build a society responsive to the needs of everyone, and should be recognized as unique individuals rather than put into stereotypes, because of some particular characteristic or life experience" (p. 207).

The call to action echoes through these statements of professional values. Can you hear it? The actions you take as a professional are an acknowledgment of your commitment to these fundamental beliefs. Author after author writing on social work identifies either *case advocacy* or *cause advocacy* as necessary professional skills (Dinitto & McNeece, 1989; Federico, 1984; Johnson, 1998; Meenaghan & Washington, 1980; Pincus & Minahan, 1973; Schmolling, Youkeles, & Burger, 1997; Zastrow, 1995). You will probably struggle to live up to these ideals throughout your career (Piccard, 1988). Still, it is not enough to simply agree to the importance of these values. You must act on them.

Under the Guise of Caring

What level of response is needed to effectively confront the suffering that brings people to the attention of human services professionals? Imagine that you are working in a school. The third-grade teacher brings Melody to your attention. Her family calls the '73 Impala station wagon home. She is dirty, her hair a haven for lice, the soles on her only pair of shoes threaten to abandon her at any time. She's not doing well in school, can barely read even the simplest of words, and seems unable to get along with other members of the class. What do you think is needed here?

- A new pair of shoes?
- A bath?
- A trip to the nurse's office to deal with the lice?

Take a Moment to Discover. . . . .

The following statements urging active involvement in improving social agencies and social conditions appear in the *National Association of Social Workers Code of Ethics* (NASW, 1997, p. 4). Consider each statement carefully and imagine a situation in which you would put each principle into practice.

- Social workers should work to improve employing agencies' policies and procedures, and the efficiency and effectiveness of their services.
- Social workers should not allow an employing organization's policies, procedures, regulations, or administrative orders to interfere with their ethical practice of social work.
- Social workers should promote the general welfare of society, from local to global levels, and the development of people, their communities, and their environments.
- Social workers should advocate for living conditions conducive to the fulfillment of basic human needs and promote social, economic, political, and cultural values and institutions that are compatible with the realization of social justice.
- Social workers should facilitate informed participation by the public in shaping social policies and institutions.
- Social workers should engage in social and political action that seeks to ensure that all persons have equal access to the resources, employment, services, and opportunities that they require in order to meet their basic human needs and to develop fully.
- Social workers should be aware of the impact of the political arena on practice, and should advocate for changes in policy and legislation to improve social conditions in order to meet basic human needs and promote social justice.
- Social workers should act to prevent and eliminate domination, exploitation, and discrimination against any person, group, or class on the basis of race, ethnicity, national origin, color, age, religion, sex, sexual orientation, marital status, political belief, mental or physical disability, or any other preference, personal characteristic, or status.

The National Organization of Human Service Education (1996, pp. 14–16) also requires a firm commitment from human services workers to social justice and to strengthening service delivery.

- Where laws are harmful to individuals, groups or communities, human service professionals consider the conflict between values of obeying the law and the values of serving people and may decide to initiate social action.
- Human service professionals keep informed about current social issues as they affect the client and the community. They share that information with clients, groups and community as part of their work.
- Human service professionals advocate for the rights of all members of society, particularly those who are members of minorities and groups at which discriminatory practices have historically been directed.
- Human service professionals participate in efforts to establish and maintain employment conditions which are conducive to high quality client services.

- A note sent home to the parents of all the other kids warning them of the possible lice infestation at the school?
- A referral to the school psychologist?
- A call to Child Protective Services alerting them to the possibility of neglect?
- A visit to the classroom to see how her classmates treat her?
- Arrange temporary shelter facilities for her, her siblings, and her mom, with the hope that her father can find space in the men's shelter program?
- Establish a shelter care program for families?
- Establish a transitional housing program that would help families like Melody's get back on their feet again?
- Establish a homeless people's organization to advocate for decent housing and the provision of support services for the homeless?
- Take action against the very forces within your community that lead to homelessness?

There is a lot that you can do, isn't there? How much will you actually do? Where will you stop? Who carries on from there? What determines your answers to these questions?

You are mulling all this over. There is a knock at the door. The fourth-grade teacher wants to talk with you about Sam. He has a black eye. His dad got drunk last night and hit him. One more child. One more set of problems. And now what is really going to happen to change Melody's life?

Perhaps all you think you can do is help Melody in her struggle with the problems brought about because she has no real home. Are you actually going to go one step beyond responding to the immediate situation? Are you really going to do anything to reduce homelessness?

If we respond to the presence of disturbing social conditions within our midst by working primarily to soften the pain they cause, does this imply a tolerance for their existence? We appear to be so caring in our efforts to respond to Melody's problems, scurrying about helping this Melody and that one, never confronting the evils that caused Melody to need our aid. We are so busy with all this caring that we have little time or inclination to do anything else. Does the shallowness of our attention and our action guarantee that there will be many a Melody in need? We must ask ourselves, What is the real effect of all our busyness?

Make no mistake about it, the actions we take do lessen the discomfort and bring some relief to those who are affected. However, we may be insensitive to the fact that our limited actions indicate an endorsement of, or at least an acquiescence to, these conditions that call for all our hurry and scramble. Under the guise of caring, we have reached a point of acceptance of conditions that produce the pain we try to ease.

Imagine that you are a worker for Child Protective Services with a caseload of 29 clients. Yet, for ongoing cases like yours, the Child Welfare League of America recommends an optimal *maximum* caseload of no more than 17. Your supervisor walks into your office with another case. You handle 20 cases competently and professionally. You handle 25 with some degree of effectiveness. How much real, constructive service do you provide to a caseload of 30?

You cannot say no to number 30. Why did you say yes? Are you truly caring for having done so? Would you have been reprimanded for refusing? How did you and your colleagues end up in such a situation? Does your acceptance of this unreasonable burden demonstrate your dedication and service to those who need you? How much benefit do they really receive? Under the guise of caring, you just can't say no. You stay busy doing your best to keep patching things up. You feel so overwhelmed. Do you really have no other choice?

If you believe your efforts matter, that they do in fact improve people's lives, should you accept limitations on your effectiveness and the consequent reduction in the benefit people will experience? Will you just be thankful for whatever kind of support you get? How will you participate in making decisions on how effectively you can provide service? Or, is that none of your business? Whom do you want to leave these decisions to?

You have learned how to juggle; in fact, you are pretty good at it. You are able to juggle 5 balls at once. All of them are safe as you toss them into the air—but 5 is the limit. What happens if someone tosses you number 6? What is the effect on the first 5? What happens to all your other cases when you say yes to number 30?

Social work and human services are hemmed in by suspicion and lack of community support. We do not practice in a vacuum. Jansson (1997, p. 8) reminds us that social workers are "more subject to social policies that control, restrict, and regulate their practice" than are most other professions. Meenaghan and Washington (1980) recognize that our careers are continually shaped by changes in the social welfare institution. They point out that it simultaneously helps, limits, and shapes the ways we deal with people in trouble. Should we as social workers and human services professionals attempt to shape this institution that shapes our practice?

I believe you do have options for challenging the circumstances that lead to the problems you confront. And I believe you have options for creating conditions that permit you to do effective work. In my experience, workers who have acted thoughtfully and purposefully to confront and resolve systemic problems have produced many positive results.

It isn't simple. It isn't impossible. Like any worthwhile professional activity it is challenging, engaging, periodically frustrating, yet often satisfying and potentially exhilarating. Simply putting up with problems is hardly ever gratifying, and although it seems safer, it is not easy. You will receive a fuller measure of professional satisfaction by promoting changes that both you and your clients deserve.

Picking the Hills You Are Going to Fight On

No matter what your primary area of service may be, you will encounter situations that will challenge you to extend your change efforts beyond the immediate problem situation to produce fundamental change. The examples just discussed illustrate the two most likely types of challenges you will face. The first involves pursuing a problem to broader levels to address factors external to clients that contribute to the discomfort your clients are experiencing. This is similar to what a therapist commonly does when pursuing or exploring intrapersonal issues and establishing a therapeutic relationship. Knowing that the "presenting" problem may well not be the "real" problem, he or she must probe deeper to discover the actual source of a client's dissatisfaction, just as you must explore a broad range of external issues that ensnare your client and contribute to dissatisfaction. The second example calls for you to challenge the limitations placed on your ability to perform at the optimum level. If the demands of your job far outweigh the resources you have to do your job (including such intangible things as time and authority), both you and your client have little hope of success. The ongoing frustrations of this situation will eat away at whatever effectiveness you may have—and at you as well.

With every single client you encounter and in any practice environment in which you work you will face problems that need to be addressed through organized action for systemic change. This is a sobering and somewhat intimidating thought. Once you recognize the effects that larger forces have on your clients and the effectiveness of your practice, you will discover many opportunities to participate in meaningful change activities. But guess what? You can't do them all, not even most of them. As a wise professor once told me, "You have to pick the hills you're going to fight on." You do have to fight some battles. At least, I believe you have to.

But be selective about the battles you choose to fight—the decision to fight must be followed by the decision to fight effectively. Taking on all challenges will leave you more exhausted than successful. To say a bona fide "yes" to something means you have to say "no" to something else.

So, how do you choose? Here are some guidelines. Choose an issue you are genuinely interested in (both intellectually and emotionally). Choose a situation you commonly confront. Evaluate whether you can make a meaningful contribution of time, talent, or wisdom. Structure your effort so it has some likelihood of success. Address the problem in an effective way.

Remember that changing one regulation or one agency policy can have far-reaching consequences. You are not responsible for solving all the world's problems, but you can contribute to the resolution of a few. There are a lot of hills out there. Pick yours.

You Have the Theoretical Base

A biologist, Ludwig von Bertalanffy, is credited with being among the first to describe the importance of understanding the interactions among the parts of an organism and between the organism and its environment as keys to understanding the organism itself (Napier & Gershenfeld, 1993). This body of thought has come to be known as systems theory, a way of understanding an organism through the "reciprocal relationships between the elements which constitute a whole" (Barker, 1995, p. 375). The configural approach mentioned earlier in this chapter is one expression of systems theory.

Systems theory has had a tremendous impact on our understanding of human behavior and social development. Prior to this a "mechanistic" approach, rooted in simplistic cause and effect explanations, was often employed. Brill (1998) points out that human services workers have recognized the usefulness of the concept of the individual *in the situation.* However, a fascination with psychoanalytic theory drew attention away from this approach to practice. Brill notes that current perspectives have moved away from these static diagnosis-and-cure concepts to a greater awareness and understanding of the usefulness of the people-in-systems model.

As described in Chapter 2, a systems orientation is fundamental to understanding communities. The framework for action outlines a clear way to analyze situations and make decisions about what you must do as a professional practitioner.

Major Features of a Systems Perspective

A system is a whole made up of interrelated parts (Brill, 1998). These parts exist in a state of balance or equilibrium. When a change occurs in one part of a system, compensatory changes take place throughout the system to establish a new balance. As a result, systems are characterized by dynamic tension—a constant adjustment between the status quo and change.

Each system has a measure of independence but is also linked to larger and smaller systems in a variety of ways. When a change occurs in one system, it will also affect other related systems. When a system fails to receive sufficient inputs, it will go into a state of decline. Conversely, if a system receives too much input, it may be overwhelmed. Both occurrences result in breakdown of the system. Maintaining healthy systems requires constant feedback and adjustment.

Think about some of the systems in which you operate. In addition to your primary system—yourself—you also routinely participate in four broader levels of systems described by Cowan and Egan (1979) as the microsystem, the mesosystem, the exosystem, and the macrosystem.

The microsystems, or personal settings, are the small immediate systems of our everyday lives. These include our family, friendship groups, work settings, and classrooms. The mesosystem, or network of personal settings, in-

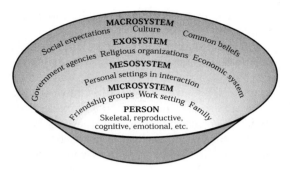

Figure 3-4
Extending systems model

volves interaction of our immediate systems with one another. What happens in one personal system has an impact on other systems. For example, what happens in your family can affect your participation in the classroom. The exosystem, or the larger institutions of our society, does not directly and immediately envelop us but does influence our personal systems and our network of personal systems. The exosystem includes institutions such as government agencies, religious organizations, and the economic system. These systems also interact with one another while they influence our more immediate systems. The macrosystem, or culture, influences all the other systems of our lives and includes our common beliefs, acceptable forms of behavior and social relationships, and our expectations (see Figure 3-4 for a graphic depiction of this model).

A systems orientation is so much a part of social work that it has become part of the definition of that profession: "The practice of social work requires knowledge of human development and behavior; of social, economic, and cultural institutions; and of the *interaction* of all these factors" [emphasis added] (National Association of Social Workers, 1973, pp. 4–5).

When you approach a situation ask yourself these questions:

1. What are the boundaries of the system or systems with which you are dealing?

2. What are the patterns and channels of communication both within the individual system under consideration and among the related external systems?

3. What are the explicit and implicit rules that govern the relationship among the parts, both internally and externally, particularly with respect to input (openness to new ideas or materials), processing (working with all the materials), and outgo (feedback or results of this work)? (Brill, 1998)

Recognizing that clients and client problems are parts of a whole will increase your understanding of client circumstances and your ability to provide help. The basic point to all this is that while systems are affecting people, people also affect systems (Cowan & Egan, 1979).

Applications of a Systems Perspective

All this may sound a little mind-boggling. Here are some ways these basic concepts could apply to situations you might well encounter.

- It may help you to understand that individuals' difficulties can stem from their interactions with other people or other systems and the ways they internally process or handle these interactions.
- It may aid you in working with individuals to process or make use of their interactions with the world around them in a new or different way to help them regain a better balance and achieve growth.
- It may show that people not only can process differently but can also behave differently toward their environment.
- It also shows that individuals can affect their environment, not just be affected by it.
- It explains that the situations clients face are dynamic, not static, and can help you identify opportunities to capitalize on forces working for change to assist clients in using these forces to move the flow of events in the desired direction.

- It may help you in analyzing the interrelationships clients have with their world and in discovering areas in which these interrelationships can be improved; you can then identify various points and various methods of intervention.
- It will enable you to see that a larger, apparently more powerful system can be changed if feedback from subsystems demands it.
- It will remind you that this larger, more powerful system interacts with other systems, equal or even more powerful, and that this also affects the system's balance.
- It will help you to understand that you are part of a system too, a helping (and at times not so helping) system that provides you with both resources and obstacles—a system the client has engaged.
- It can help keep you from being overwhelmed by providing a practical framework for making sense out of what is going on.

When you understand the forces at play, you will uncover many opportunities for beneficial change, including assisting clients to change conditions around them. Your awareness of systems will guide you in selecting the proper context for your action or the points at which you may intervene to help resolve the situation in a way that best meets your client's interests. This may call for you to work toward community or policy change.

You Have the Skills You Need

The notion of promoting community change may sound pretty intimidating, even if you do understand the need for it and its place in professional practice. This may be particularly true if you see yourself as primarily working with individuals or families and you are more comfortable doing that type of work. You may not be confident that you can pull off change in a larger system. You may think you need to develop a whole new set of skills, quite different

from those you use in working with individual problems.

This is a legitimate concern. Which skills, if any, do human services workers commonly have that can be useful in promoting community change? A review of basic skills drawn from a number of social work and human services texts should shed some light on this question. While reading through these lists, consider how each skill could be useful to you as you work for community change.

Schmolling, Youkeles, and Burger (1997, pp. 214–219) identify several characteristics of effective helpers:

Empathy—the ability to see things from another's point of view

Genuineness—the expression of true feelings

Objective/subjective balance—the ability to stand back and view a situation accurately but without becoming detached from personal feelings

Self-awareness—the quality of knowing oneself, including the knowledge of one's values, feelings, attitudes and beliefs, fears and desires, and strengths and weaknesses

Acceptance—the ability to view the client's feelings, attitudes, and opinions as worthy of consideration without necessarily approving of the client's behavior

Desire to help—enthusiasm in promoting the growth and development of others without creating unnecessary dependency; includes a basic belief that those being served do have the fundamental ability to change

Patience—the ability to wait and be steadfast, understanding that different people do things at different times, in different ways, and for different reasons according to individual capacities

Brill (1998, pp. 158–161) identifies six basic skills for effectiveness:

Differential diagnosis—the capacity to understand the uniqueness of the client and the situation and adapt techniques to this uniqueness

Timing—the ability to establish the proper tempo in working with the client, matching the pace of activities with the client's ability to use them, and selecting the crucial point in time to apply interventive techniques

Partialization—the ability to assess the whole situation and break it down into manageable units and help the client think about and decide where to begin

Focus—concentrating both the worker's and the client's efforts on the significant aspect of the situation that requires work and retaining focus until some conclusion has been reached

Establishing partnership—clarifying the association between the worker and the client so that each understands the role and tasks of the other

Structure—establishing the setting and the boundaries that are most conducive to the work that needs to be done and the utilization of an orderly, yet flexible process of problem solving

The National Association of Social Workers (1982, pp. 17–18) has offered the following inventory of skills that are essential to the practice of social work:

- Skill in listening to others with understanding and purpose
- Skill in eliciting information and in assembling relevant facts to prepare a social history, assessment, and report
- Skill in creating and maintaining professional helping relationships and in using oneself in relationships
- Skill in observing and interpreting verbal and nonverbal behavior and in using knowledge of personality theory and diagnostic methods
- Skill in engaging clients (including individuals, families, groups, and communities) in efforts to resolve their own problems and in gaining trust
- Skill in discussing sensitive emotional subjects in a nonthreatening and supportive manner

- Skill in creating innovative solutions to clients' needs
- Skill in determining the need to end therapeutic relationships and how to do so
- Skill in conducting research or in interpreting findings of research studies and professional literature
- Skill in mediating and negotiating between conflicting parties
- Skill in providing interorganizational liaison services
- Skill in interpreting or communicating social needs to funding sources, the public, or legislators

These skills define your talents as a social worker or human services professional, but they do not define the context of your work. They do not imply limitations on what you can do. Just the opposite.

You may easily see yourself applying these skills in helping individuals and families. You may view this activity with some degree of confidence but look with uncertainty on applying these skills to work for community change. Take heart. You don't suddenly lose your abilities. They don't abandon you when you address problems that have larger implications. In fact, the fundamental skills you need to work at the individual level are the same skills you use when you work for community change.

Your ability to use systems analysis will help you make sense of this larger arena of practice. The larger system behaves in much the same way smaller systems do. Your understanding of the principles underlying systems will clarify what you need to do no matter what the size of the practice arena. The way you use your capabilities may vary according to the change effort you are pursuing, but the same fundamental competencies will guide you in your work. Just like any area of practice, your increased experience will help you discover more and more about what you are doing. You will accumulate your own bundle of tricks, and you will borrow some from other change agents. As you enter the arena of community change, you will find that the fundamental skills you possess as a human services worker will help you get the job done. You just need to make the decision to enter, even if only every now and then.

Conclusion

As a human services worker, you will assist people in their efforts to lead full and satisfying lives. You will encounter many obstacles that interfere with that purpose. But, if you take the time to look, you will discover many opportunities that can aid you as well. Efforts directed to community or policy change can remove obstacles and utilize those opportunities for change. These efforts help to further accomplishment of important social welfare goals. Engaging in change efforts is consistent with basic professional practice methods. Your professional values not only support such activity, they call for it. You have the theoretical knowledge to make sense out of the situations you face and to determine effective avenues for intervention. Your training provides you with the skills to initiate and even to pursue action.

You will be challenged to take action. That much is certain. You may not know how you will respond to those challenges, or even if you will allow yourself to recognize them. But if you do so with a sense of purpose and an intent to be effective, you in turn will offer a challenge to conditions that limit human potential.

CHAPTER 4

Putting Yourself in the Picture

Chapter Highlights	

"Things have to change, Ben," Melanie says, staring at the phone, not even looking up. "Babies born so sick, so tiny . . . they just lie there in the hospital for months bonded by tubes to unknowing machines . . . and some just die. In a city like this, how can it be that pregnant women don't get or can't get the medical care they need?"

"Because people allow it to happen, Mel."

"Don't give me that, Ben. What am I supposed to do? Jump up, put on my do-gooder hat, and get things all straightened out?"

"Maybe."

"I'm a single parent with two kids. That's a job in itself. I have plenty to do on my paid job right now. And I work at a place that doesn't believe staff should be dealing with community problems anyway."

"That's right."

"'That's right,' you say, standing there so smug. I hate it when you're like that, Ben." After a moment she looks up at him. "OK, hotshot, I suppose we should start working on this."

"We?"

"Well, you didn't think I was going to do this all by myself, did you?"

———

In Chapter 1 some of the primary elements for understanding the subject of community change were presented. Chapter 2 provided a framework for making use of the underlying principles for promoting change. In Chapter 3 we looked at how this business of promoting community change relates to the profession, its theoretical base, its skills, and its values. Where do you fit into the picture? Can you see yourself working on small or large community change efforts? What do you need to take into account as you take on this challenge? What do you see getting in your way? You will confront a host of questions as you consider initiating change. Your ability to answer these questions will determine whether or not you move past "considering" and on to action. And the way you answer will govern how satisfying your efforts are when you decide to act.

Ben and Melanie have to choose between accepting conditions as they are or putting themselves into the action. Either choice has consequences—for their clients, their families, and themselves, professionally and personally.

Their feelings of satisfaction with the work they do will be influenced by how they handle these decisions.

In this chapter we will explore issues you will routinely address as you engage in the process of change. This is kind of like a video game, with each new situation ready to rob or to increase your power to meet the next challenge. Handling these issues well will increase your sense of accomplishment and add to your effectiveness. Handling them poorly can discourage you from continuing the game.

The simple fact is that when I talk about promoting change, I am talking about you, not about somebody else. You are not just out to understand what this process is about. You are out to understand how you can take part in it. So you need to answer some questions for yourself, questions you will keep answering as long as you actively pursue or avoid pursuing change. All this boils down to your ability to act effectively and to gain a measure of satisfaction from your actions that will enhance, or at the very least not detract from, your personal and your professional life.

Taking Action

You, a human services worker, a change agent. How does it all fit? What does this process require of you?

Five conditions must be met for you to take and sustain action:

1. You have to know that an action is needed.
2. You have to know what action can be taken.
3. You have to feel competent to perform the action.
4. You have to feel relatively safe to do so.
5. You have to receive sufficient encouragement or fulfillment to continue to take needed actions.

Meeting these conditions involves a set of beliefs and abilities, but it also requires thoughtful management of a number of personal matters that can motivate or interfere with your desire to take action.

Recognize the Need for Action

It is hard to act on something unless you see the need to do so. This is a pretty simple concept, but a fundamental one. You could spend your time delivering services oblivious to the fact that things should and can be different. Don't laugh, it happens all the time. Some workers plod along with some vague notion that things just aren't right, but that is as far as they go. They do not have a grasp of the politics involved in selecting the types of services and programs that exist, the extent to which those services are provided, or the manner in which they are delivered. All of these are potential problem areas. If you never consciously stop to think about these things, it is not likely that you will recognize unmet needs with a degree of clarity sufficient to move you to action.

Although it is hard to imagine, some workers just do not perceive that there is a problem to be solved. Others learn to avoid looking or to avoid thinking about what they see. This ability to keep recognition outside conscious awareness requires a degree of work at first. After a while, however, you can become quite good at it, and it will become second nature. Sad perhaps, but common. Recognizing issues means that you will have to identify the current situation as unacceptable, and then you will have to respond.

Responses to Unacceptable Circumstances

Once a problem situation has been identified, you have four options for action (see Figure 4-1). First, you can change your perception by identifying the situation as acceptable. Then you can accept it. Your second option is to leave the situation. This can be done by emotionally withdrawing or by actually leaving. Your third

Take a Moment to Discover . . . .

Think about how you commonly handle problems, even routine problems. The tires on the old Chevy may have little tread left. The landlord promised, for the third time, that he would fix the roof. The people working at the college financial aid office seem to be having a good time joking with each other while you sit, and sit, and sit a while longer. You look at the coins in the palm of your hand and realize that the cashier didn't give you the right change; you are 50 cents short. How do you handle situations like these? How do your various responses leave you feeling?

. . . .

choice is to identify the situation as unacceptable and then try to accept it. This is a common approach—one that leads to a lot of complaining, demoralized workers. Finally, you can

identify the situation as unacceptable and act to change it. Each option has very real consequences, both for you and for your clients. If you allow yourself to see possibilities, there is an implied challenge to do something. Not everyone is comfortable with challenges like that.

You cannot become equally involved in rectifying all the problems you see. Remember, you have to pick the hills you are going to fight on. As you acknowledge the efforts you do make, you will learn what you can work on and what you should let go. Your ability to manage your responses to the situations you encounter is an important skill you will continue to refine. This goes hand in hand with your ability to recognize problem situations in the first place.

Give Yourself Permission to Act

Few halfhearted attempts will be more than halfway successful. If you are going to act on a problem, you have to decide to do so. Allow yourself to believe that you can be successful and behave according to that belief. You will then make the commitment to do the things you think you need to do to accomplish your goal. Remember that you can have several levels of goals, from bringing the matter to the attention of someone in a better position to act to building an organization that will empower people to solve this and other problems. Once you decide to act, you will not just try to do things—you will do them.

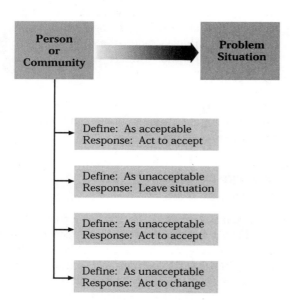

Figure 4-1
Choices for dealing with problem situations

Recognize Your Ability to Promote Change

It is common to think you need to do more than you really have to do. You may feel that you are not up to the task. You may even feel overwhelmed. In fact, a common mistake in both perception and strategy is to think you need to do it all yourself. Sitting here reading this you know that isn't true, yet somewhere down the road you may trick yourself into believing it. For those times ahead, let me offer this reminder: You do not own the problem by yourself, nor should you take sole responsibility for solving it.

Most problems have a number of contributing factors as well as a certain history. You need other perspectives and other resources. That means you need other people. Keeping that in mind, let's consider what you can offer. You have basic helping skills. Build on your strengths, and you will quickly add additional skills that fit this particular circumstance. You really don't need to know everything to get started. You will learn.

The most difficult things to master are the subtleties of empowering others, developing strategy and tactics, and negotiating and maintaining agreements. Perhaps you can think of this as the artistic side of being a change agent; everything else is pretty much a matter of information. You will gain what you need through experience as long as you adhere to two principles. First, cultivate and unlock your creativity. Second, actively seek to discover your ignorance so you can replace it with knowledge.

A particularly valuable set of skills are leadership skills. You may feel confident about your leadership abilities, or you may not yet be able to clearly see your leadership potential. In either case, your leadership abilities will grow with experience and will be important contributors to your success. However, it is also important to recognize that these skills are available in most groups of people. An essential skill you will continue to develop is the ability to draw these leadership qualities from those involved with you in the effort to promote change. As long as you remember that your abilities complement the talents other people bring to the production, you will recognize that you have a multitude of skills at your group's disposal.

Developing Sanction

A critical issue you will face as a change agent is that of gaining sanction for your efforts. This

Take a Moment to Discover . . . .

You can sabotage your own efforts with the things you tell yourself. Or, you can embolden them. Do you really believe you have the *right* to act powerfully? Do you think you have the *ability* to do so? What do you tell yourself about this? The way you answer these questions will dictate what you do. Your actions are a direct response to the messages you send yourself. What are they?

Think of a difficult situation you are currently facing. Identify all the things you tell yourself that could undermine your resolve. Now, identify all the things you can tell yourself that will strengthen your resolve.

Which set of messages do you hear?

• •

involves both the perception that your efforts are legitimate and credible and receiving the approval necessary for you to proceed. Without sanction, your efforts will be met with disinterest or with opposition. First, sanction must come from the people you are organizing. Next it must come from those who have some say over your actions, especially if your activities deviate from what you routinely do or are expected to do. This usually means your employer, if you are doing the work on company or agency time, or your family, if you are doing it on family time.

Gaining Consent from Those Who Must Move to Action

Frequently you will not have sanction when you begin working for change. Two elements are key in gaining sanction. The first has to do with your *standing* and how you project yourself and your intentions. The second involves gaining a measure of *endorsement* from those whose opinion matters to those who will be drawn into the change episode.

What right do you have to take up the issue in the first place? If you are a member of the affected group, you have standing almost automatically. However, if you are not a member, you may need to answer some questions regarding your credentials.

If you take your issue seriously and demonstrate a sense of purpose, you are much more likely to get a favorable response than if you approach your concerns apologetically or doubtfully. You don't have to and shouldn't communicate that you know all the answers, but you should communicate that you think answers can be found and that you are willing to help find them. Further, you need to show that this pursuit is not simply intended to resolve your own personal discomfort. You need to frankly demonstrate your genuine attention to the issue at hand and to the interests of the others involved.

The second step is to find people receptive to your idea and work with them. Obviously, you must start with whomever is available and interested, but the more credible these people are within the group whose sanction you need the better off you will be. These supporters can guide you in establishing a working relationship with others whose backing will be important to the effort. The display of endorsement by opinion leaders can help ease the concerns of the skeptical.

Don't worry about convincing everyone of your sound moral character and the seriousness of your intent. Focus on the people you will be working with or who otherwise are aware of your efforts. In some change efforts this may well involve only a handful of people.

Integrating Your Change Efforts with Your Job Responsibilities

Gaining support from your supervisors and coworkers will make life a lot easier for you (Russo, 1993). If you believe that your efforts are a legitimate fulfillment of your professional agency responsibilities, treat it as part of your job. I realize that this may be more easily said than done.

There are different ways to gain acceptance. One way is to get explicit permission for your involvement. Or, you might try doing some work related to the change and then seek permission for what you have already started. You may become engaged in implementing change without ever getting permission—your role just evolves and becomes accepted. There are potential gains and losses from each approach. You will have to figure out what would work best for you and your situation.

When I can choose equally from these three options, my personal preference is really behind door number two—I like to be able to show something real rather than seek support for an idea. It is easy for supervisors to say no if they don't really know what you are talking about and no real interest has had time to develop. Once some work is under way and the idea has gained some momentum, it is more difficult for a supervisor to turn down a proposal. So I like to get something started.

I also like to get support when I can. It is helpful to have support for your activities if for no other reason than it is less stressful, but it also puts more resources at your disposal. Gaining support from your supervisor is a four-step process.

The best place to start is with what your supervisor is likely to hear.

1. Outline the problem as you see it. Use statistics, specific incidents, and case examples to clarify and dramatize the situation. You want to provoke attention and show that you have done your homework. This is a critical step. If your supervisor doesn't share some of your perception that a problem exists that needs correcting, it is not likely that you will receive support for your efforts to correct it.

2. Describe the response you see as appropriate to resolving the problem, including a description of your role in the process. Briefly identify a few of the obstacles you will encounter and show how your approach addresses them. You do not need to have the exact answer to every conceivable problem, but you do need to demonstrate a willingness to acknowledge and deal with legitimate concerns. In fact, it is usually wise to invite your supervisor to be part of the problem resolution process.

3. Emphasize the philosophy behind your intent to tackle the issue and demonstrate the benefits of your involvement. You may want to show how your proposal relates to the agency mission and your and perhaps your supervisor's professional values. You certainly want to point out how the effort benefits the agency and the clients the agency serves. The more specific and down-to-earth your description the better.

4. Enroll your supervisor in the effort, if only intellectually. You may want to ask for ideas about making the change effort more effective. (Hint: Don't ask what's wrong with your ideas, or your supervisor just may tell you. Your purpose is to get everyone thinking about *how to* do things, not *how not* to do them.) If there is a role for your supervisor to play in the change effort, you may want to identify it.

Anticipate questions and be prepared to respond to them. Throughout your presentation consciously avoid falling into the possibly very attractive trap of showing how your supervisor is ignorant and wrong whereas you are knowledgeable and right.

Be careful about being so committed to a particular course of action that you cannot entertain any different way of doing things. Your supervisor will probably offer some ideas. Remain flexible. This may be a way for your supervisor to put his or her mark on the project, giving your supervisor an investment in its success. Often, suggestions do not pose an either/or dilemma. You can usually incorporate new ideas along with those you had planned to act on. Certainly, don't discount the possibility that you can learn something, that a different perspective can improve on your approach. If you are not open to this possibility, you run the risk of diluting if not rejecting the support you need.

If you really believe the project is a good idea and you need the consent of your supervisor to pursue it, don't take no for an answer. Over time you will develop a variety of skills to keep the process going until you get the answer you want. You will acquire phrases such as: "It looks like I've got a few more things to work on before I come back to you again," or perhaps, "I'll do some more thinking on this over the next week or two before we talk about it again." You may have to get another person or two to repeat the request at another time. You may even need to force the issue through the use of pressure. If it is important, you will learn how to be persistent.

Given that it is helpful to garner support if you can get it, remember that it may be appropriate to pursue your change effort without receiving formal approval. It may be unnecessary for you to seek approval, or the effort to gain approval may be such a major hassle that you end up creating another considerable obstacle that saps your energy and stands in the way of your success.

There may be circumstances in which you not only engage in change-producing activities without permission but do so in a covert or "underground" manner. The fact is that unobtrusive means are often used in promoting change, particularly within organizations. As Brager and Holloway (1978) point out, it is considered acceptable for an administrator to use more indirect means to introduce change, but it is no less ethical for a worker to do so simply because his or her place in the hierarchy may be lower. Brager and Holloway offer some guidelines to help you weigh the appropriateness of your use of covert influence to promote change, particularly within your own agency:

- Unobtrusive means should be used only when the problem the worker has identified compromises the needs and rights of clients or potential clients.
- The actions undertaken by the worker must adhere to the values of social work and other human services professions.
- Workers should employ unobtrusive measures only when the formal organizational mechanisms have already been exhausted

or when, on the basis of past experience, it can be inferred that these formal mechanisms will result in failure.

- Workers must be aware as they begin the change effort that they carry responsibility for any negative consequences that flow from it. The only risks permissible are risks to themselves or risks that clients and colleagues understand and have agreed to share.

Whatever approach you take, it should be a conscious choice based on an honest appraisal of your work situation. Just don't con yourself.

Juggling Your Immediate Duties on the Job

Now that you have decided that your change efforts are a legitimate part of your job and you have gained agency support, you have to fit this in with your other assignments. This usually involves fitting more work into the same amount of time as well as some degree of job restructuring. You may ask colleagues if they are willing to take on some of your duties, but remember you may want them involved in the change effort too. You may decide that certain other aspects of your job will have to wait or not get done at all, otherwise work on the change effort won't get done. You will have to become more efficient at managing your time, but you have to recognize that your involvement requires an investment of time. If you don't acknowledge this and deal with it, you are going to end up feeling frazzled, and you may become unpleasant to be around instead of being the charming person you are now.

Keeping Your Personal Life Happy and Healthy

Promoting change is a fascinating and at times seductive process that can distort your sense of your own importance and the importance (or lesser importance) of other people and other aspects of your life. One of the sad yet common images in this business of promoting change is the portrait of a person gung ho to save the world while losing his or her family in the process. Relationships can suffer through inattention or irritation with conflicting demands. But they don't have to. Relationships may be strengthened, but this requires attention to their importance in both word and deed. Most of the change agents I have known are vital, interesting, and curiously self-centered people. Their vitality and enthusiasm for accepting and meeting challenges make them enjoyable to be around. However, they seem to lose perspective on the importance of commonplace concerns as much of their world revolves around their community activities. This can become tiresome.

Some change efforts, particularly more complex ones, are an imaginative and challenging break from the ordinary. They can take on a life of their own and make the dull, routine matters of everyday job and life a little, well . . . dull and routine.

Organizing a change effort means that you are bringing something new to life. It requires attention and nurturing, involving a new set of relationships or perhaps old ones experienced in a new way. You are already affiliated with a number of groups, each of which demands something of you. Negotiating your way through these competing and sometimes directly conflicting demands is tricky business, especially while you are absorbed with a new set of tasks and relationships. You need to have a sense of which relationships or affiliations are most important to you and which most need your attention. It also means that you need to think about the type of attention each needs.

Situations are dynamic. You can't pull out some magical calculator and precisely assign each group its proper share of your emotional energy and time. Nonetheless, from time to time you should reflect on these various memberships and determine whether your response to them reflects what you believe about their relative importance.

Take a Moment to Discover . . . .

You have a job, you go to school, you spend time with your friends, and maybe you even volunteer a few hours a month. How do you do all this and keep a smile on your face? Well, sometimes you aren't smiling.

Think back over the last year at how many times you had to juggle various responsibilities to do what was important to you. Pick a time when things were going smoothly. During this time, what were you doing or not doing that helped? Now consider a situation when all these activities seemed to be more trouble than they were worth. What were you doing or not doing that was different? What would you like to change about how you act in these situations?

Nobody is going to hear your answer to these next questions but you, so you can be simple, clear, and direct. What do you like to blame other people for that is really your responsibility? And, what do you blame yourself for that is really someone else's responsibility? What would you like to change about how you act in these situations?

You might want to write down your answers.

• •

Common Pitfalls

Handling multiple memberships is certainly not an impossible task; you do it all the time. But it may be helpful to consider some of the familiar hazards to integrating your change efforts with your personal life.

Taking yourself for granted.   You may be used to taking on anything that comes your way, so you decide to take on a little bit more, maybe a lot more. You may find yourself always thinking of things that need to be done. You are too busy

to eat lunch. You don't just sit and visit with people because you feel that you can't afford to spend time not accomplishing anything. You don't learn and retell any new jokes. You stop singing in the shower. And you worry—a lot—about wasting your time.

Maybe you worry about what other people are thinking, and you wonder how you could do more to please them. You stifle your own thoughts lest you be thought of as disagreeable. You respond to others' requests for help but rarely ask for any yourself.

Or, maybe you sell yourself short, measuring your own standards for excellence against those of others who have grown stagnant. You may end up bringing your own standards down a notch or two, conceding to the prevailing mediocrity. You may fall into an attitude that says: "As long as we are doing something, well, that's alright; there is so much to do." Perhaps, then, it is not only your standards you sell short but your capabilities as well.

Taking other people for granted.   This can cut two ways. The first is that you expect others to be as interested and committed to the change effort as you are. They should just naturally understand what you need and provide it, probably immediately, whenever you ask. You project a kind of "drop everything you are doing and take care of me" attitude. Although this is undeniably rude, those around you are usually pretty good at helping you see what you are doing so you have a chance to make some changes.

The other perhaps more common way of taking people for granted is insidious and may be more destructive. This is the practice of ignoring people and not asking them for assistance and input, really not expecting much of them. In the personal realm, this involves not including them in your enthusiasms or fears as well as keeping yourself apart from their world.

Spreading yourself too thin.   After you have gotten a taste of involvement in community change, you see and respond to opportunities everywhere. Your work leads you to other active people who invite you to take part in this or that project. They all seem interesting and important. It doesn't take long before you are up to your hip pockets in commitments. You do a lot of a little bit, scrambling to hold up your end of the deal, without really grabbing hold of anything. You find that you are distracted a lot of the time and your effectiveness suffers, though you can probably continue to put on a good show for a while.

Impatience with routine duties.   If you are not careful, you get to thinking you are pretty doggoned important—if not you personally, at least your work certainly is. You become irritated at heretofore common responsibilities and even at the people who expect you to perform them.

Losing track of your commitments.   You forget that you scheduled an important meeting at the same time you promised your spouse that the two of you would finally take the time for dinner and a movie, with the promise of something more exciting to follow. So much is going on, sometimes so quickly, that your attention becomes focused on the demands immediately before you. Other matters fade into fuzzy afterthought.

Avoiding the Traps and Benefiting from the Experience

Being involved in efforts to promote community change is invigorating. Blending these activities with other important aspects of your life should mean more than just keeping yourself out of trouble. The following hints are basic reminders of things you probably already know. Just remember that they are easily forgotten.

Self-awareness is a prerequisite.   The most valuable thing you have to offer is yourself. The more you are in tune with yourself, the more you can refine and improve your ability to contribute to and benefit from participation.

Pay attention to how you act in and react to various situations. How do you feel about things? What do you think is important? Daily you have many chances to discover a little more about yourself than you now know. Decide to take advantage of these. You will know yourself better next month than you do now, and less well than you do next year. Be willing to learn and relearn. You will need to do both.

Take what you do seriously, but don't take yourself too seriously.   Make no mistake about it, you are important to the success of the enterprise. Things probably won't go "just as well without you." Thinking otherwise may well be an excuse for wishy-washy commitments. Your participation does mean something, but it's not the only thing.

You are going to foul up a time or two, or maybe more. When this occurs, accept the fact and don't waste a lot of energy pretending that you have everything under control and that you always know exactly what you are doing. You don't. Act fully on what you believe in and what you value, according to the best of your ability. At the same time, be able to laugh at yourself. Learn from other people, and keep your contributions in perspective.

Consciously remind yourself of what is important in your life and act on it.   Family, friends, mobile home racing, or whatever is important to you still deserves an active place in your life. You need to spend time on these things. Depending on the particular challenge of the moment, one thing or another will receive more of your attention, but overall the balance of your time should be spent in accordance with what you believe to be important. The way you budget your money is a clear indication of what you value. The way you budget your time is as well.

Understand the demands each membership requires of you.   Each group holds expectations of what membership means. Make sure you know what these expectations are and that they are the same ones you hold for yourself. If not, you may need to negotiate a new set of expectations. Before you take on new responsibilities, consider how new demands on your time fit with your current affiliations.

A couple of reminders could be helpful here. People tend to forget things that they really don't want to believe in the first place. Be prepared to remind others what the extent of your involvement can be. Don't just talk about what you can't do, but do clarify the limits of what you can do.

You may have to clearly decrease your participation in some of your memberships, or end them altogether, at least temporarily. If you are adding a new, significant activity, something has to give. What will it be?

Develop the ability to be in more than one place at a time. Figure out what a group needs from you, and see how they can get it, even if that means they don't get it directly from you. This includes seeing who else can do the things you assume that only you can or should do. (This is an assumption that should be routinely challenged.) Give some thought to what you, and you alone, really need to do and where opportunities exist to involve others. Some tasks really are routine and don't require any special expertise to be handled adequately. Sure, no one can do quite as conscientious a job as you (I hope you don't seriously believe this), but somehow the group will muddle through. When you take on something that someone else can do, particularly someone with fewer responsibilities in the organization, you not only unnecessarily burden yourself but you close off openings for others to contribute, thereby losing the chance to expand the organization's base.

Picture how things that are important to you and to the success of your effort can get done if, either by design or happenstance, you just aren't able to do them.

Resist becoming overinvolved. Once you become active in your community, a number of things will lure your interest. You will be invited to take part in many good and appealing causes. At first you may think this or that is just too good to miss. In fact, a few things are, but not many. Understand that many opportunities will come your way. You can let a few pass by.

Write things down. When you agree to do something, jot it down. Then and there. You will swear at the time that you won't forget, but let a day or two go by and you may well notice this queasy feeling that you are supposed to be doing something but you just can't remember what it is. Keep your tasks and commitments before you in a way that you will remember them and pay attention to them in a timely manner. The easiest way to do this is to write things down.

A brief note here about priorities. You write down or schedule those things that are nonroutine. If you are scheduling things that should be routine—for example, time with your kids—take a second look at what has become routine in your life and what you are trying to fit in.

Avoid Burnout

Effectively integrating your change activities with your personal life will go a long way toward preventing the dreaded disease of burnout. Going through the motions after you have lost a sense of appreciation or worth for those motions and what they are to produce is burnout. It is the loss of the will to challenge or find valued meaning in a situation. Edelwich and Brodsky (1980) describe the phenomenon of burnout as "a progressive loss of idealism, energy, and purpose" (p. 14). Bryan (1980) says that burnout "kills the motivating spirit" that causes people to get involved in social change work in the first place.

Pretty chilly thoughts, aren't they? Is burnout a natural consequence of working in human services? I don't believe so. Avoiding burnout involves managing factors that are within your control and recognizing those that are outside your control. In fact, accepting ambiguity and the need for flexibility may be

SUDDENLY, BILL, WHO TYPICALLY TRIES TO DO EVERYTHING HIMSELF, STOPS SMOLDERING AND SPONTANEOUSLY COMBUSTS AT HIS DESK... LEAVING THREE MORE PROJECTS UNFINISHED.

more healthy than expecting clarity and control in all parts of your job (Meyerson, 1994). Knowing this is one thing; practicing it, another.

Arches (1997) points out that responses to burnout in human services have too often focused on the individual, leading to the perception that the phenomenon is private trouble. Because it affects more than just the individual worker, burnout not only has public consequences but may well be caused by conditions in the workplace and public policies that workers have not effectively challenged. She argues that alleviating burnout requires commitment to social change, a change that invites workers to help one another understand the political nature of their frustration. Working together, in collaboration with the people they serve, human services professionals can create vehicles for instituting change. "Burnout is a call for action" (p. 60).

There are many useful strategies to help you maintain your sense of purpose and renew your spirit. Here are some ideas to consider:

- Develop, recognize, and be able to rely on a strong value base from which you can draw strength. Find meaning and importance in what you do.
- Develop the skills to address the situations you routinely face.
- Develop some "perspective taking" abilities. Don't overvalue your disappointments or undervalue your gains and victories.
- Take care of the things that are important to you personally. Confront what is bothering you.
- Get a life apart from your job or a particular change effort and attend to it.
- Do what you need to do to experience success. Get your work done. You will probably be more intolerant and frustrated

with other people when you don't feel good about your own efforts.

- Make mistakes.
- Don't own others' mistakes.
- Have fun. Enjoy the challenge and the people. Capitalize on the energy the tasks and relationships bring. Every now and again take the focus off the "things that need to be done." Take advantage of opportunities to laugh, be a little silly, or just play.
- Look forward to dessert. Put things in your life that you can look forward to. If you can't see anything really enjoyable in your very near future, a stressful present can be more troubling. But if you know that at the end of the day you are going to a basketball game with your buddy, or going out to dinner with a friend, it will be easier to make it through the green beans the day might pile on your plate.

Corey and Corey (1998, pp. 340–345) provide some additional thoughts:

- Look at your behavior to determine if it is working for you. Setting realistic goals means asking yourself if you are really doing what you want to be doing.
- Look to colleagues and friends for support. Don't try to internalize all your concerns and deal with them alone. And remember, you sometimes get support for yourself when you give support to others.
- Create a support group. You can take the initiative to organize your coworkers for the purpose of listening to one another and providing help. But don't get caught in the trap of using these meetings as mere gripe sessions. With your colleagues you can collectively come up with alternative ways to approach problems and think of new ways to find hope. You can also use this time to get to know your colleagues on a personal level, to have fun with them, to talk about light subjects unrelated to work, and to simply share whatever is on your mind and in your heart.

A final tip comes from Blumenfeld and Alpern (1986):

- Purposefully develop the skill to discover humor in the situations you face.

Some Keys to Personal Effectiveness

You may well be surprised at how much you are able to accomplish once you decide to take on the challenge of change. You will also discover, no doubt, that many people don't play this game very well. They just can't seem to use themselves effectively. You will be surprised at how quickly you can be taken seriously. Some practical pointers can direct you to more productive involvement. You might call these the elemental do's and don'ts for personal effectiveness. These notions refer only to you—to your attitudes and conduct. They are uniquely within your control. They tell you how to use yourself.

Don't set arbitrary limits on yourself.   Plenty of people will tell you what you can't do; there is no need to add to the list. You may give yourself messages that keep you from acting powerfully. These are self-imposed shackles, and they may not be easy to change. (It is likely that you have repeated them to yourself so often that you believe they are true.) By acknowledging disempowering messages ("I don't know anything about this." "I can't do anything about this.") and by repeatedly giving yourself new, more powerful messages ("I know some pretty useful things." "There are a number of things I can do about this."), you have a start. Just remember, the moment you believe you are powerless you will indeed be powerless—emblazon this on your heart.

Don't make excuses.   Aside from the fact that excuses are irritating, they seduce you into a "can't do" mentality. You can easily get used to looking for reasons to explain why you aren't doing what you need to do. This places the control on forces outside yourself, robbing you

Take a Moment to Discover . . . .

Your ordinary ways of looking at, thinking about, and responding to situations provide patterns that can severely restrict your actions. This is a pretty common human condition. You eliminate a host of possibilities simply because you never allow yourself to consider them. And nobody but you did this to you. Furthermore, don't be surprised if you routinely make up rules for yourself about how things work or what you aren't allowed to do. Check to see if barriers are of your own creation. Get in the habit of asking yourself: "Who says so?" To help you get beyond the confines of too rigid thinking, use some creative thinking to solve the puzzle of the nine dots. Can you connect the nine dots below with four straight lines without removing your pencil from the page or retracing any line?

```
•   •   •

•   •   •

•   •   •
```

Did you solve the puzzle? If not, the answer appears at the end of the chapter.

Source: Based on Napier and Gershenfeld, 1993.

• •

of the ability to direct your own actions. If you look hard enough, you can always find a reason you can't accomplish something. Be honest with yourself. "I can't" often means "I won't." Take responsibility for things, and get on with it. You will take yourself more seriously and others will too.

Accept the fact of certain conditions but not the inevitability of them. You can acknowledge the presence of problems or obstacles without giving in to them. "That's just the way things are" can be a self-defeating statement, implying

a kind of permanence about particular circumstances. "That's just the way things are *right now*" provides a much different orientation. Alinsky (1972) reminds us to be realistic radicals—to take the world as it is, not as it should be. Your job is to help move it to where it should be.

Prevent yourself from contracting the disease of being right. Undoubtedly, you will make a strong stand for your beliefs from time to time. You may use the appearance of intransigence as a negotiating ploy. You may secure the high moral ground in an effort to distinguish yourself from an opponent. These are purposeful actions that may well lead to success, but they are different from the disease of "being right." Those so afflicted are unable to consider a perspective different from their own. Their actions are not purposeful so much as they are reflexive. So invested are they in "being right" that adopting a different idea or behavior equals "being wrong," a possibility that is truly frightening and must be avoided at all costs. A lot of energy is wasted in an effort to be right. You usually have to make other people "wrong" in the process. Not only does this limit your learning but it also cuts off the possibility of generating potentially useful agreements. And it definitely makes your company an unwelcomed event. Get in the habit of listening as aggressively as you speak and identifying areas of potential agreement. You can then decide how you want to proceed, and you can act on purpose.

Remember why you are doing what you are doing. Understand that your purpose is to be effective: not cautious, though this may be important; not loud, though this may be necessary; not fired, though this may be fruitful. Your purpose is to be effective.

The Final Five

Aside from all the (possibly) bright ideas this chapter and this book may have to offer, there are five simple things you can do to quickly establish yourself and maintain your credibility: adopt a success attitude, be prepared, follow through, acknowledge people, and say thank-you. Follow them, and you will be far and away more influential than most people you encounter in this business of change. You will notice this quickly.

Adopt a success attitude. You do this all the time in other areas of your life. Maybe you are shopping for that particular birthday present that will bring a look of joy to your child's face. You don't know exactly what it looks like, but you know you will find it. So you keep shopping until you do. Maybe the darn car won't start. You are not sure what is wrong, but you know that if you tinker with this or fiddle with that, you will eventually get the thing going again. You expect to accomplish these things, and things just sort of naturally work out. Assuming you will prevail provides a potent orientation for approaching the challenge before you. It creates a forceful self-fulfilling prophecy that helps you take setbacks in stride and keep going. This is true whether you are shopping, fixing your car, or making things better in your community.

Be prepared. Have a clear picture of the outcome you intend to achieve from each activity in your change effort—a rally, a meeting, or even just a telephone call. Think through what you need to do to achieve that outcome, and get ready to do it. If you need to communicate with someone, don't hesitate to practice what you need to say. You will be much more confident when your message feels right. Often you will need to get information or mull over some facts. Do your homework. When you sit down at a meeting, you will be far ahead of those who are thinking about these things for the first time.

Follow through on your commitments, thoroughly and on time. You will hear the refrain "it's in process" more often than you will ever care to recall. Roughly translated, this usually

means: "Shoot, I forgot I was supposed to get that done until you just now reminded me. I'll get working on that pretty soon, I think." Don't learn that phrase.

Acknowledge people and what they say. This is one of the most eloquent things you can do. By providing people with individual recognition, you meet an important human need. Your ability to acknowledge others enhances you both. As you take others more seriously, you in turn are taken more seriously yourself. It is almost unavoidable. You don't have to agree with someone to acknowledge their point. It is helpful to repeat the message and your understanding of its importance. If you are asked a question, it is a good idea to check with the asker to be sure you answered the question.

Learn people's names and use them.

Say thank-you. Not very complicated, is it? But surprisingly not often consistently done. A "thank-you" allows you to respectfully complete an exchange, and it is noticed and appreciated. It will set you apart.

True, there is more to the business of change than these five simple points, but more than anything else I can think of, paying attention to these points or ignoring them seem to set apart those who accomplish a lot from those who accomplish little. If you remember and put into practice these elementary precepts, you will develop a significant amount of influence and encounter at least a fair amount of success.

Conclusion

Congratulations, you are no longer shouting from the safety of the sidelines. You are in the game. Your commitment reflects your recognition that you have some of the necessary skills and an understanding that new opportunities will help you to learn more. You have decided whose endorsement of your actions is needed, and you are getting that support.

This whole business of promoting change is about doing. It isn't about wishing, though you will have a few wishes. It isn't about hoping, though your hopes will guide your actions. It is about doing, about acting positively to produce a desired result.

You are a change agent. That is a noble thing to be. It truly and unapologetically is. But you are more—an employee, a parent, a partner, a person who likes to sit in the sun with a good book or play yourself into exhaustion on the basketball court. All these personas are important, and you must balance your involvement to nurture them all.

What you offer to any change effort is you—your information, beliefs, insight, intelligence, emotions, and actions. Regardless of the manner or level of your participation, you should reflect on the principles that will guide your involvement in the most powerful and effective way. After all, investing your own time and talent is the most meaningful contribution you can make; you will want to be sure it is well spent.

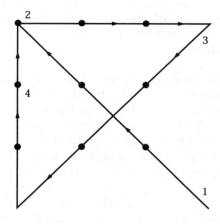

Answer to the nine-dot puzzle on page 76.

Putting the Pieces Together

It will be cold again tonight, maybe more snow. Things look so pretty all covered over with clean, fresh snow. Sarah gazes out her office window at the few remaining patches leftover from the storm three nights ago. Most of the snow has turned to slush— dirty, wet, looking colder. Maybe it will all turn to ice by this evening. The drive home could be dangerous.

What must it be like not to have a home? Where do those people go when the weather is like this? Is the ice better for them or the slush? Sarah shivers, glad the heater in her Chevy will take her warm to her apartment. Some apartments have no heat, she knows. Bills unpaid. Service shut off. In some homes family budgets will keep the heat turned down so low that people keep coats on indoors.

Yes, some people will spend the night in cardboard bedrooms, and some will be hungry, and some will be sick, and some will get drunk, and some will get hit tonight by a "loved" one. Sarah knows what's out there. Sometimes it seems too much.

She thinks about "her" old people. She has been a case manager for over a year now. Almost all her clients are elderly, and almost all of them are alone. All of them used to be children. They used to be teenagers. Back then did they ever think of growing old, of living alone, of being afraid of teenagers? Sarah wishes she could do more for them and for all those problems she can see out her window even with her eyes closed.

How else could a worker spend her time dealing with any one of these problems, she

wonders. If she tried, would she have to squeeze more work into the same number of hours? Could she find a way to make adjustments in her work assignments? Would it all be a burden, or would it be exciting? For a moment she imagines herself working to change things. The picture isn't quite clear, but she can tell she is doing something new. She envisions the faces of some of her old people, and she can see them smiling. Why? What's different? Sarah notices that she too is actually smiling just thinking about it. Why?

Picking up the ringing phone, Sarah dismisses the thoughts. It's time to get back to work. The response to her hello comes from Greg Danory, another case manager.

"What's up, Greg?"

"I've been talking with Jo Ann Handford, a counselor at

Davis Junior High. She wants to work with us on a program to have some of the junior high kids visit some of the elderly people in the neighborhoods around the school. They might do a little yard work and some shopping from time to time. Or they might just visit. She would like to meet next week to talk about it some more. What do you think?"

"Well, Greg, I think that's a start."

After a few more minutes of conversation, Sarah puts the phone down and once again looks outside. Even though the scene appears bleak, Sarah is glad she has an office with a window.

———

Maybe Sarah will work to bring junior high school students and elderly citizens together in a way that benefits both groups. Maybe she will work to change utility company policies to keep families warm on cold winter nights. Maybe she will develop socialization activities for people who otherwise would have almost no human contact. In undertaking any of these efforts, what would Sarah need to know if she is going to work to bring about change?

Part 2 will provide a number of answers to that question and give you a strong foundation to build on. As a worker involved in promoting community change, you will learn quite a lot simply by experience. However, having a foundation to build on will make learning easier and success more likely.

Learning how to acquire information quickly, use information, and connect with other change agents can provide a solid foundation to your efforts. Chapter 5, Taming the Green-Eyed Monster: Using Information and Communication Technology, provides an overview of the Internet and the World Wide Web and shows you how to use these resources. You will be introduced to a number of applications that can help you keep records, mobilize people, and make effective presentations. You will see how technology can help you keep members of your group in touch with each other, and how to make your presence felt.

It is helpful to know about your community. Chapter 6, Knowing Your Community, contains a number of perspectives on communities and key community characteristics. You will increase your awareness of how communities function to meet their needs. Methods for discovering unmet community needs and unrecognized resources will be offered, and you will understand the importance of recognizing a community's capacity to change.

Change is produced by the use of power, and it is helpful to know that you can develop and use power responsibly. Chapter 7, Power, describes the concept of power and its use in promoting community change. You will learn how to recognize who has power in a community, and you will be introduced to techniques for building your own power. One essential aspect of community change, empowering others, will be examined in that chapter.

Chapter 8, Powerful Planning, explores the importance of planning and shows you how to prevent planning from being a colossal waste of time. Each step in the planning process is described with an emphasis on making planning activities useful in the real world. You will learn to identify and deal with potential pitfalls to effective planning.

Chapter 9, People—The Most Valuable Resource, will examine ways to attract people to your change effort and ways to maintain their participation. Because most people involved in community change efforts volunteer their time, working with volunteers will be discussed. You will be offered some perspectives on the importance of recognizing and valuing cultural differences while acknowledging similarities among people of all cultures. You will be presented with some reflections on how people respond to various challenges inherent in working for change, which will help you anticipate problems and strengthen commitment.

Chapter 10, Raising Other Resources, looks at how you can obtain needed items or services for little or no money and how you can raise the money you do need. You will increase your understanding of methods for generating support from individuals and organizations. Particular fund-raising techniques will be explained, including a description of writing and submitting grant proposals.

Chapter 11, Getting the Word Out, details various methods of communication with the members of your own organization and with the public at large. You will learn how to use low-cost publicity techniques, and you will be provided with guidelines for working with both print and electronic media.

Chapter 12, Building the Organized Effort, takes you through the steps of developing an organization. You will learn the importance of issues and how to use them to provoke and maintain action. You will understand how much structure your organization needs and how you can modify or replace unproductive procedures. (*You* may mean not only you as an individual but also all the people with whom you are working. Also, you don't own *your* organization, but it is an organization of which you are a part,

perhaps a very important part.) Much of the work of organizations is really the work of small groups, so significant attention is given to matters of group process. As a change agent, you will conduct many meetings, and guidelines for running effective meetings are offered. You will examine different types of organizations and their purposes, and you will learn about the process for formally incorporating an organization.

Chapter 13, Taking Action—Strategies and Tactics, is the final chapter in the section. Basic strategies and tactics for implementing action are described along with a discussion of the strengths and limitations of various approaches. You will consider some fundamental ethical issues involved in your decisions to take action or to refrain from action. You will gain some insights on the strategies and tactics that may be used against you by an opponent. A final list of "commandments" is presented to keep you on the right track.

In actual practice many things occur almost simultaneously to build and strengthen an organized change effort. Involving people, acquiring other resources, and developing issues are all part of the process of putting together an organization that can make its presence known and take action. You really won't be working on one aspect of the effort in isolation from another. All these elements relate to one another. Artificially separating these elements provides us with a chance to give each element closer inspection. This tends to be how things work in textbooks. Understand that this is not how things work in the world in which textbook readers live.

What may have started out as a vague dissatisfaction, or even outrage, will, as a result of your commitment, turn into something more important and more potent. As you move toward accomplishment, you will notice that you will have brought something into existence, given something life. You will cultivate a group of people who will be involved in doing things on purpose. The way that they relate to one another and the way the things they do relate to each other will produce change.

CHAPTER **5**

Taming the Green-Eyed Monster: Using Information and Communication Technology

Chapter Highlights

- ✥ Basic benefits of using information technology
- ✥ Introduction to the Internet and the World Wide Web
- ✥ An adequate computer
- ✥ Other helpful equipment
- ✥ Learning about your community
- ✥ Learning about your issue
- ✥ Question the validity of information you find
- ✥ Mailing lists
- ✥ Database programs
- ✥ Spreadsheet programs
- ✥ Record keeping
- ✥ Personal information manager

- ✥ Making presentations easier and more compelling
- ✥ E-mail
- ✥ Networking with other activists
- ✥ Electronic discussion groups
- ✥ Newsgroups
- ✥ Electronic forums
- ✥ Chat rooms
- ✥ Making your own Web page
- ✥ Tactics for impressing an opponent
- ✥ Establishing a hot line
- ✥ Helpful publications
- ✥ Training

Befuddled and fiddling with the knot on his unaccustomed tie, Ben looks at the keyboard, stares at the blank screen, and looks back at the keyboard again.

"I understand that you can get those things to work much better if you turn them on, Ben." For the last few minutes Melanie has been standing at the doorway watching Ben's flirtations with the computer. "A tie even. Goes well with your jeans. Did you get all dressed up just to ask your new computer to dance?"

"No, I've got a presentation to make to the board this afternoon, and I thought I'd get on the Internet to see if I could find out what other people in the country are doing," Ben replies with more than a hint of testiness. "In a brief moment of optimism I thought I could use that presentation program you're always talking about to make some fancy overheads too. You make it look so easy. I guess, I'm not sure how to get started."

"Well, actually, for what you're talking about it is pretty easy. Want me to show you a few things?"

"Yeah, as long as you promise to use English, or at least some language that regular people actually speak."

"OK. It's good to see that you are finally trying to expand your horizons. You'll be surprised at what you are going to be able to accomplish. Not that you have ever had any doubt about all the marvelous things you can do."

"Could you please just explain how this thing works?"

———

To a large extent, information is power. Your ability to acquire, manage, and use information will fortify your endeavor and help clarify your direction. Information technology provides you with tools to gather and communicate information, sort through and analyze information, use information in decision making, and store information for future use. You can use technology to automate and simplify your work. In so doing, your efforts will become more focused and efficient, and you will be better equipped to create new collaborative relationships and strengthen existing ones.

Ben is about to acquire a whole new set of skills to add to what he already can do. He is like a lot of people in human services who are a little wary about all this technology stuff. At one level he knows it will help him tremendously. At another, he doesn't want to take the time to learn and risk looking foolish in the process.

Some of you may be very familiar with computers and other information technology, but others of you still regard the computer as the green-eyed monster. In this chapter I will discuss some very basic information and communication tools. For those of you who are practiced in their use, this material will serve as a reminder of the power you have at your fingertips. For those of you who are still a bit uncertain, this chapter will introduce you to the potential benefits of mastering a few simple steps that are easy to learn.

One unique feature of information technology is that many of these tools actually teach you how to use them as you go. Help and instruction is provided while you are using them, and you can ask questions to help you figure things out. Few hammers and screwdrivers come so equipped. It is easy to get started, and you can save a lot of time once you master some very basic skills.

Information technology can benefit you in a number of ways. For instance, information technology can:

- Help you learn more about your community
- Help you understand your issue better
- Assist you in keeping good records
- Aid in decision making
- Help you network with other like-minded individuals
- Increase the frequency and clarity of communication among members of your group
- Brighten your public presentations with more sparkle

Computer and other information technology products are expanding rapidly, with new discoveries ushering forth almost daily. Even those who work exclusively in this area can't seem to keep ahead of it all. How can you possibly keep pace? In this rushing history of our information age, what is most important is that you get started—if you haven't already. If you learn the basics of how your efforts can be strengthened through the use of technology, you have taken a huge step in effectiveness. You can continue to develop your knowledge and skills when the need and the interest arise. As a community change agent, you don't need to learn all there is to know just because it's out there. That's impossible anyway. But you will be a more effective change agent if you take time to learn what you need to know.

You can learn a tremendous amount on your own just by doing your work and by playing around and trying out a few new things. You will also see that it is pretty easy to find someone more expert than yourself who is willing to show you a few more tricks. Of course there are more formal sources of information, such as training and publications, which are briefly described later in this chapter.

Using technology to gather ideas and information through the Internet or by communicating with other change agents throughout the country is a powerful asset. It complements, but does not replace, other methods of discovery and communication. The library still stores valuable resources and employs full-time guides (called librarians) who can make your search easier. Conversations with community members will yield insights you won't find written anywhere at all. And daily or weekly newspapers remain an easy way to keep up with current events. Information technology provides some very powerful tools to add to your collection, which can make some of your old tools work even better.

Introducing the Internet

The number of people using the Internet continues to increase dramatically. Installation of second phone lines in homes—largely to provide access to the Internet—is growing at more than 20% per year, and by the year 2001 almost 30% of all U.S. homes will have second phone lines installed ("Zoom," 1997). Estimates place the number of Internet users in 1997 at 120 million people worldwide, a dramatic

A FEW WEB SITES TO GET YOU STARTED

The Well at *www.well.com* is one of the best sites for wide-ranging information on activism. Whitehead and Maran (1997) also provide a list of useful Web sites. Here is a sample of contacts you can make.

Libary of Congress: *lcweb.loc.gov*
EdLinks: *webpages.marshall.edu/~jmullens/edlinks.html* (This site provides links to a tremendous variety of educational sites.)
EnviroLink Network: *envirolink.org* (This site provides a wealth of environmental information.)
Greenpeace: *www.greenpeace.org* (This site links you to information provided by one of the world's most activist environmental organizations.)
Recycler's world: *www.sentex.net/recycle* (This site provides information on recycling.)
World Wide Web Resources for Social Workers: *http://pages.nyu.edu/~holden/ gh-w3-f.htm* (This site connects you with an incredibly extensive array of social work related information—advocacy groups, professional literature, schools of social work, and much more.)
PCL Map Collection: *www.lib.utexas.edu/Libs/PCL/Map_collection/Map_collection.html* (This site links you to a huge map collection.)
www.policy.com (This site provides access to policy positions of think tanks, advocacy groups, business, and government, along with links to chat rooms and bulletin boards, which allow you to make connections with other advocates.)
U.S. House of Representatives: *www.house.gov* (You can get information on legislation as well as on House committees.)
U.S. Senate: *www.senate.gov*
Thomas Library: *thomas.loc.gov* (This is a great source of information on legislation.)
White House: *www.whitehouse.gov*
Centers for Disease Control: *www.cdc.gov* (This site will provide you with information on specific diseases and other health issues.)
The Body: *www.thebody.com* (This is a good source for information about HIV and AIDS.)
World Health Organization: *www.who.ch* (You can get more information on health-related issues.)
Top 100 Newspapers: *www.interest.com/top100.html* (At this site you can get connected to the nation's top 100 newspapers.)
USA Today: *www.usatoday.com* (You can get national news of the day here.)
Yahoo! News: *www.yahoo.com/headlines/current* (This is a source for current news.)
CNN: *www.cnn.com* (This site provides updates of current news as well as video clips.)
Simpsons Archive: *www.digimark.net/TheSimpsons/index.html* (Check out this site in case you miss Bart and the gang.)

---

increase from the 18 million users just four years earlier (Simons, 1996).

The number of users continues to grow, and so does the amount of information available. The World Wide Web was adding more than a million "pages" of content each month as early as 1996 (Flynn, 1996), and the Internet was doubling in size every three months (Egan, 1996). The pace of growth on the Web is leading to a reworking of the Web's mechanism, and is even leading to proposals to develop a new Internet (called Internet II) for the scientific and research community (Randall, 1997). With all this information and so many people ready to make use of it, the Internet and the World Wide Web have become extremely valuable to people hoping to make a difference in their communities. In fact, it is possible that the Internet will be the dominant political medium by the year 2000 (Sussman, 1996).

The Internet is a network of fairly large computers connected through phone lines and satellite links that handles traffic from the smaller computers you and I use. Educational institutions, corporations, governments, and other Internet providers have computers with tremendous capacity and incredible speed. You have access to the Internet when your computer connects to one of these large computers that is already connected to the Internet (O'Neal, 1996).

Technically, the World Wide Web is not the machinery but the graphical tools and philosophy of making information available to a worldwide audience (O'Neal, 1996). The notion is that, like a giant spider web, any particular point or node is connected to every other node. So everybody is connected to everybody. With use of the World Wide Web, essentially the graphical portion of the Internet, becoming more commonplace, the terms *Web* and *Internet* have become almost interchangeable.

If you don't particularly like the notion of webs, imagine that you have been dropped at the front door of a huge mansion with room upon room upon room of things you might want. You have a map of the basic rooms and what you will find in each, so you start looking in various rooms. Each room has a number of doors that open into even more rooms with more goodies and yet more doors. You may only need to go into one or two rooms to get everything you need. After all, if you just need to go into the kitchen to get a frying pan or something from the fridge, you don't have to go looking in the bathroom or searching the

upstairs bedroom. Then again, you may have such a good time seeing what you can find in each room that you spend the entire afternoon just looking around.

You can get from a room on one side of the mansion to another miles away (it *is* a very big mansion) either by going from room to room or by taking one giant leap that brings you to the place you want in an instant. This magic allows you to jump from one thing you want to the next to the next, and so on, skipping everything in between that you don't want. This is similar to looking specific things up in a book's index. You find that your topic is discussed on pages 193 and 407, and you may need to read only those passages to find what you want. You don't have to read the whole book.

By the way, don't worry, you probably won't get lost. Along with your basic map you get a new map with each room, and one of the doors always leads to the outside, and one takes you right back to the last room you were in. So you can leave at any time.

A Web browser serves as the window that opens to the treasures of the Internet. NetScape and Internet Explorer are the two major Web browsers. (For all practical purposes any Web browser can connect you to any information available on the Web.) The Web browser can connect you directly to a specific site if you know the address for that site. Each site has its own address on the Web, which appears as a series of letters separated by periods (for example, *www.brookscole.com*). This address is called a URL (short for "uniform resource locator"), and it allows you to gain direct access to that site. This is really a numerical address, but to make things easier for you and everyone else to remember, letters are used in place of the numerical code your computer actually reads. The suffix for each address identifies the type of operation involved. For example, *.gov* means government, *.com* means company, *.edu* indicates an educational institution, and so on.

If you do not know a specific address or if

you just want to explore, your Web browser can connect you to one of the search engines that can take you to any of the sites that deal with the specific topic you are researching. These search engines are basically giant indexes that organize information. They are really just another Web site that performs this specific function. Some of the larger ones go by names such as Alta Vista, Excite, Infoseek Guide, Yahoo!, or Lycros. They are constantly combing through the Web identifying and indexing new sources of information that are being born. Search engines help make this vast amount of information much more manageable by providing various subject categories to better guide your journey. They also include a number of small, specialized search engines that organize information of a particular nature.

There is a burgeoning number of search services, some fairly broad and some that serve very specific interests. There are even some sites, such as Search.com (*www.search.com*) and All-In-One (*www.albany.net/allinone*), dedicated to identifying and organizing these various search services for you (Egan, 1996). It doesn't much matter which search engine you use; they all serve the same purpose, although you may find one that has features you like more than others.

Once you have connected to your search engine you can go to one of the subdirectories to explore a particular category, or you can type the name of the specific topic you would like to investigate. If you request a specific topic, you will be shown a list where information you are looking for may be found. These sources of information are known as Web sites. They are like the rooms in that mansion. The list of Web sites will include a brief description of the information you can find at that site, the title of the site, and the address for contacting the site directly. In addition to the address for each site, you will get the home page title. (A home page is a one-page introduction to the Web site, similar to the table of contents of a book, and it can also give you links to other home pages.) You can also get to Web sites by following the options offered to you through the search engines.

All you need to do is look over the list of sites and decide which sites are likeliest to provide the information you want. Then point to the site and click to see what they have there. Each site can guide you to more and more specific points of information.

You will probably find a number of favorite Web sites. Both Netscape and Internet Explorer have an easy way to keep a list of these sites, saving the address so you can go to them quickly without going through the steps you took to find them in the first place.

Getting Started

To connect to the Internet you need four things: an adequate computer, an Internet connection,

---

Basic Information Technology Toolbox

Computer hardware:
computer, keyboard, printer, monitor, mouse, CD-ROM player, fax/modem
Other useful components:
scanner, voice recognition

system, video camera
Computer software: word processor, communications software, Web browser, personal information manager, personal money

manager, database, spreadsheet, presentation graphics
Internet service provider
Telephone
Messaging service

an Internet service provider, and communications software with a Web browser. Before we take a closer look at each of these elements, you should know that making this connection can be as simple as getting a decent computer and modem and subscribing to a company that links you to the Internet, using software that is provided for that purpose. To fully utilize the potential of the Internet and the World Wide Web, it is nice to have your own connection and equipment, but that may not be within your reach. If you cannot bear the expense, it is very likely that you can gain access to the Internet through your public library. Connections to the Internet through public libraries are increasing rapidly (Freierman, 1997), and college students generally can link up through their computer center or library.

An adequate computer.   Somehow this seems like a quaint concept. It is hard to pin the label "adequate" on a tool as complex and as rapidly changing as a computer. With advancements in technology accelerating at a dizzying pace, both new software and computer users themselves are placing more demands on the machines. The types of uses you anticipate for your computer and the speed you expect figure into the determination of what is "adequate" for you. Factor in cost and you can make the search a little more challenging.

For our purposes an "adequate" computer for browsing the Internet and doing basic record management is one that can load and run popular software without your feeling that you could take a lunch break between screen changes. It is a good idea to choose a computer that can be upgraded for more complex future uses. Finally, though it may wound your finances a bit, choose a computer that doesn't cost you an arm and a leg. If you were to walk into a computer store to purchase that adequate computer, you would find two basic choices and a variety of features you might ask for:

Choice A

Microsoft Windows® 98 operating system
Pentium/166 processor
16mb of RAM (memory)
1.2gb hard drive
SVGA monitor
2mb video RAM
CD-ROM player with soundcard and speakers
28.8k fax/modem (56k may become the standard)
Keyboard
Mouse
Color Ink Jet Printer

Choice B

Macintosh® operating system 7.5
PowerPC/80 processor
16mb of RAM (memory)
500mb hard drive
Apple Monitor
CD-ROM player (soundcard and speaker are built in)
28.8k fax/modem (56k may become the standard)
Keyboard
Mouse
Color Ink Jet Printer

Although less of a configuration would work and more is certainly better, either of these computer packages would provide a basic comfort level to start with.

Like beauty, cost is in the eye of the beholder. If you cannot get an adequate computer system or parts of the computer system donated, an entire ensemble, such as the ones assembled here, can be purchased for around $2,500.

You may decide to add some other helpful, though nonessential, pieces of equipment to your package. A scanner can save or send text from a book, for example, so you don't have to type long passages. A scanner will also allow you to store and transmit pictures. Some full-service copy centers offer scanning services; this may be less expensive than buying a scanner if your need is only occasional.

The modem that comes with your computer also operates as a fax machine, so you can fax documents already on your computer and use a scanner to send other documents. Your fax/modem also receives faxes, which you can view on your computer screen. Then, using your printer, you can print those messages.

Another nice item is a voice recognition system, which allows you to speak into your computer rather than having to type your words of wisdom. Those among us who are keyboard challenged may find this relatively inexpensive device an important help in using a computer.

An Internet connection. Now that you have your computer, you need an Internet connection. For most people this means having a modem, which has become a standard item on computers. A modem allows your computer to send and receive data along telephone lines. A modem is analogous to the phone you have sitting on your desk. Your voice sends signals into the mouthpiece of the phone. Those sounds are converted into signals that can be sent along telephone lines to the phone of the person you are talking with. Then those signals are reconverted back into the sounds of your voice, which can now be heard through the receiver your friend is holding to his or her ear. A modem converts computer signals in much the same way so that they can be sent along the telephone lines and reconverted by the receiving modem back to signals recognized by the receiving computer. In this way computers can talk with each other. If your modem is slower than 28.8 kilobits per second, you may spend your time waiting around as you try to use the Internet. It may well be worth it to spend some money to replace a slow modem.

Using telephone lines to transmit data may soon pass into history because telephone lines are much slower than coax or fiber optic cable lines, which are supplied by your local cable television company. Unless telephone companies improve their technology, many home computers will probably be connected to TV cable fairly soon (Egan, 1996; Gitman, 1998; Hoye, 1997b; O'Neal, 1996; Thomas, 1997; Wichner, 1998; Wiener, 1996).

If you use a computer at work or at school, you may have a *direct connection,* which eliminates the need for a modem. More work-places are being wired for direct connections as are most colleges.

An Internet service provider. Your computer and modem need to be linked to an Internet service provider (ISP). The ISP provides the computer link to the World Wide Web. Some ISPs, particularly those serving a local area, simply provide you with the link to the Internet, whereas others provide a more comprehensive array of services. The largest full-service ISPs are America Online (AOL), CompuServ (owned by AOL), Prodigy, and Microsoft Network (also called MSN, which requires Windows 95.) Like a cable television company, each of these will have a package of basic services along with a package of premium services. Many charge a flat access fee per month. These companies also have the added benefit of providing customer support to help you when you encounter problems.

Communications software with a Web browser. The last piece you need to make all this work is communications software with a Web browser. Most individual users subscribe to one of the full service ISPs mentioned here. Each of these supplies their own software package, which includes a Web browser.

Once you have these pieces in place, you are ready to connect to the Internet. All you have to do is turn on your computer, click on the icon showing on your screen, and begin surfing.

Learning About Your Community

Typically each local government will have a home page Web site that describes government functions as well as how to directly contact the particular service you might need. Budget information, city services, and even agendas of upcoming meetings are routinely provided. Some communities have detailed and very

Take a Moment to Discover . . . .

Search the Internet and see if you can find the following things in 20 minutes:

- Agenda for the next city council meeting
- Name of the person in charge of the city or county budget
- Number of registered Democrat, Republican, Libertarian, and Green party voters in your county
- Names of three organizations in your community that deal with an issue that concerns you
- Names of three religious organizations, each a different faith
- A map that shows exactly where your house or apartment is

. . . .

useful information, whereas others provide only a general overview. However, each will lead you to other sources of more specific information.

You can easily get maps of neighborhoods or of the entire community. You can locate businesses, schools, or places of worship. History, community events, and key environmental features are typically available. Some cities provide detailed descriptions of neighborhoods along with the names of neighborhood leaders and ways to contact them. You can find out about various community organizations and associations, major employers, and current community issues. Hunting with your faithful mouse can lead you to quite a bit of information. Using any one of the search engines mentioned, you can get a good start just by typing in the name of your community.

You can obtain valuable data on the makeup of your community by linking up with the Census Bureau (*www.census.gov*). If you want to find out more about candidates running for federal and state offices, including campaign finances and ratings by various interest groups, see what the nonpartisan Project Vote Smart (*www.vote-smart.org*) has to offer. Other useful sources of information for most communities include the local Chamber of Commerce and colleges and universities that serve the area.

Change Agent Tip

A number of regional Web guides can lead you to new discoveries about your own community. Though most seem to have an entertainment orientation, they also provide some useful facts and news items. Regional guides fall into two categories: content providers or link aggregators. Content providers use their own editorial staffs to produce their own reviews. They provide a sense of local character to the information they offer. Link aggregators, such as those offered by search engine companies like Excite, Lycos, and Yahoo!, connect you to a variety of sites, giving you a broader range of information, although perhaps less depth. Most content providers focus on a few major cities, whereas some link aggregators can direct you to any ZIP code area in the country (Lidsky, 1997).

Some of the regional guides you may want to check out include:
CitySearch
   (*www.citysearch.com*)
City Sites by CIM
   (*www.cimedia.com*)
CityView (*www.cityview.com*)
Digital City (AOL keyword: Digital City
   [*www.digitalcity.com*])
DiveIn (*www.divein.com*)
Excite City.Net (*city.net*)
Lycos City Guide
   (*cityguide.lycos.com*)
Pacific Bell At Hand
   (*www.athand.com*)
Sidewalk (*www.sidewalk.com*)
Yahoo! Metros
   (*www.yahoo.com*)
(Bannan et al., 1997)

Change Agent Tip

Caution: A few words about all that information. Not all of it is valid. That is to say, not everything on the Internet has been held up to any standard of rigorous scrutiny. So be careful and be willing to confirm information you are using to support your position or to justify a particular project.

Learning About the Issue

The Internet is also a powerful source of information regarding the issues you are working on. Somebody else out there has probably thought about, worked on, and written about the same kinds of things that challenge you and your organization. Using the subject categories to get you started, you can track down reams of information on most topics. For example, you may want to know about efforts to prevent juvenile delinquency, how Regional Development Authorities work, or ways to increase the number of prenatal visits for high-risk pregnancies. You have access to these and thousands of other topics with a few well-placed clicks of your mouse.

Some Web sites provide valuable statistical information. For example, the federal government offers statistics gathered by 70 agencies on a diverse range of topics. You can start mining that wealth of information by linking with *www.fedstats.gov.*

To save time and get the kind of information you can use, remember the experts you have right around you. Although it is helpful to get and review a sample of information available through the Internet, a few conversations with people who have had some experience in the area will help you make better sense of the information you are able to obtain. These conversations will also help you organize your questions so that your search along the Web can be more focused. There is a tremendous amount of information available, and you can spend a great deal of time—and more than a little

frustration—trying to sort through what might be helpful and what is not.

If you can continue your conversations with more expert or experienced local people in tandem with your Internet explorations, by all means do so. You can continue to refine your search, make sense of the information you receive from them as well as from your computer connections, while building important relationships with people who can give you guidance.

Not only will you be able to gather new insights and information but you will be able to identify very good sources of information as well. These sources will be individuals and organizations who will have more to tell you than what you can read on your computer screen. You will be able to get a number of valuable phone numbers and addresses (E-mail and Pony Express) to give you direct access to people in the know. Pick up the phone. A 15-minute conversation is an inexpensive way to gain insights that can't be found in material written for a more general audience. It also gives you a chance to get your specific questions answered. Personal contact with others involved in similar concerns has an added encouraging and energizing effect.

The various search engines will use different techniques for narrowing your search. Do a little experimenting and playing around. You will soon pick up a number of tricks to get you to your target more quickly.

You need not go tromping along the information super highway to get information about a subject that is of fairly routine interest to you. For example, those interested in local, state, and national legislative action may subscribe to services that will let them know what legislation is being introduced and will track legislation as it moves through the process. Most of these services deal with a particular level of government action, such as state legislative action. Some will have a particular issue focus, such as education. Others will include everything. Numerous national organizations send out daily or weekly updates on developments affecting their area of concern. And some customized, personal services will keep you updated about particular topics you specify.

You can subscribe to on-line newsletters and other on-line services to keep regularly informed. Organizations use automatic mailing list managers such as LISTSERV, Majordomo, and Listproc to keep in touch with those interested in their issues. This feature allows an organization to disseminate information to those on their electronic mailing list. Many advocacy organizations utilize this technology. For example, the National Education Association (NEA) has a biweekly bulletin that provides news of important bills passing through Congress. To get this bulletin you must subscribe by sending a one-line E-mail message to *majordomo@cet.nea.org* that simply says: *subscribe hecongress.* The National Association of Social Workers has a free mailing list to inform their constituency of advocacy efforts related to government relations, political affairs, policy, and practice. Again a two-word E-mail message sent to *list@discuss.naswdc.org* can get you plugged in. To subscribe you send the message: *join advocacy.*

It would be worthwhile to check with advocacy groups dealing with your issue, particularly state and national organizations, to see if they have such a service. Many of these are free, although some charge a subscriber's fee.

Most mailing lists allow you to send and receive messages. But some, such as those often distributed by organizations, only let you receive information.

Take a Moment to Discover . . . .

Subscribe to one advocacy organization's mailing list. In the first two weeks after receiving information from them, work one thing you have learned into three different conversations.

Other forms of information technology can help you get a better handle on issues and guide you in your organizing efforts. You can use database software to make comparisons among sets of information that you might gather through surveys or other means to help you identify issues around which you might organize. It can also help you target your organizing efforts. For example, you can collect information on the various concerns of members of a community to find out which issues affect the most people or which issues people feel most intensely about. By comparing information from the respondents to information on issues, you will be able to determine which issues affect certain groups of people more than others.

Let's say that you are organizing in a certain area of town. You might discover that although most of the people living in the area are concerned with loud parties and crack houses, what they really get fired up about are speeding cars. You may discover that women in particular feel strongly about this, as do residents living on a certain set of streets. This information can give you some clues about which issues you might want to start working on.

In that same area of town you might be able to uncover other clues to problem situations. Maybe you associate certain problems with certain property characteristics. You realize that most of the run-down properties are owned by the same landlord, who can become the target of organizing efforts. Or maybe you can show the city council that problems such as vandalism or burglary are clearly associated with the presence of abandoned buildings.

Linking issues or preferences with certain

groups of people, you might attract the interest of funding sources or other groups outside the immediate community whose support you need. Your data, for example, may demonstrate that certain conditions more keenly affect older people, or that teens share a common view about new directions the community could take. Your ability to demonstrate these relationships could bring you new insights, new allies, and new dollars.

These are but a few of the many ways you can use database programs to help you recognize and analyze issues, assets, and other factors that can shape your community. Gathering and comparing fields of information will yield a picture of what is occurring or might occur within your community.

You really can get a picture. Once the data have been summarized and you have established the relationships you want to look at, spreadsheet programs can turn the numbers into a variety of charts and graphs to help you visualize what the information may be telling you. All you have to do is put in the information you want, choose from a multitude of chart types, and click. In an instant you will get a picture of your data presented on the screen. If this picture doesn't grab you, select another chart type. You have many, many to choose from.

Database programs sort, query, and report on large amounts of information. Microsoft ACCESS and FileMaker Pro (for Macs) work well. Spreadsheet programs, such as Excel (for both PCs and Macs), work well for numerical calculations and for making graphic displays. Spreadsheet programs also come with a myriad of statistical functions built in.

Using programs like these does require familiarity with computer terminology and routine functions. Though a novice might find these a little intimidating, more experienced computer users will be able to learn how to use this software fairly easily.

None of this is really magic, of course. The quality of your analysis is affected by the quality of the information you gather to begin with. It is also affected by the nature of the questions you ask of the information. Technology will help you come up with answers quickly and represent them more clearly, but it cannot determine what data to collect. Nor will it collect the data for you. But it can count it, compare it, and display it much easier than you can do with your quadrille tablet and trusty number 2 pencil.

Record Keeping

You are sitting there trying to remember the conversation you had about a month ago, or was it two months ago? You remember it was pretty important at the time. You got some key information that you knew would come in handy down the road. Well, today is down the road. But you can't quite remember what you talked about, and you can't find that scrap of paper you scribbled some notes on. You'd call the guy back, but you are not quite sure what to say. Besides, you don't know where his phone number went. Something like this ever happen to you? More than once?

Keeping track of things is an important aspect of any change effort, and using technology can make this much easier. Certainly you want to be able to store and retrieve all that information you have been gathering about your community and the issue you face. That is a fairly simple matter of using your word processing program. You probably understand that your computer is like an enormous file cabinet and that your word processing program allows you to make new files, add things to existing files, and arrange files so that you can have easy access to them. It is also easy to transfer information from the Internet into your word processing program or to a disk for future reference. (Transferring the text is easy, but you may not be able to transfer the pictures you see on the screen when using the Internet.)

In addition to storing this newly acquired information, there are at least four other routine types of information you want to remember. First, you want to record the actions you have taken. Second, you want to keep track of the contacts you have made. Third, you want to be able to keep accurate membership lists. Finally, you want to monitor your money.

The first three activities can be accomplished using software designed to serve as your personal information manager (PIM). These programs use predefined templates that are likely to meet your needs. That is, the program comes equipped with methods to collect information you want to keep in a consistent, organized manner and provides quick retrieval of that information when you need it.

A journaling feature allows you to record actions you have taken on specific tasks. For example, you can enter the names of the people involved in a meeting, what was discussed, what agreements were reached, and what assignments were handed out. You can easily make notes on other types of actions you have taken and their actual or anticipated results as well.

You will continue to meet new people whose knowledge, talents, or position can be valuable assets to your efforts, and you do not want to lose touch with them. PIM software can help you keep up with your expanding network of contacts by helping you keep consistent records of phone numbers, E-mail and postal addresses, the name of the organization the person is associated with, any special designation you want to assign this person to allow you to classify particular types of contacts (for example, elected officials, members of the media, and so forth), and several other features. It will also give you an opportunity to record the contents of any conversation or the results of any contact you have made with this person. That is only a sample of the kinds of things you can put on file. Obviously, you can be as detailed or cursory as your circumstance requires.

Imagine how helpful having all this information at your fingertips can be. If you want a

Change Agent Tip

Allow some time for entering data, and do it consistently. Develop a routine for regularly entering information, and decide on a data entry standard so similar data is entered in the same way and can easily be found. (Pay heed to the old notion of GIGO—Garbage In/Garbage Out.) Make this as simple as possible, and record only the information you need. Otherwise, this too will become a burden, another thing left over from yesterday, and the day before, and added to your "to do" list for today. Paying haphazard attention to recording information won't make these record keeping tools useless, but close to it. It will probably also add another layer of frustration that you don't need.

Caution: Having all this information doesn't mean much of anything unless you use it.

list of all contacts with a certain set of characteristics, say, female business owners who live within a certain ZIP code area, your program will "filter" or sort through all your contacts and come up with that list for you. If you want to recall just what agreements you made with that school district official you've been working with, you can find out in seconds. You can even give yourself reminders to send birthday cards to special people if you are so inclined.

You can keep track of your organization's members just as you do your contacts. Create a special category or "field" just for these individuals, recording basic information, such as address and phone number, for each member along with more specialized information. Note each member's level of activity, special interests, abilities, or other assets. It can be a simple matter to filter your membership list to see who is involved in particular teams or committees, who has agreed to take part in public demonstrations, or who can help put out the newsletter.

These programs typically have other features as well. To manage all those things you have to do, the program comes with a daily "to do" list that will help you organize your day by asking you to estimate how much time each task will take. It will further allow you to remind yourself months in advance of something you need to take care of. When that date arrives, the item you had noted will appear on that day's list. You can use the system's calendar to help you schedule and keep tabs on all those upcoming attractions in your active life.

Most PIM software will let you filter any part of your record keeping system—your journal, contact and membership lists, even your calendar—to help you identify key information in seconds. Knowing exactly where to look and what you will find when you get there definitely beats the hodgepodge of notes stuffed in a file or committed to an uncertain memory.

Keeping your financial records straight can help you make better plans and decisions and may even keep you out of jail. A number of personal money manager programs (such as Quicken for Macs and PCs) meet most routine needs for a typical community change project or organization. For example, you will be able to monitor the income received from various sources, including grants, individual donors, or specific income-generating activities. Further, you can note the dates you received or expect to receive the funds.

You can also keep track of your routine and variable expenses to see what you are spending your money on and how that relates to your income. You can print a summary report of all your activities or of just a few designated categories (such as printing or postage or bank accounts). It also comes with built-in charts and graphs to aid in organizing and presenting information.

You can use this information to make projections and to make decisions: Can we buy that fax machine? If so, when? What is costing so much money? Where can we reduce expenses if we need to? Can we afford to hire some staff?

With good record keeping you can account for how you have handled all the funds you have received from whatever source. Sloppy record keeping has been the source of many, many rifts in organizations, and it has led to the loss of valuable dollars from external funding sources. Organizations involved in controversial issues are always open to attack. A favorite tactic of opponents is to point to financial mismanagement as a way of destroying a group's credibility. Smaller organizations often do not keep track of their money very well, and most cannot afford professional bookkeeping services. With a little training, and conscientious dedication to putting in the necessary data, your use of simple personal money manager software will provide a good picture of your organization's financial health and protect you from unnecessary vulnerability.

Ah, the smell of freshly baked cookies, the lure of banana bread, still looking tasty under its cellophane wrap and, of course, the little squares of marshmallow krispies to remind you of your younger years. Ready for the rush of customers, these and other goodies are set out on the folding table behind which you and a few other members of your group sit ready to take cash and make change. Another bake sale. By day's end you have raised $73.12. (Where did that 12 cents come from?) How much did this cost you?

Record keeping can be helpful in increasing the effectiveness of your fund-raising efforts. Some organizations put a lot of time and some actual money into projects that produce a pretty small return. Using your personal money manager program, you can get a better sense of which endeavors seem to work best for you. At the very least you can identify each fund-raising activity and note how much you spent (or are spending) on each, how much you have received, and the different rates of return on your investment in each activity. Much of the cost of fund-raising efforts for volunteer organizations is the use of volunteer time. Assign a dollar figure for each hour of volunteer time to get some measure of cost. Then you can make some comparisons of the value of the return you get from different activities related to the value of what you put into them. For example, you might decide that volunteer time is "worth" $7 an hour. So, if 10 volunteers put in 2 hours each for a particular effort, that effort "cost" you $140 (10 volunteers × 2 hours × 7 dollars per hour). How much did you really "make" on that bake sale? Could other activities bring in more dollars for the same cost, activities that are just as easy and that people actually will do?

Some fund-raising activities have purposes beyond producing income—attracting community attention or establishing a sense of camaraderie among participants, for example—but you should know the costs of these activities as well. Good financial data can help you figure out which efforts need more attention and which should be discontinued. If your organization gets too large or too complex, you can add more sophisticated accounting or spreadsheet software.

Keeping accurate records gives you a good handle on what you have done and where you have been. This will help you decide where you can go from here.

Making Provocative Presentations

Your palms are a little sweaty and you're beginning to question the wisdom of that sardine sandwich you had for lunch. Five minutes to go before your presentation to the board of directors. You are really hoping to make a compelling case so that the board will loosen the purse strings and fund the project you and the young people from the high school have worked so hard to lay the foundation for. At this point you are very glad you have discovered presentation software.

Striking visual images will sharpen your audience's ability to hear the message of your spoken words. Presentation software makes this easy. Literally in minutes you can create a series of images combining text, graphic displays, and pictures to tell your story.

Programs for Macs and PCs, such as Microsoft Powerpoint or Adobe Persuasion, have numerous combinations of backgrounds, print styles, colors, and art to visually highlight your presentation. You can select from any combination of templates to depict information. You don't need to draw anything or make any complicated arrangements. You just type in a few words, bring in a chart you have stored in a file, or select from the bank of art. Almost everything you want is already there for you. With just a couple of clicks you can create a highly professional-looking visual message.

You can turn these images into overhead transparencies, handouts, or slides. To really put on a show, hook your computer up to a projection system and run the entire presentation with your computer. A projection system can bring your images to life, with words marching into position across the screen or one image fading into another. This is not difficult, although a projection system is a pretty pricey item. Education and government settings and even some social service agencies may have projection systems you can use if you are making a presentation in their facility.

Now that you have an audience ready to listen, be prepared to help them hear.

Using Electronic Mail (E-Mail)

You hear the neighborhood dogs barking. The letter carrier must be on the loose. You check your mailbox, and sure enough, you have been visited by your postal service representative who left a small package from Aunt Cecilia. She has sent you a picture of the new baby along with a letter describing the wondrous new developments in the child's life. She even sent you a recording so you can hear for yourself "just how smart" the tyke is, although it isn't clear how a series of random gurgles has migrated from "cute" to "smart." She could have sent you all that by E-mail.

E-mail stands for "electronic mail," a system that allows you to send or receive messages over the World Wide Web to anyone in the world within seconds. You can send words, pictures, sound, and even video if you want to. Instead of addressing an envelope, finding a stamp, and carting your letter down to the mailbox, all you have to do is type a much shorter address and press a button. Your parcel of words or pictures or whatever is deposited into the receiver's electronic mailbox.

You can send your message to one person or to many people at once. Imagine all the possibilities E-mail opens up, simply by making communication so easy.

Networking with Other Like-Minded Individuals

One of the tenets of community organization is to connect people who know with people who need to know. You need to know. You also know some things that could benefit others. A few of you might want to talk with each other.

By this time you have begun identifying people within your own community who share a similar interest, and you have talked with a few. Now you ask the indispensable question: "Who else should we be talking to?" As you search the Internet, you will identify some very good sources of information, often included is a way to contact specific individuals. Build a list of contacts you would like to develop, and talk to them. Avoid assuming that people with more experience and know-how are too busy and too important to talk with you. Yes, some individuals will act that way, but at least an equal

Take a Moment to Discover . . . .

Send an E-mail with a question to five different activists or advocacy organizations. See how long it takes for you to get a response.

. . . .

number will be willing to offer you the benefit of their experiences. You may well find a mentor among this group.

Electronic discussion groups.   As you begin to discover contacts, both locally and nationally, you will get a pretty good feel for who might like to continue exchanging ideas about mutual interests. Ask your colleagues if they would like to participate in a discussion group. With E-mail this is a fairly simple thing to set up.

Create a distribution list; that is, a list of people to whom you want to send the same message. Store everyone's E-mail addresses under the name you give this distribution list. This allows you to send the same message at the same time to all of these people. Let's say you have 10 people in your group. Instead of making 10 different phone calls or addressing 10 different envelopes, all you have to do is type one address and push a button. Your message will be sent to each member of your group instantaneously.

When members check their E-mail, they all see the same message posted. They can write a reply at any time. They can send the reply back to the entire list, or they can send a message to one or two specific individuals by using personal E-mail addresses. The beauty of an electronic discussion group is that everyone can talk with everyone else without anyone interrupting or feeling pressed for an immediate answer. Also, you don't need to have everyone available at the same time to participate in the discussion.

Each member should have the same distribution list, and it is likely that you will add or lose some members over time. It might be wise to appoint a "list manager." This person keeps accurate track of the members of the discussion group and their addresses. Once a month or so, the list manager sends everyone the current list to make sure everyone has the same roll.

You can develop your own methods for conducting discussions. Some groups are pretty freewheeling, with members posting questions to the rest of the group whenever they are stuck with a problem or encounter a moment of brilliant insight they want to share. Other groups add a little structure. For example, each week or each month a different person takes the lead in posing a new question, problem, or issue to the group to stimulate discussion.

Electronic discussion groups can be a simple, entertaining way to gather insights and build new relationships. If you are new to the game of community action, participating in such a group and being accepted as a peer will increase your confidence.

Keep your group fairly small, no more than a dozen individuals. (You can start with only a couple of people, and add as you go.) If the group gets too large, you will lose the personal feel that adds to the enjoyment of the discussion.

Mailing lists.   Certainly you can have larger, less intimate discussion groups. If you want to reach a lot of people, consider utilizing a mailing list of your own in the same way that national organizations do to keep people informed of their efforts or to carry on discussions. To use a large mailing list effectively, you will need an Internet service provider, as will the other members who participate. However, participants can use different providers, they don't have to have the same one.

To create your own mailing list operation, contact your ISP or contract with one of many companies who specialize in setting up mailing lists. There will likely be an administrative set-up cost and an annual fee based on the number of subscribers you have on your list. You can literally have thousands of subscribers if you want. Even at that level your fees likely would run just a few hundred dollars per year.

The mailing list provider company will maintain your subscriber lists and help manage the operation for you. You invite people to "subscribe" to, that is, participate on the list. They don't pay anything to subscribe. All they have to do is send a simple, standard message (usually just a few words) to the mailing list address indicating their interest in joining. This is just like the national mailing list examples described earlier.

With a mailing list you, or a person from your group who has been authorized to do so, can send a message to all subscribers on your list. Subscribers become recipients of updates or information, but this is really one-way communication. You can create options for any subscriber to send a message to all other subscribers on the list; in this way discussion can occur.

If you are interested in joining an ongoing discussion group rather than creating your own, there are indexes of mailing lists for selected topics. By contacting *www.listz.com* you can look for lists that address topics that interest you. Or try *www.neosoft.com/internet/paml* for another index of mailing lists (Whitehead & Maran, 1997). By 1998 there were almost 75,000 lists, and the number is growing.

Newsgroups. By participating in a Usenet newsgroup dedicated to a specific topic you can cast your ideas out into cyberspace and see who might bite. *Usenet,* a term that predates the Internet, refers to "User's Network"—all the computers connected to circulate newsgroup information (Grimes, 1996). There are tens of thousands of newsgroups, loose collections of people who regularly post and respond to messages around a particular topic. The difference between newsgroups and mailing lists is blurry. They both serve similar purposes and function in similar ways. However, articles in a newsgroup aren't distributed to people who have signed up but are posted for people to read. You may think of a newsgroup as the world's largest bulletin board. Some messages posted on a mailing list are also posted on the related newsgroup, and vice versa (Levine, Baroudi, & Young, 1997). Many newsgroup participants provide good information in their part of the

Change Agent Tip

Using E-Mail for Alerts or to Swamp the Target with Mail

E-mail is a powerful tool to quickly notify your members of an action that needs to be taken immediately. Maybe you need a large number of supporters to contact an elected official just before a key vote or to turn out for a public demonstration of solidarity. At times it may be important to flood a local television station with protests over unfair coverage.

Distribution lists and mailing lists are useful tools for these action alerts. A strong immediate response capability will impress opponents and supporters alike.

E-mail is also a valuable tool to direct messages to a particular target. Most people in positions of authority now use E-mail (or their secretaries do), and it is not difficult to get the address of someone you want to influence. Three Web sites might help:

Four11 has access to millions of E-mail addresses. (*www.four11.com*)
WhoWhere might also be able to help. (*www/whowhere.com*)
Switchboard is yet another possibility. (*www.switchboard.com*)

Your concerns will be hard to ignore when your target flicks on the screen to find that 40 or 400 messages addressing your issue have appeared overnight.

How to Find Newsgroups on Your Issues

These sites provide lists of newsgroups (Hoye, 1997a). Maybe a few can introduce you to some intriguing ideas:

www.dejanews.com—A great site for finding newsgroups dedicated to the topic you have in mind.

www.listz.com/news—Similar to dejanews; a searchable list of newsgroups.

www.dejanews.com/info/primer1.shtml—A newsgroup primer that attempts to explain the medium.

www.dejanews.com/info/primer2.shtml—A rebuttal to the previous primer. (This is the Internet, remember!)

www.ph.tn.tudelft.nl/People/pierre/anchorman/Amn..html—A list of newsgroups. (Note the double period between Amn and html.)

www.cyberfiber.com/news—Another list of newsgroups.

library.airnews.net:89/newslist—The ultimate list of newsgroups.

---

discussion, so you can learn a lot. However, some do not. Some newsgroup conversations are not overly concerned with matters of politeness, but you will be able to sort out those that are the most useful.

The thousands of newsgroups are divided into several categories: "comp" groups are dedicated to computers, "rec" groups are dedicated to recreation, "biz" groups are dedicated to business topics, "soc" groups are concerned with socializing and some social and political issues, "courts" groups are related to court issues and events, and "alt" groups cover a broad range of topics (Grimes, 1996; Hoye, 1997a; Levine, Baroudi, & Young, 1997; Whitehead & Maran, 1997).

You get in touch with newsgroups through your Internet service provider. Although ISPs may differ in the way they provide access, it may be as easy as clicking on Usenet. The amount of information sent to newsgroups every day is about equal to a set of encyclopedias. Articles posted to a newsgroup are removed after a few days or weeks, so you may want to print or save an article you find interesting. Also, you may want to "lurk" or just read the articles of a newsgroup for a while before you post any. It is a good way to find out how members of that group communicate. It is helpful to read the FAQ

(frequently asked questions), a document listing questions and answers that often appear in the newsgroup. This is intended to prevent new readers from asking questions that have already been answered (Whitehead & Maran, 1997).

Electronic forum. You can also hold a discussion with all participants involved at the same time. This is sort of like having an electronic conference call except, instead of speaking, you're typing. Most ISPs offer this service and provide instruction for the steps you need to take.

Chat rooms. People have been using the Internet for casual conversation for years. Chat rooms are for real-time conversations—that is, all of you chatting to one another at the same time. You can use either Internet Relay Chat (IRC) or Web-based chat. You need to connect to an IRC server to use the IRC system. Some of the more popular networks you can connect to include EFNet (*www.efnet.org*), the largest of all IRC networks (and a fairly rowdy one), or Undernet (*www.undernet.org*), a smaller, friendlier version of EFNet.

To use the Web-based system, all you need is a Web browser. The Web chat rooms may be easier to use. Some key sites there include

WebChat Broadcasting System (*www.wbs.net*), which offers chat rooms hosted by experts, and Ichat (*www.ichat.com*), an easy system to use (Whitehead & Maran, 1997).

Web page. Remember how you became connected to other activists by discovering them through their Web pages? Other people can discover you the same way. Your organization can create its own Web page and receive queries from other individuals and organizations who are concerned about the same matters.

You can have as simple or complex a Web page as you would like. This project requires your organization to undertake a new set of tasks, particularly if you want to maintain your page by updating it with current information. However, it also offers benefits by providing some members an avenue for using their skills, increasing the credibility of the organization, and keeping the organization on top of issues.

Setting up a Web page can be a fun, creative exercise that helps a group feel it has become real, and it is no longer a very difficult task. Web pages use a particular language called hypertext mark up language or HTML. This is a universal language your Web browser interprets to display information in a graphical format. Writing something like this used to be daunting, but no more. Web development software now allows you to lay out text and graphics as well as create links to other pages within your site without learning the underlying programming commands. You use this software much like you would use your word processing program. Working within this program you create the words and pictures you want. The program automatically converts this into a language that can be read by any Web browser.

A number of Web page authoring programs are available. Frontpage will cost you about a hundred dollars, but you can also find shareware programs such as Hotdog. You can try out shareware programs for free, and then pay a minimal cost if you like them and intend to keep using them.

Another option for converting your work into HTML is a software package such as Microsoft Office 97, which provides a conversion function with little more than a click of your mouse. This feature makes updating your Web page really easy.

Once you have created your Web page, you need to make it available on the Web. You do this by copying it onto your account with your ISP. When you open an account with an ISP, you have the capability not only to get information from the Internet but to create a presence for yourself as well. Your ISP can show you how to copy your creation to a space within your account so that your Web page is now available to the world.

As long as you have such a big audience, you might want to consider creating a *monthly newsletter* of your exploits and information on your issue. This is a good activity for your members, and it helps circulate your group's name and information.

You can sit back and let some search engine discover you, but it might be better to introduce yourself to your worldwide audience. This can be done by making a posting to a search engine. Most have a simple way to invite you to add your Web site to their list, providing an icon or button to click on. You click on to that spot, follow the directions, and you are now on stage.

Include the fact of your Web page and its address in your mailings, newsletters, and in any other slow-moving conversations. Your organization will soon reach farther than you had ever imagined.

Caution: If you ask people to contact you, they just might. You can get swamped with E-mail and other requests for your time and attention. Are you prepared for that?

Communicating with Members of Your Organization

Almost nothing is as effective as face-to-face communication, however it has never been a timely way to regularly send and receive information. People working for community change need to see each other from time to time, and smaller working groups certainly need to do

Change Agent Tip

The simplicity of current communication methods can allow your group to make its presence felt in a big way, with very little work on your part. For example, you might want to try a *redial party* or a *fax flood.*

A redial party is a fun way to make a big impression. Essentially you gather a group of people who each leave a voice mail message saying the same thing. Each person also gives the names of two other people who support this position. If you have 20 people making the phone call, the names of 60 supporters are registered. The whole process of calling takes less than 15 minutes. Here's how it works.

First, select a target whose attention you really need to grab, probably someone who has been resisting your group. The target needs to have an answering machine or some voice mail service, which you call during non-business hours to be sure you can leave a message rather than actually getting a live person. Next, invite a number of people over for a potluck dinner and a phone call, asking each to bring the names and phone numbers of two other people who would be willing to support a message on behalf of your organization. Then prepare a very simple, short script for each person to read when it is their turn to make the call. The script goes something like this: "Hello, (target's name), this is (your name). I'd like you to (state the action you'd like the target to take). Two of my friends (or neighbors or colleagues) also want you to do this. Their names and phone numbers are (state the names and phone numbers for the two other people). You can call them if you need to. Thank you for helping us make progress on (state your issue in just a few words)."

Once everyone has gathered, spend a little time enjoying each other's company and talking about the issue to heighten enthusiasm. When it's time to start, one person goes into another room where it is likely to be more quiet, dials the target's phone number, and reads the prepared script into the voice mail. This person hangs up, walks out of the room, and hands the phone to the next in line. That person hits the redial button on the phone,

so with some frequency, but other forms of communication can keep members routinely informed and connected.

E-mail and, in particular, the distribution or mailing list option, is a very effective way of allowing members to post messages to each other as well as to large or small groups. In this way teams of members or the whole organization can be informed and participate in discussions.

This works great for those members who have access to E-mail. What about those who do not? You don't have to be sitting in front of your computer to make use of other forms of information technology. The good old telephone is a simple way to communicate to all your members—establish a *hot line.*

By calling the hot line, members of the organization, or anyone else you invite to call, hear a prerecorded message generally consisting of: (1) a welcoming message; (2) facts or insights about the organization, its issue, or purpose; and (3) updates on the organization's activities and other news. A 90-second message can contain a lot of information. The hot line also invites callers to ask questions or leave comments, along with their phone numbers. The caller should be told what happens to those comments and when they can expect someone from the organization to get in touch with them.

and repeats the process. Pretty simple. All anybody has to do is hit a redial button, read a script, and pass the phone to the next person.

A couple of hints to make things go smoothly: Use a phone (preferably portable) with a redial button. Have each person practice the script out loud before making the phone call. Finally, to keep track of progress, have each caller check his or her name off a list once the call has been completed.

It is helpful to prepare a one-page background sheet for each person whose name is going to be used. They should know the issue and be able to state a position in the very unlikely circumstance that they would be asked to.

A *fax flood* accomplishes a similar purpose. Select a target who has a fax machine. Next, collect signed, two-sentence statements regarding the issue from members and supporters of your organization. (Collect a dollar or two from each person to cover expenses and to have them feel more a part of the activity.) Once you have a good number of statements (25 or more), take all your messages to a company that sends faxes. Have the company fax all of your messages, preferably at a particular time, one after another. This has the effect of interrupting the recipient's flow of faxes from other sources, adding to the pressure. (A fax company that is friendly to your cause will work with you a little better.)

You can increase pressure by having each statement request a reply. You can combine a fax flood with a redial party by having participants each bring a couple of signed fax messages and dollar bills.

In my experience these tactics work best when directed at someone who has some other person he or she needs to report to or to buffer from public pressure. You let this person know that all these calls or faxes are a sample of what you can do. Tell the target that you are directing this activity to him or her with the hope that progress can be made, otherwise you will use this tactic on the person they do not want contacted.

Setting up the hot line is a simple matter of getting a phone line and an answering machine or messaging service through the phone company. For a few extra dollars a month you can add additional mailboxes or prerecorded messages; by pressing different numbers the caller can be informed about a number of topics.

Hot lines are a very easy, fairly inexpensive, and very valuable way of heightening interest and keeping people informed, but they do require attention. First, you need to promote the existence of the hot line among your members, and you need to do this periodically. Every flyer or newsletter should have the hot line number. Keep the messages fresh. Messages should be changed weekly, particularly the news and information items. Someone must monitor the line to record the number of calls and the comments or questions made by callers. Each caller who requests a response should be contacted within a week. As you can see, it does take a little organization.

Caution: Once you distribute your hot line number, you can expect that some people who are not supportive of your efforts or who may even be active opponents will call. Some may leave messages that are "unkind." Others will see if they can get some of your inside information. When you record your messages, understand that some opponents may be listening in, and when you listen to your messages, understand that some are intended to rattle you.

If it is difficult for people to get together because distances are too great or schedules too hectic, a conference call is another option, but it can be an expensive one. If your organization's work involves a public agency, you may be able to use their teleconferencing services. If not, and you really require a conference call, you can find the names of companies specializing in teleconferencing in the yellow pages of your phone book. It is worth a little of your time to shop around because prices vary significantly. Whether you set up your call with a public agency or through a teleconferencing company, things work pretty much the same. An operator will assist in setting up the call and

tracking down people who haven't yet made the connection.

Many phone companies offer three-way conferencing as part of the package of services they provide to their customers. This is fairly inexpensive, and a member of your group may already have this service. It is possible, though cumbersome, to use this feature to conduct a conference call among more than three people at a time. Your telephone company may have other communication services that can benefit your effort. Ask about them.

Caution: Teleconferencing services through private companies can be very expensive, up to $100 for a half-hour conversation among six people. Shop around, and use this option wisely.

People still do read the printed page, and

Learning about Information Technology

The journal *New Technology in Human Services* is dedicated specifically to the use of information technology in human services practice and education. Although few articles have related directly to community change, topics of general interest may be useful.

The "dummy series" (for example, *Internet for Dummies*) are the most readable books on this topic. IDG Books Worldwide has also put together a simple guide to the Internet and World Wide Web using clear, colorful pictures and brief text descriptions. Titled *Internet and World Wide Web Simplified,* it is probably the best book for beginners.

Que Corporation publishes

books at different levels of sophistication, and they do a fairly good job of avoiding jargon in introductory texts. Que also publishes a series called *10 Minute Guide to . . .* [*the Internet and the World Wide Web,* for example]. It is very task-oriented, teaching you the "one best way" to do things rather than leading you through all the different ways to perform the same function. On the back of each of these guides is a thermometer-type bar identifying the user level from "new" to "expert" so you can select a guide that fits your level of sophistication.

Microsoft Press, a division of Microsoft Corporation, has a series of books covering Microsoft products, and

Sybex Publishers offers books on various computer topics and applications software.

PC Magazine and *MAC-WORLD* are published monthly. Each covers a wide range of new developments in computer technology. They also provide question-and-answer sections to assist you with problems you may be having. Their product reviews and comparisons are useful in making decisions about upcoming purchases. Beginners will find it a little difficult to wade through some of the jargon.

Your computer itself can give you a lot of direction. Don't forget to use the "table of contents" or the "help" screens.

Take a Moment to Discover . . . .

Think about a time when you finally mastered something you never thought you'd learn. Maybe it was using a stick shift or playing a musical instrument or finally asserting your point of view about something. Picture yourself when you were caught in your feelings of frustration. Now picture yourself today, when success has become routine. As you were reading through this chapter, was there anything you thought you might not be able to master? Picture yourself once you have mastered this yet-to-be-learned skill.

. . . .

they probably will for some time to come. You can produce some pretty nice printed pages for the members of your organization to read. Newsletters, flyers, and other forms of printed communication are important ways to strengthen affiliation and keep your members informed. You don't have to be an artist to dress up your newsletter with eye-catching graphics or to get your articles to fit neatly into columns. Put the felt marker back in the box because you can design a really nice-looking flyer in a few clicks. Most word processing programs now come with options that make all this simple.

It is easy to get into the habit of using some of the methods of communication described here. Not only can they be fun, but they also provide opportunities for members of your organization to perform important roles. Keeping people in your group in communication with each other is one of the most significant things you can do. This process will reinforce the group's sense of legitimacy while increasing the effectiveness of its planning, decision making, and action.

Training

Training normally centers around one of four areas or a combination of them: a general introduction to computers, understanding and using a particular software package, application of technology in a particular professional field, or how to use the Internet.

Training is available from many sources. The place you buy your computer or software may very well provide training. Sometimes this is included along with the purchase; sometimes it is an added expense. As interest in using information technology grows, many community organizations have responded by providing training opportunities at little or no expense. You may have to hunt a little, but it is likely that you can learn how to dance with your computer without putting much of a dent in your pocketbook. Your credit union or local parks and recreation department may sponsor classes. Sometimes the local public school offers computer literacy classes for adult neighborhood residents. Various community social service agencies, particularly those with a community development or prevention component, offer training from time to time for community members. You might even be able to take part in training that a service agency offers its own staff. Major employers in the community often support volunteer organizations. You may be able to arrange some computer training for your group with one of their volunteers. (The relationship you form with the volunteer group is an added benefit.) Community colleges commonly offer a range of credit and noncredit courses for beginning and advanced users. These are just a few of the opportunities you are likely to find in your community.

It should be pretty easy to find someone who can guide you through the basic functions, someone you can call when your computer doesn't seem to be cooperating no matter how much you plead with it. The role of "resident computer genius" may be perfect for someone in your organization who wants some very specific form of involvement. If none of your current members is able to accept this title, recruit someone from among friends, family, or members of the community. This is also a great opportunity to bring young people into the work of your organization. Children today are growing up as accustomed to the keyboard and the drag and drop as most of us were to dragging a sharpened point across a sheet of paper.

If there is a college or university nearby, your organization may very well find help from students studying computer science or management information systems. Many schools now promote service learning—a way for students to learn by developing their knowledge and skill through some form of community service. Your organization can benefit from this trend. Don't be surprised if your budding expert takes a special interest in your issue and remains available to offer help after the specific project is completed.

Conclusion

Information and communication are core components of any successful community change project. Using technology to strengthen these aspects of your effort can affect everything you do. Learning about your community and the particular issue you are dealing with will solidify your command of the matter and help you determine your course of action. Your

ability to analyze data will lead you to better decisions. Communicating with other activists and with members of your own organization keeps you connected to sources of insight and allows you to build strength. Your ability to use these tools tactically to establish your presence and to cultivate involvement in efforts to vitalize your community will increase the power of your organization. Present your ideas dynamically and encourage people to take note and take action.

Technology does not replace your ability, nor should it replace other useful forms of communication and information gathering that lead to community building. Technology can make you more effective by making the things you need to do simpler and more productive.

The more you use the various tools, the more intrigued you will become. Once you get a few basics down, you will find yourself discovering a little trick here, another helpful function there, and maybe even a whole new set of uses. You will learn from just playing around. A computer is just like a musical instrument, you get better just by playing it. Because you can notice results so quickly, you will probably keep playing—even if what you are really doing is work.

CHAPTER 6
Knowing Your Community

Chapter Highlights

- Importance of working with your community
- Definitions of community
- Geographic and interest communities
- Subcommunities as subsystems
- Close community
- Need or benefit community
- Action community
- Target or response community
- Peripheral communities
- Basic community characteristics
- Functioning of a community
- Basic community needs: physical, social and emotional, political, economic, education and communication
- Unmet community needs
- Needs assessments
- Community resources
- Community capacity for change
- Information gathering versus action
- Utilizing library resources
- Organizations as sources of information
- Individuals as sources of information
- Guided personal discussions
- Focus groups
- Surveys and questionnaires
- Informal methods
- Collecting lists
- Newspapers are more than just news

"I shouldn't have opened my big mouth, Melanie. I've got enough to do without worrying about trying to do something else."

"Yeah, you're right, Ben. That Brady Bunch Reunion movie is on tonight. It's only the third time it's been re-run. You'll probably be real busy." For the third time she takes some of the fries left unguarded on his plate.

"You thief. I suppose you want some of my hamburger too."

"No, the fries will do. Think about it for a second, Ben. It will be fun to get something going, and this is important."

"It's all important, Melanie, but why start a prenatal care center? Aren't there enough people doing this kind of work in town?"

"Ben, if there are, they just aren't getting the job done. Too many women, particularly young women, are falling through the cracks. For whatever reason, they aren't getting the care they need. Everybody's too busy, got important things to do. Right, Ben? Do you know what this costs? I mean not just to them, the women, but to the community, to the state?"

"No, I don't, and come on, Mel, don't get hot. I'm not against women getting care. You know that. I'm just not sure starting a center is such a great idea. Isn't it just a matter of coordinating the services we have now?"

"I really don't think it is, Ben, but we'd better check it out. We should find out who has an interest in prenatal care. We'd also better figure out whose toes we're stepping on by doing this. You know some of these people are more interested in protecting their turf than anything else."

"You're right. I hate to think about that, but I guess we have to. Then, again, there are people who can help us with this too. We've got to start talking to them, whoever they are. It would help if we know what we are talking about. What does a prenatal care center look like, and who are all these women who aren't getting the care they need?"

"Well, Ben, I guess we'd just better find out."

Almost any change that amounts to anything requires that you get other people working in the same direction. By now you know that. These other people are part of a community, and knowledge of the community is fundamental to your effort to promote change. How you approach your community will be based on what you know about it. It is that basic.

Melanie and Ben recognize that a good idea doesn't live apart from the community in which it is to be implemented. They recognize that there is much more they need to find out to see if their idea is really practical and useful. They need to know what response to anticipate from various parts of the community and where they might get opposition or support. They know the community is where all this will happen, so they had better find out more about it.

The community is a contributor of resources and allies and a provider of pitfalls and opponents. You want to know where these are—where to go to get what you need and who or what to avoid. The community is, after all, where the need for change, the effort to make that change, and the resistance to change coexist. In fact, it is itself slightly or significantly changed by your efforts. This is where the game is played. You need to know the size and shape of the field and what the other players can do.

Perspectives on Community

Just how much you need to know will depend on the nature of the problem, the size or extent of the change being pursued, and the kind of organization you want to put together. Three ways of looking at your community are important to your understanding. The first involves perceiving your community *as* a community. The second examines the component parts of the community, acknowledging that it is made up of several smaller "subcommunities." The third focuses on those groups drawn into your arena of action.

Your Community as a Community

There are a number of ways to think about what a community is. The first, most obvious way is to think about it as a geographic area, a place with defined physical boundaries. If you were flying over the area in a small plane, you could actually see these boundaries. Certain streets mark a neighborhood's borders. The limits of a mobile home park or an apartment complex can be clearly determined. The most fundamental characteristic of these *geographic communities* is that they are places of residence. People are familiar with them because they live there.

Some communities are defined by individuals' shared interests, activities, affection, or common identity. These characteristics differentiate them from others. These *interest* or *identificational communities* might be called food stamp recipients, single parents, laryngectomy patients, or members of the Barry Manilow fan club (Longres, 1995). Where these people live does not determine their membership in the community.

People are usually members of geographic as well as interest communities. Perhaps you live in an apartment complex in a certain city and you attend college. You have some common interests with people who live in the same place you do. But you also share some things in common with other students at your college. At lunch, after the exam has been rehashed, you and some other students may talk about good or not so good landlords or apartment managers. Some of your classmates also rent. So here you are. You reside in a particular city. You live in a particular apartment complex. You are a renter. You are a student. Already you are a member of four distinct communities, two geographic and two interest or identificational.

The notions of geographic and interest or identificational can be seen in these definitions for the word *community.*

- Community: a group of individuals or families that share certain values, services, institutions, interests, or geographic proximity (Barker, 1995, p. 68).

• Community, or a "sense of community," exists when two or more people work together toward the accomplishment of mutually desirable goals (conditions) (Lofquist, 1993, p. 8).

• A community is a territorially bounded social system or set of interlocking or integrated functional subsystems (economic, political, religious, ethical, educational, legal, socializing, reproductive, etc.) serving a resident population, plus the material culture or physical plant through which the subsystems operate (Bernard, 1972, p. 163).

Some observers describe community as a state of being that provides the community and its members with a context for empowered development. In this sense, community is both a process and a desired outcome. Palmer (1993) suggests that community is found at the intersection of the inward and outward life. "Community is a place where the connections felt in our hearts make themselves known in the bonds between people, and where the tuggings and pullings of those bonds keep opening our hearts" (p. 88).

Peck (1987) tells us of the difficulty of establishing a community, but makes it clear that the attempt is well worth the effort:

> Community [is] a group of individuals who have learned how to communicate honestly with each other, whose relationships go deeper than their masks of composure, and who have developed some significant commitment to "rejoice together, mourn together," and to "delight in each other, make others' conditions our own." . . . Genuine community is not easily achieved or easily maintained; its avowed goal is to seek ways in which to live with ourselves and others in love and peace. . . . Once a group has achieved community, the single most common thing members express is, "I feel safe here." (pp. 59, 163, 67)

And Lloyd-Jones (1989) points out the benefits that accrue from coming together to form a community:

> Individuals both enlarge and restrict their own freedoms by joining such a community. But whatever restriction results is far surpassed by the individual's and the group's ability to achieve established goals while at the same time creating mutual support and pride. (pp. 2–3)

You may view community through a variety of lenses. It may be considered a *place,* a *set of interests,* an *identity,* a *purposeful grouping of individuals* into a common whole, a *fundamental capacity* of our humanness, a *state of being,* a manner of *people relating* to one another, or a *provider of benefits* that result from effective interaction.

To work with a community, it is important for you to picture it in terms of distinctness—the clear common characteristics that connect its members. These connections provide the potential for a variety of benefits, particularly if members can recognize them and act on them. For our purposes then, a community is:

> *a number of people who share a distinct location, belief, interest, activity, or other characteristic that clearly identifies their commonality and differentiates them from those not sharing it. This common distinction is sufficiently evident that members of the community are able to recognize it, even though they may not currently have this recognition. Effectively acting on their recognition may lead members to more complete personal and mutual development.*

Communities and Subcommunities

Another way to consider the community is to examine it from its broad level to its more immediate level. Each geographic, interest, or identificational community of even a few hundred people is likely to have subcommunities

within it. You may think of these different levels as subsystems of a larger system.

Communities operate on a variety of levels. Recall the discussion of systems theory from Chapters 2 and 3. A systems perspective is helpful in understanding various component parts and levels of communities, from the broad to the very immediate. Using a geographic community as an example, the broad community has a name like Seattle, or Des Moines, or Flagstaff. If you look on a map, you see the name printed next to a circle or maybe just a small dot. You may live near the town, but not really in it. Perhaps your kids go to school in Oakwood, but you actually live on a farm several miles away. Still, you see yourself residing in the Oakwood area, or at least in Vermillion County.

A second level of your community consists of smaller divisions that describe sets of people within the broad community. Neighborhoods, the business community, the farming commu-

nity, gangs, and the medical community are all types of second-level communities that may exist within this broader community. Some of these smaller communities are clearly defined. Their members frequently associate with one another, and they clearly understand their affiliation with other community members. Various rituals, boundary lines, or other cues remind people of their membership. If you go to school in Pocatello, you know you are a member of the university community because you go to the Idaho State University campus several times a week. You see other students or other faculty and talk to them as part of your day-to-day life. You easily identify yourself with the university community.

Other second-level communities are not so readily identifiable. Perhaps you are a single parent. There may be quite a few single parents in Pocatello, but you don't know who they are. You don't routinely get together as single

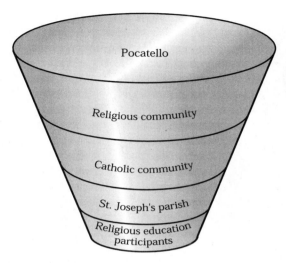

Figure 6-1
Levels of community

parents. No one issues you an identification card that certifies you as a member of this community. Yet you most certainly do share many things in common with other single parents in Pocatello. This second-level community is real, but the relationships among its members are much less clearly defined.

The more that members of a community relate to one another or to an identified place, institution, or activity, the more likely they will be to recognize their membership in the community. The relationship among members is likely to be more patterned as well.

These subcommunities can be divided into even more specific levels. Back in Pocatello (first level) you have the religious community (second level); within that community you have the Mormon community, the Catholic community, and the Baptist community (see Figure 6-1). If you need to, you can break these communities down even further into wards, parishes, and congregations. The more you break things down, the more likely you are to come to affiliations that are directly meaningful to individuals. People usually find their immediate group to be significant in influencing what they

do and how they think about what they do. Think about yourself as a student. Your college and the particular department you are affiliated with in that college influence how you spend your time. However, the particular class you take *really* influences how you spend your time. Your class is a much more immediate group than your college.

You will probably want to work at some particular level of community with which you identify, whose functioning affects your interests enough that you notice it, and where you believe your actions can have some degree of impact. This set of people and institutions close at hand is called your *close* community.

Do you need to keep dividing things down until you personally know everyone in the whole city? No, you don't. But you do need to understand that these various subdivisions exist. These smaller, close communities can be either interlocking (fitting together so that action is coordinated), overlapping (sharing some common feature), or independent from one another. Each of these configurations has some degree of power and is a potential source of support or opposition. Knowing how your community breaks down and what sets of relationships exist within it gives you some insight regarding whom you may want to involve and how. It will also alert you to potential forces of resistance and guide you in ways to reduce that resistance.

Communities in Your Arena of Action

Most of the changes you work on will provoke the interest of only a small segment of the broad community. The more important a group or segment of the community is to your effort, the more you should know about it. The less important it is, the less you need to know.

The immediate community or communities you need to know about are those involved in your particular arena of action (Kettner, Daley, & Nichols, 1985): the need or benefit community, the action community, and the target or response community. In some cases these component parts will be actual communities of people. In other instances you might more easily think of them as *systems,* a concept presented in Chapters 2 and 3.

The need or benefit community includes those people who currently experience the problem or could benefit from its resolution. Their endorsement of the change effort is a precondition for action. There are few exceptions to this general rule. Only in emergency situations or in cases involving members of a benefit community who are simply unable to give their consent, for example infants, would this rule not apply.

The action community consists of those who recognize or could easily recognize that a problem exists and are willing to work to resolve it. This includes the principal change agents as well as all those others who could contribute to making the change.

The target or response community encompasses those whose policies, actions, or inactions somehow perpetuate the problem. This community controls the resources the benefit community needs. For worthwhile change to occur, members of this community must change their practices. Sometimes they are very willing to do so; sometimes they are not. The more carefully you pinpoint this group, the more effectively you can focus your strategy.

You may not find three distinct community groups in your arena of action. For example, if you are working with a neighborhood to develop a program to visit elderly residents who live alone, the neighborhood itself is the community that is mobilized, that benefits, and that must respond for change. Or, maybe you are working with that same neighborhood to pressure banks to provide more loans to residents. The target of your effort is the banks. The neighborhood is both the action community you mobilize as well as the benefit community. If you mobilize school teachers on behalf of homeless teens to put pressure on the city government to provide shelter facilities, three distinct need, action, and target communities can be identified.

Although your main focus is on your arena of action, information on *peripheral* communities—communities whose interests your actions may affect but do not now affect directly—is also important. Peripheral communities are not currently in the game: They are standing around on the sidelines, some watching what is going on, some not paying the slightest attention. Even if you can't take time to find out much about them, you should identify who they are so you can stimulate support or quiet or counter opposition. In the example of teachers working on behalf of homeless teens, peripheral communities could include social service providers, neighborhoods adjacent to the proposed shelter facilities, and the police department.

The complexity of the issue, its size, its potential for controversy, and the range of communities it will probably affect will tell you how much community knowledge you need to have. As you come to know more about your community, you will become more confident about what you can do to make it better.

What to Look for in Your Community

There's a knock on the door. "Dadgummit!" you hiss, then quickly look around to see if anyone caught you uttering such an uncharacteristic obscenity. It seems like every time you sit back to watch Vanna turn those letters, you get interrupted. It's never during the commercial, never. Oh well, better see who it is. No one else ever gets the door.

"Hi, Vern Kadukey, cousin of Floyd Kadukey, of the Oklahoma Kadukey's. Glad to meet you," comes the greeting.

"Vern Kadukey?" you ask.

"That's right. Just moved in across the street. Thought I'd come by and get to know you, find out what sort of family lives here, and check out the house. You mind?"

"Uh, well, no, I guess not. Come on in."

Stepping across the threshold, Vern trips on the curled up edge of the rug. "Sorry, Vern, I guess we're used to that. Let me move the laundry off the couch so you can sit down."

"No, that's OK. I'll just stroll around a bit. Hey, your faucet's dripping. Don't you know how to fix a leak?"

"Uh, well, I was going to get around to it." Geez, if I knew this guy was coming over, I would have cleaned the bathroom. Maybe I'd better steer him to the garden. At least that's been weeded.

"Want to go see the garden, Vern?"

"Sure, why not. Say, what's this on the fridge?"

"That's the list of who's supposed to do the dishes and take out the garbage. You can see it's not my week." Why the heck am I explaining to this guy?

"No, I mean the little pig magnet. The one eating the ice cream. It says 'Do you really need this?' It's not holdin' up nuthin.' What's it here for?"

"Look, Vern, maybe you should come back another time. I was just in the middle of something pretty important. OK?"

"Sure. Hey, look! The Wheel's on the tube. Mind if I stay and watch?"

Oh, God. . . .

What did Vern see? What did he begin to know about you and your family? About the place you live? What would he be likely to notice that you wouldn't see? What conclusions would he reach? How accurate would these be? What could he do to make them more accurate?

If Vern spent a little more time in the place you live keeping his eyes and ears open, asking questions, and doing a little outside investigating, he'd have a pretty good working understanding of your household. He'd figure out how big your living space is, how things are structured to accomplish certain goals, how people feel about certain things, and a host of other household factors. To some extent that's what you are doing when you walk into a community and start looking around. Looking at a community is not a whole lot different from looking at a house and a household unprepared for visitors. Thinking about your community as

a household will give you some clues for understanding it better.

Let me stress that you can and should get moving on your change effort before you have each and every piece of information available on your community. You can spend a lifetime studying and still not know everything you would like to know. You have to balance your need for action with your need for information.

Some of you will want to use lack of information as an excuse for inaction. Others will want to dive in headfirst without checking to see how deep the water is. In actual practice, you gather *some* information (you need to determine how much), and then act. Then, you keep gathering information while you are taking action.

The better informed you are, the more efficiently and effectively you can use your time.

Take a Moment to Discover . . . .

Walk around and through your house. See it through the eyes of someone who doesn't know you. What clues are there to help you understand the residents of this little community a bit better? What do you notice that could help you answer some of these questions about these people?

- What inconveniences do they take for granted or have they adjusted to?
- What do they enjoy or don't enjoy doing?
- What values do they hold?
- How do they communicate information?
- Who does what work?
- What work isn't done?
- What do the residents do together?
- How do they generate income?
- How many residents are there?
- What else could you find out about these people?

This increases your chances for success and reduces the role of luck, especially bad luck. But you are not primarily a researcher, you are a change agent, maybe even an activist. Just be an informed one. The information you need about your community can be organized into five categories:

- Basic community characteristics
- How the community functions to meet its needs
- Unmet needs
- Community resources
- Capacity for and disposition toward purposeful change

As you take a closer look at each category, remember that your community could be your school, the agency for which you work, the congregation of your synagogue or church, as well as your city. Although these are distinct categories, they sometimes overlap. Think of them as lenses through which you look at your community. These categories represent general things to look for; you will have to determine the specific information you need based on the problem you are confronting.

Basic Community Characteristics

The information in this category is chiefly objective; that is, it consists of facts. You could get much of this information by riding around in a helicopter (great fun) or by reading (moderate fun). You may not have to set foot in town. A sampling of questions is provided to give you some guidance in understanding your community's characteristics and the way it functions.

One of the first things you'll want to know about are the physical features of your community.

- How big is it? What are the dimensions of this community?
- Where do people gather? Are there common places where people meet, either coincidentally or on purpose? This could be the train station, the synagogue, or the office bathroom.
- Are there key landmarks or points of reference? In Cuernavaca everyone knows the Zócalo. In Washington, DC, the Washington Monument is hard to miss, and in Atlanta most people can find their way to Turner Field. This could, however, just as easily mean the park, the junior high school, or Mr. Smedly's office.
- What does this community look like? Is it dirty or clean, old or new, well maintained or in need of repair?
- What are the natural features of the community? Perhaps there is a flood every spring. Maybe there is an abundance of water, trees, and mosquitoes. Water might be a scarce resource, and cacti may dot the landscape. The fact that your community is hot or cold, rainy, dry, or mountainous could have an effect on what people do.

Of course, a community isn't a community without people. What do you know about these folks?

- What is the population of this community? Does this number fluctuate? In some communities there are 10,000 people in the summer and 40,000 in the winter. There may be 100 people during the day and none at night. Perhaps the members of the community (for example, most students at a college) only stay for a certain period of time and then move on.
- What is the demographic breakdown? You may want to know how old or young the people are. Whether or not they are married may be important. Income, educational background, and ethnic diversity could be significant.
- How long have these people been a part of this community? Someone who arrived a month ago will have a different perspective than someone who has been around for 23 years.
- What do the families look like? A community in which there is a predominance of

two-parent, one-marriage families with an average of five children is likely to be different from one in which the typical family consists of two unmarried adults living together without children.

- What is the population density? Are there a lot of people in a small space, or a lot of space with few people?

Looking at the characteristics of a community gives you a picture of the significant aspects or component parts of the community. This is like a snapshot. You see the parts, but you don't see them doing anything. If you were capturing the community with a video camera, you would be gathering information in the second category—you'd see how the community functions.

How the Community Functions

How a community functions is in a way its very essence. One way to look at functioning is to examine how the community endeavors to meet its needs. There is a difference between needs, wants, and problems, and for our purposes needs are those things a community requires to meet its goals and to sustain itself. These are routine, ongoing challenges the community must address. As such they are different from problems, which are needs that have not been properly addressed.

You must be thinking that there are a ton of community needs. How are you going to know what to look for? It's really not all that complicated. Most communities have about five kinds of needs: physical needs, social and emotional needs, political needs, economic needs, and educational and communication needs.

As you examine how current needs are being met, ask yourself, "How did things get to be this way?" Understanding history can be an important key to deciphering the present.

Physical needs.   Perhaps the most basic needs are physical. This set of needs includes those

that help us take care of our bodies as well as those that deal with the things we make or build.

- Do people have consistent access to adequate food, shelter, and clothing?
- Is adequate medical care available on a timely and affordable basis?
- Are roads and other transportation systems adequate for getting people to and from their destinations in a timely and safe manner?
- Is the air clean to breathe and the water pure to drink?
- Are the waste and drainage systems adequate to protect health and maintain visual attractiveness?
- Are all the systems routinely maintained to prevent problems?

Social and emotional needs.   Just like individuals, communities have social and emotional needs. Forming and maintaining relationships is an integral function of the community. A feeling of well-being and confidence in the future are necessary if a community is to achieve its potential.

- Do members of the community feel safe and secure?
- Do members take pride in the community and their membership in it?
- What are the sources of pride (Go Tigers!), embarrassment (It will be fixed soon.), fear (I hope it doesn't blow up.), joy (I knew we could do it!), and other feelings?
- Are members confident of their own and others' abilities, including the ability to recognize and resolve problems?
- Do members feel a part of the community and cared for by other members?
- Do members feel free to contribute to the community and to achieve personal goals?
- What groupings occur within the community? People like to get together and feel they are part of something, or they need to get together to accomplish something. It's hard to play baseball by yourself, so Little Leagues are formed. Rotary clubs give

businesspeople an opportunity to see each other every week. A myriad of associations, clubs, and organizations exist within your community. Many of these have names and rules of membership. Knowing about these groups can help you understand how your community works and provides you with better access to people.

- How does the community handle its deviants?
- How do members spend their time and money? Looking at what people do and how they commit their resources will tell you what people value.

Political needs. Community life requires a continuous series of decisions on matters that affect its members. This process involves forming policies that manage resources and relationships. Each community faces a set of political needs, and it will develop a governance or decision-making structure if it intends to respond to those needs. Governance structures usually have clearly spelled out procedures for gathering information, making decisions, developing rules or laws, describing those rules or laws, and enforcing them. These procedures describe who is allowed to participate in the process and how (Fellin, 1995).

- Do members of the community have the desire and the ability to work together?
- Do members believe they have a right to participate in policy making?
- What is the formal process for making community decisions? What are the limits and the extent of this process? That is, over what matters is it empowered to decide, and what matters are none of its business? Which services or functions does local government or the local administration see as its responsibility?
- What are the formal governmental structures? What are the formal positions of leadership and decision making, and who holds them? These are the people authorized or acknowledged by the community to

provide direction. Community members often recognize them by their titles: Mayor, principal, supervisor, and board member are a few of these titles.

- What are the informal processes for making community decisions? Each formal process has an informal one that operates within it or outside of it. The formal process often relies on this informal process or is made irrelevant by it. A description of the informal process is the answer to the question: How do things really work? You'll need to dig a little deeper to discover this process. Be on your guard against cynical paranoia as you do your digging. Informal processes usually depend on relationships or convenience and inconvenience. Frankly, few decisions, though admittedly some, are important enough to warrant development of grand conspiracies.
- What are the informal positions of leadership and decision making, and who holds them? These positions usually don't have titles or the power is greater than the title. The people to whom formal leaders commonly look in fear, or for support and ideas, are likely candidates.
- How do people recognize problems? Some communities rely on official reports. Others acknowledge problems when somebody throws a temper tantrum. Some communities have structures for discovering problems, whereas others have patterned ways to avoid looking.
- Who is expected to be quiet, and who is allowed to speak up?
- What are the likely bases of power? In each community there are some things that give people a better chance at getting what they want. Find out what these are. (Power will be explored in more detail in Chapter 7.)
- How are community decisions carried out in practice?

Economic needs. The community's economic system provides a way for its members to develop the means to acquire things that are important to them. Usually, this means money. Each community has some economic needs.

- How do you get access to goods and services?
- What are the income and occupation levels of specialized populations; for example, women, people of color, and so on? What barriers to equal opportunity exist for these groups?
- Are opportunities plentiful or limited?
- What untapped economic resources exist?
- How is money earned and produced in this community? What are its major industries and services? Is it in growth or decline?
- Do members make their money outside or within the community?
- What forces outside the community influence its economic health?

Educational and communication needs. "Cogito, ergo sum," said René Descartes: "I think, therefore I am." People think and ponder. They want and need to know more. A community needs to know about itself and the world in which it operates. The community has to have information and methods for developing, transmitting, and receiving that information. This set of needs can be called the community's educational and communication (information) needs.

- How do members of the community learn what is going on in the community? In the world?
- How do people decide what is true?
- Whom do people listen to (bishop, radio talk show host, shop steward)? Who has acknowledged credibility?
- What schools and training programs exist for community members? How good are they? What is the degree of community control over these? How is access to them determined? How much financial support do they receive?
- What is the philosophical and editorial bias of the major formal providers of news? This could include newspapers, radio, television, employee newsletters, staff meetings, and other mechanisms set up to provide news. How reliable are they?
- What are the informal methods of providing news? What philosophical and editorial bias exists there? This could include the grapevine or rumor mill, the underground or alternative press, unofficial memoranda, and other methods people use to communicate their perceptions of "what is really going on." How reliable are they?
- What important information doesn't get communicated to community members? How do you know this?
- How interested are community members in communicating with one another?

The more interested you become in your community, the more you will want to understand it and what it requires. This is not a major project. You will simply begin to look at and think about your community in a different way. One sage observer of baseball noted that a team needs to do five things well: hit, hit with power, run, catch, and throw. The average baseball fan knows this. When, as they often do, fans consider the fortunes of their favorite team, they think about these needs and how they are being met. How solid is the pitching staff? Do we need a good late reliever? They worry that the fancy fielding shortstop can't hit a lick. Would we be better off if we traded that good base stealer for a power hitter?

You are like a baseball fan, but instead of a team you have a community. Start thinking about what the community needs and how it could improve. As you proceed you will ask more questions, and you will gain a deeper understanding of the community's assets and needs and the extent to which these assets are recognized and the needs are or are not being met.

Assessing the Community's Unmet Needs

Ideally, a community meets the needs of all its members. Of course, this ideal functioning hardly ever occurs. Needs are often undiscovered, undeclared, or considered unimportant by those who could do something about them. Part of your job as a change agent is to reverse that situation. You will work to discover community needs and help the community effectively declare them so they will be considered important enough to be met.

When a community cannot meet its goals or sustain itself, the community has unmet needs or problems. Goals don't have to be clearly written down. They can be commonly understood. For example, teen parents don't get together and write down the goal: "To have healthy children." Common sense will tell you such a goal exists. If medical care is required to meet this goal and if members of the community don't receive medical care, then adequate medical care becomes an unmet need, a community problem. You will be attempting to discover such unmet needs, those sources of frustration or barriers to a community's ability to flourish.

You want to do something to solve a particular community problem, an unmet need. You even have a pretty good idea how to do it, and you are willing to put your ideas to the test. Hold on. You might take a moment (or a month) to make sure you have a good understanding of the need you are trying to meet. That is, you should probably take time to do a needs assessment.

Usually when people say that needs exist, what they are really talking about is unmet needs. A needs assessment measures unmet needs. Some look at service needs or unprovided services. By the way, this does not always mean social services. "Services" can be either formal or informal forms of assistance. In most cases a needs assessment looks at community needs that are not being met or necessary services or activities that are not being provided in the community.

A needs assessment is a process for identifying the range of a community's needs or for more clearly understanding a particular need. In either event, it is intended to result in a "re-

duction of uncertainty" (McKillip, 1987, p. 19). Instead of getting an overview of the community, you are taking an in-depth look at one of its aspects, its unmet needs. In addition to an examination of the *extent* and *intensity* of need, the assessment should examine *how often* the need is felt and for *how long*. Finally, you also want to know *who* actually *feels* this need.

A needs assessment can include a large population group; for example, a city, a six-county area, or even a state. Or it can look at the unmet needs of a smaller population; for example, a neighborhood, a church congregation, or workers in an agency. Further, it can be designed to uncover any unmet needs or only those in a certain area, say mental health or recreation (Lewis, Lewis, & Soufleé, 1991).

Needs assessments are generally performed for one of three reasons:

- To see if there is any need for action
- To help design or direct some already contemplated action
- To confirm what we already know and to justify an already decided action

The first case forces us to look at a situation we might have been ignoring or simply are oblivious to. In the second case, problems have come to our attention, but we don't have a solid grip on their dimensions. Because we want to increase the odds that our actions will be effective, we take some time to consider what actions are most required. In the third case, we don't really intend to learn anything, so we usually don't. The purpose is to show the correctness of a course of action, so we really only pay attention to information that supports that claim. This approach is geared more to public relations than to discovery.

To design your needs assessment, you need to determine six things:

- The community whose unmet needs you intend to clarify
- The range of needs you intend to examine
- The process for getting the information you need

- The method you will use to interpret the information
- The time and money you have to do this
- How this information will be used

The first two points and the last two are pretty easy to figure out. Thinking about these things probably prompted you to do a needs assessment in the first place.

The other two, getting and interpreting the information, are a bit trickier. Frankly, it is possible to invest a great deal of money, time, and frustration in these two activities. A general caution is to avoid overdoing things. You can get so bogged down in hairsplitting details that you end up hating the process and don't want anything to do with the findings once you are done. It is possible to design a process that is creative and stimulating, one you look forward to doing. Taking a close look at something that hasn't received its due attention can excite people.

Gathering information about your community and its needs is an essential step in community change, and much has been written about the various methods for accomplishing that task. The following approaches to obtaining information about your community's needs (as well as some of the more general steps for gaining a better insight into your community described later in the chapter) are drawn from the work of Kahn (1970); Lewis, Lewis, and Souflée (1991); Lotspeich and Kleymeyer (1976); Martí-Costa and Serrano Garcia (1995); Neuber, Atkins, Jacobson, and Reuterman (1980); Warren and Warren (1984); Warheit, Bell, and Schwab (1984); Berkowitz (1982); McKillip (1987); and Zastrow (1995).

A beginning step in the process is to look at information that already exists. *Existent* or *extant data* are contained in statistics that have already been collected and analyzed and in reports that have been written.

At the beginning you may be unsure about just what information you need. That is alright. Most projects start out that way. Get some of the information you *think* you need, and then review it. This will help you focus future inquiry. To augment this extant data, get the views of members of the community. This step involves deciding how many members you need to hear from and who those members are. Thinking this through will help you determine how to approach them. Do you talk with people individually or in a group? Do you extend an open invitation to anyone who is interested (for example, hold a public hearing), or do you select participants? Do you mail out a questionnaire or meet with people face to face? These are some of the questions you need to answer.

A couple of additional points should be made regarding this aspect of your data collection process. First, get the perspectives of people who feel the need as well as those who could potentially feel the need. Second, have an eye to the future. Gather information from people whose support you will need down the road as you respond to the needs you identify. Collect the information in a way that strengthens the likelihood of their future involvement. Two sets of people are important for future contacts. One set includes the people who will decide on the course of action in response to the recognition of unmet needs, including those who have influence on these decision makers. The second set includes those people who will implement the action.

Once you have gathered opinions and information from community members, you need to address the second problem area; that is, you need to figure out what it all means. Think about the credibility of your sources, the intensity with which the information is offered, and how frequently it is mentioned.

Decide whose facts and opinions carry the most weight with you. Statistics and reports give factual information but are often devoid of feeling, that special human quality that rounds out our understanding of an issue. Conversely, those who feel a problem or who feel intensely about it often lack objectivity. You need to determine which sources give you valid and meaningful information.

Next, decide how to gauge the intensity of

the information. There are opinions and there are strongly held opinions; there are feelings and there are strongly held feelings. It is important to weigh the depth or intensity of the opinions and feelings you receive. Some problems will be felt mildly by many people. Some will be felt intensely, though by fewer people. Acknowledge this intensity and decide how you will account for it in your response.

The frequency with which an unmet need is mentioned by multiple sources is a good indication that you need to pay attention to it. If today on the train, at work, at the store, and at home different people have told you that you have your shirt on backward, there might just be something to it.

A needs assessment is the beginning of your planning process. It helps you identify barriers to community health, uncover possible issues, and raise community consciousness and commitment to action. A very important caution must be voiced here: *Do not define the community according to its unmet needs or its problems.* To do so is discouraging and self-defeating. The purpose of a needs assessment is to provide a focus to promote action; simply cataloguing a list of maladies does not do that. Later, as you plan your response, you will consider other dimensions of the problem, including what produces this situation of unmet needs, what keeps needs from being met, and how long this has gone on. These questions are really further extensions of your needs assessment. They lead to decisions for action. Planning will also help you understand the resources available to meet that need.

At this beginning point, your main concern is to clarify your focus. You want to start off on the right track. You also want to know that what you are doing matters. A needs assessment will tell you this.

Community Resources

As you answer questions about community needs, recognize that the community has many resources available to meet these needs. The fact that needs are not adequately met does not necessarily mean that resources don't exist to do the job. Part of the problem has to do with decisions on how resources are allocated. Another part of the problem involves our ability to recognize and develop resources. Though some additional help from outside the community may be required, you will discover that you have a lot more going for you than you thought.

Each community has unmet needs. That is true. It is also true that no matter how poor or frightened or lacking in immediate power, each community has resources to meet many of these needs, including the most important resource, people. In fact, a crucial element for success is your ability to recognize and build on actual and potential capabilities that exist in your community. This, not concern over limitations, will be the foundation of your work. An overemphasis on liabilities is a serious error that colors problem solving in shades of inadequacy and dependence, undermining any attempt at empowerment.

If you remember from the discussion in Chapter 2, the entire process of developing communities depends on your ability to recognize and build on community assets. A needs assessment provides valuable information but yields only a limited view of the community. To complete your work you need to do a resource assessment. A needs assessment can help give you a focus; a resource assessment gives you the energy. You can use the same approaches for a resource assessment as you do for a needs assessment: gather extant data, get information directly from community members, and make and record observations. The methods for community data gathering described later in this chapter can be applied to discovering resources.

Almost anything is a potential resource. Part of the trick is to start seeing things as potential resources. In one sense, resources can be classified according to the needs they meet. For example, if people need to eat, food is the corresponding resource. If people need access to community decisions, the courts could be a corresponding resource. But confining resources to distinct need categories is a tricky and mistaken business. Most things can be used in many ways. The last thing you want to do is limit the use of a resource or limit your thinking about it.

Books, for example, are great resources. You can read them and acquire knowledge. You can also prop up a slide projector with them. They are great for putting on a stack of papers to keep them from blowing away. You can drop a big book on the floor and wake up half the class. Books are a great resource.

A complete catalogue of your community's resources would be a lifetime's work. Focus your attention on what you want to accomplish, then think of all the resources that could apply. The process of discovering community resources never ends. Each time you take an action, you use resources. If you track these assets, you will have an updated inventory of physical, human, and social capital available to the community (Kretzman & McNight, 1993).

To discover your community resources, ask yourself these questions:

- What natural resources exist in your community? Examples are land, water, and trees.
- What tangible human-made things exist in your community? Examples are cars, bridges, and libraries.
- What systems have developed to serve members? Examples are democracy, employee grievance procedures, and games.
- What relationships have members of this community developed? Examples include family, friends, or business associates.
- What are the major institutions in your community? Churches, synagogues, schools, and government centers are examples of important institutions.
- What forms of currency are available in your community? Examples include money, barter, and favors.
- What human qualities and values exist in your community? Examples are honesty, determination, and passion.
- What skills and talents exist in your community? Examples include artistic talents, carpentry skills, and computer programming abilities.
- What information and knowledge is available in your community? Examples include scientific knowledge, historical knowledge, and inside information.
- What resource, asset, or potential contribution do you possess?
- What resources could serve more purposes? For example, a house can also be a meeting place; a church can also be a shelter; an office softball team can also be a mutual support group.
- What resources do you have a personal connection with?
- What resources can be combined to produce new resources? For example, what could be produced with a storage room and a dozen employees who each own 100 books?

Kretzman and McNight (1993) provide another useful framework for looking at community resources. Their community assets checklist includes:

Capacities of individuals: The talents of individuals in the community provide the fundamental bank of assets for the community.

Gifts of "strangers": When the contributions of marginalized citizens in our midst—the young, the old—become habitually recognized and integrated, the process of community building becomes inclusive.

Associations of citizens: Associations such as faith communities, ethnic organizations, Boy Scouts and Girl Scouts, and groups of citizens working together empower individuals and amplify gifts.

Local private, public, and nonprofit institutions: These institutions represent significant concentrations of resources, including facilities, materials and equipment, purchasing power, and technical skills.

Physical assets: Land, buildings, and streets, for example, are assets that enhance the community and, if underused, might be more fully developed.

Capacity finders and developers: These are the community leaders who are clearly oriented to finding and mobilizing assets, particularly encouraging ways for resources to be linked to each other.

Many resources go unacknowledged because people don't think they are important. When you begin to see the potential value of things, you will discover resources you never knew existed. Over time, instead of wondering "What can we do about . . . ," you may find yourself asking "What can we do with all these things we have?" This is a very different question.

Capacity for Change and Disposition to Change

All communities have some capacity to change, though some have more constraints than others. Some of the constraints are real. For example, the law may limit the political involvement of certain public employees. Some are practical; for example, single parents may spend most of their time and energy taking care of day-to-day job and family challenges. Many are attitudinal; people believe that nobody else cares or that things simply can't be changed.

Each community also differs in its disposition to change. Some communities are happy with things just the way they are. Others have grown used to things, tolerating what they don't like. Still others are ready to do something—anything—that might make a difference, now. The desire for change often involves correcting injustices, but it is not limited to this. It can also involve providing new opportunities or challenges, escaping the boredom of the routine, or just doing something fun.

Understanding your community's ability to challenge constraints that are real, practical, or imagined and its desire to do something different are crucial in directing your activities as a change agent. Capacity and desire for change can be evaluated by asking these questions:

- Are there legal limits on activities that apply specifically to your community?
- How much discretionary time do people really have?
- What really rankles people in your community?
- Do people complain about things? Do they complain publicly or in private?
- Do people talk about how they wish things would be? To whom do they talk?
- Are people who voice a desire for change criticized and put down or encouraged and supported?
- Are people intimidated by those in authority positions?
- Do people recognize when they are not doing what they want to do or when they are doing what they don't want to do?
- Have change attempts failed or succeeded in the past?
- Do people go outside official channels to solve problems?
- Is anyone exploring change in any way right now?

As you answer the questions posed here, and the ones you will surely add, you will build a storehouse of information that will make things a lot smoother for you now and help your change efforts.

How to Find Out What You Need to Know

You should now have a better idea of what you need to know about your community. In this

Take a Moment to Discover . . . .

See if you can find someone in your office, class, or neighborhood who can provide, for free or below normal cost, one of these skills or resources either themselves or through someone they know.

gourmet cooking
computer skills
grant writing expertise
political lobbying
fund-raising experience
a musician
a juggler
a plumber
a news reporter
a mechanic

section, a number of specific sources of information are described together with some ideas on how you can use those sources.

Valuing the Library

Welcome to the library. Step inside. It is comfortable, peaceful (unless it's the college library the week before papers are due), and packed with information. Take a break from whatever you are doing and spend an afternoon at the library. Your public library has a treasure trove of information about your community, so does your college or university library.

Prepare some questions in advance. This will give the librarian a better idea of how to help you. It will also help you focus your inquiry. Even if you think a vertical file is a tool for sharpening saws, do not dismay. Most librarians are very helpful. Not only do they know books and where to find them, but they enjoy helping people uncover information and discover the other wonders of their library, such as audiovisual resources, computer data banks, and much more.

You should be able to accomplish several

things during your visit to the library, especially if you come prepared with specific questions. Certainly, you want some specific information about your community. Particular facts, figures, names, and background information will help you answer some of the questions you have. It is also important to become familiar with the sources themselves. You will never be able to write down or remember everything that is potentially valuable. That's why we have libraries—so you can go back when you need the information.

A typical library will have many publications describing aspects of your community. Some of these will be national publications, some state, and some local. Some will be put together by the government, including special reports, such as a report by a special task force on homelessness. Others are put together by private groups, perhaps banks or special interest organizations. Most libraries can borrow from other libraries. They also purchase or accept material from organizations if there appears to be sufficient demand for it.

Check to see if one of your local libraries is a depository for the Government Printing Office or for the Census Bureau. If not, see if you can find out where one is. A depository houses some or all the publications of these two government agencies.

If you can't find something, don't be shy about asking the librarian for help. Here is a sampler of material that could well be in your library.

Census Bureau data. You are likely to find the *County and City Data Book* as well as the *Statistical Abstract of the United States.* Information on ethnic diversity, average household income, family size, and many other pieces of demographic data are contained in these publications. Although these data have some limitations, they provide a comprehensive statistical breakdown of the place in which you live.

City directory. This gives you the names, addresses, occupations, and phone numbers of the people who reside in your area. Many people who aren't in the phone book will be in here. It is usually cross-listed by address. In a neighborhood campaign, this can be a valuable asset.

Community profile publications. Generally published by an agency such as a commerce or tourism department, these profiles give a one- or two-page glimpse of most cities and towns in the state. The profile is chock-full of information. In many communities, the local United Way also has a comprehensive community profile.

Newspaper file. The library should have current subscriptions and files of major local newspapers. This includes recent back issues of the paper itself as well as older editions on microfilm or microfiche. From time to time, newspapers publish special reports that provide extremely valuable background information. Typically, these reports treat some aspect of the community in depth; for example, profiling the most influential people and community groups or discussing major economic forces affecting the community.

Community overview reports are also common and describe the history and key characteristics of the community. From time to time the newspaper issues special topic reports, providing an in-depth look at a particular social concern such as education, teen pregnancy, crime, or child abuse. Included in these accounts will be the range of the problem, efforts being made to solve it, and the people active in these efforts.

In larger cities numerous minor newspapers serve specialized populations. These are usually published weekly or monthly for specific areas of the city or for special groups such as downtown businesspeople or retirees.

Local magazines. Most larger cities have a magazine named after the city that caters to upper-income readers. Publications for local businesspeople, supporters of the arts, or people losing sleep wondering if they are living the appropriate regional "lifestyle" are also common. Features on local peo-

ple, politics, power, and persiflage are found here.

State yearbooks. Most states have an annual publication that provides a guide to state government, including descriptions of state agencies, legislative processes, history, important organizations in the state, and other information.

Human resource directories. These are extremely helpful in getting to know what services are provided in your community and the names of the organizations, agencies, and people providing them. One comprehensive directory may be published by the local information and referral agency, but directories that address specific topics may exist as well (for example, resources for divorced persons or for teens).

Impact or issue publications. These are special reports prepared by public interest groups. Your local Community Action Agency or Sierra Club, for example, might produce such a report. (If no report of this type is on the library shelf, contact the organization most likely to author such a report.)

Political directories. Several groups publish these directories, most commonly, the League of Women Voters. In some areas, the telephone company publishes an excellent directory. If no directories appear in your library, call the League of Women Voters or your local political parties.

Encyclopedia of Associations. Arranged by topic and cross-listed by state, this wonderful encyclopedia lists thousands of organizations in the United States. It also provides a paragraph or two about the organization with addresses and phone numbers. It may be helpful to know not only about the organizations in your state but also ones in other states that are working on the same issues you are.

Lists of local clubs and organizations. Many communities publish a comprehensive list of all local groups, including phone numbers and the names of officers. If your library does not have this, check with your local Chamber of Commerce or visitors' bureau.

Travel or tourism books. You will be surprised at how much you can find out about your community in these books. Larger cities usually have their own book. Smaller communities may be listed in a state guide book. The latter is usually not that helpful to a resident. Remember that these are written for outsiders and tourists, so they are likely to contain "points of interest" information with a little exaggerated local history and color.

Economic profiles. Put together by banks, local development corporations, or the business or economics department of the local university, economic profiles describe the economic sectors of the community and their health. Indicators of economic activity are frequently provided. Again, if this is not in your library, check with a major bank or other likely source.

Community trend profiles. Focusing on how people in the community appear to be spending their time and money, established and emerging community trends in major categories (for example, leisure time) are described. Check with the marketing department of a college or university in your area if your library doesn't have this.

Other publications that might be helpful include labor market analyses and statistics, your state's statistical review, national ranking of cities (for example, *Book of World City Rankings: Places Rated Almanac* and *Retirement Places Rated*), *Municipal Yearbook, World Chamber of Commerce Directory,* and the *Commercial Atlas and Marketing Guide.*

Special Libraries

Special libraries may exist in your community. Not all areas have these, so check with your local public library to discover special libraries in your area.

Newspaper libraries. These special libraries primarily provide background information to the newspaper's own reporters. Their basic source of material is the newspaper itself. They also have a general reference collection. These

Take a Moment to Discover . . . .

Spend 30 minutes in the library. See how many of these pieces of information you can get.

- the salary of the mayor
- the rate of teenage pregnancy
- the latest unemployment figures
- the principal area industry
- the local head of the Republican party
- the percentage of voters registered as Democrats
- the number of hospital beds
- the names of two union officials
- the average annual rainfall
- the record of one high school football team
- the story behind one historical landmark
- the names of the area's three most influential women
- the names of the area's three most influential men
- the hours the library is open

libraries are not commonly open to the general public, but their archives are now available in some communities via the Internet. Others can be accessed through national computer databases such as DIALOG, Dow Jones, or Lexis-Nexis, which index major newspapers. These database services may be subscribed to by public and academic libraries. If this service is available at your library and your paper participates, you have a wealth of local background information on almost any subject. If your paper is not part of this database, you still may be able to find out how your issues are handled in other cities.

Law libraries. These special libraries exist for the purposes of legal research and are usually part of a university law school.

Specialized government libraries. Local and state planning departments often have their own libraries. Various community plans can be found here along with valuable background data on community makeup and growth patterns.

Most state capitols have state government libraries and archives that provide library services to state legislators and other government decision makers. They routinely provide background information on issues to state politicians and agency people. Although you can go in person, it is usually helpful to go through your state legislator with a request for information. Local governments often have their own reference libraries serving city or county staff and elected officials.

Check to see how accessible these library services are to the general public. You can usually have someone, a staff member or public official, make the request for you (especially if they know you) if you can't make it easily on your own. Their wide access to information and electronic mail makes these libraries a potentially valuable resource.

Issue Research

Libraries are valuable resources for issue research as well. Reference libraries can be particularly helpful in guiding you to sources that can give you a solid grounding in the matter your group is working on. As described in Chapter 5, a lot of information can be found through the Internet and World Wide Web, though, again, be cautious about its validity. Even with the information available on-line you may still want to go to the library and pick up a book or an article.

Take a Moment to Discover . . . .

Identify an issue or topic in which you are interested. See how many public or private community groups and organizations exist that might deal with this issue.

. . . .

Leaving the Library and Looking for More

You have this sneaking suspicion that there may be more to finding out about your community than sitting in the library. Suspicion confirmed. Actually, you could go crazy with all this and never get any other work done.

So, where else? Your next stop would include various agencies, organizations, and interest groups that know something about your community. These include government agencies and private groups, both profit and nonprofit. Some of these (for example, government agencies) might not actually be physically in your community. However, most state and federal agencies collect information about groups of people such as elementary school children or geographic communities such as Durham, North Carolina.

What kinds of organizations could provide useful information? Look for organizations that do at least one of the following things.

Sell your community. Economic development corporations, visitors' bureaus, tourism organizations, chambers of commerce, convention bureaus, and travel organizations know about your community.

Sell in or from your community. Franchise organizations (for example, McDonald's), radio stations, homebuilders associations, real estate associations, banks, and newly arrived major employers are examples of organizations that need to understand the retail or labor markets of your community.

Serve your community. Councils on aging, the United Way, social service providers, religious organizations, and schools become aware of your community's needs through their day-to-day service activities.

State a particular concern about your community. Public interest organizations such as environmental organizations, anticrime organizations, minority affairs organizations, and business organizations all have particular issues they advocate and around which they generate information.

Study your community. Associations of counties, leagues of cities and towns, state and federal agencies, universities, planning and marketing companies, and consulting companies may collect or generate information about your community.

Once you have established a good general understanding of your community, you will probably want more specific information on some particular aspect of it. Perhaps you want to know more about subcommunities within your broad community (for example, mobile home communities). Or maybe you want to know more about specific conditions within your community (for example, childhood illness). In fact, you will probably move very rapidly to this level of inquiry.

Unless you intend to mobilize your entire broad community about something, you will study the broad level only to understand the setting or context in which your close community operates. Though you continue to improve your understanding of the broad community, you will acquire more information about your close community and the situation it faces. Review the five sets of organizations that have some particular knowledge about the broad community and select those most likely to have the kind of specific information you need.

What are you likely to get from these sources? First, personal perspectives—talk to people. Most people are happy to tell you just what they think. Ask them. These added viewpoints of people who work in an area that is of interest to you can fill in the blanks you find in written material. A further advantage is that this gives you the chance to start building a personal relationship with this source, which could be helpful in the future.

Next, get statistics and other data. Some of this will be descriptive, and some will be numbers, charts, and graphs. All are pieces of

the puzzle. Taken together they will help provide you with a picture of your community.

Prepared reports may also be available. Somebody has taken the time to sit down and write about what is going on in your community. They have collected and analyzed information for you. You might as well make use of this effort.

Will any of these sources just give you information if you ask? Can you waltz into McDonald's, order a Big Mac and fries and say: "By the way, may I also have an analysis of projected population growth to go?" No, but you can get the burger and fries.

It is generally pretty easy to get information from government, educational, and social service agencies. Information from those that sell the community and from public interest groups is also generally available. Private for-profit firms are less willing to offer what they know, especially if information is something they sell or if it is accumulated to give them a competitive advantage. However, just because a firm is private, don't automatically assume that it only collects information for its own purposes. Many do publish reports to the community.

Because it is so easy to get information from available sources, you may not want to waste your time trying to get something from a reluctant source. It should take no more than a day's worth of work to get all the beginning information you need from these sources. Spend about half an hour figuring out what you need to know, half an hour figuring out who might know it, and half an hour looking up phone numbers. After an hour and a half of phone calls, you will probably have all the initial information you need on its way to you. Unless you came to work late, it is not even lunchtime yet.

You will more than likely spend a few more hours in the next couple of days following new leads, following up on messages, and talking to people on the phone. After a total of 8 hours' work, you will have quite a fat file folder. (Remember, you do have to read this stuff.) As

Change Agent Tip

A simple guide for discovering the real leader of a community is to ask members of the community two simple questions. Number one: "Who would people in general say the leader of the community is?" Number two: "Personally, who do you think the real leader of this community is?" If the same person's name pops up frequently in answer to question number two, you have a better idea (not a definite answer) of who the real leader is.

time goes on, you will refine your questions and get more precise information.

You have spent some time in the library and you have received information from organizations, but you are still not satisfied. Alright, what now? "What about regular people?" you ask. "Shouldn't I get some information directly from individuals?" Yes, you should, but which ones?

You don't want to spend the rest of your life doing background. Whether you are talking about your broad community or your close community, there are three groups of people whose ideas you can solicit.

People from the *leadership group* could provide you with important insights. These are opinion leaders (people whose point of view helps shape other people's points of view), action leaders (people who can get other people to follow or do things), and representative leaders (people who represent the community to people outside the community). It is a good idea to ask leaders whose help you may need down the road.

The next group is the *knowledgeable group,* people who are likely to have either general or specific knowledge about the community. These people have a particular area of expertise (for example, traffic engineer), are particularly involved in the community (for example, community activist), hold a particular belief about the community (for example, a political columnist), or hold a position that gives them a somewhat unique perspective (for example, police officer).

The final group is the *at large group.* This consists of members of the community in general with no particular regard to who they are, what they do, or what they may know.

You have a range of folks from which to choose. Here are some basic ways to get the information, ideas, and opinions people have to offer.

Guided personal discussions.   Ideally this is a face-to-face discussion, although it can take place over the phone. These conversations are generally pretty easy to set up if you know the person, and still quite possible even if you don't. Simply call and ask if you can have 10 to 15 minutes of their time to discuss the topic. It is hard for people to legitimately deny a 10- or 15-minute request. Most will end up giving you much more time. Even if they don't, you can get quite a bit done in 15 minutes. In advance prepare six basic questions you would like to cover. You can allow the discussion to flow; just make sure your points get covered.

Active participation in the life of your community is valuable because this involvement puts you in a position to know and to be known. Two benefits flow from this: You learn more about the things you come in contact with, and you increase your network of personal contacts. Each person you meet also has a network of personal contacts. This provides you with much easier access to information and resources. People are more willing to go out of the routine to help a friend, or the friend of a friend, than they are to help a stranger.

Focus groups. This creative atmosphere for gathering information and building interest in a topic is comprised of people who bring particular perspectives to discussion of an issue. The group explores the topic with guidance from a moderator. It is usually a good idea to get a mix of people from all three groups previously mentioned—leadership, knowledge, and at large. You don't necessarily want only people who already agree with each other.

A focus group provides a lively exchange of ideas and opinions. Although the group may arrive at a generally agreed-on point of view, this is not required. Key questions around a certain topic (focus) are prepared in advance. The questions are structured to allow the conversation to flow yet remain on track. Some questions are simple and straightforward; others require more thoughtful consideration.

A moderator or facilitator asks the questions and directs the discussion, making sure all participants have an opportunity to add their two cents worth. Acting as facilitator for a focus group can be a good role for a nonprofessional community member (Krueger & King, 1997). The facilitator will see to it that an atmosphere of open discussion prevails. For example, although disagreement is appropriate, intimidation is not. A policy of nonattribution is sometimes followed to encourage frankness. This policy means that although the overall results of the discussion may be used no particular remark or opinion will be attributed to any participant.

Surveys and questionnaires. This is a good way to get detailed, specific, and consistent information. Surveys can be administered in person, over the phone, or through the mail. The more personal the approach is, the more success you will have in getting the survey completed.

A survey can be used to collect information, such as a catalogue of the skills of individuals or the nature of the contributions they would like to make. You can also use a survey to identify interests or concerns or to gather opinions. These types of surveys require a little more care.

You can design a scientific survey process that is highly reliable (it can be repeated over and over with the same degree of accuracy) and valid (the information you receive is a correct and meaningful reflection of the group represented in the survey). You are the judge of how scientific you need to be, but six important factors should be considered.

1. *Population to be surveyed.* Are you asking the right people? If you want to know which school activities high school students like best, don't ask the teachers, ask the students.

2. *Sampling.* How many from the general population do you intend to ask, and how will they be selected? If you know the people you want to talk to and their number is small enough, you can ask each one. However, you may want to know what a lot of people think. In this case, your survey group should accurately reflect the general population. If you ask only three high school students about their favorite activity, you might hear things that most other students aren't interested in at all. So sample size is important. You also need a good cross-section of the population. If you surveyed 100 students, but only the male freshmen, junior varsity, and varsity football players, you might have a good sample size, but their opinions might not accurately reflect those of the entire student body. Some method of picking people at random is needed. This means that selection of a person to be surveyed is left entirely to chance.

3. *Design the survey instrument.* Figure out what you really need to know and devise questions that will give you that information. Most often you are better off if you can ask *closed-ended* instead of *open-ended* questions. Closed-ended questions are those in which respondents pick from choices you already offer. All they have to do is circle a letter or a number, or write down a letter, number, or single word.

They don't have to write down their own ideas. They merely react to the choices offered.

At times it is a good idea to ask one or two open-ended questions to give respondents a chance to add their own ideas. A more personal method of administration gives greater opportunities for open-ended questions. Generally, though, the fewer questions of this type the better. Open-ended questions often put people off. They may not want to take the time and energy to respond. Further, the more you ask people to write, the more time you will spend trying to read the handwriting and guessing what the respondent really means.

Be careful not to let bias creep into your questions. For example, asking "Do you encourage keeping our children ignorant and unprepared for the future?" may not yield accurate information on how a person will vote on a school bond election.

The length of the survey is also an important matter. A survey that is too long will turn people off. If people don't complete the survey, it doesn't do you any good. During your pretest (described next), time people to see how long it takes for them to complete the survey. You can then let future respondents know how long it will take them to complete it. On the top of the survey itself you can write: "This survey takes only 5 minutes to complete."

4. *Accuracy and clarity.* One of the great fallacies in communication is that people know what we mean. After all, we are always so clear—aren't we? Did you ever get frustrated trying to figure out just what a professor was asking on an objective test? You know, if you look at it one way, the answer is "A"; if you look at it another, the answer is "C." Believe me, you will run into the same problems with your survey. So after you have written it, do a *pretest*—administer your survey to a handful of people who are not in your survey sample. See if they clearly understand what you are asking. Did these questions, even if clearly understood, provide you with the information you wanted? You will find that most of the time you have to revise some survey questions.

5. *Administering the instrument.* The way you conduct the survey is important. Several problems can sneak in. For example, a survey administered by an interviewer, someone who verbally asks the prepared questions, is open to bias. Interviewers should practice beforehand and be critiqued to make sure that none of their mannerisms, including tone of voice, tend to promote certain responses. Surveys conducted by mail have problems as well. Respondents to a mailed survey are likely to be those most interested in the topic. Their ideas may not represent the entire population. You have put a lot of work into preparation of the survey; make sure it is conducted properly. Try to anticipate problems and prevent them.

Finally, respondents need to feel safe to answer honestly. You may need to explain how the results will and will not be used. You may also need to guarantee that the survey will be answered anonymously.

6. *Compiling and analyzing the results.* How you look at the pieces of information and how they relate to each other will help you get a more complete picture. Ask questions that give you clear data so you don't have to guess what the respondent means.

In summary, for your survey to be helpful you need to ask enough of the right people the right questions in a way that makes it likely they will accurately respond to the survey, giving you information you can interpret and use.

Informal Methods

If you *intend* to find out about your community, it is almost impossible not to. All sorts of tidbits of information on your community are out there all the time. Anything from the way streets are named and the number of locks people have on their doors to good and bad gossip will tell you something. Once you have decided to notice things, you will. Here are a few ways of keeping your eyes and ears open that will be particularly helpful to you.

Take a Moment to Discover . . . .

Walk into some public building; for example, City Hall. Spend 15 minutes walking around, looking at signs, reading what is on the walls, perhaps even talking to a few people. Now go outside, sit down, and write down every new piece of information you acquired.

. . . .

Collect Lists

You can start building a kind of who's who in your community from lists. Who is on the board of directors of the theater company or art museum? Who are major donors to the ballet or symphony? Either because they need to look good, have the time and money to do so, or because they genuinely want to influence the culture of the community, supporters of the arts are often important people. Other lists are important as well; in fact, almost all lists of names can be useful. If you get a list, keep it.

Here are some types of lists you may find useful:

Membership lists. Members of country clubs or other private clubs, the chamber of commerce, or professional organizations, such as the bar association, are potentially useful. Any organization that has members will probably have a membership list.

Donor lists. Programs for special events such as a dinner, groundbreaking ceremony, or special recognition ceremony often list major contributors who made the event possible. Political candidates have to file statements identifying their contributors. These are available through the Secretary of State's office. These lists can come in handy.

Lists of officers or boards of directors. Business, civic, and social service organizations often seek strong people to serve as board members or officers. Many organizations list their officers, board members, and other supporters on their letterhead. Save these. Usually these people are at least moderately important and have some interest in the issue their organization addresses.

Officers of political parties. These lists include people who have clearly decided to become involved in community affairs. They want to be around power and perhaps be seen as powerful. To some extent they shape the direction of their parties and influence the behavior of officeholders. The local party headquarters or someone active in party politics will have this list of names.

Create your own lists. One of the best ways to do this is by keeping track of announcements for things such as recent hirings and promotions and recipients of awards or other honors. These can usually be found in the local paper.

Take advantage of any opportunity you have to get a list. Keep them all in a file for easy reference.

The Newspaper Provides More than Just News

News is, of course, important. Read the local news section of the paper to keep abreast of what is going on in your community. You can track the progress of particular issues or particular groups this way. In addition to the general news, pay attention to other sections as well. The editorial point of view of the leading paper usually reflects the prevailing political philosophy of the general community. Pay attention to the editorial position on issues as well as the paper's selection of syndicated columnists.

The section related to business or money often features articles or brief announcements on current or up-and-coming community business leaders. Stories on the community's economic health or particular sectors of the economy are found here too.

Letters to the editor help you identify controversial issues of the day, as well as what people think about them. And the classified section provides clues about the types and number of jobs available, as well as wage rates.

You can also get a good indication of the cost and availability of certain goods and services, such as housing and child care.

When you look at the newspaper, read more than the news. Clip and save those articles you find valuable. Your files on these will serve as good future references.

Strike Up Conversations

Be willing to ask people about their perspectives on the community. People waiting around for something, like a bus or for the machine to finish the rinse cycle at the laundromat, are often willing to pass the time in conversation. People who hear other people talk, such as barbers, hairdressers, and bartenders, often don't mind sharing a perception or two. The letter carrier often has good insights on the area he or she serves; so does the person working the cash register in the cafeteria. These are not interviews, just conversations, perhaps a sadly forgotten art. By just shooting the breeze, you might get a good idea of how the wind blows.

Observe. Walk around. Ride the bus. Get on your bike. Heck, drive your car if you have to. Even if you don't go out of your way to consider your agency, neighborhood, or city from a different perspective, see if you can learn just one new thing a week. That is not a lot to ask. After a year you will have learned at least 50 things you wouldn't have otherwise, and probably many more than that.

Conclusion

As you move from "I" to "we," you will involve people in a way that results in all of you working together to accomplish the goals you share. Depending on the situation you face and how you intend to approach it, you may be working with a handful of people or thousands. These people may come together to work on a specific issue, having little sense that they are a community, or these people may already be involved in a well-established community, strengthened with traditions and recognized by a name. Whoever these people are, you should know about them.

Your community extends from broad to specific groups. It includes geographic and interest groups, some of which are highly structured, whereas others may never actually get together as a community. Based on your general understanding of your community's dynamics and directed by the issue at hand, you need a better awareness of the communities you will mobilize for action, those that will benefit from that action, and those from which you demand a response.

Get to know the basic characteristics of the people in your community. Grasp how the community functions to meet its needs. Identify unmet community needs, perhaps by doing a needs assessment. Your needs assessment will help you understand what improvements may be needed as you go about making a difference in your community. It will give you some indication of what the problems are and how severe and widespread they appear to be. Evaluate the resources the community has on hand as well as ones it could develop. This information will help you to better gauge its capacity to work toward change.

Rely on a variety of sources and techniques to increase your understanding—but don't get stuck in the information gathering phase and forget about taking action. By discovering the wealth of information in the library, gathering reports from community groups, or just talking to people, you will see your community as alive and fascinating. Of course, the best way to learn about your community is to be involved with it. You can get to know basketball by reading up on it and watching it on TV, but you really learn basketball by playing it. The more you play, the more what you read and watch will make sense and be enjoyable. The way to understand your community is to participate in it—take part in its life.

CHAPTER 7

Power

Chapter Highlights

- Power, fundamental to change
- Types of power
- Definitions of power
- Attitudes about power
- Elements of the power relationship
- Why you need power
- Power and the status quo
- Fear of power
- Demands of power
- Bases of power in a community

- Bases of power in a group
- Identifying who has power
- Assessing your own bases of power
- Strategies for building power
- Sources of personal credibility
- Becoming part of powerful circles
- Using information
- Rights, responsibilities, and consequences of using power
- Empowering others

"It's not going too well, Mel," Ben says as he sinks down into one of the two extra chairs in Melanie's office. "How about a little counseling?"

"You can probably start by telling me what 'not too well' means," she replies. "Don't tell me that the old Redondo charm has lost its dazzle."

"Maybe I'm just rusty. Or, then again, maybe I'm just not very important. I can't seem to get any of the big shots at either St. Joan's or at Newbury Medical Center to give me the time of day. The best response I got was from the medical society, and that was only a 'we'll get back to you.' I'm feeling a little humbled."

"Humble? You? Not a chance. Discouraged, maybe, but I doubt humble. So, what you're doing isn't working. What else can we do to get them to respond?"

"Sure would be nice for our group to have a little power, Mel."

Power. The word itself provokes reaction. We need it. We use it. It often slips unsolicited into our daydreams, at times with pleasure, at others with vexation. Whether or not we are willing to acknowledge the role power plays in our actions, it will affect what we are doing at any given moment.

In an escape from proper etiquette, I will speak frankly of power, for nothing is more central to promoting change than your ability to generate and use power. You cannot promote change without using power. It is as simple, and as difficult, as that.

In Chapter 6 you were introduced to the importance of knowing your community, and you were given some steps to help you in that endeavor. You need to understand the circumstances in which you are building and applying power for its generation and use to have focus and be effective. Melanie and Ben have come up against the fact that they need power to provoke a response. They will need to figure out how they can increase their ability to take part in community decisions and to influence those decisions. They are recognizing that having a good idea is only a start. Now they need the power to turn hope into reality.

What is power? Why do you need it? Who has it? How can you get it and use it? And, how can you empower others? In the following pages

I will provide some basic answers to these questions and examine other issues pertaining to power that merit your attention.

There are many notions of power, ranging from abstract formulations of power as a force that produces a change, to practical notions of power by which machines make available energy more efficient, to personal notions of power over one's self. Of all these various types of power, I will be concerned primarily with political power—the power to make or shape policies that have an impact on people—and what might be called relationship power; that is, the power to influence how people relate to one another.

What Is Power?

In the field of community change, power is the capacity to move people in a desired direction to accomplish some end. Robinson and Hannah (1994) describe power as "the ability to realize one's values in the world" (p. 77). Rubin and Rubin (1986) suggest that power is "the ability to accomplish one's will with or without opposition" (p. 13). Building on Bertrand Russell's perception of power, Dennis Wrong (1995) adds a social dimension by implying that power necessarily involves relationships between people. He defines power as "the capacity of some persons to produce intended and foreseen effects on others" (p. 2). These definitions all suggest that power is something a person possesses and is willing to use. Power involves some sense of purpose or intention. We expect to meet some need or receive some benefit through the use of power. So, having power means that you can get what you want, or what you think you want, by having people behave or respond the way you want them to.

Sounds pretty devious and self-serving doesn't it? Perhaps it is more devious to be coy about power and more dishonest to deny the fact that we have intentions we act upon. Much like the youth with a flashlight and magazines, we have hidden our notions of power under the covers for far too long. It's time for an open assessment of power.

Power is not dominance. Dominance is the way some people use power. Collaboration is the way other people use power. You can powerfully participate with other parties to create mutually acceptable solutions, even parties whose interests are different or in apparent conflict with yours. You may combine your power with that of another group to bring something new to life. You can use your power to force an opponent to end exploitive or destructive practices. You can use your power to work with others to improve a condition. You can use your power to create.

The use of power does not have to be manipulative, but it can be. It does not have to be noble, but it can be. It may be used for evil just as well as for good (Wartenberg, 1990). If you notice the use of power and like what was accomplished, you will probably think that power is fine. If you disagree with the purpose and the application, not only will you be upset about the use of power but you will probably notice it more as well.

Power does not imply stiff resistance. Nor does it require a struggle or a fight. Yet this is how we often conceive of power: people being forced to do something they don't want to do by someone who can make them do it. This is neither a healthy nor an accurate picture of power, but those images haunt the corners of our understanding of this basic concept.

The more opposition that exists, the more the use of power will be seen, simply because there is a clash of power. If a win-lose brawl ensues, things could become ugly. Here, it is both the clash and the manner chosen to resolve the differences that call attention to power and shape our reactions to it. It is not simply the presence of power.

Power can be used in a spirit of cooperation as easily as it can occur in a climate of conflict. If you and your friends are trying to decide where to go for pizza, you may rely on the recommendations of one or two members of your group. Hearing their strong endorsement of Juan O'Grady's as the best place in town to get pizza, you willingly go along, even though you have reservations about the name. The pizza turns out to be as good as promised. Power was used—someone moved a group of people, quite literally, in a desired direction. The fact that there was no difficult conflict does not mean there was no power used.

In and of itself, power is neither good nor bad. It is simply, and importantly, the necessary element that provides the impetus in the process of making things different. That it may be used to dignify or demean depends on the user, not the tool.

Does power derive from the person? Are some people simply more powerful than others? Or is there more to it than that? Power, like many other things in life, depends on the situation, although particular people can have power in many situations. The basic question is: Can you get these particular people to behave in this particular way at this particular time? The relative degree and location of power in a situation is determined by the interplay among the individuals and groups involved. By changing who the respondents are, what they are supposed to do, or the context in which the behavior is supposed to occur, the power of a particular individual will necessarily increase or decrease.

A classroom teacher may tell students to complete a number of math problems in the next half hour. The students are expected to comply or face some sort of sanction. An hour later, the same teacher is in the middle of a faculty meeting on budget cuts and makes the same request of fellow faculty members. The teacher's colleagues might not respond so readily. In fact, they might well think this teacher needs a little time off and a little help . . . and not with math problems. The same request produced different results in different situations. In the first instance, the teacher is considered powerful. In the second, the teacher is considered disturbed.

Basically, power involves a relationship between people. For example, if someone were to influence you, the power flows from your perception that someone has control over resources (for example, time, money, information, freedom, affection) that are important to you and that that individual is willing to exercise control to your benefit or detriment. Thus, you behave in a way to achieve the gain or avoid the loss you believe will be caused by being provided with or denied these resources. The more you are dependent on an individual for those resources, and the more important the consequences of their use or withholding are to you, the more that individual is likely to influence you.

If you need food stamps, you may do what the food stamp worker tells you to do, even if this means you have to do things you ordinarily wouldn't do. You may answer questions about your private circumstances or gather documentation that proves your need for assistance. You do all this to make sure the worker provides the food stamps that keep you and your family from going hungry. If you are working in collaboration with a group from an adjoining neighborhood to clean up graffiti in the area, the time and location of your first project may be influenced by your need to use one another's tools, paint, and volunteers, along with your desire to establish a cooperative relationship that may benefit you on other matters. Each group working by itself might have made a choice different from the one required by the relationship. The key here is the perception that someone has control over resources you believe to be important. Whether or not they actually do have control or whether or not those resources are really important is not significant. If you believe this to be the case, you will act; if not, you won't.

What occurs in relationships between individuals also holds true in relationships between groups. An individual or group who desires influence must somehow communicate the potential for controlling resources. Further, to be effective this must be done in a way that provides an opportunity for those being influenced to perform the desired behavior. These pathways to power are shown in Figure 7-1.

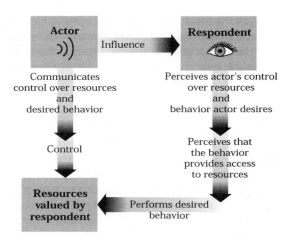

Figure 7-1
Pathways of intentional influence attempt

As an example of how this could work, imagine the plight of Earl Blern. Earl is an agency director being urged by members of the community to change certain agency procedures community members believe restrict access to service. A program designed to benefit women who work outside the home operates from 9:00 A.M. to 4:00 P.M. Monday through Friday. These hours are convenient for the agency but make it impossible for most women who are to benefit from the program to participate. After all, many are at work during those hours.

Earl is fearful that this well-organized community group will go directly to his board of directors and pressure them to fire him if he does not make the changes they want. So Earl complies with the group's demands and changes the hours.

Earl perceived that the community can, through their contacts with the board and the pressure they can bring to bear, control a resource that is very important to him, namely, the board's favor and, ultimately, his job. The group has power. It was able to accomplish its purpose by changing Earl's behavior from refusal to modify the program's hours of operation to acceptance.

What if this group weren't really organized? What if they not only didn't know anyone on Earl's board but they didn't even think about talking to the board at all? It doesn't matter. Earl's perception of the situation governed his response.

What if the situation were completely different? What if Earl perceived the group as being poorly organized with no plans to talk to his board or that no one would listen if they did? He would probably continue to resist. Even if Earl's perceptions were way off base, the group would have no power with him until he got a different message, one that changed his perception.

Finally, what if the group immediately put pressure on the board, and Earl was fired? The group would have been powerful over Earl, but they would not have accomplished their goal. By denying Earl the opportunity to change his behavior in the desired direction, by giving him the message too late, the group would not have been effective with Earl. Maybe the next director will comply, but it is a little late for old Earl to remedy the situation.

Why Do You Need Power?

If you want people to move in a particular direction, you have to use some form of power to get them there. It is as basic as the laws of physics. To change the direction of something or to overcome the inertia of the status quo, some force (power) must be applied to accelerate motion in the desired direction.

You will learn over and over and over again that simply because an idea "makes sense" has little bearing on what happens. You have probably learned this a time or two already. Do you ever have trouble getting around to paying your bills, or doing your studying, or maybe even losing a recalcitrant pound or 20? Did you find that the discovery or introduction of good ideas, ones that were reasonable and "made sense," just wasn't enough to change what was happening? It is not that we lack good ideas. It is

not that we don't know how to do things more effectively. It is that we don't often move past talking about ideas to acting on them, to implementing them, powerfully. Old habits, old beliefs, and old fears get in the way. These must be overcome to bring something new into existence.

The purpose you intend to achieve will require that people do things differently from the way they do them now. Some of these people won't mind—in fact, they may want to change—but other people will resist. Some force must be applied to awaken support, to get supporters acting in concert, or to overcome opponents.

Understand that somebody's interests are being met by the way things are at the moment. The bigger your issue, the more somebodies we are talking about. They are used to things the way they are. They may not want them to be different. Further, some of these people are much more used to getting their way than to giving way. They are used to telling other people

what to do. They don't like being told. These people aren't going to like what you are doing. They may not even like you. They are going to try to stop you. Big surprise. These people will use their power to protect and to further what they see as their interests. How do you intend to deal with that challenge? How are you going to use your power?

Fear of Power

Bob is 60 years old. He's been an engineer for 30 years, a very good engineer. Why does he need this headache? He pretended he understood. He even acted like he was happy when they told him that along with everyone else he would be using a computer. If he could, he wouldn't go near the thing, but he knows he's expected to, required to. He's not quite ready. Not just yet.

You are on a lonely stretch of highway, and

the car sounds like it's going to conk out. Do you get sweaty palms, do you get irritable, or are you pretty confident that you can figure out the problem? You are driving into San Francisco for the first time, and it is rush hour. Between you and your downtown hotel are a maze of one-way streets up and down those maddening hills. Not quite like your home in Santa Fe. Feel a little uncomfortable, a little testy?

When we are not accustomed to something, especially if that something makes demands on us, we tend to fear it some. Where will it lead me? What if I get it all wrong? So, we get our defenses up.

You can learn to use a computer. You can discover how to fix your car. Maps can guide you through a city. But power? Who ever instructed you on that? Is there anything else so fundamental about which we received so little training? Yet we are expected to use it, daily. Parents are helped with their concerns about children's obedience. Teachers are instructed on classroom management. Supervisors are trained to get the most from their staffs. Where in any of this is there an honest discussion of power? Yet when are issues of power absent from any of these situations?

When was the last time you had a serious conversation about power? About how to get it, how to use it, how to engender it, even how to recognize it? Have you ever? Is it any wonder then that many of us feel so uncomfortable, so inept, when it comes to dealing with power?

Power makes many demands on those who hold and use it (Bermant & Warwick, 1985). Handling power in an appropriate manner must be done with respect for the rights and legitimate interests of others. This requires that you be aware of others and pay attention to their rights. It means that you must wrestle with the perplexities of what constitutes "legitimate interests." Using power, you have to accept the risk that you will make mistakes and that these mistakes will have consequences. You must be responsible for your actions and accept accountability for them.

Significant change is often attended by significant conflict. In fact, there will always be some degree of conflict in a situation of community change, even those largely cooperative in nature. Some of this conflict can be handled creatively and amicably. Some of it will bring anger and the vexations that accompany hostility. At times, people may not only resent what you are doing but resent you personally. People may not like you, and you may not like them. Using power will expose the conflict and bring it more clearly into focus.

If you intend to develop power and put it to use, you must let go of convenient old excuses that explain away the presence of intolerable conditions. You must cast off the rhetoric and habits of powerlessness. When you act powerfully, you must learn not to horde power but to invest it in others as a means of producing more.

If you fear power, you may actually wish to avoid the responsibility, work, conflict, or other demands it brings. However, if you deal realistically and honestly with power, if you continue to learn more about it, you will become more at ease with its use. Whether your efforts involve an office, a classroom, a city, or beyond, you will feel more alive and you will discover a profound sense of personal fulfillment simply from knowing that you are willing to take part in making a difference.

Who Has Power?

In a community, power involves control over resources considered important to the members of the community. Getting a fix on how power is rooted in your community can give you a sense of how and why things happen. Your actions will cause repercussions that may help some and frustrate others. Understanding the bases of power that may be affected by your actions will help you spot potential opponents and allies. Finally, your awareness of sources of community power will help you figure out where you and your associates may lay claim to some.

Several bases of power exist within a community. Although the bases I will describe

CAPTURING CONCEPTS

Bases of Power in a Community

Information. Those who control the symbols of information and the interpretation of those symbols are likely to be among the most influential individuals.

Money. People with money can get their way in exchange for their money.

Laws. Determining and applying the rules can determine who wins the game.

Constituencies. Power over people in a group as well as the power to mobilize a large group can have a significant influence on the community.

Energy and natural resources. The more concentrated the energy source or the more

limited and locally valued the natural resource, the more powerful those who control these resources will be.

Goods and services. The more important a product or service is to the local economy, the more powerful those who control these products will be.

Network participation. Having a lot of connections in the community provides access to resources and an increased ability to mobilize people.

Family. Special favors and inside information are often offered to family members, and the community may defer to members of well-known families.

History. Knowing a community's history, how it has approached similar issues, and where the skeletons are buried can be used to powerful advantage.

Status occupations. Occupations that draw prominence and deference give power to the individual or group of individuals currently holding that position.

Illegal actions. Illegal activity expands the scope of the game, giving power to those who go beyond the accepted limits or rules of play.

Personality. A personable or intimidating style can extend an individual's power by charging the atmosphere.

relate to a common city or town, these bases exist to some extent in the subcommunities and interest communities within the city or town as well, such as a neighborhood, a school, or a professional group. If you are promoting change in this type of community, keep its characteristics in mind and you will see how the bases of power apply to it as well.

The more bases of power you have, the more you are perceived as being willing to exercise power, and the greater your personal credibility, the more likely it is that you will be powerful. Don't forget that "you" can refer to your group or an institution such as a church, not just to you as an individual.

Common Bases of Power in a Community

There are a dozen bases of power common to most communities. The larger the community, the less likely control over a particular power base will be concentrated in a few hands. In these communities, power may be more fragmented and shifting as competition and the dynamic complexities of the community result in an ongoing ascendancy and descendancy of various individuals and groups. With so much going on at the same time, one particular individual's power in a particular sphere of community activity may be great, but relative to other individuals and other spheres it may be much less overall. Although more and varied forces are at play keeping larger communities in motion, remember that all communities are in some state of change.

Power relationships are based on *perception* and *dependency.* De Jouvenel (1958) describes power as having three dimensions: It is *extensive* if the respondents are many, it is *comprehensive* if the actor can move the respondents to a variety of actions, and it is *intensive* if the actor's bidding can be pushed far without the loss of compliance (p. 160).

In your consideration of power bases, keep in mind that a person must be willing (or be perceived as willing) to use power for the power base to be meaningful. Bases provide the *opportunity* for power; they don't guarantee it. Let's look more closely at some of these bases of power.

1. *Information.* Possession of knowledge and the ability to control what other people know gives tremendous advantages. Information is the currency of tactical action. People who have a lot more information than others certainly have a clearer perception of what they need to do. In an information age, those who control the symbols of information and the interpretation of those symbols are likely to be among the most influential (Luke, 1989). Power is rooted in perception, so this is a very strong base indeed.

Examples of people with this base of power include: newspaper editors, talk show hosts, educators, gossips, gatekeepers (those who control the flow of information to decision makers), preachers, computer wizards, and political confidants.

2. *Money.* If it is not true that anything and anyone has a price, then it is darn close to being true. Money provides the single easiest access to other things. Those with a lot of money can buy much of what they want, or they can tie things up so that other people can't use them. Moneyed people can buy land or products, contribute to candidates or the United Way, hire attorneys or

public relations consultants, and still have enough left over for a cup of coffee and a doughnut.

Most people want money. To get money, they have to go to the people who have it. This creates quite a dependency on those who have money or can provide access to it. (Recall that dependency is the other basic component of power relationships.) People with money can get their way in exchange for their money.

In a culture obsessed with money it is worthwhile to acknowledge that people are fascinated by the rich as kind of cultural superstars. They defer to the affluent simply because of the status wealth confers.

Examples of people with this base of power include: rich people, bankers, investment coordinators/deal makers, employers, and community foundations.

3. *Laws.* The ability to make, interpret, and enforce the policies governing a community confers a great measure of authority. Determining and applying the rules can determine who wins the game. Rule making within a community includes formal law, agency or business regulation, as well as company policy. More often than not, laws are designed to maintain the prevailing orthodoxy rather than to challenge beliefs or redistribute power or other resources. To the extent that redistribution is done willingly by those in power, it is often a stratagem to raise the stakes against more radical protest.

The ability to exercise a degree of influence over who fills rule-making positions is a formidable function. Of course, those who influence the rule makers themselves have power. To a large extent this is what community power is all about.

Examples of people with this base of power include: key players in legislative bodies (mayors, city council members, county commissioners, state legislators, members of Congress), campaign strategists, workers, contributors, members of selection committees, chiefs of police, county sheriffs, attorneys, judges, members of regulatory bodies, lobbyists, and community executives (mayor or city manager, school principal, or chief executive officer of a company).

4. *Constituencies.* The ability to influence the lives or behavior of large groups of people provides significant power in a community. This includes power over people in the group as well as power of the group. It may also refer to the power that occurs because the interests of many people in an identifiable group are involved.

If the people in the group are dependent on someone for something (for example, a job or a degree), that individual has influence over those people. The power of the group is demonstrated when others are dependent on the approval of the group itself for something (for example, votes or purchases). Community members may act on behalf of the interests of a large group if there is a perception that harming the group's interests harms the community as a whole.

Examples of people and groups with this base of power include: major employers, labor leaders, community organizations, business and professional associations, community activists, religious leaders, local political party leaders, and college presidents.

5. *Energy and natural resources.* This refers to the ability to control the use of or regulate access to energy produced by means such as natural gas, coal, nuclear sources, water, oil, and maybe someday the sun and wind. This may include the power company or the gas station (particularly if it is the only one in town). Control over specific natural resources such as land, water, timber, and the like are included in this category as well. The more concentrated the energy source or the more limited and locally valued the natural resource, the more powerful this base will be.

Examples of people with this base of power include: utility company executives, environmental activists, real estate developers, members of resource regulatory bodies, gasoline distributors, farmers, and water users' associations.

6. *Goods and services.* The more important the product or service is to the local economy the more noteworthy this base of power will be. Also, those dealing with high-priced yet common products (cars and houses) tend to be more powerful. Again, the more limited the access to the good or service, the more powerful those who control it are likely to be.

Examples of people with this base of power include: department store owners/executives, new car dealers, grain elevator owners, construction company owners, hospital executives, mental health executives, cable television executives, and economic developers.

7. *Network participation.* The good ol' boy network does exist, and the good ol' girl network is emerging. Having a lot of connections in the community provides ready access to resources and the ability to mobilize select groups of people quickly. It plainly helps to know a lot of people.

In addition, each member of a particular network participates in other networks. Through this process, a person's name, reputation, and influence can begin to grow. There is an assumption that if everybody knows so-and-so or hears the name pop up frequently, this must be an important person (or group).

Networks include formal organizations such as the Chamber of Commerce as well as informal affiliations such as business associates. Members of certain groups with select admission criteria are often accorded more influence within the community. Their members may look out for one another a little more to affirm group identity.

Examples of people with this base of power include: those who have taken part in numerous community activities, members of civic and service organizations (Rotary, Lions, Soroptimist), active members of churches or synagogues, members of agency/organization boards of directors, owners of businesses, members of country clubs and other private clubs, and members of local leadership groups (2001 Committee, Phoenix Forty).

8. *Family.* Blood usually does run thicker than water. Family members have a sort of "preferred customer" status with one another.

Special favors, inside information, and similar advantages are offered to members of a family in ways they are not routinely offered to those outside the family. Family membership generally grants immediate access to relatives who play important roles in the community. Family members are part of a fundamental network.

The longer standing, the larger, and the more influential a family is, the more opportunities it provides. This includes deference by others in the community to those who are simply members of important families as well as the relationships prominent families often develop among themselves.

Examples of those with this base of power include . . . how about members of influential families.

9. *History.* Knowing the traditions of a place, what has gone on before, and where the skeletons are buried can provide insightful advantage for understanding current philosophies and actions. Though history doesn't exactly repeat itself, certain trends do cycle. A clear understanding of a community's history can increase credibility. By directly or indirectly relating proposed actions to past patterns, common spoken and unspoken beliefs and fears can be used to great advantage.

Examples of people with this base of power include: reporters, local historians, and long-time active community residents (especially school, religious, business, and political leaders).

10. *Status occupations.* Certain occupations draw prominence and deference. Some provide a kind of community celebrity that attracts interest and even fawning attention. More weight is attached to the words and actions of these people either because their occupation endows them with a degree of expertise or morality believed to be the province of a select few or because the recipient feels favored by the attention.

Examples of people with this base of power include: rabbis, bishops, physicians, head coaches, attorneys, and professional athletes.

11. *Illegal actions.* Some people just don't play by the rules, or perhaps they play by a different set of rules. The standard limits on action just don't apply to the game they are playing. If the consequences of resisting are acceptable to the resister, resistance is likely to continue. However, assessing the likely consequences usually involves a circumscribed set of possibilities based on assumptions of legitimate behavior. When those assumptions no longer apply, the consequences become difficult to determine or are unmanageable. Resistance begins to break down. The whole idea of overcoming resistance is to make the consequences for resisting less attractive than accepting the proposed action. Removing the limitations of legality or morality can provide an individual with a vast array of options to develop strategies and overcome resistance.

If someone says, "Do this, or we'll see you in court," that can be a difficult but understandable dilemma for which you can prepare. However, if you are told, "Do this, or we'll have someone break your legs," and you believe them, that gives a different feel to the situation entirely.

Illegal activity provides an expanded game. The potential use of violence is just one form it may take. If one person is willing to use rational argument, whereas another is willing to use argument, bribery, and threats of violence, the latter simply has more weapons. Dealing with this situation is not always as easy as going to the police. Sometimes the illegal participants are the police.

Examples of people with this base of power include: gang members, members of traditional organized crime families, drug dealers, neighborhood bullies, and backroom deal makers.

12. *Personality.* Some people have developed a personal manner that attracts enthusiasm, support, and respect like a magnet. They project a sense of purpose and confidence in their own and others' ability to accomplish goals. They spark in others a belief that problems can and will be addressed. Others have developed an intimidating presence. They act like they should be taken seriously and use confrontational techniques to discourage opposition. Still others are just so likable and persistent that it is hard to say "no" to them.

Regardless of the particular approach used, individuals with this base accomplish what they want through dint of their personality and a single-minded belief in what they are doing. They have an air of assurance and are not intimidated by others. The best of these can utilize a variety of styles and match them to the situation. They have made getting their own way into a kind of performance art.

Though this base of power is different from the preceding ones in that the only resource is one's self, it is nonetheless an important one. Ultimately, the atmosphere created determines success, and personality can be an instrumental force in establishing the right atmosphere.

Common Bases of Power in a Group

Much of the real action of community change occurs within small groups. It is here that most of the work and most of the decisions take place. The basic aspects of power—perception of dependency within relationships—certainly apply to small groups, especially since it is the relationship among members that is the essence of a group. Johnson and Johnson (1997) discuss six useful categories of power within groups.

Reward power occurs when an individual responds to the behavior of other group members by dispensing valued positive consequences or by removing negative ones. This results in group members wanting to gain his or her favor and strengthen the relationship between them.

Coercive power is just the reverse. This exists when an individual can respond by punishing other members. Members feel forced to go along to avoid discomfort.

Legitimate power is based on the group's belief that the individual has influence over them due to that member's position. Thus, the treasurer may have some authority over

dispensing group funds or the chairperson may manage group discussion.

Referent power is established when others want to identify with or be like a particular individual—or even want to be liked by him or her. Sometimes group members comply out of respect, sometimes they do so to seek approval from a popular person. Remember how people sought the approval of the most popular person in high school? That is one example of referent power.

Expert power flows from those who have unique knowledge or abilities that are honestly offered to the group for its benefit. However, if people begin to feel inadequate around such an individual, her or his power can diminish.

Informational power is similar to expert power. In this case, the group is influenced by the individual's particular access to information and her or his ability to think and communicate clearly. (pp. 373–374)

These bases of power address the dynamics of what is occurring within a group and how its members relate not only to one another but also as members of a group. They also apply to how the members relate to the objectives of the group.

Determining Who Holds Power

Power fluctuates within a community as new actors and new issues present themselves for consideration. This occurs even in fairly small communities, such as a hospital or a school. New problems, new opportunities, and new personnel create shifts in power.

A good way to determine who has power is by talking to people, especially the more active members of your interest community. Ask these people who influences them. That is, find out whom they do or would respond to and why. Then ask them who their most difficult opponents and most effective (not just nice, but effective) supporters are. Get some idea of what makes someone difficult or effective. Next, get a picture of whom they see influencing other people and how this influence occurs. Finally, ask whom they think *others* would say are powerful and why, and then find out who would be on *their* list and why. This process will lead to many an interesting conversation, a number of good insights on community power, and a beginning assessment of the power present in your arena of action.

Recall the value of lists. Get lists of every group, organization, or event that involves community power. See whose names appear frequently and where. If you can, note who seems to associate with whom or how tentacles of power reach out into the community and come together again (Male, 1993). Obviously, you can put a lot of time into this, but once you have a base of information you will pick up lists as a matter of habit. Be sure to review them to keep up to date. While you are gathering lists, make up a few of your own with your perception of who is well stationed in the various power bases in your community.

Remember that local newspapers and magazines commonly prepare community power analyses and feature stories on prominent community leaders as well as rising stars. Special reports on sectors of the community (for example, a review of major employers) can come in handy. Keep on the lookout for these.

Those with power are often more comfortable directing the action from behind the scenes than they are being on center stage. Watch what is going on in your community in general and with regard to your issue in particular. Is more attention than normal being given to a particular area of town, a particular industry, a particular ethnic group, or a particular issue? Why? Has the normally outspoken critic of this or that grown uncharacteristically quiet? Is there a new road being built to a vacant piece of land? Hmmm . . .

Pay attention to where and how limited resources are allocated. Which schools get additional space? Which programs get expanded? Notice how undesirable issues are handled. Whose budget gets cut? Where does the new hazardous waste get dumped?

Look also to see who responds to whom. Who is asking the questions? To whom do people turn for answers? Who seems to take direction; who seems to give it? Who asks permission? Who provides it? Who can call people to a meeting for tomorrow at 10:00 A.M. and be sure that everyone will show up?

Finally, analyze all this good information. What tentative conclusions can you reach about who is benefiting by plans, decisions, and actions? Who is losing? Who is gaining? Who is paying? People may tell you that they are afraid to do things "because of the risks involved." What is seen as a risk? Who controls the negative consequences if things don't work out? What are they? Asking questions such as these will help you determine who controls the limits of the action and who establishes new boundaries.

By gathering information, keeping your eyes and ears open, and calculating who seems to be getting their way and under what circumstances, you will have a good gauge on which actors hold the power in your community.

Assessing and Building Your Own Bases of Power

Never forget that the moment you believe you are powerless, you are indeed powerless. Action itself implies the use of power. How will you respond to the opportunities before you? Maybe you don't have all the power you need. But you want to accomplish something, and you recognize that you do have some tools to start with. What could they be? Let's take a look.

One thing you probably have is a good perspective on the problem situation. You know that people are unhappy or hurting and that the condition is unacceptable. A certain power comes from being on the right side of an issue. It may not be enough by itself to win, but it can get you and others going, help sustain you through the tough times, and put your opponents on the defensive. Knowing all you can about a problem, its harmful consequences, and the moral issues involved can be real assets.

Review the bases of power within your community. Which of these are available to you at least to some degree? Do you have any expertise or information not commonly held in your community? Can you speak with professional authority or on the basis of a sound grasp of the particular subject with which you are dealing? Do you hold any position of authority or leadership? Here is a tough one: Does anybody like or respect you?

Take a look at the resources at your disposal. Can you mobilize a constituency, or at least begin to? Can you talk to a community group to help shape their thinking, or can you get a favorable story on the six o'clock news? Does anyone from whom you need a response depend on you for anything, or perhaps depend on you *not* to do something? Can you deliver votes? Are laws or regulations in place that can serve your interests? Can you embarrass any important person or group? See Kahn (1970, 1991) and Amidei (1987) for more on these topics.

One of the fundamental resources at your disposal is cooperation or compliance. To go along or to "do what you are told" involves a series of actions you can take or withhold. The possibility of many people acting together in organized noncompliance offers a potentially potent advantage (Sharp, 1973b).

You probably have some claim on at least one base of community power if not more. Take a good look at the possible power capital you possess. Be sure to include your own personal assets. You probably routinely overlook or undervalue a few of the things you have going for you. Now look at those who are or will be working with you as you build an organized effort to promote change in your community. What emerges when each person takes stock of his or her own power inventory? This evaluation should provide you with a more encouraging picture of the means you and your group can use to get the upper hand.

Establishing your own ability to influence

Take a Moment to Discover . . . .

When you are faced with a situation that really bothers you, one you would like to change, what are some of the first things that go through your mind? How do these thoughts lead you toward or away from purposeful action? How do they help or hinder your effectiveness?

• •

the flow of events involves three basic strategies: making use of existing power, building power through organization, and developing personal power.

Making Use of Existing Power

The purpose of this strategy is to provide you with well-positioned allies. Two avenues are available for using existing power. First, you can purposefully recruit powerful community members who may be willing to support your aims. (I will refer to those individuals who hold power as influential community members or ICMs.) Second, you can form alliances with existing power blocs, particularly organizations sympathetic to your cause or those that share a common enemy with you.

The first step in involving those who already have power in the community is to take stock of the connections you and your supporters have. Next, get in touch with those ICMs whose help you think you will need. Obviously, this is easier if a relationship already exists. You may need to spend some time reaffirming your relationship, even while you are asking for assistance. Don't hesitate to approach ICMs you don't know if you believe they may be interested in your cause. Working together could be the start of a valuable relationship.

When recruiting the support of ICMs, invite them to understand your problems and, once they have a good grasp of the situation, ask them how, not if, they would be able to help out. Be prepared to ask them for a specific type of involvement. Generally, ICMs can serve your effort in one of three ways:

1. Influential community members can serve as window dressing to provide a certain credibility to your endeavor by signing a letter supporting your position, appearing with you in public, or allowing their names to appear on your letterhead. In this case, ICMs do little more than lend their names and stature to your cause.
2. ICMs may go to bat for you on specific problems, using their personal relationships or their position in the community to intervene on your behalf. This may provide immediate benefit while helping you to be taken more seriously in the future.
3. You may recruit ICMs as ongoing participants in your work. You benefit from their direct involvement and get plugged into the current of community power.

While considering which powerful individuals to call on for support, also see which groups or organizations can lend you some of their strength. You may be outgunned as a single neighborhood contending with an insensitive city hall, but if the powerful neighborhood coalition from across town endorses your operation, the scope of the conflict becomes much different. Look to groups outside your immediate conflict, especially those who will

regard your struggle as a reflection of their own. Figure out which organizations have issues, interests, or people similar to yours. Are any of your members also members of one of these groups? Forming alliances with other organizations is an important, ongoing component of the development of power. Supporting organizations can provide you with the same type of help you can get from individuals, although because of policies and internal issues they usually cannot respond as quickly.

Whether your added support comes from powerful individuals or organizations, receiving the backing of those who already have power can get you right into the game. A caution should be sounded, however. Using the power of ICMs and other organizations may not help you build your organization. The more you rely on them for success, the less you rely on yourselves.

Building Power Through Organization

The most significant and enduring strategy for effective community change is to create a base of power for yourselves. By mobilizing the interest, action, and power of others, you can develop an organized constituency, an authentic base of power. Organizing is a fundamental approach open to any community change agent. When individuals concentrate their power by acting together in planned, purposeful ways, much can be achieved. Chapter 12 contains a

Change Agent Tip

Give each member of your action group an index card. Ask each person to list the three most powerful members of the community they would be willing to ask for a favor. Though few of the names you get may be among the very most powerful, you will begin to discover your organization's access to higher levels of community clout. These connections will help you establish a bank of power from which you may draw, and it may also provide you with names of potential new members of your action group.

detailed examination of the process of developing an organization.

In most situations you will quickly confront the limitations of your own power and the limits of your own time and energy. You simply need other people, and they need you. This is not only a matter of effectiveness but also one of ethics. It is unlikely that you alone have such a command of the issues that you can speak for all concerned. It is hard to know what really is best for everyone. People are not commonly so anointed, though some may act like it. If you are doing all the talking and all the work, you leave no room for anyone else. You deny them the prerogative and responsibility to act on their own behalf. Frankly, what gives you the right?

Developing Personal Power

Each person in your action community has the potential for increasing her or his power. Personal power flows from three sources of credibility:

Credibility as a person: Do you do what you say you are going to do? Can people rely on you? Do you take control of your actions? Can you be trusted?

Credibility of your information: Is your information accurate? Is it timely? Does it consider a different point of view? Is it comprehensive, or is something left out, perhaps purposefully?

Credibility of your power base: Will others actively support you? Do you have any resources to withhold or deliver?

Increasing your power requires strengthening these various sources. How do you do this? Let's look at these issues in reverse order.

Putting Yourself in the Power Loop

Insinuating yourself into powerful circles involves placing yourself in position to be known and positively regarded by people with community influence so that you may affect community decisions and utilize the new relationships you develop to assist your continued efforts to improve the community. You do this by building your credibility in a situation in which people with power relate to you as a person who is capable and at least equal to others they value in a situation they take seriously. Now I don't want to give the impression that you can waltz in and become fully accepted in any group, nor that there aren't some very exclusive groups that may never include you as a member. Still, you can be integrated into some pretty vital groups without too much difficulty.

Where do you start? You may have more opportunities than you think. Influential community members gather in a variety of groups to work on community issues. Certainly these gatherings serve other purposes for ICMs, such as relationship building and exchanging gossip. They can serve the same purposes for you too. The community issue focus, however, provides working contact with people who possess more power in the community than you do. Keep in mind that if you act like you belong, people will tend to treat you that way. Groups that can be found in most communities include:

- *Local agency boards of directors* generally include a number of ICMs. Because you are not joining a board just to meet people, focus on those agencies whose mission reflects your own interests. From the work you have done so far you may have established contacts in the community or in the agency itself who can recommend you as a candidate for the board. If so, you have already started the process of becoming included in community decision making. If you don't know someone who could "sponsor" you, make contact with the agency director, board chair, or head of the board's nominating committee and let them know of your interest. Spots on agency boards come up routinely, and you stand a decent chance of being selected if you show a genuine interest and can communicate what you can offer to the organization.

- *Community action, problem-solving, or issue groups* often attract community leaders and provide opportunities for "unknowns" to shine. The major requirements are to show up, start talking, and start working.

- *Political campaigns* are always looking for responsible workers. With your willingness to take on tasks and your competence in performing them well, you will find a steady increase in responsibility and recognition. The more campaigns you work, the more campaign expertise you will develop, and the more your assistance and input will be sought. The relationship you develop with the candidate can be beneficial when he or she takes office. Working closely with the candidate's staff, advisers, and active supporters is also helpful as they themselves may be or may become important community figures.

- *Public boards and commissions* can provide you with a position of influence. Some state and local governments are fairly littered with such bodies; a number of them even do important work. The clerk of each governmental jurisdiction (for example, state, county, city, or town) should be able to provide you with a list of the various boards and commissions and their vacancies, along with information on the appointment process.

Other possibilities could include groups that plan and coordinate special events, like an annual parade or fair; various task forces on topics of immediate community interest; and United Way committees. Don't be shy about inviting yourself into something that attracts your interest and the interest of other key members of the community.

Because much of the work in these situations takes place in face-to-face group activity, you have a good chance to make a favorable impression. This is especially true when working in newly formed groups where leadership vacuums exist and relationship boundaries haven't yet been established. Prepare yourself to perform capably, speak up, and take the time to get to know people. You will soon find that you will have accomplished something important simply by demystifying your perception of people who hold power. Those with measurable clout are not markedly different from anyone else. Some are friendly, some obnoxious; some are dynamic, some dull; some are easily open to new relationships, and some are reticent.

Unknown commodities are a little suspect. You are too if you are an unknown. So get known. You don't need to be accompanied by a brass band. If you are noticeably competent, and even likable, you will be recognized, and you will find yourself included in more discussions of greater importance.

Using Information

Having solid information will assure you a measure of credibility. People give more weight to the words of someone who knows what they are talking about. Don't you? Doing your homework involves not only collecting pertinent information but also organizing it in a way that speaks to what is on the mind of your listener. Of course, this means you had better get a good idea of what actually is on that listener's mind.

Know your topic sufficiently well that you can cite a few specific references or note specific facts. Then check to see what is missing. See if you are uncomfortable discussing any particular aspect. This might indicate that you don't really know something you think you should know. Or, look at your argument from the opposite point of view. Can you identify where it is vulnerable, where you cannot really use data to justify what you believe to be true? Once you have done this honestly, you will have a good grasp of the subject and be able to communicate it clearly.

You can undermine your credibility by misrepresenting the particulars of the matter. If certain details don't support your position, you are better off acknowledging them and comparing them against the prevailing strength of the information that does support your claims.

Having a good feel for your topic and for the situation in which you are discussing it will give you confidence. You will also give confidence to those who need to determine a course of action by supplying them with a good foundation of information on which they can support a decision. When people depend on you because of the reliability of your information, you have a lot of influence.

Inspiring Confidence

Act powerfully. How you set the stage for action and how you act can influence the immediate progress of events. It is far better to be the driver than to be taken for a ride.

Quite a few books have been written on the subject of building personal power. Some promote the use of intimidation; others stress cooperation. Regardless of the strategy you choose, certain fundamentals should be observed to use and maintain your personal power. These apply particularly to situations in which your organization's efforts are being resisted.

- *Act on purpose.* Be in charge of your own behavior. Make sure your actions relate directly to the effect you want to produce. If you do not have an intentional outcome for what you are doing, you will probably end up responding to someone or something else.
- *Act unapologetically.* You believe you have a right to your position and that you deserve the benefits you seek. Communicate this. If you aren't convinced of the legitimacy of your interests, why should anyone else be? If you are convinced of this, why would you communicate that you aren't?
- *Set the agenda.* You determine what will and will not be discussed as issues. Don't get sidetracked; stick to the essential points. If other items are brought up, acknowledge them. If these are genuinely important to the other party, you will need to attend to them in the course of your efforts to reach a productive resolution. However, don't allow these other matters to substitute for your concerns.
- *Don't impose arbitrary limits on your own behavior.* Your choice of actions should be measured against ethics and effectiveness. Ask yourself if you are keeping your possibilities for action open and creative. Be willing to be outrageous and unpredictable. You have enough rules to live by. Don't waste your time making up new ones.
- *Don't get locked into one pattern of behavior.* Be willing to change your approach while holding firm to your goal. You limit your effectiveness by becoming too predictable.
- *Consider your short- and long-term gains and losses.* The way you handle the situation today will have consequences for tomorrow. Remain attentive, and be honest about what you are doing. You can easily rationalize compliant behavior, thinking you are making things easier to handle at some indiscernible point in the future, when you really just want to avoid a fight. Of course the reverse could also be true. You may just want to fight now and ignore the consequences. There is no simple answer here. Consider how you can produce an immediate gain in such a way that long-term gains become more likely.
- *Be on the lookout for areas of agreement.* If the emphasis is on disagreement, that will be the only result. The whole point is to forge an agreement, one that serves your interests. Be aware of common interpretations, beliefs, and values. Observe when the other party is willing to move in a direction acceptable to you. Though the agreement may not be so much a formal declaration as a change in behavior, you had better be able to detect signs that can guide you to a satisfactory outcome.
- *Acknowledge others' need for influence.* Each person needs to feel some measure of influence in a relationship. Know that this exists. If you do not intend to allow an opponent any influence, realize that this will increase resistance. Providing room for another party's influence in a way that does not detract from your interests increases the chances for a satisfactory conclusion.
- *Hold 'em accountable.* Whenever you reach an agreement in word with another party, make sure you have a way to see if it is being

Take a Moment to Discover . . . .

Think back on a time when someone was able to silence you, someone who acted like you did not have the right to raise an issue or voice disagreement. How did this happen? How did you feel about your response? How could you now handle a situation like this differently?

• •

honored in deed. Then pay attention to see that it continues to be. If you allow the other party to ignore an agreement, it doesn't really exist, and you send the message that you are not serious about the agreements you reach. Don't accept excuses for breaches that could have been controlled.

• *Remember that all behavior is purposeful.* What is the other party telling you by its response? How do you use this information? How are you responding? How do you use this information?

• *Ask forgiveness, not permission.* How often have you seen people give up their own authority to act by first asking for someone else's approval? You may have done this yourself. Don't lightly give away your authority to act. If you determine that something needs to be done, do it, understanding that there may be some consequences you will have to deal with later. Frankly, most of the time this involves an apology for not consenting to someone else's control.

• *Don't make excuses.* Accept responsibility. Blaming others is not only irritating but communicates that others determine your fate, not you.

Using Your Power

Does pursuing your interests faithfully mean that you have to stop being friendly? Of course not. You can be friendly while firmly holding people to their agreements. You can be thought-ful of others while not being dissuaded from what your organization needs to accomplish. Acting powerfully does not imply that you become a less pleasant person, just a more intentional one.

Every change effort involves a "statement about why particular people at a particular time may be ready to challenge power, how they can, and why they should" (Cox, 1987a, p. 241). When you use power, you are respecting your rights and the legitimate rights of others. Many of the opponents you will encounter want to maintain policies and continue behaviors demeaning to whole classes of citizens. They do not have a right to do this. Although you must acknowledge their interests, you need not accept them as legitimate. It is too bad that change may be painful for those who have grown used to having things their way at the expense of others. However, it is not your responsibility to ease their discomfort by pursuing your goals with a diminished sense of purpose. You are not called upon to protect the nonlegitimate interests of others, no matter how entrenched or long-held they are. The interests of those who struggle with you deserve far more respect.

When you battle *powerful ignorance,* you are likely to meet resistance from those who want to hold onto their practiced ways of understanding things or from those who do not have enough concern to listen to what you have to say. This can be frustrating. It is almost like you are trying to get people who are standing still to start moving, and moving in the right direction. When you take on *powerful interests,* your struggle is more difficult. In this case, you are trying to turn or move past people who are pushing you backward.

Whenever your pursuits challenge the advantages of powerful others and the routines that support those advantages, your own legitimacy to act will be criticized. Whether parents or teachers or bosses or mayors, people with power often believe they have a right to do exactly what they are doing. When you come along to challenge this notion, you are almost automatically seen as acting improperly. A common tactic is to attack your very right to question (Staples, 1984).

Somewhere along the line someone may well call you naive or misguided or even pigheaded. Maybe you will be called trouble-maker or rebel or even radical. Some of you are not used to being treated this way and may find these charges upsetting. That is understandable. Those of you who intend to make a career out of promoting change will get used to this. As long as your picture of yourself comes from you and from the people working alongside you, this won't be much of a problem. If, however, your perception of yourself and your organization's legitimacy comes from those you are confronting, you may begin second-guessing yourself.

In a community conflict, you often need to promote your group's right to challenge accepted practice. You may have to inoculate the community (and your supporters as well) against the tactic of discrediting your efforts by predicting that it will occur and by clearly articulating your message.

When you use your power to get a response from those who do not share your goals, information, or values, you are likely to meet some opposition. This is a predictable part of the process, one you must address with a clear sense of purpose and a secure belief in the validity of your interests. Your use of personal power to influence elements in a situation should be directed toward advancing the interests of your group. Effective use of personal power aids in developing the power of your organization.

Empowering Others

A fundamental task in promoting community change is developing the power of others. The success of your effort requires it. More than anything else, your limits are defined by a lack of power. The more people your organization has who are capable of acting powerfully, the more you are able to erase limitations. An organized effort with many people acting powerfully and

confidently in concert is far more effective than one with a strong leader and a lot of hopeful followers.

Empowerment involves overcoming sets of beliefs, oppressive structures, and stifling routines that keep people and their concerns isolated from one another (Friere, 1973; Gutierrez, 1995). Recognizing interests held in common with others in similar circumstances and the ability to connect with one another in purposeful action builds a foundation for strength (Crowfoot, Chesler, & Boulet, 1983; Parsons, 1989). In fact, Wenocur (1992) argues that an emphasis on helping ordinary people gain sufficient knowledge and skill to make systems respond to their needs is the highest priority in fields such as social work as it is essentially related to the fundamental value of self-determination. Gutierrez and Lewis (1994) emphasize the importance of helping people make the "connection between personal problems and political issues" (p. 31).

"Oh, great," you're thinking, "I not only have to become more powerful myself, but now I have to worry about how to make everybody else more powerful too. How the heck am I supposed to do that?" Well, rest easy. It is not your job to *make* everybody powerful; you probably couldn't even if you tried. It is your job to *encourage* the process. It begins with the idea that people will work together to overcome obstacles, and it is first expressed in the way you work with others. Not only does this not require a lot of effort, but it will actually save you some.

Empowering others requires that you look for guidance to some of the basic notions of power. Recall that power involves possessing resources, influencing others, and determining direction. Many opportunities exist for those involved in your effort to discover and use resources they have and to develop new ones. Members can influence one another as well as those outside the organization. Each member will determine what steps he or she will take to further the cause, and each will have occasion to shape the direction of the overall effort. All these opportunities exist. You just have to recognize them and take advantage of them while promoting the notion that others do the same. The catch is that you have to value these opportunities to even see them in the first place.

You reverse the process of empowerment when you deny opportunities to other participants or when you accept or even encourage their giving opportunities away. Don't kid yourself, this will happen. As soon as you get in the habit of thinking "I can do it better myself," you are closing off chances for others to do as well as you, or to learn to do as well. (By the way, just because things are done differently from the way you would do them does *not* mean they aren't done as well.) And, yes, people do routinely give away the power they have. How many times have you heard "Oh, I'm not really good at anything" or "I don't know, it's up to you"?

Once people begin to believe in their own power, they value and make more available their contributions. The result is a richer and stronger organization. Clearly, you alone are not responsible for increasing the power of other participants, although the greater the role you play in the change effort, the more attention you need to give this concern. A number of simple steps can help you create and take advantage of openings for others to step forward. These steps include:

• *Ask questions and ask for input.* By seeking information you don't have and by valuing another's ideas, you reinforce something very fundamental. You counteract a common powerful fear people have of being thought of as stupid, as somehow less. You can always acknowledge what someone says, if only by restating the comment to demonstrate that you have clearly heard. Accepting every part of every viewpoint is phony, though you can generally find something of value in a response. Learn to disagree without putting down an idea or the person who offered it. Recognize good ideas and their originator, and allow other people to have better ideas than yours.

• *Reroute questions.* Feel free to pass on questions asked of you to other people. An occasional, "I don't know, what do you think, Hank?" can draw in more people.

• *Promote access to decision making.* Decisions reflect the will of those who have power. If decisions rest on the ideas of a few, only a few will be powerful. If they rest on the input of many, many will be powerful (Brown, 1991).

• *Give recognition and credit whenever you can.* A simple "Good idea, Gladys" or "Thanks for helping out at the meeting yesterday, Zach" can be valuable. Commenting on contributions in the presence of others provides a nice acknowledgment. Formal recognition, such as including names in a newsletter story, awarding certificates, and even humorous awards, can be useful too. Let people take credit for the work they have done, but don't tolerate members fighting over credit. If this occurs, it can be devastating. Such squabbling is usually a symptom of too little credit being given out, not too much.

• *Rarely accept statements of inability.* "I can't" or "I don't know" will probably be declared more often than you care to hear. Don't buy it, at least not easily. Be willing to ask questions like: "If you can't do this, what can you do instead?" or "Can you think of just *one* thing?" When you stop believing in people's inabilities, you will learn a number of techniques to encourage their abilities.

• *Promote the distribution of responsibility and authority.* There is plenty to do in a change effort. Help spread the tasks around. Ask for help yourself. If someone takes on a project, let that person handle it without you hovering, and certainly don't redo it all after they think they are done. Although coordination of effort is important, there are many things people can be in charge of, especially if they have a clear understanding of expectations and a chance to shape them.

• *Promote the acceptance of mistakes and acknowledge your own.* Few things are as debilitating as the fear of making a mistake that is going to be made into a big deal. People learn from their mistakes. Sometimes they learn not to try again. They can also learn how to improve by building on what they have done. Look first to compliment, and question the need to criticize. Include yourself in this too. Acknowledge and learn from your own mistakes without making a big deal about them.

- *Encourage the development and awareness of resources.* Recalling the relationship of resource use to power, your group needs to do more than increase members' sense of their own personal competence as they shape the nature and direction of the change effort. The organization must cultivate resources that may be used to increase its power. As part owners of these resources, members of the organization experience an expansion of power.

- *Promote the relevance of actions.* Actions members are expected to take in the name of the organization, especially those that challenge authority, must fit their picture of how the world works. It must make sense to them (Cox, 1987a).

- *Promote the recognition of success.* Your organization will win victories, some minor, some major. Pay attention to them. Empowerment occurs through success and the confirmation of effectiveness success implies. This is true for the successes individuals achieve on their own as well as for those they achieve as members of a group.

Just by pulling together you are all going to feel and be more powerful. Yet you will have done even more if the process you use in bringing people together helps them discover and believe in their own personal potency. The most powerful organizations are made up of powerful people. When people feel empowered, they see themselves differently, as more capable, more responsible, and more willing to shape forces rather than be shaped by them. This has consequences far beyond the immediate events.

Conclusion

Every relationship embraces power. It is the very root of all our relationships. Every relationship involves people responding to one another. With no response there is no relating, no relationship. Relationships, between lovers, between students and teachers, between competing interests in the community, are all marked by the interchange of expectation and reply. To be in a relationship is to influence and to be influenced.

Power affects everything we do. It is not only a useful thing, it is essential. Power can be used to enhance the parties in a relationship or to exploit them. If one or more of the parties are dissatisfied with what they are receiving from the relationship, they must use their power to change things for the better. But they can only do this if they believe they have the ability and the right to do so.

If you are going to promote change, you need power. If you are going to be powerful, you need to decide if you are going to be purposefully powerful or accidentally powerful. If you are going to use power, you must do so knowing that others may not like it. If you intend to be successful, not merely self-important, you will cultivate the power of your partners. Both power and impotence impose choices and consequences. When you make the choice to act with power, you help set the direction. No longer will you just be told where to go.

CHAPTER **8**

Powerful Planning

Chapter Highlights

- Planning as a waste of time
- Planning as necessary
- Definition and description of a plan
- Basic steps in the planning process
- Planning as a process
- Reasons for planning
- Degree of planning necessary
- Importance of participant interest
- Four levels of planning
- Time available for planning
- Nature of the change effort
- Complexity of the change effort
- Available planning resources
- Range of planning elements in an ideal plan

- Images of potentiality
- Brainstorming
- Criteria for good goals
- Relating systems theory to planning
- Force field analysis
- Recognizing and using assets
- Stakeholders
- Importance of pacing your activities
- Indicators of job completion
- Difference between monitoring and evaluation
- Recognizing pitfalls in advance
- Obstacles to effective planning and ways to deal with them
- Consequence avoiders
- Risk avoiders

The coffee is hot and the donuts and the conversation are good. Ten people have come, fewer than had "promised" to be here, but still a good turnout. A pretty good sampling it is too. Two businesswomen active in the community, a school counselor, a public health nurse, a couple of self-styled health care advocates, and even a member of the state legislature. Only one very young woman has come, though, one of the agency's clients, and she is sitting off to the side. Does she want to be noticed?

Where are the "consumers"? Ben ponders. Aren't they what this is all about? Maybe. There will be other opportunities for planning. We'll have to try something different. We're still learning. His thoughts are broken by Melanie's welcome to the group.

" . . . and so we have a good idea of the unmet need and some of the barriers to meeting that need. . . . "

She still sounds like a social worker, Ben muses.

Melanie continues, "Over the past few months, everyone here has been involved in sifting through a number of ways to deal with this. We have come to the point now where we believe that establishing a comprehensive prenatal care clinic is the best way to go. How do we make that happen? What do we have to do?"

The group stares back in response.

"So, how do we get from here to there?"

Now three people speak at once. And now the vision is a little, no, maybe a lot closer to becoming a reality.

———

Planning is a waste of time. You put in hours of endless discussion. You argue over subtle nuances of five-letter words buried in the middle of the third paragraph on the second page. And then, when you are finally done, the plan sits on the shelf, never to be looked at again. Planning is a waste of time. Don't you agree? Well, if this is what planning is, then yes, it is a waste of time.

Then again, lack of planning will almost certainly be a waste of time. Ben and Melanie recognize that talking about what you want to do is not enough. You need to make decisions about what "better" looks like, and actions must be taken to get you there. They recognize that you need to hear the voices of the people who have a stake in the outcome, particularly the voices of those whom the change is intended to benefit.

So, what to do? Let's start by recognizing that planning is necessary but that it can also be a colossal waste of time. To understand planning as a useful activity and to use it to increase the effectiveness of your change effort, you need the answers to a few questions. First of all, just what is a plan, and what, for that matter, is planning? Next, why should you plan at all? What benefit does it provide? Assuming you have gotten sufficiently good answers to encourage your further inquiry, you will probably want to know how much planning you need or don't need to do. Now down to brass tacks. How do you plan? What are some useful planning models? What are some basic obstacles to planning, and how do you confront them? And, finally, what else do you need to know or at least think about when you are getting set to plan? Let's take a shot at each of these.

What Is a Plan?
What Is Planning?

The community is the context of your action, and power gives strength and purpose to your concerns. Planning, the topic of this chapter, helps put that concentrated power to use by providing the approach and direction for your actions. The approach to planning described in this chapter refers to the steps you take to initiate and implement a community change. The procedures used in planning for the continued development of an existing social service agency may need to address other factors beyond the scope of this text, although certain perspectives offered here may have some benefit in those situations as well.

A plan is a set of decisions made on actions to be taken to reach a goal. It is the product of the process of planning, an active process that is the opposite of simply allowing events to unfold. A plan can be said to exist when a point in the process has been reached where a coherent set of operations designed to meet a given goal has been determined with sufficient clarity that they may be acted on (Mayer, 1985; Perlman & Gurin, 1972; Weinbach, 1990). Whew! Let's take that apart.

Because the planning process doesn't really have an ending point, a plan isn't just a final product. You have a plan as soon as you have decided what to do about the situation you are facing. As the process proceeds, your plan continues to be modified. You don't have to wait until your planning is "done" before you have a plan. Determining a coherent set of operations to reach a given goal means that you have made decisions on a number of things to do (and not to do) and that these actions are related to one another and are directed to whatever it is you want to accomplish. These actions need to be sufficiently clear that you know just what to do. Therefore, you have a plan when you have proceeded far enough in your consideration of possible courses of action that you know what it is you need to do to accomplish your purpose and you are ready to act.

A plan can be a very formal document, or it can simply be the clear understanding of the actions you are to undertake. If it is at all possible, it is helpful to write down your plans. Berkowitz (1982) points out that the very act of getting something down in black and white can clarify your thoughts. Seeing your ideas on paper can also make them seem more real to you, thus strengthening your own motivation.

Planning is the process, the series of steps you take to gather information and make decisions to determine your plan. These steps include:

- Deciding what you want to achieve
- Selecting actions to be taken within a given period of time to overcome obstacles and move you in the desired direction
- Determining specific tasks
- Assigning responsibility
- Analyzing the outcome of your intentions and actions

I should probably clear up an important point about planning right now—you never stop planning. Of course, you are not going to spend all your time planning. Aside from the fact that such a prospect is dreadfully dreary, it isn't very productive. You are, however, going to continue to spend part of your time in planning. Planning is an ongoing process. The only way to get a plan "done" is to get all the information about your situation and then keep the world from changing at all. Of course, this is impossible. So you will always be tinkering with your plan, modifying it to meet changing conditions and additional information. Your plan is a living document. You can't plan for everything, so don't try to and don't pretend to try to.

People who try to do their planning as one stage, and their action as the next stage, encounter several serious problems. First, group members want to and actually need to do something to maintain and develop their interest. You can easily choke off the excitement by overemphasizing the need for a detailed problem analysis and a methodically detailed blueprint. You can only sell planning as action for just so long. A second problem involves the fact that you are always working with incomplete information. Once you think you are "done" with planning, it is much more difficult to incorporate new information into your plan. And third, the ever-changing nature of situations means that the world in which the plan was originally developed is different from the world in which it is implemented. If you try to base all your actions on a plan that is somewhat out of date, you will be frustrated in your efforts to force the real world into the one you envisioned by your plan. You may find this sufficiently irritating that you throw out the plan altogether.

Once established, your plan will be shaped and reshaped by new forces and new information you discover as you proceed with your action. Planning involves vision, discovery, decision making, and action. It is a purposeful way of looking at the future with the intent to shape it.

Some Basic Reasons for Planning

Why plan? Well, for one thing, it is almost impossible not to. Almost everything we do relates to some sort of plan, either implied or explicit. This morning when that blasted alarm went off, why did you get up? Why not just lie there in bed? OK, so you did for a while, but why not just stay there? My guess is that lying around in bed would not have helped you accomplish your goals for the day. That is, it would have been incompatible with your plan. Somewhere along the line you decided to go to work or to school today, probably because that fits into an even larger plan. You determined a set of activities that will help you achieve your goal. Set the alarm at night. Get out of bed in the morning. Take a shower. Make the coffee. Grab your backpack or briefcase. Go catch the bus. You get the idea.

Sometimes, especially when dealing with matters a little less routine than trying to get to work or school on time, it is easy to forget to do something important if you don't do a little thinking ahead. Look at the example above. Is there anything important you left out in your hurry? Good planning can keep you from overlooking an essential task, say, something like remembering to put your clothes on before catching the bus.

Take a Moment to Discover . . . .

Think of a time when a group you were involved with decided just what needed to be done, and then let it go at that. No one actually agreed to perform any specific task. Perhaps this occurred in your family, or where you work, or at school, or with a community action group. What was the result? Was the goal accomplished in a timely manner, or at all? How were the relationships among the members affected?

. . . .

The importance of thinking ahead certainly applies to your change effort. If you want to achieve your goals, here, too, you need to plan. A plan will help you to use yourself and your resources in the most intentional manner. You simply will not accomplish your goals through a random series of actions. You know this. The actions you take must be those necessary and sufficient to accomplish the identified purpose, they must relate to the goals as well as to one another, and they must be in proper sequence. You don't have unlimited time and unlimited resources; therefore, you need to use these in the most effective way possible. You need to plan.

Powerful planning creates both a sense of urgency and confidence in moving toward your goals. Simply by removing confusion, participants feel more capable. This feeling is further strengthened by the knowledge that they have made purposeful decisions from a range of alternative choices. Making necessary tasks clear and relating them to the accomplishment of important goals creates a tension that calls out for action. People feel the need to move, to get on with it.

As you move forward, things are going to get in your way. Your plan will help you see many of those twists, turns, and occasional chuckholes in the road ahead and prepare for them. Your plan will help you identify and marshal resources. One view of planning is that it is a way of solving problems by making the very best use of resources (Keller, 1983). Planning will guide your actions to be effective (productive in accomplishing your purpose) and efficient (done with the least time and effort) in achieving your goals.

Did you ever notice that in trying to solve one problem you end up creating another, perhaps even larger, one? Bad but unintended consequences are often the legacy of good intentions coupled with little forethought. A good plan produces thoughtful action and minimizes the likelihood that your efforts will simply generate new problems.

Good planning involves identifying both the promise and the difficulties that exist in any situation. Good planning goes beyond problems; good planning enables you to create opportunities.

How Much Planning Is Needed?

Basically, you need to know where you want to end up and how to get started to get there. The two most difficult problems most change efforts face are knowing what success looks like and actually taking the first step to get there.

Planning to implement community change is similar to the process of writing a paper. Most often, the most difficult words to write are the first ones, aren't they? If you don't really know what you want to say or what points you want to make, you are going to have a tough time getting started. You sit at your desk, pencils all sharpened, paper neatly in place, beads of sweat on your forehead, the clock ticking away, closer to the date the paper is due. If you make things up as you go along, your paper may not cover the essential issues and may ramble on without focus. Using this approach, you are plain lucky if you hit all the important points because you probably don't even know what they are. Having a picture of what the paper should look like when it's finished, together with an outline to guide you, surely would help.

The time you put into your initial planning effort is important, but it should not be exhaustive. You do need to start with *some* planning. In fact, start with about as much as the participants in your effort can stand. No matter what stage of development your change effort is in, at the very least you need enough planning to know where you want to end up, where you are going next, and what you need to do to get there.

At some point you will notice that your planning efforts have become tedious. People may become bored with it. When this happens, they may agree to anything just to get the job over with. Planning then no longer serves its purpose and may become counterproductive. When you can't stand it anymore, stop doing it.

Participant interest is a critical driving or limiting force for your planning efforts. You may need to do a little educating on the importance of planning before you actually begin. If people don't see the value of planning, it will be hard to get them to do it with any enthusiasm. People often confuse "planning" with "inaction." (On the other hand, sometimes they do know that this is exactly what planning means.) If this is the case, don't use the word *planning.* Call it something else, like "figuring out what we've got to do." Some people may be very willing to engage in planning as long as you call it something else.

You may also discover that some of your group's members value the contribution of planning and see it as a kind of game: outlining strategies; identifying enemies or other obstacles; looking for friends, alliances, and other resources; and figuring out how all these things fit together. As long as they don't get too carried away with overplanning, they can be very helpful in keeping your group looking ahead.

Levels of Planning

You cannot make a detailed plan for everything, and you cannot be so vague that you don't really know what to do. Is there some sort of happy medium? Can you be a little detailed and a little vague? Yes, there is a way around this dilemma, but it is not by striking a balance between being detailed and being vague. The trick is to plan in levels—four levels to be exact (see Figure 8-1).

Your plan will proceed from the broad to the specific. You start with where you want to end up out there somewhere in the future and then move closer and closer to the present, becoming more and more specific about what you need to do. When you have completed the four stages of the plan, you know not only where you are ultimately headed but exactly what you need to do tomorrow to start getting there. No matter how you arrive at these basic components, your plan needs to include:

- A sense of the ultimate desired condition
- A specific target that represents significant movement toward that condition

- The major activities you need to accomplish
- The specific steps to get you going

The first step is to establish the overall intent for your effort (Mayer, 1985). Here, you identify your vision for the future, the end result of what all your work is intended to achieve. For example, if you are concerned about prenatal care, your vision might be: "Every pregnant woman in Atlanta receives adequate prenatal care."

The next stage is to select an action-oriented target or goal that will help fulfill that vision. Using prenatal care again, your goal might be: "To establish a multiservice prenatal care clinic by (a specific date)."

At the third level you establish the framework for your effort, identifying the major components of your plan. These describe the various sets of activities that must be undertaken to accomplish your purpose. Although you do not identify all the activities themselves, note what each set of activities is supposed to produce. These will be your principal objectives. At this level you also want to get some idea of the order in which you need to achieve these objectives. This tier represents your best thinking of where in general you want to be headed and might include selection of the clinic site, determination of the range of services, securing funding, or establishing community support.

The final level puts some meat on this skeletal plan, identifying which sets of activities you need to begin acting on and identifying what needs to occur within each set of activities. You are also figuring out a sequence for these activities and their relationship to each other. These specific action plans clarify what you are going to do over the next one to three months. For example, you may decide that you first need to build community support and that this will lead to involvement of people who can help you determine the range of services, which will set the stage for your fund-raising activities. Later on you can begin to identify possible sites.

Start by identifying steps you will take to gain community support, your most immediate concern. These steps could include contacting

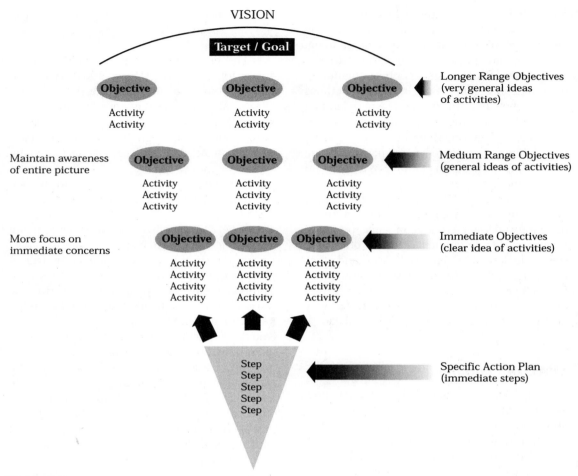

Figure 8-1
A four-level plan for action

the Health Department for statistics you can use to describe the problem, identifying other individuals and organizations who have an interest in the issue, contacting a particular news reporter to do a story on the issue, and other specific actions.

Plans at this level should look no further than three months ahead. In fact, the shorter the time frame the better. This level of planning represents actual, concrete decisions and specific steps. As a practical matter, these immediate plans can usually be determined in monthly (or, if appropriate, quarterly) meetings. Keeping

in mind the activity sets you have already selected, at each meeting ask these questions: "Are there new or different objectives we need to accomplish?" and "What do we have to do next?"

Planning for a relatively short but defined period of time allows you to be very specific and to keep the tasks close enough at hand so they have some sense of urgency or real purpose. When you plan too far down the road, you con yourself into thinking things are so far away you don't need to worry about them. So usually you don't, and they usually don't get done. At this final, specific level, the series of actions extend sufficiently into the future so that you have a sense of direction and progress, yet they are close enough at hand that you actually pay attention to them. As you execute your immediate plans, develop new information to incorporate into your next planning cycle.

As you begin acting, continue planning; keep looking ahead. This routine requires that you keep your focus on exactly what you are going to do over the next month (or so) and on making sure that those actions relate to the sets of activities (objectives) you need to be working on at the time. Continue to make sure that you have very clear steps to take and that each of these steps relates to movement toward the goal. With this ongoing, action-oriented approach to planning, you are constantly reexamining the relative importance and timeliness of each set of major activities, perhaps modifying them, perhaps eliminating some and adding new ones. Your plan stays fresh, relevant, and clear.

Basic Planning Elements

If you lived in a textbook world and could devote all the time necessary to develop the perfect plan, what could you do? You could explore each of the planning steps one by one, seeing each to conclusion before moving on. If anyone seriously suggests that you really do this, tell them to go back to their reading or whatever it was they were doing, because they certainly have not tried to produce change in the dynamic world in which both you and I live.

So, if things don't work this way in the real world, why learn about it? This is a good question. When you need to do some planning, you want to do as many of the right things as well as you can. As much as possible you will select from the ideal to meet the demands of your current real-life situation. It helps to know what the ideal is. So open your textbook and step in. Look around; things are peaceful, quiet, and cozy here—and, yes, a little dull. Now that you have become acclimated, let's get to work.

These basic planning elements are present to one degree or another in all planning considerations. Sometimes, either because of other demands or the inattention of those doing the planning, they receive only a flicker of notice. However, each of these elements should be given some considered thought.

Identify current areas of unmet needs or discomfort. Something brought you to this situation of change. Just what is it that people are upset about or dissatisfied with? By uncovering instances of unmet needs, you give yourself a picture of the current situation that requires some fixing. This helps you identify your starting place or your focus.

Remember, you want to distinguish between *needs* that are going unmet, the *causes* of the problem, the *symptoms* of the problem, and the *solutions* to the problem. These are four different things. All of these are important, and you will eventually make some determination on each. But as you do, maintain an awareness of how your own values and perspectives can color your perception of these various factors (Ellsworth, Hooyman, Ruff, Stam, & Tucker, 1982). Looking at causes (forces that interfere with people getting what they need) and symptoms (that which indicates people don't have what they need) is valuable in helping you understand the unmet need as you move toward a solution (Kettner, Moroney, & Martin, 1990). Initially, though, zero in on whatever it is that people need but don't have. To get a better feel for this, ask yourself basic questions such as: "What don't people have that they need to feel happy, or good, or at least satisfied?"

Now that you know what "unhappy" looks like, it's time to get a view of happy.

Identify your vision for the future. What do you want to accomplish? What does "good" or "happy" look like? Your vision is your picture of what should be happening instead of what is now happening. It is the complete realization of your efforts stated in positive terms and clear, simple language. It is a strong declaration of your intent.

CAPTURING CONCEPTS

Planning Elements

These planning elements are present to one degree or another in all planning considerations. In an ideal situation, you should give each of these elements some considered thought.

- Identify current areas of unmet need or discomfort.
- Identify your vision for the future.

- Identify your target using images of potentiality.
- Identify factors in the future environment.
- Identify current obstacles and resources.
- Identify stakeholders.
- Identify actions to mobilize or use existing advantages to overcome obstacles.
- Identify the sequence and relationship of actions.

- Identify necessary time frames.
- Identify people who will handle necessary tasks.
- Identify indicators that show planned tasks were completed.
- Identify measures of effectiveness and indicators of trouble.
- Develop methods of acquiring new information.
- Perform identified tasks.

Identify your target using images of potentiality. What are you actually shooting for? Images of potentiality, a concept developed by Eva Schindler-Rainman (1977), provides a simple, yet powerful way to identify the specific outcome you desire. There is much truth to the saying, "If you don't know where you are going, you will end up somewhere else."

A problem is simply the difference between where you are and where you want to be. Closing that gap is the intention of planning (Nutt, 1985). This method helps you see clearly just where you want to be. Using images of potentiality, you project yourself into the future and visualize what things will look like once you have responded to the unmet needs. Here is how it works.

- Pick an imaginary date in the future far enough away to give you sufficient time to work to accomplish your goals but not so far that the sense of urgency to act on the issue is lost. For some changes you seek, two months in the future would be appropriate. For others, a year or two would be fitting. Still others may require you to look five years down the road.

- Now, pretend that this future date is the present. So "today" is . . . whatever date you have selected. You are there now. Visualize the situation today. Go ahead, look around. What do you see?
- Describe everything you see now that the problem is solved and you have accomplished everything you had set out to do those months or years ago when you first started. Identify clear, visual images. For example, you can't really see "people getting along better" but you can see "people playing softball in the park." It's hard to know just what "things look better" means but "all the walls have a fresh coat of paint" gives you a good picture.

If your group is just getting started, it should concentrate on turning only one or two images into reality. Trying to do more than that can fragment your group and stretch your resources past their limits. Or you can end up with the same bunch of people trying to do too much and getting burned out in the process. The images you select to turn into goals should present you with a moderate challenge. Images of potentiality is a powerful way to make your goals for the future more real. When goals come alive, it is easier for people to commit to moving from where they are to where they want to be.

The goal you select should be one that people are enthusiastic enough about that they are willing to work to make it happen. That is, people pick the thing they really want to work on. This may or may not be the "most important" item on your list of images. A common mistake groups make is to select the item everybody agrees is the most important. Often, this is something people really don't feel capable of dealing with, or even if the matter is important, it's not really very interesting. To start with, it is much better to pick interesting over important. Make sure everybody knows this from the start.

The criteria for a good goal should be kept in mind. First, it should be feasible; that is, the resources needed to accomplish the goal must be available. Second, it should generate some excitement. Third, it should be clear enough

that it gets you all headed in the same direction and you can easily tell when you have reached it. Fourth, the goal should be something your organization will make happen. Finally, the goal should be consistent with the reason that brought you all together in the first place (Dale & Mitiguy, 1978).

Identify factors in the future environment. You are planning today to institute something that will be in place some distant, or not too distant, tomorrow. You have an idea of what today looks like, but how about tomorrow? You should consider how your efforts today relate to the future environment.

Recall that any specific plan you prepare is somewhat out of date the moment it is "done." New developments will occur, and you will need to respond to some of these. Which forces will help or hinder your efforts at the time they are actually taking place, not today when you are *thinking* about doing them? What will occur in

Change Agent Tip

It is helpful to take advantage of brainstorming techniques when a group is generating ideas. A few simple rules for brainstorming sessions include:

- Write everything down
- Everyone offers an idea
- No criticism of any idea
- No discussion of ideas during brainstorming
- The wilder the idea, the better
- Stress the quantity not the quality of ideas
- It is acceptable to repeat an idea

- Build on one another's ideas

You can build on people's enthusiasm as they create the world they will eventually work to make real. While you are brainstorming, though, some people will catch on to the idea of clear images much better than others. In the spirit of brainstorming, you don't want to tell people that their ideas aren't good enough, yet you do want sharp images. To get around this obstacle, create two columns: one headed

IMAGES and the other headed IDEAS.

Encourage everyone to offer their ideas, even if they are not yet sharpened into images. People will soon get the hang of things, and some good ideas that otherwise might be silenced will find their way into the IMAGES column. Planning that is purely rational is limited. Let your intuitive side come out of hiding and into the bright light of planning. Allow it to influence your actions as well.

that future environment that makes it more receptive or more resistant to what you want to do? What new opportunities does the future hold for your organization? It is in this world, a month, a year, or five years from now, that you will be working. Do you know much about it?

There are a few things you can do to give yourself a glimpse of the future. Similar to images of potentiality, an exercise called "creating the future" allows you to envision future conditions that may have an impact on your project. Select a specific date in the future and act as if that future date were the present. Then ask participants to consider the following question: "What is going on today that can in some way influence our success in (whatever change you are attempting to implement)?" Some of these factors will be economic, some political, some technological, and some plainly off-the-wall.

Recalling the discussion of systems theory presented in Chapters 2 and 3, start with the broadest system likely to have an impact on your efforts and narrow your field down to the one in which your members participate.

It is helpful to develop this picture of the future over two separate occasions. On the first occasion, create the future for the broadest arenas likely to influence your success. Then, about a week later, do the same for your more immediate spheres of action. (If you don't live in a textbook world, you may have only one opportunity to do this. If that is the case, reduce the number of levels you examine to no more than three.)

It is helpful to familiarize yourself with publications that forecast future developments. Proceedings from community conferences that attempt to gauge future developments, information from various government planning bodies, and community trends publications should prove helpful. The World Future Society prepares two publications that may provide you with some helpful perspectives on the future: *The Futurist,* a monthly magazine, and the *Future Survey Annual,* a compendium of data and projections related to the world of tomorrow.

Identify current obstacles and current resources. You've dealt with the future; now you need a picture of the current environment—the arena of action in which you are going to promote change. These are the forces that have an impact on what occurs in the system in which you want to make changes. This requires your attention to its interaction with other systems that affect it.

A number of years ago Kurt Lewin (1951) described a technique known as force field analysis. Figure 8-2 diagrams a simple force field. A number of contending forces operate in your arena of action. Some of these forces drive you toward your goal; others drive you away from your goal. A state of tension exists, producing a dynamic situation as forces act on one another. At any given moment these forces are in relative balance; this balance represents the current state of affairs. (For an excellent discussion of force field analysis, see Brager and Holloway, 1978.)

Using this method of viewing the current situation can help you determine which forces you can mobilize and which forces you must counter. To get this snapshot, brainstorm all the forces now present that may help or hinder your success. These forces may be tangible items, such as people or meeting rooms or backhoes, or intangibles, such as apathy or personal connections or skills.

First, list all those things that may be getting in your way. Remember, you are listing currently operating forces, not those that may develop. Some common restraining forces include inhibiting policies or procedures, history of failed effort, lack of information, intimidating opponents, ingrained attitudes, and a lack of money. There are, of course, many more, some of which are unique to your circumstances. Generating this list will give you a good idea of the obstacles you are facing.

Many groups think only of the obstacles they must face or the difficulties they will encounter and fail to regard equally the forces operating to benefit them. This leads to discouragement and lost opportunities as well. By

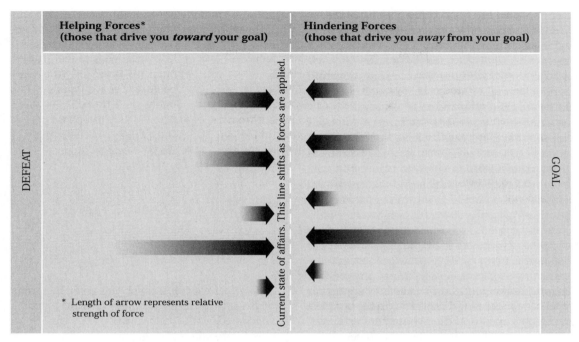

Figure 8-2
Simple force field based on Lewin's technique (1951)

examining your helping forces after you have considered your hindering forces, you generate confidence and build on the discovery of resources by beginning to look for them much more actively.

Force field analysis holds that driving and restraining forces are in relative balance. You do have a lot going for you. Unless the situation is rapidly deteriorating, some things present in the environment are keeping the situation from getting much worse much quicker. What are these things? The most obvious asset any community has is its people. This is so evident that it is frequently overlooked. Other common forces include dissatisfaction or anger, helpful laws and policies, leadership, money, talents, personal networks, and physical resources. What else is there? If you imagine the opposing forces as the bad guys, what's holding them in check? These are some of your helping forces.

After the forces present in your arena of action have been identified, it is a good idea to get some notion of their relative power. You may, for example, assign numerical values to designate how much influence each force wields. This doesn't have to be a precise measurement, but it will give you an indication of the more important forces you need to think about. As you begin to move to action, remember that you can combine a number of smaller forces to make a more potent one. For example, a lot of people, a small room, and a couple of television cameras can add up to quite a powerful force.

Using force field analysis, you can discover a lot about your current situation in less than an hour. It is a good idea to repeat this exercise from time to time to keep your picture of the present, its dangers and its opportunities, up to date.

Change Agent Tip

Asking some basic questions can shed light on stakeholders, those who may have a powerful influence on your change effort. The answers to these questions will help you discover the stakeholders your change effort must take into account.

- Who currently feels the problem? How?
- Who benefits from the current condition? How?
- Who could benefit from a changed condition? How?
- Who currently makes decisions on this issue? What is the nature of these decisions?

- Who else needs to feel the problem? How? (or) Who needs to behave in a different way? How?
- Who is likely to oppose you? Why?
- Who is likely to support you? Why?

Identify stakeholders. *Stakeholders* are people who have a stake in what you do. In the broadest sense this means those whose interests your actions could benefit or threaten. Their influence is so powerful that they deserve their own category.

Mason and Mitroff (1985) identified stakeholders as having purposes and strategies that support or resist your efforts. Those who are supporting have goals generally compatible with your goals and are moving (or would like to move) in the same general direction you are moving. Resisters, whom they characterize as nonsupporting, resisting, or actually opposing, provide barriers to your success or move in the opposite direction.

Take an extra minute or two to think beyond the obvious resisters to identify all those who have a stake in or benefit from the current situation. You cannot ignore them, for they will surely make life difficult for you as you pursue a change that threatens their interests.

Some people benefiting from the current situation may seem to have interests similar to yours, but they are currently getting something (for example, funding or good press) as they pursue their activities. Your presence can threaten their piece of the action, their turf.

Remember that as soon as you enter the arena of action the scene changes. You may not be welcomed with open arms. This can be a surprise to you, so be prepared.

Now think about those with interests similar to yours but who would not be threatened by your success. Think for that extra minute or so about those who would be genuinely happy or who would breathe a little easier if you succeeded. You may be able to uncover some unanticipated backing.

It is essential to move supportive stakeholders to the role of *investor* by involving them in planning in a meaningful way (Benne, 1985; Ellsworth et al., 1982; Kettner, Daley, & Nichols, 1985; Lewis, Lewis, & Soufiée, 1991). It is necessary that they develop ownership of the goal. When individuals have a strong attachment to the goal, their personal need to accomplish the goal leads to a strong commitment to the success of the entire group (Horwitz, 1954). Playing a role in the development of the goal is probably the best way to promote this strong acceptance. Key stakeholders cannot be limited to information-giving roles. They need to participate in strategy determination, task accomplishment, and decision-making capacities.

Identify actions to mobilize or use existing advantages to overcome obstacles. Now that you have a picture of what needs to be changed, what the desired conditions look like, what future forces will influence your efforts, and what forces are now present that will affect your success, it is time to identify what you can do to get to where you want to go.

Decide which obstacle you want to overcome first. Look over your list of helping forces or resources and decide which of these can be used to counteract whatever is working against you. Generally, pick assets that are easiest to use, although other criteria such as developing broader participation and keeping yourself from becoming too predictable should be considered. A clear picture of actions you can take will emerge from reviewing your assets. If there is time, test a number of alternative actions as you decide what to do. Sometimes less than the best is better. As you select actions that hold the best chance to get you to where you want to go, make sure these are actions you can actually see yourself doing. Selecting the best activities (as if we know what they truly are), but ones you know you are not really going to do, is about the same as selecting no activities.

Next, identify the particular steps that need to be taken (such as making phone calls, distributing fliers, or cooking tacos) to activate the resource.

Identify the sequence and relationship of actions. Which of these things do you do first? The best way to answer that is to consider what comes last. By working backward, you can better determine how the steps you plan to take relate to each other and to what it is you want to accomplish. You can also figure out how specific actions can bolster or interfere with one another.

Identify necessary time frames. The great philosophers of our times, stand-up comedians, understand that the secret to life is good timing. Deciding when something must be done is pretty important. Don't assume that this is commonly understood. Make your time frames clear.

One thing you will probably notice is that everything apparently needs to be done by tomorrow, if not the day before. Unless you are dealing with a scheduled event whose timing is outside your control, it is likely that you can pursue a less frenzied schedule. If a frenzied schedule is not really required, it won't be sustained anyway. People will normally do things about the time they think they need to be done. So don't drive yourself crazy worrying about getting everything done well in advance, and at once. If you jam up the first few months with most of your activities without rest or pacing, participants may feel worn out as soon as the first set of things is completed. You will

Change Agent Tip

Homan's Rule of 33: Things will be 33% different from what you think they will be, generally on the downside. For example, if 12 people tell you they are coming to your get-together, expect 8.

One of the most common "surprises" is that things will take 33% longer to do than you thought they would take, even if you are generous in your estimate. Think about all the papers you have written or the assignments you have done. Didn't almost all of them take longer than you had thought?

probably discover that many things don't get done on schedule thereafter. This can lead to discouragement and to unnecessary conflict. Give yourself some leeway for things running over schedule.

Identify people who will handle necessary tasks. Here's a radical thought: Things don't get done by themselves. Designate who is responsible for seeing that each task gets completed. There is a key phrase here—"seeing that a task gets completed." Individuals taking on the responsibility don't necessarily need to do the job themselves. They just need to make sure that it gets done. Sometimes no one in your group has the necessary time, talent, or interest to perform the task, but one of you can usually find another individual, perhaps from outside the immediate group, who does. This may result in bringing a new member into the fold. However you go about this, see that the individual has a sense of investment in the task and a sense of personal responsibility. Things no one is willing to commit to usually don't get done.

Identify indicators that show the planned tasks were completed. It is sometimes difficult to determine whether a task is completed because we don't really know what completed looks like. By selecting indicators of job completion, you can more clearly determine whether or not you are doing what you said you were going to do. These also help to clarify or make more specific just what the task involves.

If your task involves holding a meeting, one indicator could be the minutes of the meeting, another could be a sign-in sheet. If your task involves developing media attention, an indicator could be a record of news stories aired. If fliers are to be distributed, the fact that you have a flier and a list of the distribution points and numbers distributed could be indicators. Indicators are simply your response to the question: How do you tell that you got it done?

These indicators help you monitor your efforts. You will be able to determine what you did and when. Not only will this help keep you

on track but it will also help you determine your effectiveness. Evaluating your efforts is important, but before you can determine whether your effort is working, you need to determine just what work you have done.

Identify measures of effectiveness and indicators of trouble. To *evaluate* your endeavor means checking to see if it is producing the desired results. When you evaluate, you ask yourself: "Are we accomplishing what we want to accomplish? Why, or why not?" This is different from *monitoring,* which asks the question: "Are we doing what we said we were going to do?" Monitoring asks what is being done; evaluating asks whether or not it is working (Kettner, Daley, & Nichols, 1985).

Just as you have indicators of task completion, you should have indicators of task effectiveness. These are your responses to the question: "How do we tell if this produced what we wanted it to produce?" If a meeting was to lead to increased money from a particular source, your indicator would be more money from that source. If your intent with the news media were to influence the vote of the city council, your indicator would be the council's actual vote.

These are pretty simple indicators, but they give you a sense of how you are faring. Some occasions demand a more sophisticated approach to evaluation. For example, you may need to clearly identify the relationship between actions and their consequences. You may need to determine not only if this particular action directly produced this particular consequence, but maybe also how or why. No matter how superficial or thorough your evaluation procedures may be, you still need to know what your indicators of success are; that is, what outcomes you expect to produce.

In any effort there are signs of your accomplishments, your growing success. By knowing what some of these are, you can recognize and celebrate their attainment. Maintaining an awareness of your victories great and small can keep you driving forward and help

Change Agent Tip

Sometimes no one is willing to volunteer to take responsibility for getting a certain job done, although everyone agrees that it is necessary. There follows an uncomfortable silence in response to the question: "OK, who's going to take care of this?" Let's hope you catch yourself before you volunteer to take on another thankless job that nobody else wants to do. Otherwise you and the two or three other people who can't stand silence for an answer will come to be seen as the "main people" in the organization—the ones who really are going to worry about getting things done. The other people then get to become less "main" and understand that they have an acceptable role of being less committed. They can then come to expect less of themselves as they come to expect more

of you "main people." Unfortunately, you will soon come to share these expectations.

So, what to do? The thing still needs to get done. If you have noticed a pattern developing, talk to the other "main" people beforehand. You can agree to take on your fair share of duties, but none of you will jump to rescue the organization by doing whatever no one else seems willing to do. The first thing you can try is to just sit there and accept the silence. It should be long enough that there is some noticeable discomfort. Eventually someone will speak up . . . maybe. If that hasn't produced an eager soul, something a little more direct may be in order. Try saying something like this: "Well, it looks like we don't think it's all that important that we

get this done." This usually produces protestations to the contrary. If it doesn't, and people just sit there, then drop it, let it go. You may need to risk squandering a few opportunities before people get the idea that the work really is going to be spread around, or it's not going to get done.

If people agree that the job is worth doing and they say so, then ask again: "OK, who's going to take this?" After a second you may need to invite someone by saying something like, "How about you, Gus?"

An alternative approach is to ask: "What will happen if we don't get this done?" Then ask: "Is that OK with everyone? How about you, Gus?" These questions usually encourage some members of the group to agree to take charge of the task.

you overcome the myriad setbacks that can stymie you.

Just as there are signs of success, there are danger signals too. You had better have an idea of what these look like so you can heed their warnings.

Develop methods for acquiring new information. Leave bread out for a while, and it gets stale. Leave plans untouched for a while, and they get stale too. You need to keep an eye on

your plans to keep them fresh, up-to-date, and relevant to your situation. Whenever plans no longer effectively relate to current conditions, they become deadweight. They also convince people that planning is a waste of time.

To keep your planning useful for meeting current demands and giving direction to the future, you have to keep informed about current and likely future conditions. Identify the sources you will use to get new information and how you will incorporate the information provided into your planning and decision

Change Agent Tip

Here is yet another case where you can benefit from a look at the future. We all know the accuracy of 20-20 hindsight: "Looking back on it now, I would have done things a bit differently" or "If I had only known then what I know now." You have probably used phrases like this a time or two yourself. I know I have.

Why wait until that day when the problems you should have foreseen smack you in the face? Why not bring them forward in time to do something about them? That is what a technique called "projected 20-20 hindsight" is intended to do.

Toward the end of your planning, take a little time to talk about pitfalls in the road before you and how important it is to try to identify them. Then take your imaginary leap to that date you have targeted for reaching your goal. Ask the group to take a look back on your effort "today" . . . because you failed. Then ask: "From this vantage point, what did we miss in our planning? What happened that caused us to fail? What faulty assumptions did we make? What did we do that we shouldn't have done? What didn't we do that we should have done?" It is a good idea to have separate sheets of paper for each question you ask, or separate small groups to work on each question.

Pick a few of these answers and develop responses to them. For example, an important one could be: "We ran out of gas." If you think that might really happen to you (by the way, it usually does), think now of how you will recognize the signs that this is occurring and determine what you will do when you recognize those signs. You don't have to develop a strategy for dealing with each possible pitfall, but recognize them as warnings. Have some fun with the process. Take the lists out every now and then to look at. If you are aware of pitfalls, they will be much easier to avoid, and you will be more confident because you realize what could have happened if you weren't looking.

---

making. Do you need to keep in touch with certain individuals? Do you need to read newspapers, memos, or other written material related to your area of interest? How will you use your indicators of task completion and indicators of effectiveness?

From time to time get together with the people who helped develop the plan to review and modify it. If you are in a fast-paced situation in which important conditions really do change daily, your plan will require constant attention and fine tuning. The less rapidly changing your conditions are, the less frequently you need to review your plans, and the less likely you probably will. However, the less frequently you review a plan, the more thorough you need to make your review. Don't wait too long between reviews, however. If you find that each review involves a rediscovery of your plans, then you have waited too long and your plans have probably become documents that no longer inform your actions.

Review dates should be built in to your planning process. Depending on your situation, this could be every afternoon, every three months, or every October.

Perform identified tasks. All this planning doesn't amount to a hill of beans if you don't actually do anything. Although performing tasks may not technically be seen as part of the planning process, let's not forget that action is what this whole business is about. Consider, too, that action and planning are occurring at the same time. You cannot just stop everything you are doing to plan, and you cannot wait until you are done planning before you act.

Obstacles

Pretty easy stuff, isn't it? Just follow the cookbook, turn up the heat, set the timer, and out pops a plan. I don't know whether it would be nice or boring if it were that easy, but rest assured, it isn't. Let's look at some of the things that can get in the way—and maybe even consider a thing or two you can do to face these obstacles.

An unpredictable future. One of the simple facts about the future is that you don't really know what is going to happen. By planning you increase the odds that you can predict and influence the future, but you cannot fully know or control it. Accept that simple fact and be willing to be surprised. A misplaced belief that you are able to control all forces will leave you unnerved and unprepared when you discover that you can't. Anticipate the fact that some unanticipated things will occur. You can and should develop some contingency or backup plans. Most important, though, you should be willing to roll with the punches if you get hit by something you didn't plan for, and you should be ready to take advantage of some unexpected opportunity.

Lack of skill. Most planning situations in community change do not call for sophisticated skills. If you feel hampered that your planning process can't move forward because your data collection, data analysis, and consequent decision-making methods are not sufficiently

complex, you might be overdoing things a bit. Hagebak (1982) calls this problem the "bog of sophistication." Check also to see that this lack of skill is not simply a justification for not getting started. Large, highly complex change efforts require some sophisticated planning, but most changes are really not all that complex.

Every day each of us answers the basic questions involved in planning: "What do you want to have happen? What do you have going for you? What is getting in your way? Knowing this, what do you need to do?" We do this so often and so easily, whether it involves driving to the store or figuring out dinner, that we don't even notice we are planning, but indeed we are. You need to recognize that you not only have the fundamental skills but you use them all the time. All you have to do is apply them in a different arena.

What you already know is probably enough to get you started. If you need to know more, ask a planning expert for some direction or some time. Colleges, public agencies, and some social service organizations have planners. You can generally find someone pretty good who can give you a hand.

Lack of interest. Most of us are not interested in doing things that are boring and have little value, especially if we don't think we are good at them. Planning is no different. If you want to involve people in planning, you have to confront these three obstacles. To promote a little more interest in planning, first of all you have to make it interesting. There is a natural excitement for doing or creating something new; capitalize on this. Don't wear people down with the mechanics of planning. Build on their enthusiasm. Also, give a little attention to the setting. Consider doing this over pizza or in a cabin on a weekend retreat, or somehow making things a little different, a little unique, a little fun.

Second, you will probably have to confront people's previous experiences of fruitless planning. Allow them to point out how they will make sure that doesn't happen this time. You probably won't convince the reluctant by talking

about the importance of planning. You have to approach the process as if it is important and clearly directed to improving the problem situation. Avoid making planning appear too grand. This often generates skepticism. When planning takes on a life of its own, it becomes irrelevant and cannot live up to its lofty promises. People realize this right away. While they will go through the motions of planning, they won't make an investment in it.

Third, the way you present planning will give people the message that this is something they can do. Calling planning "figuring out what we need to do," for example, will go a long way toward bringing things down to earth.

Take your planning process one step at a time. Providing a rough overview of the process can be helpful. However, if you go through an exhaustive list of everything that needs to be done and all the things not to do, you will end up confusing people. Guiding people through the steps one at a time keeps them on track and gives them something specific to do. From time to time show how a particular step relates to what you want to accomplish so participants know why they are doing what they are doing.

Thirst for action—don't want to take the time to plan. When emotions are running high, people want to act. They don't want to mess around with this planning business. They certainly don't want to hear the learned voice of reason telling them to calm down and think this through thoroughly. That's all right. Plan a little bit. The energy they now have for action is probably more valuable anyway. (The exception to this is if what people want to do is clearly so shortsighted that they will cause more problems than they are solving. Then you might have to get them to stand back for a minute to take a broader look before acting.) If you can, get some agreement on where you want to end up, and then just worry about what you can do right now and how you can do it. After a period of initial fervor, the group is usually ready to determine some longer range strategy.

You do have a delicate balance to strike

here. You don't want to get into the habit of not planning, but by the same token, you don't want to dampen enthusiasm and cut off spontaneity. Community change does require some discipline, and not everyone wanting to be an activist is ready to accept that. Over time, certain roles will emerge with some people acknowledged as providing strategic leadership whereas others can be counted on for taking needed action. As long as both aspects are valued, the group stands a good chance of achieving some success. Problems occur if none of the activists want to seriously think ahead. Some people in leadership roles would rather be active than effective. They rather like their images as activists, and it is in serving that image that they are mainly interested. You will have to watch for this in yourself as well as with other members of your group. It leads to a resistance to considering the consequences of your actions because the consequences are really not important, just the action is. It is vital to keep a sense of purpose. The value of planning is to provide action with a sense of purpose.

Another group of *consequence avoiders* are those who shy away from planning because an honest look at things may call into question the effectiveness of a preferred course of action. They just want to do what they want to do. It may be comfortable, exciting, or whatever. Taking a good look at the most effective approach may require a change in preferred tactics. If the tactics themselves are really more important than the outcome, planning is an irritant and irrelevant.

If all you want to do is have fun, go find something else to do. If you are mainly interested in commanding attention, rob a bank—you can scare a lot of people, it is exciting, and you will probably get on the news.

Planning to avoid action.   At the opposite end of the spectrum are the *risk avoiders* who are hesitant to take action and so plan the thing to death. Risk avoiders want to make sure all risks are identified and minimized before any action is taken. Some want actions to come with guarantees. Sometimes the effort to plan is easier than the work involved in implementing the plan. After all, you can control the plan; you can't control everything that happens when you put things in motion. Testing your great ideas is a lot harder than declaring them. All contingencies must be accounted for and every detail considered. As the situation changes and new information becomes available, risk avoiders keep retooling their plans. They could do this forever, and probably would, if something didn't come along to give them a push. (Something usually does.) The sad thing is that despite all their planning they aren't really prepared for action because they don't really want to act.

If you suspect that this is going on, you must confront it. Some of the following questions might be helpful for bringing the concern out in the open: "When will we have enough information to act? When will we be ready to act? Are we really afraid of action? Are we more afraid of failure than we are willing to take a shot at changing things? Are we afraid of the work that we will have to do if we actually start acting on our plans, or are we afraid that our plans won't work?" This can lead to some productive discussion, and it can lead to action as you realize what you have been doing. Be careful not to demean or ridicule people for their fears. That approach will just lead to denial and divisiveness. It really is all right to feel uncertain. If that is what is going on, accept the fact that you feel that way and accept, also, the fact that you still need to get going.

Belief that plans won't be followed or have an impact on decision making.   There is a game that goes like this: person in authority asks subordinates for their ideas; gives them the impression that they are really being listened to; makes them feel part of this *shared* process; and then goes ahead and does what he or she wanted to do all along.

Has this ever happened to you? Probably. You feel like a dupe, don't you? It has probably happened to others in your group as well, so don't be surprised when you encounter this sort of skepticism. And don't encourage it by playing the same game yourself. Sometimes an idea someone else offers may be less perfect than your own, but it may still be acceptable. Accepting this "less perfect" idea may be the wiser course, especially if it is workable and others have a strong investment in the proposal. Broad ownership of the plan is usually more important than perfection anyway.

Encouraging people to take some responsibility for implementing their ideas (if the group agrees that they are worth doing) is one way to show that you take the suggestion seriously. With this approach, the person can make sure that the action will be handled in the way he or she wanted. If you ask people for information for planning, let them know how the information will be used and what purpose it will serve. Also, let participants know how the information will benefit them and the change effort.

Forgetting to include people in planning. Leaving people out of the planning process can be deadly. Some may passively or aggressively attempt to sabotage the direction you decide to take. Others may simply have little interest in pursuing a course they did not help set and may not fully understand.

Take stock of who should be and who would want to be included or at least invited to help determine your future goals and actions. Look at those who operate in the relevant systems your change effort engages, particularly those stakeholders in the need, action, and target communities. (These communities, which constitute your arena of action, were discussed in Chapter 6.) Try to figure out roles for those who want to be involved.

It may be appropriate to exclude someone from developing your plans. However, if you do, make sure you honestly examine your reasons for doing so, and also make sure you have considered the cost of their exclusion.

Defining the problem in terms of the solution. Defining the outcome you want to achieve and defining the means for achieving that outcome

are two different things. For example, children in your neighborhood are threatened by cars speeding down a busy street they must cross on their way to school. This is something the neighborhood wants to take action on. Someone pipes up: "The problem here is that we don't have a street light at the intersection." The room positively flutters with the simultaneous bobbing of many heads. Hold it right there, don't move. You are in danger of defining the problem as a solution. Sorry, folks, but your problem is not the lack of a street light. The problem is that your kids may get killed. The street light may or may not be a good solution, but if that is all you think about, you will close yourself off from thinking about any other approach to achieving your goal. If you put in the street light and your kids still get hurt, you haven't accomplished your purpose. However, if your kids are safe without a street light (maybe you put in speed bumps or a crossing bridge instead), you have solved your problem. Which is more important, your children's safety or a street light? Now, which do you want to work on?

When you are defining the outcome you want to achieve, ask yourself: "If the situation were different only in this way, would we be satisfied?"

Planning to produce a predetermined approach. Planning in the purest sense involves no assumptions. Pure planning doesn't exist. We all start off with some assumptions, often including a preferred way of handling the situation we face. If you already know what you want to do about a situation, you have to ask yourself what your purpose is in planning. You have to distinguish between planning that intends to discover and then implement the best approach and planning that intends to discover the best way to implement an approach you have already decided on. Generally, the "discovery" method is better. Frankly, there are times when you don't have much time for discovery, the problem is pretty clear and simple, or the solution is so self-evident (be careful, you can be fooled by this) that you may just decide to go ahead and figure out how to best do what you think you need to do.

If all you are really doing is shaping the process to support a conclusion you have already reached under the guise of discovery, you are manipulating information and ideas; you are not using them to discover. You have a vested interest in protecting a position; therefore, you will not consider all the information equally. You will approve of those things that support your approach and disapprove of those that challenge its wisdom. The effect is not much different from defining the problem in terms of a solution. You end up cutting yourself off from considering other options, and you may leave some of your partners feeling a bit burned.

Now it is all right to have an idea of how to deal with a particular issue; in fact you probably will. You can use your planning processes to test this idea against others. If you can do that objectively, which is difficult, you will end up with an approach you have confidence in.

Groupthink. Many groups establish norms that prevent the free expression of ideas. In these groups, there is pressure to maintain an agreeable atmosphere free of dissension. The primary goal becomes promoting a shared perception of reality rather than discovering and shaping that reality. Conformity is stressed and accomplished more often by subtle than by direct pressure. Gentle reminders are given to members that the group has things under control and that expressions of doubt are expressions of lack of faith in the group and its leaders. The group conspires to ignore signs of trouble. Open disagreement is seen as an attack on the group and its prevailing wisdom. To suggest that there is a better way or that the group is overlooking something important is just not done.

Participants are not willing to be seen as deviants or troublemakers who upset the group's illusion of unanimity and control over events. To protect themselves and the group from this discomfort, participants censor their own thoughts. People keep their misgivings about a proposed course of action to themselves, sometimes taking potshots later on a failed course of action. Janis (1982) has labeled this process *groupthink.*

You can see how dangerous this process can be to a group. Their unreal view of reality can have some very real consequences. Agreements that are superficial can fall apart when put to the test. Things that have been ignored can rise up to knock down the group's efforts. The sad thing is that groups often aren't aware of their use of groupthink, and they are left confused about what went wrong.

Keep on the lookout for signs of groupthink and bring it up if you think you may be closing off discussion to force group agreement. A good, simple question to ask is: "Is there anything we don't want to look at?" When you have the time to use them, techniques such as brainstorming, force field analysis, and projected 20-20 hindsight should give you a good rein on groupthink tendencies.

Conclusion

Planning requires that you acknowledge and accept the fact that you will have to change your behavior. If planning doesn't help you figure out what you want, determine what to do, prepare you to do it, and keep you on track, planning is a waste of time. But if planning increases the chances you will do the right thing at the right time in the right way to get what you want, and you put it to use, then it has been time well spent.

Powerful planning not only gives you direction but builds commitment, enthusiasm, and confidence. Planning is a vision of a better future made more possible by the determination of purposeful actions. If you grab hold of that vision and make it yours, if you take those actions in the present to shape the future, if you continue to pay attention and keep your plans alive, one day you will look around at what you have accomplished—and it will feel good.

CHAPTER **9**

People—The Most Valuable Resource

Chapter Highlights

🧩 You are not going to do it all by yourself

🧩 Few participants will have sustained involvement

🧩 Organization is both a process and an outcome

🧩 Involve people from all parts of the arena of action

🧩 Purposeful recruiting is important

🧩 Levels of participation in an organization

🧩 Participants may change their level of involvement

🧩 Clues to identify those likely to be more involved

🧩 People need to recognize opportunities for involvement

🧩 People will respond at their level of awareness, interest, and self-confidence

🧩 Talents and assets the organization needs

🧩 Each person has something to contribute

🧩 People can commit to the issue, the organization, or each other

🧩 Share your talents wisely

🧩 Personal characteristics of influential members affect the organization

🧩 Particularly beneficial personal characteristics

🧩 Steps for involving people in the effort

🧩 Ways to maintain member involvement

🧩 Meet basic needs of membership

🧩 Relate members to each other and to the task

🧩 Recognize progress

🧩 Recognize the use of volunteer time

🧩 Typical circumstances for using paid staff

🧩 General considerations for working with volunteers

🧩 Acknowledge the initiator's special degree of commitment

🧩 Cross cultural lines

🧩 Learn about yourself and others

Six weeks and nothing has happened. One meeting, some scribbled notes to add to the collection of yet other similarly written brilliant ideas trapped in a file somewhere, and a couple of conversations about the next steps, still untaken. That's about it. Melanie and Ben are starting to feel like this grand idea of theirs is destined to be stuck in neutral. It seems that there are too many other things that steal away the time and too little encouragement to keep moving ahead.

"We can't do this all by ourselves, Melanie. We're not getting done what needs to be done."

"No foolin', Ben. It's not my idea to drive myself crazy, you know. I do have other things to do around here."

"Yeah, I know. Doing something like this isn't part of your job or mine, but we have kind of taken this on."

"Look, Ben, why don't we just get some help? We know some of the things that need to be done at this point. Why don't we work on getting some other people to be part of this, spread things around a bit? I'd rather work on that instead of working on only a few of all the things that we haven't really been doing anyway."

"It would be nice to have some other people involved. I don't know. I guess it would seem more real if it weren't just you and me. Maybe I'd take it more seriously. Give it more time."

"It's not just the time. Believe it or not, there are some people who know things that we don't know."

"Shocker, ain't it. OK. I know Donna Sanderson is interested in this sort of thing. I'll ask her. You want to check with Kurt Nicholas over at the Health Department? I'm sure he'd know a lot."

"I'm not too sure what I should be asking him. Oh, that's an excuse. Never mind, I'll figure it out. Yeah, let's get started. It's time we got moving again."

You are not going to do it all by yourself. Any change that amounts to anything involves other people, maybe even a lot of people. Although few people will have sustained involvement over the life of the change effort, many people will play a role in its success. These people aren't just sitting around offering advice (well, maybe a few are), they are *doing* things to accomplish a specific purpose or set of purposes.

Melanie and Ben are coming to grips with the fact that the originators of an idea cannot keep it to themselves if they hope to get anything done. Not only do they have to share the idea but they need to share *ownership* of the idea as well. They realize that success requires the time, talents, and perspectives of many other people. They also know that all these people aren't going to flock to the cause. You have to go out and get them.

In previous chapters in Part 2 you have learned to better understand your community and how power operates within it, and you have been given some suggestions on how to plan your actions to produce the desired results. Yet, unless you are capable of being in several places at the same time, nothing significant is going to happen unless other people become involved. This chapter looks at how you involve people, how you develop and keep commitment, and how people's talents and energies can be put to work.

Much of the work in a change effort is commonly done by people who are not paid to do it. This requires special attention. The nature of voluntary activity, particularly when complementing the work of paid staff, is an important consideration. Finally, as you work on various change attempts, you will find yourself reflecting on why people do the things they do to help or hinder. Here are a few observations to set you to thinking even more.

Organization is fundamental to your success. Organization means *people working in concert.* It is both a process and an outcome. You do things through organization, and you build an organization as you do things. Whether you need 2 people or 2,000 people, you need to understand them and understand how they can relate effectively to one another and to the challenges that beckon them in the process of change.

What Do You Need?

Remember that there are three types of communities affected by your attempt to make a difference: the need or benefit community, the action community, and the target or response community. Taken together these are called your arena of action. There are times when these are three different communities, and times when they are one in the same. Ideally, you want to have people from each type of community to aid you or even to make up your organization. There may well be conflicts among and even within these groups. Gaining a clearer understanding of these differences and how to negotiate among them will at the very least require some information from those who will be affected by your decisions and actions (Patton, 1987). Of course, if the need, action, and target communities are all the same, this is a little easier. If they are all different, you face more of a challenge.

If you have decided to bring people together in a grand scheme to save the planet, or at least to clean up part of the neighborhood, does it matter whom you involve? If you just get a bunch of people together, won't that do to get started? The answers are yes and yes.

Yes, at first you make do with what you have. Enlist the support of anyone who is interested. From that group you will be able to get a lot of what you need.

And yes, it eventually does matter who participates. Over the long haul, any random group of people probably will not do. Unless your random group is so large that you are bound to find what you need within it, you need to be more intentional in your recruiting. In Chapter 8, I stressed the importance of involving people who are affected by plans and decisions in the process of making planning decisions. This notion applies to *all* of the organization's activities. This ethic is fundamental. As you consider the various ways of generating, utilizing, and maintaining the human resources of your organization, understand that those affected by the organization's actions, particularly members of the benefit community, play a critical role in determining actions and in taking them (Fawcett, Seekins, Whang, Muir, & Balcazar, 1982).

In a similar vein, your organization will benefit from the participation of those who have a role in implementing the change you are seeking. Without their involvement you run the risk of the change being sabotaged once agreement to establish new, more beneficial conditions has been reached among the parties who comprise the interest community. If the change does not make sense to those charged with implementing it, it will likely be greeted by passive resistance at best. Conversely, if this group has an investment in the change, particularly through participation in its design and the actions to bring it about, there can be a substantial payoff. They will want to see the change work, and they may well extend themselves to see that it does. Because these are the people who will actually end up doing what needs to be done, it is their actions that ultimately determine the effectiveness of the change.

Involving people is a purposeful, ongoing process that addresses three essential considerations. First, the number of people and level of their commitment and participation must fit the demands of the situation. Second, particular talents and assets must be found among the participants. Third, participants who bring positive personality characteristics will be particularly valuable to the effort.

Sometimes you will find one person who can offer all these things to the organization, but this is rare. Generally, if an individual can give any one of these things to the organization, it will benefit, and you should try to get him or her involved.

Let's take a closer look at each of these attributes.

Level of Participation

What does participation or involvement mean? Does everyone have to operate at the same level of intensity? No, involvement can occur in many different ways. Everyone does not have to have the same zeal. Making fervor a requirement of partnership would eliminate a lot of potential help and power.

There are actually six different opportunities for participation available to those interested:

- Leadership, the core group participants
- Workers, ongoing active participants
- Assisters, occasionally active participants
- One-shot participants
- Advisers
- Inactive, general supporters

As a matter of practice, people will change their level of involvement from time to time. Even if they move from a more active to a less active role, they may still feel a strong affiliation with the effort if communication with others in the organization continues to occur.

Leadership

The core group, that handful of people who worry more, plan more, and provide more direction for the project than others, offers the most active level of participation. The organization and the changes it seeks are important in these people's lives. Even when alone they think about it, trying to understand more of the dynamics of the situation and what should be done to deal with them. These are the people who keep in close contact with one another to talk about what is going on. They meet more frequently than required by the routine schedule. They expect to participate in meetings, not just attend them. They make many of the decisions about what needs to be done and understand, for the most part, why. These are the people for whom the organization and its agenda really matter, who want to keep things alive and moving. It is they who feel anxious about the organization's support and strength and who feel a real sense of loss should the effort dwindle and die.

The core group usually consists of 6 to 10 people, rarely more than that, especially for new organizations. The need for core group members to keep in steady communication with one another tends to limit its size. Members expect to be part of all major decisions and frequently feel a little hurt—or maybe even very angry—if left out.

Members may be elected, self-selected, or specifically recruited. They are often the products of the winnowing process that eliminated the initial big talkers and the only moderately interested from this role. The core group goes by a variety of names, including the steering committee, the planning committee, the Friday morning group, or the board.

Workers

Ongoing, active participants support the organization and its aims but choose not to take part in all the deliberations. They are willing to follow the leadership of core group members. These participants maintain a steady interest in the organization and take part in many of its activities. Along with the core group, they do much of the work of the organization and may even have particular responsibility for a major set of functions.

The difference between them and the core group is that participants at this level do not have as clear a picture of the overall program of the organization as it evolves, nor do they really care to. They either don't want to or can't currently attend all the meetings, consider and develop strategy, or worry about things in general. They only occasionally play a part in decision making. These workers may trust the members of the core group and the general direction things are taking, lack the self-confidence needed for deeper involvement, or be too busy or otherwise not that interested. You may well find potential (as well as previous)

leaders among these workers. An effective organization will look for opportunities to groom new leadership and make sure that participation in the core group is open to people willing to make that kind of commitment.

Assisters

Occasionally active assisters do things when the mood strikes them or when they are specifically asked. Having a moderate interest, they would like the effort to be a success and will lend a hand, but they really don't want to get blisters. Other occasional assisters have periods of high activity interrupted by stretches of apparent indifference. Their interests run hot and cold. Organizational matters can hold their attention for only so long before their enthusiasm fades. Don't fuss over these members, but do maintain communication with them. Although their participation is sporadic, it can come in handy. It is often available when asked for, and over time some assisters develop a stronger affiliation with the organization once they discover their particular niche.

One-Shot Participants

This category includes those who do something only once or are involved for only a short period of time and then disappear from the scene altogether. These are people who soon learn that they have overestimated their interest or underestimated the cost of their participation. Some discover that the change effort isn't what they thought it was. Others simply flit from one thing to another, not quite sure what they are looking for, maybe never really finding it. Still others have a *sneeze experience*. Drawn by the excitement that a change effort offers, they step out of their ordinary roles to do some things, maybe even a flurry of actions they consider dramatic. Once they get this excitement or drama out of their systems, they return to the safety of their normal routine. These sneezers get a big bonus. For the next 25 years (and perhaps well beyond), they can talk about the time they were "radical." (For a previous generation, this spawned talk usually preceded by, "Back in the sixties, I . . .")

Over time these tales can grow to rival the fabled "one that got away."

Even one-shotters can be a benefit to the undertaking. They may take part in organizational activities that require a high level of intense energy for a short period of time. Or, they may be willing to join in a show of force and stand as part of a crowd. You may need people to do this. Although it would be nice to have more ongoing involvement, even these limited acts can be useful. Just don't waste a lot of your time trying to reenergize previous participants if it is pretty apparent that their batteries have gone dead.

Advisers

Advisers give little sustained attention to the workings of the organization, yet they can be valuable. These are people who can provide particular insights, ideas, or technical information. They are the people you go to when you want to hold a press conference but aren't sure how. Or, they might tell you how to get a particular action started or how to influence a particular official. Maybe they can give you pointers on how to strengthen your organization.

Most often you seek out advisers because of their experience in similar situations or because they have expertise in an area about which you know little. These supporters are usually more effective if you initiate their involvement by asking for some guidance. True advisers are different from those self-appointed saviors of the cause who just want to tell you what to do but don't want to sweat themselves. Frequently, members of the organization resist unsolicited advice as meddling or uninformed. Frankly, it is often just carping from the sidelines.

Many of those whom you will tap as advisers don't consider themselves to be members of your organization. In fact, their distance from the organization might bring some very helpful objectivity. Even though remaining somewhat detached, once they have contributed to what you are doing, they will develop an interest in your success, particularly if you report back on how their counsel was used. Due to the natural resistance most of us have to advice, you may need to legitimize the adviser's role within the organization before it can be effectively used.

Inactive General Supporters

You may enlist the support of community members who have a high degree of visibility and credibility but who may not do much actual work. Their assistance comes in the form of an endorsement of your effort. Questions regarding your intentions and legitimacy will be asked—not always out loud—and the support of influential community members can help calm these uncertainties and, in fact, signal particular groups that you should receive active support. Participation by these individuals usually comes in the form of an agreement that their name may be used in conjunction with your effort.

Other general supporters are people whom you may never know. They don't show up for any meetings or work assignments. They probably don't even feel that they are part of the change effort. They watch what you are doing and wish you well. As long as you make an effort to let people know what you are doing, you can trust that these supporters will be out there.

So what good are they? Even though they do not participate in any specific activity of the organization, they may contribute importantly to its success. Through many subtle means, perhaps talking to a friend, maybe writing an unsolicited letter to a public official, or simply voting a certain way, they help create a climate of change. Whoever makes decisions with regard to the change has to pick up signals that the change will ultimately meet with general acceptance, if not approval. Though inactive in your organization, these general supporters help transform the atmosphere in which it operates. Foster this support.

With six potential types of participants, how do you know who is going to be what type? You really don't. That clears things up a lot, doesn't it? Here are some clues that may point you to those who are likely to be more involved. Look for people who have made some *investment* in the effort or who have some special *relationship to the issue* the organization is working on or to the *people* working on it. Next, notice the ways people *respond to requests* to help out, as well as the extent to which they *initiate actions* or *offer suggestions* on what they can do. These are probably good candidates for active involvement. Those who don't follow through on their agreements or their own offers to contribute will probably be marginal participants.

Remember that only those who know about the organization can participate at all. Provide potential members with knowledge about your goals, activities, and other members. And be sure to provide clear opportunities for involvement. People unsure of your desire to include them or how they can be included may be hesitant to help out. You may mistake this hesitancy for lack of interest. Check to see that opportunities for involvement are real.

The best advice is to pay attention to people; listen, resist snap judgments, and be patient. When opportunities are real and communication is maintained, people will respond to their level of interest and self-confidence. Over time you will get a good sense of who wants to participate in a meaningful way and who is looking for something else. Those who are really not interested won't do much. Don't waste your time trying to change that. Figure out how their level of interest can benefit the organization and make use of it without pretending it is different from what it is. Those who really are interested will keep trying to help out if you give them half a chance. Sometimes capable people can't quite figure out how they fit in, but they want to. They may need to try out different kinds of activities before they hit on the right ones. Help them discover how they fit into your organization.

Talents and Assets

At different stages of your organization's life it will need people to do different things. When

your organization is just getting started, you need people who can inspire and motivate others. Later, when you are trying to overcome resistance from those who oppose you, you would benefit from people who have strategic skill or influence with the opposition. Although your group will more than likely have to meet most of the essentials on the following list, understand that you will not always have to have all these things available at the same time. Recruit what you need when you need it.

Numbers. If you can hold all your meetings in a telephone booth, you are in big trouble. The right number of visible participants will depend on the change you are working toward. Attempting to make a change within a private social service agency may require the visible involvement of only half a dozen workers. Making a change in a large public school system may involve hundreds or even thousands of people.

Numbers give credibility and a sense of confidence to participants and outside observers as well. People may have to see that others are making the decision to join in the action before they feel good about their own decision to become involved. Those you are trying to impress, particularly the opposition, will take you more seriously if they believe you are more than just a handful of idealists or complainers. Numbers also give you access to other resources your organization will require. People bring skills and talents and community connections that can benefit your effort.

Doers. The people in your group will have to do things, not just talk about them. Some of these things are tedious and time consuming. You need people who are responsible in making commitments and following through. This includes those willing to take their share of the load without having to be pressured into it. Just as important, they have to let others take a share as well.

Opinion leaders. If Merle Kaduke, whose idea of high fashion is wearing socks of the same color, attempts to advise you on new acquisitions to your wardrobe, you may just hesitate a second, or forever, before you follow his suggestion. However, if your good friend Monique Tres-Chic, contributing editor to *Vogue,* recommends just the accessory to complete your ensemble, you may find yourself the proud new owner of an overpriced trinket. People, especially when unsure, frequently look to a select few to help inform and shape their perceptions. You know who these people are in your arena of action. Get them involved in your organization, or at least on your side. They give you credibility and an avenue of communication to others who may be uncertain about joining in.

Potential organization leaders. Leaders provide the organization with energy, confidence, and direction, along with a host of other things. Without leadership, nothing will be accomplished. The organization will fall apart. Leadership is an essential requirement for any organization.

Different types of leadership are needed at different stages of the change process, and not all leaders will sustain their interest. Further, leaders who were helpful in early stages may become difficult obstacles later on. As a result, your organization will experience a turnover of leadership, probably in the first six months if your effort lasts that long. This is natural; don't be surprised when it happens. Creating a pool of potential leaders and purposefully developing new leadership is absolutely essential if the organization is intended to have an extended life. You cannot develop the organization without developing new leadership. It is that basic.

One of your primary challenges as a change agent is to identify people who can perform leadership functions. Involve them in the organization and groom their leadership abilities. Remember, all current leaders were once potential leaders. Check to see who among those currently involved, perhaps in a minor way, has some potential for leadership.

A brief note here about leaders and leadership. Leaders aren't necessarily those people who are always in the spotlight. There are many different leadership functions. Some of these valuable roles include strategists, coordinators, public speakers, problem solvers, and those who help improve communication and understanding among the members. Trying to find one person who can perform all these actions will probably be a waste of time; find several people who can each perform a few of them.

Motivators. Things will drag. There will be times when progress seems slow or nonexistent. People will lose sight of what they are trying to accomplish and why. People will become discouraged.

After an initial burst of enthusiasm, the newness and excitement will probably wear off. Other demands will be made on people's time and attention. Members will get distracted and maybe even lazy. You need someone to fan the spark of interest—to help participants see the chance for success and its importance and to encourage them not only to stay involved and working but to want to. Motivators know how to keep the energy going. They know how to have fun. Deadly serious organizations generally die. Motivators keep things lively.

Influence connections. You need people who have some influence in the benefit, action, and target communities. If you can recruit an influential person who is actually a member of the community to be influenced, your effectiveness will be enhanced.

Those with influence may act as translators. That is, they can explain your organization's goals to others, possibly resistant others, in a way that produces a response. They know the right code words and the right concerns and can better communicate within that frame of reference. Understand that this type of communication can require some special knowledge or skill. Some individuals with influence will be able to get people to want to go along. Others will make people (again, this usually means opponents) go along, even if they don't want to.

Determine what kind of influence you need, and try to get people who have it.

Specialized skills or talents. Any organized effort requires skills in certain areas such as writing, planning, negotiating, and running meetings. Chances are that these basic skills will be present in any group of a dozen people, so check first within your current membership to see who has these skills to contribute or who can more fully develop them. If your organization is large (or you intend for it to be) or the issue it is tackling is complex, you will probably need some additional skills.

This doesn't mean that one person always gets stuck doing the same thing. Some skills can easily be taught to others, or new members with particularly needed skills can be recruited. Generally, the most effective recruiters of new talent are current members who possess the same skill to some degree. They know what to look for, and they are often motivated by a desire to get some help. Perhaps one of the single most critical skills, and one which is often over-looked, is the ability to run a meeting effectively. Take pains to find someone who has this skill and let them run your meetings or *purposefully* teach the "chair" how to do it.

Access to other resources. In addition to people, you may need a variety of other resources (meeting rooms, printing, computers) to get the job done. Look for people well-connected to a particular resource you need, to the community in general, or to a bank vault. These individuals may be willing to use their contacts or their own resources to help the organization get what it needs.

Each person has something to contribute. Everyone who participates in the change process you are undertaking has something to offer, be it a skill, particular knowledge, personal connections, or other qualities that can benefit the organization. Keep an eye out to discover what each person can do and be willing to ask them to do it when the time comes.

Get to know people on a personal level. Through the process of relationship building, you can discover the abilities participants bring to the organization. Equally important, this approach strengthens commitment to the organization. Participants develop a commitment not only to resolving the issue at hand and to the organization forming to address it but also to one another.

Wouldn't it just be easier to ask people what they can do? Certainly this question should be asked of each participant, but don't count on it to yield all the information you need. Some people may be new to participating in a change effort and simply don't know what they have to contribute. Even veterans of other change struggles often don't see how their skills in other areas fit with what the organization is trying to accomplish. And some are too shy, modest, or otherwise reluctant to let their talents be known.

You will constantly be amazed at how people undervalue their abilities. We are taught this devaluing process from kindergarten on. As a change agent, one of your most important challenges is to encourage people to unlearn those crippling messages and instead to acknowledge their competence, trust in it, and act on it. This means that you have to believe in the fundamental ability of people to do some things well—this includes you too.

Don't keep your talents secret from either yourself or the organization. However, disclosing what you can do is a delicate process if you are in a leadership role. You want to let other participants know your capabilities but at the same time give them room, in fact encourage them, to let you know theirs. If you are one of the initiators of the change effort, you have established a sense of ownership in the process. The mere fact (actually it is quite a significant fact) that you have gotten the ball rolling required a special investment on your part. You begin your participation in the group with a significant attachment to the organization and its purpose. This is not true of other partici-pants. Their attachment will be different from yours, so you need to give theirs room to grow. If other people can make a contribution by doing something you are capable of doing, let them do it. If you could have done it better, keep quiet. You really don't need to let anyone know. You can lend a hand in the future if a similar situation should arise.

If you have some particular knowledge or ability you intend to use to benefit the effort, let this be known early on in a matter-of-fact way. Then, when the time to make use of your contribution comes, it is expected and valued. Otherwise people can come to resent your involvement and become discouraged that you are taking over.

The Right Stuff

The organization cannot be divorced from the personal characteristics of its more influential members. They will affect relationships among the participants and shape the personality of the change effort itself. Look for these important attributes in the people you want to have actively participating in your organization. Hardly anyone will have them all.

- *Roll with the punches.* This ability is one of the most important qualities to look for in people who are going to play an important role in your organization. Every member of your core group should possess this trait. It may not surprise you now to know that not everything is going to go perfectly as you proceed to implement the change, but it may surprise you when it happens. Even if people are not purposefully gunning for you, your plans will get knocked around a bit. That is one of the few things about the change process that I can guarantee. You want to have people working with you who know this and can handle it when the time comes. Stupid little things will happen: equipment will break down at a crucial moment; someone will forget to follow through on an important and simple task; it will snow on your Fourth of July rally. Big things may well happen too. When setbacks occur, many people get flustered. You need someone who can stand in

there. People who roll with the punches have a sense of optimism. They believe that things will eventually work out and that they will help make that success happen. They are able to keep things in perspective and not get rattled by the unexpected. If you have a few of these folks involved, you will be able to make things happen.

- *A good sense of humor.* A lot of what happens will be funny. People who can recognize this and help others to do so as well are extremely valuable. Humor energizes, releases tension, and gives us a clearer perspective on the situations we encounter. Along with this, you want to have people who are playful. You've got to introduce some play into your work, or people will find something more interesting to do. Just because what you do is important doesn't mean it has to be gloomy.

- *Tenacity.* Tenacious people won't let go of a project until it is finished. My mother used to call this stick-to-it-tiveness, an antidote to the disease of give-up-itis. Change very often requires that you keep the pressure on those who are improperly using their power (Alinsky, 1972). Tenacious people won't back off at a few (often empty) conciliatory gestures; nor will they let confusion or uncertainty defeat them. No one will be able to talk these people into quitting when things get tough.

- *Risk-taking ability.* Becoming involved in a change effort in the first place involves some risk. Change means going from the known to the unknown. Risk takers are able to try something new, give unconventional ideas serious thought, and do things beyond what is ordinarily expected. Effective change often demands that this be done. An effective risk taker is neither ignorant of nor overly worried about possible consequences. She or he is personally willing to accept the same risks asked of others. This type of person usually has a healthy quality of irreverence. Some people are intimidated by the contrived trappings of power, but not the risk takers. They know that people are people, and they are not afraid of them. Risk takers are willing to stand up for themselves because they know that not doing so may involve an even greater risk.

- *Regard for others.* As people work on the issue, they will be working with each other. Careful attention to both the task at hand and the people working on it are requirements for success (Johnson & Johnson, 1997; Napier & Gershenfeld, 1993). People who can recognize and respond to what is important for other people are a must. Those who have true regard for other people have true regard for themselves. Because of this, they understand that some people will see things differently from the way they see them. This allows them to handle, even encourage, disagreement effectively. They can assert their own point of view without attacking people who think differently.

- *Self-reliance.* There are no blueprints, no handy guides to show you each thing that needs to be done. You need people who are aware of and trust in their own abilities to figure things out. People who can look to themselves and believe that they have some answers or can at least find them will give confidence to others. This is particularly true if they can acknowledge their own uncertainty and have the confidence to confront it.

- *Desire to learn.* The process of change is the process of discovery. Once your organization stops learning, it starts dying. People who are eager to learn more give your organization a better understanding of what to do. Learning is not only a prerequisite for action, it is the result of it. Action puts ideas to the test and produces new ideas. A true learner knows that you can't wait until you know everything before you do anything. You will be learning by doing. A learner delights in challenges, seeing challenges as opportunities for discovery. People who know everything can't evaluate or easily redirect their actions. They need to limit or ignore contradictory information; they need to make others wrong. This can get old very quickly. A learner knows he or she doesn't know everything. Thus, they don't have to limit themselves by pretending to know. Quite the opposite. Learners don't place artificial limits on themselves.

- *Responsibility.* Responsible people understand and accept the requirements of their participation. They get things done. They expect that they will take care of the commitments they have made. They don't expect other people to do it for them, nor do they expect other people to be incapable of following through on commitments. They make mistakes, but rarely make excuses. Responsible people take initiative and accept authority, knowing that both are requirements of responsibility. They make and receive suggestions because they value what they do.

- *Decision-making ability.* Progress depends on a series of decisions. Indecisiveness leads to organizational stagnation. The organization needs to have people who know how to make decisions, who are aware of different styles of decision making, and who know when to use each appropriately. Some situations call for consensus, others are best served by a vote, and yet others may require an individual with authority to make the choice. In making decisions, these people recognize the require-

EVERYBODY, SOMEBODY, ANYBODY, AND NOBODY

This is a story about four people named Everybody, Somebody, Anybody, and Nobody. There was an important job to be done, and Everybody was sure that Somebody would do it. Anybody could have done it, but Nobody did it. Somebody got angry about that, because it was Everybody's job. Everybody thought Anybody could do it, but Nobody realized that Everybody wouldn't do it. It ended up that Everybody blamed Somebody when Nobody did what Anybody could have done!

Source: From a cartoon titled: The Facts of Life.

ments of the situation, including the importance of maintaining relationships among people in the organization and the members' willingness to support and implement the decisions that are made.

Participants will contribute other qualities to the organization, but the ones I have mentioned here are basic. Without them, or with too many people who act in the opposite manner, the organization will get nowhere and fall apart. No matter what else participants provide to the organization, they all give a bit (or a lot) of themselves. Who they are and the qualities and the characteristics they share will shape the character of the organization itself.

Getting People Involved

Maybe you are thinking: "All right, so there are a variety of roles people can fill, but how do I get them involved in the first place?"

Ask them. The simple fact of the matter is that although people may be expected to join

something, not many are clearly asked to do so. You may be surprised with the response you get when you take the time to ask.

A number of things can increase the likelihood that your approach will yield helpful, reliable members. This process involves four steps:

- Contact people
- Give people a reason to join
- Ask them to join
- Maintain their involvement

Contact People

For people to respond at all, you need to bring your organization to their attention. They need to know that you exist and want their involvement. If they don't know about you, they can't do anything with you. All active members, particularly the leaders, need to understand the importance of developing the membership of the organization. This is fundamental. One of the most important aspects of the leaders' job is to keep on the lookout for people who could be

LADDER OF COMMUNICATION EFFECTIVENESS

There are a variety of ways to reach people; the more direct ways will bring you greater likelihood of success.

One-to-one conversation
Small group discussion
Large group discussion
Telephone conversation
Handwritten letter
Typewritten letter
Mass-produced letter
Newsletter
Brochure
News item
Advertisement
Handout

Source: Howe, 1985.

invited into the effort. Initiators of the change effort, in particular, need to fight the very real tendency to keep things to themselves.

Where do you find all these people? First, look around you. Your current contacts with individuals, particularly those with whom you work or who are involved in other community activities with you, will provide you with the best possibilities. When others working with you in the change effort also use their affiliations, the list of potential members can grow dramatically. This only works, though, if you are consciously looking to recruit new participants. I cannot overstress that point. Regularly assess what you need and stay on the lookout to invite those who can help to join your effort.

Second, understand that you may need to make repeated attempts to contact people. You have to become part of their consciousness. People have many things to think about other than the change effort in which you are involved. If they do notice you, they may soon forget. More than one attempt will probably be necessary, particularly if your contact is not face to face.

Third, use more than one method to contact

potential members. Again, the more indirect your methods, the more likely that frequent as well as varied approaches will be necessary.

Fourth, when making contact with an individual, listen to their concerns as well. See if you can identify some problems or other circumstances you both have experienced (Max, 1980). Finally, the more personal and direct your contact is, the more likely you will be to receive a favorable response.

Give People a Reason to Join

In addition to believing in the importance of the group's goals, people join groups for a variety of reasons: they like the task or the activity of the group; they like the people in the group; or the group, though not directly satisfying the person's needs, can be a means to satisfying his or her needs elsewhere (Napier & Gershenfeld, 1993). People who believe in what you are doing, enjoy the activities you do, like some of the people involved, and see that participation can benefit them are the strongest candidates for membership. Understand that any one of these reasons could be sufficient to encourage a

Take a Moment to Discover . . . .

Over the past year, if you stop and think about it, you have probably had the chance to join several groups or partici- pate in some group activity. These may have been social groups or perhaps they involved more formal organizations. Maybe you were personally invited; pos- sibly you just received a form letter or heard an ad on the radio.

Which of these, if any, did you de- cide to take part in? What in particular attracted your interest or encouraged or discouraged your involvement? How did the way you were asked affect your decision?

. . . .

person to join. Both what you represent and the way you represent it are important. You have to establish credibility with people before they will join your effort.

Ask for Participation

None of us like rejection. Whenever you ask someone to do something or participate in something, you risk rejection. That's why some people don't ask at all. This is an entirely effective strategy for avoiding rejection. Unfor- tunately, it also avoids developing participation in your organization.

To want to soften the potential blow of rejection is normal. However, it is very difficult to soften the blow without sending the message that you expect it. If you tell people you expect to be rejected, that is probably what you will get. Another pitfall is the apologetic approach. It goes something like this: "I know you are real busy and I hate to take up more of your time, but I want to ask you something, if you don't mind." Inspiring, isn't it? Usually, someone asking in this manner is simply unsure of the response he or she is likely to receive. Unfortunately, what this may be interpreted to mean is that the asker is not sure of the work he or she is doing or why.

There is no simple, handy way out of this. Recognize that many people are reluctant to take part in something that may cause them to alter their routines or their perception of "the way things are." They may have conceded to the burdensome conditions they currently face, and working to change conditions requires rejecting the investment they made in adapting to them. They may feel that they may not be able to measure up to the demands involvement may make of them, perhaps exaggerating in their own minds just what those demands might be (Mondross & Berman-Rossi, 1992). Other people legitimately have other interests. They may genuinely be unable to give time now, and they may say yes later. Accept the fact that no matter how important the issue or how effec- tively phrased the request, some people will say no to you. This does not devalue you or your concerns. Other members, ideally all members, need to be involved in recruiting. Depending on the size of your organization, you may want to have a group of members whose major respon- sibility is recruitment of new members.

Here are some suggestions that should improve the likelihood that people will decide to work with you.

• When you make a request of someone, make sure you provide an easy way for the person to respond to you. This is particularly important when the request is indirect, say made through a newsletter, because the re- sponse is not immediate. Ask yourself: "If people decide to say yes, how do they let me know, and how do they know that I got their message?" Further, if they do communicate an interest in participating, ask yourself how they know what their next step is. Remember that involvement means action. If you merely say "thanks for your interest," you have not really promoted their involvement. You need to be certain they have received your response to their intent to take part and now know what to do.

• Your request or "message package" should communicate the following elements:

the purpose (aims or goals) of your organization; its importance; what it does; that it needs people; the types of things they can do; and the way they can let you know their decision to participate. Include in the activities they can do things that are fun (for example, social activities), things that are simple (for example, making phone calls, typing, or giving money), and things that are "important" (for example, meeting with legislators or appearing as a guest on a talk show). Based on your relationship and the nature of your contact (face-to-face versus a letter), you can modify these elements to best suit the situation.

• Phrase your request (unapologetically) in the way likely to promote the best response. For instance, people may not want to join, but they may be willing to help. Joining may be perceived as involving endless meetings wrangling over subtle nuances in the bylaws. Helping may be perceived as doing some specific things to benefit the effort. Others may be willing to join by paying a few bucks to be a member, but not be willing to help, which may imply doing a lot of work.

• Ask specifically for what you need or for what you would like people to do. Make a clear request for a specific action or set of actions. Include clear options for participation.

• You may run across potentially valuable individuals who are only a little interested in participating at the present time but may well develop a stronger interest in the future. Ask them to do a few little things at first, and over time ask for more as their interest and feelings of competence develop. Even these initial simple requests should represent a level of participation slightly higher than these individuals would otherwise have considered for themselves. This will make their affiliation with the effort more real.

There is an important caution here. Do not mislead people by saying, "The only thing I want you to do is . . ." or "All you have to do is . . . " if you have more that you intend for people to do. Clearly stating one level of expectation while intending another will eventually create resentment. Though subtle, this is significantly different from increasing affiliation by making more important requests when there is more interest. Purposely misleading people tricks them when there is no real interest. Asking people for more participation should be based on developing interest. In this case, you are making a direct request for a new level of involvement. Don't ask people to do what they really are not interested in doing.

If someone you are grooming for greater involvement flat out asks you, "Is this all you want me to do?" you simply answer, "Of course, I'd like you to do more in the future, if you are interested, but this is how you can help out now." Expectations should be mutually clear and moderately challenging.

When you start out, there will be people aware of what you are doing who are not yet willing to make a commitment to join you. They may be waiting for you to prove yourself before they agree to work with you. These can be some of your future most valuable members. They are discerning people. They are only going to participate in something that means something (Von Hoffman, n.d.).

Then there will be others whose participation you would dearly love to have but who don't have any real intention of making a commitment. They may even lead you on a bit about helping. At some point you need to say to yourself that they know where to find you if they want to. If you have honestly made requests and created opportunities for participation that remain open and your desired recruits are aware of your organization, you probably have done enough. If you are spending your time falling all over yourself to get someone to participate, you have to stop and ask yourself why. You may want their participation because you somehow think you need their stamp of approval before you can truly take yourself seriously. When this is the case (as it really often is), you end up second-guessing yourself rather than doing the work you need to do. Believe me, you don't need the people who are just not interested. There will be plenty who are and plenty of things for you to do.

A number of people will simply seem to find their way to you and pitch in. That is encouraging, and you will experience it. Just remember, though, that some people never help because they're never asked.

Maintain Involvement

Once people have expressed an interest and they're ready to go, you want to keep them going. You can talk someone into joining, and you can talk them into staying one time, maybe twice. After that, there had better be more to it because they'll walk before you can do any more talking.

Several ways to promote continued affiliation revolve around some very basic human needs—needs for inclusion, control, affection, recognition, accomplishment, and altruism (Johnson & Johnson, 1997). Maintaining involvement is a matter of responding to these needs, recognizing that their importance varies with each individual and perhaps even with each cultural group (Latting, 1990). Here are some suggestions for keeping valuable members involved in the effort.

Make a special effort to help newcomers feel welcome. According to Napier and Gershenfeld (1993), because most people feel uncertain in new situations involving strangers, anxiety is the prevailing and dominant emotion at the start of any group setting. Change agents need to be aware of the stages of group development (covered in more detail in Chapter 12), particularly the uncertainty and wariness that accompany group beginnings (Mondross & Berman-Rossi, 1992).

Give people something to do, the sooner the better. When people respond favorably, put them to work right away. Give participants things to do that they can see as both meaningful to the undertaking and that generate a personal investment on their part.

You will, or should anyway, have a good

idea of the types of things that need to be done. Often, you will have recruited someone with a specific task in mind. So, of course, this is what you will ask them to do. Still, it is usually a good idea to let them know about other things that need to be done that you would want their help on.

Your aim here is to offer participants a range of tasks that to some degree match your perception of their level of skill, interest, and time. Tasks that are short-term and specific are usually better in the initial stages of involvement. Let them make the choice of what they want to do. They are more likely to do a better job on things they choose to do. Job satisfaction and involvement are important elements enhancing commitment (Dailey, 1986). Also, they become aware of other things the organization needs. This in itself communicates that they are needed in the organization, and it gives them things to think about doing in the future.

Give clear directions and adequate preparation. Whenever we are new at something most of us are a bit unsure of ourselves. We feel more vulnerable and are more easily frustrated. We also like to make a good first impression. Even if you are working with people you already know pretty well, this change effort may be a different experience. It is new. This creates the opportunity and the anxiety of a new impression.

By giving people the necessary background on the task they are to perform (for example, why these phone calls are important or a brief review of what the issues are) and making sure they have clear, complete directions, you will help people feel more confident in their abilities to do the job. They should also know whom to contact if they do have questions. This gives people permission to ask for added clarification if they need it.

Increase the responsibility of the work. Increased responsibility generally leads to an increased sense of ownership in the undertaking. It also increases the person's sense of value to the organization.

Show how the work relates to the overall

Change Agent Tip

Try different methods of asking people to do things. Asking people at a regular meeting hits the same group over and over. That might not be desirable. Making a general request to the group itself tends to get the hand-raisers to respond, the same people who always seem to volunteer or get stuck with the work. The sit-backers lose opportunity and responsibility (they may want this, you understand). You may lose them.

Try passing around a sign-up list with check-off columns for most needed actions. Next to their names, people simply check which one of three or four tasks they'll help with.

Another approach is simply to ask specific people to do specific things. Don't ask for volunteers.

The point is to purposefully spread the tasks around to increase the number of participants and decrease the number of burnouts.

effort. People want to feel that what they do has a purpose. Tell people the reason a certain task needs to be done and why it is important.

Give participants a chance to say "no" to some things. This is important, especially if someone has been doing a lot for the effort. This is more effectively done by acknowledging the contributions the individual has made and then letting them know that someone else can do the job if they say no. This will strengthen the "yes's" you receive. By the way, giving people the right to say no while making them feel guilty about exercising that right isn't giving people a chance to say no.

Have people work together. Affiliation with others involved in the effort is important (Floro, 1989). Working together helps people get to know one another better. By relating to other people as well as to the task at hand, members strengthen their bond to the organization.

On short-term projects, like addressing envelopes, it is often good to have people get together as a group. On long-term tasks, like doing background research, it frequently helps to have people work in pairs.

Doing work with others usually increases motivation and accountability. Members are conscious about meeting the expectations of other participants, so they may do a little more than if they were doing things alone. Work doesn't have to be the sole focus. The social aspects involved in doing things with other people make the tasks more enjoyable and more attractive. Isolation diminishes enthusiasm and contributes to people feeling lost. Try to avoid this.

Help people to feel they are part of the group, an insider, not an outsider. To a large extent, working with others will accomplish this, but other steps should be taken or, in some cases, not taken. First, a "not taken." Watch out for inside jokes, stories, or perceptions that are mentioned in public but hold meaning for only a select few. Actions such as these convey that some people are more in the know than other people. The others feel less valued, less a part of things. It's no fun being an "other." Include others so they can join in the joke and in the group's shared history.

A number of steps can be taken to strengthen the sense of group affiliation and identity among the members. If your organization grows large, it may become less personal. Make a special effort to remember people's names and know how to spell them correctly. Invite participants to activities such as social get-togethers, parties, picnics, or going out for pizza. Members who are new or perhaps unsure of their status in the group (you will know who these people are) should receive a personal invitation in addition to any general announcement made.

Depending on the type of organization you develop, you may have membership cards, put together a newsletter, send out an occasional update letter, or do any number of things that promote a sense of alliance.

Get to know people on a personal level. Personal relationships are the glue that holds the organization together. People are able to see that they themselves, not just their interest in the particular issue, are important to the organization. In turn, they communicate this to others. It is important to know people as individuals, not just as partners in a common cause. This provides greater opportunities for members to establish a connection to one another, strengthening their commitment to the enterprise they are working on.

Ask for ideas and opinions. This brings members into the creative process of the organization, deepening their commitment. People value highly the things they create. (Don't forget those laminated bookends you made in shop.)

A couple of cautions are worthy of mention here. First, it is not a good idea to ask people for ideas about what other people should do. Most of us are quite happy to tell other people a lot of things that would seem sensible and easy to do—as long as we don't have to do them. When you invite suggestions about the direction to

Take a Moment to Discover . . . .

Think about your laughter. When we're by ourselves, we rarely laugh out loud. We laugh a lot harder when we're with other people. It feels good to share something with another. Think about something you would like to change. How can you share this project and involve others?

take, let members know you are looking for them to take part in putting the ideas into action.

Second, if you have an opinion or preferred course of action, don't ask someone else for theirs. They may tell you something different from what you're thinking. This can put you in a situation where you end up trying to discredit an idea you sought. If you want feedback or support for an idea you have, ask for it. That will put the discussion where it belongs.

Support opportunities for people to work on their particular interests. Individuals may discover their particular niche within the organization. As long as this does not close off opportunities for other people or detract from the primary work you are doing, it can strengthen allegiance.

Keep in contact. Out of sight, out of mind—out of action. This may stun you at the time, but the change effort you are working on isn't the single most important thing in the lives of other people involved in the organization. Believe it or not, other concerns will demand or distract their attention. You want to increase the chances that the effort is something they continue to pay attention to, so stay in touch.

True, people have a responsibility to maintain contact on their own, but matters of the moment can easily waylay the best of intentions. The organization has to do its part to communicate with its participants. This increases the chances that the effort is one of the many things they will give thought to.

Acknowledge people and their contributions. Recognize and thank people publicly for their interest and work on behalf of the organization. This doesn't demand an annual awards banquet (though that would be nice). In fact, informal methods can be more significant. During a meeting, for example, or in a newsletter, it is nice to mention an individual and the work they have done. Look for simple, sincere ways to draw attention to people and the value of their participation. In addition to public recognition, a private acknowledgment can be very powerful. This makes the message more

Take a Moment to Discover . . . .

Sometimes it is difficult to notice small gains as you labor to implement a change. Nothing is so discouraging as to put forth some energy with little to show for it. Especially if this involves taking a risk, why keep trying?

If you have ever tried to master a new skill, you know what I'm talking about. Remember when you were trying to learn how to play the guitar, or use a computer, or cast a fly rod? From time to time you had to take notice of how you were improving. This helped you deal with some of the frustration, didn't it? Some of us couldn't see the progress quickly enough, so we still can't play the guitar worth beans. How can you use this experience to provide encouragement to others?

. . . .

personally offered and more personally received.

Routinely let members know the progress the organization is making. Gardens don't grow overnight unless, of course, we're talking about the weeds in them. Each day's growth seems small, each month's significant, each season's wonderful. Until the first bloom of fruit appears the waiting can be tedious. If you've grown gardens before and had success, you are patient and confident. If you haven't, you may wonder if you'll ever have a harvest.

Change usually results from a series of minor shifts rather than a sudden dramatic turn of events, although dramatic changes will occur and they are exciting. However, these are not so much events in and of themselves as they are the culmination of the actions of the organization.

Every so often you need to step back and note the progress you are making. This needs to be communicated clearly to those involved along with you. Identify specific achievements, whether that be meetings held, decisions

reached, money raised, conditions improved, or whatever. Develop your ability to see these gains. You may have to look for them; they may not hit you in the face. Be able to compare how things were three months ago to where they are today. There will always, forever, be things not yet done. Give yourself and your organization a periodic break from those concerns. Learn to value and communicate to one another how far you have come. People like to be associated with a winner. They feel good about themselves and seek closer identification with the source of this good feeling. Paying attention to progress will keep a winning focus.

Progress involves a sense of direction. It is easier to go boldly if you have a good idea of where you are going. An uncertain future leads to hesitancy, which undermines commitment. As you report on the distance you have traveled, be sure to remind participants that they also know where all of you are going; your organization will move with a more confident step.

As you endeavor to maintain the involvement of those working toward change, remember to take into account basic human needs. See that the organization responds to these needs. Above all, promote the importance of the things people are doing and their value to one another.

Working with Volunteers

Most change efforts depend primarily on people who are voluntarily spending their time on the project (Schindler-Rainman, 1975). People are bound to the effort through their interest in the issue and the commitment that follows from this. They are not specifically paid to bring this change about.

Even if you are working with others in your agency or profession to promote some specific agency change or response to a community problem, you will probably be doing a number of things on your own time. Some activities will take place during nonworking hours or will be shoehorned in with other responsibilities.

Most of what has been said so far in this

chapter relates to this typical situation. However, there are times when paid staff are involved in the process of promoting change. Four situations in which this commonly occurs are:

- A paid staff person (perhaps you) works in an agency and incorporates change activities into her or his job routine.
- An agency staff person has designated responsibilities for developing various projects aimed at community improvement.
- Paid staff are specifically hired to help coordinate and direct the change effort.
- The change effort may involve creation of a formal, ongoing organization or even a new agency, and in the process of institutionalizing the change, staff are hired to continue a change begun by volunteers.

In all likelihood even these situations will call for extensive use of volunteers. When volunteers work alongside existing program staff, you need to be sensitive to a set of concerns particular to this situation.

Before you recruit your first volunteer, you should have a pretty clear idea of just what the volunteers will be doing. It is important to include staff in the determination of the role of volunteers and the identification of tasks volunteers will perform. If the organization is large enough to have administrators in addition to other staff, they should be included as well. It is necessary that staff and administrators be committed to using volunteers and know how to do it. Volunteers who feel unwelcome or who just show up and then sit around with nothing meaningful to do, don't keep showing up (Lauffer & Gorodezky, 1977; Wilson, 1980).

It is easy for relationships between staff and volunteers to turn sour even when both parties are initially eager to work together. Volunteers sometimes begin to resent the fact that they are working hard to further the cause yet they don't get paid for their time, while others do. Or maybe they are relegated to jobs that are nothing but leftovers or seem too simple or are

even demeaning. These are jobs nobody else wants to do. After a while they may come to feel like exploited, second-class citizens.

Paid staff sometimes feel threatened by volunteers. They may fear that their jobs may be given over to a volunteer someday, leaving them high and dry. Or, if volunteers are performing similar tasks, they may come to believe that the value of their work is undermined and that even their wages are affected by the available volunteer help. It is not surprising that an uneasy tension can develop if these concerns go unrecognized and unaddressed. Utilizing volunteers to complement paid staff requires thoughtful consideration.

Working with people who volunteer their time necessitates regard to other considerations as well, whether or not these people are working alongside paid staff. Here are some things to keep in mind as you develop your volunteer workforce.

Volunteers cannot be held accountable in the same way as paid staff. Rarely does a contractual obligation exist for people who donate their time. Their help is not offered in exchange for something; for example, a paycheck, which would normally hold parties to their commitments and provide a constraint on both parties to encourage fulfillment of mutual agreements. Because volunteering is a decidedly one-sided affair—that is, little of real value is directly offered to the volunteer for his or her services—the conditions that usually influence a working relationship don't exist.

Situations in which there are problems in performance or other areas are best resolved by straightforward communication sensitive to the interests of the parties involved. This includes an honest discussion of how the member's actions fit with the nature and goals of the organization. Most of the time, this clarification of matters will effectively resolve conflicts. It may also lead to a decision by the member to leave the organization, if he or she determines that what is expected of members is not personally satisfying. Certain behaviors outside the ethical or moral boundaries of the organization may result in your asking the member to withdraw from participation.

If a member is not performing adequately, check to see if he or she understands the level of performance expected. Also see if the member has sufficient training, information, and tools for effective performance. Finally, find out if the member's interests match the requirements of his or her responsibility. Attention to these matters can improve the quality of the member's participation and his or her sense of fulfillment.

Scheduling a group of people who are contributing their time and energy can be a difficult business. Other responsibilities take up the bulk of the members' time. It is often difficult to have people's free or open times match. Winning the lottery may be easier than getting full attendance at a meeting.

If routine, predictable work needs to be done by volunteers, specific people need to be scheduled for specific times to do the work. Don't just hope people show up. That won't work. Also, expect that about one third of the people scheduled to help out will find themselves preparing excuses for why they "couldn't make it" when you expected them. Do overbook.

If a group of people are scheduled for a particular activity, be sure things are prepared so they can get started right away. Waiting until people show up before you figure out what to do can waste time and make you appear unorganized. Take a few minutes to prepare your directions and any necessary materials. Doing so conveys a sense of respect for the volunteers and the task they are to perform. It also gives them a feeling of confidence in knowing what they are to do.

People don't automatically know they are appreciated for their efforts. Develop formal and informal methods to recognize individuals and the contributions they make.

Some orientation to the organization and to the role the individual is expected to fill can provide answers to questions that might go unasked (Lauffer & Gorodezky, 1977). Newcomers generally spend some anxious time guessing at things veterans take for granted. For one thing, without trying to sound like your parents, do watch your language. Imagine walking into this conversation: "You know, Hank, with these cutbacks in WIC and the confusion over TANF, even stretching any FEMA funds we might use to cover only food purchases, we'll be in the red months before the end of the fiscal year. Then, if we can't come up with the matching portion of the foundation grant. . . . Well, you know what *that* would mean."

The level of a person's intended involvement in the change effort and the complexity of their tasks will suggest how much orientation and training is required. Take care to see that people know what is going on and how they fit in.

Sometimes screening volunteers is called for. If this is the case, develop a clear set of screening criteria truly appropriate to the matters at hand. Then develop an effective method to determine whether or not the criteria are met.

As much as anything, a change agent is a manager. You want to bring together the talents and energy people have and direct these to the purpose of change. When you are working with people, recognize true good effort, even if (especially if) the outcome isn't all that good. If people make a good effort, that's usually a sign that they care that things turn out well. Attacking the results serves to discredit their intent. It is a waste of energy, because you will have to go back and rekindle, reassure, and reestablish confidence in the relationship—not always easy to do when people are giving their time.

By acknowledging good intent and good effort, you are in a better position to discover what needs to be different next time. Respected people can more easily tackle tough problems, including their own mistakes. If you act toward people as if what they do matters to them, it most probably will.

Most of the people you will be working

Change Agent Tip

When arranging meetings, first try scheduling them for 7:00 A.M. Most of the time, the only conflict you will have at that time has to do with pillows or child care. People can usually make these morning meetings. People are also fresh at this time of day. By the time people get to the meeting, they have been up and going long enough to kick-start the brain cells. If the reason for the meeting is important to them, people will usually make it.

Just maybe, morning meetings will not be greeted with eager enthusiasm. Is there another option? Yes. It should work too. Using a simple method developed by Richard Fridena, mark a sheet of paper with seven vertical columns, one for each day of the week. Next, draw horizontal lines across the columns for half-hour blocks of time, starting at 7:00 A.M. and ending at 10:00 P.M. Give each meeting participant a copy, asking them to darken the blocks of time when they cannot meet. Emphasize that this doesn't mean don't really want to meet, or would find it a little inconvenient—no, it means *can't* meet.

After you have collected them, put them all together in a stack. Now, here comes the tricky part. Hold them up to the light. Wherever the light shines through, that's a time when you can meet. This usually saves about 19 hours of trying to find the right combination by the "how about Tuesday at 4:00 P.M.?" method. You can modify this little gimmick to fit a variety of situations.

with, perhaps all the people you will be working with, are giving their time to something they believe in. Not everyone has the same amount of time; not everyone has the same strength of belief. Still, the relationship all these people have to the organization is a voluntary one. Nurturing this relationship requires careful attention.

Challenging Cultural Differences

One limiting phenomenon you may encounter is the difficulty you or others in your organization have crossing cultural lines to develop support. Bound by discomfort in relating to whomever the "thems" might be (those in some way different from "us"), you may draw from a circle of support that restricts what the organization could become.

So what will you do? Will you stick to your own group, leaving members of other groups as undiscovered allies? Will you label them as "uninterested" for not responding to an invitation not extended or, worse, view them as enemies because they are not on your side?

Of course not, you say. I hope you are right, but don't be too hasty. In a confusing situation, one in which we are uncertain of our control, it is common to feel a need to affirm our particular construction of reality. We tend "to turn for support to those we believe share our own views" (Napier & Gershenfeld, 1989).

There are all sorts of cultural lines if you stop to think about it in a broad sense. You are familiar with an awareness of diverse ethnic cultures. Certainly you should be aware of any rationalizations you or members of your organization use to justify not involving people of a different racial or ethnic group. That is pretty obvious. But how about people who occupy different economic positions in the community or different positions in the hierarchy of the place where you may work? We all know that upper-level administrators are just do-nothing paper pushers, and the secretaries' biggest challenge is to see how long they can stay on break. This knowledge should keep us from trying to include anyone from these groups, right? What other "highly enlightened" things do we know?

Do you treat some people with more respect than others because of the job they hold or their social class? Do you think that because a person is a member of an identifiable group, like the city planning department or the board of directors or maybe the police department, that he or she holds exactly the same views as every other member of that group? Napier and Gershenfeld (1993) call such mistaken notions attribution errors: "People committing an attribution error assume that the actions of the group reflect the particular attitudes of individual members and that knowing something about how a group behaves means knowing something significant about subgroups or individuals within it" (p. 14).

It is normal to get used to being with a certain set of people, to stay with the familiar. It is simply easier to spend time with people who have similar interests, similar routines, and similar methods of communication. Some of us feel a bit inadequate dealing with people with whom we are not familiar. Yet the need for change probably touches people who aren't part of your familiar set. The ability to respond to that need probably exists among them as well.

Don be afraid of anybody. Don't be afraid, for example, to ask for or expect help from a bureaucrat, just because the person is a bureaucrat. Don't immediately write off someone because of your own biases and fears.

When you begin to take action on things that need to be corrected, you will start with the people you know pretty well. The question is: Will you extend beyond this? Are you willing to challenge your own notions and anxieties about people of different groups? Or will you remain comfortable with people of your own group, whatever group that might be?

You may have to make a special effort to get to know other members of your community with whom you don't commonly associate. The time to begin doing that is now, not because some special situation calls for your attention and their help but because you believe that this is a matter of basic importance.

THE COMMITTED VISIONARY

Few, if any, people in the organization will be as committed as those (you?) who initially recognize and act on the need for change. Even in situations that might seem minor, the visionary, the originator of an idea and its required action, will be more dedicated than anyone else. He or she sufficiently and personally felt the need to act before anyone else. That attachment to the reason for acting is not easily forgotten or dulled. It allows the visionary to weather the storms of doubt, confusion, and temporary setbacks better and longer than anyone else. Moved unaided to action, he or she has a greater fullness of involvement and often a greater need for success. Lack of success or abandonment of the effort comes much harder. Abandonment seems to repudiate or at least de- value those initial beliefs that were sufficient to risk rejecting complacency. Only success justifies the initial urge, the risk of taking action.

You need to understand this fundamental principle. Few will share, in quite the same way, your belief in the importance of what you are setting out to do. To ignore this invites misunderstanding and disappointment.

Some Reflections on People

We don't spend enough time considering people—the raw material of the organized effort. What are they like? Why do they do what they do? What do we need to know about them?

These are questions libraries of sociology and psychology texts attempt to answer, so I'll not presume any definitive conclusion here. Still, there are some things I think it would be helpful for you to consider. Many of these notions are based on my own observation and reflection on people with whom I have worked in the business of promoting change.

This sampler of observations includes some points that are plainly obvious, but don't be fooled. It is usually the obvious things we ignore or want to dispense with, and it is usually just such things that are at play.

Here are some things to get you started. The statements offered here are about people in general. They refer to most people much of the time. There are ample exceptions to these generalizations, but in my experience, they have been accurate often enough to be worth your consideration. See what you can add to this list.

- People are basically good, and want to do good things. If given half a chance, they will.
- People are willing to provide help, given the right circumstances.
- People want to be accepted and liked.
- People fear being seen as incompetent, foolish, or stupid.
- People need to feel worthy and able, confident and competent.
- People need to save face.
- People need acknowledgment more than they need agreement.
- It is not easy for people to break out of routines.
- Lots of people won't ask for help. Consider the barriers to seeking help faced by a person who is generally competent, who wants to appear competent, yet who needs help with something he or she thinks others think he or she *should* know.
- People tend to take things more seriously when they are accountable to other people.
- You can't hold people accountable for things they don't know.
- People hear what they want to hear and remember what suits them.
- People need to feel connected with others yet prized for their uniqueness.
- All human behavior is designed to meet needs; it is purposeful, not accidental.
- People will do only what they believe to be in their best interest to do, often their financial self-interest.
- People need a sense of hope. To act, people need to believe that something beneficial will result from their actions.
- If people can't feel anything, they won't do anything.
- People operate within their immediate frames of reference, acting on what they can understand and what is important to them right now.
- People can only see what their vantage point allows them to see. Vantage points are shaped by values and experiences.
- People tend to wait until the last minute to get things done or at least do things relative to a deadline. It is the deadline that makes the task real.
- People fear the unknown. They are unwilling to commit to it.
- People are spurred to action by enthusiasm and anger. They are immobilized by fear and confusion.
- People are open to influence when they are distracted (Johnson & Johnson, 1997).
- People are less open to influence when they have been inoculated against it (Johnson & Johnson, 1997).
- People who are confused will generally say no.
- People who are unconvinced of an action or are in the initial stages of involvement need

Take a Moment to Discover . . . .

What motivates you? Excites you? Induces fear in you? anger? action? What do you try to hide or show?

Using these musings, what might you guess about other people? How are they the same as you, how might they be different? Are you ever truly unique? Are the reasons for your reactions ever limited to you, and you alone? Watch other people. What do you see? What does that make you think about? What conclusions do you reach? Which should you challenge?

Develop this practice. Think often about what you can learn from your own behavior, attitudes, and emotions. Watch others and think about what you can learn from their behavior and what you guess their emotions could be. This is an imperfect process, but as you continue it you will find that you learn quite a lot about people and what makes them tick. You will learn a lot about yourself too.

Fundamentally, this is what change is all about—your ability to work with or against other people to get something done. If you know yourself and other people better, you will get a lot more done.

• •

to see immediate results to justify their investment of time.

• People need to know their role and the importance of their actions in the scheme of things.
• People don't like to think their time is being wasted, especially by someone else.
• People want freedom and direction—simultaneously.
• People relate far better to a problem or an

issue with which they have had a direct, personal experience.

• Under stress, people will often vent their frustrations on the nearest available object, which might be a person, even a friend.
• Don't bad-mouth people. Some people are jerks, true, but it doesn't really benefit you to broadcast the news of a person's shortcomings to one and all. The world will probably discover this without your help anyway.
• You need people to take action; you need action to get people.
• Organizations, which are just collections of people, will act pretty much like people do.

Conclusion

Working with people to produce a needed change is a satisfying and sometimes exciting proposition. It will have its trying times too. To get through periods of frustration, notice the progress you all are making toward your goal. The work you are doing to improve conditions will by itself attract people and the skills they possess. Most of the time, though, you need to go beyond this natural attraction and actively seek the people you need. Learn how to involve people and how to keep them involved. Acknowledge and further develop the interest people demonstrate, thoughtfully strengthening their relationships to one another and their connection to the work that must be done.

Don't be intimidated by distinctions between groups of people. Seeing the value of people and what they can offer, you will reap the benefit of working with people from a variety of economic, social, or ethnic groups. Understanding that most people are giving their time, show respect for them and their contributions.

Continue to learn more about people; reflect on what frightens them, emboldens them, and moves them to action. Recognize that the human capital of an enterprise is its most valuable resource. With this understanding, you will promote change in a way that gives others a stake in the outcome and the efforts to achieve it.

The change effort requires the involvement of a number of people besides yourself. Pay attention to the people who comprise the organization and value them. For, as much as you value the work that must be done by the organization, as much as you value the goals it seeks to achieve, you know it is the people of the organization who will accomplish its purpose. Without the people, there would be no organization, no success. With them, so much is possible.

CHAPTER 10

Raising Other Resources

"Amazing," Melanie says as she hangs up the phone. Shaking her head she walks into Ben's office to find him working on the quarterly reports. Before she can say anything, he looks up, exasperated. "I wonder sometimes if this Health Department contract is worth it. It seems those bureaucrats would rather pay you to write reports than to actually spend time with the people who need help."

"I know what you mean. Maybe this will brighten things up a bit. I just got off the phone with Dr. Renfro. She says she's willing to give 4 hours every two weeks. That's not all. She said she knows a couple of her friends whom she can talk into giving some time too. Ben, this thing is really taking off."

"Yeah, I know, things really are falling into place. I was worried about whether any of the medical people would really pitch in."

"They are, but I'm afraid we need to get going or we'll lose their interest. I'm glad that people are willing to donate their time, but we've got to give them things to use. I mean, where are we going to get all the equipment we need, and the supplies?"

"It would be nice to make sure that we had a place to do all this too. I hope St. Joan's comes through. But remember, Mel, we did plan for this. We did know that it takes more than just people."

"I know, Ben, but now that it's moving I'm starting to see things I didn't really think of before, like a waiting room. Shouldn't we get some furniture? We've got to have something, and not just broken-down old folding chairs either. The way the place looks sends a message to these young women. It should be nice, not dumpy."

"Well, I know one thing I'm getting right now."

"Yeah, what's that?"

"A headache."

"Be serious, Ben. Really, how do we get everything we need?"

Good question, well-phrased—"everything we need," not "money for all of this." You may or may not need money. Granted, money can make things easier, at least it certainly seems that way if you don't happen to have very much of it, which is, of course, the case for most change efforts, especially in their early stages.

Melanie and Ben will have to generate

a range of resources to accomplish their goals. They will need to build a budget and determine what they can get for free and what they will need to purchase.

In Chapter 9, the focus was on people as a resource, the most important resource available to the organization. In fact, the organization is people. It can get by without some other things, but it cannot exist without people. But the members of the organization may need other resources to aid them in their effort. In this chapter, I will discuss what some of those other resources could be and how you can get them.

Most of the time people think that the first thing they must do is go out and get money. Some of the time this is true. But most of the time you can get a lot of what you need without spending a cent. How? "Thou shalt hustle," one of the fundamental commandments of change.

Hustling means to keep moving, keep probing, always being ready to gain ground. It also means getting things for free or very cheaply. Money is one way to get things you need. Hustling is another. A good change agent will know how to get things for free and how to get money for things that aren't.

Before you can begin to do either, though, you have to figure out what it is you really need. Determining just what resources you have to have is usually called building a budget.

The three fundamental tasks of raising resources are:

- Determining what you need
- Hustling what you can
- Getting money for the things you need to buy

Building Your Budget

Building your budget is an ongoing process. You need some things to get the change effort under way. Next, you may need to find more resources to implement the change. Finally, you may need ongoing (and perhaps even greater) resources to institutionalize the change, to make sure that what you started continues.

For example, a group of you may identify a need to develop a support system for students at risk of dropping out of school. You may need some resources to create an interest in the effort and select the best approach (getting under way). Next, you may need resources to establish such a system in a particular school (implementing the change). Finally, you may need to identify resources that will allow the support system to stay in place for years to come (institutionalizing the change).

In practice you will always be finding out that you need this or that to keep you going. Your budget needs will be somewhat different in each phase of your change process. Something that may be important very early in the game may not be needed at all later, and vice versa. Also, you may find that you only need some item or service for a particular occasion.

In the very early stages of your change effort, your focus is on generating enthusiasm and building support for your idea. You don't want to get bogged down in a lengthy analysis of the resource requirements of the change effort. You may not really even know enough at this point to determine what you need. At the beginning it is common to discover as many needs through your actions as through your planning. However, as time goes on, you will want to give more advance consideration to your organization's resource needs.

There are seven basic categories of things you may need now or that you will need in the future. These are:

People: time, skills, talents

Communication: printing, postage, telephones, copying

Equipment: computers, video cameras, furniture

Supplies: pencils, paper, coffee cups, refreshments

Space: meeting places, office, storage

Transportation: air travel, use of buses, rides to and from out-of-town meetings

Special or miscellaneous needs: day care, security, or a band for a fund-raiser

Spend some time talking about each category. You will probably want to skip some categories and concentrate on others because you readily see needs in one area and not in another, or you can see ways of getting some things and not getting others. Go ahead and start with whatever categories you want. But don't stop there. You will need something, fairly early on, from each category. Bet on it. So, start where you want, but spend time on each category.

Take a look at what you need now or will need soon. Brainstorm the possibilities. You don't necessarily need to own anything or have exclusive access to it. You just need to be able to use what you need when you need it.

Hustling for the Things You Need

Hustling is just what it sounds like, moving around quickly and thinking ahead. In the broad sense, this means always looking for opportunities or ways to create them, being quick to make use of a change, thinking a few steps ahead, taking those steps while others sit back, and remaining ready for action. Rather than looking at the limits of your situation, see the possibilities. In regard to resources, make sure you get what you need free or at very little cost. You will get many things from places most people don't, generally because they don't even try. You will get people to give you things, often things that other people have to pay for.

When people, businesses, or organizations give you things or services you need instead of money, this is called an in-kind contribution. Soliciting in-kind contributions is an important part of the hustling process. Receiving contributions in forms other than cash might help you in your efforts to attract grant funding because in-kind contributions demonstrate community support (Robinson, 1996). Further, it helps establish a partnership between you and the contributing company, one which may provide direct financial support later (Picker, 1997). Businesses are encouraged to participate for their own benefit. In fact, many businesses, particularly larger businesses, have some sort of public involvement program. Dove (1983) points out that an effective public involvement program can benefit businesses by putting their internal resources to work at minimal cost, either as a supplement to or an alternative for cash contributions. Walker (1987) asserts that for businesses, in terms of marketing and measurable results, much more can be said to support in-kind contributions than cash contributions.

Companies contribute an estimated three dollars of in-kind support for every one dollar of donations (Breiteneicher & Hohler, 1993). In-kind gifts, like any gifts, are good for both the giver and the receiver. More corporations are providing in-kind support; see how your needs and the resources of businesses and corporations in your area match up (Sinnock, 1995).

You may be thinking, "I'm not a con artist; I can't do this." Right and wrong. You are most definitely not a con artist, or at least you shouldn't be. A con artist tricks people into giving up something they usually can't afford to give up, often using misrepresentation. So, if you think you're not a con artist and you're not going to become one . . . Whew! That's where you are right. The world doesn't need more con artists.

A change agent does need to hustle. True, the term *hustler* has some seamy connotations. My choice of the term probably harkens back to a youth spent spearing line drives and lunging at curve balls. "Hustle," on that field of play, was a wonderful verb. If you prefer "go-getter," feel free to substitute.

If you think you can't be a go-getter, you are mistaken. The fact is, everybody asks for things, and everybody gives things away. You simply need to learn how to ask for things that your change effort needs, from people who have some reason to give them to you. Though practices may vary from one region to another, in general your organization will benefit from products and services you can obtain for little or no cost.

Change Agent Tip

There is a salesman in Texas who sells cars. He sells a lot of them. In fact, a few years ago he sold more cars than anybody else in the country. He didn't even work too hard to do it. He just knew that people knew people, who knew people.

If you buy a car from Ol' Tex, he tells you to send your friends to him. If you do, and your friend buys a car, Tex will give you a very substantial finder's fee, cold cash. If you encourage a few friends to buy from Tex, you can make a tidy sum. Tex makes an even tidier one. Pretty soon everybody is buying cars, making tidy sums.

Tex operates on the principle that everyone knows 200 people. Somebody among those 200 people wants to buy a car. You and Tex are a lot alike. Tex needs customers; you need something else, say, the use of a backhoe for a weekend to help plant trees or a band that can supply a little music for your fund-raiser Friday night. Somebody from among the thousands of people the members of your group know is likely to be able to help you out.

Each person who is active in your organization should fill out a personal resources card. This activity is best done in a group, especially after some discussion of hustling. You should provide opportunities at a later date to update your cards, because people will always think of more to add and they are also developing access to more resources.

So what goes on this card? Names and resources (see Figure 10-1 on page 210); that is, names of people who can do something, and what they can do for your change effort. On the front of the card have the person write her or his name, phone number, and address. Then in each of four columns (two on the front and two on the back), provide space to respond to one of these four requests.

1. Name the three most important people from whom you would be willing to ask a favor, especially a political favor, or the use of his or her influence.

2. Name the three richest people you'd be willing to ask money from to help this effort.

3. Name three people you'd be willing to ask to give something other than influence or money. (Write what you'd ask for.)

4. Name three skills or talents you'd be willing to contribute to this effort.

That's it. You now have an immediate resource bank.

You will have to offer some guidance on filling out this card. The immediate reaction of a few might be, "But I don't know any important people." Calmly explain that you just need the three most important or richest or beneficial people that they *do* know. That may be a kid brother, a neighbor, or a local paint dealer. Any of these can contribute one dollar, one letter to a legislator, or help in painting the office. We all know people we can ask to do a little something for the cause. Take no more than 10 minutes to fill out the card. Any more time than that will make the process too tedious.

To give you an idea of how powerful this little resource bank can be, consider this. If you have only 10 people involved in your effort and the average contribution they get from each of the "richest" people on their list is $10, you have immediate access to $300. Most attempts to get something accomplished don't start with that much in the kitty.

(continued)

Change Agent Tip

Side One	
Name _____ Phone (home) _____ (work) _____	
Address _____	

Three most important people from whom I would ask a favor, particularly a political one.	Three richest people I would be willing to ask for money to help this effort
Name _____	Name _____
Position or Significance _____	
_____	Name _____
Name _____	
Position or Significance _____	Name _____
_____	Any additional names?
Name _____	Name _____
Position or Significance _____	
_____	Name _____

Side Two	
Name _____	

Three people I would be willing to ask for something other than influence or money	Three skills or talents I would be willing to contribute to this effort
Name _____	Talent/skill _____
Ask for _____	_____
Name _____	Talent/skill _____
Ask for _____	_____
Name _____	Talent/skill _____
Ask for _____	_____

Figure 10-1
Personal Resources Card

In human services training, we're not told to go out and get things. We're told to write grant proposals. Grants are nice, I will even talk about them later, but they are only one way of getting what you need. We in human services tend to act apologetic and even a little guilty when asking for things. If you stop and think about it, it's a little crazy to apologize for asking people to help out.

To some extent this is a game, and it is fun to play. You'll enjoy being inventive, discovering creative ways of getting, despite what your Aunt Emma has said, something for nothing.

There's a bit of a trap here. You can end up spending more time on this process than you should, even making more work for yourself. Yes, you can even start hustling things just to see what you can get. This doesn't really happen very often, because you can usually use just about anything you get. However, if this does happen, you've missed the whole point and are wasting time and manipulating people, hardly a laudable endeavor.

Most of the time you will find plenty of resources readily at hand, generally wherever you spend a good deal of your time—at work, home, school, places of play, and places of worship. This means not only you, but everyone else working on your change effort as well.

You can turn your need for certain items into an opportunity to develop support for your undertaking and an investment in your success. By making it easy for people to find ways to give to the effort, you increase your supply of investors. Whenever someone gives something, you get not only the particular resource they contribute but a little bit of them as well. They become a little bit more a part of the effort, a little bit more interested in its success.

Two warnings should be sounded here. First, don't ask people who can easily give a lot to give little. You can leave out the smaller contributors and lose out on some big items if some of the potential major givers feel they have met their contributing obligation. Second, refrain from the habit of taking a few bucks out of your own pocket to cover incidental expenses,

unless this needs to be done in a hurry. Otherwise you (and usually others around you too) start using this approach as the way to get the things you need. You cut yourself off from other investors, start feeling a little resentful, and out-of-pocket yourself right out of lunch.

When you and your partners in action have gotten to the point where you are looking for a particular service or item, ask yourselves whom you know who has it or has ready access to it. If you don't have the resources you need at your disposal, you or the people joining with you in this effort probably know someone who does. In fact, if a group of you spend no more than 10 minutes talking out loud about this, you will almost always come up with at least two or three ideas.

Those resources that are not immediately around you, ready to use, tend to be services, special knowledge or skills, or expensive equipment. Usually, even these are not too far off, although you may have to ask someone outside the membership of your organization.

To help you think about this further, consider some likely sources. First and foremost, consider who among the community you want to organize has ready access to the resource you need. Need a flier done? Is there a printing company in the neighborhood? Need some artwork? Is there an art department in your school? Need legal services? Are any of your colleagues attorneys or married to one? Start within your own community. This strengthens the ties to the community, gives people a specific way to help out, increases the number of people who have a stake in success, and sets in motion a way for the community to begin thinking of and relating to itself. In fact, a lot of people will be miffed or feel left out if you don't ask them. They may be even harder to involve down the road if you overlook them now.

"Thou shalt hit them in their self-interest!" is another commandment that serves as the basis for a lot of what you do in promoting change. Your adherence to this direction will cause you to consider whose self-interest is or could be involved; this is the second group you look to. Two powerful motivators are economic self-interest and prestige.

Many times people will give you things free or at a reduced cost in hope of receiving some other returns later. These returns could include better access to a new group of customers, your continued business, and referrals for business.

People's sense of personal prestige can be used to your advantage as well. Does helping you out make someone look good? Does turning you down make someone look like a lout? Does anyone's stature increase or diminish according to whether or not they respond to your request? People who see themselves (and are seen by others) as "doers" love to be able to deliver; they also hate thinking that other people think they can't get something done. Do you know any of these?

Other likely sources have some degree of self-interest but may have other motivations as well. People and organizations who are philosophically disposed toward you have resources of their own that they may be willing to share with you. In almost every community, at least one or two groups share your general concerns, even though their specific emphases may be different from yours. Consider how your success benefits the things they are working on. By now you have done your homework on your community, and you know who these people are.

For example, if you are involved in developing a neighborhood tree planting program, consider the number of environmental, conservation, and beautification organizations that exist in your area. If you are undertaking an effort to keep teen parents in school, think about the various organizations working on education, child abuse, economic development, mental health, or a host of other issues related to teen parenting. Nongovernmental citizens groups are the most likely sources of help, but don't rule out public and private agencies in your quest for the things you need.

Places where you spend your time and where you spend your money are places where you have built a relationship. They probably want to see you again. They may have some-

thing you can use. Ask for it. Among these are organizations to which you belong or hold events that you attend. These can be religious, civic, or social, from your synagogue to your aerobics class.

Also on your target list should be businesses or dealerships you regularly or have recently patronized. Where do you buy your insurance, where do you have your checking account, where do you get your tomatoes? Any or all of these might be willing to help you meet some specific need. Your presence or your hard earned dollars are an investment in the success of these enterprises. You can certainly ask them to invest in yours.

Finally, there are relatives, friends, and acquaintances. Even if no one in this personal network of yours can offer what you are looking for, they might be willing to help find someone else who can.

Ask for What You Need

Now that you have determined what you need and considered who might have it, it's time to figure out who will be doing the asking and how. Then, you need to ask.

The simplest direction is that whoever has the best connection to the most likely source should do the asking. Most of the time this will work. However, sometimes you will need to spread the asking around a bit. Otherwise, you may find that you have the same two or three people doing all the asking. Having a number of people involved in acquiring needed resources helps create an attitude that we're all looking for ways to add to the effort. Further, success in this endeavor will solidify the person's attachment to the change effort. This last point is particularly important. A person will usually take some particular pride in this accomplishment and feel closer to the organization that has benefited from it.

Exactly how you ask does depend on the situation. Regardless of the situation, though, there are a few things to keep in mind to improve your chances. First, the more personal the request, the better. Talking with someone face-to-face will usually get you a lot more than writing a letter. Second, show how the giving helps the giver. Everyone has some personal interest involved, even if it's not economic self-interest. Be able to identify and show how giving meets the giver's interest. Third, show how the giving benefits the recipient. Each of us likes to know that when we do something it matters. Be able to describe clearly what a particular gift will do for the change effort. Finally, close the deal. You are not asking someone to think about helping you. You are asking them to actually do it. Get a yes or a no when you ask. At the very least, get a time when you'll hear the yes or no. Then follow up.

Don't be afraid to ask. You and the issue you are working on are worth it. The worst thing that can happen is that someone will say no.

After a while you will have developed a kind of hustling state of mind, a way of thinking that believes that what you are doing is good and that there are lots of people out there who are able and willing to do something to keep things moving ahead. You won't think twice about asking for things you need. It will be routine. It will begin to affect the way you go about things in general. And, if you have gotten a good group of people to think and act this way, you'll be very hard to stop.

Commonly Needed Resources

Following is a list of the most commonly needed resources you can usually get for nothing or next to nothing. See who has what you need, and ask for it. Make sure you are aware of any possible benefits, including tax benefits, the contributor can receive. Be ready to describe benefits to potential contributors, and do so accurately. All of these suggestions depend to some extent on your ability to show a connection between the interests of your organization and the interests of the contributor.

- *Printing or copying.* Most print or copy shops will do small orders, especially if the

printed material identifies the shop that donated the printing. Large social service agencies, hospitals, and most units of government have print and copy capabilities. Some local governments actually do printing routinely for certain types of community groups. Check to see if this exists in your area.

College and technical school graphic arts or advertising students are sometimes looking for projects. The schools may also do the required printing.

Union print shops will do "labor donated" small orders. You pay only for the paper. If you have to bring your own paper, try to get some other agency to donate this to you. If you need to buy it, make your purchases from paper wholesalers. You'll save a lot more money than buying it from the printer.

If you just can't find someone to do the whole thing for you at no cost, you can usually find someone who can prepare the work for printing. Many professions have the skills you need. Graphic artists, drafts people, landscape architects, and others are usually able to do this work. Check your organization's network or check with schools that offer this training.

- *Consulting.* Unless you are seeking a major consulting project, especially one requiring a lot of writing, you will find that many experts in the community are willing to offer you a bagload of helpful tips or a guiding hand. Generally speaking, the best bet is to go directly to the source. If you need some ideas on setting up a lobbying campaign, go talk to a lobbyist. If you don't know any, there are many public interest organizations that can put you in touch with one. If you want some direction on working with the media, ask someone who works in the field. Reporters and editors won't usually tell you how to handle a particular story, but they will offer some general and very helpful guidelines.

Many experts and consultants will respond to your request for a one-time get-together or presentation. Ask her or him to bring materials. Then arrange for some access to your consultant a couple of times a year to discuss particular problems. You'd be surprised how many will work for a lunch or a few beers after work.

- *Attorneys.* Before you set out to get legal assistance or representation, try to determine what type of help you are seeking. You should ask yourself, "What do we need an attorney for?" This question will be asked by others, so do ask it of yourselves first. Overall, the best bet is to get your own attorney. If you do not personally know an attorney well, search your organization's network for possible connections. Many law firms do a percentage of *pro bono* (for free) work.

If you do not know any attorney who is willing to give you free legal assistance, there are still other avenues you can explore. You can call the bar association in your county and explain your circumstances. The bar association should have the names of attorneys or firms who do *pro bono* work. Some local bar associations have programs that help fledgling organizations with routine legal concerns (for example, preparing articles of incorporation). Generally, the more political or controversial the organization is, the more reluctant the bar association is to offer help.

Other public interest legal organizations may be willing to give you assistance. These would include the American Civil Liberties Union or a public interest law organization. These organizations exist in each state. If your legal assistance needs don't fall within their scope of activities, they are usually willing to direct you to other sources who may help.

You can also contact the Alliance for Justice in Washington, DC, for further direction. The alliance is a national association of public interest law groups. Their staff will help you think through your situation and assist you in uncovering legal resources that could be available to you. The alliance publishes a helpful directory nationwide (*Directory of Public Interest Law Centers,* 1997).

Local legal aid offices may be another source. However, be aware that you will usually be met with a long waiting list and income eligibility criteria. Again, though, you may find legal aid to be a good source of referral to helpful private attorneys.

State and local governments often have divisions that handle certain actions, such as consumer affairs matters or cases of discrimination. These may be appropriate for you to contact.

If there is a college of law in your area, it is possible to approach the school for some assistance. Under the direction of a professor or a mentoring attorney, a law student group could undertake a project to research legal issues of importance to you. Because law students are not practicing attorneys, they cannot represent you in legal action. However, the research they do is valuable. If you can't find anything for free, you generally can find an attorney who will let you use his or her name as your attorney but not charge you unless actual legal work is done. You can negotiate the cost and extent of the work when you need it.

- *Other specific talents or skills.* An effective way to garner some much needed expertise is to use staff loaned to your effort from another organization or business. Loaned staff will generally be provided on a temporary basis to work on a specific project (Walker, 1987). Your request must be clear and specific, including the estimated number of hours required. Be able to show how the partnership will benefit your effort, the community, and the contributing organization.

- *Space.* Your space needs will probably fall into three categories: occasional use (for meetings and workshops), office use, or storage. Recent concerns over liability have made arranging for the use of space a little more difficult, yet you still have a good chance of getting what you need for free.

Schools, hospitals, churches, and synagogues will probably give you a place for a meeting or workshop. In fact, almost all medium to large organizations have this capability. You need to figure out where your connections are and what meets your needs. Storage is usually a matter of finding out who has what kind of storage capacity that you need and asking for it. You might have to be a bit creative, using space in a way that's different from how it's normally used. For example, one food bank uses a beer distributorship to provide refrigerated space. Liability problems are a bigger obstacle than finding the storage place itself.

Office space is more difficult to come by. To get this without cost, you may really need to hustle. Check out your connections with property management companies and real estate brokers. Other sources are religious organizations, shared space with like-minded organizations or large institutions, such as banks and universities who have holdings in real property. All of these provide free office space, but it's not common.

• *Equipment.*   Equipment, or the temporary use of it, is one of the easiest things to get without spending any money. See what connections you have with people who sell, rent, or use the equipment. For example, auto dealerships donate used cars (not clunkers either), construction companies can contribute the use of a front-end loader and operator for a day, real estate offices will let groups use their phones for a couple of evenings, and rental firms have an extra set of posthole diggers to help you get blisters.

What might be used or outdated equipment for some can be perfectly adequate for you. Things taken as trade-ins might not be good for resale, but they may make for a great (and usable) contribution.

• *Shared computer time.*   Corporations are now well equipped with computer support, and a number of companies are now providing computer time as a means of in-kind assistance (Breiteneicher & Hohler, 1993).

EXPLORING THE RESOURCE JUNGLE

Get to Know Your Community's Resources

Though the items and services mentioned here are the most common resources change efforts seek, your own situation will no doubt require other things from time to time. Your success will depend in large part on how well you know your community, how many people you know, and how many people know you.

You're well on your way now to getting the things you need to conquer the world, or at least to improve your part of it. Will you need to spend any money at all? Yep. Hmmmm . . . you knew that was coming.

Getting and Spending Money

Yes, you will have to spend some money. Some things you can hustle may be more wisely bought. Some things you can get for free or cheap look that way. Sometimes that's all right, sometimes it isn't. Your effort has a certain image it wants to project. Some of the things you may be able to get for free won't fit the image you are trying to project or just won't do the job, so you may have to pay for them. For example, maybe for one special all-day get-together you need a very stylish conference room and all you can get free is the church broom closet. Or perhaps you have reams of donated low-quality paper, but you want your letterhead to look classy. Some things are worth paying for.

Staff, an Expensive Item

One of the most important things you may have to pay for is people. Certainly people are the most valuable resource. They are also the most costly if you need to pay for them, and there are times when you definitely should.

This is an expense you normally don't incur until you are in the implementation or institutionalization phase of the change process, if at all. Paying for staff is the single most expensive item for almost any organization. Unless the organization is engaged in raising funds for things it gives away (for example, a food bank buying and then giving away food), most of the money it raises will be spent on people who work for the organization. All the other expenses taken together will rarely outweigh the expense of staff.

If we don't have to pay anyone to do the work, we'll save a lot of money, right? Absolutely. So the best approach is to get someone or even several someones to donate their time and work for free. Well, not necessarily.

If all four of the following factors are present, the use of nonpaid staff for ongoing support makes pretty good sense. However, all four factors must be in place.

1. The work doesn't need to be done according to a tight schedule. Certainly, a specific amount of work doesn't need to be turned out every day.
2. The work doesn't place a high number of unusual, unpredictable, or inconvenient demands on the worker. People won't commonly be asked to go out of their way to do something.
3. You don't have to worry about the worker's ability to do the job properly. The work does not require a set of sophisticated skills, and there won't be much confusion about whether or not the job is being done right.
4. The worker is fairly easy to replace if he or she should lose interest or need to drop out for one reason or another.

If any of these things aren't true, there will probably need to be paid staff somewhere on the scene.

Although it may mean that you need to raise more money, hiring staff can make very good sense. Paid staff usually have a stronger sense of obligation. They expect to be and can be held accountable. Even if the contract is not written, both parties know that one exists. There is an agreement that provides mutual benefits. A paycheck not only provides benefits to the worker but it also affirms the agreement he or she has made.

One of the key duties of the paid staff is to generate more support for the organization, including more funding. Generally, the position should be able to pay for itself and generate additional revenues. This certainly doesn't rule out the use of volunteer help. The use of donated time will always be important. Paid staff should be able to enhance the effectiveness of this kind of contribution.

Your decision to hire employees will take into consideration the size, nature, and purpose of your organization. The intended length of the organization's life will also be considered. The longer you expect your organization to last, the more likely you will be to hire people to help run it.

Other personnel costs come in the form of specialized services you just can't hustle. These will frequently be in the area of legal or financial services; for example, bookkeeping and filing financial reports and documents. The more ongoing or pressing your needs for specialized services are, the more likely you will have to pay for them. Also, if the activity involves a significant use of one person's time (for example, an attorney pursuing a lawsuit or an accountant conducting an audit), you can expect to incur some costs.

Keep Some Money in Reserve

In addition to whatever personnel costs you have and the necessity to purchase items you can't or decide not to hustle, you will need money to cover a variety of unanticipated expenses. It is a good idea to have an adequate contingency fund available. You can't be certain when you will need to have some extra dollars on hand, just be certain that you do. It is a good rule of thumb to have enough money in the bank to provide operating costs for six months over and above any anticipated income. The size and the nature of your particular organization may dictate a smaller or larger backup fund. Still, you should plan to have something in reserve.

Filling the Coffers

If, after all, you do need some money, how do you go about getting it? To answer this question you first have to answer a couple of others. The first critical question is how much do you need? A variety of techniques will yield you hundreds of dollars. These are great if you need hundreds of dollars; they are a waste of time if you need tens of thousands of dollars. Next, you have to consider whether you need a steady income or an occasional infusion of funds. Generally, the larger your budget, say over $10,000, the more predictable your income base needs to be. These are the two basic questions. They will set your general direction. As you begin to select various options you will need to ask more specific questions.

There are two different approaches to generating money in your program. One is called *fund-raising*. The other is called *resource development*.

Fund-raising activities occur on a smaller scale with the intent of an immediate payoff. Bake sales, raffles, and events fall into this category. This is appropriate for organizations that can get by with a short-term financial approach. Fund-raising usually involves a number of activities, each of which has a beginning and an ending point. When the need for more money becomes apparent, a new fund-raising activity is dreamed up and implemented. It is the sense of an upcoming need that spurs the fund-raising action. The organization lives off the proceeds from one activity to the next. Over time, you may plan so that these activities become more predictable, but you never really build a permanent financial base.

The resource development approach takes a longer and broader view. With this method, there is an intent to develop a predictable and growing income base. Here, income is seen as the result of an ongoing process, not a specific activity. Expansion of donor lists, establishment of trusts, and planned giving are examples of the development approach. Organizations that plan to be in business for a while, that are visible in the community, and that have large budgets are usually better served by using resource development techniques.

One more proviso is worth mentioning. Getting money will cost you something. Whether that is postage, printing, hamburgers, or your time, it will cost something. Think this through. You want to be pretty sure that what you are likely to get is worth what you had to spend to get it.

Further, no matter how you approach the business of getting money, you will have to invest your own thoughts, time, and energy. You need to plan and to take action on your plan. You have to monitor activities to make sure that you are doing what you intended to do. Finally, you need to evaluate your approach to see that you accomplished your goals and that whatever investments you made in the process were worth it.

Figuring out how to get money is a fun, creative, even exciting process. Granted, actually doing what you've figured out isn't always quite as fun, but it can be made more so when you allow the enthusiasm of your imaginative planning to carry over.

Options for Bringing in Dollars

There are two basic paths you can travel to get to the rainbow's end. The first involves asking individuals to give you their own money. The second involves asking individuals to give you other people's money. In the first instance, people make decisions on behalf of their own interests. In the second, people make decisions on behalf of the interests of a group, organization, corporation, foundation, or government agency (Breiteneicher & Hohler, 1993).

Each change effort or organization will use a different approach based on the amount of money it needs, the types of activity in which it is involved, the current level of community acceptance, its need for short- or long-term support, its level of skill and interest in pursuing different approaches, and the time and money it can spend to raise more money. If you seek money from individuals, you will soon see that there is an almost endless assortment of ways to get individuals to give you money. You might even make up your own way.

Although getting money from corporations, foundations, and the like has its own twists and turns, these organizations usually share one thing in common: a written proposal or grant application will probably be required. The length and nature of these will vary, but it is likely that you will be doing some proposal writing for all sources other than individuals. Developing grant writing skills is well worth your time.

Contributions from Individuals

Decisions made by individuals will determine whether or not as well as how much money you will get from any source. However, this particular category involves getting money directly from people with no intervening structure. I'm talking about people giving you their own money, not somebody else's.

This category deserves special attention not only because there are so many ways to go about it but also because more money comes from individuals than from any other non-governmental source. Of all the money given each year in the United States for charitable causes, 80% comes directly from individuals. It's not a paltry sum either. In 1993, individuals gave almost $118 billion to support causes they believed in (Hodgkinson, 1996, p. 86). With each succeeding year, this figure continues to rise.

Religious organizations definitely get the lion's share of all this generosity, receiving almost half of all dollars contributed. However, human services receive about 25%, and causes that provide public and societal benefits receive about 10%. This is a significant slice of a very large pie. All this money doesn't come from the very wealthy. Although the average American contributes about 2% of his or her personal income, those of modest means actually contribute a higher percentage (Hodgkinson & Weitzman, 1996b). What does this mean to you? Although middle- and upper-income individuals

TEN QUESTIONS, PLUS ONE

If you want money, you need to answer ten questions, plus one.	• When are they in a giving or spending mood?	• How do you acknowledge and nurture people for the future before and after they give?
• Who has it?	• What message do they need to hear?	• What resources do you have to direct this effort?
• Who is likely to give it to you?	• How do you send that message?	Plus one:
• Where do you have a connection with these people?	• Who sends that message?	• What other questions do you need to ask?
	• How do you make it as easy as possible for people to respond?	

may give more total dollars, all members of your community are potential contributors, real financial investors in your effort.

Six Basic Steps

Getting money from individuals involves six basic steps, no matter what approach you use. By breaking it down into steps, I run the risk of making the process seem pretty complicated. In actual practice, you will be able to mentally check off each step (and you should do this) once you have repeated the procedure a few times. The more experience you gain in asking for money, the simpler and more routine this process will be for you.

First, it is helpful to know whom you are asking. *Identifying your prospects* is a fundamental step. "Who" comes before "how" (Breiteneicher & Hohler, 1993). Understanding how much you need and when as well as whether you are looking for a nonrenewable gift or building a substantial base of income will guide you in your selection.

Second, you need to *nurture* these *prospective givers.* Once you have identified the prospects, establish some type of relationship with them. This includes developing their awareness and interest in your efforts (Baird, 1997; Brakeley, 1997).

Third, think about and *prepare a message* that will be most effective in producing a

favorable response. You need to take into account what this particular individual needs to know and feel to decide to contribute money. You need to put together a message that will provide that information and stir those emotions.

Fourth, you need to *deliver that message.* Think of how and in what circumstances you can most effectively communicate your message to the people who need to hear it. The more direct your communication and the clearer your request, the more effective you will be. Recalling the "ladder of communication effectiveness" described in Chapter 9 should give you some ideas on techniques you can use (Breiteneicher & Hohler, 1993; Freyd & Carlson, 1997; Reinhart, 1990).

Fifth, after you have sent your message, *follow up* to see that your message has been received and that any pledges made were kept (Baird, 1997).

Finally, *say thank-you.* In many situations, particularly when you have made a direct personal request, a thank-you is an important step, even if you did not receive a contribution at this time. Remember, there is always tomorrow (Baird, 1997).

Direct Requests

The most effective way to ask someone for money is to do it directly, face-to-face. The more

Take a Moment to Discover. . . . .

Many of us are uncomfortable when asking people for money, so we tend to put a lot of distance between the asker and the giver. We are often more concerned with taking care of our discomfort than with getting what we're asking for. We usually end up with good protection from discomfort when we do this but with not many more dollars than we started with.

Think about how often we ask people, friends, relatives, coworkers, and the like for money for routine requests. We commonly ask for money for stamps, gas, snacks, and pop—or at least we expect people to chip in. Sometimes we also ask people to spend money to go out on a Saturday night to attend a basketball game or a movie.

Reflect back on the last week or last month. How many times have you asked or expected someone to give you money for something, regardless of what it might have been? How many times have they asked you for money?

Think about the circumstances surrounding the request for money. What can you learn from thinking about the times you ask people to give you money, or to spend money to be with you, or when they ask you to give money? How would you ask any of these people for money to support your change effort?

Today, ask one person to give you money for something, ideally for some worthy cause you support.

. . . .

money you are asking for and the less experience the prospect has in giving to a cause like yours, the more you need to be prepared when making your request. Even if you are making a minor request from a friend, don't assume that preparation is unnecessary.

Here are a few things to know and do that might help you.

Know Your Prospect

- Gauge how much the prospect is capable of giving.
- Determine the prospect's likely motivators and to what facts and emotions he or she is likely to respond.

Prepare Yourself for the Contact

- Know in advance what you will say. Be able to clearly and simply describe what you need and why. Practice out loud so it doesn't sound awkward.
- Describe why you think the undertaking is important to the prospect and what his or her contribution will mean.
- Be willing and able to answer questions.

- Determine if anyone else needs to be involved in making the request.
- Arrange the right time, place, and people to ask the prospect.

Make Contact

- Make your request.
- Get the money then and there, or at the very least arrange a time when you can pick it up.
- Thank the prospect.

Tips

- People give to people. The asker's relationship to the giver is important (Breiteneicher & Hohler, 1993).
- Promote personal involvement. Some ways to do this include inviting prospects to take part in lectures or public meetings, personal issue discussions, presentations to other groups, and to volunteer. Nonprofit agencies particularly want to make sure they are grooming a new generation of investors (donors) and that their fund-raising techniques increase civic engage-

ment rather than keep donors distant (Burlingham, 1997; Hall, 1996; Reinert, 1990).

- People are more likely to respond when asked to give an immediate contribution than when a delay between the request and the receipt of the donation exists (Reeves, Macolini, & Martin, 1987).

- People are more willing to help out someone who has done them a favor or who has given them something (Regan, 1971). Consider buying your prospect dinner, lunch, or a soda. Have you done anyone a favor recently?

- Discuss common opinions and values at some point in your conversation. This provides a shared frame of reference and a recognition of affiliation that makes the request easier to state and easier to meet.

- Major donors will often contribute to exciting programs with their hearts more than their heads. Exciting means bold or visionary more than controversial (Panas, 1989).

- You never offend a person by politely asking for too large a gift. Most are flattered that you think they could give that much (Reinert, 1990).

- Reward or in some way recognize contributors, paying careful attention to provide special rewards to major givers (Baird, 1997).

- Using emotion can help. Pride, outrage, guilt, affection, and fear are common emotions that promote a response.

For those of you who know better, I apologize for what I'm about to say. (Since you do know better, you also know this must be said.) Your ethics will guide you in all of this. Obviously, you are not going to ask someone to do what he or she cannot do. You are not going to play on people's emotions simply because you can do so. You are responding to feelings that are legitimately present in the situation. You are not making your relationship dependent on a contribution. You will understand that increasing your effectiveness within ethical bounds may itself be ethically required, or you wouldn't be doing this in the first place.

Pitching to Groups

If you can't directly ask an individual to give you money, your next best bet is to ask them in a group, the smaller the better. Groups can achieve a shared or group view of a situation and exert peer pressure on their members to respond appropriately. Groups can be addressed as a unit to solicit funds from the group itself as a single contribution, or contributions can be requested from individual members of the group.

When preparing to make your pitch to a group, consider many of the same things about the group as you did with individual donors—estimate their ability to give, their giving history, and get some background information on the organization itself. Understand, also, that most groups are worried about your legitimacy, especially if you are a new organization. Your approach to them must take this into account.

Receiving money from the group itself, rather than from the members of the group, requires a different process. Many groups and organizations, especially those that routinely make donations of over $1,000, have a formal process established for handling requests. The larger and more formal an organization is, the more extensive the process is likely to be. The more you know about the process, the greater your chances of receiving funds. This process generally requires a written proposal together with a short verbal presentation in support of the proposal. Follow the guidelines described later in this chapter on funding from organizations.

Tips

- It is sometimes helpful for you to have a couple of people present in the audience who have already agreed to give you money. Yes, you may call them shills. These shills should demonstrate their support and their contribution in a way that best stimulates participation by other members. For example, if you are "passing the hat," these supporters can be among those who first receive the hat. Seeing your friends drop in their checks or dollars can encourage others to do so as well.

- Your local Chamber of Commerce may have a list of all the clubs and organizations in your area. For a modest cost, usually less than $10, you can purchase this list, which includes the name of the club or organization, its phone number and address, and the name of the chief officer or contact person.

Memberships

Requesting an annual membership fee from participants in the organization is a simple, effective way to raise money and increase commitment. This approach tends to make your organization a more formal one, bringing more expectations and responsibilities. If you want to keep the relationship among members purely informal, you may want to skip this method.

In your effort to "recruit" members, start with individuals who by word or action have expressed an interest in the organization or its goals. Each of these people should receive a personal request that they become members.

It is easier to ask for a membership than for an outright donation. You are acknowledging interest and inviting participation as well as asking for money. Potential members have the opportunity to gain a sense of affiliation. They have a choice to belong. As members, they are not considered nor do they consider themselves outsiders who are asked to give to "you." Instead, they become part of "us" and to some extent become recipients of the contribution as well as makers of it. By asking every person who has expressed an interest in your effort to become a member, you can quickly add to your coffers. Even though the amount you raise from this group is likely to be relatively small, it's worth the modest effort.

After asking everyone who has shown some support for the effort, the next step is to contact those who are potential beneficiaries of the organization's work. Again, a personal, face-to-face request is far more effective than any other

method. A simple plan should be worked out to reach as many people in this group as possible. At the very least, when anyone from the organization has contact with another person who could gain from what the organization is doing, that person should be asked to be a member. This is a habit that should be consciously developed among the members of your core group. If only a handful of members routinely recruit and you have no other plan for approaching these potential contributors, you will still steadily build the organization and provide new income.

The third step in developing a member base is to invite people to join whenever your organization contacts the general public. This, too, should become a habit, and it is an easy one to acquire. Membership forms should appear in all newsletters and be available at all public events. Each public speaking opportunity should be accompanied by a call for people to become members.

Members should receive something in return for their contribution. Membership cards are easy and inexpensive to produce. They should not look cheap. Attractive, plastic laminated cards that fit easily into a wallet or billfold are the best.

Newsletters are important in reaffirming participation. Each membership organization should have one. It is important to remind people that they are members and why. If it is easy to provide other benefits, do so. Special event invitations, discounts, or other rewards available to members only are helpful. However, do only what is easy to do. If you make the process too complicated, you turn a simple technique into a time-consuming one.

Members become the source of future funds and friends. Each year you ask members to ante up. Although not all continue, most will, providing the organization with a predictable source of income.

Periodically you should make a special appeal to members for additional donations. This should be tied to a special situation or challenge to the organization. Although you don't want to barrage members with these requests, you will be able to draw money as well as goods and services from members in addition to their membership fees.

Tips

- Keep membership dues low, below what people are able to give. Membership dues simply get people involved in the organization; you can ask them for other help later.
- Consider having several levels of membership with different privileges and benefits for each level (for example, voting and nonvoting). The higher the level, the higher the fees.
- Your membership form should be simple to fill out and return. If you can collect it on the spot, you will get a much higher rate of return.
- Include the line "make your check payable to" on the form. If the donation is tax deductible, say so.
- You can also ask for other information such as special knowledge, skills, community contacts, or interests. Don't require this information, otherwise the form may become irritating to fill out.
- If you are asking for members during a speech or presentation, do so toward the end of your talk. Forms should be passed out right after you make the request during, not after, your presentation. Get it into the hands of your listeners; don't make them come up and get it. If you can work it in, take a moment before you conclude your remarks to allow people to fill out the membership form.
- Have a modified form, used for presentations, that requires only essential information. Also have a box that says, "I can't pay you now, but I will later." Though this may lose you a few dollars that you could get then and there, it will rope in enough fence-sitters to more than make up for it.

Indirect Requests

Indirect requests from individuals include all techniques other than a face-to-face request for a contribution. These are primarily requests over the phone or by mail.

Indirect methods produce a much lower response rate but have the advantage of reaching many more people. Even if individuals don't respond to one particular indirect request, their awareness of the organization is increased and they may respond at another time.

Further, those who do respond become part of your donor base. You will resolicit these people from time to time for additional contributions. Most people who give once will give again, usually at least two more times. A good rule of thumb is that as long as you cover the initial costs of your solicitation campaign you will eventually make money if you have a planned resolicitation campaign. For larger mailings a return of 1% or more is considered acceptable (Klein, 1992). Ideally, you want to do more than just cover your costs. You want to make money the first time. Understand, though, that *resolicitation of identified donors is where the real money is.* Your rate of return on resolicitation is a great deal higher than that on your initial request.

Some groups do what is called *prospecting.* This means that their initial contact is done mainly for the purpose of discovering prospects (the gold in this game) to add to their base of donors for future contacts and additional dollars.

Keep accurate and thorough records on all donors. Building your donor base is a basic concern. You don't want to start from the beginning each time you go out to ask for money.

Telephone Solicitation

This method involves calling people at home and asking them for money to support what your organization does. The better your organization or the problem it deals with is known, and the better you know the people you are calling, the better will be your results.

This approach has the advantage that you speak directly with the potential contributor. It has the distinct disadvantage of pestering people at home along with a host of other callers offering dance lessons, water softeners, and tickets to the local police ball. This is particularly true of cold calling (that is, when people are not expecting you to call). You run the risk of turning them off to your organization. You also have to be concerned about the volunteers doing the calling. They may be treated rudely. You could lose a few this way. If you think you can get past this interference, using the telephone is definitely worth it.

Telephone fund-raising campaigns come in all sizes. You can call 100 people or 100,000 people. The number of telephone lines at your disposal will play a large part in this decision. Equally important is the number and the enthusiasm of your volunteer callers.

Tips

• Finding ways to maintain the enthusiasm and esprit de corps of your callers is essential. It is far better to have too many callers for the number of calls to be made than vice versa. A good standard is to expect that each caller can complete 40 calls per night and be willing to work for two nights of calling. Therefore, it will take 12 committed callers for you to complete about 1,000 phone calls.

• Turn your telephone campaign into news. Let the community know who is calling and when. Who has donated the use of the phone and where the callers will be when they are making the calls can be news too (Ardman & Ardman, 1980).

• Get lists of people who will be likely to give. Contributors to organizations similar to yours, names of potential beneficiaries of your efforts, friends and acquaintances of your members, and memberships to exclusive clubs and organizations are good places to start.

• Make sure the lists are neat and are complete with names, addresses, and phone numbers before you start.

• Develop a short, written script that will guide what you say. The script should include your responses to the things the person at the other end is likely to say. The script should mention your name and the name of the person you are calling early in the conversation. Read the script out loud a few times before you make the first call. This will get you comfortable with the message and help make sure that it sounds natural, not phony. You will also be able to hear if your request is clear. The script should have the respondent answer "yes" to a couple of short-answer questions before asking for the contribution (for example, "Are you aware of _____ ?" "Do you think _____ is a problem in our community?"). If calling friends and acquaintances of members, use the member's name in the script. Get permission to do so.

• Arrange for a small group of people (six or so) to call from the same location. The location should have a phone line for each caller. Social service agencies, insurance agencies, and real estate offices are likely candidates. It is important to do this as a group. Individuals who call from home hardly ever complete the task.

• Complete all calls by nine o'clock.

• Have letters and any related materials available in advance to follow up each call. One letter goes to those who have agreed to send their contribution, thanking them for their contribution. This letter should include the amount pledged. Another letter goes to the people who are thinking about contributing, thanking them for their interest. The third letter goes to those who have said no, asking them to consider it at a later date. Make sure envelopes and stamps are available and that a letter is prepared after each call. A personal handwritten note is included from the caller on each letter.

• Acknowledge any likely resistance to the call.

• If the requests are met with a noncommittal or a "no" response, suggest a small amount.

• Consider having the volunteers get together for dinner before the calling begins; after dinner meet for a half-hour training session. These activities can stimulate group spirit and help give callers confidence (Ardman & Ardman, 1980).

- Have fun. Have refreshments. Most people are reluctant to make phone calls, so add as much social enjoyment as possible to the task. For example, set pizza goals. Whenever the group achieves a certain total in pledges, send out for a pizza. Keep a scoreboard of totals and cheer when certain amounts are reached.

- There are firms specializing in telemarketing. Check the percentage of money that goes to you and to them before you decide if you want to hire them. Some offer token items like trash bags or light bulbs in exchange for contributions. Check on the reputation of the firm by getting a list of clients and talking to them.

Telephone Support for Small Mail Campaigns

The telephone can be a useful tool to increase the impact of a letter sent to a select group of potential donors. A mailing of 500 can easily be followed by three nights of calling. This will measurably increase the number of contributions the letter could generate on its own. This approach incorporates features of broader telemarketing and direct-mail methods. Due to its smaller scale, it is simpler to do and easier to manage.

The letter should be signed by an individual who has some favorable status in the eyes of those receiving the letter. Ideally, he or she should be a member of the group receiving the letter, known personally by members of that target group, and be identified with the issue. For example, a successful home builder who has spoken publicly on the issue of homelessness could be a good letter signer for other home builders asking them to contribute to an effort that works with homeless people.

Sometimes an individual who is outside the immediate target group but held in high regard by those in the group will make an effective letter signer. The highly popular coach of the university basketball team, writing to those same home builders, or a nationally respected environmentalist, writing to a local environmental group, may produce a good response.

On some occasions, particularly if your organization is not well known, you may want to have several people sign the same letter. Having several signatures on the same letter gives the impression of broader support and increases the chances that those receiving the mailing will respond to the name of a person they trust. The disadvantage to this is that you can lose the more personal touch that a single signature provides.

It is particularly important to get good lists when using this technique. The names you select should be those who are much more likely than the general public to respond to both the issue at hand and to the person or persons signing the letter with the amount of money you need.

Tips

- Write the letter for the signer. Most signers don't want to take on the job of composing a letter. Provide an opportunity for the signer to review and modify the contents to reflect his or her personality. Make sure the essential elements are retained.

- Use facts and emotions in your letter to which the target group is likely to respond. Frame the message in a way that makes the most sense to them. This is usually not the time to get people to agree with your political or philosophical view of things. Your main purpose here is to get money.

- Mention that this mailing is going to only a few people.

- Include a P.S. on the letter saying that someone will be calling in a few days.

- Include a self-addressed return envelope with the letter.

- Ask the signer if he or she would be willing to make a few follow-up calls. If so, you can indicate this in the P.S.

- Follow the same procedures involving telephone solicitation discussed earlier. Additionally, make sure you remove from the calling list names of those who have responded to the letter before you begin your calling. There's no need to bother them again. Also, include a copy of the original letter when you send your follow-up letter to those who are undecided.
- Personalize your outside envelope. Handwrite or type the address. Save mailing labels for some other time (Brentlinger & Weiss, 1987).
- Use an envelope of high-quality paper.
- Have the signer's name and mailing address as the return address, or use a mailing address with no name. Do not use your organization's name in the return address. After all, they are responding primarily to the contents of the letter and the signer, not to your name.
- Send your letters with first-class postage. Use stamps, not metered mail.
- Handwrite a code number or the person's name on the return envelope you have inserted. This reminds people that you are paying attention to who is responding, and who is not.
- Have the letter signer actually sign each letter.
- Have the letter signer write a personal note on as many letters as possible. Something like "Don, I hope to hear from you" would be sufficient.
- Using another name, have your own address and phone number included on the list so you can see how the process is working.

Direct Mail

Direct mail is effective for prospecting and resolicitation. Unless you have a hot list, one that is likely to provide a high percentage of contributors, or a huge mailing, you will probably not make a lot of money on your first general request. In fact, you may well lose money on the first go round. However, continued resolicitation of the contributors who do respond can bring you a profit in the long run.

So don't give up on your donor list too quickly. Direct mail is best used as part of a long-term process for building a constituency base (Klein, 1992; Lautman, 1997). Of course, if you are holding some lists that just sizzle in your fingers, you might want to give this a try. Be aware that the quality of your list is the most important ingredient in this type of fund-raising (Barnes, 1989). Also, be aware that with increasing costs and increasing competition (12.2 *billion* pieces sent in 1995) the value of this form of fund-raising is decreasing (Craver, 1995; Hall, 1996).

In addition to costing you money, direct mail requires considerable time and energy. You need to gather lists, design your mailing piece, stuff and address all the envelopes, gauge the best time for sending all this out, and check your supply of aspirin. For these and other reasons, most smaller or new organizations do not use direct mail. Larger, well-established organizations do find this profitable. They have the resources to put into it.

This method exists because if you have the resources and you do it right, it can make money, lots of money. Some companies specialize in direct mail and can run your whole campaign for you. Others specialize in selling lists (for example, the list of all subscribers to *Ms.* magazine who live in a certain ZIP code area). Others, including sheltered workshops and organizations serving developmentally disabled citizens, will take your addresses, envelopes, and materials and prepare the mailing.

Direct-mail techniques have become increasingly sophisticated. If you believe your organization would benefit from pursuing this method of fund-raising, check to see which firms in your area can help you. Again, see if you have any special connections that could lead to some free or low-cost consultation. Remember, it is important to be sure the firm is reputable before you do business. Do your homework.

Events

Need money? Hold an event. It's almost a knee-jerk response. Imagine a small group sitting around fretting about money. Before too long someone will very likely pipe up with, "Hey, let's hold a (dance, fun run, basketball game, concert, all of the above)." Be sure that your community, especially likely donors, and your members who are to organize the event have sufficient interest. Special events are becoming increasingly more difficult. In many communities both donors and organizers are getting burned out on them (Sinnock, 1995).

Event fund-raising usually means that you are introducing an activity into the community calendar that is interesting enough that people will want to give you money to join in the fun. Even if you are capitalizing on an existing community activity, you are introducing a new element in the bargain.

There are four basic types of events: those requiring attendance and ticket sales, those requiring participation and registration fees, those that other groups do on your behalf with a select community of potential contributors, and those that serve as a promotion of your organization as well as some other product or service.

Some events can be considered as much people-raising events as fund-raising events. In this case, you try to get as many people to take part in the activity as possible while making just a little bit more money than you need to cover your costs. Here, the cost to the participant is very low because you are more concerned with bringing out a lot of people than bringing in a lot of money.

If you use this approach, you had better make sure you know what you want to do. Many groups are disappointed when they have a great turnout and little money to show for all the work. If you make a $2 profit on every person who shows up, you will need 500 people to attend to make $1,000. Making $1,000 after many, many hours of work can be deflating. Getting a crowd of 500 people can be a tremendous boost to your organization. Just make sure that your purpose is clear.

You have to have a number of things going for you to hold a big event that raises a lot of money. First, you have to have a lot of resources to put into planning and organizing and promoting the event. This usually means people (and their contacts) and money. Second, you need to have plenty of time in advance of the scheduled date to work on the project. Six months or more lead time is a good rule of thumb for larger affairs (Allen, 1997; Ulin, 1997). Third, your event should be sufficiently unique or attractive to a large group of probable respondents. This requires that you have access to a lot of people who would truly consider taking part. Finally, your organization, or at least the issue on which you are working, must have strong credibility in the community. The members of the community have to know about you and your issue and care about your success.

Smaller events are obviously much easier to organize. However, even small events have the same four demands, just on a reduced, perhaps a much reduced, scale.

There's no doubt about it. Events require creativity, attention, and hard work. They can drain an organization's resources, deflect from its primary work, and set members up for disappointment. They can also energize and excite members, provide a clear set of activities for members with the promise of tangible results, provide a vehicle for attracting new members, help communicate your organization's presence and work to the community, and raise money to boot.

Remember to collect names, addresses, and phone numbers of those attending each event. These names can be added to your contributor or support list, which you may resolicit for future income (Klein, 1992).

Ticket Events

Paying, usually in advance, to attend something a little bit out of the ordinary is the essence of this approach. Contributors don't have to do anything but be there. Food and entertainment are the common features of these fund-raising events. Dinners, plays, concerts, famous and semifamous speakers—all are used as ticket events.

This is another area in which competition and costs are increasing. Some communities have literally hundreds of these events per year, and it is not surprising to have costs run up to 80% of your total take (Freedman, 1996).

This fund-raising method requires some sort of drawing card, some enticement for people to add yet another activity to their day-to-day routine. Not only are people asked to put something else on their schedule, they are asked to pay to do this as well. They need to buy a ticket.

There are two important elements for success. First, select a drawing card that is sufficiently interesting to prospective contributors. This may include the other people in attendance. People may not want to miss an important social occasion that all the "right" people attend. It's fair to say that socializing is the main event at a major benefit (Brentlinger & Weiss, 1987). The more out of the ordinary your request, the more special it should be. For example, coming up with something to lure people out on a Tuesday night is more challenging than getting people to eat a midweek lunch.

The second necessary component involves selling all those tickets by setting the right price for the event and getting those tickets into the hands of contributors and getting the money out of their pockets. Although tickets are frequently sold at the door, it is the advance ticket sales that normally determine your success.

Tips

• Don't count on your drawing card to sell most of the tickets. Ticket sellers usually sell far more tickets than the event itself would.

• Get a *very* detail-oriented event manager to coordinate the work (Allen, 1997; Ulin, 1997).

• Consider getting corporate sponsorship to underwrite the event, but recognize that sponsors need benefits such as visibility or high-end clients attending the event (Freedman, 1996; Ulin, 1997).

• Promote your event to groups and individuals most likely to attend. A good invitation list is essential. Any advance publicity about the event is helpful. Figure out how your drawing card is newsworthy. Fliers, mailings, telephoning, and newspaper notices should be used. The strategy here is to keep the event in the public eye and build a sense of anticipation (Brentlinger & Weiss, 1987; Ulin, 1997). This is particularly important for major events.

• Make it easy for contributors to buy a ticket even if no one asks them to purchase a ticket. Have a phone number they can call, an order blank they can fill out, or some other way of getting in touch with you.

• Ticket sellers should be grouped into teams of five, with team leaders. Team leaders check weekly on team members' progress. This need not and should not be heavy-handed. Each member should expect to be contacted about progress. Team leaders need to follow through.

• Team competitions motivate ticket sellers, and especially team leaders. You'll be surprised to learn how important it is for some sellers to get "credit" for a sale. Winning teams should get some prize or recognition.

• Provide other incentives for ticket sellers. One free ticket for every ten sold is often a good idea, especially since not all ticket purchasers will show up anyway.

• Depending on their financial wherewithal, consider having ticket sellers buy whatever they do not sell.

• People often buy tickets mainly to please the ticket seller. The nature of the event and the cause are important, but the ticket buyer's relationship with the ticket seller or the organization the seller represents is usually more important.

• Encourage some people to buy a block of tickets, not just one. For example, business people sometimes buy an entire table of tickets for a dinner event, giving seats to employees or clients.

• Send "save the date cards," a notice mailed as much as six months in advance, to prospective patrons. Their purpose is as much to stake a claim to the community's attention as it is to reserve a spot on the calendar (Brentlinger & Weiss, 1987).

- Whenever possible, get news coverage of your event. You will have to determine some newsworthy angle that will attract coverage. Remember, your event can give more than money. Milk it for all that it's worth.

- Get meaningful donated items to be used as door prizes and include a mention of these on printed tickets and in your promotions. A weekend for two at a nice resort is a good door prize.

- Publicly, formally, and clearly recognize all volunteers who made the event a success. This includes acknowledgments in the event program, a personal letter, and mention to the audience on the day of the event.

- Prepare and follow a checklist of things to be done. This requires advance planning. Have a checklist for things you need to do in the months, weeks, and days leading up to the event. One organization has a 101-point checklist for one of its major events, including everything from developing the planning committee to checking the room temperature on the day of the event. The length of your checklist will relate to the size and complexity of your event (Allen, 1997; Brentlinger & Weiss, 1987; Ulin, 1997).

- Do what you can to keep your expenses down. The lower your costs, the higher your return. Know what all your expenses are, and find ways to reduce them. Shopping around will lead you to bargains. One caution: Don't look cheap and tacky. A fancy, high-class event should look and feel that way.

- Using celebrities may be a good idea for your event. Many celebrities will waive their appearance fee if they believe strongly in the issue. They will also attract immediate attention to your organization and issue. Be careful of hidden costs, however. Airline tickets, hotel rooms, and fees to members of the celebrity's entourage can be very expensive. Make sure you know all the costs in advance (Fisch, 1989a; Freedman, 1996).

- Many people who buy tickets to the event don't show up. This varies with the type of event. It is not uncommon to have a third of the ticket purchasers absent. It is acceptable to oversell the event. It will probably make you nervous, but go ahead and do it anyway.

Registration Events

These events are similar to ticket events, except that the contributor is asked to do more than just attend. The contributor pays to become a participant, not just an attendee. Such events usually provide some benefit that lasts beyond the event or the opportunity to engage in an enjoyable activity. Workshops, conferences, and seminars are examples of the first type. Bicycle tours, fun runs, and golf tournaments are examples of the second.

Registration events are commonly targeted to a specific group such as counselors, day-care operators, golfers, subatomic nuclear physicists, and other everyday people. This makes it somewhat easier to select an attractive activity. The challenge is to design the activity in such a way that it stirs interest and effectively meets expectations.

Registration events have a further benefit in that they capitalize on what people do anyway. Professionals attend conferences as part of their work routine, golfers golf, and runners run. Registration events don't ask people to do much out of the ordinary or add much to a busy schedule.

You won't have to go through all the bother of selling tickets, but you will have to promote registrations. Except for the ticket-selling process, registration events require about the same things as ticket events. You need to promote the event, do advance planning, make a checklist, and keep your costs down. Because registration events deal with a narrower potential contributor group, they are often a little more manageable.

Tips

• Most registrations will come in during the week prior to the event. Don't sit back and wait for this to happen, but don't get panicky too early and call off the event.

• Figure out in advance how to make the event look and feel successful even if you only get half the registrations you expect. How you arrange seating in a room and how you design where people congregate at the beginning of the event are two ways to do this.

• Make sure you have direct access to your target group and involve them in planning the event. You shouldn't try to attract librarians if no one in your group has ever shelved a book; don't try to involve basketball players if you all think Magic Johnson is famous for card tricks.

• For conferences, you can make money by renting space to vendors who hope to sell products or services to those who attend.

• If your event involves something measurable, ask participants to "sell" pledges or sponsorships. Participants ask their friends, neighbors, and innocent passers-by to contribute a certain amount, say 50 cents or $5, for every run scored, every mile run, or every basket made. Sponsors can also contribute a flat dollar amount. This can be as high or low as they please. Participants who bring in a certain amount in pledges above the entrance fee may have the fee reduced or eliminated.

• Send a letter to prospective participants. Enclose with this letter two sponsor sheets for the participant to fill out. The reason for sending two is that the participant may need more than one if he or she fills the first sheet with sponsors. If the participant does not need the second sheet, suggest that it be given to a friend (Petersen, 1979).

• Understand that you'll need to devise a simple money collecting mechanism and that not all those who have pledged will make good on their promises.

• Send a thank-you letter acknowledging your receipt of the registration fee.

• Provide participants with some mementos of their involvement. Baseball caps, T-shirts, and pens printed with the name of the event are good souvenirs. These can serve as enticements as well.

• Get high-profile people to take part in your event. Featured speakers, local elected officials, or local athletes can serve this purpose.

Events Coordinated by Other Groups

Many groups hold activities for their members that serve as fund-raisers for community service activities. This often involves something like an athletic tournament, a barbecue, or some modest entertainment. The sponsoring organization will usually split the proceeds with you. They do most of the work, and the event is directed to their members. The community service orientation of the organization is fulfilled in a way that gives their members something enjoyable to do.

Tips

• Get out your list of local clubs and organizations and send a letter to each group on the list whose assistance you would want. The letter should include examples of things the group could do to benefit your organization and how the two of you would work together. Follow up the letter with phone calls to the organizations most likely to respond.

• Have clear, written agreements about what each of you will do and how money is to be collected and divided. Keep this simple; after all, they are doing you a favor.

• Unless the sponsoring group has a well-established community activity they do as a community service fund-raiser, you should shy away from events that go beyond the membership of the sponsoring group. These are usually pretty small-scale events and are best kept that way by having the sponsoring group work with the people and the activity they know best.

Promotions

Take advantage of what is going on in your community. Is there a grand opening about to happen? Is the attendance at the movie theater down during the middle of the week? Can you help the local nine attract more fans to the ballpark?

Businesses are now linking with nonprofits on cause-related marketing, tying the business with the issue the organization is working on. This usually benefits more established and less controversial organizations, but check to see if such a partnership is possible for your group (Goldstein, 1993; Sinnock, 1995).

Often businesses will include an organization in a special promotion to boost their product and their image in the community. This usually involves your organization getting a percentage of the sales; for example, 25 cents from every Morty's Mega Monster Burger sold today will go to your organization.

Tips

- Prepare in advance to describe your ideas to the sponsoring business or organization and be able to show how both parties can benefit.
- Go to your Chamber of Commerce and ask them about any grand openings or other special events businesses are scheduling.
- Watch for new construction of business and commercial complexes and talk with the owners.
- Keep the type and amount of work you do reasonable compared to what you are likely to gain and consistent with your own organizational goals and image. After all, you want to be seen as more than a hawker of Morty's Megas.
- Periodically send a letter and follow up with selected phone calls to likely sources. They may not bite the first time, so give them other opportunities to think about a mutual project.
- Don't be pushy or demanding or riddle prospective partners with guilt.

Nonevents

As a variation on the direct-mail and registration event approaches, some organizations find that asking people *not* to do something works well. Using a lighthearted approach, contributors are told they can participate in an event without having to do anything, without even having to leave their homes.

A nonrun for people who hate jogging, a stay-at-home tea for people who just can't get the hang of holding a tea cup with their pinky just so, or a don't-weed-the-garden Saturday can hold a lot of appeal.

You act as if this were a real event, but, of course, no "participant" has to do anything. Registrants should receive something to acknowledge their involvement. A packet of flower seeds or a tea bag can be enclosed with the original letter. Or a T-shirt claiming that the wearer definitely did NOT run on the hottest day of the year can be sent to those who send in the registration fee.

Tips

- Hold the nonevent at the same time every year.
- Do some buildup. As the time approaches, let people know that the nonevent is coming up so they can plan not to take part.
- Send humorous thank-you letters with your receipt of the registration fee or contribution.
- Have fun!

Sales

Selling a service or a product is a pretty standard way of raising relatively small amounts of cash. Bake sales, car washes, and yard sales are the most frequently seen examples of this approach. Each of these could be the subject of a booklet describing "How to hold a successful _____ ." There are a variety of little tricks that can increase your profits.

Nonetheless, the basic notion is to put as good a product or service in front of as many people who are likely to spend money on it as possible.

So, if you're holding a yard sale, begin collecting items early from as many sources as possible to make sure you have a lot of good things to sell. Hold your yard sale at a house in an affluent neighborhood. (Yard sale junkies are inclined to shop where they think rich folks are getting rid of some good stuff, cheap.) If it's a bake sale you're holding, make sure you have a variety of goodies at a range of prices. Then select a spot where people who have the munchies are likely to pass by. Outside the college cafeteria or right outside the church or temple after services are good bets. If it's cars you wish to clean, try to corner the busiest intersection in town.

Selling products made especially for you (for example, T-shirts or baseball caps) is a little trickier. You usually have some initial investment to make, or you get a small percentage of the overall price of the object. If you think you can sell a lot of these, it may be worth doing. Your best tack is to sell items on a variety of occasions to a captive audience of potential supporters. Rallies, conferences, and other special events provide captive audiences.

Sales of candy and nuts and other dentists' delights also require a high volume to make a profit. Items that sell for a dollar or less make it easy for someone to "contribute" to the organization and get something in return.

Organizations that have a lot of kids have, along with them, immediate customers—the kids' relatives. Kids are usually more willing than adults to go to neighbors or to stand in front of the local grocery store to sell their goods.

Because success requires a lot of people selling a lot, a lot of organization is required as well. Sales teams with team captains and clear accounting methods to keep track of the product and the money are essential. The companies that provide the products can usually instruct you on how to set up your promotion and keep track of your sales.

Holding an auction is another method of sales. You have to spend time and energy locating quality donated items for sale, promote the auction effectively to attract a good number of buyers, and then conduct the actual auction so it runs smoothly and gets you as much per item as possible. This includes selecting the best order for auctioning the items, holding an auction preview, and preparing a program. A professional auctioneer is generally well worth the money for the directions he or she can provide as well as his or her skill in working the buyers. Some auctioneers will volunteer their services for nonprofit organizations. Many professional auctioneers are members of the National Auctioneers Association. Contact that organization's local chapter for help in obtaining the services of an auctioneer. Before you hold an auction, attend a few on your own to see how, and how well, they work.

If an auction doesn't suit your fancy, how about selling pizza? Occasionally you will be able to find a restaurant or stadium concession that will let you have a large share of the receipts in exchange for providing workers. You may not make a lot of money, but this is quick and easy. About all you have to do is schedule some of the members of your organization to show up to work and make sure they do it. The work usually involves working the cash register, waiting on tables, or bussing tables. You don't have to do the cooking.

Although you may be able to use this method on a routine basis, say once a month, make sure more than enough of your members are willing to work before you agree. People can quickly get tired of this duty, so it is generally better to make this a fun, special occasion.

Other sales approaches such as bingo or opening your own thrift store are potential money-makers. They require a tremendous amount of commitment on the part of your organization. A thorough explanation of undertakings such as these requires much more space than I have here. To find out more about them, talk with someone who manages such an enterprise for an organization.

Generally speaking, the smaller or younger your organization, the more likely you will benefit from a project that is short term and involves selling a product or service you have readily at hand. What you choose to sell and how you choose to sell it are limited only by your creativity, the resources you have to put into the effort, and, of course, the legal restrictions you may face.

Planned Giving

Much of the information on planned giving is drawn from the Nonprofit Counsel (1986) and Moerschbaecher and Dryburgh (1997). The concept of planned giving means a gift that is of sufficient magnitude that making it is integrated with the donor's personal financial plan or estate plan. The way the gift is made is designed to benefit both the giver and the receiver. Obviously, gifts of this type come from the more well-to-do. This method of developing an organization's resources is on the rise and can provide tremendous financial stability for formal organizations.

Generally, planned giving has been seen as an avenue only for older and larger organizations. Experts are now saying that every formal organization, no matter how small or how new, should have a planned giving program.

What does such a gift look like? Probably the most common is a bequest in a will. However, the gift can take on many forms such as trusts, pooled income funds, or other mechanisms designed to increase both the ease of making contributions and their value. Some of these methods will provide income to your organization soon, whereas others will have an impact many years down the road.

This all sounds pretty technical, doesn't it? Well, it is. That is why you should seek the assistance of an attorney, a bank trust officer, an accountant, or another professional knowledgeable about planned giving if you intend to pursue this approach.

The income potential of a planned giving program is huge, but confusion over how to get started causes many organizations to ignore this approach altogether. It is also a source of conflict and tension between the staff of an organization and those whose job it is to court wealthy donors. A clear understanding of the role planned giving can play within an organization, even a small organization, should be developed before you pursue this option. If you can afford to ignore thousands and thousands of dollars, you can disregard this source of support. However, if you have an incorporated organization that plans to be around for a while, you'll probably want to see how you can get some of these gifts directed your way.

Looking in Nooks and Crannies

A broad range of options for relieving your money woes should be explored. Did you know that placing coin collection canisters by the cash registers of 100 restaurants can bring you $20,000 a year? Or that you can easily make $75 just by having 20 members of your organization save aluminum cans for about a month? Hard work, isn't it?

How about pennies? There are untold creative ways for collecting pennies. A local bank might sponsor a "bring us your pennies" week on behalf of your organization (Goldstein, 1993). Or, you might have a radio station promote a penny week. Maybe a "collect the mayor's weight in pennies" drive, or a "mile of pennies" promotion (that would be 84,480 pennies). You can dream up all sorts of ideas. Besides all the pennies you get (which, of course, do turn into dollars), you can get tremendous publicity, lots of dimes and quarters, and, yes, even dollars from people who want to support your creative cause (Lynn & Lynn, 1992).

Look for every chance you can to raise money. If pursuing a particular opportunity does not distract you from your main purpose, take advantage of it. Some things should become routine, second nature. Every one of your newsletters should include a way for people to give you money. Many a community presentation will provide you with an opening to ask for financial help. Make use of it. As you incorporate this perspective in your continued efforts to strengthen your organization, you will worry less and be able to spend more.

Securing Funds from Public and Private Organizations

You now have a pretty good idea of how you can get money from individuals. If you want to consider all the options, where else can you look? Getting money from other groups and organizations, including the government, is another potentially valuable approach. This involves negotiating an intervening process, which serves as a kind of barrier or filter between you and the people who make the decisions. Almost every potential funding organization has some process you must follow.

This means at least two things to you. First, understand the procedures for each particular funding source and follow them well. Second, understand that, even with this approach, it is people, acting as individuals or as a group, who make the final decisions. Their decisions will be based on objective reasoning as well as a variety of other influences. Get to know the funding procedures and get to know the people as well as you can.

The process for approaching funding organizations for money has many similarities to the way you approach individuals. First, *identify* prospective sources of funds and then *target* those that are most likely. Second, *establish contact* and *nurture* prospective sources. Third, *prepare* and *submit* a *written proposal* to the funding source, and *follow up* on that submission. Fourth, *prepare* and *offer* a *verbal presentation* to the funding source, and follow up on that presentation. (Though this step is not always required, it is helpful to be prepared.) Fifth, *say thank-you* and nurture future relationships.

Identifying Prospective Sources

Increasing your awareness of all the possible sources of funds is an ongoing process. First of all, look at groups whose interests or goals are compatible with yours. Next, consider professional groups that may be interested in your concerns. Third, find out all you can on community service groups and their funding priorities. Following this, think about the businesses and corporations that serve your area. Federated funding programs, such as the United Way, would be the fifth set of potential contributors. Foundations are another possible source to consider. Finally, get to know how the various levels of government can be involved in funding your operation.

Spend some time brainstorming the possibilities. Then make some educated guesses on what your best bets are. Follow that with some research on the sources you consider most likely. After that, keep your eyes and ears open to other possibilities. You may discover something that changes a low-ranked source into a suddenly hot prospect. Maybe your best friend's brother just got elected chair to a wealthy community service organization. Maybe the county government just received a federal grant to fund organizations such as yours. Things change. Be aware, and be flexible. This will provide you with a lot of opportunities.

It is helpful to know a little more about each type of funding source, from those whose processes are likely to be informal to those whose procedures are increasingly formalized. The more formal and large the funding source is, the more formal and complex their process is likely to be; also, the more likely they will be to fund formal, incorporated organizations. Smaller, local funding sources tend to be more flexible.

Like-Minded Groups

These are groups that share values similar to yours. They may well be promoting an issue that is similar to yours. Groups that see themselves as working on the same issue, trying to mobilize or influence the same constituency, will also see themselves in competition with you. If this is the case, they will probably be more interested in protecting their turf than in giving you money. However, groups that have a related political or

Change Agent Tip

The Internet is already a helpful aid to your fund-raising efforts and may become even more so. Certainly the information you may get to help you discover sources of funds or learn more about fund-raising can be very helpful. A few sites suggested by Morth and Collins (1996), Robinson (1996), and Lewis (1997) might be worth exploring:

The Foundation Center (*fdncenter.org*) has a wealth of resources on how to write proposals, a directory of grant makers on the Internet, and links to many other valuable sites. You also get connected to the *Philanthropy News Digest.*

The Grantsmanship Center (*www.tgci.com*) provides the current day's grant announcements from the Federal Register and has links to grant-making organizations. Also, the full text of the *Grantsmanship Center Magazine* is provided.

The National Society of Fund Raising Executives (*www.nsfre.org*) offers information about the soci-

ety and has links to other fund-raising sites. This is another extremely helpful organization.

The Catalogue of Federal and Domestic Assistance, available at the General Services Web site (*www.gsa.gov.fdac*), lists sources of federal funds.

You can also go to your search engine and click on "grants."

The National Network of Grantmakers (NNG) publishes the *Grantmakers Directory* (1998), a periodically updated list of over 160 funders of social and economic justice work and 20 foundation resource organizations. It is extensively indexed with useful information on each source. You can contact NNG at *www.nng.org* or (619) 231-1348.

There are several directories and databases available on CD-ROM, though these can be pretty expensive. Check your public library to see if they have any that you can use, especially FC Search.

Fund-raisers are still not quite sure how to use the Internet to get to donors directly, but they are working

on it. (Check the sites listed here to see what seems to be working.) Some are putting donation forms on-line. Others are using them for silent auctions. Still others use their Web sites to promote events. And some organizations are linking with corporations as the sponsored cause of the corporation, using the company's Web site to help them reach an audience and raise funds. Certainly this medium will help organizations connect with a new generation of givers, and some experts think the interactive potential of the Internet will increase donor affiliation with organizations (Hall, 1996; Moore, 1995; Sinnock, 1995; Warwick, 1994).

Using the Web can be another way for you to get across the message of your issue and your work. You can offer those who contact your site a number of ways to support the effort, one of which is contributing money. Your presence on the Web and your invitations for support can assist the other fund-raising efforts you undertake.

issues agenda may welcome another group into the playing field by making a contribution to get you going or to help with a special need.

The process is likely to be informal, usually

involving your making a direct request to the group during one of their meetings. Ask for a specific amount for a clearly identified purpose, and show how their contribution promotes your

Understanding the Terminology of Funding

Knowing the common language of the funding process is important. Here is a brief overview of the terms you are likely to hear.

An **RFP** is a **request for a proposal.** This means that if a funding source, often some branch of government, is sending out an RFP, it is seeking proposals from community groups to provide a particular service. Often, your proposal will be in response to an RFP.

Matching funds are dollars given to an organization if it can come up with some additional dollars elsewhere. Often, the match is expressed in terms of a ratio. For example, a three-to-one match means that for every dollar you raise elsewhere, the funding source will give you three dollars. So, if you raise $250, the source would give you $750, for a total of $1,000. There are frequently minimum and maximum limits on matching funds.

Pilot programs and **demonstration projects** are somewhat experimental. Usually, a funding source will give you money for just a couple of years to get the program up and running. The premise is that if the program has merit, other funding sources will pick up the tab after the initial funding

has run out. It may also be intended that the program be used as a model for others to follow.

The **funding cycle** is the time during which a funding source accepts new proposals and awards grants. Different funding sources have different funding cycles.

A **fiscal year** is a budget year. It describes a 12-month period during which money is spent on an organization's program. Different funding sources use different fiscal years. Some follow the normal calendar year, beginning January 1st and ending December 31st. Another common fiscal year, one often used by state and local governments, begins July 1st and ends on June 30th. The federal government's fiscal year runs from October 1st through September 30th. As you can see, receiving funds from various sources that use different fiscal years can create some complications for your organization.

When a government funding source decides to award a **grant** to another organization to provide funds to enable the receiving organization to perform a specified set of functions for an agreed-upon dollar amount, it usually formalizes the relationship through a **purchase of service agreement** or **contract.** This contract sets forth the terms of the

relationship, including the nature and extent of the services the receiving agency will perform, the amount of funding the purchase agency will provide, and a schedule of payments.

If your organization is incorporated and pays staff, you may want to prepare a **case statement,** a centralization or documentation of all information describing your organization: needs, goals, objectives, strategies and tasks, staff, facilities, budget, institution plans, financial history, and staff competence to serve the mission or the cause the organization represents. It is a database.

This is a massive document, requiring many hours of staff and volunteer time. Aside from its helpfulness in organizational management, it is an essential tool for seeking large contributions, especially from corporations. If your organization is not pursuing this type of major funding, your time is probably better spent doing something else. Putting together a good case statement requires a lot of work. Do it when it is worth all the effort.

These are the basic terms to know, though you will hear others from time to time. You will develop a greater mastery of the vocabulary with experience.

mutual concerns. Do your homework before the meeting by getting to know a member or members of this group. Find out how much the group would be willing to give. Ask for an amount in that range when you make your pitch.

Though the contribution is likely to be modest, rarely over $250, this can be an important step in fostering alliances that will be helpful down the road. Be willing to return the favor to other groups when your ability to help out is developed.

Professional Groups and Associations

These organizations exist to promote the interests and the issues relevant to a particular profession. Dentists, nurses, accountants, social workers, and turkey farmers all have professional organizations. Many of these will have local chapters in your area. Some of the things you are working on will be a natural for two or three of these groups to support. If you are developing a program to assist victims of AIDS and their families, for example, check to see if any of these groups have expressed a particular interest in this topic. These would be the first groups to approach.

These organizations exist to serve the issues of concern to the profession, the image of the profession in the community, and the self-interests of the members of the profession. If your request can reinforce the group's issues, its image, or the self-interest of its members (ideally all three), you can reinforce your chance for a favorable response.

Professional associations normally want you to put your request in writing. Most often this works to justify to their membership any support given to you. The decision to give you money will probably be based more on your initial discussions and verbal presentation than on your written proposal. The organization's local board or steering committee will hear your request. Try to get a commitment from them at that time. A delayed decision or one routed through their committee structure may mean that enthusiasm for your request is lacking. This may be a signal for you to develop more support.

The amount of money you receive will probably be less than $500. Even associations of the wealthier professions don't often give more. Again, check beforehand to determine how high you can realistically make your request.

There are exceptions to this. Some organizations see their support of community efforts as a routine function. Where this is the case, you may receive more money. However, the process is likely to be more complex, with your written request carrying more weight.

Community Service Clubs and Organizations

These clubs and organizations, such as the Lions or the Soroptimists, are formed to give their members status, opportunities for socialization, a mechanism for providing service to the community, and recognition for that service. Take these factors into account when approaching service organizations.

Most of these groups have a pretty well-defined area of interest, and the recipients of their help must be seen as worthy of support. Therefore, children, the physically challenged, or those struggling to overcome serious obstacles may be favored. Getting the support of the organization's leadership beforehand will smooth the way. A well-prepared, factual, and emotional presentation will play an important part. It is sometimes helpful to make a purely informational presentation to the general membership that spurs interest several months before you make any request for money.

These groups will give by taking on something as a project, making a modest one-time contribution, or by "passing the hat" at a meeting, usually a breakfast or luncheon. If your request clearly falls within the group's special project interests, you may be able to receive up to a few thousand dollars. If not, don't count on more than $200.

A particular set of community service groups have raising and dispensing money as one of their main purposes, if not their primary purpose. Chief among these is the Junior

League. Other groups that are unique to a particular community serve this function as well. These organizations follow a fairly structured funding process. Their grants can range into the tens of thousands of dollars.

Businesses and Corporations

Larger corporations that are major employers in your community will almost always contribute to the community in the form of donations. Smaller businesses frequently will as well. Corporate giving is big business. In 1993, corporations contributed $5.25 billion to charitable causes (Hodgkinson & Weitzman, 1996a, p. 119). Providing funds to support community efforts demonstrates social responsibility and is good business practice as well. *The Corporate Giving Directory* and the *National Directory of Corporate Giving* are two excellent resources for identifying corporations that contribute money. Information about the corporation, its funding priorities, and the number of dollars it contributes is provided. A contact person for each source is identified as well.

Strategic philanthropy, a term coined more than 20 years ago by Nina Kaiden Wright, describes an approach corporations use to evaluate the most effective way to spend their donations (McKay, 1988). The intent is to promote the corporation that promotes the community project. John L. Mason, president of the Monsanto Fund, uses the phrase "investing for results." Those responsible for fund investments must be able to demonstrate that the fund supports the objectives of the corporation (Mason, 1988). Contributions are often tied to corporate marketing strategies, with many donation dollars coming from marketing budgets (Hunt, 1986; Picker, 1997). Some observers characterize corporate giving as enlightened self-interest, a belief that contributions benefit the businesses in the long run by promoting a healthier community and business climate (Picker, 1997; Zippay, 1992).

Corporations usually have special priority areas (for example, hunger or education) and they tend to target their contributions to projects that address their priority interests. Often, the chief executive officers or members of corporate allocations committees determine funding priorities based on their personal interests and social contacts (Zippay, 1992).

Another important concern is geographic (Morth & Collins, 1996; Picker, 1997). Corporations with large numbers of employees in regional offices or plant locations throughout the country tend to target their giving in local areas (Webb, 1982). Remember to mention any volunteer support your organization receives from the company's employees (Breiteneicher & Hohler, 1993). Mason (1988) says that geographic considerations are their first priority: "We seek projects that involve the communities, large and small, where Monsanto operates" (p. 380).

The larger the business and the more distant the ownership from the community, the more complex the sequence of activities to secure funding is likely to be. The reverse of this is true as well. The smaller the business or closer to the community the ownership, the simpler your request can be. This includes, believe it or not, just walking in and asking.

Newspapers in many communities publish an annual list of the largest employers in the area, with a description of the company and the names of the chief executives. This is an excellent source of likely prospects. If your newspaper does not have such a list, check with your Chamber of Commerce.

Your case statement will serve you well in approaching businesses, particularly large ones. A large request should be based on a well-thought-out strategy. Identifying and wooing the right corporate officer with the right people is a must. This is an aboveboard process that promotes donor understanding and involvement with your organization and its request. Whenever possible, schedule a personal, face-to-face meeting. Chances of receiving funding are estimated to increase by 70% if a proposal is preceded by personal contacts (Picker, 1997).

Recognize the potential benefits important to the contributing corporation (Breiteneicher

& Hohler, 1993; Morth & Collins, 1996). Strengthening its ties to the community is a major consideration. Explore the tax advantages to the corporation as well. Though this is normally not the compelling reason for the contribution, particularly from small businesses, tax benefits can add to its attractiveness. Be aware that some donors are insulted by the implication that tax write-offs are their only concern. Also, understand that the paperwork necessary for the business to get some tax breaks may not be worth the trouble.

Employee matching programs can be a valuable source of funds for your organization. In these programs the company matches gifts given to you by their employees (Picker, 1997). Ask each contributor if his or her company has such a program. Don't assume that the contributor has thought of this.

The number of nonprofit organizations competing for corporate dollars will undoubtedly increase. The organization that does its "homework" properly—research, cultivation, and planning the best approach—will be the one that gets its share (Webb, 1982).

Federated Funding Programs

Federated financing refers to campaigns conducted by one agency for others. Usually, the fund-raising group is itself a nonprofit agency or an arm of another body such as a corporation (Mirkin, 1978). Federated campaign organizations commonly have four functions. First, they develop membership from participating agencies. This involves screening new applicants as well as monitoring current members to assess the appropriateness of their continued involvement. Second, they raise money for their members through a combined appeal. Third, they assess a range of community needs. Fourth, they allocate funds to their members based ostensibly on the determination of community needs and the members' ability to meet them.

Catholic Charities, Federation of Protestant Welfare Agencies, and United Jewish Appeal are some well-known federated campaign organizations. The largest and best-known federated campaign in the United States is the United Way of America, parent organization of local United Funds. It has been in existence since 1887 and operates in many communities throughout the United States.

Because of the tremendous amount of money and publicity it generates, the United Way demands your attention. It funds formally incorporated agencies with strong community support, political clout, and a decent track record. It may be difficult for new members to break into the United Way club. The same agencies tend to receive funding year after year. Older, more traditional agencies that don't rock the political boat are favored. Your development of a program within such an agency may give you access to United Way dollars. This may help you get your foot in the door.

Receiving United Way dollars usually means accepting some limitations. Pursuing other sources of funding (for example, approaching corporations) may be restricted. You may also be prohibited from soliciting funds from the community during the months of the United Way campaign. An agency's appeal in the community and its consequent ability to help the United Way attract funds may be an important reason for its inclusion in United Way membership. Therefore, agencies that become controversial give United Way executives headaches, and they may find themselves outside the club. Think about this before you apply for membership.

The United Way has a very formal process, including submission of a written proposal and a verbal presentation, sometimes two. Get as many members of your agency's board as you can to attend these presentations. Those individuals who make funding decisions like to see clear demonstrations of board involvement and support.

Begin building social relationships between members of your organization and volunteer members of the United Way Planning and Allocations Committee. Though you should properly stay within the prescribed process when making a request for funds, it doesn't hurt

Change Agent Tip

One of the most helpful organizations to assist your fund-raising efforts is the Foundation Center. The Foundation Center offers a huge amount of information through more than 200 Cooperating Collections throughout the country, at least one in every state. These collections are housed in public libraries, and in addition to providing a wealth of resources, they provide excellent guidance to assist your efforts. Here's a list of what you can find in their Cooperating Collections. (Contact your local library to see which Cooperating Collection is nearest you.)

- Reference librarians experienced in finding information on funding sources
- Free orientations to the collection
- Copying facilities for a nominal charge

- Copies of Foundation Center publications, plus other directories of funding sources, newsletters, fund-raising journals, guides to fund-raising and grant writing, program planning, nonprofit management, and almost anything else short of the exact combination to the bank vault
- Foundation and corporate annual reports, press clippings, and application guidelines
- On-line bibliographic database (*fdncenter.org/lnps/index.html.*) of about 15,000 listings, many with abstracts of books and articles relating to philanthropy
- FC Search, the Foundation Center's database on CD-ROM

I believe FC Search, the Foundation Center's database

on CD-ROM, to be the Crown Jewel. This database covers more than 45,000 U.S. foundations and corporate givers, includes descriptions of almost 200,000 associated grants, and lists over 183,000 trustees, officers, and donors. This is a very easy-to-use tool that will help you customize your search, and a well-targeted search is the key to grant seeking. Even first-time grant seekers will easily figure out how to use this database to narrow the search to the likeliest prospects. And remember, there is a reference librarian there especially to help you!

This is a *fantastic* resource. If you are looking for grant funding, you just have to check this out!

You can also reach the Foundation Center and its links to other sites at its Web site (*http://fdncenter.org*).

to have people who like you making the decisions. Few awards from the United Way fall below $1,000, and typically they are several times that amount.

Foundations

Foundations exist to give away money and promote certain interests. In 1993 the 37,571 U.S. foundations provided $11.11 billion in grants (Hodgkinson & Weitzman, 1996a, p. 106). You won't be the only one who knows this, so you are likely to face stiff competition.

Foundations most often target their giving to a specific geographic area, a particular issue, or some combination of both. The primary guide to foundations is the *Foundation Directory,* which lists the major foundations in each state. This directory is very comprehensive. It lists 7,960 foundations with at least $2 million in assets or $200,000 in annual giving, though this is fewer than one fifth of all active grant-making foundations in the United States (Tuller & Cantarella, 1997). It provides information on the amount of funds the foundation has, the average size of its grant award, the number of awards it gives, names of contact people, and other pertinent data.

A lot of homework on your part is essential prior to approaching any foundation. This point cannot be overstated. Using the *Foundation Directory* and other publications, computerized databases, and indexes in your library, you can narrow your search to perhaps a half-dozen foundations that make grants in your field and your geographic location (Pendleton, 1981; Robinson, 1996).

Foundations can be divided into five categories (Allen, 1981; Pendleton, 1981):

General purpose foundations. These are the particularly large and well-known foundations. They have a wide range of projects and operate with relatively few restrictions. Generally, they are interested in very large projects.

Special purpose foundations. These foundations restrict their funds to a geographic area or a specific field of interest.

Corporate or company foundations. These foundations are established by corporations or companies to handle most of the funds donated by the company. Some corporations donate funds through the corporation in addition to their corporate foundation. Also, many corporations will match an individual employee's contribution to a charity of the employee's choosing, but only if the employee brings it to the attention of the corporation by filing the proper forms.

Family foundations. These are usually small foundations under the control of the family that set them up. Their grants fall within their areas of personal interest. Many of the smaller family foundations are not included in published listings.

Community foundations. This type of foundation operates with many small funds centralized under community management. Grants are usually restricted to a particular geographic area. However, many of these local community foundations do have large assets and a broad range of interests. This makes them a good potential source for your community change effort.

Your approach to foundations starts by sending a letter of inquiry to each foundation on your target list. Express your interest and describe your organization, including a list of other groups that support you. Ask for more information on the foundation, including award procedures. After about two weeks, follow up your letter with a personal phone call. Always make personal contact unless you are explicitly told not to. You should quickly acknowledge receipt of any information from the foundation with a personal response.

The decision to make an award to you will generally be based on the strength of your proposal. Verbal presentations are not often required. Gifts range from hundreds to hundreds of thousands of dollars.

Public Funding

Government funding provides a good percentage of the budget of most social service agencies. Some private agencies are almost totally publicly funded. Though government agencies rarely give money to organizations that are not incorporated, small agencies and new programs in existing agencies do receive government funding.

"Government" really means governments. Your organization may work in an area that cuts across various city and county government lines. Each is a potential source of funds. These local governments sometimes combine to form a *council of governments,* which serves as a mechanism for funding community programs. State and federal governments are certainly potential sources of funds. So when I say *government,* the term does not refer to just one government body. Different layers or levels of government exist, each with its own organizational structure and procedures.

Strings are usually attached to public funding. The higher the level of government, the more and the stronger those strings may be. Some might be considered ropes. Some programs become addicted to government money and the resulting government control. They stop looking to other sources of funds from the communities they serve. This can turn into a bad habit. Think about it.

How do you get money from the government? Good question. The answer is complicated by all those various levels of government and the various programs each government operates. Still, a few guidelines should help point the way.

Get information.   Find out what funds various levels of government have to deal with social concerns such as yours. Discover through which mechanisms, departments, and programs they give this money.

For example, the federal government publishes the *Catalogue of Federal and Domestic Assistance,* which should be available in your public library. This describes federal programs approved to receive funding and for how much. This does not necessarily tell you if the particular programs actually were given the money for which they received approval, but it is a good start.

Every business day the federal government publishes the *Federal Register.* You can subscribe to this or trek on down to city hall or your library once a week to look at the latest issues. In these you will find the most splendid examples of bureaucratic jargon known to man, woman, or child. You will also find requests for proposals for a variety of projects. You will have to wade through pages of regulations to find those requests. After you have looked at this publication a time or two, you will understand how to read the publication and your wading will only take about 5 minutes.

The Commerce Business Daily is another federal publication that publishes requests for proposals. Occasionally, along with requests for military hardware and training Peace Corps volunteers in Honduras, you may find a request for a proposal that addresses your interests.

The most helpful process is to establish yourself with contact people within government funding agencies. Call them. These individuals know what is going on and can alert you to upcoming opportunities. Also, agency policy makers can help you discover money stashed in various bureaucratic hiding places and find ways to make this available to you. This could be done, for example, in the form of a highly specialized proposal request directed to your organization (Sladek, 1981).

If you don't know anyone in a particular government agency of interest to you, start with the community information or community relations department and go from there. Discover and make use of notification procedures used by government agencies. Get on a list to receive requests for proposals. Then start building those contacts.

Develop a rudimentary understanding of the budget, particularly the budgets of local governments. The more you know, the better. You don't have to drive yourself crazy, but do understand where and on what the money is intended to be spent. Review the most likely budget categories. This will give you some indication of how much money is available in your interest area. Also, you can use your agency contacts to find out if and how some of this money can be directed to support your organization's endeavors.

Get help.   Develop a relationship with politicians and their staffs. They are helpful in identifying possibilities and supporting your requests. Politicians who can get credit for delivering the goods to their constituencies have additional motivation.

Supportive administrative staff in government agencies can give you information and direction. Government operations should be public knowledge, so this will not compromise public service.

Get public attention directed to your issue. This will be helpful in making requests to state and local governments. One of the functions of government funding is to keep people quiet. Attracting community awareness and concern to your issue can attract government money as well. Another role of government is to promote and support helpful private efforts. If your organization becomes recognized as a valued community resource, government funding sources may be happy to show their investment in your mutual success.

Get involved in the budget-building process. Find out how the various departments of your state and local government participate in development of the budget, and work with them to include funding in the new budget to deal with your area of concern. It is easier to get money if it is there in the budget in the first place.

The submission of a formal proposal is usually part of the funding process. Get a well-written proposal describing an effective approach to addressing a recognized problem into the right hands on time. Don't be afraid to ask for guidance as you are preparing your proposal.

If money is available in the budget to respond to a recognized community need, if timely and valuable information regarding the funding process is given to you, if you have internal, political, and community support, and if you describe an effective approach in a well-written proposal, you will stand a good chance of getting government funding. Purposefully work to put all these elements in place.

Get to Know the People Involved

Regardless of the type of organization from which you are seeking funds, be it the federal government or the local PTA, you will be dealing with people. Establishing your relationship with individuals from the potential funding source is a critical step. You cannot overlook this. The personal relationship that develops might be the most important factor affecting funding (Webb, 1982).

Establish a good, friendly, and appropriately personal rapport with the individual or individuals who serve as your contacts within the funding sources you court (Schumacher, 1992). Follow his or her advice and direction. Ask questions. This gives the contact a little bit of a stake in your success.

Yes, politics is involved. The process isn't pure. Yes, it is often whom you know. Yes, people do help one another with favors. This isn't as seedy as it sounds, though. Frankly, most of us would rather work with someone we know, in whom we have confidence and trust. Grantors are no different.

Knowing your funding source means knowing the people at your funding source. Inside advocacy is a big part of the game. By spreading your network of personal contacts, you increase the chances you can win occasionally when you play.

Make use of opportunities to meet grant makers, and cultivate those relationships. Treat them as colleagues, do not act subservient. Some foundations or groups of foundations have a "Meet the Grants Makers" event. Take advantage of this. Also consider attending the National Network of Grantsmakers conference to get to know the people who may give you money (Robinson, 1996).

Proposal Writing

I have frequently referred to a written proposal. You have probably sensed that this item must be important. It is. Skill in proposal writing is a valuable asset in your organization's efforts to acquire money.

Your proposal is your record of what you want to do and how. It is the passkey to many a treasure vault. On many occasions, it will be the one element that gives all the others meaning. But it does not stand alone.

Once you have identified a possible funding source, then, to the extent possible, prepare that funding source to receive your proposal favorably. Next, clearly think through just what the program or activity you are describing in your proposal is intended to accomplish. After this, figure out just what you actually have to do to meet that goal; that is, effectively plan your activity or program, including its likely costs and evaluation procedures. These steps warrant a significant investment of time and creativity. What you write in your proposal is the product of this effort. Consequently, it is well worth your time to take this preparation phase seriously.

It is only when you have clarified these matters related to your purpose and approach that you actually sit down and write your proposal, following the guidelines provided to you by the funding source itself. You now need to organize the information and ideas you have in a way that is most meaningful to the funding source. Although each funding source will have its own preferred format and areas of emphasis, there are some pretty standard components to a proposal.

After the proposal is written, packaged in an attractive, easy-to-read manner, and submitted (on time!), you need to muster the appropriate support to reinforce its positive reception.

Written proposals vary in length according to the requirements of each funding source. In some cases, a written proposal of one page will suffice. In others, you may need more than 100 pages to provide all the information requested.

Your written proposal essentially responds to four questions.

- What problem are you trying to resolve?
- How do you intend to solve this problem?
- How much will this cost?
- How can you tell if your program works?

These four questions can be broken down into as many as 15 distinct proposal categories, which I describe next (Allen, 1981; Cavanaugh, 1980; Coley & Scheinberg, 1990; Decker & Decker, 1978; Geever & McNeill, 1997; Golden, 1997; Long, 1979; Mitiguy, 1978; Morth & Collins, 1996; Pendleton, 1981; Picker, 1997; Robinson, 1996; Shellow & Stella, 1989).

The complexity of your proposal will be governed by your particular funding source. Though I am describing many categories, you may not need them all, or a few may be merged

into one category. Most funding sources provide a clear set of guidelines for you to follow in preparing your proposal. Do follow these *precisely* (Smith, 1989). One of the major reasons proposals are rejected is simply their failure to follow prescribed guidelines. There is no need to make your proposal more complicated than required, and doing so may work against you.

Your proposal may include some or all of these pieces.

- *Cover letter.* Keep this brief, rarely beyond one page. In this letter you tell the funding source who you are, what you intend to do, and why. This should be on your official letterhead and be signed by an officer of your organization.
- *Title page.* This states the title of the project, to whom it is being submitted, the date of submission, the name and address of the organization submitting the proposal, along with the name of a contact person (or proposal author) from the submitting organization.
- *Abstract or proposal summary.* This brief summary is one of the key elements of your proposal. In it you clearly and concisely describe your response to the four basic questions mentioned previously. In addition, tell the funding source a little bit more about your organization. To some extent, this is an expansion of your cover letter. Still, this should be kept short, no more than two pages, generally much shorter than that.
- *Introduction.* In this section describe your organization in more detail. The purpose here is to demonstrate your credibility as an organization capable of pursuing a project. You may also include particularly interesting aspects about your organization as they relate to the project you are proposing.
- *Problem statement.* In this section provide some background information on the problem you intend to address. You may describe how long the problem has persisted in your area, how this problem is manifested (symptoms), and other efforts that have been undertaken to solve it. Describe the range and

depth of the problem, both through your use of statistics and in narrative discussion. You want to communicate to the funding source that this is an important issue that demands attention.

• *Goals or proposed response.* Here you describe what needs to be done to address the situation or what long-range goals you seek. Do not describe your specific activities in this section; instead, clarify the broad accomplishments expected by your effort. You may also phrase this section in terms of solutions; that is, what broad solutions does this problem require?

• *Statements of objectives.* A program objective is a statement of a concrete, measurable result of your program within a specific length of time (Cavanaugh, 1980). These objects relate to your goals. You cannot be vague here, clarity is important.

• *Implementation or methodology.* In this category tell the funding source exactly what you will do, and when, to accomplish your objectives. Tell the funding source how you will use your resources, including facilities, equipment, and personnel, to achieve your desired results.

• *Personnel involved.* The people who will be working on your project are important. Provide a brief background description (one paragraph will suffice) on each person who will have an active role in the project.

• *Budget.* The funding source needs to know on what you intend to spend the money you receive. Prepare a line-item budget reflecting the various expenses required to undertake this project. Often, the budget section lists other sources of revenue and indicates which expense or portion of expenses will be covered by the source from which you are seeking funds.

• *Budget narrative.* In this section briefly describe the expenses listed in the line-item budget. You may also provide a brief explanation or justification of the importance of these expenditures.

• *Future funding.* If your project involves more than a one-time activity, the funding source will probably want to know how you in-

tend to continue the project after this particular grant runs out. Commonly, funding sources provide money for a limited period of time. If they intend to make an investment, they will want to know that you are currently preparing to keep the program (and their investment) alive.

• *Monitoring.* It's important that you keep track of your activities to see that you are doing what you said you were going to do. In this section, clarify how you intend to keep tabs on your proposed activities.

• *Evaluation.* The funding source will want to know how you will go about determining whether or not you have met the stated goals, and why or why not. Show how you define "success" (Cavanaugh, 1980).

• *Appendixes or addenda.* Put any information in this section that does not fit into any other category but is still important for the funding source to know. This could include endorsement letters from other organizations or noteworthy individuals, the names and titles of members of your board of directors or other active community supporters, a letter from the Internal Revenue Service verifying your tax-exempt status, news clippings regarding your organization, affiliations with other organizations or other funding sources, and additional statistics or other supporting data.

Many organizations find it helpful to develop a boilerplate proposal, a standard proposal addressing all 15 proposal categories. This way you will be well prepared to respond to requests from potential funding sources. Do not merely send along your boilerplate proposal. It is simply a background document that will assist you in preparing a unique proposal to a particular identified funding source.

Tips

• Do your homework on prospective funding sources. This can never be said enough. At the very least know who the key players are, what the source is looking for, and how they want you to relate to them.

Take a Moment to Discover. . . . .

A proposal can have a number of elements. The complexity of a proposal is related to the complexity of the project for which funding is sought and the requirements of the funding source. The following list reviews seven different elements for a standard proposal. Put yourself in the place of a proposal evaluator. Critically look at each element of your proposal. Score each element from 1 (very poor) to 6 (superb). What would your total score be? What weaknesses did you discover? As it stands, would your proposal be funded?

Summary	Clearly and concisely summarizes the request
I. Introduction	Describes the agency's qualifications or "credibility"
II. Problem Statement or Needs Assessment	Documents the needs to be met or problems to be solved by the proposed funding
III. Objectives	Establishes the benefits of the funding in measurable terms
IV. Methods	Describes the activities to be employed to achieve the desired results
V. Evaluation	Presents a plan for determining the degree to which objectives are met and methods are followed
VI. Future or Other Necessary Funding	Describes a plan for continuation beyond the grant period and/or the availability of other resources necessary to implement the grant
VII. Budget	Clearly delineates costs to be met by the funding source and those to be provided by the applicant or other parties

Source: The Grantsmanship Center.

• •

• Brevity beats verbosity. Keep your writing short and to the point. If you are not sure if something belongs in your proposal, it probably does not. Proposals to corporate givers and small foundations are typically short.

• Write in a straightforward, person-to-person style. Remember, these are people reading your proposals, not computers. Use active voice.

• Send your letter directly to the proper person, and do double check the correct spelling of names. Do not send "To Whom It May Concern" or "Dear Sirs."

• Avoid jargon. Funding sources are more impressed with what you can do rather than how you can sling the lingo.

• Humanize the proposal. Let the voices of those who will benefit come through.

• The proposal summary is the first thing most reviewers look at. This is your key. Make it work.

• The title of your proposal should be clear and grab interest. Don't make it cute.

• Ask questions. If any part of the guidelines is unclear, no matter how small, be sure to ask for clarification so you know exactly what to do (Smith, 1989).

• Throughout your proposal, make sure you clearly demonstrate how your project effectively furthers the goals of the funding source. Your goals are important, but so are theirs.

• Point out the strengths of your organization, not just the needs it has.

• Avoid the common problems that lead to proposal rejection: not clearly identifying and substantiating a significant problem, and lack of clarity about how monies will be used for project activities. Other common problems include: methods do not suit the scope of the problem, no clear evaluation plan, objectives are not clearly measurable, and time schedule is unreasonable (Coley & Scheinberg, 1990).

• The proposal will be reviewed by several people, so don't make them tear apart some fancy binding to make copies. Most prefer that the pages of your proposal be clipped together. Some don't even like staples.

• Make sure your proposal is easy to read, with lots of white space and type not smaller than 12 point.

• Follow up. Do not sit around for weeks or months waiting for a reply. Unless you are instructed to do otherwise, contact the funding source about two weeks after you have delivered your proposal. Then ask when would be a good time to recontact. You want the funding source to know that you are taking the proposal seriously, but you do not want to be a pest. Also, this provides you with an opportunity to offer additional information that would be helpful in securing the grant or to clarify any misunderstanding. Further, this strengthens the personal relationship between you and your contact person at the granting organization. Strong personal relationships are often as important as strong proposals.

• Say thank-you (yes, again). Even if you do not get the grant, it is important to express your appreciation for having been considered for this grant. You do hope that you will have an opportunity to work together in the future. Your "thank-you" helps foster future opportunities regardless of the outcome of this particular proposal.

Verbal Presentation

Occasionally a verbal presentation may be required. Sometimes groups believe their work is done when the written proposal has been completed and submitted. They spend little time on the presentation figuring that "we know all this stuff, and anyway it's only a 15-minute presentation." After spending weeks writing a

proposal, some aren't willing to spend a couple of hours preparing a verbal presentation as compelling as possible. Then, again, some are.

Some presentations will occur before the proposal submission. These may provide you with an opportunity to receive an invitation to submit a proposal. Others follow upon delivery of your proposal. These presentations allow the grantors to meet with you and discuss the merits of your project.

Tips

• Use an interactive process. Ask and ask for questions. Two-way communication helps build a relationship and allows you to discover and respond to what the grantor is thinking.

• Anticipate objections, even draw them out. This gives you a chance to openly discuss whatever reservations may exist in the grantor's mind. If you don't do this, your side may never be clearly heard (Crompton, 1985).

• Know your program, what you intend to accomplish, and how.

• Be straightforward. If the grantor feels you are being deceptive or beating around the bush, he or she may think you really do not know what you are talking about, or worse.

• Be well organized. Your presentation should flow logically from one subject to the next. Rambling around may cause the grantor's interest to wander away.

• Bring audio or visual enhancers to your presentation. These would include films, slide presentations, charts, or photographs. Use these to support your presentation, not substitute for it.

• Put materials into the hands of the people who are hearing your presentation. Again, this could include charts and graphs or photographs. You may want to do this toward the conclusion of your presentation so that during your presentation the audience is looking at you, not the materials in their hands.

I have seen groups turn a probable "no" into a "yes" with a well-handled presentation. I have also seen the reverse happen as a result of a poor presentation.

Collaboration

The notion of organizations working with one another rather than against one another to get funding goes against the grain of common practice, but it may truly be beneficial. Your organization can benefit from forming partnerships with other organizations, using your combined resources to seek out and secure funding. By dividing the work, both in getting funding and in completing the project, a lot more can get done. Many donors, from individuals to foundations and government agencies, look favorably on collaborative efforts. Demonstrating community leadership on issues as sensitive as funding enhances the image of your organization to funders, constituents, and other key community players. More important, it may help stimulate a new way for organizations in your community to relate to each other, allowing you to accomplish much more (Fallon, 1993).

Strings Attached

There are many treasure chests out there, some are large, some are small, and some are very well hidden. To discover any of these requires work (sometimes a lot of work), some ingenuity, some fiscal accountability, and some entanglements with the inevitable strings attached to each. Don't kid yourself. Each source of funds comes with strings attached. Some are threads, some steel cables. If you depend on contributions from the general public, you must keep the trust of that public and continue to demonstrate your worthiness. If you receive money from the federal government, you may find the regula-

tions governing the use of those funds make sense in Washington, DC, but seem a little crazy in Tacoma. If United Way dollars support what you are doing, you may be expected to avoid controversial activities, especially those aimed at one of their large contributors.

Acknowledge that the strings are there and that you'll have to keep on good terms with the puppeteer, or be willing to run the risk that some of what you want may be left dangling.

Conclusion

No matter how big or small, old or new your effort is, you will need to generate additional resources. Many times you will be able to directly receive needed goods or services. Sometimes you will need to raise money to acquire them. Regardless of the approach you use, you will be asking other people, either as individuals or as representatives of organizations, to provide the resource support you need. Target your efforts to those most likely to respond favorably. Develop and nurture relationships with those who may be able to invest in your success and ask them to do so. Your request may take any number of forms: a direct person-to-person request, a letter, an organized presentation, or even a formal written proposal. Thoughtfully and purposefully prepare and deliver your request to increase the chances of a rewarding response. Acknowledge and thank the people who have considered contributing to the realization of your goals.

The various techniques described in this chapter should give you some direction toward your pot, or at least your cup, of gold. More than that, however, they should spark your own thinking, your own ingenuity. In your own unique fashion, refine the methods described here and come up with some creative ones of your own.

CHAPTER 11

Getting the Word Out

Chapter Highlights

- Awareness can promote interest; ignorance inhibits action
- Education is insufficient for action
- A knowledgeable, supportive environment assists the change effort
- Credibility is essential to your success
- You need to communicate with supporters, targets, and the general public
- The Three Holy M's: message, medium, market
- Sending information by word of mouth
- Presenting to other groups and organizations
- Newsletters, brochures, and position papers
- Speakers' bureau
- Fliers and posters
- Four categories of low-cost publicity
- More than one person can deliver your message

- Receiving assistance from other organizations
- Public service media and PSAs
- Capitalizing on radio and television talk shows
- What news gets reported?
- Key personnel in the news media
- Building relationships with members of the news media
- Becoming a news source; understanding and providing good information
- Participating in a news interview
- Preparing and using news releases
- Holding a news conference
- Event coverage
- Weekly and specialty newspapers
- Editorials and letters to the editor

Friday morning, yesterday's coffee still in the pot, phone ringing down the hall, no one answering, of course, and Ben sitting at his desk, more drooping than sitting, poring over the box scores. Friday morning, everything in its place.

Setting her purse down, Melanie peers over Ben's shoulder. "What are you up to?"

"Just reading the paper." He looks up. "There was an article I saw earlier that started me thinking. It's about a report the university just released on health care costs related to prenatal services. It says that insufficient services cost the taxpayers millions of dollars."

"That's pretty surprising, Ben."

"Well, it shouldn't be, Melanie, that's what we've been saying all along."

"No, actually, I meant the fact that you were reading the paper and that you started to think. But the stuff about the report is pretty impressive too."

"Thanks. You know, I was thinking, here we are putting together something that will deal with just what this report is talking about and nobody called to ask us our opinion. I get the feeling that a lot of people don't even know we exist."

"Well, we certainly have been talking to people, Ben. What do you want us to do? Get on the news?"

"Yeah, I think so. Or at least some way of reaching more people than we obviously have."

"I don't know anything about the news business, Ben. I'm not even sure who it is we're trying to reach."

"So, we learn. And people learn a little more about why we need this center."

"Well, I wouldn't mind getting to know Jeff Johns from Channel Seven. Maybe there's a way we can use the attention that report is getting."

Some things just shouldn't be kept secret. The need for the change you are seeking and the attempts to change fit nicely into this category. Getting information to people and getting information from them are crucial activities in your march toward change.

Melanie and Ben are recognizing that to get on the community's agenda of issues the community needs to know they exist. As change agents, they need to go beyond their professional circle of supporters and begin to foster community awareness and dialogue. Certainly they will need to keep in contact with the people working with them, but to build needed community support they must also reach out and inform people who don't know much about the issue and may never even have thought about it.

Earlier, we looked at ways to get information from and about your community. In this chapter we will look at reasons to get information out as well as some of the ways you can reach people who can use the information to aid the cause you are working on.

Regardless of the size of your community—a social service agency, a neighborhood, or even an entire city—your ability to effectively inform others will be a great asset. Some methods described in this chapter (press conferences, for example) are more appropriate for informing larger audiences. Yet you can apply the basic concepts for reaching people with your message to all the different communities you focus on in your change efforts.

Importance of Making Your Efforts Known

Drawing attention to your actions and the need for them serves several purposes. Why you are communicating to people will affect how you choose to do it. Let's look at several of the major reasons to get the word out.

Let People Know You Exist

Your organization is a new force in the environment. It will move people in new directions, sometimes in directions they do not want to go. This movement is caused by people reacting to what you and other members of your organization are doing. But you will have no reaction, you probably will have no members, if no one knows you even exist. This is the starting point

and the first reason to publicize your intent and your action. People have to know that there is an interest in changing things before they can decide what to do about it. If people don't know you exist, they can't work with you or oppose you. Spreading the word will give some people hope and enthusiasm and other people worry.

Stir Interest

People hear that old ways are going to be challenged. People start talking. People start thinking. In some cases, people even start acting. Provoke people. You don't have to get people mad, but you do have to get them thinking differently and thinking about behaving differently so they will begin to believe in the possibilities.

You have to overcome the inertia of inaction or acquiescence. The rumblings of interest begin to alter the circumstances in which you are operating. With your help, interest will build on itself, setting things in motion.

Expose the Issue and Educate for Action

It is easy, and fairly common, to take refuge in ignorance. The security that comes with not knowing is a powerful force in keeping things as they are. Bringing the issue into focus shakes people out of their complacency.

It is sometimes safer to pretend a problem doesn't exist, especially if you feel powerless to do anything about it. When people begin to see what is really going on (at least from your perspective), they begin to understand the various aspects of the issue and, most important, how it affects them. Awareness makes it harder to tuck things away out of consciousness.

Ignorance is not always a purposeful choice. Sometimes people simply don't know. So many things compete for our attention that we scarcely notice some things, but we might be willing to do something about them if we did.

Those who are responsible for maintaining

the problem would just as soon keep other people unaware. They especially don't want their own roles noticed, nor do they want to be held accountable for their actions, or lack of them. By exposing the ramifications of the problem and who is involved, you can agitate people and counter the very powerful process of ignorance.

Education, however, is not sufficient for action. Don't be fooled into thinking it is. Too many groups make the mistake of assuming that if people know about a problem they will act on it. They even have "education" as the major goal. Education may be a precondition for action, but it is not action. Merely knowing about something does not guarantee action on it.

Once people have a clearer picture of a situation, you can introduce them to ways of putting their awareness into action. Help people see that they can act, and probably should. Show them how and what steps they can take. This is a necessary part of the process of educating to promote change. People who are aroused want to know what they can do. Don't leave them hanging. Take advantage of the opportunity you have created.

Education will help create a climate for change. Not everyone will be so concerned about an issue that they will want to spend their time working on it. Still, they may be supportive of those who do. You need this kind of support. A hostile or insensitive environment will make things harder for you and aid those resisting change. A more knowledgeable, supportive atmosphere affects the tone of the contest. Potential resisters may see the handwriting on the wall and make a less than concerted effort to maintain the status quo.

Attract New Support

Building the organization involves building membership in it. The message you send out regarding the need for action will bring people into your organization. People who care enough to move ahead will be glad to know that others are involved in the issue. Your organization gives them a way to express their interest.

Strengthen Affiliation

The notoriety the organization receives increases the attachment of those who have already enlisted. It contributes to a feeling that they are part of an alliance to be reckoned with. As members of such a group, they feel more important or more powerful. As other people come to regard the change effort more seriously, its participants are reinforced for their commitment. This bolsters resolve and enhances motivation to press forward with the work of the organization.

Credibility

I will frequently mention credibility or allude to its importance. It is a central element necessary to your efforts to promote change. Are you real? Do you have the power you say you have? Is your information accurate? Your credibility will be challenged both directly and indirectly throughout the life of the change effort by supporters and opponents alike.

You are asking people to believe in what doesn't yet exist. This is not easily done. Whether for members, those you hope to influence, or the public in general, uncertainty is hard to act on. For you or me to commit to something, we need to let go of some fairly natural restraining tendencies. We require at least some evidence that letting go is a good idea. The less credible or believable something is, the more reluctant we are to affiliate with it. The more we are able to believe that something is for real, the more willing we are to respond to it.

If handled correctly, your efforts to communicate your presence, your purpose, and your progress will provide you with this most powerful benefit. Credibility establishes the foundation for all the other benefits. It makes them possible.

Identifying the People You Need to Reach

You will be communicating different types of information to at least three different groups:

- Your supporters, whether active or general
- The target or response community
- The general public

It is most important that your membership be kept informed. Your participants should be apprised of the progress of and particular challenges to your operation. Tell them what's going on. Be sure your direct supporters are well informed about the issue or problem you are trying to rectify. Keep the issue before them to keep them in touch with the purpose you share and to deepen their understanding and commitment. From time to time provide a motivational piece. These are intended to maintain, and periodically heighten, enthusiasm. Finally, let participants know about specific organizational needs they may be able to meet.

Continue to educate other constituents of the action and benefit communities regarding the problem, the goals, the activities of the organization, and the sources of resistance. Keep them aware of roles they can fill.

Positive change results when people who have a good idea also have the power to implement it. Two fundamental things you need to communicate to the target community are the strength of your ideas and the strength of your support. Regardless of whether or not the target community actively opposes the changes, you will have to overcome some forms of resistance, even if that just happens to be old habits.

The target group should know what it is you expect them to do; that is, what and how they are to change. Extend opportunities to them to participate in solving the problem. Finally, they should be aware of the important activities of your organization, including its large and small victories, that enhance its position in the eyes of other community members.

On some issues it is important to have the general public take notice. There are times when even relatively small changes would benefit from broader community awareness. When you communicate with the general public, you usually do so either to gain broad approval and sanction for your activities and concerns or to rouse it to action. Inform the public of the validity of your concerns and the unreasonableness, if not the downright perfidy, of your opposition. You want the public to understand how your success will benefit them and that your failure will be their loss. Finally, you want the general public to know that you are alive and kicking. Let them know some of the things you are doing, and periodically remind them of your issues.

The Three Holy M's

Figure 11-1 shows the relationship between the Three Holy M's:

- *The market:* the recipients of your message, the people from whom you want to get a reaction
- *The medium:* the technique or device you use to get the message to the market
- *The message:* what the market needs to hear to respond

The basic reason you communicate with someone is to get a reaction from them. You want them to think or to know something, do or not do something. Therefore, you take care (or at least you should) to prepare the proper message. The disappointment of many change efforts can be traced to a lack of attention in preparing and sending an effective message. When we fail, it is often because we start by saying what we want to say without giving adequate consideration to who is going to hear it and how. We get things backward. The message is the last thing we should consider. The market is the first. The medium fits in between. I call these the Three Holy M's.

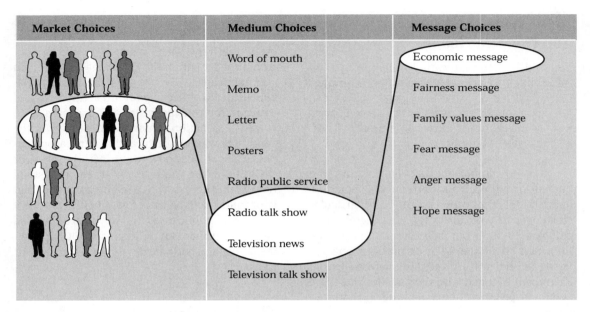

Market Choices	Medium Choices	Message Choices
	Word of mouth	Economic message
	Memo	Fairness message
	Letter	Family values message
	Posters	Fear message
	Radio public service	Anger message
	Radio talk show	Hope message
	Television news	
	Television talk show	

Figure 11-1
Example of relationship between the Three Holy M's: pick the right market, select the right medium, and send the right message

The entire process of getting the word out is driven by the reactions you want to get from the market. It is as simple and as complex as that. The more that other things become important, such as feeling self-righteous, the less effective you will be. Paying attention to how the message, the medium, and the market relate to each other will strengthen the impact of your communication. Just who are these people you want to influence? What response do you want from them? What do they need to hear to trigger that response? Do they respond to facts, emotion, or intellectual argument? In what ways do they receive information? Which methods do they trust? Which of these can best carry the message you want to send? Which methods would the market consider to be appropriate for your message? You will probably want to consider other things as well, but this is enough to get you started.

The market—the people you intend to influence, and therefore the messages you send—will no doubt vary from one change project to the next; so too will the vehicles you use for delivering the message to the market. Nonetheless, there are some standard methods you will more than likely use. This chapter will focus on increasing your understanding of a variety of approaches for sending your messages.

Techniques for Sending the Message That You Control

Some methods for getting the word out are under your control or largely under your control. Your group is responsible for preparing and sending the message rather than having to convince or rely on someone else (such as the news media) to do that for you.

Take a Moment to Discover . . . .

Today you will probably pass by quite a
few signs that beckon your attention
to a community event or to an item of
information someone thinks you should
know. Will you read any of these?
Maybe a few, but not most. What do
you think determines this? What can
you learn from your answer?

. . . .

Word of Mouth

Talk it up. People involved in your effort should
tell everyone they know (and a few they don't)
just what they are doing and why. It has long
been said that word of mouth is the best form of
advertising. This is because people regard as
truth or near truth the things they hear from
those around them. Think of the power of gossip
or the rumor mill. If something is repeated often
enough, it becomes true whether or not it
actually is. Presumably, you will be spreading
the truth, which should increase the believabil-
ity of what you say.

When you talk with people about the
situation you are facing, especially people who
are unfamiliar with it, be sensitive to their level
of interest. Plant seeds, don't give lectures. Build
curiosity, don't assume it. Avoid turning people
off by giving them more than they want to know.
It is usually better to tell people a little less than
they need to know rather than a little more. The
type and number of questions they ask will let
you know how interested they are.

One effective technique involves asking
questions and then listening. Set people to
thinking about how they feel about the issue,
and see if they can relate it to themselves in
some way. Try to pick up on that feeling. Guide
people to reach their own conclusions on the
matter. They become more attached if these
judgments are their own beliefs, not just yours.
You should have a few standard points you want

to make. You can even have a few standard
phrases handy to rely on if you like.

Consider a more formal campaign in addition to spur-of-the-moment conversation. This
may include a planned strategy with specific
individuals "assigned" to those you particularly
want to influence. Or, you may assign teams to
directly contact individuals in certain groups or
areas in your community. A door-to-door approach in a neighborhood is an example of such
a campaign.

Meetings

Obviously, the people involved in your project
will be meeting from time to time to plan,
exchange information, and make decisions, but
other people meet too. This provides you with
an opportunity to spread your message. Concentrate on groups and organizations whose support you would like to cultivate. This is a good
way to build allies too. Most groups will give you
the 5 or 10 minutes you ask for to make a
presentation. Make your points clearly, using
examples and facts to back them up. That is, be
prepared. Using a little emotion often helps,
even with the stuffiest groups.

Let the members of the group know what
you want from them. Ask for it, clearly. Then be
quiet. Wait for the response. Remain for any of
the group's discussion on the matter. You may
be able to inject some insight, and it will be a lot
harder for them to turn you down when they are
looking at you.

Always leave some written material behind.
A one-page summary of your points and your
request or a brochure are usually all that is
necessary. Make sure that whatever you leave
has your organization's name, if you have one,
and a way for people to contact a specific person
in your group.

Newsletters

A regular means of communicating to your
members is necessary to keep everyone linked to

the effort. If your organization has more than a handful of members and these members don't see each other regularly, you might want to develop a newsletter. Newsletters enhance the feeling of legitimacy and permanence of an organized group. They help supporters keep in touch with the organization and its agenda. But newsletters take time to produce, and if you need to pay for printing and mailing, they can cost money.

A few simple suggestions will help your newsletter accomplish its purpose of communicating to supporters and strengthening their sense of affiliation: keep it simple and personal, keep it regular, and keep one person in charge.

First and foremost, someone, a responsible someone, needs to take on preparation of the newsletter as his or her major contribution to the organization. If nobody really wants this job, don't try to put out a newsletter. You would only get a couple of issues out before it would fizzle. Fizzled projects aren't good for organizations.

Next, make sure it is published on a regular basis, preferably monthly. Sporadic or hit-and-miss publications give the impression that other efforts by the organization are sporadic or halfhearted.

Finally, remember that you want people to read the thing. Rarely should it exceed four sides in length. (There are, of course, exceptions to this, particularly for newsletters whose purpose is to examine a range of community issues.) A basic line-up of articles would include these regular columns: news, editorials, featured personality, and upcoming activities or events. That's about it.

Don't forget that your organization is made up of people, not just issues. People like to see their names in print. So print lots of names. Look for ways to spread credit around when describing gains the organization has made. When featuring an individual, profile the personal side, not just the professional side, and always mention some reason why the individual is supporting the cause. Use humor, cartoons, or simple graphics, and keep the articles short. Solicit articles from supporters to distribute the workload and promote a sense of ownership.

Newsletters are good for reaching outside your organization as well. Include people on your distribution list who are not active in your effort but who should be kept informed about your organization, particularly members of the news media. Features in your newsletter can become the basis of news stories.

Brochures

There seems to be a natural desire for some people to want to develop brochures. Before you do, stop and ask yourself who is supposed to

---

Change Agent Tip

Everybody goes to the bathroom. Most of us also spend time standing in line or cooling our heels in waiting rooms. And while we are there, what do we do? . . . besides the obvious, I mean. We look around. We read what is on the walls—signs and graffiti. Or we peruse copies of *Field and Stream* that were new in the spring of 1983 or become fascinated by the latest in *Modern Dentistry*.

Places where people are bored are wonderful places to post or leave materials you want people to read. Elevators, grocery store checkouts, laundromats, doctors' offices, food stamp offices, and buses are some of my favorites. Of course, nothing really beats the back of the door in the stall of a public restroom.

read this brochure, how will they get it, and what are they supposed to do once they have read it? If you can't come up with good answers that justify the time and possible expense of printing a brochure, you shouldn't produce one. Unless your change involves establishing a permanent program or alliance or organizing a significant conference, you probably don't need a brochure.

If you decide you need a brochure, there are some basic things you should know. Most brochures are simply a standard 8½-by-11-inch sheet of paper folded in thirds. This arrangement gives you five panels for graphics and information and a back panel for an address if it is to be mailed.

The purpose of your brochure will be either informational, answering questions and conveying pertinent details, or invitational, arousing curiosity and encouraging some steps toward participation in something. Decide which emphasis you want and stick to it. If you want people to read it, keep these tips in mind as you develop your brochure:

- Think space; brochures with too many words are rarely read.
- Keep your sentences short and avoid jargon.
- Use a hook to grab attention and get people to peek inside; bold statements or questions often do the trick.
- Use high-quality paper; a cheap presentation often isn't worth the money you save.
- Work with an experienced printer; most will provide you with valuable guidance.
- Consider using a union printer; aside from philosophical reasons to do so, some groups will scrutinize your literature wanting to see the union label.

Position Papers

If your group has taken an official position on a particular matter, you may want to prepare a clear written statement that convincingly articulates your position. This is particularly useful in communicating your point of view to government bodies, community task forces, and the news media. A position paper provides an explicit statement of your beliefs and protects you from people who want to misconstrue your position. It also provides you with a good tool to help shape the development of policy, especially if you are trying to influence the decisions of a working group looking into the matter. Other groups will rely on the work you have done, sometimes using your work in place of work they would otherwise have to do for themselves. It allows you to convey your points in a clear, direct, and fully explained manner, which increases the chance they will receive thoughtful consideration. If you only offer your viewpoint verbally, you have to trust that your comments will be remembered, and remembered accurately. Quite an act of faith. A position paper can serve as a backup to amplify the points you make when using other forms of communication.

The length of a position paper will vary according to the complexity of the issue you choose to address. It may be as short as a single page, or it may be 25 pages long. The paper should outline why the issue at hand is relevant to your group, what your position is, and how you support your position. Your support should demonstrate philosophical, rational, and factual justification.

If you are preparing a paper that exceeds five pages, provide an abstract that summarizes the entire paper in two or three paragraphs. Use headings and subheadings to highlight key sections. Supply a bibliography showing the sources you used to develop your position. For particularly long papers, it is also generally a good idea to include a table of contents. As with any written material, make sure it is attractive and free from errors of spelling, grammar, and punctuation.

Speakers' Bureau

Making presentations to other community groups or at a community forum is a useful way to shape the community's perception of your organization's concerns and establish the climate for change. This affords you the opportunity for a face-to-face discussion with people who are themselves part of an organized power base or who are interested in community affairs.

To make a speakers' bureau work, you need to identify people who are interested in making presentations, train them, and solicit invitations to speak. Each of these elements is important.

Not everyone is interested in public speaking, and certainly not everyone is good at it. Ask your supporters to volunteer for this assignment and also ask them to identify people they think would be good speakers. Then make a particular effort to recruit people who have a special expertise. This is not something you want to talk people into doing. Only use people who like, or at least don't mind, this type of activity. They won't back out of engagements and will probably represent you more effectively.

Training is an important component of your program. Each speaker should be comfortable with her or his standard presentation, be well versed in the organization's goals and positions, and be practiced at handling questions, particularly the tough ones. Each speaker should learn how to relate your group's concerns to the concerns of the audience.

Seek out opportunities to make presentations. Many groups use guest speakers. This includes college classes, civic and fraternal organizations, community affairs groups, religious groups, and others. Libraries, hospitals, and major employers often sponsor community lecture series. Look in the community events calendar in the newspaper to get an idea of the type of speaking possibilities typical of your community. Then send out a letter to appropriate groups announcing your availability and respond quickly to the invitations you receive.

Your speakers' program should be part of a purposeful campaign. It is more effective if you target particular constituencies you want to influence. Personally arrange opportunities to address specific groups whose members may play a role in any community debate on your concerns.

Fliers and Posters

Fliers and posters can be inexpensive ways to notify a lot of people or foolish ways to waste a lot of paper. By giving thought to just a few things, you can improve the quality of the ones you produce. The first point to think about is how you are going to distribute your material. If you produce 500 fliers, you want to make sure that 500 end up in public, not neatly stacked on somebody's desk. You can't hand people a fistful of fliers and expect that they will distribute them for you. The process must be more purposefully managed. This matter should be cleared up before you print your first piece.

The next point concerns where you post your information so people will notice it. Places where people go to look for information are obvious, though not always the best, choices. Too many bulletin boards are so cluttered with outdated information that nobody really pays attention to them. Most of the time people will not stop to read a poster, so it is a good idea to put them in places people are moving toward or where they are already stopped.

Your message has to capture attention. Striking design and sharply contrasting colors do this. One dramatic word or picture will command more attention than several. Think space. A few easy to read words is far better than an essay. Finally, tell people what they need to know. If you can do this in a provocative or clever way, all the better; the reader will remember more.

Review of Methods Other People Control

Some people are in the business of communicating information, and at times you will use them to help get the word out. You can pay public relations and advertising companies to help you with this. Among other services, they will help you design materials and develop and buy advertising. If you have oodles of money, you may want to buy their expertise. Check around to determine what professional assis-

tance and paid advertising can do for you and which agency can best serve your needs.

Most change efforts, however, aren't beset by the problem of what to do with all that extra cash. They need to figure out how to do things for little or no money. Some people in the communication business will help you publicize your concerns for little or no cost. These fall into four categories: other groups and organizations, public service advertising, entertainment and public affairs programming, and news media.

Again we get into this "you" business. As I have pointed out, you includes not only you, yourself, but other people in your organization as well. This is particularly true when it comes to communicating outside your group to the rest of the community. If your mug is always in front of the cameras, if your words are the only ones quoted in the press, people outside your organization and, sadly, also those within it will begin to think that the organization is pretty

much just you and a bunch of followers. Worse, it can affect you this way too.

Make a special effort to have a number of faces for the public to see and a variety of voices who can speak on the issues you (all) are facing. To establish easy access to your group it may be effective to identify a particular individual whom those outside the organization may contact to get your group's views and reactions to issues or events. The contact person may then help connect those who have such requests with any one of a variety of the organization members who are prepared to respond. It may be appropriate to have one contact person, but it is most definitely not right to feel that only one person really knows what is going on, that only one person should have the limelight. A number of people can represent you well if representation becomes an expectation and a responsibility. Some members will be better than others, yes, but some are definitely better than one.

Other Groups and Organizations

The main ways other groups can help you are by allowing you to make a presentation to their members and by providing you space or coverage in their publications. Think of all the publications in your community in addition to the regular newspapers: church bulletins, employee newsletters, social service newsletters, and community interest group mailings to name a few. Most of these are potential vehicles to carry your message to a specific constituency. This is particularly true if the group's interests are similar to yours or if a member of another group is involved in your project.

Personally contact the individual in charge of the publication. Be ready to explain how information on your project would be valuable or of interest to their readers. Ask for publication guidelines and deadlines. You will be surprised at how frequently your request for publication is accepted.

Groups who share a similar viewpoint can assist you in other ways. On some occasions, say, at a news conference or a public hearing, other organizations may offer public statements on your behalf to lend emphasis and credibility to your assertions. They can also help by making routine announcements for you to their own constituencies. When you thank the assisting organization for their help, let them know of any reaction or benefit you received as a result of their assistance.

Public Service Advertising

Many change efforts use this form of communication to enhance their efforts to reach the public. The standard approaches include free billboard space, newspaper community announcement columns, and radio and television public service announcements.

Billboards. Outdoor advertising companies often donate billboard space to community groups for special projects or events. Usually, this also includes the cost for putting up the signs. The signs are posted on a space-available basis. This means that some of your signs may stay up for a long time in some very out-of-the-way location or for a short time in a prime spot. Customarily all you have to pay for is printing. The billboard company can direct you to printers who handle this type of work, and the outdoor advertising company will show you how to design a billboard, including some tricks that will help you reduce your printing costs. Be aware that your sign should have no more than 10 words on it. Also, the sign company may not be sure just when there will be free space to hang your sign, so make sure you give them plenty of lead time.

Newspapers.   Newspapers run several community announcement columns. Typically, one column provides information on upcoming community events, whereas another describes services or resources available in the community. Each column appears regularly on a certain day, say, every Sunday or every Thursday. Watch for the section in which the columns run, and then contact the editor for that section. The editor will let you know what you have to do to get your information printed.

Radio and television public service announcements.   Some of the following suggestions are drawn from information prepared for the United Way by Ruby and O'Brien (1978). Public service announcements (PSAs) are not the same thing as news stories. They are, in effect, commercials for your project. They are handled by different departments at the station and are seen as a service to the community and to the organization featured. They usually describe a service the organization offers, a need the organization has, or an upcoming organization activity.

Radio PSAs are pretty easy to prepare. It is helpful to contact each station to find out if any particular format is preferred. This serves a number of purposes. First, it establishes contact between you and the station. Second, it helps you provide the station with material that is easy for it to use. Third, it gives you a good reason to do a follow-up contact with the station to ask if your materials were in the proper form and if they have any questions regarding the content. You are really doing a follow-up to remind them of who you are and to reinforce the importance of your announcement. Follow-up contact is important whether or not you made a previous contact. Now, most public service directors will tell you that this isn't necessary, that they will air whatever they can fit in. In actual practice, though, they do develop certain preferences, whether they know it or not. They tend to air more frequently those announcements that are easy for them to handle, that are well written and well prepared, and that help people they know and like. I have seen significant differences in results between groups who simply send out material and hope it gets played and those who put in a little extra effort to establish contact and prepare their material well.

Make no mistake, this is a very competitive business. Radio stations routinely receive many requests for "free advertising." You need to do something to make yours stand out from the rest. Here are some guidelines to help increase the odds that your message will get on the airwaves.

- Write your message in a way that sounds good when it is read out loud. Most radio PSAs aren't prerecorded, though some are. The deejays don't want to read a statement that sounds too awkward or stilted. Read your announcement over a few times and modify it until you get the right sound. Though the deejays will probably change it a bit themselves to suit their own styles, the less work they have to do, the better.

- Time your announcement. Standard spots are 10, 15, or 30 seconds in length. Each station will have its preferred standard. At the end of each announcement, note its length. Remember that professional announcers can read with emphasis faster than you can. A general rule of thumb is two and one-half words per second.

- Type your announcements in large type using capital letters only. If you have proper names, spell them out phonetically as well. Use double or triple spacing and wide margins. Some stations that use shorter PSAs prefer that the announcements be typed on index cards.

- Include some sort of hook to get the listeners' attention. People don't remember boring messages. Probing questions, humor, and dramatic statistics are good devices. Some stations like announcements that have some emotional content (but refrain from being too melodramatic), whereas others prefer those that are purely descriptive or factual. If you haven't discovered preferences while doing your "homework" on the stations, then send two versions of the same announcement.

- If you include a phone number in your announcement, it should be the last thing in your announcement. Repeat the number if you can.

- Some stations will let you record your own PSA. This personalizes the message more. Using your own name in the announcement ("Hello, I'm Carl Kadukie of . . .") further individualizes it.

- If you have an ongoing need for public service air time, consider using a three weeks on, two months off airing schedule. Periodically rewrite your messages. This schedule keeps your messages fresh with both the audience and the station, while it gives the impression that you are always around.

- Enclose a brief cover letter with your material. This should describe who you are, mention the importance of the announcement to the community and your program, and ask the station for their help in informing the public.

- If you can make the time (and you really should try), it will help your cause to hand deliver your announcements to the station. This is particularly true the first few times you work with a station before you get to know the people at the station and they get to know you.

- Send a follow-up thank-you to those stations who were cooperative in airing your message. Note any response you received from the community that could be related to their support.

The process for television public service announcements is similar to that for radio. The major difference is that television PSAs have both the benefit of and the requirement for visual support. You can make your production as simple or as complex as your time, skill, and budget will allow. Television stations prefer to air announcements that are well made, so even if your production is simple, avoid looking cheap.

There is a lot of help available to assist you in producing your spot. Community access cable television stations will train you in the use of video equipment. Students from the media or public relations departments of the local college may be able to help you as part of a class project. Advertising companies occasionally donate their services to the right cause if requested to do so by the right person. Even the local network affiliate station may produce your announcement at very little cost if a key person at the station takes a real interest in your project.

Here are some suggestions to help you get your message across.

- Get to know the public service director at each station. The person who fills this role will also have other duties at the station. She or he will give you helpful directions on how to work effectively with the station. Because each station may have some unique procedures, ask for directions and follow them.
- The written format of a television PSA uses two columns. The left column provides the directions for the video (for example, if you are using slides, it would show the sequence in which they should appear) and the right column provides the directions for the corresponding audio.
- If you are using slides to convey your point, use clear 35-mm slides with a horizontal presentation. Remember that a television screen has a 3:4 ratio, so any artwork you prepare should conform to that ratio. Your slides will

probably be cropped, so take this into account when selecting pictures. Pictures that convey action are usually better than those showing someone's face, unless the face communicates a certain drama or elicits an emotional response. Use one picture for every 8 to 10 seconds of audio. Too many different visuals are distracting.

- Having a local personality as a spokesperson can give you credibility and recognition. It also makes producing the spot a relatively easy matter. (Do not use a media personality or your spot will only run on the station for which the individual works.) Avoid the talking head approach; cut away from the speaker a couple of times to show some other action, or have the speaker involved in the action.
- Your visuals will tell your story. Thoughtfully consider what you want your viewer to feel. Then choose images that will produce that response. In fact, turn the sound off when you are reviewing your PSA. If you are getting your point across well by the visuals alone, you have done a good job.
- Prepare an audio script, perhaps including music, that evokes a response from the viewer and complements the video portion of your spot.
- Standard television PSAs are either 10, 20, or 30 seconds in length. Ten- and 20-second spots have a better chance of airing. There may be more open time slots for these lengths and, since most PSAs are 30-second productions, there will probably be fewer spots with which yours will have to compete.
- You need to get a signed release from each person seen in your announcement.
- You may have a better chance getting your spot aired on independent stations. Though their audience may be smaller, this may be offset by the fact that your announcement is shown more often. It is worth it to make a special effort with these stations.
- Most stations are willing to make a dub (a copy) of your PSA and to send the dub to other stations.
- Get to know the traffic manager at each station. This person slots the paid commercials

and the PSAs and, in some cases, has discretion in deciding which PSAs get aired and when. If there is some open time that can be filled with PSAs, and they know you and like your project . . . Well, you get the picture.

Entertainment and Public Affairs Programming

Essentially this approach involves appearances on talk shows. Community talk shows have long been the staple of local television Sunday programming, competing with the roosters for the attention of early morning risers or the drowsy late afternoon viewer after all the day's games have been played. The weekday mid-morning slot also finds an occasional audience. Not exactly prime time. The main thing, though, is that there is an audience. You will reach some people who have an interest in your community, and you have the opportunity to educate and build a relationship with one of the station's on-camera personalities, even if he or she is not yet one of the stars. An additional benefit is that it makes your supporters feel good. There is something about being on TV that makes people seem and feel important. It also hones your skills in representing your project to the public. What you receive from an appearance on one of these programs is certainly worth the small effort they require.

Radio talk shows are quite a different matter. These programs continue to gain in popularity and influence. Often looking for controversial topics, they provide an ideal medium for your message. Since many of these shows are of the call-in variety, you have the chance to interact with your audience to directly influence some perceptions and to get people talking about what you are up to and why.

A number of simple steps can help you take advantage of the potential these television and radio programs offer you.

- Do a little homework on the show itself. Watching or listening to the show a few times before your appearance will give you a sense of

---

Change Agent Tip

Orchestrate call-in shows. This is a simple way for you to influence the direction of the conversation in a way that puts your efforts in the most favorable light. You have taken some pains to get air time and to prepare yourself well. Now complete the job. Use the air time fully to your benefit. I am surprised at how rarely this is effectively done.

You need just a handful of supporters, each prepared with two questions. Each person has a primary question and a backup question in case an "unscheduled" caller phones in with a question that is close to one of your prepared ones. Use good judgment. Don't overdo things, and don't ask a question that has already been asked by someone else.

When you prepare your questions, include some that appear to be hostile to or in opposition to your point of view, but ones for which you have a good answer. Also, write them in the way that people really talk. Perfectly proper grammar and a two-dollar vocabulary are not commonplace on call-in shows. Establish some kind of order or time schedule for your supporters to call in.

"I'd feel a little silly doing this," you might be thinking. Don't worry, most people do. In fact, that's usually enough to get them to waste this golden opportunity to communicate their ideas and shape a part of the community's perception. Is that important to you? It's your call.

the program's flavor and an understanding of how the host approaches topics and works with the guest. You may pick up on the host's biases, way of asking questions, or a propensity to do most of the talking or to let the guest have a free rein. Most hosts want to set their guests at ease because a comfortable guest is a talkative and engaging guest.

• Get the facts straight. Your use of statistics or ability to cite a particular study communicates that you are well informed on the subject and deserve some consideration. A simple technique is to prepare an index card that outlines the points you want to address. Next to each, note a statistic or reference to jog your memory. When doing a radio show, you can keep your index cards right in front of you as well as any other material you want to use. If you are doing a call-in show, you are likely to hear from people who disagree with you or who don't fully understand your perspective. This gives you a wonderful opportunity to show the strength of your ideas. While preparing, review your list of points and imagine that you are on "the other side." What would your objections be? Consider how your facts and reasoning could counter those objections. You can add these notes to your index card as well. This exercise will help you communicate to supporters and opponents alike.

• Provide background material to the show host. When you schedule your appearance, ask the host how much in advance he or she would like this information from you. Usually a week in advance is sufficient. You can suggest this. Provide the host with a small packet of information regarding your effort that includes a one-page description of your group, what it intends to accomplish, and why. Also, provide a set of sample questions that address points you would like to have emphasized and that can guide the host in developing additional questions. Clearly indicate that these are sample questions; don't imply that the host is incapable of coming up with inquiries of his or her own. (The less controversial your project, the more comfortable the host will be in using these questions.) Other elements can include newspa-

per stories on your project, position papers or statements you have produced, a list of your goals and objectives, general project descriptions, or brochures. Don't overwhelm the host. Just pick from whatever you have that would give someone a good understanding of your concerns and your organization, and use a marking pen to highlight key sections.

You want to make things as easy for the host as possible. A well-prepared host invigorates the discussion and helps you emphasize important topics. The easier you make the host's job, the more willing he or she will be to work with you. It is also more likely that you will be invited back.

Be interesting, using stories, examples, and humor to illustrate your points. Data in monotone is the scourge of the talk show. The only demon nearly as scary is the guest who can utter only the words "yes" and "no." You don't need to be Eddie Murphy, but you do want people to take an interest in what you have to say. The simplest direction is to tell your story in human terms. There is a lot of truth in the saying that the death of a thousand people is a statistic; the death of one man or woman is a tragedy. How can your audience see themselves, their family or friends, or the things they value in what your organization cares about or what it is doing? What can they find funny or frustrating or moving? Guests who are engaging, well informed, well prepared, and who make the host's job easy are welcome ones. They are often welcomed back.

Talk shows give you an opportunity to personalize your organization and its concerns. They give recognition to your efforts, a boost to your supporters, and help you reach people with whom you would not ordinarily have direct contact. They can attract a few new supporters, quite a few opponents, and encourage the climate for change.

News Media

She lowered the microphone from my face, and then paused so I could fully appreciate her point. "Mark," she said after a moment, "this is a news interview, not a public service announcement. If you want to make a public service announcement, contact our public service department. If you have a news story, we can keep talking." I wonder if my red face, which did fortunately make an appearance on the news that evening, caused anyone to adjust the color on their set.

What is news, and how do you get the people in the news media to report it, preferably in a way that furthers your interests? News is something that has just happened or is about to happen. It is unusual, affects a lot of people, affects someone generally considered to be important, or affects someone the audience can identify with. If it happens in the immediate vicinity of the audience, it is especially important. Some of the information in this section was drawn from Rathbun (1986) and materials developed by the editors of the *Arizona Daily Star* (1988), Daun (1991), Kimble (1991), Johnson (1991), Cross (1992), and Lefton (1992).

News is something you would be interested in even if you were not involved with the story. If you don't think you or the people you know would be interested, it probably isn't news. Publicity isn't news either. Publicity is designed to promote a person or a group, not to inform the public. True, there are gray areas, and promotion does on occasion pass for news. However, an organization that is intent only on promoting and not informing will soon wear out its welcome with members of the news media. Some of these items can be news for an organization:

- Election of officers
- Opening of an office or headquarters
- Issues and events
- Significant projects
- Actions that attract attention or have consequences for the community
- Significant community meetings
- Benefits
- Important speakers, important visitors
- Resolutions passed at business meetings

- Release of the results of studies or fact-finding activities
- Special awards won or given
- Member participation in national or world affairs
- Unusual fund-raising ideas
- Community classes offered

For news to be reported it must first, of course, be news. It must also meet the criteria of interest and accuracy. News needs to be of interest to a good portion of the audience, and the facts must be correct.

What you read about in the paper, hear on the radio, or watch on the six o'clock news is a combination of hard news and feature stories. Hard news mainly includes events and occurrences, whereas features touch on stories of human interest or offer more in-depth information on a subject rather than on an incident.

For news to be reported in a way that furthers your group's interests, you must provide good, accurate, informative facts that put your group's concerns in a good light and respect the professionalism of the people in the news media. Your major local newspaper or journalism society, or perhaps a public interest group, may publish a manual to assist you in working with the media.

Let's take a look at how this game is played. Getting in or on the news is essentially a business of form, of information, and of relationships. I'd have to say that good relationships are surely as important as anything else.

Building Productive Relationships

Just who are these news people, and how do you get to know them? Almost anyone who makes decisions on what gets printed or aired as news is a potentially valuable person to know. For the print media, mainly newspapers, the key people are the city editor, the assignments editor, feature and editorial page editors, editorial writers, and reporters, both the beat reporters and the general assignment reporters. The beat reporters will probably be the most important among this group. Of course, it doesn't hurt to know the managing editor and the publisher either, but they are not as immediately involved with writing and preparing stories and editorials.

For the electronic media (that is, radio and television) the cast is about the same. Most radio stations have pretty lean news operations. In addition to the news director, radio stations also have people who read the news, and some have full-time reporters. The news and talk stations have larger news departments, but even these are pretty small except in major news markets. Local affiliate television stations and some independent stations have standard news departments. You will notice different levels of commitment to the news operation even among stations in the same city. The most important personnel for you to know in television news are the assignments editor and the producer. Also helpful to know, but of lesser importance to getting your story on the air, are the reporters, the news director, and the anchor people. Both radio and television stations have station managers who set the general policies of the stations, but they are not typically involved in the day-to-day production of newscasts.

Editors make the basic decisions in news operations. For example, they decide what types of stories they are looking for, which stories will be covered, the amount of attention the story will merit, and which reporter will be assigned to a particular story. Editors have most of the formal power, but they work behind the scenes. The people with whom you will have the most face-to-face contact and with whom you will most likely develop a relationship are the reporters. Reporters can influence editors' decisions, and they do the most critical job on the news team—they report the story. Reporters gather information, decide what is important (the angle), and communicate their impressions through the story they prepare. Television news producers are becoming more influential in deciding what they want to air and the story angles. Though the editors decide which stories get covered, reporters can and do suggest story ideas. Don't forget that your current reporter friend may one day become an editor.

To identify reporters who may be interested in your issues, watch the news and read the paper. Notice which reporters seem to cover which types of stories. Newspapers have some reporters assigned to a particular beat. These reporters look for and report stories on particular subjects; for example, the goings-on at City Hall, crime, health, or economic matters. They also have general assignment reporters who are not tied to a specific area. However, even these reporters do have some areas of interest, though they may not always be free to pursue them. A few television reporters have a specific area on which they concentrate, but most work on general assignment with some particular areas of interest and expertise. By paying close attention to the reporters and the stories they cover, you can begin to get to know them.

Of course it helps to meet them. The basic ways are pretty routine. The most likely way you will meet a reporter is by contacting her or him directly about a story. This may result in an interview, which gives you the opportunity to get to know the individual better. If the work you are doing in your change effort has attracted media attention on its own, you may be contacted for an interview by the reporter. Another opportunity is the talk show. Some reporters also serve as hosts of talk shows. Your appearance on the show gives you an excellent chance to begin building a relationship with the reporter.

So, once you meet them, how do you build a relationship? Essentially you do this the same way you would with anyone else you would like to know better. Being friendly is a good start. Yes, there is a bit more you can do.

- Be well prepared for your interview. Assist the reporter in getting a good handle on the story. Have your facts straight and at your fingertips and be able to convey the essential elements of the story. If there is an opposing view, acknowledge it, but show how yours is better by comparison.
- Be straightforward. Evasive people don't gain much favor with reporters. Certainly you

will represent the facts in the way that best supports your position, but don't misrepresent them. You want reporters to be able to count on your information. You will only burn somebody one time.

• Be polite. Even if the reporter seems unfriendly, maintain your courtesy. This does not mean you should be apologetic for your concerns or your actions, nor does it mean you have to act as if you are in any way less important than she or he is.

• Though you may make suggestions about things, like other people to contact or ways to visualize an issue, never tell them how to do their job or imply that they don't know how.

• Invite them to make a presentation on the news media to a group in which you are involved. This could be a college class, a professional organization, or a church group.

• Get together with them for lunch or after work for some refreshment. Get to know them on a more personal level. You may ask for a meeting for the purpose of discussing an issue or a potential story. This allows you to help the reporter more fully understand the complexities behind a situation. It also gives you the chance to get to know one another better. If the invitation was purely social, do *not* use this time to discuss your particular agenda, except in the broadest of terms. If the reporter wants to bring up a particular question, fine, then you can talk about things more specifically.

• Be seen as a good resource. Let reporters know the things you are involved in, but don't be a name dropper. If you have expertise in particular areas, let them know. Call them from time to time with potential stories they may be interested in. You will find that you will be contacted for assistance with other stories. Often this will involve helping the reporter identify a person with knowledge of a particular subject. Or, it may involve some specific information. If you don't have the information they need but you think you might be able to get it, tell them you will work on it for 10 minutes and get back to them. Then *you* make some quick

phone calls. This is much better than giving the reporter more phone calls to make or saying "I don't know."

• Put reporters on your organization's mailing list. This keeps them aware of what you are doing and gives them some story ideas.

• Never, ever ask them to do you a favor by running a story, and never tell them that they have to do a particular story.

• Once you have gotten to know a particular reporter, keep in touch.

Providing Good Information

Good information is, first of all, accurate. The facts you provide are reliable and give a suitable representation of the situation. Assuredly, you want to paint a picture that serves your purposes. Draw attention to factors that support a point you want to make or that distracts notice from a situation you don't want examined. Though you may stress certain details over others to emphasize a circumstance, do not exaggerate your case by overstating specific facts. For example, if 100 people showed up for an event, you may say that you were excited that so many people attended, but do not say that the crowd was over 250.

Good information is interesting and relevant. Try to draw a connection between yourself and the reporter's audience. The audience should be able to see themselves in what you experience. Stories related to recent news items are easier for the audience to associate with.

Good information is unusual. Show how the condition you are describing is not commonplace or not acceptable.

Good information is important. Demonstrate that what is happening or has happened affects a lot of people or some particular person or thing the audience highly values. An increase in taxes or the destruction of a historic landmark could be considered important information.

Good information is thorough, yet concise. The information you provide touches on the classic "five W's and an H": Who, What, Where, When, Why, and How. Address these fundamental points in as succinct a manner as possible. Clearly underline important factors, but do not lecture on them.

Many times you provide information through an interview. When responding to a reporter's questions, try to give distinct, direct, 10- to 15-second answers, and throw in a few quotable lines. Long responses with no pauses make it harder to hold the reporter's attention and leave you to the mercy of the reporter or the editor who must capture the chief points of your message.

This is particularly true of television, where news stories are rarely more than 90 seconds long, and usually less. Before taping your interview, spend a couple of minutes going over the essential aspects of your story with the reporter. This will assist the reporter in asking you the right questions, and it will help you get oriented so you can distill the main ideas you want to communicate.

Remember that anything you say to a reporter can be used in a story unless you clearly state *beforehand* that what you are saying is "off the record." Even then, some reporters will try to figure out how they can use the information. A good caution is: Don't say it unless you can handle reading it. If the reporter cannot use the information, you have to ask yourself why you are bringing it up in the first place.

Using the Proper Form and Style

Initial contact.   Knowing whom to contact for a story is the first step. If you have established a relationship with a reporter or an editor, that is a good starting point. If you haven't, it is proper to start by speaking to the appropriate editor. When contacting a television station, ask for the assignments editor. For newspapers, talk to the city editor or the city desk when you have a story involving hard news. If you have a feature story, speak to the proper feature editor or tell the city desk that you have a story intended for the "feature side." They will direct you to the right person.

Selling your story involves thinking about it

from the editor's perspective. Why would the audience care about this story? How does this idea relate to recent news? You would also want to know what the caller has available to help get this message out. Dealing with these concerns will help you sell your story. Remember that you have two audiences. You must convince your first audience, the media, that your story has merit to get to your second audience, the general public.

Many reporters have seen it all. The ways that most groups present information is so routine that when reporters or editors see something new they flock to it. Further, if you can convince the reporters of the validity of your position on the issue, they will make your point for you.

Objectivity is a rarely achieved condition in news reporting, and it may be rarely intended. Here are some ideas that will help you get your story noticed:

- Always think visually, especially for television. Find a way to tell or reinforce your story using images.
- Tell the story through the eyes of the person most affected. If there is a victim, let her or his voice tell the story.
- Don't lay it on too thick.
- Jar the media out of their preconceived idea of who you are. Show a side of yourself that they don't know.

Carefully study the newspapers and the TV news for a week or two. You will learn quite a lot. You will see how stories are handled and what gets attention. Most of all, you will see what reporters are looking for. Give it to them.

News releases.   Communicating with the news media by means of a news release is common practice. So common, in fact, that an editor may have to wade through dozens before getting to yours. It is important to recognize that you are in competition with others who want attention. Taking a little extra effort to prepare your release properly may help yours stand out from some of the rest. Write the release as if you were

NEWS RELEASE
(The words "News Release" should appear in large, bold print at the top of the page.)

Name of your organization:	Contact person(s):
(if you don't have stationery)	*(with titles)*
Address:	Phone, fax, E-mail:
Today's date:	For Immediate Release
	(or For release: date)

Sample News Release Format
(Start almost halfway down the page with a 3- or 4-word slugline that says what the story is about.)

Begin the text of your story a few spaces below your slugline. Remember to use your five W's and your H in the first paragraph. You should double or triple space your text and use wide margins. This enables the editor to make changes.

Use standard 8½-×-11-inch white paper.

If you have to go to a second page, write the word "MORE" three times across the botton of the page.

MORE   MORE   MORE

Sample News Release Format/Page 2 of 2

Start the new page with a new paragraph. At the top left of the second page write the slugline and "Page 2 of 2." Do not exceed two pages for a news release.

At the conclusion of the release, put the number (30) in parentheses or put a series of pound marks ###### or put the word "END" three times across the bottom.

Because your release goes to the electronic as well as the print media, use the words "news release," not "press release."

(30)

Figure 11-2
Sample news release

the reporter. Pay particular attention to the lead or beginning paragraph. It should sound like news.

Generally, a news release has four essential elements: a title and date, contact information, release date, and text. Figure 11-2 provides an example of a standard news release. When writing your release, put all the important information in the first paragraph, ideally in two sentences. This includes the who, what, when, where, why, and how. This is your "lead." Your lead should entice the reader to want to know more. Since editors cut from the bottom, make sure that your most important information is at the very beginning of your release. Each subsequent paragraph should have information that is of decreasing importance. Use short words, short sentences, and short paragraphs,

usually no longer than two sentences. News releases are straightforward pieces, so avoid humor and cute phrases. Using direct quotes from individuals can spice up your release, but clear the quote with the person before using it. Try to keep your release to one page.

Unless there is some reason you want to work exclusively with one particular news outlet, you should get your release to all news providers. It is far more effective to hand deliver your release. If your release concerns an event, you should deliver it 7 to 10 days before the event. Then follow this up with a reminder call within a week of the event.

You may want to send a photograph along with your news release. Newspapers use black-and-white glossy photographs. Attach a "cut-line" to the bottom of the picture describing the photograph. If you are identifying people in the picture, do so from left to right. Attach the cutline to the picture by taping it on the back near the bottom so that the words appear just below the picture.

Put some time into planning your headline and your photo. Make them so irresistible that the editor cannot pass them up. Editors know that most readers look only at the headline and the photo, and maybe the first couple paragraphs of the story. If you can tell your story in a headline and a photo, you have a real advantage.

With the rapid growth of information technology, more and more editors are relying on E-mail. In some newsrooms, editors don't even check the fax machines frequently. In fact, a fax machine can go through an entire roll of paper before anybody notices.

If your organization has a Web site, put your news releases and news stories there in addition to sending your notices by E-mail. Some newsrooms have individuals who comb through local Web pages for stories.

Call the news outlet before you send your release to alert them to the fact that it is coming.

News conferences. When your organization has a particularly compelling story or announcement to make, a news conference may be in order. This is an effective approach for attracting a lot of attention to your concerns. Since news conferences are for special occasions rather than routine stories, you should use them sparingly. Giving attention to a few special details can help your news conference run successfully.

Send a teaser news release a week in advance. This release announces the news conference and promotes interest in it. All the essential details regarding time and location are included, along with a description of the purpose and the participants. In describing the purpose, state things in a way that will spark the curiosity of the editor receiving it. For example, you might say that information will be provided showing that a major state agency is operating in violation of federal law and is in danger of facing millions of dollars of sanctions. Or, you might promise to show how over 100 children died last year because of the inadequacy of prenatal care services and how this problem is costing the state millions of dollars. You want to whet their appetite without giving away your story.

Call the media people you have invited on the day after they received the release. The stated reason for calling is to answer any questions regarding the arrangements for the conference. Do not answer any questions about the substantive issues you plan to discuss at the conference itself. Of course, the real reason you are calling is to heighten their awareness and interest. Call again the morning of the event as a reminder.

There may be times when you want to call a quick news conference to rally attention to an immediate issue. The sense of urgency can promote reporters' interest in the event. These types of conferences may be useful in calling attention to a controversial community development before an opposing side has determined how it is going to handle public discussion on the matter.

Don't answer questions about the subject of the conference before it takes place. You may get a call from a reporter who is trying to pry the story from you. Resist the temptation to give it away. Once the story is out, there is no reason to hold a news conference, and no one would attend anyway.

Generally, the best time to schedule a news conference is Monday morning at ten o'clock. News builds during the week as stories develop and compete with new stories. Things start more or less fresh on Monday; it is a slower news day, and all the news crews are at full strength. Ten o'clock is the beginning of the work day for many reporters. Scheduling your conference at this hour draws their attention before other stories emerge throughout the day.

Hold the news conference at a familiar or particularly significant and visual location. Reporters and editors don't want to waste time figuring out how to find some out-of-the-way place. They want a location they can get to easily and that underscores the issues being discussed. This adds to their ability to cover the story. A strong visual image captured in a photograph or on videotape can heighten the impact of your words.

Have adequate parking and easy access. This may strike you as pretty self-evident and a little silly, but I have seen film crews drive around a location for a news conference a couple of times and then keep on going because there was no place to park their van. I have also witnessed reporters wandering around a complex for a while before figuring out which building and which room the conference was being held in. They were not in a good mood when they finally arrived. Don't let this happen to you. It's a simple matter to take care of.

Prepare news packets. Include in the news packet the text of your presentation along with a news release describing the conference. Also provide a one-page fact sheet and any supporting information that may help reporters understand the issue more fully or give them an additional angle on the story. Pass these out halfway into the conference. (You don't want to give them the story before the conference starts or have them sit there reading, not paying attention to what you are saying.) Personalize the packet. Make labels with the reporters' names, and stick them on the packets right before you hand them out. It's a small detail, but it is one of those things that shows you are a class act.

Start the conference 15 minutes late. Even reporters arrive late to functions. You want to have as complete an audience as possible, and you want people to mill around a bit to increase anticipation. This is also a good time to begin to set up postconference interviews.

Have a prominent speaker. A familiar and important face lends credibility to your cause, attracts attention, and makes your conference more newsworthy. Do not have more than three speakers.

Make the presentation brief, followed by questions and answers. The main prepared remarks should not exceed 15 minutes. Shorter is better than longer. Prepare yourself to anticipate reporters' questions so you have good, pointed, concise responses. If attendance by nonreporters, supporters, or the general public could be considered appropriate (and it usually is), have them sitting or standing where they will be caught by the camera.

Arrange for interviews immediately following the formal presentation. Let the reporters know who is available for interviews. More than one person should be prepared to be interviewed.

Give some thought to the setting. Have about 12 feet between the speakers and the first row of chairs (if seating arrangements are necessary) to give photographers enough room to operate. If you are indoors, the photographers may need to set up lights. This means there must be an adequate number of outlets and sufficient space to set up their equipment.

Have good visuals. In addition to what the location has to offer, you may have models, displays, large charts, or other visual aids to help with your presentation and to reinforce your comments.

Have good munchies. Coffee and donuts go a long way toward establishing goodwill.

Provide dramatic information. You have a captive audience; send them a strong or provocative message. Have them leave wanting to tell other people what you had to say.

Event coverage. Your organization will be involved in other newsworthy events. Protests, important meetings, and community service functions might be good events for calling out the news media. Many of the steps involved with a news conference apply here as well. Send out an advance news release, give thought to the location, have people prepared to be interviewed, and have printed material to distribute to reporters. You can probably forgo the donuts.

Your material and your comments should focus on the purpose of the event, not the event itself, since event activities should be self-evident. Show how the activities relate to the purpose; don't just emphasize the activities themselves. Although reporters may not use the news release you hand out at the event, they may well feel naked without one. So do have one available, and remember to keep it to one page.

Reporters value their time, just like you do. They like the concept of "one-stop shopping"— that is, all the people who they want to talk to are there: the public official, the victim, the organization's spokesperson, and so on. Make sure you know what the story is. Don't make the reporters try to figure that out. In advance, think about what's really going to get in the story and concentrate on that. Keep it simple. And remember those visual images.

Weekly and specialty newspapers. In your efforts to work with the news media, remember that there are many players, not just the major ones. A medium-sized city will probably have a dozen or more newspapers that reach smaller or specialized markets. Many of them have small staffs and are starved for news and attention. It is common for smaller papers to allow you to submit your own articles for publication. Get a list of the ones that exist in your community, and make use of those that can help you spread the word.

Editorials. Editorial support, particularly from the community's major newspaper, is

Change Agent Tip

Using a few carefully placed letters, you can generate plenty of community discussion and turn a small issue into an important one. You can also keep an issue going, preventing it from fading from public view. In addition, you can stimulate the interest of the news media and generate further coverage of the matters you are working on.

Here is how it works. Invite people over for a letter writing party. You only need about five people. Each person writes a letter addressing the basic subject. This is the first group of letters. These are mailed a couple at a time, with a few days between each mailing. Then, on the assumption that a couple of those letters from the first group will be published, a second group of letters is written as responses to the first. These are drafts that await only some specific references to the published letters to which they refer. These response letters are written in a way that they can apply to any of the letters in the first group; a few can even take oppositional points of view. A couple of these are typed up and sent soon after the first letters appear. Then the process is repeated in response to the next letters published. Make a few of your letters provocative so they will stimulate this additional community response. You will notice that other people in the community will begin writing letters as well.

You want different signers to the letters you have generated, so get permission from several people to use their names on letters your small group writes. Read the letter to the person whose name you are using for her or his approval before it is sent, and send the person a copy, especially since the paper may call to confirm. Notify the "writer" when the letter is published. Also use different types of stationery.

By the time you are finished, it will look like this issue has sparked a great deal of community reaction. And all it really took was five or six people having fun working together for an hour or two one evening.

extremely valuable. It says that what you are doing is not only important to know about but also that it merits approval. Contact the editorial page editor or one of the editorial page staff about their writing an editorial in support of your concerns or allowing you to prepare a guest editorial. Arranging a face-to-face meeting is preferable, though not always necessary. Unless the editorial board is very familiar with the topic, spend some time educating them about the importance of your issue and the strength of your position. Providing documentation of your points is particularly important. It is helpful to understand the editorial slant of the paper and to be able to show how your agenda relates to specific positions they have taken in the past.

Letters to the editor. One of the most widely read sections of the paper is the letters to the editor. They offer you a useful vehicle for generating community discussion of your concerns and for influencing community opinion. Not all newspapers print all the letters they receive, and the ones they do print are often edited. A few hints will strengthen the likelihood that yours will receive attention. First, keep your letter under 200 words. Next, recalling that editors cut from the bottom up, put all your essential details in the first few sentences. Refer to some story that has recently appeared in the newspaper or the letters to the editor column. When providing your name, also add any title that can lend credibility to your words. Send your letter neatly typed and free from grammatical or spelling errors. Finally, include your phone number.

Deadlines and other details. The more you know about how to make the job easier for members of the news media, the more they will want to work with you. You will learn many of these things by doing. You will learn when you have to reach a reporter to make the evening paper. You will learn that two thirds of the people get their news from television and that television news gets many of its stories from the

newspaper. You will learn that it is not really a community issue until it has been in the paper.

You will learn by your mistakes too. You will learn, as I did, not to call a reporter just before the evening news airs. She was busy putting the final touches on a story and . . . Let's just say that my phone call was not a welcomed diversion.

You will learn that timing is important. Get to know the deadlines for the newspapers and the broadcast schedule for television. Generally speaking, you can call in a breaking news story at any time. However, for planned events or to drop a tip, call television stations between 9:30 A.M. and 3:30 P.M., but do not call within 45 minutes of a newscast. Deadlines for morning newspapers are around 9 P.M. and 11 P.M. (for early and later editions); for afternoon papers, 7:30 A.M. and 10 A.M. are probable deadlines.

You will learn to provide brief, written material emphasizing important facts and views whenever you are working on a story. This is particularly helpful when working with television news, since the station may send only a photographer to capture your event. When there is no reporter on the scene, your written material will help the station put the story together more easily and more effectively, increasing the chances it will be aired and covered well.

You will learn that you enjoy working with the news media. You will learn how good it feels when your message goes out and the community begins paying attention to the importance of the things you are doing.

Conclusion

People should know about you and what you are doing. If you remain unknown, your road will be difficult, if not impossible. Good skills in publicity will make it much easier for you to accelerate your progress toward success. You cannot take advantage of the potential benefits if you rely on a haphazard approach. You need to manage this task with a sense of purpose.

Take purposeful steps to communicate with your supporters, your targets, and the community at large. The means of communication you choose and the messages you send will be geared toward your understanding of the market, those people you intend to influence.

There are many methods at your disposal. Some, such as word of mouth, newsletters, brochures, and position papers, are largely within your control. Others require assistance from people outside your organization. These may include the use of billboards, public service advertising, appearances on talk shows, or getting your efforts and issues described in the news.

When you get the word out about your organization, you attract much more than just attention. You pave the way to new supporters and the resources they can provide. You establish the credibility of your issue and your efforts to resolve it. You awaken the community's interest and get it to recognize that the need and the possibility to improve the community exists. You start moving the momentum for change in your favor and in so doing make it much harder to try to make your organization and its concerns go away.

CHAPTER 12

Building the Organized Effort

Leaning back in his chair, staring at some thought apparently trapped halfway between the tip of his nose and the ceiling, Ben hears a chuckle that causes him to turn around. He sees Melanie standing at the doorway to his office looking mildly amused.

"Sorry for breaking up your reverie, pal, but I didn't think you could ever work up enough energy to have one. What've you been contemplating?"

"I was just thinking how far we have come, Mel. Things are really moving."

"I know what you mean, Ben. When we started out, I didn't have a clue about what we were supposed to do. Don't smirk. I know you didn't either."

"Well, maybe not. To tell you the truth, though, I really didn't think we could get this many people interested and working, not to mention working in the same direction. I really feel good about what we all have done."

Melanie nods her head. "Yeah, I feel like somehow I'm a little more in control of things. I don't just sit around and complain anymore."

"Yes you do." Ben laughs. "I know what you mean, though. There is more to this job than putting up with the baloney."

"Nice to know, isn't it? You know, it has been a good time, well, most of it anyway. Sorry to disturb you, go back to your pleasant thoughts."

As she walks away, Melanie thinks back on the conversation six long months ago. It seems like yesterday that just the two of them had this thought about starting up a prenatal care center. Just the two of them. Funny how many other people are now involved in bringing this idea to life. Maybe a lot of people really had the same idea too.

———————

"Some assembly required." Daunting words these. You begin to feel a little gnawing uncertainty in the pit of your stomach. You open the box. Pieces spill out over the carpet, and you wonder if any got swallowed by the deep pile.

Oh, well, if you want to go anywhere, you have to start putting this bike together. You look at the pieces, sigh, and reach an uncertain hand for the directions. They're written in Korean.

Putting together an organized change effort

can be a similar experience. You have to have enough of the right pieces to begin with, a few tools, a fair amount of patience (it doesn't come together all at once), and an understanding that those who write the directions may be using a different language. The challenge is to get all the pieces working together so that the thing, bike or organization, moves forward with those who climb on board.

Over time Melanie and Ben moved past complaining to seeing issues to taking action. The two of them started the action. However, a successful change effort needs much more than a couple of initiators. It needs a number of people working together, using their knowledge and talents and time in an organized way, and it needs issues to get and keep things moving.

To build your organization you first need to gather some of the parts: people, information, other resources, issues, and some time. Then you put these parts together in a way that allows them to work with each other, using the potential of each to produce a desired result with the least amount of wasted energy. Making this happen requires *organizing, structure,* and *flexibility.*

Organizing is the process of obtaining and putting the necessary pieces together to accomplish your purpose. Structure refers to the deliberate, agreed-upon methods for handling predictable or routine activities and tasks. Flexibility is the ability to change tasks, responsibilities, and structures to better achieve your goals according to the particular demands of your set of circumstances. It is the lubricant that keeps the whole thing running smoothly. Together, all these elements comprise the organization.

Building an organized effort requires your attention to all those matters we have discussed thus far:

- Using information
- Understanding the community
- Generating and using power
- Planning purposeful action
- Involving other people
- Generating and using other resources
- Communicating to the community

These are the gears you must mesh to bring progress.

How much organizing do you need to do, and how much structure needs to exist? These are two of those questions with the infuriating answer of, "It depends." Some of the factors on which these depend are your purposes for organizing in the first place; the number of people involved; the nature of the issues on which you are working; the number, complexity, and relationship of your tasks; and the intended longevity of your organization.

If your intent is to develop an organization that will provide a large number of people with a permanent base of power to contend with a range of fundamental issues, you need to pay a great deal of attention to the organizing process and the development and maintenance of supportive structures. But if your goal is to rectify a specific concern, and you are bringing people together only for as long as it takes to deal with this particular matter, less attention is needed for crafting your process and establishing your structure.

A handy way of thinking about these differences is by asking yourself the question: "Is the organization itself more important than the particular problem we're working on, or is resolving the problem itself more important than putting together an organization?" Or to put it another way: "If we lose on this matter but strengthen the organization, is that good or bad?"

General questions of organizing and structure apply to all types of organizations, and in this chapter I will look at the basic procedures for putting together an organized effort, whether it be temporary or ongoing. However, most people who attempt to promote changes within their communities do not see themselves building a permanent, multi-issue, broad-based organization to amass and wield power, so I will not focus on the particulars of that approach.

A word of caution about structure. Keep

looking for the right balance. Too much or too little structure can scuttle your efforts. If you "just let things happen," you may end up spending a lot of time going nowhere until a few more compulsive or impatient souls start telling everyone else what to do or end up doing it themselves. This is not a good prescription for organizational success. However, if you assume you have to create procedures for any eventuality, you are going to bog your work down with a lot of unnecessary rules and regulations that don't fit the situation you are facing, and you will not know how to handle unpredictable or unplanned occurrences.

As your organization develops, you will start feeling a need to make certain matters more routine. For example, you may need to determine who calls meetings, who runs them, and who keeps track of what you are doing. Having people agree to hold certain positions within the organization may be a way to provide some management of these items. As you grow, more separate tasks need to be done, and you may notice that having everybody doing everything gets confusing at the very least. Maybe it would be better to work in teams, each with certain areas of responsibility. If each decision—from the color of your stationery to the menu for your community luncheon—must be fully approved by every member, you won't be making many decisions. Perhaps you need to agree on who needs to make what type of decisions and how they are to go about doing so.

Generally, a good practice is to allow your structure to emerge in accordance with the emerging needs of your organization. This means that you have to be attentive to the needs of your organization. Some of these needs can be easily anticipated; some have to be discovered. When you notice things that require routine attention, clarify responsibilities or develop procedures to take care of them. Be willing to modify and improve those procedures. This may mean getting rid of them altogether.

Becoming more organized helps you build and focus the interest of participants and other resources. However, organizations are not built out of thin air. They must have a reason for being. When enough people are concerned about something to move toward action, there is the beginning of organization. Organizations are brought to life by issues and are built by working on them.

Organizations Are Built Around Issues

Something has to demand your interest and grab the attention of others. Something has to spark a surge of effort to overcome the many reasons not to bother to make things different. Something must sustain your drive and give meaning and purpose to your use of power. You need *issues.* Issues provoke action. Issues give you energy and a reason to move.

What Are Issues?

Issues help us see and get a handle on the problems or conditions we are facing. Issues are rooted in controversy (Williams, 1989) and disagreement (Kettner, Daley, & Nichols, 1985). They focus on a proposed solution to a problem (Staples, 1984) or underscore the consequences of not acting. Issues bring an undesirable situation into focus in a way that leads to action. An issue is tied to something specific; it is not just a general dissatisfaction with the way things are. Issues serve to crystallize feelings by attaching them to a specific circumstance, condition, or set of behaviors.

Issues are different from problems. As Robinson and Hannah (1994) explain, "problems are common gripes which are discussed in general terms, characterized by overall agreement that they need to be addressed, but in fact, lead to no action. Issues, on the other hand, are specific, selected aspects of a concern dissected into manageable parts of solutions that can be acted upon" (p. 82).

Issues are developed by change agents to attack a problem. They come in layers—from

Take a Moment to Discover . . . .

Think back to a time when you confronted an issue or volunteered your time to help out with something. Perhaps it was a simple issue like not getting the correct change from a cashier. Maybe it was more substantial, like helping out on an elementary school fund-raiser. Whatever it was, you didn't ignore the matter. You did something. Why? What prompted your involvement? What interests were at stake? What does this suggest to you about what motivates people to respond?

- Issues are a way to define, perceive, understand, or give focus to a situation.
- Issues are an expression of dissatisfaction about a situation.
- Issues are produced by obstacles or resistance to improvement.
- Issues imply action or contain proposed solutions to difficulties.
- Issues shape people's responses to the situation and serve as rallying points.

Though issues may contain the seeds to solution, they also hold some traps for the unwary problem solver. Understand that the way you analyze a problem suggests methods for solving it. Be careful of defining the problem in such a way that only a limited set of solutions can be seen. You can overcome this potential shortcoming by discovering how other people see the issue. It also helps to have a clear understanding of the kind of issue you are working on.

superficial indications of things gone awry to fundamental sources of chronic destructive conditions. Issues have a number of basic elements.

Types of Issues

Not all issues were created equal. They come in a variety of types and serve various purposes. Though you will be more concerned with developing particular issues for the direct purpose of generating action, issues also commonly describe extensive concerns. Certain *fundamental issues* provide the starting point for consideration and action. Hunger or poverty or mental illness circumscribe a set of problems or questions that appear on the social landscape. They provide the broad context for action and speak to basic concerns that we have as citizens. Because they are so broad, they are not sufficient to provoke action. But they do provide the foundation on which more specific issues

are built. They give us a framework to identify, examine, and give meaning to these more specific matters.

Specific issues are those clearly identifiable sources of frustration or barriers to accomplishment that call for purposeful, distinct action. They are compelling and exciting (Staples, 1984). Specific issues fit into three categories: mobilizing or recruitment issues, long-range issues, and maintenance issues.

Mobilizing or *recruitment issues* strike people's self-interest and attract people to the organization (Staples, 1984). They seize attention, generate dissatisfaction with current conditions, and spur people to action. Mobilizing issues help to illustrate the problem and give people something to do about it. They act like

---

CAPTURING CONCEPTS

Good Issues, Bad Issues

Distinguishing good issues from bad issues is important. Good issues will move people to action; bad ones won't. Here are some characteristics of issues to keep in mind when you or your organization defines issues for action.

Good Issues . . .

- Are simple to comprehend
- Suggest concrete action
- Suggest immediate action
- Are ones you have a stake in, where self-interest is involved and relates to people's experience
- Involve emotional and intellectual attachment
- Offer the beneficiaries a way to participate
- Promote community unity
- Respond to the needs of the organization

- Provide a moderate challenge
- Limit the risks of failure
- Capture the imagination

Bad Issues . . .

- Are vague, abstract, or theoretical
- Have no clear resolution
- Have future or delayed action
- Are outside the community's frame of reference

- Involve only an intellectual attachment

- Limit participation to a few individuals
- Promote divisiveness in a community
- Respond only to an immediate situation, ignoring the needs of the organization
- Are difficult or insignificant
- Entail high costs for failure
- Are dull

Pick your issues carefully and be sure people have enough power to act on them. Power is a precondition for action. An issue is not a real issue until the group has the power to act on it.

a magnet by showing people that joining with others is a good way to work on the things that bother them. These issues tend to be immediate and pressing. Action on them can produce direct results in a relatively short period of time.

Long-range issues require sustained efforts on several fronts over a span of time. Although they are still specific, people are less inclined to jump on board either because the payoff is too far in the future or because the challenge just seems too big or difficult. Still, these issues are important to nourish the organization and help it to achieve more significant benefits for the community it serves. Mobilizing or recruitment issues can be used as building blocks for achieving success on a long-range issue.

Maintenance issues are aimed not so much at drawing people out or resolving a particular matter as they are directed to promoting the organization itself. For example, this may involve taking a strong public position on a community controversy or endorsing another group's stand. They can provide mileage by establishing new allies, increasing visibility and credibility, and developing new skills (Staples, 1984).

Working on the fundamental issue of hunger, you may have a long-range issue involving low Food Stamp benefit levels. You may unnecessarily tackle exasperating application procedures and demand elimination of a ridiculous application form as mobilizing issues. Your public endorsement of a civil rights group's report charging patterns of racism in the operation of a particular Food Stamp office can provide a good maintenance issue.

Issues and Organizations

What kind of issue is used and how it is used will depend on the kind of organization promoting the change. Management of the issue will vary with the purpose of the organization, its intended longevity, and its stage of development. Let's look at some different types of

organizing efforts and their resulting relationship to issues.

Temporary, single-issue organizations. Some organized efforts are temporary ones. They are put together to deal with a particular situation and to bring about a distinct and limited change. This is a fairly typical approach to promoting change. Once the issue that has prompted a group to form has been concluded, there is nothing to keep the group active, and people return to their routine activities. Most temporary, single-issue groups don't give much thought to developing the organization beyond the resolution of their particular problem.

Ongoing, single-issue organizations. Some groups work on a rather large "single" issue over a long period of time. Usually this is a more fundamental issue like hunger or education. They are not so much single-issue organizations as they are organizations with a limited focus restricted to a set of related issues. Their primary purpose is to deal with a persistent community problem, with less intention on empowering the organization itself. They draw people interested in this one issue and make no real effort to attract people with other interests. Since they intend to be around for a while, they must address two distinct continuing goals. First, they must accomplish the purpose of the organization to rectify certain community problems. Second, they must build and solidify the organization itself in the process. Their use of issues must further both these ends.

Multi-issue, power-based organizations. Even though multi-issue organizations attract a lot of attention in the literature on community change, they are probably less frequently developed than other types of organizations. They are established to contend with an array of issues affecting people in a similar constituency.

Multi-issue organizations cast their nets much further than single-issue groups, hoping to snag a broader array of issues and bring in people who are attached to them. These organizations use issues as a way to achieve progress by improving conditions while at the same time attracting new members. Alinsky (1972) has said that "the organization is born out of the issues and the issues are born out of the organization" (p. 121). Issues are beneficial in building the organization so it can confront other issues down the road and fortify its ability to be an ongoing community influence.

Although these groups confront a range of issues, at any given moment they are likely to have a particular focus. In addition to improving specific community conditions, these organizations intend to alter the established balance of power in the community. They are concerned not only with firming up the organization but also with expanding the power base by attracting new members and giving those members a real feeling of power.

Issues and Organization Development

You will use issues to move the organization along. Different types of issues are called for at various stages of an organization's development. A newer organization requires a more immediate and compelling type of issue than a more mature organization does. (Though it is important to remember that immediate issues should not long be absent from the scene.)

The way you assess a situation, select issues, and proceed in your action is similar to the shape of an hourglass (Figure 12-1). You may proceed from the very broad to the specific as you conceptualize the problem and focus on an issue, preparing to move people to do something about what disturbs them. Those narrow, specific issues will propel people to action. Then, as members gain some experience and confidence grappling with immediate issues, they become ready to take on broader challenges.

In a similar hourglass fashion, some change agents float a number of issues, purposefully blurring the boundary lines between distinct

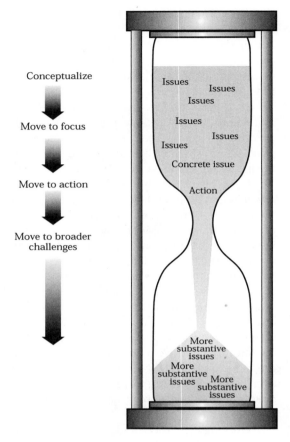

Figure 12-1
Issue hourglass. As with any hourglass, you can flip over the issue hourglass to repeat the process on increasingly more substantive issues.

issues to attract a greater number of people to the change effort (Gates, 1980). This broader array of issues is used in a mobilizing phase to stir interest. As the group moves to a decision-making phase, a clear, concrete issue must be defined. If this specific issue can represent an array of concerns, the organization has a better chance of maintaining the enthusiasm of its various members. If the issue relates only to a narrow set of concerns, the organization runs the risk of losing members who may become disenchanted, feeling that the organization has been unresponsive to their problems. Once the group successfully tackles the specific action issue, it feels more capable of addressing other, perhaps more substantial problems.

Selecting Issues for Action

What is it about an issue that will cause people to change their habits? A number of factors affect how people respond to issues. Issues should be immediate, something that people are currently bothered about; specific, something clearly identifiable; actionable, there are some specific things people can do; and realizable, people are encouraged by the prospect of victory (Alinsky, 1972). The most important principle to keep in mind in the selection of issues is that good issues move people to action, whereas bad issues don't (Kahn, 1991).

To see if the issue helps accomplish your purpose, ask yourself the following questions. Does this issue move people to action? Does it help people feel that they have gained something? Does it attract new members to our effort? Does our organization gain in credibility? Does it continue to develop our organization's

skill? Is it appropriate to the stage of development of our organization? Does it strengthen our organization's overall functioning?

The whole point of developing issues is to get people doing something or doing something differently to make things better. You have to shake them out of whatever they are doing that keeps things the same. Things will be different only when a sufficient number of people start acting differently. The issue will challenge people to do just that.

Here are some ideas on how to get the ball rolling.

- Highlight aspects of the issue that make people feel angry, guilty, excited, or almost anything. People won't do anything unless they feel something, so—get them to feel.
- Challenge people with the issue. Show how it puts something they value on the line or provides a test.
- Increase the discomfort with the present situation by emphasizing the negative side of the issue. Bring out the irritating details or the harmful consequences of current conditions.
- Rub raw the sores of discontent. Use the issue to prod and poke at the things people are

---

Change Agent Tip

Once a group is really rolling with their litany of complaints, you want to get them to think about acting to make things different. A few key comments can turn the conversation from impotent frustration toward action. Essentially, you want to get the group to focus on a choice between hanging onto their frustrating situation or acting to make it different. There are many different things you can say to change

the direction of the conversation. The point is to keep your comments or questions short. Some examples are:

- I guess we could hang onto being so frustrated or we could do something. Which should we do?
- Now that we have gotten all this off our chests, are we going to just sit back and let things stay the same?
- It feels good to finally get

this all off our chests, doesn't it? Maybe it feels so good that we can keep meeting like this without ever doing anything to make things different.
- I don't suppose we actually want to *do* anything about this.
- Sounds like we are ready to make some changes around here.
- Where can we start making changes?

already upset about (Alinsky, 1972). Prevent people from salving their discomfort. Keep people upset. Remind them that they are upset, and remind them why. Grind. Irritate. Do this until almost any action toward change is a relief.

• Thou shalt have a quick initial victory. Take action on one simple aspect of the issue that people can identify as a success. You might make this item seem a bit bigger than it really is and the victory a little more clear-cut. Don't exaggerate too much, or you won't be credible. Just don't be bashful about dressing things up a bit. Giving people a taste of accomplishment can whet their appetites for bigger challenges. They begin to believe in their capability and are encouraged to continue their efforts.

• Thou shalt hit them in their own self-interest. Help people see how the issue affects them. Point out details that show they have a stake in the outcome.

• Make them live up to their own rhetoric. People with high-sounding phrases and low-level actions are hard-pressed to keep ducking the issue when you persist in holding them to their words. This method can be a withering tactic when used on opponents or a kind of kick in the backside to sluggish supporters (Alinsky, 1972).

• Stimulate a vision of what can be accomplished, what can replace the reality people have to deal with today. Get people to consider the possibility of an ideal alternative to what they are currently experiencing (Schaller, 1972).

• Adjust the issue to reflect the fact that people's values are inconsistent with the current condition and their own behavior. Clearly show the difference. Communities, like individuals, sometimes just drift along in their routines not realizing that they have developed habits out of sync with their important beliefs. At one time or another we all plod along like this, not noticing, at least not until something or someone hits us pretty squarely in the face with the disturbing truth. This approach is complicated by the fact that there are often competing values present in any situation. To use this technique, take the

high road, and take it first. Accentuate overarching values that emphasize people's goodness as well as their tradition of fair play and active help for one another. Paint your issue with the brush of these values and show that they are superior to petty or mean-spirited notions that may also be operating. This helps to put your opponents on the defensive.

• Personalize the issue. Use a particular victim or villain in the present situation who characterizes the elements of the issue you want to underscore. You can, in fact, make a person the issue. It may be easier to get worked up about little Joey Balefuleyes or rude Carl Callous than about the Department of Health Services. This can dramatize the concern or put people on the spot. Don't let scoundrels hide behind anonymous regulations, corporations, or vague consequences. It is much simpler to take note of and monitor the actions or the plight of an individual than of some impersonal system.

• Plant seeds if the situation is not yet ripe for action. Sometimes you need to be patient. Nurture a developing interest by bringing up the issue from time to time. Ask people for their ideas and opinions on it. Let them stew on it for a while. After some time of sorting things out on their own, potential participants may become more attached to the issue and more receptive to pursuing it further.

• Keep the issue in front of people's faces. Issues not seen or felt are easily ignored. Don't mistake an initial burst of enthusiasm for long-term commitment. It is too easy to get distracted, lose heart, or forget the original provocation. Keep the issue and what it means clearly in focus to serve as a motivator and a guide for ongoing activities. By the same token, don't get too discouraged if the early response is underwhelming. People practice ways to insulate themselves from a difficult reality. It may take a little while for them to shed their reluctance to take a chance that things could be better. By keeping the issue before them and keeping it from growing dull, you begin to wear down that resistance.

Change Agent Tip

You may want to get a sense of what is bugging people. Maybe, though, you or other folks in your group find it a bit hard to just walk up to people, especially if they are strangers, and ask them what's bothering them. How do you start this conversation? How do you get people to open up? There is a simple method to break the ice and get good information.

Construct a simple survey asking people to respond to three specific issues you have selected. (Make sure you leave off a couple of good issues.) You can use a simple ranking system from "extremely upset" to "don't mind at all." The point here is to keep it short. The survey is mainly a tool for getting at other things that are annoying people.

Once you have your survey put together, go knocking on doors, sitting in laundromats, stopping by offices, or wherever you will find the people you need to talk to. When you make contact with people, ask your three questions to get them started. Then ask them to identify two other things that aggravate them and why. Talk about these items, and ask a few follow-up questions. You will find that people like to give their opinions, especially if they don't have to prove they are correct.

This approach will accomplish three basic purposes. First, and most important, it will help you discover what is on people's minds. Second, you can use it to stir them up a little. The discussion will bring some irritants to the surface, prompting people to recognize that everything isn't just hunky-dory and getting them a little restless to do something. Third, it will help you and the other participants make contact with people and get to know them better.

Regardless of the approach you take, use the issue as a tool to force the hand of the opposition and to move the minds, hearts, and, if need be, the hindquarters of those who could support you. Find the edge of the issue that cuts. Cut through the excuses. Cut past the fears. Cut down through layers of defenses until you pierce a nerve. Cut so that people can feel.

The most fundamental method for getting a response aims a message at people's immediate self-interest. With this as your reference point, a number of particularly compelling themes can be used to communicate your issue and prompt a reaction:

- Children
- Pocketbook issues
- Family issues
- Fairness
- Beating up the bully
- Frustration
- Prevailing values

Whichever theme—and there are many others—you find useful to frame your issue, remember that your concerns not only make sense but are just and good as well. If you take the high ground, your opponents will have an uphill struggle.

A direct or personal affiliation with the problem is the most fundamental reason people respond. In fact, it is fair to say that some degree of personal attachment to the issue or the change effort is necessary for an individual to maintain involvement. If everything else is equal, the more directly the issue affects you, the stronger your attachment will be to the effort to resolve it. Whether the connection to the issue is direct or indirect, it must be a personal one. People with little investment in an issue will probably not ride out the rough spots.

By selecting an issue you give people a way to identify what is troubling them. You help people begin to get a handle on the problems they face and to grapple with them.

Once you have focused people's attention on an issue, you can begin to build an organization that will take action. Although each organization is unique in some ways, most organizations progress through some basic stages.

Bringing the Organization Along

Sequence of Typical Organization Building Activities

No two change efforts are quite the same, so it is with some hesitance that I suggest a "typical" set of organization building activities. Yet it is helpful to have guidelines that can provide some sense of how to go about the process. Keep in mind that although an organizing effort typically follows these steps, your particular situa-

tion may demand a slightly different order or timetable. Remain flexible, and tune in to the needs of your change effort.

Identify what's bugging you.   What is it that you seem to keep coming up against? What is it that sets your blood to boiling, makes you shake your head in disgust, or leads you and your associates to complain? Try to put your finger on what it is that you wish were different. Recall that identifying the issue is not the same as identifying the solution, which refers to how you can make things different.

This step particularly relates to change episodes you initiate as someone who has a personal interest in an issue. If your intent is to organize people rather than to solve a particular problem, you will need to identify what is bugging them.

Think about it for a while.   Now that you have a good idea of what is irritating you, see if you can figure out why. Think about what makes it so annoying to you and maybe to others. Now is

---

CAPTURING CONCEPTS

Initial Hurdles

The first set of hurdles you need to clear in developing an organization are those questions regarding your own credibility and the credibility of your interest in the problem situation. Some of these questions relate to you personally. Some relate to your *standing,* a concept discussed in Chapter 4. Who are you? What kind of person are you? Can I rely on what you say?

Will you do what you say you're going to do? Why do you care about this problem? What can you possibly know about it?

The more important or risky the change or the more that involvement in working toward change represents a departure from what people are used to doing, the more seriously these questions will be asked.

The second set of hurdles

involves your attitudes about other potential participants. You will have similar questions about them.

The third involves assumptions about your ability to shape the future. You must develop a belief in the potential success of your effort to sustain your motivation and to perform the necessary actions to achieve it.

a good time to sit down with one or two people who might feel the same way you do.

Based on what you know, try to diagnose the problem. What seems to cause it? What seems to keep it going? Who gains from keeping things the way they are? Who would be inconvenienced by a change? Spend some time mulling it over. Try to focus in on the issue you want to address.

Do a little homework. Test your assumptions. Doing some sort of preliminary needs assessment is beneficial. If there are facts and figures to be gotten, get them. The more you know about the issue, the better you can communicate your concerns. You will also be more credible to those who must consider whether or not they will respond to you, and you will feel more confident about what you are doing.

Part of your homework should include talking to other people about their perceptions of the issue, especially those most affected by it. If you can, find out not only what they think about the issue but also how they feel it or experience it. You will never really stop doing homework, but you should not wait until you know everything before you act.

Identify other interested individuals. Thinking about the issue and the homework you have done will help you identify groups of people as well as specific individuals who are affected in one way or another by what is going on. Make a prospect list of these candidates and add to this list as your change effort evolves. Just because someone should care doesn't mean that they will. First, approach people you feel most comfortable with and who will take the least amount of convincing.

Figure out how to communicate what you know, think, and feel. Express yourself clearly and succinctly by organizing your thoughts. There is nothing wrong with jotting down a few phrases and saying them out loud to hear how they sound. You don't want to prepare a script, but you do want to be able to make some poignant comments.

Start talking to likely candidates, one or two at a time. This builds on conversations you have probably already had with people as you have attempted to get a better grasp on matters. Much human services work, whether that be individual therapy or community change, occurs through development of effective relationships. Spend some time getting to know your potential partners a little better if you do not know one another well already. Gaining confidence in each other and firming your understanding of what you each think and feel about the problems you face will help you deal with the uncertainty inherent in working for change. Throughout this process, you need to strengthen the belief that you can actually do something to improve your situation. The less well you know each other, the more time you should put into building these relationships. This is a crucial time in building the organization. Your ability to attract initial encouragement and actual support will probably persuade you to continue your efforts or convince you to forget the whole thing, at least for the time being.

Most of the time you will start by working with people you already know. You will work with them because you feel comfortable with them and have some confidence in them. They will work with you for the same reasons. Generally, it is better to talk to one or two people at a time; the more natural or more a part of your routine this is the better. You don't have to have a meeting to talk to people. Meetings sometimes imply a degree of formality or commitment that people may not be comfortable with; casual conversations can be more helpful at this point.

Eventually you do need to ask for a commitment. Something like "Let's do something about this, OK?" followed by, "What do you think we should do?" is helpful not only to get people to agree that they will somehow be involved but also to get them thinking about what they will do. They must put themselves in the picture of action.

Identify others who are willing to do something. Every conversation should include a question like, "Who else should we be talking to?" Remember, you don't just want a small group of friends who tell you how right you are, you want to build some sort of an organization. Go back to your original prospect list. Are there any individuals on that list to whom you should now be talking?

By this time you may have only three or four accomplices. You and your co-conspirators should each agree to get a commitment from one or maybe two additional people. Letting these new recruits know who else is involved usually provides some reassurance.

You don't need to go from 2 people to 200 overnight. You can get quite a lot done with six or eight people.

Have a small group meeting. The main purposes of this first meeting are to reinforce your feelings about the issue and to strengthen your commitment to each other and to solving the problem. Other important concerns include shaping and clarifying the issue you will address, providing leadership opportunities for people other than yourself, and figuring out what your next steps should be.

Two potential dangers should be avoided at this initial get-together. The first is just sitting around complaining about the situation and not making any concrete decisions on what to do about it. Although this may help confirm your own intelligence and moral rectitude, it releases energy that should be spent working on getting rid of the problem. The second is trying to make detailed plans for all the work that needs to be done, with an implication that it all needs to get done right away. This can lead to a beginning burst of creative energy followed by a feeling of being overwhelmed. Members may feel drained just thinking about all the additional work, and spend the next few days crafting excuses as to why they can't be involved after all. The fact is

that you survived this week without all the work being done. You will probably survive the next one even if things are not markedly different. There is a lot you can do to improve this situation; you don't need to do it all at once.

Do the simple things right away. Generally, it is more difficult to start doing things than it is to actually do them. So make it as easy as possible for people to start. By the way, simple does not necessarily mean unimportant.

You need to find some balance between confirmation of your beliefs, directions for the future, and specific tasks to complete in an identified period of time. In fact, all meetings should include identification of *specific tasks* to be done by *specific people* by a *specific date.* Keep the number of things to do reasonable and *useful.* They should yield some clear perception of progress. Further, all meetings should allow you to get to know each other better and to enjoy each other's company. (If you don't, you probably won't keep working together.)

Finally, two items for consideration at your first meeting will become routine matters for future discussions: Who else should we involve, particularly someone with leadership potential; and what else do we need to know?

Recruit, do your homework, and complete your identified tasks. During the time between your first and second meetings, you should be active in moving the effort forward on your immediate objectives. Sounds pretty evident, but you would be surprised at how many change agents use this time to wait for the next meeting. Complete any assignments you agreed to do.

Although you may use interviewing to prospect for new members, it is often better to ask a new recruit to help you with some particular task. Now that things are beginning to roll, this allows you to say "join us" in a clear, simple way. Even though some people may hesitate to "get involved," they may be willing to help out with some identifiable job.

Continue doing your homework on the issue and the community, especially the community in your arena of action. Find out how similar communities or groups have dealt with this problem. Obtain a more accurate understanding of who is likely to support or oppose you and why. Begin to discover who benefits from the current situation and how they profit. You also want to uncover the costs involved in maintaining these conditions and who has to pay them. Do they pay in dollars, in anguish, or in lives? This is the time to more fully develop any needs or resource assessments that may be required.

Hold your next get-together(s).   In addition to the ongoing purposes of strengthening your resolve and continuing the development of leadership, this meeting should focus on an analysis of the problem situation. Define your issue focus and plan for action. Begin to develop broader strategies and tactics. A lot of the homework you have been doing will be used during this meeting, so information sharing is critical.

The answers to some basic questions should help you understand what you are facing and provide some direction for your action. The first set of questions centers on principal members of the community. Who are the actors in the play? Who makes decisions on this issue? What are the nature and consequences of these decisions? Who feels the problem? Who else needs to feel the problem; that is, whose behaviors need to be different? Who is likely to oppose you and why? Who is likely to support you and why?

The next set of questions relates to the actions you would consider taking. Knowing who needs to feel the problem, how can they feel it? To what will they respond? What do you need to do to get the right people behaving in the right way? You may not get complete answers to all these questions at this meeting, but you should make substantial headway. Answering these questions will help you develop strategies and tactics.

Your planning efforts should start taking shape, moving forward with the processes outlined in Chapter 8. If your objective is to resolve problems rather than to establish a broad power-based organization, you should focus most of your planning attention on actions to produce the desired change, not (for now) on building the organization. Look for opportunities for some easily completed mini-projects or quick, initial victories.

Depending on the issue you are tackling, all this may be a lot to accomplish at one time. If you notice that members are getting weary of the process, take a break until the next time you get together. This next meeting shouldn't be too far off anyway if you want to sustain the momentum and complete some basic work. In the meantime, make sure there are a few specific things you and your associates can do to keep a sense of progress. For example, this may be the time to begin raising other resources or exploring alliances with other groups.

At the completion of this stage you have clarified your goal and the major areas or sets of activities you need to work on. This will suggest some areas on which members can concentrate their energy. This is a very important development. By breaking the overall enterprise into practical packages, participants can better understand and manage what they have to do. With the emergence of this division of labor, you can help participants make sense of what needs to be done and how their efforts fit into the overall picture. The result is less confusion and more efficiency.

Although it is helpful for members to have a clear set of tasks on which they can focus, allow for the fact that members may want to take on new duties from time to time. The fact that members have particular responsibilities does not mean they should always be stuck doing the same things. Members should always have opportunities to develop their skills and commitment by undertaking new responsibilities.

Do what needs to be done.   It is a good idea to work together in teams, even if the team has only two members. Working in teams allows for a creative exchange of ideas, helps prevent members from being disconnected from the effort or from each other, and provides motivation as individuals usually want to be seen as responsible contributors to team success.

Members and teams need to keep in communication with each other. Make sure the various teams get what they need from one another and that their work fits together. It is usually necessary to have a liaison committee or a steering committee to serve this function. Members of this group regularly communicate with each other to be sure that the work of the teams is coordinated and that necessary information is exchanged in a timely way. Also, they are commonly empowered to make decisions that don't require full discussion by the entire organization or that need to be made within a very short time frame. With each team having an identified liaison, any member of the organi-

zation has easy access to other teams. (Notice that a structure is starting to emerge.) It would be a mistake, however, to require that teams only communicate to each other through the liaison. Such arbitrary rules can become a source of unnecessary conflict and can hamper communication.

It is also about time to appoint a "Nag." Finally, you should start thinking about what you want to call yourselves. Understand that most of the work of the organization does not occur at meetings, but between them. Teams should get together as needed.

Get together again.   Celebrate your accomplishments and your victories. This is a valuable exercise. If you only look at how far you have to

Change Agent Tip

The Nag
Most of us intend to do the things we commit to do but the distractions of the everyday world often leave our well-intended promises locked in the I'll-get-to-it-when-I-can closet. How can action groups deal with this very normal dilemma? Appoint a "Nag." Or if the members of the group haven't developed a sense of humor yet, you can call this person the "follow-up coordinator."

This is an extremely valuable position and one that every group should have. The key point is that this role must be understood, formalized, and mutually accepted;

that is, the group needs to clarify what the job is and agree to select a particular person to do it.

Basically, the Nag does three things:

1. Records everyone's commitments during the meeting.
2. Reads back the commitments (along with completion dates) at the end of the meeting to make sure that everyone has the same understanding.
3. Calls the responsible person a few days before a task is to be completed to check on his or her progress. Although the Nag may help the re-

sponsible person figure out how to complete the task, the Nag does not assume responsibility for doing the work. This is really a very friendly reminder call; it brings people's commitments back to their attention so they can act on them.

When the role is agreed upon and understood, the Nag's duties help reinforce the idea that the organization is working and that people are doing what they are supposed to do. This job is so important that the Nag should rarely take on any other responsibilities for the group.

go or the work you still need to do, you will soon feel worn out. By this time in your organization's development, you have come a considerable way. Turn around and look at the ground you have covered. Paying attention to your gains is energizing.

Look for ways to incorporate some easily arranged social activities into your work. Perhaps a "no business" get-together is in order about now, or maybe a combination potluck/ working session.

Although you need to continue refining your action plans, you now begin seriously discussing matters pertaining to the organization itself, not just to the work of the organization. Make decisions on formalizing the organization. Are there any positions that need to be formalized and filled? Do you need a treasurer, a secretary, a chairperson? Do you need a bank account? Do you need routine meeting schedules, agendas, minutes, and other formal procedures? Do you need to establish bylaws that delineate the formal procedures of the organization, particularly who gets to vote on matters affecting the organization? The answers to some of these questions rest with the decision on what kind of organization you want to be. Later on in this chapter I will describe various types of organizations.

If you anticipate that your organization will grow so big that all the members can't get together to discuss concerns and make effective decisions in a timely manner, a specific policy-making group will be needed. Usually called a board or a steering committee, this group will make the fundamental decisions that determine the direction of the organization and the way it is to function. It will also oversee the activities of any staff hired to carry out these policies on a day-to-day basis and make decisions regarding significant expenditures of funds.

These are all items you may discuss during this meeting mainly given over to matters of the organization's growth and development. A special team should begin working on those mechanisms critical to enabling the organization to operate smoothly while aggressively

pursuing its goals. This team's recommendations should be proposed for adoption at the next general meeting.

Finally, select a name. A name gives you identity and solidifies you as an organization. It signifies to you that you have actually brought something to life. You become more than "a bunch of us who want to do something." Your name should be easy to say and to remember, and it should let people know what you are about.

Go public. Promote the fact of your existence. Announcing yourselves puts your name and purpose into people's awareness. Proceeding quietly can be counterproductive and confusing to potential participants. Are they being encouraged to participate or not? People are a little suspicious about secretive or unknown groups. Regardless of whether they are supporters or opponents, it is hard to reckon with something they don't know much about, which appears to have little broad support, or which perhaps doesn't have enough confidence in itself to clearly, publicly state its case. Going public will make an opponent more worried about the attention, interest, and support you will draw. A supporter will be encouraged that helpful actions are being taken and that you are real.

There are different levels of going public. Some of these, like purposefully spreading the word, being open about your intentions and your actions, and posting fliers promoting the issue and inviting participation, might be done at an earlier stage. Press conferences, public demonstrations, and other acts can be used as forceful coming-out events. Any activity that seeks recognition of your group as an entity in the community should stress what the issue is and what you have been doing about it. Plans for future actions and invitations for participation should also be announced.

Hold a formalizing meeting. The purpose of this meeting is to adopt recommendations regarding key aspects of structure and procedure, familiarize new members with your purpose and program, and reinforce your collective will to succeed. It is here that you approve the bylaws and elect officers to formally establish yourselves as an organization. Not every organized change effort needs to reach this stage; only those requiring sustained action over a period of time will need this degree of formality.

During this meeting you have to strike a delicate balance between having things well organized and ready for decisions and remaining open to suggestions. Because there are likely to be new members who aren't really certain about what is going on, leave some clear opportunity for them to ask questions and contribute ideas and leadership. You cannot simply allow for this, you must encourage it. Otherwise it all looks like a "done deal" cooked up by a few insiders who will reduce everyone else to the role of spectator. Provide background on what has occurred to date, who has been involved, what you intend to achieve at the meeting, and why. Leave some nonpivotal leadership positions open to nominations from the floor, and solicit the participation of newcomers to fill them. By taking steps such as these, you can let both new and old members know how they fit in without having to throw all the work you have done out the window and start all over from scratch.

Though this meeting will emphasize matters pertaining to the organization, it must not be devoid of action items. You need to decide on a number of actions to further your agenda to keep you directed to your business and to sustain your momentum.

Begin indirect recruitment. Up to this point, recruitment efforts have been personal, generally face-to-face. If the issue you are tackling requires a larger organization, you now need to reach out beyond your personal networks to a larger audience, inviting the participation of people whom none of you know. Although your personal efforts will continue, you need to extend your welcome much further. The suggestions contained in Chapters 9 and 11 will help you attract and utilize new members.

Keep working, monitor progress, and confirm the actuality of the change. Continue to move your agenda forward by identifying and completing tasks, particularly those that institutionalize or make permanent the changes you seek. Understand that once the change has been agreed to you will need to monitor its implementation. You may discover that you will need to keep the pressure on to ensure adherence to agreements that are to result in changes.

Implementation will not be easy. Unanticipated problems and other setbacks will occur. Those who resisted the change may attempt to undermine its genuine realization. It is not uncommon for changes to be temporary. A situation that appears to have been changed may well revert to the previous condition once the pressure to pursue new directions has been removed. Maintain vigilance and an unmistakable willingness to take action until changes are incorporated into the day-to-day life of the community (Kettner, Daley, & Nichols, 1985).

Developing Your Organization

Develop leadership. You cannot separate building an organization from developing leadership. Even if your effort involves only 10 people working together for six months, this subject requires your purposeful attention. The larger you aspire for the organization to grow and the longer you intend for it to be around, the more critical this concern becomes.

Developing leadership entails more than looking for the one leader to replace you. It means looking for several leaders to work alongside you, some of whom may assume aspects of your role when it is appropriate for you to leave the scene. Leaders are those people who routinely demonstrate the ability to influence others in an attempt to move the group forward. Leadership more accurately refers to the behaviors that provide the influence. The reason for making the distinction is that by seeing leadership more in terms of behaviors than as people you open up the possibilities for leadership to be expressed by any number of

Take a Moment to Discover . . . .

Think back to a time in your experience with someone who was a leader, especially after the leader had been absent for a while. Maybe this was your teacher, a member of your choral group, or your star pitcher, someone in whom you all had confidence. How did you feel and perform when that person was gone? How did you feel when that person returned?

All of you in the class, in the group, or on the team had work to do or contributions to make that the leader didn't take away from you. Yet, in his or her presence you all seemed to perform better. Who could offer that type of leadership in your organization?

• •

members in the organization. This keeps the group vital and self-reliant rather than dependent on a few.

Particular types of leadership roles are important to the organization. At least six basic needs for leadership exist in organizations. These include leadership in:

• Guiding strategic and tactical decisions
• Inspiring and motivating others to encourage accomplishment of tasks
• Providing direction and coordination of efforts
• Representing the organization to the public
• Negotiating the organization's interests with other individuals, groups, and organizations
• Addressing internal relationship issues

Different people can fill each of these roles; you don't have to worry about finding someone who can play them all.

Potential leaders possess some degree of commitment and capability. Both of these attributes can be strengthened over time. You can start developing leadership by encouraging the people who are currently participating in the

organization who demonstrate a willingness to provide some leadership. Some of these individuals will turn out to be effective leaders, and some of them won't. Some potential leaders will hold back, so you may not notice them at first. Perhaps they are a little unsure of themselves, or perhaps they are a little unsure of the organization, its sincerity, or its prospects for success. These potential leaders may take a little while to survey the scene before deciding if making a greater effort would be worth it. There will also be some individuals who are not currently members of the organization, but whom you will deliberately recruit because of your awareness of their leadership capabilities.

One implication of this is that you will probably experience a turnover in leadership. The people who are eager to get something going may not be good at sustaining their own efforts, much less the organization's. The organization has different needs in different circumstances and at different stages of its development. Don't be disappointed if the early leaders drift away from the organization. In fact, it is very likely this will occur. That is one of the reasons you need to be on the lookout for new leaders.

How do you develop these potential leaders into actual ones? A good beginning is to let other members know that you don't have all the answers, that you are finding your way too. One of the best ways to kill off emerging leadership is to convey that it is not needed or not wanted. To counter that possibility, actively encourage others to take a greater role, see to it that opportunities exist, and then get out of their way.

A beginning means of encouragement is soliciting ideas, especially as they relate to the six basic areas of leadership. Leadership involves some degree of risk taking. The potential leader must feel sufficiently safe before he or she will demonstrate real leadership. Safety levels vary among people. Some establish confidence pretty easily, whereas others take a while. By asking for ideas you get some gauge of capability while inviting a small leadership commitment in a nonthreatening way.

You may notice that one or two members of your group, perhaps including yourself, are seen as the arbiters of which ideas are good and which aren't. If this pattern persists, your efforts to develop new leadership will seem phony and remain superficial. You need to demonstrate your trust in the judgment of emerging leaders if your efforts to develop leadership are really going to mean anything. By deferring judgment to others and following their lead, you send a message to everyone that there are more than just a handful of people capable of providing direction.

You may need to do more than provide encouragement and opportunity. You may need to provide some conscious mentoring, working closely with those who seem capable of and interested in assuming a greater leadership role. Pass on what you have learned through your own training and experience, particularly your experience in this effort.

Natural turnover. After an early period of enthusiasm, a few of your number will disappear. Don't be surprised if half of your initial group is gone after six months. Don't be worried either. (Well, do be worried if these individuals haven't been replaced by others or if overall interest and participation is steadily dwindling.) Some loss is natural. There are many reasons. It is harder to keep something going than it is to start something. Some people get discouraged by not seeing immediate results. Others may find that they are not really very interested in the issue after all or can find nothing very meaningful to do about it. Some would rather talk a good game than play it. Yet others will move away, get a new job, fall in love, fall out of love, or have some other experience that takes them away from the action.

As long as your issue is sufficiently important and you make an honest effort on some basic fronts, your numbers will be sufficient to do the work. Some things you can do to cut down on the loss of membership are:

- Help members find specific ways to contribute
- Offer encouragement to the unsure

- Provide opportunities for leadership
- Establish a sense of overall direction
- Strengthen relationships
- Recruit and involve new members

Things to avoid doing are wasting energy worrying about who is no longer active and wasting time chasing after people who really aren't going to maintain their involvement. While some absences could have been prevented, and you can learn something by doing some reflecting, most of your turnover can be accepted as natural. You will continue to grow if you focus your energies in a positive direction.

Get people doing something right away. All that early energy and enthusiasm needs some focus to keep it from dissipating. An activity that is a stimulating change from the routine can serve important functions of unifying the participants and providing them with an opportunity to enjoy working together. A specific project or event people can undertake quickly works best. This is not an activity that is carefully thought out and then patiently explained to the group. No, these are best born of the spontaneous ideas that just seem to pop out of group discussion. The best ones are tangible, like painting a mural, creating a banner, conducting a food drive, or digging in for a Saturday neighborhood tree planting. Even something social like a barbecue, a weekend campout, or a fun-filled retreat could work. Really, almost anything that will get people going and confirm their identification with the effort will do.

This focal activity becomes an enjoyable experience that attracts the interest of new members, becomes part of the group's history, and, by moving the group forward, introduces it to a range of other possible activities.

Things will take longer than they should. We all know that change takes time, but we tend to throw that understanding out the window when dealing with our own efforts to make change. Though your work should and will accelerate the process of change, maybe even significantly, it will not make it immediate. Sorry. If you can maintain the odd state of eager patience, you will be effective while still being pleasant to be around.

Decide if an easily achieved gain will be better than one gained from struggle. You may be able to pick up the phone, call a friend, and easily solve a problem your budding organization is facing. Is this the best thing to do? Not always. Often it is more beneficial for the organization to gain a sense of accomplishment by achieving something through hard work. Your decision is based on what, at the time, the organization needs most.

Accept the reality of unearned dividends. An improvement in the community will benefit everyone, not just those who helped to bring it about. If a neighborhood park gets built, people who never worked on the project will swing on the swings or play a little three-on-three on the basketball court. This can cause resentment and create divisiveness. Do not presume to know why each nonparticipant does not become involved. Instead, focus on those who are involved, and create honest, ongoing opportunities for people to become involved according to their abilities. Then just accept unearned dividends as a fact of life.

Move past reaction. During the early phases of building your organization, you may be responding primarily to some discomfort experienced by the members of your community that is caused by an outside authority. You may initiate action by trying to stop something from happening or by trying to end a harmful practice. These can be effective motivators.

At some point, if your organization is to grow beyond an immediate issue, you will need to *promote your own agenda.* Go beyond a series of essentially defensive struggles to assert your own program of action. When this occurs, you are much more in charge of your own destiny. You are provoking reaction rather than acting provoked.

General Stages of Organizational Development

It is normal for your organization to go through certain stages or phases in its development. Though these periods of growth are fairly predictable, the length of time it takes to pass from one stage to the next will vary with different organizations. At every stage, your organization has the opportunity to move forward toward growth or stagnate and eventually pass away.

There are seven common phases of organizational development and maturation: introduction; initial action; emergence of leadership and structure; letdown, loss of members, and floundering; recommitment, new tasks, and new members; sustained action; and continued growth, decline, or termination.

Introduction
This marks the very beginning of your effort. You recognize your (or the community's) frustration with current conditions and begin to talk to each other about it. You begin to understand the issue more clearly, get to know one another better, understand your feelings about the situation, and decide to do something to make a change.

Initial Action
This stage is characterized by a handful of original members doing an armful of tasks. Common tasks include contacting potential supporters, gathering information, preparing written statements, and holding meetings to figure out what it is that you want to do and how to go about doing it. Enthusiasm, energy, and regard for one another are usually high.

At this stage, groups often make their first presentation (often unsuccessful) to those who are in a formal position to do something about the problems the community faces. They soon realize that more work needs to be done to secure significant change.

Emergence of Leadership and Structure

As the next steps are being considered, members frequently turn to a few leaders for direction, clarification, and encouragement. A need to make decisions and organize work more efficiently is recognized, and procedures are established. Work proceeds as members gain a clearer picture of what they need to do. A clearer sense of purpose begins to take hold.

A few of the original cast drop out as the early period of inspired activity gives way to more routine work. Another common deterrent to maintaining participation is the tendency for some early leaders to focus on their own agendas, seeing only their own solutions to problems and generally ordering others around. Even though these "leadership" actions may be done with apparent politeness, they soon wear thin. Leadership struggles may well occur as the group continues feeling its way.

Letdown, Loss of Members, and Floundering

It is not uncommon for organizations to go through a period of doldrums. The early energy has waned, and nothing seems to be happening. Members may become emotionally fatigued. If no concrete gain can be seen or if no interesting action has taken place, people may lose focus and question whether the effort is going anywhere. The organization will lose some members, and those who stay may vacillate between being angry at the defectors and struggling to keep their own faith.

This is a critical time for the organization. If no visible activity involving a substantial number of members occurs or no identifiable victory can be claimed, the effort is likely to wither. If the organization can make it through this period successfully, it can take future occasions of listlessness in stride more easily.

Recommitment, New Tasks, New Members

Leadership asserts itself during this phase to motivate members and assure them of the value of their involvement. Work is broken down into coherent, manageable assignments, and mem-

bers feel good knowing what they have to do and how their work fits in with the overall scheme of things. New members are recruited, and they bring vitality and new ideas. If members can point to a particular accomplishment, they begin to feel good about themselves again and renew their belief in the organization. A more genuine sense of purpose is realized.

Sustained Action

The organization's program moves forward, and members can readily acknowledge gains on several fronts. Setbacks are seen as temporary, not terminal, and a sense of confidence, and perhaps even pride, takes hold. Many of the early leaders play less active roles, and new leaders step forward. New projects are considered and undertaken. These new ventures occupy the time and devotion of only some of the members. Everybody doesn't have to be involved with everything.

As the organization continues to grow, more formal means of communicating among members are developed.

Continued Growth, Decline, or Termination

Scenario 1. The work continues, but nothing new or interesting seems to happen. Leadership remains in the same hands, and the same verses keep getting repeated to the same songs. Those who have the most investment in the effort struggle for a while to put the best face on things while not really doing much to refresh and restock the organization. They may work harder on their own responsibilities and take over other people's jobs. After a while they, like the rest of the members, run out of gas. People stop showing up, work is done sporadically and less well, and for all practical purposes the organization exists in name only, if at all.

Scenario 2. The work of the organization is completed, and it is time to go home. Sometimes when this occurs the members aren't quite sure what to do with themselves. There is a little restlessness as members still get together to try to figure out what to do next before it finally dawns on them that they are, in fact, done. This is a good time to deliberately recognize accomplishments. Holding an event that celebrates the group's successes and declares an end to the effort allows members to feel a sense of achievement and completion, enabling them to move on to other things. In the absence of a commonly proclaimed conclusion, members just drift off into other interests with vague feelings of being unfinished.

Scenario 3. New projects and new challenges bring more members and continually recharge the interests of participants. Periods of stagnation or confusion are recognized and managed. New leadership urges the organization forward. The authority of the organization's reputation paves the way to further accomplishments. The community and the individual members feel strengthened by their affiliation with the organization.

Small Group Processes

The work of organizations is largely the work of groups. Most of the stuff of organizing for change—discussing, plotting, planning, decision making, and camaraderie—occurs in groups. Building a successful organization demands an understanding of the functioning of successful groups. Purposefully building around the support and close communication a small group affords can be a helpful method of organizing (Breton, 1994; Gutierrez, 1995). The information in this section dealing with small groups has been drawn from Tuckman and Jensen (1977); Tropman, Johnson, and Tropman (1979); Konopka (1983); Napier and Gershenfeld (1993); Zastrow (1997); Brown (1991); Johnson and Johnson (1997); Home (1991); Mondross and Berman-Rossi (1992); and Sachs (1991).

Task and Relationship Dimensions

Two basic levels of group operation require continuing attention. The first of these, the *task*

component, is directed toward accomplishing the group's purpose. The group puts forth energy to determine which steps must be taken to accomplish the goal, to take the necessary steps, and to keep moving forward. All those actions that conduct the group toward these achievements are called task actions. If the task component receives little attention, the group won't accomplish very much.

The second principal element of a group's operation is the *relationship* or *maintenance* component—the ability of group members to work well together, to effectively manage their conflicts, to maintain their involvement, and to feel good about themselves as individuals and about the group as a whole. All those actions not directed at the work of the group but directed at enhancing harmony among individuals and between the individual and the group are called relationship or maintenance actions. Maintenance activities are most important for organizations that intend to stay together for a while. Taking care of relationship issues after a sequence of intense task activities is especially vital to the organization's continued health. If the relationship component receives little attention, the group will probably fall apart.

Any action that strengthens the group on either the task or relationship level can be considered a leadership action. Johnson and Johnson (1997) identified a number of specific leadership actions that can promote group effectiveness. Task actions include:

Information and opinion giver: offers facts, opinions, ideas, feelings, and information.
Information and opinion seeker: asks for facts, opinions, ideas, feelings, and information.
Direction and role definer: calls attention to tasks that need to be done and assigns responsibilities.
Summarizer: pulls together related ideas and suggestions and restates them.
Energizer: encourages group members to work hard to achieve goals.
Comprehension checker: asks others to summarize discussion to make sure they understand. (p. 195)

Among the relationship or maintenance actions are:

Encourager of participation: lets members know their contributions are valued.
Communication facilitator: makes sure all group members understand what is said.
Tension releaser: tells jokes and increases the group fun.
Process observer: uses observations of how the group is working to help discuss how the group can improve.
Interpersonal problem solver: helps resolve and mediate conflicts.
Supporter and praiser: expresses acceptance and liking of group members. (p. 195)

Effective and Ineffective Groups

Johnson and Johnson (1997) have identified characteristics of effective and ineffective groups (see Table 12-1). Ongoing attention to factors present in effective and ineffective groups will help you monitor the functioning of your own group. This will help you identify specific areas where improvements can be made. Johnson and Johnson have developed a simple, valuable model that will help you maintain awareness of essential issues.

Four other critical factors for group effectiveness have been identified by Kaner, Lind, Toldi, Fisk, and Berger (1996). They are:

Full participation: all members are encouraged to speak up and say what's on their minds
Mutual understanding: members need to understand and accept the legitimacy of one another's needs and goals
Inclusive solutions: members take advantage of the truth held by all members, not just the quick and the powerful but the slow and the shy as well
Shared responsibility: members recognize that they must be willing and able to implement the proposals they endorse

Take a Moment to Discover . . . .

Think of yourself in a situation in which people are trying to accomplish something. This may be planning a party, preparing for a class presentation, or even cleaning the house. Review the lists of task and maintenance leadership actions and put a check next to those you see yourself routinely providing. Next, put a star beside those you seldom do.

Now look at what you have marked. What does this suggest to you about your leadership style and what you think is important?

Stages of Group Development

Like organizations, groups go through stages of development. These occur not only over the life of the group but to some extent whenever the group gets together. There are many descriptions of the sequences of group growth. Tuckman and Jensen (1977) provide a handy way to remember these periods of development, describing them as forming, storming, norming, performing, and adjourning (pp. 419–427).

During the *forming stage,* members are unsure of themselves and the group. They try to figure out where they fit in with these new relationships. The *storming stage* is characterized by rebellion as members assert their individuality and resist authority. In the *norming stage,* members establish procedures and a sense of how they should act in the group. Activities become more predictable and routine work becomes easier. The *performing stage* is marked by a concentration on the tasks of the group. People grow more comfortable with the roles and relationships within the group and become more flexible in their approach to getting things done. Finally, as members approach completion of the work, the group enters

Table 12-1
Characteristics of Effective and Ineffective Groups

Ineffective Groups	Effective Groups
Members accept imposed goals; goals are competitively structured.	Goals are clarified and changed so that the best possible match between individual goals and the group's goals may be achieved; goals are cooperatively structured.
Communication is one-way and only ideas are expressed; feelings are suppressed or ignored.	Communication is two-way, and the open and accurate expression of both ideas and feelings is emphasized.
Leadership is delegated and based on authority; membership participation is unequal, with high-authority members dominating; only goal accomplishment is emphasized.	Participation and leadership are distributed among all group members; goal accomplishment, internal maintenance, and developmental change are underscored.
Position determines influence and power; power is concentrated in the authority positions; obedience to authority is the rule.	Ability and information determine influence and power; contracts are built to make sure individuals' goals and needs are fulfilled; power is equal and shared.
Decisions are always made by the highest authority; there is little group discussion; members' involvement is minimal.	Decision-making procedures are matched with the situation; different methods are used at different times; consensus is sought for important decisions; involvement and group discussions are encouraged.
Controversy and conflict are ignored, denied, avoided, or suppressed.	Controversy and conflict are seen as a positive key to members' involvement, the quality and originality of decisions, and the continuance of the group in good working condition.
The functions performed by members are emphasized; cohesion is ignored, and members are controlled by force. Rigid conformity is promoted.	Interpersonal, group, and intergroup behaviors are stressed; cohesion is advanced through high levels of inclusion, affection, acceptance, support, and trust. Individuality is endorsed.
Problem-solving adequacy is low.	Problem-solving adequacy is high.
The highest authority evaluates the group's effectiveness and decides how goal accomplishment may be improved; internal maintenance and development are ignored as much as possible; stability is affirmed.	Members evaluate the effectiveness of the group and decide how to improve its functioning; goal accomplishment, internal maintenance, and development are all considered important.
"Organizational persons" who desire order, stability, and structure are encouraged.	Interpersonal effectiveness, self-actualization, and innovation are encouraged.

Source: Johnson and Johnson, 1997

the *adjourning stage*. The group concludes its work, which results in a change in the relationship among its members.

Napier and Gershenfeld (1993) describe five stages in the evolution of working groups: the beginning, movement toward confrontation, compromise and harmony, reassessment, and resolution and recycling.

Before members ever enter the group they have some idea about what is going to happen. These ideas color their perceptions during the *beginning stage,* which is a time of watching, waiting, and testing out how to act. After people have dropped their polite façades and begin acting more like themselves, the group moves into the next stage, *movement toward confrontation.* Questions arise over who makes decisions and how. Concerns over matters of control and freedom are expressed, and leaders are criticized. Members try to firmly establish their place in the group, seeking prestige and influence. This is bound to cause some conflict. After a while, members realize that if this continues the group will disintegrate.

This recognition ushers in a period of *compromise and harmony,* during which the group tries to reverse destructive trends through attempts at reopening communication and drawing members together. A period of goodwill ensues with tolerance for different behaviors and more acceptance of individuals. Collaboration is increased, and competitiveness is reduced. Though openness and honesty are encouraged, members are careful not to step on one another's toes, and there is a subtle pressure to preserve the spirit of harmony. As a result, resistance goes underground, making it harder to make decisions. Feelings of confidence and relief give way to increased tension. The group realizes that a kind of superficial fellowship needs to be replaced with some other approach.

During the period of *reassessment,* the group may try to impose greater restrictions in an attempt to streamline procedures and increase efficiency. Or it may delve more deeply into its problems. This can lead to the group realizing how vulnerable it is to personal needs, suspicions, and the fears of its members. Members come to see how these issues affect the ability of the group to accomplish its goals. By establishing mechanisms for appraising its operations and making adjustments, the group can build on the foundation established in the previous phase. It legitimizes the expression of feelings that are not always positive or that may

produce conflict. The group realizes that its survival depends on increasing shared responsibility as well as personal accountability. This, in turn, increases trust and individual risk taking.

Finally, during *resolution and recycling,* the group realizes that periods of conflict and periods of harmony are normal, and conflicts are handled easily and quickly.

Groups can get "stuck" at various points as they move toward maturity. Also, they may regress from time to time to earlier stages of development. It is helpful to understand these phases so you can recognize events occurring within the group as signs of normal group development. With this understanding, you can help guide the group as it matures and be patient with events that might otherwise appear disturbing.

Common Pitfalls for Groups Promoting Change

Not surprisingly, every organization will experience some problems as it tries to get organized. A number of probable trouble spots can make the road a little rougher than you would like it to be. Keep your eye out for these problems. Each problem is followed by a list of symptoms to watch out for.

Inflexibility

- Overinvestment by individuals in their ideas, positions, and plans; unwillingness to see how changes to ideas, positions, and plans offered by others can help the group achieve its goals.
- Failure to see early plans as tentative.
- Inability to "roll with the punches" and take setbacks in stride.
- Defining problems in terms of solutions instead of in terms of needs.
- Lack of contingency plans; no "spare tire."

Intolerance for Confusion

- Beliefs that things won't or can't work out all right.

- Premature need to have complete answers to all questions; belief that these answers will never arrive.
- Need to know what everyone else is doing, and why.
- Lack of belief in one's own ability to figure things out.
- Need for guarantees.

Poor Group Process

- More talkative members not *actively* withholding comment and inviting or allowing less talkative members to participate.
- No purposeful effort to assist less talkative members to develop confidence in their ability to make verbal contributions.
- Less talkative members not accepting invitations or opportunities to contribute.
- Lack of clear, mutual understanding about what the group intends to accomplish; lack of clear and agreed-upon expectations.
- Members' inability to state what is important or what needs to be done to achieve success.
- Lack of summarization; lack of checking to see that members understand decisions.
- Development of a "repository of all knowledge"; that is, an individual who is supposed to know everything so other members are relieved of their responsibility to know.
- Decision making by just agreeing with me, or decision making by agreeing with whatever you say.
- Over- or underemphasis on task demands.
- Lack of purposeful attention to group process, or too much attention to matters of group process (including the "heavy duties"; that is, every little problem becomes a "serious issue that I think we need to discuss").
- Expecting someone else to solve something you see as a problem.
- Not taking time to enjoy each other's company.
- Believing that having fun is a waste of time; viewing tasks as work only.

Inadequate Communication

- Exaggerating or understating the importance of issues, concerns, or problems.
- Inability or unwillingness of members to declare needs in a way that people can act on them.
- Belief that everyone thinks things are as important, as good, or as bad as you do.
- Inability to listen to what is important to other members; inability to "go past the words." (Hint: Could you write down two things that are clearly important to each person with whom you are working and clearly state how each sees that these are being met?)
- Making inexplicit agreements.
- Lack of understanding of how the actions of one team or group within the organization has an impact on the agenda, matters, or concerns of the others.

Lack of Distributed and Developed Leadership

- Communicating that the less active members are not concerned or not intelligent.
- Decision making by just agreeing with me (or with you).
- Current leadership is too directive.
- Current leadership states opinions as facts.
- Leadership invested in "experts."
- Unwillingness by members to assert leadership.
- Whining by members who are less involved in leadership actions.
- Inability of leaders to promote leadership skills of others; lack of purposeful distribution of leadership tasks; lack of purposeful development of new leadership.

Lack of Follow-Through on Tasks

- Lack of honest understanding that "didn't have the time" often really means "didn't take the time."
- Inability to break tasks down into manageable units. (Hint: You can make phone calls in 10-minute blocks.)

- Too many excuses. (Hint: If you "hear" yourself fashioning or rehearsing an excuse to other members, let that be a signal unto you.)
- Frequent statements that things are "in process" or "being worked on."

Turning Fears into Anger

- Communicating that less involved members are not concerned or not intelligent.
- Intolerance of another's peculiarities or well-intentioned mistakes.
- Your fears are greater than your faith in others.
- Making up problems that don't really (or as yet) exist.
- Assuming or imposing arbitrary limitations on what you can do.

Poor Development Efforts

- Lack of purposeful recruitment efforts.
- Lack of purposeful fund- and other resource-raising efforts.
- Lack of purposeful development of new leadership.

Most of these problems can be nipped in the bud just by members recognizing them and deciding to handle things differently. A group that routinely assesses how it is working is able to acknowledge and deal with its internal problems. With such an orientation established from the very beginning, periodic general reminders will take care of most of the problems.

Still, some individuals don't get the message. Even after a group discussion of behaviors that can promote or hamper the ability of people to work together, they persist in acting in a counterproductive way. This needs to be brought to the attention of the errant members, ideally in a way that does not cause embarrassment. You can call direct attention to things when they happen without attacking an individual. You can help by saying something like: "Hang on for a minute, Ed. You just interrupted Sandy. He may not be finished." Or if need be, it

can be discussed in private. If it is truly a problem, though, it cannot be neglected. Dealing with these situations in a matter-of-fact manner before they get to be persistent problems will minimize the chance that an angry confrontation will be needed to clear the air.

Two final points are worth making here. First, you aren't the relationship sheriff who has the job of keeping everyone on the cooperative straight and narrow. Every member should be encouraged to deal with things that are getting in the way. Second, obviously, not every little mistake needs to be pounced on. Some things that are really not part of a pattern can be ignored.

Meetings That Keep the Momentum

Meetings that produce nothing but future meetings can be the death of the movement (O. M. Collective, 1971). A seemingly endless series of reports, hit-and-miss conversations that randomly address items of importance, discussions that spend too much time on minor concerns and too little on major ones, matters routinely held over for yet another meeting—you have been to this meeting, haven't you? You have seen these characteristics in "action," and you have winced at the thought that tonight you have another meeting to attend.

You may well have attended more bad meetings than good ones. This shouldn't and doesn't have to be the case. Too many meetings accomplish too little, waste time, or are just plain dull. One of the great ironies is that most of us have frustrating experiences at meetings most of the time, yet the notion that just anyone can run a meeting persists unquestioned. The title of "chair" does not by itself confer magical powers that enable its holder to handle a meeting well. A poor conductor will inhibit the performance of an orchestra; an ineffective chair will hamper the productivity of a meeting (Tropman, Johnson, & Tropman, 1979). Meetings should provide or revive energy, not sap it.

Tips for Effective Meetings

Actually, learning how to run a meeting effectively is much easier than many people make it out to be. By using your time, your participants, and yourself purposefully, you can accomplish quite a lot by bringing people together. Keep your focus on the goals for the meeting, pay attention to both the task and maintenance needs of the group, use a little common sense, and you will have meetings that maintain interest and inspire action.

Running meetings will quickly become routine for you. The danger is that it can become so routine that you become sloppy. Going over a mental checklist before each meeting is a good habit to get into. The more you are primed to get the most out of your meetings, the more you will produce, the more time you will save, and the more momentum you will build. (See the box on pages 304–305 for suggestions to help make your meetings productive.)

Types of Organizations

Not all organizations are the same. Distinctions are based on type, design, and purpose. You have a variety of organizational configurations from which to choose to bring people together to work for change. Some common types of organizations include: membership organizations, open organizations, coalitions, networks, core groups, and steering committees.

Membership Organizations

Membership organizations are characterized by having a prescribed method for individuals to establish their affiliation. Normally this consists of paying dues. Organizations may establish other criteria as well. These can include setting minimum qualifications for membership, nomination and selection procedures, written agreements detailing the rights and duties of membership, a code of ethics or conduct, and other policies that more strictly define membership.

In addition to codifying requirements for membership, some organizations develop a number of symbols and rituals that serve to further strengthen the members' identification with the organization and their bonds to one another. These range from a Shriner wearing a fez to the Girl Scout promise sign to a member of the Lions Club having to pay a fine for not shaking everyone's hand before the start of a meeting. Use of special signs is more commonly the case when group affiliation itself is a particular value.

Of course, all organizations develop some set of symbols or norms that convey a sense of uniqueness. Yours will too. Since you normally want to cultivate a broad membership and an unintimidating atmosphere, more restrictive admissions practices and elaborate customs are probably both unnecessary and unhelpful.

Dues are perhaps the simplest and the most effective method to distinguish formal membership. One of the main reasons for establishing dues is that in so doing you ask someone to explicitly declare support and affiliation. You literally confirm the member's investment in the organization's goals. Since your intent is to both strengthen and increase participation, it is a good idea to keep the cost of dues low. Though you can raise money through the payment of dues, doing so is usually a minor consideration.

Because they have taken steps to confirm the individual's connection to the group, membership organizations can generally depend on a stronger commitment from their participants than can less formal groups. Defined membership makes it much easier to identify, contact, and mobilize proponents of an organization's point of view. These organizations also have a better gauge on the degree of support they have and, if need be, can point to their roster as evidence of that support. They can unequivocally assert the fact that they are speaking for a genuine constituency.

Open Organizations

Most membership organizations intend to be permanent, and over time they will pursue an array of interests. In contrast, open groups tend

Twenty Suggestions to Help Make Your Meetings More Productive, Plus One

1. Know why you are having a meeting, and design your procedures to accomplish your purpose. If your proposed meeting doesn't clearly and logically relate to action or increased group cohesion, don't have it.

2. Pay attention to matters of scheduling. First, select a date that gives you enough time to implement the decisions you make at the meeting. It does no good to come up with a brilliant idea that you just cannot act on because you have left yourself so little time to do anything. Second, select a date and hour that allow for as many of the key participants to attend as possible. Next, give yourself enough time during the meeting to take care of the needed business. Finally, select a site that is convenient and appropriate for the nature of the meeting and the size of the group.

3. To the extent possible, make sure participants know and understand the purpose and type of meeting beforehand. Send out pertinent information in advance of the meeting so individuals can start off mentally prepared. (Though you should encourage participants to read over the material you send, don't expect that everyone will do so. You had better briefly review the key points of the material before you begin a discussion on it.)

4. Prepare yourself well with material, information, and any supplies needed to conduct the meeting. Review minutes of previous meetings and reports related to the topics under review to get your bearings straight before the meeting begins.

5. Develop an agenda that allows for the major items to be discussed. It is generally better to place important issues at the beginning to make sure they receive their due attention rather than rushing through them in the closing minutes. Know how much time should be spent on each item. If more time is needed as the meeting progresses, negotiate for it, clarifying that other items may get little or no time. Do not have the meeting go longer than advertised unless you have negotiated for the extra time. If more time is needed on an issue that can wait for resolution, ask a few people to work on it and provide a recommendation for action at the next meeting.

6. Decide how long the meeting should last. People can usually meet for about an hour and a half before their minds begin to wander to things more interesting. Marathon meetings that go on for hours can be useful at the beginning stage of the organization when enthusiasm and a sense of mission are running high or when preparing for some critical event in the life of the organization. They can make the circumstances seem more dramatic and the people involved in them more important.

7. Don't try to do too much at one meeting. Your preparation for the meeting should include a review of the topics for presentation and an assessment of participant interest as well.

8. Establish group sizes appropriate for the degree of discussion necessary. A large group may be broken into smaller groups for discussion with time allotted for reporting back to the entire group.

9. Pay attention to matters of structure and space. Whenever possible, participants should sit in a circle. Leave an extra chair open for a late arriving member, but otherwise try not to have too many open seats. Too much space between people decreases the energy and the potential for group cohesion.

10. Have fun. Meetings that are deadly serious can be deadly. A little playfulness can be an important element. For example, asking participants to bring snacks can contribute to a more congenial and relaxing atmosphere and increase involvement.

11. Use the talents and the interests of the participants. Unless you are simply giving information to a passive audience, remember that each participant is a resource.

12. If all members do not know each other well, take time for introductions. "Icebreaker" activities may be helpful in building new rela-

tionships. These can be as simple as having each person say a little about themselves and state what they intend to get out of the meeting.

13. Clarify the intended outcomes at the start of the meeting. During the meeting, periodically check with the participants to see how you are progressing toward their accomplishment.

14. As you begin the discussion of items, bring people up to date with recent developments. This can be particularly helpful to new members.

15. Purposefully keep the discussion on track, periodically summarizing the key points and identifying areas of emerging agreement. This can be done gently. Don't be heavy-handed.

16. Make explicit, specific decisions that are clearly understood by everyone. Don't let a lot of talk about something that needs to be done substitute for definite decisions and assignments about doing it.

17. Follow the general ground rules for effective discussion: pay attention to

spot those who are trying to speak and encourage them to do so; invite comments from the more quiet members; acknowledge contributions of members; encourage controversy in a climate of respect, recognizing that which is important to one another.

18. Use decision-making methods that are appropriate to the importance of the topic; for example, consensus on important items and majority vote on minor ones.

19. When a matter is settled, move on.

20. Close the meeting. Summarize the main points and decisions made during the meeting, identify the next steps to be taken, and recognize progress being made by the organization toward its goals.

Plus One

21. Jot down your understanding of matters immediately after the meeting, including impressions, next steps to take for the direction of the effort, and specific tasks. Make sure you write down your own assignments.

to be more focused on current issues and often do not plan to solidify the organization's development. Those involved are more likely to identify with the issue than with the organization. Building the organization is done primarily to accomplish a specified purpose rather than being a goal in itself. Thus, codifying membership policies is less of a concern. There are few barriers to membership. In organizations of this type, whoever says he or she is a member is a member.

Open organizations readily accept new participants. With concerns related more to the organization's agenda of change than to its procedures, prospective participants find it easy to become involved in the organization and its work. This can be an asset for a group working on a specific concern, especially one that can be resolved in a matter of months.

Since participants have little actual commitment to the organization itself, it is often difficult to sustain allegiance. Members tend to come and go unless the program of change is very specific and time limited. It is pretty common for work to be fragmented and for many projects to be dropped before completion. Of course, this can also be true of membership organizations. It is just more likely to occur when the participants' ties to the organization are loose and when no one is quite sure who is really involved. Open organizations certainly can structure their procedures, though a spirit of informality is more common to these groups.

Some open organizations have a very specific focus and concentrate most of their energies on accomplishing a defined objective. A political campaign or a group working together to change a particular agency policy are examples of such groups. Groups that work to resolve very limited issues are often called *ad hoc groups*. Another type of organization with a narrow focus is a *task force*. This variation describes a temporary collection of people who commonly have some special expertise that is particularly helpful in dealing with the problem at hand.

Not all open organizations have a restricted scope. Some have a broader agenda. The main function of these organizations is to provide an opportunity for people with similar concerns to have access to one another. They are loose confederations of like-minded souls. In these cases, the organization's agenda becomes a part of the community's ongoing register of concerns, while from time to time members focus on specific projects. A local committee on homelessness or an AIDS awareness council may fit this description.

Coalitions

Coalitions are organizations of organizations (Figure 12-2). They are created when a group realizes that its power base is too small for it to successfully pursue an important issue, so it joins forces with others who are affected by the same issue. When these various organizations agree to work together, the coalition is born.

Many coalitions are of the ad hoc variety, formed to address a particular concern and disbanded once that particular matter is resolved. Others become more permanent organizations, usually with a single broad focus such as health care, hunger, or reproductive rights (Checkoway, 1987; Cox, 1987b; Dale, 1978; Kahn, 1991).

Putting a coalition together provides a number of benefits to the change effort. One particular advantage is that the coalition has ready access to resources that have already been organized. Each member has something already in place that is of value to the coalition. This may be volunteers, money, good relationships with lawmakers, or leadership ability. Also particularly important is the ability to inform and mobilize a large number of people in a fairly short period of time. Each member probably has staff, a board of directors, and a constituency it serves. That could represent quite a horde of troops. Coalitions often have an easier time gaining identity and acceptance in the community. Many of the participating organizations bring established community credibility; their names and their leaders are recognizable to the media and to other members of the community. Finally, involvement by a variety of

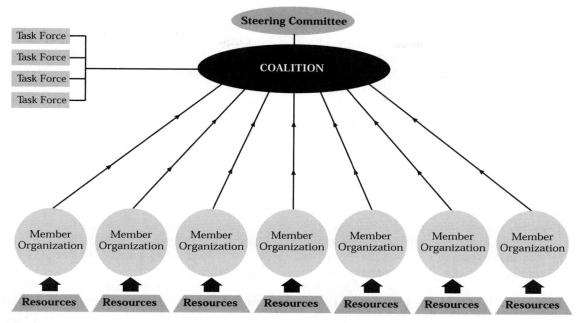

Figure 12-2
Model of a coalition

groups working on the issue gives it an almost immediate degree of legitimacy (Jansson, 1994).

Assembling a coalition involves a series of steps somewhat similar to bringing new members into any organization. The first step is to determine whom you would like to have involved in the coalition. The second is to contact them, emphasizing how the issue affects their self-interest. The third is to secure some commitment to the coalition from each organization. Next, you need to involve the member groups in the work of the coalition. Of course, throughout the life of the coalition, you need to maintain communication with those who are involved.

You will take several things into account in selecting potential members. The best starting place is to enlist the support of organizations with whom you have already established a relationship. After this, a little critical thinking is in order (Kahn, 1991). The first question you should ask is: Who is most likely to join? Organizations that serve people who are af-

fected by the issue or that have compatible philosophical positions are likely candidates. So, too, might be those whose particular interests, talents, or knowledge relate to your issue. Could the carpenters be interested in your community renovation efforts? Could the insurance brokers help you curb drunk driving?

The next question is: Who has what we need? In addition to the more obvious resources of expertise, numbers, and money, make sure you have members in your coalition who can relate to the different publics you intend to influence.

Contacting potential members is best done through a face-to-face discussion. This allows you time to answer questions and clarify how the aims of the coalition fit the interests of the organization whose involvement you seek. Additionally, explain any benefit the organization could receive through their participation in the coalition. If possible, bring along an individual who is well regarded by the targeted organization to help you make the pitch.

It is important to get a written agreement from those who are willing to be publicly involved. It is always a good idea to first ask the organization how they may help the effort. You can build on these ideas for further commitments. The easiest way to obtain a record of agreement is to develop a simple commitment form that spells out various general categories of commitment. Another approach is to ask for a letter of support written on the organization's stationery. Whichever way you choose, it is important to at least secure permission to list the organization as a member of the coalition. Although some organizations cannot, for reasons of their own, become official members of the coalition, they can publicly endorse the coalition and its goals. This should be offered as an option to those who decline membership.

From the very beginning, enlist other members to help with the recruitment effort. This increases their commitment as well as the coalition's field of contacts. Once you have a number of organizations signed up, it is time to hold a general meeting. Take this opportunity to build further enthusiasm for the undertaking and strengthen cohesion among members. Also, clarify members' roles and expectations and underscore the value of participation and the potential for significant accomplishment that exists as a result of those now present in the room.

You will find that a relatively small percentage of member organizations will be regular active participants. However, this core can accomplish a lot by using the many resources at the coalition's disposal. This may range from asking one or two members to perform some specific activity to occasionally mobilizing the entire membership. It is important, though, that these resources be used. Making direct requests of member organizations increases their feeling of involvement in the effort. Organizations rarely asked to do anything will lose interest and will most likely not follow through when they are finally asked. One important thing to remember is that each participating organization is concerned about many other things. One of the consequences of this is that requests for action should be made directly if at all possible. General requests of the membership are likely to go unheeded.

Communication among member groups is a crucial concern for the coalition. From simple matters like sending a follow-up note to those who agree to become members to holding coordinating meetings or sending out periodic progress updates, matters of communication must be given a high priority.

Coalitions commonly utilize committees or task forces organized around various functions to which the coalition needs to attend. These may include fund-raising, media communications, lobbying, and research. A coordinating committee composed of committee leaders and other interested members should be set up to manage the affairs of the coalition. This com-

Change Agent Tip

Have some sheets of newsprint hanging on the wall of the meeting room listing separate tasks or areas of responsibility that need to be handled. One should say something like: "Another job I am able to do." When a sense of purpose and enthusiasm has been generated, ask members to wander around the room and sign up for a task they would be willing to work on. Have a few people prepared to "prime the pump" by being among the first to volunteer. These sheets can be used to develop the coalition's task forces or teams.

mittee also helps plot overall strategy and direction. Open access to participation in this committee is vital. A general rule is that anyone who wants to be on it can be. Clear and meaningful opportunities to be involved in decision making will check the growth of divisive fear and mistrust.

In their "Campaign Handbook," the League of Women Voters (1976) offers several rules that coalitions should abide by:

- The goal should be clearly defined and stated; no one is empowered to speak for the coalition on any other issue.

- Each organization is free to act for itself outside the coalition, but not in the name of the coalition except with appropriate authorization from other members. What is required for authorization should be delineated.

- All participating groups should be encouraged to speak out in their own names, as well as under the coalition umbrella, in support of the goal.

- If everyone can agree from the beginning that success is more important than individual or organizational prestige, later conflicts will be minimized (though seldom eliminated). (pp. 1–2)

Coalitions can be very effective and can provide you with credibility and resources very quickly. Keep in mind that with so many varied interests involved, coalitions require a high degree of attention to maintenance matters.

Networks

Networks are distinct types of organizations that link people through a series of interconnected personal relationships (Figure 12-3). The intent is to establish and nurture these relationships so that each member is connected in some way to all others. Networks are not created to deal with a particular problem; rather, they are established to promote very broad goals. Networks put like-minded people in touch with each other so they can share resources and

Network

Figure 12-3
Model of a network. Members of a network are connected to all other members. Each member can contact any other member to make a request. Members bring personal and professional resources to the network.

further common interests. The arrangement dramatically increases the availability of support and practical assistance.

Whereas a coalition is a collection of organizations, a network is fundamentally person-centered. Networks usually involve people who hold leadership positions or are fairly active in the community. Many, if not most, of the participants work in human services agencies. The assumption is that these individuals are able to activate resources other network members could use. This can be something tangible, like providing space for a meeting; it may be a service, like conducting a presentation on discharge planning; it may be a skill, like helping to set up a computer; or it may simply be help in cutting through the red tape.

A network is built on the idea that people are more willing to be helpful to someone they know and trust than to a stranger. So, a principal aim of a network is to have as many people with similar interests get to know, trust, and commit to help each other as possible. Therefore, an individual is invited into the network not so much to help with a particular problem as to be available to help in general.

In addition to the emphasis placed on building personal relationships and sharing resources, networks stress the importance of circulating information. The assumption is that many of the network participants are "in the know." Members help one another keep current on developments within their areas of interest. They also assist in putting the word out when one of the members needs some special help. A particular agency usually serves as a clearinghouse of network information. Regular newsletters and routinely updated membership lists (which identify particular resources members have committed to share) add to the storehouse, as do frequent get-togethers among members.

Dosher (1977a) identified four main functions of a network. The network provides:

- Communication linkages and information channels for the exchange of needs and resources
- Participant support systems and resource sharing
- A means for coordination, cooperation, collaboration, person and program actualization, training, and capacity-building
- A means for collective action (p. 6)

Ideally, the network is established at an initial meeting conducted in a workshoplike atmosphere. Dosher (1977b) identified the key network concerns that should be addressed at this first gathering:

- The purpose(s) of the network
- Network function or goals
- Recognition of personal values
- Deepening and strengthening interpersonal relationships

- Structure and member roles
- Identification of member resources
- Future plans and responsibilities (p. 1)

A network is a process for bringing people together to advance a particular public policy or practice (advocacy network) or to assist one another and to serve mutual needs (exchange network). Members of a network are committed to sharing information and resources (Langton, 1982).

Some networks are structured simply to facilitate the connection between individuals and serve both advocacy and exchange purposes. Such a network is not formed to take a position on specific community issues, but the process does facilitate network members getting together to take action, though not in the name of the network. Because of the many connections members have made through the network, it is easier for people to join forces to organize a legislative action program, a workshop, or a bake sale. Those who want to be involved in any given project can do so, and those who do not can just sit back if they like.

Every one of us has our own personal network—those people we know and for whom we would do a little extra. A network as an organization simply brings all these networks together so people can ultimately benefit from one another's particular abilities and "connections."

Core Group and Steering Committee Organizations

Some organizations have almost no structure at all. Such groups are characterized by a handful of highly motivated participants making most of the decisions and doing most of the work as well (Figure 12-4). These groups tend to be interested in resolving particular problems rather than in developing the power of the members of their community. (The exception to this is when the community is so small that a significant portion of that community are members of the core group. A group of human services professionals who function as the core group will serve as unelected directors of the effort, probably without declaring that they comprise any formal decision-making body of the organization. Core group members usually do not hinder others from becoming involved in the inner circle, but they don't actively encourage it either. If relative outsiders are willing to jump in and work, and at the same time try to figure out what is going on, they can do so. However, core group members are commonly too impatient to spend time preparing new members for more active roles.

As the organization grows, or if it seeks increased legitimacy, active members may establish a steering committee to oversee progress. The steering committee positions may be filled by election, though this does not have to be the case. It could well be that whoever meets as the steering committee is the steering committee. As you might guess, few, if any, formal standing committees exist. "Committees" form when a few members get together to work on a specific task, meanwhile other small groups are working on other tasks. When the task is completed, so is the committee.

If the organization continues to grow, or if it decides to take on challenges in addition to those prompted by its original formation, it may well develop a greater degree of structure. However, most of these organizations do not stay around long enough for that to happen. Either they stop working when they have accomplished enough of their goals, or their lack of attention to organizational matters does them in.

Core groups can be highly efficient and can successfully address a limited agenda. Since it is difficult to sustain enthusiasm for long periods and because little effort is directed to building for the future, groups like these tend to come and go.

Incorporating

If you want to stake a claim for permanence, you may consider formally incorporating your

Figure 12-4
Model of a core group. A core group is an action-oriented organization with little formal structure. An "inner circle" of highly committed members does most of the work and makes most of the decisions. Membership in the inner circle is open to anyone willing to do the work.

working on agency employment conditions might fit this description.) Noncore group participants in the change effort have only a mild sense of affiliation with the organization, and their action is commonly limited to periodic demonstrations of support, such as letter writing campaigns or rallies.

If the number of active members of the organization stays small, it is likely that those

Change Agent Tip

Creating a paper organization is a clever attempt by a young organization or a core group to establish legitimacy. It involves a little creative use of letterhead in an attempt to look more substantial and formal than you really are. Two basic versions of what is essentially a ruse exist.

In the first case, your organization gives itself a name, mailing address, and phone number. It also names several officers and a steering committee or board. Although the organization may consist of only 12 people, each person is an officer or a member of the steering committee. Next, design formal letterhead stationery listing the organization information (address, names of "board" members, and so on) along with the organization's logo. Take this down to a good printer, and presto—new organization. The printer will even help you with the design. Use high-quality paper and conservative colors to enhance the effect.

The other technique is to get a list of organizations or individuals to endorse your effort. This is easier if you really are forming a coalition, though you can use this technique even if you are not. These endorsers do not have to play a role within the organization, they merely declare their support. Once you have a significant number of names, prepare a letterhead listing all of your endorsers. This can make a rather modest organization look very big.

Obviously, impressive letterhead is not sufficient to get the job done, but it does help get you into the game more easily. Because appearance plays such a large part in the game, tricks like these can have an influence.

organization. By so doing you create a separate legal entity with its own identity.

Benefits of Incorporating

Incorporation creates a psychological effect on the membership that all of you, working together, have created something with substance. It also provides you with recognition in the community beyond your immediate supporters. It can provide other, more practical benefits as well. A corporation can serve as a buffer between the members and an uncertain world. As a separate entity that can sue or be sued, it can provide some protection to its members in the event of a lawsuit. In fact, many states provide for exemptions from or a limitation of liability of directors of nonprofit organizations. (Nonetheless, it is a good idea to check into insurance, particularly corporate general liability and directors' and officers' liability insurance.) Taking the step to incorporate will help you get money, either by giving you greater access to funding from government organizations and private foundations or by aiding your efforts to solicit contributions from private individuals (Hicks, 1997). Incorporating means that you really are in business to pursue your mission.

You may work with a community coalition or small organization that does not want to go through the steps of formal incorporation, yet your group may want to seek grant support through foundations or government sources. In some instances an established, incorporated agency may be willing to let you affiliate with them under an arrangement that allows you to use their incorporation status. Check to see if an agency you work for or others within the community will sponsor the community group and its activities (Hicks, 1997).

Basic Steps of Incorporation

The decision to incorporate brings with it a series of additional decisions that will shape the future of your organization. It will also bring some additional paperwork. Following the guidance of an attorney and an accountant who are familiar with incorporation procedures is a wise step. Since most incorporations are routine matters, it should not be difficult to find a professional among your community contacts who can provide you with help for free. The process of incorporating includes the following activities.

Identify your purpose. Spend some time thinking about your reason for existence. Write down, in very broad terms, your areas of interest and service. In many states, a statement of purpose is required in the Articles of Incorporation. This serves to set forth your area of legal operations.

Identify the incorporators. These are the people who will take initial responsibility for getting the incorporation under way. They will play a significant role in shepherding the process until the board of directors is formally established. Frequently, the incorporators become the first board of directors.

Develop a board of directors. Though you do not need much of a board to incorporate, you do need substantial help from your board to stay in business, especially if you are doing business as a service agency. Most new organizations need a working board. Having a few board members who serve as window dressing to enhance your image may help, but you need to have a good group who will be active in helping to determine the direction of the organization and securing community support.

The board you establish at this time is a policy board, which is different from an advisory board. Policy boards hold the ultimate power in the organization. As their name suggests, they set the formal policies governing the operation of the organization. In addition, other routine duties include approving the budget, approving contracts, approving significant expenditures, and hiring or firing executive staff. By contrast, advisory boards hold no formal power within the organization. Their main responsibility is to provide community input into the direction of various programs. Although some advisory boards are very active in support of their programs, they have no formal decision-making authority.

Give some careful thought to the development of your board. One basic decision involves the size of the board itself. A board with 15 members is about average. (The laws of your state may set some limitations on the size of your board.) You will probably want to hold a couple of slots vacant in case you identify an outstanding individual whose participation on the board could make a strong contribution to the organization.

When selecting board members, start by looking for individuals who can provide one of the three W's: work, wealth, or wisdom. Then meet specific needs of the organization by recruiting community members who possess certain expertise or resources or who have access to a particularly important population. For example, do you need an accountant, someone from the construction industry, a wealthy individual with wealthy friends, or members active on diversity issues? Paying careful attention to the ethnic and gender balance of your board almost goes without saying (almost, but not quite). However, many organizations fail to include members of the constituency they serve on their boards of directors. This is an inexcusable oversight. Attention to the composition of your board is one of your most important tasks.

Select officers. You will determine which individuals will fill the positions you designate. The typical positions are president, vice president, secretary, and treasurer. These offices are normally filled by election. Some organizations have replaced the board offices of president and vice president with chair and vice chair, making the president and vice president paid staff positions.

Prepare Articles of Incorporation. This legal document establishes your organization as a corporation and sets forth basic principles. It covers issues such as the organization's name and purpose, its place of business, the handling of any assets in the event of its dissolution, its status as a profit or nonprofit corporation, as well as other matters. Obtaining the assistance of a professional is important to help you draw up these articles.

One of the important issues you should discuss with your attorney or accountant is the tax status of the corporation. You need to determine first whether or not you intend to be a nonprofit organization, and if so, whether or not you intend to be tax-exempt. The two common types of nonprofit corporations are those designated as either 501(c)(3) or 501(c)(4). These numbers refer to classifications within a section of the Internal Revenue Code. These are 2 of 27 different types of tax-exempt organizations under 501(c) of the Code, which represents quite a range of concerns (IRS, 1997a, 1997b). Some of the tax-exempt categories allow for a number of creative approaches that may well relate to interests in your community. You may want to take a look at them as well. For the purposes of our discussion, I will focus on the types of organizations referred to as 501(c)(3) or 501(c)(4).

Though both types are nonprofit, there are important distinctions between the two. Contributions to 501(c)(3) organizations can be tax-deductible for the contributor, whereas contributions to a 501(c)(4) are not. Further, claiming tax-exempt status as a 501(c)(3) organization saddles you not only with more paperwork but with certain limitations on the amount of lobbying activity your organization can undertake. (One persistent myth is that a 501(c)(3) organization cannot engage in lobbying. This is *not true*. There *are* limitations, but you *can* participate in lobbying efforts (IRS, 1997a, 1997b; Phelan, 1997; Troyer, 1991; Zack, 1997.)

Activities such as voter registration and candidate forums are permissible if conducted in an unbiased and nonpartisan manner, but 501(c)(3) organizations are strictly prohibited from engaging in political campaigns (Phelan, 1995, 1997; Zack, 1997). Consider incorporating as a 501(c)(4) organization if you intend to engage more heavily in lobbying. Such an organization can take part in political activities as long as the principal purpose of the organization is to advance social welfare (Zack, 1997).

If you find it in your interest to be heavily involved in election activities, you may want to form an organization that is expressly political. Section 527 of the Tax Code covers these organizations. That section provides for limited exemption from income taxes for political organizations such as political action committees (Zack, 1997).

Before you make any decisions regarding these various options, consult a professional who is familiar with choices for incorporation so you fully understand the restrictions and the benefits each choice provides. (A sample set of Articles of Incorporation is provided in Appendix A.)

Agree to a set of bylaws. The basic rules describing how the organization is to operate are declared in your bylaws. Their purpose is to prevent problems by establishing and making clear the basic procedures for running the organization. Common matters addressed in bylaws include:

- Leadership roles and duties
- Election procedures
- Quorum policies, voting methods, and voting rights
- Determination of criteria for membership
- Establishment of committees
- Schedules for various types of meetings (annual membership meetings, regular board meetings)
- Notification of membership regarding organization action

$$\text{CAPTURING CONCEPTS}$$

"We're a tax-exempt organization, so we can't take an active role." I have heard some variation of that sentence so many times that I believe it is important to set the record straight. You most certainly *can* be actively involved in advocating for a change in public policy, and there are many things you can do that are not even considered lobbying. That tax-exempt, nonprofit organizations cannot lobby or engage in advocacy is *simply a myth.* The only organizations that cannot engage in lobbying activities are private foundations (Phelan, 1995).

Most social service agencies and many other social welfare organizations are 501(c)(3) organizations, so let's take a closer look at what you can do. In 1990 the IRS published a new set of regulations dealing with lobbying activities for this group of organizations (Troyer, 1991). These regulations set forth a number of clarifications of what had been a pretty murky set of tax rules.

The substantive changes made at that time still apply today (IRS, 1997a, 1997b; Smucker, 1997).

A 501(c)(3) organization (except private foundations) can engage in lobbying. However, these organizations cannot engage in "substantial" activities to influence legislation. Just what constitutes "substantial" has been confusing and open to judgment. An organization can continue to operate under this vague test, or it can instead elect to operate within clear, specific limitations on lobbying activity. This election provision is covered under Section 501(h) in the Code. Not only are these limitations clear but some would say they are generous (IRS, 1997a, 1997b; Phelan, 1995, 1997; Troyer, 1991; Zack, 1997). Key provisions include:

• A charity can spend up to 20% of its first $500,000 of exempt purpose expenditures (generally this means the annual budget, with

some adjustments) on lobbying activities. That's $100,000 for an organization of such size! Even though the proportion it can spend for the second $500,000 and beyond continues to decrease, if its expenditures are large enough, an organization making an election under 501(h) can spend up to $1 million on lobbying! The organization must keep a record of its expenditures for lobbying and grassroots activities.

• Though most organizations are eligible, 501(c)(3) religious organizations cannot make election under 501(h). Check to see if your organization can qualify.

• "Lobbying" and "influencing legislation" are narrowly defined to relate to introduced bills and specific legislation. Prohibitions are not related to dealing with general legislative concepts not yet distilled to a specific proposal. Also, they do not relate to rules or actions by nonlegislative bodies like school boards and housing

(continued)

CAPTURING CONCEPTS

authorities. Communicating with a government official is not considered lobbying as long as the principal purpose of your communication is not directed to influencing legislation. Communicating with a government official is only considered lobbying if that official is a member of a legislative body or if the principal purpose of your communication is to influence legislation. Communication is considered direct lobbying if two conditions are present: (1) the communication refers to specific legislation, meaning legislation that has already been introduced in a legislative body or a specific legislative proposal that the organization supports or opposes; and (2) the communication reflects a view on the legislation.

• Only activities that involve an expenditure of funds fall under restrictions on lobbying.

• Only 25% of the money you spend on lobbying can be spent on *grassroots*

lobbying (rallying the troops) as opposed to *direct* lobbying (direct communication with a member or employee of a legislative body). Again, both grassroots and direct lobbying are narrowly defined. For example, for communication with the general public to be considered grassroots lobbying, it must refer not only to specific legislation and reflect a view on that legislation but must *also* urge the recipient of the communication to take action on the legislation. The Lobbying Disclosure Act of 1995 adds some registration and reporting requirements for lobbying at the federal level and includes attempts to influence the executive branch as lobbying.

• Expenditures related to initiative and referendum campaigns are permissible and are counted against the more liberal direct lobbying percentage.

• Electing to abide by the restrictions under 501(h) simply involves filing Form 5768, a one-page form. You

can change your mind later and revoke your election.

A number of other provisions in the Tax Code and the Lobbying Disclosure Act of 1995 describe what you can and cannot do with respect to lobbying. It would be wise to sit down with an accountant or tax attorney to go over the applicable regulations. You will find that indeed you can do very much to advocate for a change in public policy.

If you work for a private, nonprofit agency, one of the most significant steps you can take to move forward the process of change is to get your agency actively involved in shaping public policy. A social service agency has a base of power that it can put to use in partnership with its constituents. Public policies affect people. They affect your community, the people your agency serves, and even the agency itself. Knowing that your agency can also affect policy, perhaps you will decide that it should.

- Expenditure of funds
- Procedures for amending the bylaws

No set of bylaws can anticipate every possibility, but they do prevent problems stemming from misunderstanding or misuse of power. Bylaws should be written clearly so they are easily understood. Professional assistance can be valuable in developing your bylaws. (A sample set of bylaws is provided in Appendix B.)

File with the appropriate government agency. So the public can know what you are up to, state incorporation laws will probably require that your articles of incorporation be officially filed with the appropriate government office.

Publish your articles of incorporation. To give the public even more of a chance to learn about your corporation, in most states you are required to publish your articles of incorporation in a newspaper published in the area of the primary location of your operation. This may well be the major expense in incorporating, so before you give your money to the major daily, check to see what your publishing options are. Frequently, smaller newspapers in the area, maybe even in a nearby small town, can publish to fulfill your legal requirement. Their advertising rates may be a fraction of what the larger papers will charge you.

File necessary reports. You will be required to file periodic reports with various government agencies.

Now you are a full-fledged corporation doing important business in your community. You have come a long way from the days when you just sat around and grumbled about problems. You have not only accomplished something meaningful for today but you have done something for the future as well.

Conclusion

There is a lot to complain about. Sometimes it just feels good to let off steam. Sometimes it feels even better to use that steam to accomplish something. You are probably not the only one around who thinks things could be better than they are right now. When you set your mind and energy to finding some of those other people and working together to actually make a difference, change is inevitable. Your very decision to join forces and to act transforms the nature of things. The chances are that you will also accomplish some, maybe even all, of the specific changes you seek. You are moving from hoping things will change to making changes.

Every person in your organization always has some energy, but like batteries on a store shelf it may be just sitting around. Maybe all that energy is going in different directions and is being wasted. Acting together in an organized manner will bring more resources to bear on the situation and make your energy much more efficient, more focused, and more powerful.

Your recognition that problems don't have to be tolerated will move you through a series of actions that will result in coalescing forces directed toward change. Identify others who are willing to work alongside you. Gather more information on the community and the issue that affects it. You and your partners will come together to determine which steps you will need to take, and you will take them. You will experience bursts of enthusiasm when all things seem possible, and you will hit the doldrums and question the probability of your success. And you will keep moving forward.

You may start with just a handful of people, but your organization will grow. It will become more structured to meet the emerging demands it faces, yet it will remain flexible to ensure that procedures make your work easier rather than getting in the way. Some of the people working with you will drop out of the effort, but you will add new members to strengthen your numbers. Recognize that developing leadership and developing the organization are inseparable.

Since most of the planning and work will be done in small groups, pay attention to group dynamics. Particularly, help the group perform the tasks it needs to perform while enhancing relationships among members of the group.

Know that conflict and controversy are not only inevitable but hold the potential for strengthening the group and its efforts. Recognize and deal with those pitfalls that predictably face any group working for change.

And you will have meetings, large ones and small ones—many meetings. Make sure all these meetings have a purpose, that you all know what that purpose is, and that you take practical steps to see that the purpose is accomplished.

The type of organization you become will reflect the demands of your situation. It may be a small, temporary alliance of individuals working to achieve a modest improvement in the community, or it may develop into a formal enterprise that becomes legally incorporated.

This process of putting the pieces together to build an organized effort will be a challenge. You will be exasperated, and you will be excited. You will be doubtful, and you will be confident. You will get angry, and you will laugh out loud. Perhaps above all, you will take a degree of satisfaction from the fact that you were able to get something done, and that this mattered.

CHAPTER **13**

Taking Action—Strategies and Tactics

Chapter Highlights

- ❧ Recognizing temptations for inaction
- ❧ Accepting insecurity
- ❧ Adopting the will to act
- ❧ Cycle of empowerment: action, involvement, communication, decision, action
- ❧ Conditions for action
- ❧ Relationship between situation, organization ability, and strategy
- ❧ Avoid the trap of predictability
- ❧ Action is in the reaction
- ❧ Definition of strategy
- ❧ Basic strategies: confrontation, negotiation, collaboration, cooptation
- ❧ Outcomes of the change process
- ❧ Effects of strategy on the relationship between the parties

- ❧ Definition of tactics
- ❧ Factors influencing the selection of tactics
- ❧ Importance of ethics
- ❧ Recognizing mutual benefits
- ❧ Education as strategy
- ❧ Creating a receptive environment
- ❧ Partialization
- ❧ Getting the right people in decision-making positions
- ❧ Tricks for special occasions
- ❧ Strategies used against you
- ❧ Commandments of change
- ❧ Basic factors necessary for action

The polite smiles belie the tension in the air. Dr. Jim Simpson, Director of the Health Department, is already looking like he'd like to leave, and the meeting hasn't even started. Maybe it was the scene on the six o'clock news of him yelling at the pregnant teens to get out of his office that is troubling him. Maybe it's the idea that this Melanie woman refused to meet with his assistant and insisted on taking his valuable time. Maybe the chairs in the agency's meeting room aren't as comfortable as those in his plush office. Maybe it's the thought that Senator Cindrich, sitting across the table, is breathing down his neck. After all, he couldn't refuse her "request" that the parties sit down to reach a settlement on the prenatal care center. Maybe it is all these things.

After the long months of researching the issue, bringing it to the community's attention, and building a strong base of support, the time has finally arrived to actually work out a deal that will bring the center to life. Real agreements will be reached; real resources will be committed. Excited and more than a little nervous, Melanie smiles back at Dr. Simpson, nods to the others, and says, "Shall we begin?"

———

It's time to put your money, or maybe more important, your time, where your mouth is. It's time to stop talking about what you would do, or what you are going to do, and to start doing it.

Melanie and Ben have been able to build power and to strategically direct that power to produce results. The members of the organization they started have chosen their tactics and taken specific actions. Because they acted, they have now arrived at this point where the dream of a prenatal care center will take real form and be given life.

Many good efforts die aborning. The frustrations with present conditions or the excitement of creating new ones run smack up against the reality of taking action. Antennae, in search of reasons not to make a change or why it can't be done, suddenly sprout. And these are very sensitive antennae. They can pick up the murmur of a potential difficulty and magnify its volume until it can shout down the tentative notion to act. Good intentions wither into halfhearted attempts accompanied by strains of "I'll see if I can . . . " or "I'll think about doing . . . " or the death knell: "I'll try to . . . "

If you look for reasons not to take action, you will find them. You just have to decide whether these are more important than the reasons to act.

If you have actually read this far, either you have to take a test on this chapter or you really intend to make a difference. Maybe both. If you intend to act, accept the fact that uncertainty comes with the territory. Acknowledge the misgivings that tug at you to hold back. Oh, yes, there will be many little voices saying:

- You can't act until all the details are covered.
- You can't act because you might not succeed.
- You can't act because you don't know exactly what to do.
- You can't act because no one has done this before.
- You can't act because there will be repercussions, you may get into trouble, someone may not like you, or you may have to do some real work.

Those voices may fret at you, but they won't keep you from moving forward. By your action, you talk back. You are saying:

- All the details will never be covered; I can accept that.
- I do expect to accomplish something important.
- Most of what I know I have learned by doing; this is no different from anything else, and I certainly have enough basic skills and knowledge to at least get the ball rolling.
- Sure, there will be repercussions, including the fact that I can take some pride in what I am doing, I'll get to know some good people even better, and I may even have a little fun.
- There will be hassles, I can handle them.

Understand, the best you can, the realities of the situation, good and bad, and accept them. Then you can start doing things that lead to changes. It is not lack of money or support or authority or skill or any similar thing that coaxes people into sitting still. These certainly are barriers, but ones that can be dealt with. It is the lack of will to confront the barriers, real and imagined, that preserves conditions that should be changed. It is the will to act, and to keep acting, that makes the difference, a will built on the belief that things should and can be different. You can start without resources, and you can proceed when they are in short supply, but you can't do much with meager will.

Taking action is the final step, and the first one (Figure 13-1). Every change effort requires that someone begin doing something different. Every successful change is the result of action. Distilled to its essence, the process of change involves taking goal-directed action, strengthening your organization through the effective involvement of others, maintaining communication to keep the reality of the change effort

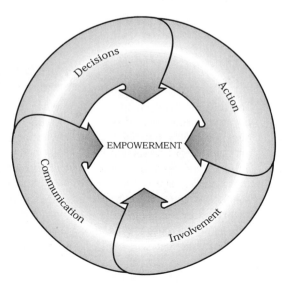

Figure 13-1
The process of change and empowerment

and the relationships among members strong, and continuing to make purposeful decisions. Action. Involvement. Communication. Decisions. Action. If you remember no more than this and adhere to it, you can look forward to numerous successes.

The decision to act and to succeed is the precondition to accomplishment. The more clear that decision, the stronger your actions will be. This decision depends on two things: that chances to gain something meaningful are sufficiently high and that dissatisfaction with the current state of affairs is sufficiently strong. To sustain action, you, as the change agent, must keep these two factors in focus, at times emphasizing the prospects for success while at others intensifying the bitterness over current conditions. You need to do this both for yourself and for the other participants in your change effort. If one or the other of these ingredients is irretrievably lost, it is time to stop beating your head against the wall and move on to something else.

It all boils down to this. None of your ideas, desires, or plans amount to a hill of beans unless you act on them. Once you have decided to act, here are some approaches that can make your actions more effective.

Major Action Strategies and Tactics

I once worked with a group of social workers who were trying to make changes within a major state agency. They kept talking about how they needed to cooperate with this person or that department. It was apparent that all their cooperating was getting them nowhere. When I questioned why they were pursuing this strategy when it clearly was not working, the person sitting next to me patted me on the knee and said, "Mark, I shouldn't have to remind you, we're social workers, and social workers cooperate." Aside from the dubious premise of the remark, it showed how a group of people had gotten locked into a strategy that was determined out of context with the demands of the situation they were facing. Though generally it is nice to be cooperative, it is hardly virtuous to be ineffective, especially if important real-life needs of clients are at stake.

"Thou shalt have the situation dictate the strategy" is a fundamental commandment of community change. Each situation you face will provide you with a set of unique variables that recommend one strategic approach over others.

A CHECKLIST FOR ACTION

The following checklist will become so routine that these questions will frame your perspective of any setting for action. Your need to answer these questions will guide everything you do, and your ability to answer them will powerfully increase the likelihood of your success.

- From whom do we want to get a response?

- What response do we want to get?
- What action or series of actions has the best chance of producing that response?
- Are the members of our organization able and willing to take these actions?
- How do the actions we decide to take lead to the needed development of our organization?

- How do our actions produce immediate gains in a way that helps us achieve our long-term goals?
- Is everything we are doing related to the outcomes we want to produce?
- How will we assess the effectiveness of our chosen approach to help refine the next steps we should take?
- What are we doing to keep this interesting?

Be sensitive to these cues as you decide on your strategy. The selection of the approach you take must be based on your organization's ability to take the best advantage of your strengths and the openings the situation offers you. The choice is driven *first* by what exists in the situation, which is then matched to your group's temperament and available resources. Both the temperament and available resources can be changed to some extent.

Avoid the trap of becoming limited in your choices, which is the result of never allowing yourself to consider different methods. Doing the same thing all the time leads you into yet another trap, that of being predictable. Especially in a conflict situation, if the other side always knows what you are going to do, they can more easily prepare to control how they respond, and you could lose an important advantage.

Tips

• The purpose of any strategy or tactic is to provoke the target into a reaction helpful to your cause.

As Alinsky (1972) points out, "the action is in the reaction" (p. 129). The person or persons from whom you seek a reaction are members of the target community. I refer to them as the *target* or the *respondent.* My use of the word "target" is not meant to imply opposition. They may or may not be in conflict with you, although in most cases there is some degree of hesitancy or resistance. The target is simply the focus of your efforts. Be cautious about your expectations. You can make a mistake by presuming that a target is either hostile or eager to respond favorably.

A strategy is the general framework of, or orientation to, the activities you undertake to achieve your goal. It is not a particular action but rather a series of actions that take into account the anticipated maneuvers of your organization as well as those of other parties, particularly the target. It is the overall approach

to action that sustains your effort by giving it a coherent direction. Erlich and Tropman refer to strategy as the "orchestration of influence attempts" (1974, p. 175) that brings together and consciously blends a variety of different components of action. They add that a strategy "takes into account the actions and reactions of key allies and adversaries as they bear upon achievement of the proposed goal" (1987, p. 258). In my experience, four basic strategic approaches can be pursued:

• Confrontation
• Negotiation
• Collaboration
• Cooptation

Confrontation involves bringing the demands of one party to the attention of another and forcing compliance. Negotiation is the process of bringing parties with different needs and perspectives to an agreement. Collaboration occurs when parties contribute resources to accomplish a common goal. Finally, cooptation results when parties share common beliefs about matters and when the success or failure of one party produces feelings of success or failure in the other.

The essential outcome of the change process is the institution of new agreements that create a change in the environment and alter the relationship among various parties. In practice, these basic strategic approaches may represent stages in an overall attempt to forge and maintain agreements between parties. Each succeeding approach envisions the parties in closer relationship. For example, when parties are in confrontation, they are usually far apart on the matter at hand; when they are cooperating, they are working together. So you may use one approach to set the stage for activities in the succeeding one if you intend to move the other party into a closer relationship with you. That is, you may use confrontation to get the other party to negotiate, which may lead to collaboration, which in turn may result in coopting your former opponent (Figure 13-2).

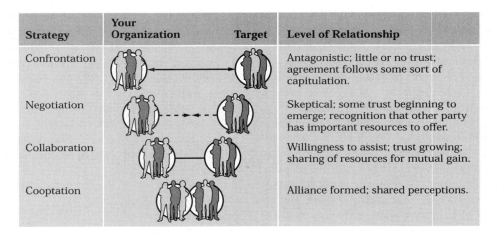

Strategy	Your Organization	Target	Level of Relationship
Confrontation			Antagonistic; little or no trust; agreement follows some sort of capitulation.
Negotiation			Skeptical; some trust beginning to emerge; recognition that other party has important resources to offer.
Collaboration			Willingness to assist; trust growing; sharing of resources for mutual gain.
Cooptation			Alliance formed; shared perceptions.

Figure 13-2
Linking strategy choices to the relationship between parties

Of course, you may neither need nor want a closer relationship. You may confront and force the other side to agree with you with little or no negotiation, and you can negotiate a settlement that does not include a subsequent series of collaborative activities. So the agreement you reach by employing one or another of these strategies is based on what you are capable of producing given the factors present in the situation at hand, the current nature of the relationships among parties, and the relationships you ultimately wish to develop.

Tactics are specific activities designed to elicit a particular response from the target within the context of a discernible strategy. They can be further defined as "an action or phase of a strategy implemented to attain a limited objective which is instrumental to the attainment of a desired end state or goal" (Connor & de la Isla, 1984, p. 245n). In selecting tactics, you need to know who the target is, what response you want, what will influence the target to respond in the desired manner, and how that response fits with your overall strategy to accomplish your purposes.

All of this means you have to do a little homework before you launch into action

(Figure 13-3). The major elements you need to study are:

- The issue
- The target
- Your troops
- The resources at hand

Using the process of force field analysis described in Chapter 8 is helpful. You need to have enough information so you can act with intelligence and confidence without getting sucked into the quagmire of paralysis by analysis.

- *Assess the issue.* Know the issue better than your target does, including the basic facts of the matter and the causes and effects of problems. Know it well enough that you can communicate it in clear and perhaps even dramatic terms. Know how the problem or issue is addressed elsewhere or what solutions have proved effective. Know the rights and obligations of the parties involved.

- *Assess the target.* Know the target system, how it acts and reacts. Know who the principal decision makers are and their particular interests. Know if the target is likely to be generally supportive or opposing of your efforts, and why. Make sure you have, in fact, selected the right target. Determine where the target has strengths to assist or resist you. Does the target have strong community or political support? Is it a master at manipulating the media? Does it have a lot of money? Recognize the target's vulnerabilities. Is it overly sensitive to its public image? Is its funding source willing and able to exert pressure? Are there superiors to which it must answer? Each system has its own Achilles' heel, a vulnerable spot in a seemingly invulnerable structure.

• *Assess your troops.* Where are your sources of strength? Do your members have a high degree of commitment? Do you have numbers? Do you have expertise? Are there important cultural norms that will inspire or impede certain actions? Where is your Achilles' heel? Are your members easily intimidated? Will they lose interest at the first sign of difficulty? Do you fight among yourselves?

• *Assess your other resources.* Know which resources are vital for your success. Which of these are at your disposal or can be developed fairly easily? Is there community sympathy for your situation? Do you have access to money or to the news media? Will other groups lend you active assistance?

Many of these homework items are easily known; some take a little digging. Be careful to avoid taking important items for granted. With the understanding you gain from your investigation, you will be well prepared to consider a variety of options for action.

Confrontation

Confrontation is the strategy you use when you need to compel a target to change its position or behavior. In these cases, the target becomes the opponent.

Situations for Which Confrontation May Be Appropriate

• The target refuses to meet with you.
• The target is unresponsive to your call for change.
• The target doesn't expect a battle from you.
• The target cannot effectively defend itself from your attack.
• The target doesn't want attention.
• You need to show that the target is vulnerable.
• You need to crystallize the issue.
• You want to dramatize the issue.
• You want to draw attention to your group.

Elements	Things to Know
Issues	Basic facts; causes and effects of problems; solutions applied in other places; rights and obligations of parties
Target	Probable reaction to specific tactic; principal decision makers; degree of and rationale for support or opposition; strengths and vulnerabilities; cohesion
Your troops	Degree of commitment; numbers; probable reactions to opponent's tactics; cultural norms; strengths and vulnerabilities; cohesion
Other resources	Awareness of needed additional resources; availability and location of resources; steps required to gain access to resources

Figure 13-3
Considerations for your selection of tactics

- You need to energize your group.
- Your members need to feel a sense of power.
- Your members are especially angry.
- You need to show that you are willing to fight.
- You need to attract allies.

In confrontation you pit the power of your organization against the power of the respondent on a particular issue, in a particular context. Rarely will your organization be more powerful overall than your opponent, but you can be more powerful in a specific instance. Define the extent of the conflict, and focus your power on a fixed area of operations. For example, you may not be more powerful than the state government, but you may be able to force the manager of a local welfare office to change procedures.

To employ this technique, set the vulnerability of the opponent against the strengths of your organization. The more carefully contrived this match is the better. It starts with understanding what the respondent is likely to be sensitive to. Your tactics increase the opponent's discomfort to the point that it becomes more palatable to agree with you than to maintain resistance. You must be able to devise an operation so that either the degree of disturbance or its duration is something you can sustain much better than the opposition can.

Confrontational methods are usually showy because you must get your adversary to notice you and to respond in some way. Also, the added attention increases the perception of community pressure and contributes to a climate of controversy that is often bothersome for the opponent.

Strengths of a Confrontational Strategy

- The presence of an external opponent that is the focus of your organization's attention significantly strengthens cohesion.
- By picking your fights purposefully and beating a formidable foe, you increase the perception of your group's power.

- You can intimidate targets, making them less likely to give you problems on other matters or more likely to be agreeable to your concerns in future situations. The mere threat of confrontational tactics in the future may be sufficient to accomplish your purposes.
- Winning provides your group with a tremendous emotional uplift.
- You may be able to catch the other side off guard, especially if they are not accustomed to being met by planned, organized confrontation from groups such as yours . . . or by those cooperative social workers.

Limitations of Confrontation

- This strategy requires a strong commitment by your members. Their commitment can be put to the test, exposing possible weak spots in your organization. Remember, some people are much more willing to talk a good game than to actually play one.
- A loss can be discouraging and emotionally draining. It can lead to internal bickering as members look to blame someone, often those close at hand, for failure.
- The other side, whether they win or lose, may become less willing to work with you in the future and may become passive-aggressive in their implementation of agreements. (This is much more likely if you don't keep the heat on them.)
- You may discover you enjoy this approach so much that you engage in confrontational methods just because you like the show, not because they are effective, and become more impressed with developing tactics than with producing outcomes.
- You may discover that you so dislike the emotional investment this strategy requires that you look for ways to avoid its use, even when it is clearly indicated.

Confrontation requires a sharply defined opponent. This can result in an oversimplification of the situation in which assigning blame becomes the easy answer. When you blur lines of responsibility to intensify the focus, you run the risk of ignoring other relevant factors that may impinge on the problem. You may forget that a major reason for confrontation is that changing your target's behavior disrupts established patterns, allowing you to move aggressively on related aspects of the situation. Your supporters may become disheartened to discover they may be just getting started; they aren't done. Further, if you think changing your target's behavior solves all your problems, you can lose sight of your own areas of responsibility and capability. This blurred view may reinforce a belief in your own powerlessness. After all, if the target is fully responsible for the situation, you are fully dependent on its actions or nonactions for your own welfare.

Tactics and Tips for Confrontation

Freezing the target. Keep your focus clearly on the target. Refuse to be distracted by others, often allies or subordinates of the target, who try to get your attention. When using this approach, your concentration is sometimes riveted to a single individual. Keep this one target in your sights and attempt to isolate it from its buffers or bases of support. You may need to engage in a series of actions to get and keep the target interacting with you.

This tactic is especially useful when the target is easily identifiable, when the target tries to get you to deal with others who have limited authority to act, or when attempting to respond to a number of allied opponents would diffuse your energy and dilute your efforts.

Personalizing the issue. This is related to freezing the target, and it essentially involves linking a particular person with the problem you are trying to rectify. The intent is to make life miserable for someone whose actions or inactions make life miserable for others. Pressure is brought to bear on the individual through a variety of means. Commonly, the target is cast as the cause or the maintainer of the problem and the suffering it produces. The target comes to symbolize all that is wrong with

the situation. Typical methods can include public ridicule, constant interference with the target's routines, as well as exposing the target's arrogance, ignorance, incompetence, or the difference between the individual's public statements and private actions.

This tactic tends to cause the target's tentative supporters to shy away for fear of becoming targets themselves or of being painted with the same brush. It will, however, tend to solidify the target's hard-core support. This may strengthen resistance, but it may also result in a small group of particularly nasty opponents becoming cut off from their support and going down together.

Your actions may result in removal of a particularly offensive individual from a position of power. However, simply removing one person from the scene rarely removes the conditions that cause the problem. Personalizing the issue sends a message to the target system regarding the seriousness of your intent and your willingness to hold those who perpetuate the problems accountable for their actions.

This tactic is particularly effective when the target has little strong personal allegiance, is arrogant or offensive, and is prone to hasty or imprudent reactions.

Getting outside help. This procedure involves seeking the assistance of others, particularly organized groups, who are outside your immediate arena of action and who are sympathetic to your cause. Ask potential allies to endorse your concerns and provide you with specific acts of assistance, such as making public statements on your behalf, loaning you volunteers, or arranging meetings with key individuals. Outside allies have access to different audiences than you do and may well have direct access to some decision makers who won't give you the time of day. It is particularly helpful to draw the assistance of a group that has broad public approval or credibility.

This tactic tends to demonstrate the breadth of your support and the legitimacy of your position. It helps you to keep from becoming isolated yourself, aids in keeping a resistant opponent distracted, and increases the resources at your disposal. If your organization is small, new, or relatively unknown, outside help will be beneficial.

Using disruptive tactics and civil disobedience. These activities generally fall under the rubric of direct action. According to Staples (1984), direct actions occur "when a group of people take collective action to confront a designated target with a set of specific demands. The group action involves people *directly* with the issue, using their numbers as a means of pressuring their opponent" (p. 3).

Procedures for handling disputes are the turf of those who control the procedures. Standard approaches may give the opponent the upper hand as these are usually designed to protect those in power rather than to accelerate needed change. So you may well be playing their game, and they are probably just as good at it as you are, if not better. You may need to change the game so your opponents have to respond to *your* procedures. This puts them on unfamiliar ground. They are not so sure how to react, and they will probably make some mistakes.

You can take a variety of actions to throw an opponent off balance and out of the comfort zone of the predictable. Sit-ins or occupations, picketing, boycotts, and mass demonstrations are among the most common forms of attention-getting activities. Because they are familiar, your opponents may know how to respond, so you may need to add some new wrinkle. However, even though they may know how to respond they usually don't want to, and they generally would like to avoid trouble.

Often the most effective disruptive tactics emerge from the situation itself. A busy office may be frustrated by an endless series of phone calls that tie up the lines and prevent any work from being done. A public agency may be hamstrung by countless requests for different public documents. Rush hour commuters may become angry at a traffic stoppage, become incensed with everyone (this includes you), and

demand that something be done to settle this. Convention proceedings may be interrupted by staging a guerrilla theater act. Be creative, and be willing to do the unpredictable.

One of the worst things that can happen is that you are ignored. Actions that attract notice at the outset may quickly become part of the landscape. Take pains to make sure this can't happen.

The usual process for engaging in disruptive tactics is to escalate the disruption in accordance with the resistance you meet. This conveys a sense of mounting pressure. However, as Kahn (1970) points out, reversing the practice by directing a major action on a relatively minor issue may prove effective by catching the other side off guard.

Civil disobedience. Defined by Rubin and Rubin (1986) as "intentionally and publicly disobeying a law and the passive acceptance of the consequences of disobedience" (p. 261), civil disobedience may take a number of forms. It may involve diverting the water from an irrigation canal, setting off building fire alarms, or refusing a court order to return to work. Perhaps the most common example is unauthorized occupation of a building or a site. If you are going to engage in civil disobedience of any kind, preparation is extremely important.

You should be well aware of the possible and probable consequences of your action and be prepared to accept them. Participants need to be well rehearsed for the actions they are to take or not take. If those taking part are likely to be harassed or taunted by those opposing the action, they should have experience role playing this situation prior to the event. Should arrest be likely, or even desired, participants must know how to conduct themselves throughout the arresting and booking process. Arrangements for bail or legal representation must be worked out beforehand. Organizers must have undertaken a reconnaissance of the area to maximize the effect of the operation and avoid problems. It is a good idea to get some special training from those who have experience conducting these actions. If you and your members know what to expect, you will be able to stand firm and make an important statement.

Use this approach when you need to grab attention from an unresponsive or delaying target or when the broad community is tolerating or refusing to take a hard look at problematic conditions. If you want to provoke people into taking sides, dramatic actions help. These methods are effective at revealing opponents as oppressors or calling attention to an unjust or absurd law, ordinance, or regulation. They can energize the members of your organization and strengthen their commitment to the cause.

Threats of action may be sufficient to produce the response you want. Often the image of the event in the opponent's mind is more fearful than the event itself. If you do make a threat, be sure you are ready to back it up with action.

Diversionary issues. Remember the old movies where captured GIs plot to escape from prison camps? They always come up with the idea of starting a fire somewhere on the compound, and while the bumbling guards scurry about trying to put out the blaze, our heroes make good their escape. Using diversionary tactics is not much different. You get the respondent worrying over a set of secondary concerns or alarming actions you might take. In their distraction, they agree to your primary point or allow you to institute a change before they can move to stop you.

One community group attempting to establish a much-needed community agency was being thwarted by established agencies who felt their turf was threatened. The community had just conducted a special drive and raised a large sum of money to deal with the problem. Representatives of the various community agencies and government bodies gathered together to address the problem as a body officially appointed by the mayor. Immediately, the advocacy group demanded it receive all the money raised. This precipitated an onrush of arguments as each agency vied with the others to lay claim to a share of the pot. In the midst of all the commotion, the advocacy group asked that the decision on divvying up the funds be put on hold for a moment while design of the proposed new agency was approved. So concerned were the participants to get back to the business of dividing the spoils that they unanimously endorsed the proposal in a matter of minutes. This was done in a packed community hall before news crews of three local television stations and both major daily newspapers. The advocates gave interviews describing the new agency and its benefits, and the event received strong media coverage. By the time the opponents realized what had happened, it was too late to go back on their agreement to support the new agency, to which they had even decided to award a token amount of money.

This tactic can work when your target is concerned with a number of issues. Exaggerating one issue may increase the target's feelings of vulnerability to that issue and keep it so preoccupied that other matters seem less important. Resistance to other matters then breaks down.

Encirclement. You can overload the target by forcing it to respond to a variety of different tactics at the same time instead of one at a time. Confront the opponent with a lawsuit, picketing, investigations by government agencies, letter writing campaigns, boycotts, or other actions to the point that the target is overwhelmed. You must have sufficient resources to utilize this method (Booth & Max, 1977).

Developing dependency on a pet project. This is somewhat like a diversionary issue. In this scenario your organization undertakes to help the respondent accomplish something of major importance to it but of minor importance to you. Because of the particular assets your group possesses (for example, credibility within the benefit community), you can assist the respondent a great deal. After the respondent has made an investment and the project is under way, ask the respondent to make a commitment to something important to your organization, usually on an unrelated matter. Knowing that you can well withdraw your support and ruin its special project, the respondent may be willing to go along with your request.

For this technique to be successful, the respondent must care more about the pet project than about the matter you want changed. Further, you have to be emotionally and ethically prepared to withdraw your support from the project and allow it to fail. This tactic functions well with a target who has been passively resistant to your efforts or who acts in a paternalistic manner toward your group.

Partners in collusion. This gambit is a variation of the good cop, bad cop routine. In that game the bad cop berates and generally mistreats a suspect. With a threat and a flourish, the bad cop then exits the room, leaving the suspect alone with the good cop, who is sympathetic and kind. The good cop then asks for cooperation so that the suspect won't have to deal with the bad cop. The good cop may suggest a dislike for the bad cop and his or her tactics, and may even hint that the suspect's assistance can be a way of getting at the bad cop. The suspect decides to cooperate with the much more reasonable good cop.

The good cop in your case would be an advocacy group that appears to be reasonable and well mannered, especially in contrast to the inflammatory rantings and public displays of a different, apparently more radical community group that fulfills the role of the bad cop. The role of the suspect in this little drama is played by the target of your intentions.

Just like the cops, the two groups are acting in accordance with a planned tactic. The "bad" group can be picketing, while the "good" group, with respectable representatives carefully chosen, asks for a meeting. After agreements have been reached, both sides can claim victory while making sure not to discredit one another. After all, you both have constituencies you need to keep happy and possibilities for future mutual actions to protect.

This tactic can be effective in bringing together two groups with similar interests but different action orientations. The target may be able to rebuff either group's approach, but the purposeful combination of the two changes the situation significantly. This approach may move the target toward cooptation by the "good" group.

Lawsuits. Being sued is almost as much fun as root canal surgery. Most people would prefer to avoid both if they could. Enter the threat of a lawsuit to get the target to pay attention to you. Although large companies and government organizations often find themselves the subjects of lawsuits, being sued is no trivial issue to them either.

Many individuals, especially those who have come to tolerate, if not accept, a condition of powerlessness, are unaware of their legal rights and their opportunities to assert them. Participation as plaintiffs in a lawsuit can bring members a sense of strength and power. Legal action allows them to assert their rights in a forum that must take their concerns seriously. Your willingness to seek redress through the courts demonstrates that your organization refuses to be pushed around. It shows that you are willing to make your claims and to back them up. It forces the target to reckon with you.

If you do threaten legal action, make sure you can back it up. Determine that you are on a strong legal footing before you make your threat, and follow through by filing a suit if your issues are not resolved satisfactorily.

Once you are in court, the proceedings can drag on and on and on. And on and on . . . especially if your opponent decides to try to tie you up or simply outlast you. Meanwhile your members' enthusiasm can wane if there are few other fronts on which you are working. This can lead to discouragement. So, as you consider this tactic, take care to become well versed in what you can expect. Know the type of resolution you are seeking, understand your opponent's options and likely responses, and ascertain the probable costs in terms of both time and money that this commitment will require.

You don't want your members just sitting around during the time it takes to settle the suit, so rarely will pursuit of legal action be the primary focus of your activity. Still, there are ways members can participate in the process. They may actually serve papers on your opponent, a rather empowering action; they may take part in the deposition process, allowing them to directly confront the target; and they can perform some research and information-gathering tasks (McCreight, 1984).

Using legal tactics requires a close coordination between the organization and its attorney. Decide whether you will include the organization in the action, use small suits to focus your case, or file a class action. You may also need to sensitize the attorney to the developmental needs of your organization and their relationship to the lawsuit (McCreight, 1984). Having an attorney as a member of your organization is a definite asset, especially if he or she agrees not to be compensated until you prevail in your litigation. If this is not available to you, there still may be ways for you to receive representation without a great deal of financial strain. A number of these options were discussed in Chapter 10.

Be prepared for the fact that as soon as you mention the possibility of litigation (or most any conflict tactic for that matter) the target will accuse you of being disruptive, as if you are the problem, not the target's policies or actions you intend to change. If they respond this way or in similar ways, such as acting as if you have harmed the warm relationship between you, take it as a good sign. You have made them uncomfortable. Still, be careful about how you present your legal options. You don't want to make wild threats, nor do you want to prematurely close off exploration of other avenues.

Lawsuits can be effective when the legal rights of your organization or its members are being abused. It can also be the tactic of choice to accomplish some other purposes. Lawsuits may be an effective way to attract attention from diverse audiences. Your action may gain the interest of regulators, the media, legislators, and other potential targets (League of Women Voters, 1977). Legal action, or the threat of it, can motivate the target to work more seriously with you on the matter at hand. Through the *discovery* process of litigation, you may be able to acquire some valuable information about your opponent that would normally be unavailable to you. The publicity or attention your suit attracts can increase your organization's credibility (McCreight, 1984).

Use appropriate channels. The use of institutionally designed appropriate channels is anathema to some change agents. Generally, they fear that this lets the target control the process and that it threatens to bog down their efforts. These fears are well founded *if all you do* is concentrate your efforts on trying to make these channels work.

There are some valid reasons for pursuing officially designed procedures, while not fully relying on them for your success. First, they may work. The shock of this may cause some major coronary damage, but it does happen. Second, by not following procedures you give the target an out for not dealing with you. The target can easily represent itself as the victim of an ill-informed if not insolent group. Such a response may be generally accepted by less involved members of the community, which may be most of the community. You may end up undermining some potential support. Third, by taking the appropriate steps, you can clearly demonstrate that you have acted in good faith, but that the procedures just don't work. You can show that the target is insensitive, arrogant, or incompetent in dealing with your legitimate issues. The target is now on the defensive.

It is important to develop a backup plan for what you will do when the prescribed procedures fail. However, don't wait until the breakdown has been proven before you try to figure out what your next steps will be. Have some point in mind at which you can declare the process to be a failure. This allows you to be prepared to emphasize your message about the ineffectiveness of the system and to switch

quickly to your backup plan. This quick change in the game is likely to catch the target off guard.

This tactic is particularly appropriate when you are dealing with a bureaucratized organization.

Cutting off support, particularly financial support.   You may be able to weaken an opponent not only through direct confrontation but also by eroding some of its major assets. Take some time to analyze factors critical to the opponent's operation. It may be more profitable to focus your actions on these critical supports than directly on the opponent itself. A good starting point is money. Generally, reducing the opponent's ability to get and use money will force it to change its behaviors. For example, a bank needs depositors and a store needs customers. If you can influence depositors or customers, especially one or two major ones, to change their practices if the target doesn't change what it is doing, you can strike a severe blow. Maybe a recalcitrant agency counts on United Way

funding, which you can hold up with negative publicity and direct lobbying. Find out where the money comes from, and you will usually find a good wellspring of power.

Other important sources of support include people whose endorsement is necessary for the target's success. Drawing these people away from the target or reducing the enthusiasm of their approval can seriously shackle an opponent.

This tactic is most appropriate when engaged in confrontation with a powerful opponent. It sends a strong message to other potential targets that you are willing to implement tough measures to achieve your goals. Consider making an example of one particular opponent if you are fighting several similar opponents. Don't forget the other side can play hardball with your support base too.

An excellent description of a host of additional nonviolent confrontational tactics is described in the series *The Politics of Nonviolent*

Action, by Gene Sharp (1973a, 1973b, 1973c). Confrontation requires acceptance of risk, clarity of purpose, and a high level of emotional energy. If handled well, it is capable of producing dramatic changes.

Negotiation

Negotiation is a good strategy to use when the response community is willing to work toward an agreement and your prospects for working out a favorable settlement will not be significantly improved in the practical future.

**Situations for Which
Negotiation May Be Appropriate**

- You can neither convince nor force the respondent into full compliance with your demands.
- Your organization can no longer effectively sustain confrontation.
- Your group needs to see progress toward accomplishing some gain.
- The respondents have indicated an awareness of the legitimacy of your concerns.
- You have identified something both sides can exchange to meet your interests.

CAPTURING CONCEPTS

Good Advice on Conflict Tactics

Greg Speeter (1978b) summarized some good advice on conflict tactics from Alinsky that will serve you well.

Rule 1. Power is not only what you have but what the enemy thinks you have.

Rule 2. Never go outside the experience of your people.

Rule 3. Wherever possible, go outside the experience of your enemy.

Rule 4. Make the enemy live up to their own book of rules.

Rule 5. Ridicule is your best and most potent weapon.

Rule 6. A good tactic is one that your people enjoy. If your people are not having a ball doing it, there is some-

thing very wrong with the tactic.

Rule 7. A tactic that drags on too long becomes a drag. People can sustain militant interest in any issue for only a limited time, after which it becomes a ritualistic commitment, like going to church on Sunday mornings.

Rule 8. Keep the pressure on with different tactics and actions and utilize all events of the period for your purpose.

Rule 9. The threat is usually more terrifying than the thing itself.

Rule 10. The major premise for tactics is development of operations that will maintain a constant pressure on the opposition. It is this unceasing pressure that results in the reactions from the opposition that are essential for

the success of the campaign. It should be remembered not only that the action is in the reaction but that action is itself a consequence of reaction and of reaction to the reaction ad infinitum. The pressure produces the reaction, and constant pressure sustains action.

Rule 11. If you push a negative hard and deep enough, it will break through its counterside. That is, every negative can be converted into a positive.

Rule 12. The price of a successful attack is a constructive alternative. You cannot risk being trapped by the enemy in his sudden agreement with your demand and saying, "You're right; we don't know what to do about this issue. Now you tell us." (p. 108)

- You can provide the other party with a gain that assists them and serves your interests.
- You want to build a working relationship with the respondent.

Negotiation is a process of reaching an agreement between or among parties through a discussion during which each agrees to use or withhold available resources or to perform or refrain from performing certain acts. (For this discussion, I will consider negotiations between two parties, although more parties could be involved. The same principles generally apply in situations involving more than two parties.) The decision to enter into negotiations rests with the perception by the parties that there is something to gain from participating or something to lose by not doing so. To negotiate, the parties have to be willing to come to an agreement. Further, there must be an overlapping range of acceptance (Rubin & Rubin, 1986); that is, what is at least a little acceptable to one party is at least a little acceptable to the other. If the ranges do not overlap, if the parties cannot find mutually acceptable items, then negotiation is not possible.

During negotiation, be aware of the interests of both parties as well as the relationship that exists between you. This helps you identify possible short- and long-term costs and benefits. For example, you may negotiate an agreement beneficial to you but that harms the other party and weakens the relationship between you. Or, you may be so concerned about maintaining a relationship that you make an agreement that provides you with very little immediate benefit.

Negotiation takes two basic forms. Negotiation can be *positional,* a process in which parties declare their positions and try to go as far as they can with their position. For example, you think you and your friend should go out for hamburgers, and your friend thinks you should eat pizza. Your position is hamburgers, your friend's is pizza. So, you try to convince your friend of the merits of hamburger while acting in a way intended to get the decision to go your way. Meanwhile your friend is doing the same

about the glories of pizza. You are both locked into your positions, and your bargaining will likely take on a win-lose quality.

The other basic form of negotiation is *outcome oriented,* a process in which you identify the broad outcomes you want to achieve based on the parties' respective needs, not their positions. Alternative choices are generated based on a clear understanding of the needs of the parties. Neither party has to devalue the other's interests. Each merely needs to value an agreement that meets the needs of both parties. Using this approach, you and your friend determine that you really need to eat something pretty soon that tastes good, fills you up, and doesn't cost very much. This opens up the possibilities. Who knows, maybe you decide to go to a restaurant where you can eat different things.

Regardless of the approach you use, both parties should be operating from similar orientations. You cannot assume that the other party will understand negotiating in the same way that you do.

Strengths of a Negotiation Strategy

- You are likely to end up in a more favorable condition, even if you don't get everything you want. Getting only half of what you want is probably an improvement over what you have now.
- You set a precedent that negotiation can occur. Your foot is now firmly in the door. When

Take a Moment to Discover . . . .

Have you ever lost sight of the importance of a relationship as you bulldozed ahead to get something that seemed important to you? Or, have you ever been so afraid of losing someone's favor that you did something that went against your grain?

What did you learn from these experiences? How can you apply that learning to your role as a change agent?

. . . .

you were little, did you ever try to talk your mom into letting you stay up an extra half hour to watch something "real important" on TV? Even though she agreed to do this "for this time and this time only," I bet you knew you would be able to negotiate again.

- You might get more than you expected.
- The other side's ability to gain something makes them more accepting of your gains.
- The opening discussion allows you to bring issues to the table that have not been formally acknowledged. Even if you don't immediately gain much on some of them, you have put them into the awareness of anyone who observes the negotiation.
- You begin to develop a relationship with the other party that is much more within your control.

Limitations of Negotiation

- You can negotiate away some non-negotiable items.
- By focusing on the wrong agenda or spending too much time on peripheral issues, you can accept the appearance of gain while gaining nothing of real value. For example, you may find yourself discussing where the road will cut through the neighborhood rather than whether it should be there at all.
- You can settle for too little and weaken the legitimacy of your call for future concessions from the other party.
- You can look like dupes to your own constituents, weakening their support and confidence. You can look like pushovers to the other party, which may lead them to take you and your concerns less seriously.
- You can damage future relationships by selfish or subservient actions.

Tactics and Tips for Negotiation

Some minor or simple negotiations require application of only a few of these suggestions. Determine the degree of importance the outcome of negotiation holds for you as well as the degree of difficulty you are likely to encounter in achieving your goals, then treat the negotiation process accordingly.

- Be prepared. Have an agenda. Know your facts and figures and have them written down. Select an advantageous time and place for conducting negotiation sessions. If the negotiations are particularly important or difficult, clarify the various roles members of your team will play and rehearse some of the probable negotiation scenarios.
- Have a clear goal in mind.
- Be willing to renegotiate.
- Find out what the other side wants or needs and see if you can give it to them. You don't have to, but see if you can. If you do, determine when and how you will do this, and possibly in exchange for which benefits you seek.
- Be willing and able to package items or issues to provide a wider range of negotiating possibilities.
- Acknowledge that the other party may need to blow off steam from time to time. You don't need to respond to everything that is said.
- Identify how agreements will be monitored and what sanctions, if any, will be applied for nonconformance.
- Get a third party involved if you are in a decidedly less powerful position.
- Confirm agreements in your own words.
- Be fresh, well rested, and eat right. (This *does* matter.)
- Be willing to break off negotiations or to take a break.
- Get to know the people on the other side; let them know you and your concerns. Be aware that people need to save face and will go to great, often unreasonable lengths to avoid losing face.
- If you spot a problem with the negotiation process, bring it up for discussion.
- Summarize frequently.

Methods for Win–Lose Negotiation

If you decide it is in your best interest to pursue positional negotiations, these suggestions can help you gain an advantage over the other party.

• Ask for more than you need, but be sensible; don't exaggerate to absurdity.

• Prepare a retreat plan that delineates how you intend to use various items in your negotiation. To do this you must clearly identify your nonnegotiable items, your important items, and your giveaway items.

• Ask more questions than you answer. Generally, let the other side do more of the talking.

• As time goes on people sometimes become more willing to agree, if only because they want to move on. You can use this to your advantage by dragging on or exaggerating minor issues, moving to more significant ones when the other side is worn down.

• Spend detailed time on items you are willing to give away. This draws attention to the item, making it appear more important than it really is. As a result, you may more easily get something important to you because the other side now "owes" you one.

A number of other authors provide additional insights on the negotiating process, for the most part reflecting a bargaining perspective. Brager and Holloway (1978, p. 196) have these points to offer.

• Relate your concerns to the other party's frame of reference.

• The more you can demonstrate commitment to a position that is credible to the other party as irrevocable, the more you are likely to win your point in the settlement. (Many others expound on this point, including Schelling, 1963; Pruitt, 1981; and Rubin & Rubin, 1986.)

Rubin and Rubin (1986) make these suggestions and observations.

• Negotiate only with the people empowered to make the decision.

• Make sure you get specific commitments, not "we'll do something about that."

• Getting the other party to meet with you is an important accomplishment, but not an end in itself.

• Borrowing from Fisher (1972), these authors suggest that bargainers attempt to find negotiating issues by *fractionating* or separating the issue into subissues to discover some points of possible agreement.

• Consider counterproposals carefully. Be willing to call for a break in the action to discuss new offers among yourselves.

Splain (1984, pp. 166–170) recommends the following guidelines.

• Insist that your organization is dealt with as the only bargaining agent.

• Formalizing the bargaining committee and thoroughly preparing for the negotiations represents a critical set of tasks. It requires a more serious detailed effort than preparation for any single action or leadership meeting.

• You must lay the ground rules. Five key ones are: all relevant information necessary to bargain in good faith must be made available; agree on the timetable (dates and times) as well as the location; identify the other side's bargaining team, and clarify any questions of authority and accountability; agree on whether bargaining is open to observers or closed; and agree whether or not any nonbargaining activity (for example, using the media) will be allowed during the bargaining period.

• Be capable of demonstrating flexibility in your range of styles. Be able to employ soft (friendly) or hard (abusive) tactics.

• Avoid getting publicly locked into a position.

• Use informal conversations to break an impasse, or let neutral third parties define a beneficial compromise.

Chester Karrass (1981, pp. 44–45), an expert in business negotiations, finds the following tactics profitable.

• Set up a negotiation schedule that allows you time to *think* about issues.

• Refuse to permit items that are considered nonnegotiable to be discussed.

• Never answer until the question is clearly understood, and do not hesitate to answer only part of a question. Allow the other person to interrupt; it gives you more time.

• Lead your opponent into examining your counterposition: "We seem to be on the same track except for . . ."

• Place the blame for errors and oversights on past policies, data processing systems, outside consultants—anybody but the person opposite you.

• Take steps to make concessions without coming off the loser. Some techniques: get the other party to put all its demands on the table first; don't be baited into item-by-item negotiations and concessions until you are sure of all the other party's demands; never be the first to make a major concession; when your opponent makes one, don't assume you have to make one of equal importance; get something in return for each concession you make; conserve your concessions, give a little at a time, make your opponent work for what he or she gets; don't hesitate to say "no" to a key demand, say it often enough, effectively enough so the other party knows you mean it; don't agree to "split the difference," try for 70–30 or 60–40 first; don't be afraid to back off from a concession you've already made, but don't try to back off once the deal is concluded; keep track of all concessions made, take notes on yours and the other party's.

• If a sensitive issue has to be negotiated, save it for last, after successful resolution of some other issues.

Methods for Outcome-Based Negotiation

One of the most significant contributions to the art of negotiating is contained in the gem, *Getting to Yes,* by Roger Fisher and William Ury (1991). The authors call their approach *principled negotiation.* The concept involves starting with a clear understanding of the *legitimate interests* of the parties. It proceeds to the generation of alternative strategies to serve those interests. The selection of the subsequent course of action must meet the tests of fulfillment of the parties' requirements in a way that can be measured by objective criteria.

Fisher and Ury contrast this with traditional negotiation, which starts from a *limited set of positions* designed to meet the interests of only one party, irrespective of the other's interests (Figure 13-4). Such a process is characterized by a test of wills, not merits, and results in invalidating the other's interests (which are tied to its positions) rather than exploring issues to discover possibilities of agreement.

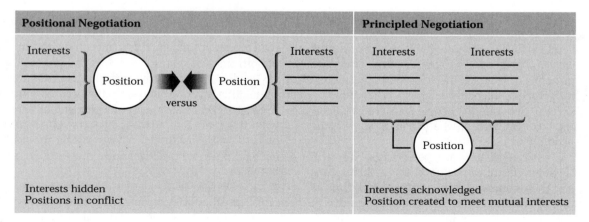

Positional Negotiation	Principled Negotiation
Interests — Position — *versus* — Position — Interests	Interests — Interests — Position
Interests hidden Positions in conflict	Interests acknowledged Position created to meet mutual interests

Figure 13-4
Differences between positional and principled negotiation

As a general practice, principled negotiation has a number of advantages, especially when you are dealing with a more powerful competitor. This style of negotiation helps to even the playing field and keep you in control of factors in the situation that are more likely to be in your favor. Items irrelevant to the issues and over which you may have little control carry much less weight in this process.

The methods Fisher and Ury outline allow you to fully commit yourself to necessary actions. As long as you think you have the right and the capability to insist on being treated respectfully (Do you?), you need not have any hesitancy about acting principled, whereas you may be reluctant to fully engage in a process that relies on being devious and clever or undermining the other party. By insisting on dealing only with the facts and merits of a situation, you don't have to accept nonlegitimate interests as legitimate.

Fisher and Ury (1991) emphasize these tenets.

• "The most any method of negotiation can do is meet two objectives: first, to protect you against making an agreement you should reject, and second, help you make the most of the assets you do have so any agreement you reach will satisfy your interests as much as possible" (p. 97).

• The stronger the other side appears "in terms of physical or economic power, the more you benefit by negotiating on the merits. To the extent that they have muscle and you have principle, the larger the role you can establish for principle the better off you are" (p. 106).

• "Separate the people from the problem" (p. 106). Be hard on the problem, soft on the people.

• "Negotiators are people first" (p. 18). "People's desire to feel good about themselves, and their concern for what others will think of them, can often make them more sensitive to another negotiator's interests" (p. 19). "On the other hand, people get angry, depressed, fearful, hostile, frustrated, and offended. They have egos

that are easily threatened" (p. 19). "To find your way through the jungle of people problems, it is useful to think in terms of three basic categories: perception, emotion, and communication. The various people problems all fall into one of these baskets" (p. 22).

• "Interests define the problem. The basic problem in a negotiation lies not in conflicting positions but in the conflict between each side's needs, desires, concerns, and fears" (p. 40). "Behind opposed positions lie shared and compatible interests as well as conflicting ones" (p. 42). For a wise solution, reconcile interests, not positions.

• Hold people personally accountable for their actions and their information.

• Acknowledge the interests of the other party as important to the negotiation.

• "Look forward, not back" (p. 52). "You will satisfy your interests better if you talk about where you would like to go rather than about where you have come from. Instead of asking the other party to justify what they did yesterday, ask, 'Who should do what tomorrow?'" (p. 53).

• "Invent options for mutual gain" (p. 56). "Four major obstacles inhibit inventing an abundance of options: premature judgment; searching for the single answer; the assumption of a fixed pie (the situation is seen as essentially either/or; either I get what is in dispute or you do); thinking that 'solving their problem is their problem'" (p. 57), an orientation that creates reluctance to think up ways to meet the interests of both sides.

• Insist on objective criteria. Don't try to settle differences of interest on the basis of will. "Negotiate on some basis independent of the will of either side, that is, on the basis of objective criteria" (p. 82). These criteria should be legitimate and practical and should apply to both sides.

• "Never yield to pressure, only to principle" (p. 88); that is the integrity of the process.

• "If you have not thought carefully about what you will do if you fail to reach an agreement, you are negotiating with your eyes closed. The reason you negotiate is to produce something better than the results you can obtain without negotiating" (p. 100). Therefore, determine your BATNA (Best Alternative To a Negotiated Agreement). "That is the only standard against which any proposed agreement should be measured. That is also the only standard that can protect you both from accepting terms that are too unfavorable and from rejecting terms it would be in your best interests to accept" (p. 100).

- "Apply knowledge, time, money, people, connections, and wits to devise the best solution for you *independent of the other side's assent* (emphasis added). The more easily and happily you can walk away from a negotiation, the greater your capacity to affect its outcome" (p. 106). This is really all about power. In other words, you will be stronger by the extent to which you do not depend on the negotiation.

- If the other side refuses to focus on the merits, just don't respond to the game they are playing. "In effect, you change the game simply by starting to play a new one" (p. 107). Still, the other party may attempt to engage in trickery. Three basic tricky ploys that may be used are: those intended to deceive, those designed to make you emotionally uncomfortable, and those that lock the other side into their position.

- "There are three steps in negotiating the rules of the negotiating game where the other side seems to be using a tricky tactic: (publicly) recognize the tactic, raise the issue explicitly, and question the tactic's legitimacy and desirability—negotiate over it" (p. 130).

- "Don't be a victim. It may be useful at the beginning of the negotiation to say, 'Look, I know this may be unusual, but I want to know the rules of the game we're going to play. Are we both trying to reach a wise agreement as quickly and with as little effort as possible? Or are we going to play "hard bargaining" where the more stubborn side wins?' Whatever you do, be prepared to fight dirty bargaining tactics. You can be just as firm as they can, even firmer. It is easier to defend principle than to defend an illegitimate tactic" (pp. 142–143).

Negotiation requires preparation, purposeful attention to detail, and an ongoing awareness of alternative choices. Further, it requires an intentional decision regarding the methods you will use to reach agreement. When used effectively, negotiation can bring about a solution to current problems in a way that fosters opportunities for future problem solving.

Collaboration

Collaboration occurs when two or more parties share resources to accomplish a goal important to them all. They go beyond the mutual acceptance of a course of action; they "co-labor." That is, they each perform some measure of work to accomplish the goal. When the strategy of collaboration is used, the target becomes a *partner* in a common enterprise. The shared goal need not be equally important to all parties, nor do they necessarily pursue it for the same reasons. For one group the particular, observable end to be accomplished may not be all that important, but the ability to establish a working relationship with their partner may be. Or, perhaps collaboration offers relief from accusations of callousness through the appearance of sensitivity that participation in a cooperative venture can bring. In fact, the partners don't even have to like each other to collaborate, though it makes things much easier if they do. Whatever the reason, the common goal unifies their respective motives and provides the impetus to work together.

Situations for Which Collaboration May Be Appropriate

- The respondent has resources you need and from which you can benefit.
- You have resources to offer.
- You need to carry forward the results of negotiated agreements.
- You recognize you can give the respondent a way to meet some of its needs if the respondent helps you meet yours.

- You want to develop a working relationship with the respondent.
- You want to show that you can get the respondent to react to you, and you are looking for ways to make it easy for that to happen.
- You want to increase the respondent's dependence on you.
- You want to educate the respondent through close or ongoing contact.
- You recognize that the respondent is agreeable and wants to work together.
- You want to establish new attitudes and practices in the community.

We talk a lot about cooperation, but most of us aren't really skilled at developing and maintaining collaborative relationships to meet community problems. It is hard enough to work together on a class project or to get five families (especially if they are related) to go on a camping trip together. Getting groups who are nervous about one another's motives or dependability to join forces is a formidable task, though it is possible if thoughtfully done.

As one strong advocate of collaboration points out, agencies and organizations don't cooperate, people do. Collaboration is *people* deciding to work together (Hagebak, 1982). Yet these people are tied to organizations each with their own policies, procedures, traditions, and formal and informal goals. These and a host of other barriers interfere with the purposeful attention to matters collaborative relationships require. Still, as Hagebak (1982) points out "when it gets right down to basics, the decision to cooperate—or become a barrier—is a *very personal decision*" (p. 33).

Some of your partners will be coerced or convinced into collaborating with you. Others, with interests and motives similar to yours, will be eager for the opportunity. For collaboration to be effective, even the most well-intentioned partners must confront a number of matters that threaten to weaken their relationship or scuttle it altogether. Doing so successfully can provide for creative, powerful relationships and a cooperative spirit, which can ultimately extend to other matters.

Strengths of a Collaborative Strategy

- The resources that can be brought to bear on the situation automatically increase.
- You may be able to move your partner into a greater appreciation of problematic conditions and their ability to have a positive impact on them.
- You can teach your partner more effective ways of serving the benefit community.
- You may increase your partner's dependence on you, thus altering the balance of power.

If carefully nurtured, collaborative relationships can establish a whole different way of addressing community dilemmas. Collaboration makes future problem solving much more efficient by taking energy away from maintaining battle lines and putting it toward improving the community.

Limitations of Collaboration

- Jealousies and other difficulties often cause partners to pull back in a posture of self-protection as soon as complications emerge. This undermines cooperative intent, rendering the effort practically ineffective and emotionally dissatisfying.
- You may become less willing to bring a partner to task on other matters for fear of reducing their collaboration on your shared undertaking.
- The partner may take all the credit for success, and blame you for failures.
- You, who may be more committed to the success of the actual project, may end up doing a far greater share of the work.
- Energy, sometimes a great deal, is required simply to maintain the relationship.
- You may lose some autonomy as you provide your partner with a degree of control.

- A breakdown in the collaborative relationship can make it much more difficult for parties to work together in the future.

Tactics and Tips for Collaboration

A collaborative relationship needs to function on both the task and relationship levels. Each of you should be clear and reasonable about what you expect to get from the venture and what you expect from your partner to achieve your goals. People aren't going to magically grasp and remember your expectations. You are going to have to tell them, perhaps more than once, and hold them accountable. Though many aspects are unique to each of these relationships, a number of general topics should be carefully examined. You need to proceed with a steady and mutual recognition of the importance of each of these items.

Communication. You need to keep talking with each other throughout the life of the project. Generally, the more personal your communication (preferably face-to-face), the better. Each partner should have a primary communicator who has the authority to give, receive, and act on information. If you just want to get work done and iron out differences, keep the number of participants at any meetings small, probably no more than three per participating partner. (Information exchange meetings can be much larger.) As the size of the group increases, the opportunity for members to participate declines and people start playing to the audience, especially if there are difficulties in the relationship. When you think you need to put on a show, you can bring in more people.

Clear agreements. You can prevent a multitude of problems by explicitly delineating the tasks to be performed and the type and extent of resources to be shared. Clear, mutual understandings also help coordinate efforts and resources. Hagebak (1982) warns that memory is imperfect, perceptions differ, and forces affecting our decisions change. So even when working with partners who are friendly, it is best to put agreements in writing.

Decision making. You and your partner need to determine over what issues each can make its own decisions and which require joint approval. If there are multiple partners, you also need to determine which style of decision making you will use. Consensus usually works best. Essentially, consensus exists when two conditions are met: each party is able to clearly state what the decision is, and each party agrees to support and implement the decision. Other methods, such as majority vote or decisions by an executive committee, may be appropriate.

Monitoring and evaluation. Believe it or not, all good intentions and wonderful ideas don't pan out. Keep track of how partners are living up to their agreements and how well plans are working. Clear agreements and plans will aid in this process. Since you cannot foretell the future, accept the fact that refinements and renegotiations are part of the game.

Recognition. Each of you needs to receive some acknowledgment from your constituencies that you are serving their interests. Stories in the local media, personal letters acknowledging your work, or appearances from other partners before your group are likely ways to get this recognition. Quotes from your partner regarding how your contributions help them and how the project helps your constituency can be useful. Be willing to provide the same sort of recognition to your partner.

Trust. A sufficient amount of trust in each other or in the strength of some external mechanism that holds parties accountable (like a contract or an oversight body) is a prerequisite for collaboration. Acting in a trustworthy manner yourself is the first step in promoting this quality.

In situations in which there is some hostility between partners, the other party might suggest that you refrain from some legitimate activities they just don't like. They may be using the relationship to get you to cut back on some of your other activities. You need to assess for yourself whether or not you are living up to the specifics and the spirit of the agreements you have made on the matter at hand.

Leadership. There has to be a force to keep the ball rolling, and rolling in the right direction. An ability to spot potential problems, bring issues and opportunities to the fore, and effectively coordinate activities is necessary. The strength of the agreements themselves is not sufficient to accomplish these requirements. People from your organization, and ideally from the other's as well, need to clearly understand the necessity of providing a leadership function within both the work and the relationship realms of the program.

Here are some additional points to help make collaboration work.

- Make sure the timetable for task completion and especially the pay-off period is realistic and mutually understood. Make sure partners know when certain activities need to be done and that they have a sense of progress. Sometimes the more tangible benefits take a while to realize. It may take some time to complete a ballfield or turn a profit on a business venture. You don't want partners getting discouraged and giving up because they had an unrealistic idea of when they would achieve returns.

- Provide opportunities to create a sense of ownership in the venture. This is especially important for reluctant associates. Involve partners in things such as naming the project or designing a logo. It will be hard to undermine a project they have christened.

- Provide public acknowledgment of the respondent's participation in the combined venture. This lets many people know the expectations your partner is expected to meet.

- Use vehicles, such as the letter to the editor column, to call attention to your partner's contributions and to encourage future ones.

- Give tangible awards, such as plaques or certificates, at a presentation before your group as well as your partner's. You can do this while you are working together in a way that suggests a future productive relationship. Don't leave recognition until everything is completed.

- Privately acknowledge good work. You can do this with a comment or in a personal letter. It is better to make reference to something specific than to make general statements.

- Work together on tedious or demanding tasks like letter stuffing or digging holes for a tree planting. You can easily introduce a social component into these activities that strengthens the relationship as you really do work together.

- If your partner is creating a problem, bring it to his or her attention in a direct, matter-of-fact manner. Nip it in the bud. You can say something like: "Jim, I've noticed _____ . As a result, _____ . How do you think that should be corrected?" Avoid the "Jim, we need to talk" approaches that burden the matter with excess emotional baggage. Wherever possible, let your partners make corrections to the problems they have created.

- Take note of what is working and the advantages each partner is reaping. It is a bad practice to focus on problems while taking good things for granted, yet it is a common one. When you pay attention to things going in the right direction, you emphasize a positive focus and build confidence in the relationship. This also helps you keep problems in perspective and deal with them more effectively. Failure to deal constructively with problems is often a sign that there is little confidence that the relationship can handle any conflict.

- Get to know one another personally. The less we know about people, the more we have a tendency to make up things about them, especially if we begin to encounter problems. Though you don't have to become fast friends with your partners, a more personal, informal relationship can help cut through artificial barriers common in more reserved relationships. Further, a built-in accountability exists among people who know each other well, as long as one party doesn't use the relationship to take advantage of the other.

Collaboration requires attention to maintaining agreements and relationships. By greatly increasing the resources available, a more comprehensive improvement in a situation can occur more easily, and the experience of collaboration can establish progressive methods for understanding and acting on future challenges.

Cooptation

Many years ago, a social psychologist by the name of Muzafer Sherif (1936) conducted an experiment in which individuals observed a fixed point of light in the darkness. Because of a perceptual phenomenon, the light appears to move. Sherif asked the participants to note how far the light moved. When individuals worked with others to form a group decision on the amount of movement, individual judgments were replaced by the group's perception of reality. What the group decided became "true," and the individuals' judgments were discarded in favor of the group's. Even when no other group members were around, the individual still relied on the group's perception as being correct.

People's perception of reality is strongly shaped by their affiliations. You may decide you can accomplish more by bringing certain actors or groups of actors into the fold than you can by keeping them at a distance. Through continued exposure to your perceptions, even opponents can begin to see things your way. In fact, this strategy is especially geared to opponents. Barker (1995) describes cooptation as a "strategy for minimizing anticipated opposition by absorbing or including an opponent in the group's membership" (p. 34). Cooptation occurs when the beliefs and attitudes others hold about a situation conform to yours.

Cooptation usually begins when a formerly antagonistic party changes its manner in regard to its opponent. This party will often appear to be more accepting of its previous opponent and in some way invite the adversary into a relationship of greater congenial contact. This may even include offering a means of formally joining the inviting party's ranks.

This gambit is frequently used by powerful resisting groups to undermine their more grassroots opposition (though it is available for use by grassroots organizations as well) (Crowfoot, Chesler, & Boulet, 1983). It is not uncommon, for example, for key leaders of the opposition to be offered jobs in the competing organization. Or perhaps appointment to a special committee that appears to carry some status or special privileges is arranged. Such tactics are intended to weaken an opponent's resolve by giving those who make the offer an appearance of being fine folks after all . . . and, in fact, their positions don't seem to be that unreasonable either. Those who have been coopted will begin to soften their opposition or risk losing this newfound acceptance by their former enemy. They may begin to justify this new moderation by finding merit in a previously scorned point of view. When this occurs, a former opponent accepts, usually unwittingly, a position of furthering the interests of the coopting party.

People are susceptible to this ploy for a variety of reasons. They may be so tired of the antagonism that they are eager to pick up on any change in attitude. They may believe that the new, more amiable relationship provides greater opportunities for influence. They may be flattered, or even simply relieved. The strategy of cooptation is usually purposefully manipulative.

Situations for Which Cooptation May Be Appropriate

• The opposing group is uncooperative and is not a good target for confrontation, perhaps because it is highly regarded by most of the community.

• Maintaining an adversarial stance will result in only isolated gains or a standoff.

• A few key individuals who have some influence within the opposing group are amenable to some sort of affiliation.

• There is a particularly vocal critic you would like to silence.

• Your group doesn't have the capability

for effective confrontation, nor does it have the resources needed for cooperation.

• You can weaken opponents by bringing them into your organization where their opinions will be in the minority (Barker, 1995).

• You will probably be in an ongoing relationship with the respondent, and you believe that a productive, working relationship can develop if purely antagonistic positions are changed or not adopted at all.

Some people are uncomfortable with the notion of cooptation. It somehow doesn't seem quite right, as if beating an opponent over the head (not literally, I hope) were a lot better. The fact that cooptation is more covertly than overtly influential makes it different from most other strategies. It does not make it better or worse. This strategy is simply another way of bringing an opponent over to your way of seeing things. You are choosing to work more closely with an adversary, providing the adversary with an opportunity to better understand your needs, rather than working from a distance with opposing frames of reference. Ultimately, any strategy is intended to persuade the respondent to accept the legitimacy of your beliefs. Cooptation is a more subtle form of persuasion in which you invite respondents into your perspective rather than directly countering theirs.

Others may not like this approach because it does not strike directly at problem-causing policies, nor does it maintain a clear distinction between conflicting camps. Points that can be made through open confrontation may be obscured; and it appears to blur the lines between good and evil.

There are times when distinctions need to be emphasized and the nature of the conflict dramatized. At these times, cooptation is the wrong strategy to pursue. However, not all opponents must always be seen as evil and kept at arm's length. The notion that opponents can never accept and act on the validity of your interests is a fairly limiting one. The question is: How do you ultimately get them there? Pursuit of this strategy is based on the belief that greater

understanding and at least a partial alliance will lead to more change than the more direct use of power.

Strengths of a Cooptation Strategy

• You can defuse a potentially harmful critic.

• You can maximize a former opponent's commitment as he or she identifies with your self-interests.

• You can gain some insights into the workings of the competition.

• You gain access to a community or organization that has been closed to you. The coopted party can serve as a kind of translator, communicating your interests with an understanding of the codes and perceptions of the other group. This person can also act as an introducer, helping members of your group gain some degree of acceptance in the other group.

• This strategy requires little investment of energy or resources.

• An obstructing group can become an allied group.

Limitations of Cooptation

• You can let a fox in the henhouse. That is, those whom you invite in may have no interest in working with you and may use information they obtain against you.

• You may inappropriately soften your stand and become reluctant to hold your newfound friends and their organizations as accountable as you should. (You become a little coopted yourself.)

• You can be transparent in your attempts and come off as insincere and manipulative, further damaging relationships.

• You can get caught up in the game of coopting people, thereby diminishing your own personal integrity.

Tactics and Tips for Cooptation

• Cooptation is a process that works over time. The target of your intentions is eased into a greater appreciation for your point of view. Be aware that respondents are likely to be at least a little cautious, so go gently. Avoid the temptation to put people down for past sins or to prove that they or their organization are wrong, or you will just promote defensiveness and maintain existing frictions.

• Absorb some of the target's concerns by making selected and acceptable changes in your organization (Mason & Mitroff, 1985).

• It may be helpful to place the target on one of your key committees, even your steering committee or board. Though the degree of responsibility you give will be based on the nature of the relationship with the group the target represents, some degree of importance must be attached to the role to ensure the individual's interest and involvement. Also, greater responsibility deepens and accelerates the process of cultivation.

• Each target should get the message that he or she is seen as a team player.

• Once targets have had some time to become acculturated to the needs of your organization, invite them to help seek solutions to the problems you face, particularly as these relate to working with their own constituency.

• Don't attempt to coopt too many people at a time. Two important targets are plenty.

• Whomever you attempt to coopt must have credibility within the opposing community.

• A good person to target is one who has cooperated with you in the past.

• Remember that the purpose is to draw in and build support, not to set someone up as a patsy who will suffer some loss because of your actions. Aside from the obvious ethical problems with harming someone, it will probably come back to haunt you.

Cooptation requires patience and a belief in the possibility that someone who has previously interfered with your success can become an advocate for your cause. It can curtail resistance and establish valuable links to key constituencies.

Other Strategic and Tactical Considerations

Adhere to a firm code of ethics. Consider the ethical dimensions of your action or inaction. If you set up an opponent, have you unfairly or unnecessarily abused another human being and cheapened yourself in the process? If you allow a serious problem situation to persist because you will only engage in polite tactics, how does your mannerly approach honor those whose suffering is prolonged?

From time to time you will hear the complaint: "That's just the ends justifying the means." Recognize these statements as specious. The fact is that all behavior is purposeful. All behavior is a means to secure some valued end. That is, all ends are purchased by, and may be used to justify, the choice of some means or actions. For example, if I choose not to engage in a certain behavior to preserve my sense of professionalism, I am simply selecting a different end, preserving professionalism, and using the importance of that end to justify whatever action I decide to take or not take.

Don't get caught up in meaningless arguments over whether the ends are justifying the means. Your time is much more wisely spent firmly rooting yourself in a fundamental code of ethics. Review your commitment to ethics and keep it alive. Your behavior may very well change from one situation to another, not, one hopes, because you lack ethics but because your ethics inform and drive every important decision you make. Your steadfast commitment to integral ethical principles will guide you to act differently as you face different challenges to your beliefs.

Recognizing mutual benefits, an overriding strategic orientation. Along with basic concerns regarding selection of a strategy mentioned at the beginning of this chapter, three overriding considerations should be kept in mind. First, you need to think about how a certain approach will help your organization accomplish its particular goals. Next, you need to consider how the strategy will aid in the continued development of the organization. But that's not all. You must also take into account the benefit the target perceives from pursuing a course of action you desire. If you have given thought only to what you want them to do and not why they will want to do it, you have only thought things through halfway. You need to consider why the target will respond, from their point of view—not yours.

People do things because it will get them something they want or avoid something they don't want. People don't readily act against their perception of their self-interest. So your deliberations on strategy must include not only what you need but what they need as well. This raises a number of questions. What's in it for them? Or, what's important to them? Will the target readily recognize a benefit, or will you have to sell them on it? Remember, in many cases the change may require that the respondent move onto unknown territory or even accept a loss of power. Remember, also, the fact that just because a course of action "makes sense" may have little bearing on the response you will get. What makes you think that the target will respond in the way you want it to?

Another fundamental commandment of change is: "Thou shalt hit them in their self-interest." The more clearly you can focus your actions on the things (rational, normative, and emotional) that are important to the respondent, the more direct and meaningful the response will be. Although this may very well mean that you select a strategy that will cause the respondents discomfort for resisting, you will generally find that the more easily the other party is able to recognize a benefit by pursuing the action you desire them to take, the less resistance to change you will encounter. The more convincing you need to do, the more resistance you can expect. By discovering a course that can provide direct benefits to each party, you weaken both the interest in and the legitimacy of opposition.

If you can identify some things each party is eager to accomplish and select an approach that provides for that accomplishment, the change effort will be fairly smooth. If, however, you are the only party to receive a direct benefit, the change effort is likely to be a more difficult undertaking.

Education as a strategy.   If the only thing in the way of positive change is a lack of information, then education is an effective method to use. Frankly, a simple lack of information is rarely the major stumbling block. Too often those who wish to promote change have their sights set on educating people (frequently focusing on the already sympathetic) as if all that anyone needs in order to act is more awareness of the situation and its consequences. When education becomes the goal, change agents too often stop short of doing all they need to do to move the process forward. There is an assumption here that knowledge is sufficient for corrective action, that if people just knew more they would automatically act to change things. My guess is that you already know the importance of a number of things—changing the oil in your car, balancing your checkbook, studying routinely, not just the night before the test. Is knowing these things enough to get you to act on them the way you should?

Do you really want people to know more, or do you want them to act differently? Education is an important part, if not a necessary part, of any change effort, but it is only a part. Certainly, people need to know about problems, their effect, and what an individual can or should do about them. Yet they generally need more. Education must be complemented by other methods that will motivate people to act in a meaningful manner.

Creating a receptive environment.   A host of elements and actors are present in any situation. In most cases, only a few of these will be directly affected by your efforts to bring about change. Those who must respond to your attempts will look for signals in the environment that favor or oppose new directions.

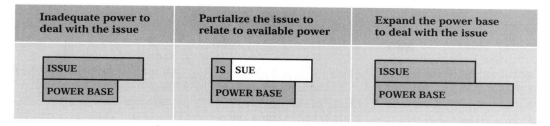

Inadequate power to deal with the issue	Partialize the issue to relate to available power	Expand the power base to deal with the issue
ISSUE / POWER BASE	IS SUE / POWER BASE	ISSUE / POWER BASE

Figure 13-5
Relationship between your issue and your power. You must have an adequate base of power to deal with the issue you confront. If your base is too small, you need to partialize the issue, expand your power base, or do both.

Prior to taking action directly related to the change you intend to make, you may take steps to help create a climate supportive of or at least nonresistant to change. This could involve an information campaign, inclusion of specific opinion leaders in your planning efforts, or other approaches.

As Julian (1973) observed, change comes about when a "significant number of people—or a number or significant people" (p. 9) agree that a problem exists. By creating this impression, you encourage acceptance of new ideas and make it easier for decision makers to respond favorably.

Partialization. This tactic essentially involves separating the goal into distinct aspects and pursuing each aspect, one at a time. (This can also refer to separating a community into component subgroups and organizing one group at a time.) Frequently this is done by breaking the goal down into its sequential steps. You then concentrate on phases of the change, taking the less risky or controversial ones first. For example, you may not be able to make all the changes you want in the operation of the local Food Stamp office. Problems exist in the way the expedite program is operated, the hours of operation don't meet the needs of the community, the application form is too long, and the staff is rude to the clients. By partializing the change episode, you may first concen-

trate on implementing a series of in-service training workshops designed to sensitize the staff to the needs and anxieties of the clients. From this may come a greater awareness of the validity of other concerns, and the staff may become allies for agency change rather than opponents of it.

Partialization may be helpful if it is likely that you will fail to accomplish the full set of changes you seek, but you can accomplish a more limited goal (Figure 13-5). This usually means that according to your analysis your organization does not currently have sufficient resources (time, money, expertise, or power) to fully institute the program of changes you seek.

Partializing helps you set the stage for future efforts. It provides your organization with the motivation of a victory while giving you a stepping stone to additional challenges. The danger is that you may settle for this initial victory and never move on to more meaningful changes. Bear in mind that the target might grant you a small gain as a type of concession to buy you off or distract you from more sweeping changes. It is necessary to keep the goal you have partialized in clear perspective.

Getting the right people in the right places. The quality of many decisions is directly related to the quality of the decision maker. If the actions of a particular decision maker are going to be crucial, it may be important not only to

Collaborative, Campaign, and Contest Approaches

Other useful formulations for strategies exist. Warren (1975), Brager and Holloway (1978), and Speeter (1978b) provide descriptions of three other ways of understanding basic methods for achieving change.

Collaborative Efforts

(Warren) "Collaborative strategies are based on the assumption of a common basis of values and interests through which substantial agreement on proposals is readily obtainable. The predominant role of the change agent is that of an *enabler* or *catalyst.* [The change agent] is not concerned about putting through their own preconceived proposal but with helping the pertinent group

reach consensus on the issue at hand" (pp. 138–139).

(Brager and Holloway) Collaboration is "characterized by open communications. Problems tend to be stated as such rather than as solutions, information regarding the perspective of both parties is widely shared and a climate of tentativeness typifies the interaction. Collaborative tactics include problem solving, joint action, education, and mild persuasion, each involving a more or less ac tive attempt to influence another party" (p. 131).

(Speeter) "People and groups work together when they recognize mutual needs and recognize that working together will help them meet those needs better than working alone" (p. 92).

Campaign Procedures

(Warren) Campaign strategies may be appropriate when there is a "lack of agreement among the principal parties that an issue exists or lack of agreement regarding how the issue should be resolved, but where in each case there is a likely prospect of reaching an agreement. [These] are strategies of achieving agreement to a proposal even among differences, by 'winning over' the other parties through persuasion. The predominant role of the change agent is that of *persuader*" (p. 140).

(Brager and Holloway) Campaigning falls "at the midpoint of the continuum between collaborative and conflict methods and contains some elements of both. Campaign tactics include 'hard' persuasion, political

attempt to influence that decision maker but to influence who holds the decision-making position in the first place. Your organization may decide to actively participate in processes to determine who will hold pivotal decision-making positions. This may mean taking part in political campaigns, search or selection committees, or confirmation proceedings.

The simple fact is that it is a lot easier to influence those whose beliefs are similar to yours than it is to influence those with whom you have some fundamental differences. This is especially true if you contributed to an individu-

al's successful effort to obtain the position. Working to get the right people in the right places could be an efficient investment of your time.

Tricks for Special Occasions

A limitless number of special techniques can be used to strengthen the effectiveness of your organization. Remain aware of the little things that are important to your success, and see if a little twist here or there can give your project or maneuvering, bargaining and negotiation, and mild coercion" (p. 132).

(Speeter) Campaign strategies are characterized by debate and "have traditionally been used to persuade key individuals or organizations to join in specific action. They have been increasingly used to hold elected officials, bureaucrats, or corporations accountable to specific citizen needs. Campaign strategies mean working to some degree in someone else's system" (p. 97), often using the legislative process.

Contest or Confrontation Means

(Warren) "Contest strategies are characterized by abandonment, temporarily at least, of efforts at consensus and employment of efforts to further one's own side of an issue despite opposition from important parties to that issue. [This occurs when] there is 'issue dissensus,' that is, a state where there are different positions which, at least for the time being, appear irreconcilable. Some contests involve vigorous clashes of opposing positions, but these take place *within accepted social norms.* Some are occasioned by attempts to *change the distribution of power* in the community. Some contests involve a *violation of community norms.* [Some] involve a deliberate attempt to harm the opponent or remove him [or her] from the issue-resolving field, that is, *conflict in the stricter sense of the word.* The predominant role of the change agent is that of *contestant"* (pp. 143–144).

(Brager and Holloway) The contest mode carries coercion "a considerable distance further, involving public conflict and pressure. [Contest tactics] include virulent clashes of position (through 'no-holds-barred' debate and public manifestos), violation of normative behavior (for example, moving out of the bounds of 'proper' behavior by means of protest activities such as demonstrations), and, in the extreme, violation of legal norms (for example, halting operations by sitting in)" (p. 133).

(Speeter) "Confrontation is a strategy of last resort" (p. 101). It is characterized by demands, threats, throwing the other side off balance, and dramatizing the issue.

cause a boost. Be inventive and have a little fun while you're at it. Here is a sample of particular tricks to address common hindrances.

Stacking a small room. The conference room where you are to make your presentation is located on the ninth floor. You could use the exercise, but it's quicker to use the elevator. Six people get on the elevator with you. At the third floor, two more people step aboard. One more squeezes in at the fifth. What brought this crowd, you wonder. By the time you have made

it to your ninth-floor destination, you are beginning to feel claustrophobic. All 10 of you tumble into the same conference room. It is a very nice, comfortable room with a large table surrounded by plush seats. Additional chairs line the walls. The place can easily hold 50. After their passage on the crowded elevator, the people separate into three little groups seeking their own places in the room apart from the others. They find seats along the walls as you go to the head of the table. You doodle on your note pad for a while. No one else enters the room. Finally it is time to begin. You look up, notice all the empty chairs, and think to yourself, "Hardly anybody showed up. What's wrong?"

The use of space can give an impression of community disinterest or create the sense that there is a movement afoot. You may want to convince dubious members of the community that everyone is on board with the project, or you may want to demonstrate overwhelming community support to an opponent. If you expect 30 people to show up, schedule your function in a room that can comfortably seat about 20. Set up only 15 or so chairs to start off. Have a few stacked up in the room and the rest easily accessible in the room next door. As people arrive and chairs are being set up, you can be "amazed" by the tremendous turnout. If people have to stand along the walls, so much the better. Even those who aren't in on the ploy won't mind having to stand as long as the show is good.

Defusing an opposing argument. Preempt the opponent's argument or plan by releasing it first. Let your audience know just what is coming, and then discredit it. This leaves the opponent offering something people have heard before and about which they have at least some suspicions. They have been inoculated against its impact. This approach allows a group to be forewarned and thus forearmed. The opponent is put on the defensive and may even be forced to abandon or alter a favored position. Of course, you may even anticipate and announce *this* likelihood.

Keeping the record straight. Amnesia seems to strike some targets when it is time to make good on promises made. It seems as though they were "misunderstood," and they didn't really mean what you thought they meant. In the course of a discussion, some outrageous statements may be made, ones which, especially if made politely, may go unnoticed or, if noticed, be tolerated. These common occurrences can be dealt with by having a member of your group volunteer to serve as a secretary who takes minutes of the meeting.

Nobody actually likes to be the secretary, so rarely will anyone compete with your volunteer for the honor. Yet the secretary is one of the most powerful people at any meeting. During the meeting, the secretary can record, confirm, and note the confirmation of promises. The secretary also has the authority to interrupt the proceedings at any point to "ask a question for clarification." This gives the secretary the chance to call attention to a comment or ask a speaker to further explain some objectionable statements. By acting in his or her official capacity, the secretary can expose points without being argumentative. As long as the individual doesn't overplay the role, the secretary can control the meeting.

The minutes should be widely distributed, making sure that key points confirmed during the meeting are underscored. You need to anticipate that some of the targets will object to the record, so be ready to effectively counter these gripes. The "volunteer" should be well prepared to perform the function. Spend a little time discussing and perhaps even role-playing this position.

Individualized petitions. A petition provides a simple way for people to voice their opinions. Twenty-five people can sign a paper attesting to their support for an idea or a statement. Still, it is only one piece of paper. Much better to have 25 pieces of paper, each one asserting the same support for the desired action. This is not the time for conservation.

In addition to the printed message and signature, each person could be encouraged to write a one-sentence personal note on the bottom of the page. Most people are willing to do this, especially if you are prepared to suggest some topics about which the individual may want to comment. You can even suggest some comments when it seems appropriate.

If you put a fold in each sheet and then stack the opened sheets on top of each other, it makes for a more impressive pile. You can present 2 pieces of paper with 50 signatures or a fluffed-up batch of 50 papers, many with personal statements. Which do you think will have the greater impact?

Strategies and Tactics the Target May Use on You

You are not the only group considering the actions it can take to gain an advantage or head off a threat. The target, particularly in a conflict situation, is trying to provoke a response from you that would advance or protect its interests. It is helpful for you to consider a few common schemes you are likely to face.

Buffer groups. Beware the formation of a committee established to "explore and seek resolution to shared concerns." Though I suppose a few of these things really work, most of them are set up by those under attack to diffuse energy. They become part of a pseudo problem-solving structure that simply adds an additional layer between you and the respondent while allowing it to establish some control over the action setting (Crowfoot, Chesler, & Boulet, 1983).

First of all, recognize the process for what it is and, even if you do participate, place your trust in other activities you control. Refuse to accept limitations on your actions as a condition of membership. Be willing to declare the process a sham and walk away from it. The opponent is likely to want to hang on to the appearance of cooperation, so you may be granted some concessions to appease your threats.

Divide and conquer. In a conflict situation, the target is likely to try to drive a wedge between you and your partners or among the members of your organization itself. This is usually done by granting some temporary favor to one group over the other, spreading rumors, or promoting an agenda likely to bring dispute to your ranks. Discuss this probability among yourselves in advance, and see if you can guess what your opponent will try to do. By making a game out of

it, you can strengthen your resolve for unity and belittle your opponent's methods.

Absence of decision makers. As a variation of the buffer group game, the target may serve up a variety of individuals who can "transmit your concerns" to those in authority. You can transmit your own concerns. If people don't have the authority to act, don't waste your time meeting with them.

Vague agreements. Any agreement lacking specific outcomes to be produced by specific actions of specific people according to a specific timetable is fluff. Common "agreements" include those to "take action" or "resolve the problem," or worse, "to look into the matter." There are a number of ways to dress up delays or inaction as agreement. Be careful to make sure that what you are agreeing to is meaningful. Acknowledge that the "agreement" represents a good starting point, but not a real agreement. Then specify the steps and the time frame acceptable for forging a true agreement.

Telling you what you want to hear. This is one of the most effective tricks in an opponent's arsenal. It can deflate the energy from your drive more quickly than air can escape from an untied balloon. This ploy is especially effective with those who are uncomfortable challenging authority, don't really want to do any more work, or who yearn to be "right" over being effective. Be prepared to hear a variety of pat responses that by themselves mean nothing. "I agree with you." "Yes, you're right." "You have raised some valid concerns." These are some of the standards. Be mindful not to let these statements reduce your impetus for useful action. Use the apparently favorable response to push for actions to back it up. You may answer by saying something like: "That's great to hear; now let's focus on exactly what you are going to *do.*"

Endless meetings. Much, if not most, of your work will be done during volunteer hours. By calling meeting after meeting after meeting, the target can simply wear you out. The time spent at a meeting is increased by the time spent thinking about and preparing for the meeting. This can add up. Quite often the people who call these meetings are paid for their time, so they may be happy to meet forever. If you suspect this is happening to your group, first confront the target about it. Then start placing more strict requirements on the justification for meeting. Make sure the intended outcome of the meeting is realistic and logically related to movement on your goals. If there is no real need to have a face-to-face conversation, tell the target you will discuss matters over the phone.

You can play this game too. Have a good supply of "alternates," so any number of people can attend meetings rather than just a few. If the alternate is not sufficiently versed to make a decision, state that decisions reached at the meeting must be ratified by the membership. If an alternate needs to be brought up to date with the current state of the proceedings, make sure the target is requested to do so during the meeting. The need for the target to regularly reorient new participants, who may be no more than message transmitters to your organization, can dampen enthusiasm for this ruse.

Don't be shy about scheduling a meeting at a time and in a place that is convenient to you but inconvenient to the target.

Requests for volumes of information. Check to see how the target intends to use the information you produce. If they cannot clearly demonstrate that information leads to action, tell them you prefer to spend your time in more constructive ways. Another response is for you to request payment for producing certain kinds of information. If they are not willing to pay for a "study," ask them how this information can be so valuable.

Withholding information. The target may promise to provide you with necessary information that is rightfully yours. They promise, but do not act. They may continue to delay to drain your momentum and to keep you from being

able to move or make decisions. Do not wait. At the time you request information, establish deadlines and methods for ensuring accountability. Be willing to make an issue over the broken promises, invoking the intervention of third parties or other parties who have power over the target. You may be tempted to withhold information or action until the target gives you what you need. This may work on some occasions, but inaction on your part may play into your opponent's hands.

Especially when you are dealing with a public institution, learn how to request information under the Freedom of Information Act and be willing to exercise that right.

Overwhelming you with information. There may be some truly important data provided in the volumes you get, but you will have to wade through mounds of relatively meaningless information to discover it. An opponent may use this tactic to say that they were more than forthcoming with their information and that they did in fact tell you of their plans, so you should not be surprised by the unfolding of events.

Your tendency will be to set things aside until you have time to read it all. It may gather an inch of dust before that time ever comes. By then it may be too late. To protect against this, have someone in your group prepared to critically pore over any information you receive. You could end up with a lot of ammunition.

Providing you with special attention or offerings. Be wary of opponents bearing gifts. Although you want to allow for the fact that people *do* change their attitudes, it is wise to consider the context in which special favors are offered. If there is an expectation that you will back off on your pursuit of issues or if you are to be seen as more important than other members of your organization, your benefactor may not be operating from the most kindly of intentions. You may decide to accept the gift and pass it along to someone else. Or, you can decline altogether.

Feigning injury or hurt feelings. Avoiding accountability is important business to some opponents. Unable to deal with the facts of their behavior, they may try to gain some sympathy by acting unjustly accused or unfairly harmed. What they are really trying to do is change the agenda and put you on the defensive. You don't need to explain yourself, nor should you feel apologetic or guilty for adhering to the importance of the facts of the matter. You can defuse the opponent's tactic by giving your opponent a clear, specific way to be a partner in problem resolution. Their refusal to do so can become an enduring symbol of their insincerity.

Commandments of Change

At various points I have made reference to "commandments" to follow in working to promote change. These have developed over the years as I have reflected on the diverse types of change efforts in which I have been involved. A principle achieves "commandment" status if its importance is consistently borne out under varying circumstances. Here are Homan's Thirteen Commandments for promoting community change. Remember them and use them to further your own change efforts.

1. Thou shalt hustle.
2. Thou shalt keep the cycle of empowerment rolling.
3. Thou shalt do thy homework.
4. Thou shalt hit them in their self-interest.
5. Thou shalt have those who feel the problem play a significant role in resolving the problem.
6. Thou shalt have the situation dictate the strategy.

Do You Have What It Takes?

As you get ready to move from talking about doing something to actually doing it, take stock of the assets your group brings to the scramble. Be sure the basic factors crucial for action are clearly present in your group. This will help you detect any weak portions in your foundation that may need some shoring up before you press the issue. Check to see that you are well supplied with these ingredients.

- *Clarity of purpose.* Your issue is clear and compelling and your sense of purpose certain and strong. You are able to articulate both your issue and your purpose.

- *Commitment.* You and the other members of your group have made a conscious commitment to do what it takes to achieve success. You are determined not only to take action but to adequately prepare for it as well.

- *Interest.* There is sufficient interest in the issue from a sufficient number of people.

- *Workers.* There are enough people who are willing to take on whatever time-consuming tasks are necessary so that one person doesn't get stuck with it all.

- *Leadership.* An appropriate range of leadership has developed so one person doesn't try to do the things other people could and should do.

- *Information.* You know what you need to know to act and to prevent unintended consequences.

- *Risk taking.* You and the other participants are willing to take risks.

- *Power.* Your organization has enough power to get a response from those from whom you need a response at this particular stage in your change episode.

7. Thou shalt have a quick, initial victory.
8. Thou shalt prevent unintended consequences.
9. Thou shalt keep thy options open.
10. Thou shalt do things on purpose.
11. Thou shalt roll with the punches.
12. Thou shalt commit thyself to learning.

And the final one, should you forget everything else.

13. Thou shalt laugh and PEA*, and thou shalt be relieved.

Conclusion

You won't put up with things the way they are. You have acknowledged a need to take action.

* Have *Persistence,* generate and use *Energy,* and take *Action.*

You involve more people, giving you the power and resources you need. You keep talking to each other, and you make decisions. With a clear sense of what you intend to accomplish, you have assessed the situation to determine the most effective strategies and their accompanying tactics to advance your goals. You have determined how the ideal selection of actions fits the real capabilities of your group. You have actually gone out and implemented your actions purposefully and evaluated their effectiveness.

You have committed yourself to the success of your venture. You are determined to be persistent. You enjoy the company of your partners. And you do not take yourself so seriously that you cannot recognize and benefit from the humor that comes as a welcome visitor to most any situation. Though maybe you are just starting out, you smile. You have probably already won something pretty important.

PART III

A Closer Look at Typical Change Contexts

Not far from where you are sitting right now, there are people who are frustrated by circumstances that seem beyond their control. Opportunities are hidden or denied. Services don't work. Insensitivity has grown from indifference to erode hope.

Not far from where you are sitting right now, people are deciding to take action to direct their future. Somebody started the process that brought these people together. Maybe somebody who two years or even two months ago never thought about challenging "the way things are."

How will it turn out for these people? Will they fail? If so, why? What will get in their way? Will they succeed? If so, why? Will they just be lucky, or will they do the right things right?

Today, what do they know about producing change? Do they know much about the community that will be affected by their efforts? How will they generate the power they need? Will they waste their time trying to plan for every possibility, or will they fail to plan at all? How will they attract others to their cause, and will they work well together? Will they be able to raise the money and other resources they will need? How will they spread the word about what they are doing and why? Will they be able to define issues to produce the reaction they want? What steps will they take to become more organized? Will the strategies and tactics they select fit the situation they face?

You know something about each of the questions they will have to answer. You are probably much more prepared to begin the process of promoting change than most people who actually take the risk to do so. If you were in that meeting today, you would have important contributions to make.

As you engage in professional practice, you will encounter many systems that have an impact on the people you serve. You will have many chances to initiate changes to remove barriers people face or to create new programs or new promise. Different arenas of action were covered in a general way in Chapter 1. In the chapters in Part 3, you will be given a closer look at three different settings where you may very well have the opportunity to develop and use your skills to promote change.

P art 3 is a little different from Parts 1 and 2. At the conclusion of each chapter you will find a story designed to illustrate the principles described in the chapter. In each story, change agents do some things well, and some things not so well—just like real life. You will be asked a number of questions about the story to see what you think about the situation and to help you figure out what you would do—maybe even what you will do—when faced with a similar opportunity.

Neighborhood change efforts may take you out of your office and into the places where people live. What occurs or does not occur in neighborhoods has a tremendous effect on the quality of life of the residents. Neighborhood change can take on many forms, ranging from more fully developing the natural helping systems that already exist to establishing neighborhood self-government and economic vitality.

In Chapter 14 we will explore the meaning of neighborhood and gain an understanding of the importance of neighborhood functioning. You will see how neighborhoods change over time and learn about neighborhood organizations. You will discover various ways to strengthen neighborhoods, and you will be given some insights on important factors that will affect your chances for success.

Organizational change skills are particularly important for professionals working in human services. Our organizations can be vehicles for delivering services or mazes in which good ideas and good service get lost. The process of improving existing services or developing new ones usually involves some change in service organizations. Service organizations are our workplace. Their degree of effectiveness or in-effectiveness has an impact on our own ability to render quality assistance. The satisfaction we derive from our work is closely related to the functioning of the organization through which we do it.

In Chapter 15 you will gain a clearer picture of the characteristics that influence the behavior of organizations. You will consider several different types of changes you can make in organizations, and you will learn more about the obstacles and opportunities that affect the change process. You will be introduced to key ingredients of organizational change, and you will be provided with a number of specific tactics that will increase your effectiveness.

Legislative change is increasingly recognized as a critical activity for social workers and human services workers. Policies that emerge from legislative bodies can set in motion an array of forces that limit or expand opportunities for the people we serve. The extent and availability of public resources is directly related to legislative decisions. Even the way services can be provided is shaped by the actions of those who set public policy.

A variety of legislative assemblies from town councils to the Congress of the United States pass laws that affect our communities. A number of avenues exist for influencing these legislative decisions. One of the most effective of these is the practice of lobbying. Specific lobbying activities become far more productive when made as part of an organized lobbying effort.

Chapter 16 focuses on efforts to influence the actions of state legislatures because these bodies are more accessible to the average worker and because the policies they establish have significant consequences. You will learn how to prepare yourself to take part in the work of affecting legislation. You will gain an understanding of the legislative process, and you will see how the essential components of a legislative action campaign work together. Basic lobbying activities and methods will be explained, and you will be given a number of tips for increasing your effectiveness.

At some stage of your career you may well find yourself working to strengthen a neighborhood, improve an organization, or influence the passage of laws. Whether you respond to the challenge of change by working in these arenas or others, you already have a strong base of information to serve your efforts. Now, as you are reading, some people burn with a desire to make things different, whereas others, who have forgotten how to even feel angry, are making daily concessions to survival, having given up and given in long ago. What will your actions mean to them, and to you?

CHAPTER 14

Enhancing the Quality of Neighborhoods

Chapter Highlights

- Quality of neighborhoods affects the quality of people's lives
- Various ways to look at and understand neighborhoods
- Different characteristics of neighborhoods
- The neighborhood as a focus of worker attention
- The neighborhood as a valuable system for meeting individual and family needs
- Social functions provided by neighborhoods
- Neighborhoods are affected by people and institutions both inside and outside their borders
- Models of neighborhood change
- Neighborhood organization is needed to produce neighborhood change
- Even workers who are not community organizers have several options for action
- The long tradition of neighborhood organizing

- Basic approaches to neighborhood organizing
- Neighborhood organizations and their relationship to local government
- Classifications of neighborhood organizations
- Activities of neighborhood organizations
- Elements of successful neighborhood organizations
- Basic change-related tasks
- Recognize, develop, and utilize neighborhood resources, especially membership
- Residents need to have a personal connection to the common good
- Neighborhood as an economic system
- Suggestions for increasing the prospects for success
- Neighborhood action, a way to confirm dignity
- Overcoming fear by realizing that good organizers are always making mistakes

All of us who live in a city live in a neighborhood. Most of us who live in a town live in a neighborhood. For most Americans, the quality of our lives is strongly affected by the conditions that exist in the area captured by the view from our front doors (Ahlbrandt & Cunningham, 1979). Our neighborhoods "form a significant part of the social environment and an important context for social work practice" (Fellin, 1995, p. 77). Our neighborhood may be a densely populated place where row houses snug against each other or a tract of suburban single-family dwellings. The boundaries of a trailer park might mark our neighborhood. Or the neighborhood might be our apartment complex.

What Is a Neighborhood?

Neighborhoods come in many shapes and sizes. Wide variations of neighborhoods exist not only among cities but within the same city. To some, a neighborhood is home to hundreds of people. To others, the term may describe an area of 75,000 people (Downs, 1981; Hallman, 1984; Kotler, 1969). Barker (1995) describes a neighborhood as "a region or locality whose inhabitants share certain characteristics, values, mutual interests, or styles of living" (p. 252). Schwirian (1983) has identified the basic elements of a neighborhood as: people, place, interaction system, shared identification, and public symbols. He defines a neighborhood as "a

population residing in an identifiable section of a city whose members are organized into a general interaction network of formal and informal ties and express their common identification with the area in public symbols" (p. 84).

Neighborhoods have been distinguished by social class, race and ethnicity, psychological unity among people who feel they belong together, family status and lifestyle, housing conditions, and social characteristics that describe the interactions of people within the neighborhood and between the neighborhood and the wider community. Various neighborhoods have particular norms and values. They hold beliefs about acceptable displays of wealth, noise, home upkeep, lifestyles, and attitudes toward outsiders (Hallman, 1984; Keller, 1968). Schwirian (1983) has combined these and other factors into descriptions of neighborhoods as natural areas, social areas, and interaction systems. Natural areas are characterized by a particular geographic area, a unique population, a social system with rules and norms, and distinguishing emergent behaviors or rules of life. Social areas are marked by different combinations of status, family form, and ethnic specialization. Interaction systems describe a series of social systems and relationships. Ahlbrandt and Cunningham (1979) have summarized a neighborhood as a community, a market possessing purchasing power, a service area, a provider of shelter, a political force, and an actual or potential level of government.

Different observers recognize different dimensions in their view of the neighborhood. For example, residents are more likely to see a much smaller neighborhood than will urban planners. Downs (1981) has described four expanding dimensions of the concept of neighborhood:

- The immediate neighborhood (which others might term the "face block") is the cluster of houses around one's own.
- The homogeneous neighborhood extends to where the market value of housing or the mix of housing types and values noticeably changes.
- The institution-oriented neighborhood describes an area in which residents share common relationships with a local institution such as a school, church, police precinct, or political ward.
- A regional neighborhood comprises a much broader area such as an entire suburb or township.

As you can see, the term resists clear definition. In fact, Downs (1981) has commented that "no one definition has come into widespread acceptance among neighborhood residents themselves, neighborhood organizations, or academic analysts" (p. 13). A couple of the most meaningful observations are in some ways the simplest and in some ways the most complex. Wireman (1984) says that "a neighborhood is the area named by residents when asked: 'Where do you live?'" (p. 38). The National Commission on Neighborhoods (1979) offered: "In the last analysis, each neighborhood is what the inhabitants think it is" (p. 7).

Although academicians, city administrators, and professional planners may argue over the proper determinants of a neighborhood, it is the residents for whom the concept has the most meaning and who ultimately define their own boundaries. Researchers have found that members of specific neighborhoods do have definite ideas about what constitutes their neighborhood, suggesting that "neighborhood" is a "vivid reality in people's lives" (Ahlbrandt & Cunningham, 1979, p. 14).

We each have our own personal neighborhood. Essentially, your neighborhood is what feels like your neighborhood. This, however, is a dynamic perception. Your understanding will be affected by your age, how long you have lived in the area and how much time you spend in it, whether and how far you have ventured on your walks, and other factors that influence the type and degree of your interaction with the various elements of your neighborhood. Think about your own neighborhood. What pictures do you see?

Neighborhood as a Focus of Attention for Professional Workers

The neighborhood is the smallest operating unit in a city above the level of the family (Doxiadis, 1968), and what goes on there seriously affects its members. Efforts to strengthen the quality of neighborhoods command the interest of those who deliver human services.

Why should we care about strengthening neighborhoods? First of all, the people living in them matter. The character of a neighborhood affects all its residents, perhaps especially its children (Coulton, 1996). Almost 4 million children live in neighborhoods that can be considered severely distressed (O'Hare, 1994). Further, underdeveloped and impoverished neighborhoods can affect the entire community, harming a city's image and its economic health. Deterioration tends to worsen and spread. By increasing the health and vitality of neighborhoods, we expand residential choice, provide for a better distribution of population and jobs, and contribute to the tax base rather than drain resources from it (Suchman, 1994). We promote conditions that encourage security, interaction, and the growth of social capital (Wagner, 1995).

The nature of social services may well change in response to the challenges of an information or knowledge society. Agencies that can incorporate a more integrated approach to serving their communities will become increasingly relevant. Wagner (1995) has pointed to the emergence of a Fourth or Community Sector, which may well replace the traditional Third (nonprofit) Sector, which he says favors maintenance and survival over client change and social impact. This new Community Sector is defined as "a loose amalgam of existing and yet-to-be-created non-profit organizations (self-help groups, neighborhood and member-based organizations) that develop new approaches and financing mechanisms to address neighborhood concerns. They link three activities: social service, economic development, and capacity building, and create a local vision and renaissance of activity" (p. 12).

Morrison, Howard, Johnson, Navarro, Plachetka, and Bell (1997) argue that differentiation among the roles of caseworker, group worker, and community organizer is not functional to a "holistic approach that emphasizes the environment as well as the person in the environment" (p. 533). Social work training should place students in neighborhood networks rather than isolating them in single service agencies.

Quality Neighborhoods

The quality of neighborhoods is surely affected by the quality of its housing stock, but there is more to a neighborhood than just houses (Ahlbrandt & Cunningham, 1979). It is naive to think that families are completely self-sufficient, particularly in this highly mobile, highly specialized nation. Assistance is not as readily available through extended family systems as it once was. Most families meet their needs through their interaction with other systems. Clearly, the neighborhood is one of those valuable systems. Neighbors can provide one another with a range of practical and emotional support. Borrowing a cup of sugar, helping out in times of emergency, establishing social contact over a cup of coffee, or helping to fix a leaky toilet are some of the common forms of assistance neighbors provide to each other. The benefits of these commonplace activities, of course, extend beyond eggs and coffee and functional flushing. These connections provide

psychological benefits by strengthening our attachments to a wider human community and by helping us recognize the reality and importance of our interdependence. More effectively functioning neighborhoods are more likely to offer their members the benefits of "neighboring" (Keller, 1968).

These neighborly activities are complemented by institutions that may provide jobs as well as a variety of commercial, educational, religious, and social services that benefit residents. Wireman (1984) describes a set of social functions that would be provided in an ideal neighborhood.

- Effective schools responsive to neighborhood needs.

- Attractive, clean, safe play places close to home for casual, unstructured play. (For small children, these areas must be within sight or calling distance.) Places and appropriate supervision for more formal play, including cultural activities.

- Adult control over neighborhood children's behavior.

- Fast access to emergency health care.

- Locally available or convenient transportation to other support services—normal health care, family counseling, special educational services, and so on.

- A variety of provisions for child care, including preschool, after school, and care during summer vacations.

- An opportunity for children to know a variety of adults as friends, neighbors, and role models.

- An environment relatively safe from crime, physical hazards, and racial or ethnic tensions. (p. 39)

Of course, not every neighborhood is blessed with an abundance of developed internal resources. If the needs of their residents are to be met, neighborhoods must work to develop internal resources and collaborate with external institutions to obtain needed assistance. They should have the flexibility to shape services to best fit the area's particular requirements. These

Table 14-1

Organizations Used to Meet Human Needs of a Neighborhood

| | Service Providers** | | | | | |
| | Based within Neighborhood | | | Based outside Neighborhood | | |
Human Needs and Services*	Private Nonprofit	Private Profit	Government	Private Nonprofit	Private Profit	Government
Employment Services Jobs						
Commercial Sale of Goods Services						
Income Support Programs						
Credit						
Housing						
Utilities						
Food						
Clothing						
Safety						
Transportation						
Education						
Recreation, Arts						
Health						
Social Services						
Governance						
Civic Participation						
Communal Events						
Religion						

*Detailed services and activities should be added under each human need.
**Individuals, families, and informal groups will also be responding to human needs.
Source: Hallman, 1984.

neighborhoods would be further strengthened by attracting resources that enable them to create and develop their own institutions (Suchman, 1994; Wireman, 1984).

Hallman has developed a chart that is helpful in assessing the presence of needed resources and services in the neighborhood and the organizations involved in meeting them (see Table 14-1). Reviewing this chart will help you see how, by whom, and where these needs are met or not met adequately. Observe that neighborhood needs are met to some degree by a combination of individuals or groups based both inside and outside the neighborhood. By taking advantage of opportunities to strengthen basic neighborhood elements, workers in the business of providing human services can significantly benefit the families who reside there.

Natural Processes of Neighborhood Change

Like any system, neighborhoods are always undergoing some degree of change. People move in and out. Some dwellings deteriorate while others benefit from the attention of paintbrush and hammer. Some trees, if there are any, wither and die while others bloom and, perhaps, new ones are planted. Forces outside the neighborhood, such as the general economy, attitudes of lending institutions, and changing local ordinances, help or hinder neighborhood improvements. Of course, the rate and direction of change can also be influenced by the presence of a purposeful change agent.

Several authors have observed the way neighborhoods change over time. Some of these descriptions of change focus on factors related to neighborhood decline, whereas others try to explain forces working in the direction of neighborhood revitalization.

Invasion-Succession Model

The invasion-succession model views changes in the neighborhood as a result of conflict that occurs when a natural area is "invaded" by socially or racially different individuals. If some accommodation between the newcomers and the established population is not reached, one of the groups will withdraw. This will lead to changes (Schwirian, 1983). If the withdrawing group takes valuable resources from the community (for example, family income, shop ownership, political clout) before these can be effectively replaced, the neighborhood is likely to decline.

Life Cycle Model

Various life cycle theories describe the changes in neighborhoods. One of the major proponents of this point of view is Anthony Downs (1981). According to Downs, neighborhoods have a life cycle from birth to death, but they may reverse the "aging" process through various forms of revitalization. Further, they may resurrect themselves. From an abandoned, lifeless space, a neighborhood may be born anew.

The life cycle model includes five different stages of change:

- A stable and viable neighborhood
- A minor decline
- A clear decline
- A heavily deteriorated neighborhood
- An unhealthy and nonviable neighborhood

A stable and viable neighborhood exists when no symptoms of decline have appeared and property values are rising. A period of minor decline may follow in which some minor deficiencies in housing units are visible and density is higher than when the neighborhood was first developed, but property values are stable or increasing slightly. A neighborhood in clear decline is marked by populations from lower socioeconomic groups. Renters are dominant in the housing market, and landlord-tenant relations are poor because of high absentee ownership. Other factors, such as higher density, low confidence in the area's future, and abandoned buildings, are also associated with this stage. In heavily deteriorated neighborhoods, housing is very run down and even dilapidated. Most structures require major repair. Subsistence level households are numerous, and profitability of rental units is poor. Pessimism about the area's future is widespread. An unhealthy and nonviable neighborhood is at the final stage of change. Massive abandonment occurs, and those residents who remain are at the lowest social status and incomes in the region. Expectations about the area's future are nil.

Downs makes the point that at any stage the neighborhood can be declining, stable, or improving. At the time he made these observations he noted that although images of severely blighted urban landscapes have been burned into our perceptions, most American cities do not contain any neighborhoods in the latter two stages of decline.

Political Capacity

The physical and economic conditions of a neighborhood send messages to the residents and to outsiders as well. Residents may see daily confirmation of the enormity of their struggle to cultivate a safe, healthy, and attractive environment. It may erode confidence in their hope of achieving personal success. Outsiders may see an area not worth saving or one easily exploited. Although these perceptions may be accurate, they may mask a vibrancy of interpersonal relationships that may exist in poor areas and be absent in more affluent ones.

Departing from what he sees as an overemphasis on physical and economic factors affecting neighborhood change, Rick Cohen (1979) has focused on a political analysis and presents his stages from the point of view of development rather than deterioration. According to his perspective, a neighborhood can be economically rich while remaining politically poor. The first of Cohen's stages is a *disorganized neighborhood,* one in which there is no organization capable of providing leadership. In these neighborhoods a change agent should act as a catalyst while nurturing people with leadership potential. In *primary institutional neighborhoods,* a few basic organizations, such as churches, schools, and fraternal and social clubs, exist. The change agent acts as a mobilizer, strengthening the linkages among families and neighborhood institutions, changing the orientation of residents from inward to outward, further developing leadership, and developing neighborhood resources. *Civic neighborhoods* are beginning to deal with issues of neighborhood interest. A group claiming civic concerns as its primary purpose is developed. The organizer's role is that of process facilitator, assisting the neighborhood by helping to get its resources and groups to work in harmony. A *networked neighborhood* has a civic group with strong support, and nearly every block is represented in the organization. There is a danger that the organization may become too centralized and

bureaucratized and that it may engage in nonproductive political tests of wills with municipal officials. The result of these conflicts could be stalemate and inaction. By assisting the organization as a strategist and negotiator, the change agent can help the neighborhood group navigate through some stormy waters. In a *mass communal neighborhood,* everyone is a member and participates in a neighborhood organization or civic group. The neighborhood is concerned about a wide range of issues, and it delivers services. High voter turnouts, widespread participation in organizational activities, many different people in leadership roles, and an increasing control of neighborhood resources are indicators of a mass communal neighborhood. The change agent acts as a maintenance assistor to help keep the neighborhood from slipping into stagnation.

As you can see, the development and status of a neighborhood organization is a stimulus to and a reflection of the state of political organization of the neighborhood. Each stage of neighborhood development presents new challenges to the neighborhood organization itself. For example, Cohen points out that many neighborhood organizations are born of controversy and opposition. The group starts off in an underdog role. When their political capabilities significantly increase and successes mount, the organization may be set adrift as it realizes that it has outgrown its original identity. It may experience some aimlessness as it searches for a new identity. A further challenge confronts successful neighborhoods. Mastery of political influence may result in the neighborhood pursuing its own interests at the expense of other neighborhoods. A lack of awareness of the interdependency among neighborhoods may lead to the NIMBY (Not In My Back Yard) phenomenon, producing destructive, selfish conflicts ultimately harmful to all.

Additional Models of Neighborhood Change

Other models have been developed in recent years to explain neighborhood change (Schwab & Ringel, 1991; Schwirian, 1983). Demographic and *ecological* theories describe changes in demand for housing supply and the changes in economic base (for example, from heavy industry to service) to identify forces that produce neighborhood change. Creation of attractive, additional dwellings outside the neighborhood may draw people away. Development of employment opportunities in the area immediately surrounding the neighborhood may lure new residents to the neighborhood. These theories also deal with issues related to the effects of crowding and residential design.

Sociocultural approaches look at changing values related to urban living. The purchase of a home is related to the availability of a number of benefits, such as cultural facilities, recreation, and social diversity. If the neighborhood provides an attractive package of elements that have current cultural value, the area is likely to grow. If these elements are missing, the area is likely to decline.

Political-economic explanations of neighborhood change emphasize forces at play beyond the neighborhood boundaries. These include the actions of a variety of monied interests (such as developers, banks, and construction companies) who work together to influence property values and government decisions regarding revitalization efforts. Their manipulation of broader community decision making results in assistance to some areas of the city and inattention to others, with the ultimate beneficiaries being the monied interests themselves. Other forces, such as rising or falling mortgage rates, taxation policies, and availability of land for development, also have relevance for neighborhood growth or decline.

Social movement explanations for neighborhood change focus on the effects of neighborhood organizing, including issue identification and development, action to achieve neighborhood goals, and citizen participation in municipal decision making. The effect of these organized activities (if successful) is certainly change. These changes may make the area more attractive to current residents as well as to a host of newcomers . . . some of whom may be considered to be "invaders."

As you can see, there is some relationship among these more commonly presented views on neighborhood change. Each should give you some clues for assessing the conditions in your neighborhood and the route you may take to improve those conditions. Though neighborhoods may undergo some "natural" stages of growth or decline, movement in any particular direction is obviously not inevitable. Purposeful action on your part could bring about changes that would improve the quality of the neighborhood and the lives of its residents.

Understanding Neighborhood Organizations

Your efforts to improve neighborhood conditions will trigger development of a neighborhood organization or assist the progress of an existing organization. You will bring people together to undertake a particular project, or you will aid in developing a permanent organization that itself will undertake diverse projects and provide other functions. Regardless of the nature and extent of the changes you seek, some sort of neighborhood organization will be involved.

As you begin to gain a better understanding of what the neighborhood needs and has, you may come to the conclusion that a concentrated and comprehensive approach to organizing is ultimately needed. If your primary professional responsibilities do not lie in the area of community organization, you may not be able to make the type of investment that the thorough approach to organizing would require.

What to do? Well, you could go out for pizza and forget the whole problem. This is probably not the most effective approach for assisting the neighborhood. At least four other choices are available to you. One course of action would be to initiate a modest but meaningful change with a definite beginning and end for your involvement. The neighborhood receives the direct benefit of the change, itself an important accomplishment, and it may awaken the residents' recognition of their capabilities and spur some of them to take some further actions. Even if no subsequent action directly follows the change episode, it may indirectly contribute to efforts further down the road.

Recognizing that continued resident action may not happen of its own accord, you may decide to take the second option, which involves purposefully using the change to develop leadership and continued interest. If you can further link the nascent neighborhood organization to other support systems (for example, a successful organization from another neighborhood that can serve as a mentor), the effect of your particular change episode may be more long-lasting. This second approach requires greater involvement than the first.

Your third alternative is to get help. There may be individuals or groups in the community who can sustain a deeper level of involvement in working with the neighborhood. Your main contribution is to discover the particular resource and help establish the relationship between the neighborhood and those who will provide organizing assistance.

Your fourth choice involves convincing your agency to become more actively involved in the life of the neighborhood.

Whether your participation is modest or substantial, an awareness of neighborhood organizations is useful.

In addition to the authors specifically identified, the ideas in this section were also drawn from and shaped by Bratt (1987); Burghardt (1982); Clay (1979); Dupper and Poertner (1997); Fantini and Gittell (1973); Fellin (1995); Kennedy (1996); Kretzman and McNight (1993); Mayer (1984); Rich (1979); Scheie, Williams, Mayer, Kroll, and Dewar (1997a, 1997b); Suchman (1993, 1994); Suchman and Lamb (1991); Thomas (1986); Wagner (1995); Warren and Warren (1977); Williams (1985, 1989); Wireman (1984); and Wolpert, Mumphrey, and Seley (1972).

Types of Neighborhood Organizations

Neighborhood organizing is by no means a new phenomenon. Examples of the establishment of neighborhood organizations have been recorded for over a hundred years. In more modern times, federal programs in the 1960s and 1970s provided the impetus and support for development of neighborhood organizations. For a period of time these organizations flourished. Even after federal support diminished, many of these groups continued and new directions in neighborhood action were taken, sometimes encouraged by municipal governments. Neighborhood organizations formed as a result of government programs certainly were influenced by the goals of the program as much as by the residents themselves.

Currently, residents seem to be showing renewed interest in their neighborhood organizations. For example, the number of neighborhood associations in the Phoenix area grew from 28 in 1990 to 522 by 1997 (Reid, 1997). Results from the annual Metro Survey by the Metro Chicago Information Center show increased participation in neighborhood organizations for all ethnic and income groups surveyed (Garth, 1997).

Fisher (1984) describes three approaches to organizing that are based on how neighborhoods are envisioned:

Social work. The neighborhood is viewed as an organism. Efforts are made to build a sense of community, particularly by providing social service organizations. This method lobbies for and emphasizes delivery of social services.

Political activism. The neighborhood is viewed as a political entity or power base. The absence of power needed to defend the neighborhood is seen as the basic problem. Efforts are made to give people more control over their lives. Strategies are rooted in the presumption of a conflict of interest between the neighborhood and those in power outside of the neighborhood.

Neighborhood maintenance. The neighborhood is viewed primarily as a residential area. Efforts are vested in protecting property and its values. Neighborhoods using this style of organizing are usually free of major problems. (pp. 9–16)

Many neighborhood organizations regularly interact with their local governments. Such a relationship may provide benefits to both the neighborhood and the government in the form of decentralization of government services or decision making. Though this may only involve opportunities for an exchange of information between the two groups, more significant collaborative efforts also occur. Some neighborhood groups receive contracts to deliver public programs in the area, and others work closely with units of government to create, develop, and operate programs benefiting neighborhood residents.

Simpson and Gentile (1986) identify three forms of neighborhood organizations related to governmental processes: advisory councils that are officially established by the municipal government, independent neighborhood groups that have claimed governmental or political powers, and groups that have been organized by or incorporated into an official government neighborhood program.

In addition to these general categories, neighborhood organizations commonly fall into one of the following classifications identified by Hallman (1984):

Neighborhood association: used for two purposes, advocacy or low-budget, self-help activities; has individual members, representatives from other organizations, or a combination; ranges from block clubs to multi-issue neighborhood organizations.

Neighborhood congress: an organization of organizations; tends to concentrate on advocacy and neighborhood organizing but might sponsor a neighborhood corporation or program operations.

Neighborhood advisory committee: usually set up by a government agency to deal with issues related to its mission; has an advisory role in program planning and possibly in program implementation and evaluation; selection of members might be by an administrator, nominees of specific organizations and interests, or a combination.

Neighborhood council: a unit with official recognition by the city or county to deal with policy issues in a number of program areas; mainly advisory authority rather than final decision making; members usually elected by residents; in some places, existing associations have gained recognition as neighborhood councils.

Neighborhood corporation: funded and staffed to operate specific services or undertake developmental activities; incorporated, usually as a nonprofit organization but might have profit-making subsidiary (or vice versa). (Note: Similar activities, especially as they relate to economic development, are performed by neighborhood development organizations or *community development corporations.*)

Neighborhood government: has legal power and authority equivalent to that of a municipality to make policy and run specific programs; has access to financial resources necessary to carry out its responsibilities; democratic selection of governing officials. (Note: Some neighborhood government groups might more accurately be referred to as *quasi-governmental organizations* in that they have some, but fairly limited, policy-making authority, often related to zoning issues.) (p. 265)

Neighborhood organizations may also take the form of a typical homeowners' association that concerns itself primarily with the maintenance of neighborhood facilities (for example, a community pool) or the preservation of the physical attractiveness of the neighborhood. Participation as a voting member is usually limited to property owners, so renters rarely have any real voice. Homeowners' associations are sometimes more concerned with regulating residents' behaviors, often done through enforcement of deed restrictions, than with advocacy on behalf of the neighborhood. They are often set up and even managed by the corporation that built the housing development. Advocacy issues are commonly related to protection of property values. It is common for the original developer of the tract to establish the association.

Tenants' associations may be considered as

a type of neighborhood organization if you consider an apartment complex or similar housing configuration to be a neighborhood. Certainly these organizations at the very least exist within neighborhoods. Tenants' organizations are primarily developed to secure and protect the rights of renters to receive well-maintained, safe housing.

Social service agencies, both public and private, may develop a neighborhood service center. (If the center is not developed, established, and operated by the neighborhood, it would not technically be a neighborhood organization.) Although the operators of the center usually defer to the authority of the sponsoring agency, center staff will, from time to time, engage in advocacy or development efforts on behalf of the neighborhood. These activities complement the provision of direct services such as counseling or job training programs. As a social worker or human services professional,

you may have the opportunity to develop such a center or to refine the nature of the programs it offers.

As you can see, no one basic neighborhood organization type exists. Organizations are shaped not only by the particular needs of the neighborhood but also by the interests of the organizers. Factors such as the extent of the organizers' interest, awareness of organizing options, and availability of time may well be reflected in the design of the organization.

Activities of Neighborhood Organizations

A brief rundown of common activities undertaken by neighborhood organizations provides some examples of the things you may be able to accomplish by bringing people, both residents and individuals and groups from outside the neighborhood—particularly local government, schools, religious institutions, social service agencies, and private foundations—together in the effort to strengthen the vitality of a neighborhood. You can accomplish a great deal to enhance the quality of life for neighborhood residents simply by encouraging and supporting the further development of natural helping networks that exist in the neighborhood. Here are some ideas that you might try:

- *Strong identity:* attractive, identifiable neighborhood boundary markers; emblems on windows of collaborating businesses; special neighborhood signage.
- *Events:* potlucks; carnivals; fairs; art shows; holiday lighting; activities emphasizing area culture; entertainment, such as sporting events, dances, or drama.
- *Facelifting:* neighborhood cleanup; minor housing rehabilitation or beautification; tree planting and other landscaping; community gardens; beautifying commercial corridors; streetscape improvements; pocket parks.
- *Social interaction:* newsletters providing information on resources, neighborhood personalities, and neighborhood and community events affecting the neighborhood; intergenerational mentoring; exchange of resources or services for mutual assistance; participation in neighborhood organization decision making, operation, or activities.
- *Community education:* forums; speakers; credit and noncredit classes.
- *Sponsorship of groups:* Girl Scouts; Little League; Alcoholics Anonymous; performing arts group.
- *Monitoring services of local government:* garbage pickup; fire protection; police protection; street maintenance and repair; sewer maintenance and repair.
- *General improvements:* traffic; zoning enforcement; neighborhood planning.
- *Security:* identification of household items for burglary protection; safety and security inspections; foot patrols; neighborhood watch; community policing in collabora-

tion with neighborhood prevention efforts; neighborhood-based public defender and mediation services; cadre of community youth workers working with service agencies and law enforcement.
- *Service delivery:* day care; visitation of elderly; shopping services; co-ops such as babysitting or food purchase; provision of emergency food; substance abuse counseling; services designed for particular groups such as children, young people, older people, or single parents.
- *Administration of public programs:* garbage pickup; job training programs; G.E.D. preparation; collaboration with public sector for program design, development, implementation, and evaluation.
- *Economic development:* anti-redlining actions; property management; property development; housing rehabilitation; acquisition of personal assets through home ownership programs like HOME and HOPE IV, and savings plans like Individual Development Accounts; small grants program, loan funds, business incubators, and business assistance centers to promote economic vitality, including development of resident businesses, such as home repair and maintenance, landscaping, house cleaning, house painting, computer services, typing services, restaurants, and retail.
- *Political empowerment:* voter registration activities; voter turnout activities; candidate forums; public hearings; participation in coalitions; organization of power base.
- *Improvement and redesign of local schools:* family resource centers, providing an array of wellness and human services; schools to function as activity and community learning centers with increased hours of operation; schools serve as resource attractors for community development efforts; neighborhood involvement in classroom activities and school decision making.
- *Neighborhood government:* zoning; permits; licensing; traffic and parking regulations; code enforcement.

A COMPREHENSIVE NEIGHBORHOOD REVITALIZATION PROGRAM

Many of the neighborhood activities described in the text can be integrated into a *comprehensive neighborhood revitalization program.* This is a long-term process that requires sustained commitment from a number of parties working in partnership with the neighborhood in accordance with a community plan. Neighborhood leaders and residents change the way they relate to powerful people and institutions outside of the neighborhood. Basic activities in such a comprehensive approach could include efforts to improve physical appearance; upgrade community facilities and infrastructure; rehabilitate existing housing and add new housing stock; revitalize neighborhood commercial assets; provide ongoing economic development and job training for residents; integrate and ensure relevance of social services; improve the effectiveness of public services, particularly schools and public safety; and develop leadership (Chaskin, Joseph, & Chipenda-Dansokho, 1997; Kennedy, 1996; Naparstek & Dooley, 1997; Suchman, 1994).

Many of these activities can easily fit more than one category. As you become more involved in the neighborhood, you will intentionally develop activities that serve a variety of purposes. The "spillover" effect of programs often produces additional positive benefits, such as intergenerational or interracial contact, development of leadership, or increased commitment to the neighborhood.

Elements of Successful Neighborhood Organizations

Certain characteristics are common to effective neighborhood organizations that have had some time to develop (Perlman, 1979). These include assets such as:

- Full-time, paid professional staff
- Well-developed fund-raising capacity
- A sophisticated mode of operation
- Various skills, such as negotiation, planning, and lobbying skills
- Issue growth from neighborhood to nation
- External support that ranges from technical assistance to organizer training schools
- Expanding coalition building

Although it is helpful to be aware of these qualities as you help direct the growth of your organization, what about those organizations that have just successfully gotten off the ground? What elements are important to getting a good start? One study identified a number of factors that helped neighborhood groups during their first year of organizing (Laird & Hoover, 1993). These neighborhood organizations:

- Felt connected to other resources, such as community agencies, schools, churches, and other grassroots organizations
- Participated in community networks that led to an increase in confidence, competence, and access to other resources
- Continued to involve more people
- Trained and empowered new leaders
- Became recognized by elected officials and were contacted by them
- Held celebrations tied to the neighborhood
- Recognized and exchanged resources within the neighborhood
- Received and made use of technical assistance
- Received modest financial support from a funding source interested in nurturing their success

Basic Change-Related Tasks

Neighborhood change is similar to any community change endeavor. For the community to act on the possibility of change, two conditions need to be present: the residents must be sufficiently unhappy with current circumstances, and they must have a sufficient degree of belief that their actions can produce a successful outcome. For the change to be made, the neighborhood must have sufficient power and resources to introduce the change and to sustain it.

The information in previous chapters provides you with a solid foundation for building and sustaining an organized neighborhood change effort. A brief review of important elements, with suggestions from Gatewood (1994); Hallman (1984); Kretzman and McNight (1993); Schwab and Ringel (1991); Suchman and Lamb (1991); and Suchman (1993, 1994) geared specifically to neighborhood change, underscores the key phases.

To get off the ground, a neighborhood organization needs an initiator, someone to get the ball rolling. This could well be you or the person who brought the interest for improving the neighborhood to your attention. In addition, a neighborhood organization needs to:

- *Promote communication.* Neighbors need to talk among themselves to recognize dissatisfaction, stir up interest, and begin building some level of trust. This may occur through informal conversations with residents, a door-to-door resident contact campaign, informal small group meetings, or by other methods.
- *Do its homework.* A better understanding of neighborhood characteristics, concerns, resources, leadership figures, needs, institutions, and other elements should begin in the early stages. Continue to develop a good information base. Essential here is the recognition, documentation, and use of the wealth of assets of individuals (including "strangers"; that is, the marginalized members of the community—the young, the old, and the labeled); local associations and organizations from stamp clubs to neighborhood organizations; local institutions, including parks, libraries, and community colleges; natural attributes such as vacant land, proximity to downtown, trees, rivers, scenic views, and historic sites; and local community leadership.
- *Develop issues.* The ability to define and articulate concerns will help build momentum.
- *Hold initial meetings.* You need to introduce the idea of an organization, begin to formalize the organization, identify beginning plans and related actions, and make decisions.
- *Take initial action.* Do something to help confirm the reality of your organization and its capability. Usually these are specific, visible actions such as placing a stop sign. Or they are beginning actions that lead to further actions such as inviting an elected official to meet with your group.
- *Celebrate accomplishments.* Draw attention to the gains you have already made.
- *Recruit members.* Attract new participants to your effort.
- *Further develop plans.* Plans can become more comprehensive. Remember to include not only the people who live in the area but those who work or go to school there as well.
- *Further develop organizational leadership and structures.* Identify potential leaders and provide them with opportunities for demonstrating initiative, influence, and direction. Clarify organizational issues through development of various committees, promulgation of bylaws and, perhaps, preparation of articles of incorporation.
- *Engage in fund-raising and acquisition of needed items.* Obtain the resources needed to operate the organization and to pursue its activities.
- *Take further action.* Engage in actions or tackle projects that have a more significant impact on the neighborhood.
- *Expand power.* Create linkages with other sources of power, join coalitions, create media attention, or undertake other activities

that promote your group's ability to influence decisions affecting the neighborhood.

This rough sequence of activities offers an overview of some of the basic tasks you will need to perform. This process is not really a step-by-step guide since some of these actions will overlap with one another or even occur simultaneously. Also, although some of these activities have a beginning and ending point, most will be ongoing throughout the life of the organization.

Additional Factors Related to Successful Neighborhood Change

Attention to a number of general principles that apply to neighborhood change and empowerment will give you a better understanding of this arena and strengthen your effectiveness.

Sources of Strength

Membership development is a key matter. Groups with large memberships are taken much more seriously by actors outside the neighborhood and by residents as well. More members means more resources, more clout, more potential leaders, and so on.

Revival, even in deteriorated areas, is possible. Though in some cases a significant infusion of external resources is required, each neighborhood has some capacities and resources that can be mobilized to promote neighborhood renewal (Clay, 1979).

Interaction develops commitment. Neighbors' interaction with one another and with neighborhood services such as the local grocery store will increase favorable sentiments toward the neighborhood. Sentimental attachment to the neighborhood is further increased when residents can participate in networks that not only meet their own needs but allow them to recognize that they have important contributions to make to others within the network. This has implications for building a sense of

community. Neighborhood changes that increase these positive sentiments may be accomplished through rather small and low-cost efforts (Kretzman & McNight, 1993; Morrison, Howard, Johnson, Navarro, Plachetka, & Bell, 1997; Putnam, 1995; Roach & O'Brien, 1982; Wagner, 1995).

"The level of satisfaction of citizens with a neighborhood and their perceptions of the direction of neighborhood change are critical in determining the commitment of people to their place of residence" (Ahlbrandt & Cunningham, 1979, p. 13). Additionally, "for revitalization to occur, residents must have confidence not only in the physical elements of the community but also in their neighbors" (Clay, 1979, p. 79).

A shared perception of threat can move people to action. Mobilization of neighborhood resources is more likely when the neighborhood is perceived as threatened (Thomas, 1986). "Neighborhood organizations, regardless of the income of their constituents, share a single overriding goal: defense of their turf" (Williams, 1985, p. 112).

Residents need incentives for action. It is not sufficient to sustain members' motivation with a focus on general neighborhood benefits. Residents need to understand their personal connection to the "common good" (Rich, 1979).

Economic Considerations

The neighborhood is an economic system. It has wealth, enterprises, and a flow of money, goods, and services in and out, and circulation within. Its wealth may be seen in buildings and physical facilities, land, equipment, and machines (ownership can be near or distant), as well as in the personal wealth, talents, and skills of its people. It has commercial and industrial enterprises and public and nonprofit organizations. All these have capital investments and goods. They hire people and give out money through paychecks and public welfare programs.

All neighborhoods have a cash flow. As an example, a neighborhood with 2,000 people with a per capita income of $6,000 has an annual income of $12 million. How much this circulates in the neighborhood or goes out of it determines how much the neighborhood is benefiting from its money input. "A net inflow of dollars adds to prosperity, a net outflow leads to decline" (Hallman, 1984, p. 83).

Lending institutions must disclose lending records. The Federal Home Mortgage Disclosure Act requires records disclosure. Neighborhood organizations have used this act and the Community Reinvestment Act to work with lending institutions to encourage lending in the neighborhood (Hallman, 1984; Naparstek & Dooley, 1997).

Diverse Perspectives

Skepticism may be the order of the day. Many neighborhood residents will take a "wait and see" attitude toward your new organization. They may have been disappointed by past attempts at neighborhood change, or they may be mistrustful of claims that "I'm from the government (or social service agency), and I'm here to help you."

In poorer neighborhoods, residents may have learned that they fall way down on the local government's and the wider community's list of concerns. They may have developed an outlook of impotence, and they certainly don't have much faith in pursuing matters through "appropriate channels," which more often leads to a runaround than to resolution (Williams, 1985).

A number of different interests affect the community. The individual resident wants some things that conditions in the neighborhood influence. Perhaps he or she wants security, maybe protection of property values, possibly social relationships. The neighborhood residents in common, as a community, also have things they want. Many of these will be the same as the individual's wants—good schools, police protection, and well-maintained streets. Some may be different. The community may want all single-family homes, whereas an individual might decide to make some extra money by dividing a dwelling into several apartments. The

community may want an attractive environment, whereas the individual may want to decorate a front yard with the remnants of 1978 Oldsmobiles.

Other actors also have intentions in and for the neighborhood, some compatible with community preferences and some in conflict. The most likely other interests are: absentee landowners; businesspeople from inside as well as outside the neighborhood, such as developers or store owners; lending institutions, such as banks; service institutions, such as churches, schools, or social service agencies; and local government (Ahlbrandt & Cunningham, 1979; Wolpert, Mumphrey, & Seley, 1972).

Enhancing the Prospects for Success

Neighborhood change and empowerment is a process of discovery and action. The suggestions provided below should help to build successes, establish neighborhood potency, and increase your awareness of this arena of action.

Tackle issues that are within your capability. Remember that the specific problems on which you intend to take action cannot be larger than your base of power and resources. If you are not faced with an immediate problem, gain some experience and develop a track record on smaller actions before you deal with bigger ones. If you do not have that luxury, expand your power base by establishing connections with community institutions and other community groups, or attempt to partialize the issue.

Many of the issues confronting neighborhoods are related to more fundamental community and social problems occurring beyond neighborhood boundaries. Your organization can ally itself with others as a way of making inroads to more fundamental problems while it takes action in the neighborhood to counter their effects. For example, you may participate in a movement promoting economic justice while undertaking economic development activities in your neighborhood.

Understand that as you address larger issues you are likely to need support, assistance, and actual resources from groups outside the neighborhood. These may be governmental units, lending institutions, or community activist groups.

Realize that not all good ideas are feasible. Some projects are just too complicated given the current abilities and clout of the neighborhood.

Move from reacting and petitioning to negotiating and mutual problem solving. From time to time you will interact with local governments to head off potentially destructive actions or to secure specific benefits for the community. Your ability to act assertively as a partner rather than a supplicant is a key distinction in the maturation of your organization.

Plan for higher level results. Link activities to outcomes that change conditions (Kibel & Miner, 1996).

Develop methods and practices to handle internal disputes. Internal squabbling and unresolved conflicts drain energy and undermine resolve. Keep clear records regarding money, a common source of conflict. Focus more on action than on arguments over arcane sections of the bylaws.

Identify neighborhood leaders. People who are visible and credible in the neighborhood, such as the rabbi or the store owner, may be able to provide leadership, particularly in the early stages. People who are known to hold professional or authority positions, such as a doctor, schoolteacher, architect, or police officer, are often looked to for direction. Get to know the various neighborhood networks. Each is influenced by an informal leader.

Try to identify those whose opinions carry some weight. In some neighborhoods there are no recognized opinion leaders because people simply don't know or talk much to each other. However, through your efforts to organize you will discover potential or future opinion and task leaders.

Understand local government systems and forms of government. Find out which governmental jurisdiction has authority over specific matters of neighborhood concern. Typically this would be city or county government. Also, discover the formal structure of authority in the local government. For example, does your city manager or mayor hold more authority? Are your community's representatives elected by ward or by a general election of the entire community?

Discover "administrative guerrillas." These are officials in local government who believe that community involvement is desirable and act that way. They can provide valuable contributions, particularly in providing you with inside information and in influencing the perceptions of other officials on neighborhood matters (Thomas, 1986).

If you are working under contract with an outside funding source, see to it that you meet contractual obligations. Make sure basic paperwork procedures, especially those having to do with finances, are demonstrably in order, particularly if you are involved in a struggle with local government or other influential community interests. Failure to comply with the terms of your contract can leave you vulnerable to those who are looking for ways to discredit the organization (Mayer, 1984).

Get the children involved. When you include children as active community members, you will find other members as well—their parents.

Get help from those who have more experience. There is no sense reinventing the wheel. Take advantage of technical assistance.

Establish mentoring relationships. Learn to benefit from the experiences of more established neighborhood organizations. Establish a mutual understanding of the mentoring relationship, otherwise the older organization may grow impatient with requests for assistance or the younger organization may feel irritated by unsolicited advice. Establish some mentoring mechanism such as once-a-month breakfasts among the leadership of both groups. You will discover that both groups benefit. Be mindful of the potential for jealousies and the mentor's need to pretend to know it all.

Some Final Considerations

Major setbacks in life can knock us down. They can demand much of our energy as we struggle to get back on our feet. Sometimes, though, what really wears at us, tears at us, a little here, a little there, is the accumulation of all those things that tell us we just don't count. Whole groups of people are written off because of where they live. Whole groups of people, even those living in more affluent settings, can grow to accept conditions that numb the spirit. Our neighborhood, our place, is so much a part of our daily lives that we cannot escape the meaning its life holds for us.

When we act in a way that says we matter, that we are to be taken seriously, that we are no longer to be ignored, we rediscover elements of dignity. Neighborhood action is a way to reclaim and confirm our dignity. Participation in neighborhood organizations affects the feelings residents have about their own lives and their environment (Downs, 1981).

You may work in a neighborhood that has enthusiasm, confidence, and a fair amount of cold cash. You may look at such a neighborhood with eager eyes and envision conspicuous accomplishments. You may look at a different neighborhood and see the violence, the decay, the fear, the faded faces of hopelessness. You may think, "What can I possibly do? Where can I even start?" The last word of your question is your first step. Each neighborhood has something, some resource or capacity that can be a starting point. Hallman (1984) makes a valuable observation. He notes that all neighbor-hoods, both those with and those without a significant presence of social pathologies (drugs, violence, bad housing, breakdown of family life, and other problems), have personal networks, mutual support, peer groups, indigenous organizations, churches, social institutions, and other attributes. Your ability to look at a neighborhood not only in terms of its problems but, more important, in terms of its capacities will give you some direction and some hope, and you will learn how to pass these on.

Think about how you plan to approach the business of neighborhood change. Do you intend to develop from within, using local strengths and visions? Do you believe the most important direction and resources must come from outside the neighborhood? The way you answer these questions will direct what you do.

Similar to your work in any change effort, you will do some things very creatively and very well. You will also make mistakes. You may fear that you will not be as good as you need to be. Burghardt (1982) has a valuable commentary on this matter. He says, "Holding onto this fear has been the undoing of many organizers, for the simple reality of organizing life is that good organizers are *always* making mistakes and being a little less effective than they ought to be" (p. 27).

As you recognize the value of learning by doing, you will recognize your increasing capability as you gain experience. Your experience may lead you to help transform a neighborhood and, in the process, transform the people who live there.

Something for the Children

Margie Ruiz studied the door. Years ago someone cared enough to cover what had been a beige hue with a coat of something close to lime green. Not her colors, but they at least showed that someone was paying attention to the place. No one had made a recent attempt. In quite a few places, the green gave way to beige, which surrendered to the weathered wood turned gray by sun and rain. Again she rang the doorbell.

Knowing that she needed to get out of her office and into the neighborhood, she knew even more clearly that she didn't want anyone to open that door. Margie didn't like talking to complete strangers, and she liked even less that the stranger might think her a busybody. After all, what was she really doing here? Even if she could stammer out an introduction, she knew that in some ways she was saying, "You people in this neighborhood don't have your act together, and you need me to help you figure things out." There was something vaguely rude about her standing on that doorstep, and Margie Ruiz did not consider herself a rude person.

Margie jumped a little as the door opened. She hadn't heard anyone coming, and whoever it was took so long to answer that she had almost turned to go.

"I'm sorry, young lady, did I frighten you?"

Margie could see that the door was still partially secured by a chain latch. She could barely make out the face that peered out at her through the small space. Embarrassed, all she could think to say was, "I don't know, maybe," which didn't seem to be a good start to the conversation. But it was.

Mabel Hughes had lived in Sunvale Gardens for over 40 years, and she had once liked lime green. The gangs and the arthritis had moved her from her tiny front yard to the chair on her front porch and, finally, indoors. Margie found out that they had not taken her wit nor her intelligence. They had not taken her memories of a nicer neighborhood nor her knowledge of who was doing what to whom today.

Through Mabel, Margie was introduced to Mr. Richards, who ran the small grocery store on the corner. She met Mrs. Metcalf, who lived two doors down, and Reverend Metton from the Baptist church. And from them she met others. It took her a while, almost six months, but Margie began to know the people who lived in Sunvale Gardens and the things that bothered them.

All this was nice, but she still had her casework duties to take care of at the agency. Yet, it was those same casework duties that led her to Mrs. Hughes's door: the young, single mothers talking about their babies getting lead poisoning from the paint peel-ing from the walls; the young men acting so tough, so cool, and looking to belong; the children falling behind in school, unable to do their times tables but able to figure out all you could buy with a month's allotment of Food Stamps. She talked to all of them about what was going on, or what wasn't, in the gloomy area called Sunvale Gardens. And she asked them what could be done to make things better. They said, "nothing," and shook their heads and laughed at her. Except for Jerome, all of 17 and twice a father, who said, "Go talk to Mrs. Hughes."

Maybe she'd better stick with casework. Six people showed up at the meeting tonight. The first *real* meeting Margie had called. She had gotten the school district to give her the cafeteria for the night. Mr. Corrigan, the principal, didn't even bother to make the short presentation he'd prepared.

She knew all the things that were bothering the people in the neighborhood. A person can learn a lot in six months. She had told them about her plans to put together an organization that would make the changes they all wanted. She had told them about the people she knew who worked for the city, and how they said they were going to help. She had put so much into this. Now, six people. She tried not to be angry, but she had to fight the urge to yell at them all, "OK, just sit there, be glad you're stuck in all this, don't even think things could be different!"

Margie didn't yell. Margie wasn't rude. She looked at Mabel, just an old woman whom she had talked into going to a meeting at night. She sighed to Reverend Metton, the minister, and she wished that prayers were enough. She saw Mr. Richards and wondered who was minding the store. The young college student Dwight Hoopes had shown up. So did Loretta Looth, and Margie wondered where Loretta found a baby-sitter for her three kids.

Margie sat down. She spread out her hands and said, "Now what do we do?" It was Mrs. Hughes who broke the silence. "I'm glad you asked us, Miss Ruiz. Maybe we could start with something for the children."

Some Questions to Consider

1. If there are no major changes in the way the change effort is being conducted, how is this story likely to end?
2. What information or assumptions led you to this conclusion?
3. If you were Margie Ruiz, what would you have done differently? What would you have done the same?
4. What can Mabel Hughes or any of the others attending the first meeting contribute?
5. What are some of the significant problems facing the neighborhood? Which seem to be the best targets for initial action?
6. What assets or resources might be available to the group?
7. What particular steps would you take at this point that would enhance the prospects for success?

CHAPTER 15

Increasing the Effectiveness of Established, Formal Organizations

Chapter Highlights

- ⟡ Organizations are creatures of human design

- ⟡ Improvements in organizations result in improvements in service

- ⟡ Resistance to pressures from outside of the organization

- ⟡ All organization members can initiate change

- ⟡ Tension between commitment to client and loyalty to agency

- ⟡ Five types of agency change

- ⟡ Organizations as systems

- ⟡ Structure, processes, and philosophy of organizations affect the change effort

- ⟡ Different perceptions among the organization's members affect the change effort

- ⟡ Overcome success

- ⟡ Overcome failure

- ⟡ Dealing with procrastination, critics, and unintended consequences

- ⟡ Link your change effort to important elements of the organization

- ⟡ Principles for increasing your effectiveness

  - know your issue well
  - involve clients
  - gain support of advocacy groups
  - capitalize on external threats and opportunities
  - create worker support systems
  - identify stakeholders, attract investors, and secure allies
  - understand the organization's culture
  - create a receptive environment
  - expect, identify, and deal with resistance
  - reduce personal risks
  - implement and confirm the change

- ⟡ Minor changes can have major benefits

- ⟡ Improving your organization is an ongoing process

In this chapter the focus of discussion is on more formal, well-established organizations; among them are the social welfare agencies that you may work within. These kinds of organizations have some characteristics not necessarily present in the less formal, grassroots organizations preceding chapters have focused on. However, they also have many similarities.

Organizations are creatures of human design, empowered by the strength of human creativity and purpose, and limited by human foibles and ignorance. Organizations can be bungling or competent. They can be shortsighted or forward looking. They can be defensive or insightful. They can be productive or wasteful. They can neglect or take care of themselves. In short, organizations are collections of people, and they tend to act, not surprisingly, like people.

Most of the work of human services professionals is done through some organization, usually a public or private agency. The usefulness of this work is, to some extent, constrained by the imperfections of those organizations themselves. Improvements in the quality of our organizations translate into improvements in the effectiveness of our work. Thus, the organizations become arenas for change.

Human services workers aren't the only ones who have noticed the need to improve their organizations. Business corporations, large and small, have been the subject of many a writer's or consultant's attention. There is much to be learned from the examples, good and bad, that the business world provides. Yet, despite their many similarities, it would be naive to think that human services organizations and private, for-profit businesses should operate in the same way. Their purposes are different, and certainly the societal demands they face are not the same. As a consultant and a practitioner in both worlds, I have seen those differences.

Many of the thoughts and suggestions I provide in this chapter have been informed by my experience. But they are not my ideas alone. You will find the perspectives of a number of writers in the following pages. I have particularly relied on the observations of Belasco (1990); Brager and Holloway (1977, 1978); Cohen and Austin (1994); Dubois and Krogsrud-Miley (1996); Frey (1990); Goldberg (1980); Gottleib (1992); Gummer (1978); Holloway (1987); Hyde (1992); Kettner, Daley, and Nichols (1985); Kirst-Ashman and Hull (1997); Litwak, Shiroi, Zimmerman, and Bernstein (1970); Lumsden and Lumsden (1997); Martin (1980); Morgan (1997); O'Looney (1993); Patti (1974, 1980); Patti and Resnick (1975); Resnick (1978); Resnick and Menefee (1994); Richan (1992); Senge, Kleiner, Roberts, Ross, and Smith (1994); Sherman and Wenocur (1983), Weinbach (1984); and Wernet (1994).

Organizations certainly respond to outside pressure. They need to and do respond to threats, opportunities, and trends in the larger political and economic environment. In fact, if they don't respond, if they don't fit, they will cease to exist. But it is not those forces alone that lead to change. Members of the organization, perhaps even you, will work to ward off direct demands for change "outsiders" may make. One likely reason is that members feel threatened by the implication that if they were doing their jobs well no pressure would need to be brought. Another related reaction is defensiveness. There is often the perception that those outside the organization "just don't understand." They don't understand the organization's mission, its funding constraints, the value of its current methods, the difficulties involved in making the change, and on and on. This increases the value of making changes from within.

All people who make up an organization are capable of initiating some change, although the discussion of organizational change issues is frequently directed to the top leadership of organizations. Executives and administrators are counseled on ways to streamline the organization, develop strategic initiatives, or manage personnel for greater productivity. Although effective action from those in the highest positions of the organization can produce important changes, the responsibility and opportunity to promote change should hardly rest there. In the course of your daily activities, each of you will be able to identify barriers to effective client service or opportunities to create even more effective approaches. Regardless of your formal position in the organization, that recognition will spark an interest in organizational change. It is to you that this chapter is addressed.

As a social work or human services professional, it is likely that you will come face-to-face with some fundamental value conflicts as you work within a service agency, especially a large service agency. You may want to promote the interests of clients, whereas the organization wants to promote its status. Your values of being readily responsive to changing conditions and promoting the value and uniqueness of each individual might be at odds with an organization interested in maintenance and predictability, one that believes in objective, impersonal relationships. Organizational values of service may run counter to your beliefs about empowerment. A host of other conflicts may also be in store.

First you must recognize that these value conflicts are likely. If you expect them, you won't be thrown off stride when they show up. Second, you need to develop attitudes and skills for dealing with them constructively. Otherwise you will end up hating your work, being angry with yourself, and, if you do not leave the organization in the hope that the next place will be magically different, you will retreat into burnout.

Change efforts initiated by workers not in formal leadership positions face a number of obstacles. Although many excellent corporations in the for-profit sector have discovered the value of fostering worker initiative, human services organizations have been slow to tap the potential of this creative force. Rarely do line staff have formal authority to initiate change. Doing so requires workers to engage in activities normally seen as outside their areas of responsibility. Further, the strategies and tactics required to promote recognition and response to a given issue may conflict with organizational norms and expectations of "professional" behavior. This is further complicated by a sort of necessary role reversal. That is, low-authority people are encouraging high-authority people to take the organization in new directions. They have, in effect, become the leaders. That is not a situation many formal leaders take lightly.

The authority embodied in professional ethics may transcend certain arbitrary limits on worker authority. A belief in professional responsibility may drive workers to seek changes that will benefit the people they serve. Many human services organizations recognize and give at least lip service respect to the value of professional ethics. You should not dismiss this practical asset. In addition, in each organization there is the likely availability of peer support as well as assistance from some who hold higher positions of authority. Together, these dedicated individuals can mobilize for change.

Still, a tension exists between the worker's responsibility to advance client interests and the worker's loyalty to the agency. Though I would argue that the worker's *primary* duty is to work on behalf of the client, no clear agreement among professionals, either in philosophy or in practice, exists on this point. This is a question you will continue to ponder throughout your career and continue to answer through your actions.

Types of Changes

As a human services worker, you may seek changes in the way the organization relates to broader systems (for example, government authority or community expectations), to its immediate systems (client groups), or to its internal systems (agency procedures or agency staff). Five basic types of changes are typical.

1. *Mobilize the organization to engage external systems for the benefit of clients or workers.* Workers may attempt to involve the agency in public policy discussions relating to changes in laws or in regulations affecting public programs. The agency may be asked to become an advocate on matters involving funding, particularly as they may affect benefit levels of public welfare programs, compensation for employees, or increases in the number of program staff (resulting in an improvement in the staff-to-client ratio). Moving a public social welfare agency to vigorously seek an increase in the number of child protective services workers to substantially reduce caseloads would be an example of this type of activity.

2. *Removal of procedures that inhibit service.* All rules at one time made sense, or at least seemed to. Unfortunately, some rules or procedures take on a life of their own and outlive any usefulness they may have had. Or, rules that make sense in one situation are applied to situations that have different demands. Or, rules are

created apart from the context of day-to-day reality. They are fashioned more out of concern with what might happen than with what actually does happen. The list could go on. The simple fact is that some rules serve neither clients nor the goals of the organization. Workers can gain relief from cumbersome or inappropriate rules and procedures by seeking to establish more helpful or empowering policies.

3. *Program or project development.* Workers may institute entirely new programs or undertake a new project within a program to better reach an underserved population. Establishing a gang prevention program within a neighborhood might represent a new direction for an agency traditionally wed to counseling services.

4. *Program or project modification.* Workers may alter the design of existing services to increase benefits to clients or to promote accessibility and utilization of services. This may involve a change in service methods (for example, from individual to group counseling). It may also deal with matters such as program relevance to client needs, program location, or community awareness of the program.

5. *Utilization of clients in setting agency direction.* Most workers would adhere to the principle of client decision making with regard to choices related to individual matters. Yet this same ethic is conspicuously absent when it comes to the design and delivery of services. Workers may redress circumstances that promote client dependence and program irrelevance by investing clients with the skills and authority to influence agency decisions. An example of this would be including a significant number of clients on agency boards of directors and other agency advisory committees.

Elements Affecting the Behavior of Organizations

A brief consideration of the framework of the arena of organizational change is in order. Why do members of human services organizations or the organizations themselves act the way they do? I will not pretend to provide you with a comprehensive answer to that question, but I can offer you a few insights to help you make sense of some of the things you will see.

Organizations as Systems

As you recall from the discussion of systems theory, communities function as systems. In this case, the community is your organization. Systems are set within even larger systems and are composed of a number of smaller systems. As all these systems act to meet their needs, they influence and are influenced by one another. You can see how this applies to your organization. The general rules of the organization, its resources, even the size of the organization itself influence its component systems (or subsystems). Those subsystems (for example, administration, various operational programs, and clients) all affect each other and influence the organization as a whole. Although the various parts of the organization and the organization itself influence you, *you also influence the organization.*

Another aspect of a systems orientation that applies to your desire to make changes is the fact that your organization is constantly responding to obvious and subtle pressures from inside and outside the organization. That is, *it is constantly changing in some way.* Your awareness of the changes taking place will help you develop and direct these forces to accelerate change in a desired direction.

A human services organization is influenced by an array of external forces to which it must respond to justify its very existence. The fact that these forces are often at variance with each other creates a tension in the organization that can produce problems. Particularly, the contradictory values and beliefs of the general society relating to social welfare are evident in conflicting directives issued to organizations and expressed through the behavior of service organizations. Imagine the various constituen-

cies an organization may try to please: diverse political interests, funding sources, professionals, clients, other agencies, referral sources, and the general public. When you consider the number of disparate interests to which it responds, you can begin to understand some of the reasons the organization does not operate with peak efficiency.

Here, again, you are faced not only with a dilemma but with an opportunity. By collaborating with interests both inside and outside the organization, you may be able to neutralize some of these forces while marshaling others. When these forces are focused on a particular aspect of the organization's functioning, you can influence both the rate and the direction of change.

The more you understand the organization's relationship to its external environment, the more you are also able to recognize opportunities to strengthen the organization. Even though your agency may be operating in the world of nonprofits, it is still operating in a competitive marketplace. Its ability to make strategic decisions to reach groups that have not been effectively served by other organizations or to better serve current "customers" can attract resources that help the organization flourish.

The Organization as a Political System

An organization is a political system. Those who have the power to set policies usually do so in a way that serves their interests, often at the expense of others. Do not make the mistake of ignoring this process or assuming that it confirms the evil lurking in the hearts of policy makers. It is a fairly normal process, one in which you probably engage from time to time in your personal if not professional life. Whoever is involved in decision making tends to make policies reflecting their own norms, values, and beliefs. In the process of involving more people in decision making, you will influence development of new norms as you mix new values and beliefs into the policy-making process.

The Organization as an Economic System

The organization provides a type of product (a service) to the larger system or community in exchange for the resources (usually funding) it receives. It also has an internal economic system as goods and services are bartered or paid for. The ability to provide or withhold funding to various programs or to staff positions within the organization affects relationships. Certain behaviors produce rewards, some others are costly. An informal exchange system of rewards and favors is also always in operation. Both formal and informal systems have a powerful influence on the nature and direction of change within the organization. You need to take them into account.

The Organization as an Ideological System

Which fundamental beliefs drive the organization? What convictions about what it should and should not do direct its actions? How does it view its mission? How highly does it value its very approach to providing service? How strong is its adherence to its history and traditions? What doctrines does it hold to be true? By understanding the organization's view of its purpose, its process, and its past, you can introduce change in a way that reduces resistance.

The Organization as a Social System

Human services organizations are different from other communities in the degree of interaction among the members and the degree of meaning members attach to their participation. In few communities do members spend a significant portion of their waking day in direct relationship with one another and with their common purpose. Neighbors may see each other from time to time, social workers meet in professional gatherings a few times a year, and cycling enthusiasts may pedal past one another on occasional Saturdays. Human services workers see each other almost every day, for hours. They work side by side or together to advance the community's goals. They assist or interfere

with each other's professional careers. The time they spend supporting or gossiping about each other is greater than the total time most of them spend in general conversation with members of any other community in which they participate.

Since so much of their time is given over to their involvement with this community, what goes on there becomes very important. Many members even derive their personal identity from their participation in the community: "I am a human services worker, a program manager, a counselor."

These are not trivial matters. They intensify the change experience. It is much easier to contact members, much easier to bring them together, and much easier for change to threaten.

Structural Characteristics of Organizations

The structure, processes, and philosophy of the organization as well as the perceptions of its members will have an impact on how you proceed to make changes. What is the size of the organization? Is the organization composed of many different programs and functional units or only a few? The more complex an organization, the more forces that can assist or inhibit the organization you will have to recognize. Does the organization have a centralized hierarchy of authority? Does your boss have a boss who has a boss who must get yet another boss to approve the change? Your assessment of whether the organization vests decision making in the hands of a few or invites broad participation will suggest the tactics you will use. Does your organization have an elaborate set of rules governing everything from hiring practices to bathroom usage? An abundance of policies usually inhibits change, although you may be able to find some policies that provide justification for change.

In all organizations people know incompletely; that is, each person has limited access to information. Those people who work at the direct service level are more able to comprehend problems encountered by clients. Those who struggle to balance the budget are more likely to know of the potential financial strain various programs impose. Organizations with a high degree of specialization or a rigid hierarchy of authority feel the burden of perceptual differences more severely.

With some people allowed access to information and others denied, or with some people attentive to their narrow concerns while others worry over very separate matters, it is likely that different if not contradictory perspectives will emerge. In these organizations, the ability to have and to hold particular information may define a person's domain. A desire to protect the domain may contribute to a reluctance to share information, thereby further impeding communication. As a change agent, you need to see that other people see the situation differently.

Additional Processes Influencing Change

See if the experiences, conditions, and possibilities described here appear in your organization. Each will affect your ability to institute change.

Overcome Success

Believe it or not, success can get an organization stuck. You only need to look at the example of many corporations in the United States to see how past successes led them to dismiss or miss new challenges and opportunities. As long as nothing changes, tried-and-true methods are functional. When conditions change, the same methods may become irrelevant or worse.

Overcome Failures

Workers may have made attempts to improve the system with little to show for their efforts but frustration. They may become jaded to new

efforts (yours) and seek the protection of cynicism. Your challenge to present conditions may remind other workers of the unpleasant accommodations they have made to put up with day-to-day problems.

Feelings of powerlessness may express themselves in a variety of behaviors. Some workers may bounce from one personal crusade to another. Some may become passive and do whatever they are told. Others may find ways to sabotage the organization. Still others may reduce uncertainty through abdication, withdrawing into their own personal little niche, retreating to the safe service of regulations, or leaving the organization altogether. Of course, many will become martyrs, working hard, but unappreciated, in the selfless cause of others.

Although many, many of your colleagues may be inspired by the potential for change, you are wise to remain mindful of the reticence or the disabling coping responses past failures have wrought. Expect that people want to do a good job. But they may be afraid to get their hopes up, or they may have forgotten how to hope after so many years of trying to quiet the urge.

Recognize Potential Problems

Throughout the preceding chapters, we have explored a number of problems associated with promoting community change. In fact, the mere thought of the potential for problems is enough to quiet to inaction the enthusiasm of many a potential change agent. Although I do not want to belabor the idea of obstacles, your awareness of certain problems due to the unique nature of the organization as a community will help you keep things in perspective.

Procrastination. Members of this community are engaged in other community projects, mainly, their day-to-day work. There is enough for them to do to stay busy and distracted with this immediate "community work," so work on the change effort gets pushed to the side. (Of course, other factors contribute to procrastination as well.) With all the time members spend with each other, you would think that more would get done. When it doesn't, you can get overly frustrated.

Relax. The problem is mainly a perceptual one. By using the techniques you have read about in previous chapters, you will keep moving forward. It is especially important to keep communicating the vision, keep making decisions, take concrete (even if minor) actions, and involve more people.

Critics.   A few people will make light of your enthusiasm or your vision. Some will find fault with your methods, if not your intention. Some will tell you directly; most will not. Because these are people you work with, their criticisms may have more of a sting.

Anticipating the likelihood of this response will decrease the irritation you might feel. Responses to the criticism? Directly invite the critics to join with you. Ignore them. Learn from the criticism. Though the content of the criticism may provide some help in improving your effort, the *fact* of the criticism will be important information. As those of you involved in the undertaking provide encouragement and support to one another, you will deal with this and other obstacles constructively.

Unintended consequences.   Because the change you are proposing will have an impact on a highly interactive system, it may well produce significant effects you did not anticipate as well. Some of these will be good, some won't. With an eye toward evaluating actual and likely results of your actions and a willingness to make modifications, you can avoid the most detrimental repercussions.

Pay Attention to Possible Linkage

The more you are able to connect your change to the organization's ideology, goals, structure, and member relationships and attitudes, the more likely you will celebrate a successful outcome.

Principles for Increasing Your Effectiveness

Kirst-Ashman and Hull (1997) have developed an easy-to-remember process for initiating and implementing organizational change called IMAGINE.

I   Start with an *Idea*
M   *Muster* support and formulate an action
     system
A   Identify *Assets*
G   Specify *Goals* and objectives
I   *Implement* plan
N   *Neutralize* opposition
E   *Evaluate* progress

Once you have made the decision to make a change, your effort will be enhanced by paying attention to these basic elements.

Know Your Issue Well

• Gather the necessary facts and figures regarding the change you propose.

• Find out the history of this issue. Has the change been sought in the organization before? If so, what happened? What lasting effect resulted?

• Has the change you are proposing been tried elsewhere? Has it ever worked? What can be learned from that? How can you use this information to garner support for your ideas?

Involve Clients

• Recognize the tendency to avoid the issue. Personally, I believe you need a better reason than "I don't know how" for excluding clients in efforts intended to benefit them.

• Appreciate the benefits of client involvement. If clients can easily see how the proposed change affects them, they can be a tremendous asset to the effort. Clients can help shape the change, increasing the prospect that it is indeed helpful and relevant to their experience. Clients can make demands on the system, both in terms of standing and tactics, that the worker may not be able to make. Further, it is hard for resisters to rationalize away problems or to justify inaction to clients.

• Promote client empowerment. When workers assist clients to recognize additional dimensions to their private struggles, when workers communicate their belief in clients' ability to act on their own behalf, and when workers indicate a willingness to learn from clients as partners, empowerment of clients has benefits far beyond the immediate change.

Gain the Support of External Advocacy Groups

• Strengthen your effect. The ability to send a message from the outside that is consistent with the message you are sending from the inside increases the credibility of the message and the chances that it will be heard. Additionally, close working relationships will decrease the possibility that groups with similar interests but with different information and perspectives will operate at cross purposes.

• Assess the organization's perception of external actors. The impact of external support (or opposition) depends on how widespread or strong the organization perceives it to be.

Capitalize on External Threats and Opportunities

• Seize the moment. Timing is critical to change efforts. Point out current conditions that will help the organization recognize how the proposed change can provide a public relations or financial benefit or ward off a potential loss.

Create Support Systems That Sustain Worker Involvement in Change

• Bolster your resolve. Workers often need each other's tactical and emotional support to become comfortable with taking and using power. An active support group can establish an empowering worker subculture within the organization that may replace a fragmented, defeatist orientation.

• Understand the purpose and functions of an empowerment group. A support group of this type is *not* developed as a temporary mechanism to deal with a particular problem. Empowerment groups are *not* mechanisms for complaining and reinforcing values and beliefs of impotence. Members of an empowerment group commit themselves to meeting regularly, sharing problem-solving responsibility, recognizing the resources each member brings, and taking responsibility for their own actions within the organization. These actions provide a constructive way to deal with frustration, reduce worker burnout, and protect against divide and conquer tactics.

Identify Stakeholders, Attract Investors, and Secure Allies

• Realize that the most critical determinant of success or failure is involvement of a significant number of people in shaping the vision.

• Know who the significant actors are. Who is interested in promoting the change? Who will directly benefit? Who has authority to approve or deny the change? Who are the opinion leaders? All members of the organization are potential actors. Though some have more formal power than others, all who are aware of the change effort make decisions to ignore, support, or oppose the change. They all will decide to get involved or refrain from involvement.

• Discover the extent, degree, location, and temperament of support or resistance. What resources will these people use to support or resist?

• Identify the stakeholders in the current situation. Where and how can they find a stake in the new situation?

• Don't ignore the needs of the staff who have to implement the change. The final features of the change will be shaped by their hands.

• Avoid alienating potential allies who may not support you in the early going.

• Recognize the resources of low-ranking people: access to information; control of information; relationships with other actors; credibility, reputation, or standing; personal skills or expertise.

- Maintain the commitment and support of critical actors. Keep people oriented to the need and what's going on to meet it. Keep people up to date with what is going on in the change effort. Remind actors of the value of the roles various people can and are playing. Determine how to use various mechanisms to communicate that the vision is working.

Understand the Culture of the Organization

- Some organizations emphasize control and allegiance to authority and procedure, whereas others, on the opposite end of the spectrum, are committed to openness and outcomes. The rhetoric of an organization doesn't always describe its true character. If you can present your change as being culturally consistent, and if you adhere to cultural norms in the way you present it, your chances for success will be higher than if you ignore cultural conditions.
- Understand alliances and antagonisms, especially among decision makers. You can gain valuable information by observing meetings, asking questions, and cataloguing complaints. Pay attention to the types of relationships that exist by noting who refers to whom, who defers to whom, and who spends time with whom.
- Determine which supporters can hold which resisters accountable.
- Understand and use informal networks of communication.
- Get to know the official documents and approved statements of the organization. Key information to collect includes: policy manuals, authority/organization charts, promotional material the organization sends out, and budgets. These can help you spot entry points for introducing change to the organization. You will be able to identify formal relationships and procedures. You will be able to discern differences between rhetoric and practice, real and phony threats, and other inconsistencies.
- Acknowledge but do not rely too heavily on hearsay.
- Ask yourselves: "Which aspects of the current culture empower us, and which aspects don't?"

Create a Receptive Environment

- Create an awareness of the need for change. Identify and thoughtfully disseminate symptoms of problems. These may include letters from clients (with their permission), data on important outcomes, positive reports on other providers or other motivating comparisons to your "competitors," and worker observations.
- Consider having a workshop (or periodic workshops) to identify opportunities for improvement. Keep this focused on a particular area of operation. Participants should include staff of different levels of authority. Use the "goals to action" process described in Chapter 8.
- Decide where in the organization to initiate discussion of the problem.
- Develop your own personal influence with respect to the problem. Take steps to increase your credibility and standing.
- Understand the mission of the organization and relate the change to it. Help the organization acknowledge goal displacement.
- Consider proposing the change as being so linked to organizational values and other activities that it represents little real change at all.
- Commit yourself to learning, and promote the idea of a learning organization, one which purposefully uses its experiences to increase effectiveness and inform its actions. All actions of the organization become connected with discovery.
- Begin by focusing on one particular aspect or area of the organization. This is less threatening. Ideas are introduced to other parts of the organization, not forced on them. In a learning organization, changes in one area become models for another.

Expect, Identify, and Deal with Resistance

- Recognize that resistance is not necessarily a bad thing. The need to test your ideas against resistance will reduce the chances for unintended consequences, and it may lead to

TEN SOURCES OF RESISTANCE OR SUPPORT FOR ORGANIZATIONAL CHANGE

Frey (1990) has identified 10 possible sources of resistance or support for organizational change:

1. *Perceived advantage.* Not all proposals will benefit all groups within the organization. Not adequately assessing the perspectives of particular groups (decision makers, implementers, staff) can lead to resistance.

2. *Effort.* The heavier the investment of time and energy on the part of various organizational actors, the more difficult it is to sustain a high level of interest and commitment.

3. *Risk.* These are the costs incurred if the proposal fails to meet its objectives. There are three types of high-risk proposals: (1) proposals that, once adopted, cannot be terminated or reversed without incurring a substantial cost; (2) proposals that must be implemented in their entirety and cannot be done in stages; and (3) proposals that conflict with the dominant values of the organization.

4. *Sunken costs.* Proposals that challenge the investments the organization has made to support certain institutional practices will be resisted.

5. *Understandability.* An inability to condense complex proposals into simple language that is compatible with the values of the particular audience will interfere with acceptance.

6. *Ability.* The organization has to believe it has the capacity to carry out the proposed change. Assume that any proposal that requires additional funds is likely to be resisted.

7. *Depth and distance.* The more the proposal seeks to change basic goals and objectives, rather than just procedures, the more resistance will increase. Also, the greater the number of administrative levels it must pass through, the greater the chances of resistance.

8. *Idea and ideology.* Innovations that have been tested are less likely to be resisted. Those that fit the

ideology of the organization are also more likely to receive support.

9. *Need.* This reflects the organization's sense that something ought to be done to fix a problem. The more that belief is shared, the more responsive the organization will be. However, just because people agree that "something must be done" does not mean there is agreement about just what that should be or how it should be implemented—another source of resistance.

10. *Generality.* This refers to the scope of the proposal. The more the proposal affects larger systems, the more it will be resisted. Proposals that affect only a small part of the organization are more likely to be tolerated.

Keep each of these factors in mind as you assess the feasibility of your proposed change and develop your strategies and tactics.

---

new discoveries. Avoid "tuning out" problems that need to be addressed.

• Recognize that bringing the change closer to reality can energize supporters and opponents alike.

• Determine the degree of similarity and difference in goals between supporters and resisters.

• Be cautious about expecting too much from your connections. Although your friendly relationship with a formal decision maker will be helpful, do not assume that it is sufficient to ensure approval of the change.

- Understand the sources of resistance. These could include lack of information or differences in information, apathy, fear, psychological investment in current operations, differing interests and commitments, lack of clarity in defining the proposed change, responses required from other components of the organization, or personal animosity among participants. Also, recognize the impact recent history or other current demands have on the organization. For example, an organization that has just recently recovered from major turmoil will be more interested in promoting stability than change. An organization in the midst of budgetary woes will not want to take on additional financial burdens. An organization distracted with other issues will probably give little attention to less significant change requests. (Although this may prevent formal approval, it may be a good time to institute informal procedures that can be formalized at another time.)
- Consider using the least threatening tactics that will produce the desired result.
- Seek resister involvement and contributions.
- Avoid responding to hostility with hostility.
- Keep a formal record of events and agreements. Clarify timetables for actions. Your group should determine what consequences will follow if timetables and other agreements are or are not kept.
- Be prepared to confront likely manifestations of resistance. Some of the more likely include high-authority actors claiming little or no authority on the issue, vague statements of support with no concrete actions to indicate support, delays, exaggerating minor or unrelated issues, or divide and conquer tactics.

Reduce Personal Risks

- Ask forgiveness, not permission. In my experience, many people involved in human services are reluctant to step outside narrowly defined roles without first getting permission from those in authority to do so. Some individuals believe that working for change goes hand in hand with experiencing some personal loss. Their fears become magnified when conditions or colleagues challenge them to take part in change-promoting activities.
- Appreciate the benefits as well as the hazards. The discussion of risks itself may exaggerate their potential. In many cases, change agents experience not only strong personal fulfillment but significant professional recognition for their actions. Even so, our fears may lead us to pay more attention to instances when working for change leads to trouble. The fact is that there sometimes *is* a risk involved, and exaggerated or not, it should not be naively dismissed.
- Understand the more likely negative consequences. Rarely does advocating change result in loss of a job. A person who is "punished" for their involvement may experience interference with career advancement within the organization, denial of requests for authority support on other matters, or receive some form of social disapproval. These punishments may range from temporary and moderate to long-lasting and severe.
- Understand that the nature of the change, the breadth of support for the change, the tactics used to promote the change, and the outcome of the change effort are all factors relating to the consequences for change agents. You may have the chance to influence these elements in a way that reduces risk.
- Recognize attempts to intimidate change agents. One of the more common methods used by those in authority who are resisting the change is to encourage general discomfort and focus attention on one or two individuals as the "cause of all this trouble." They attempt to distract attention from the issue and attribute the pursuit of change to some character flaw exhibited by primary advocates of change, reducing matters to a "personality issue." This may frighten off potential allies and those who

are hesitant to support, especially those who look to people in authority to tell them what to think.

- Anticipate the tactic. You who support the effort need to talk openly among yourselves about how you will handle the situation when it arises. Provide support to one another that is *visible* to everyone who is aware of the conflict.

- Don't have primary advocates of change who can become separated from other core group members. Have several people in visible roles. Develop a strong support base.

- Find yourself a partner who supports your potential and who strengthens you.

- Know your rights. Be prepared to clearly assert them if disciplinary action is brought against you.

- Put yourself in a position within the organization that gives you standing to promote change. This can be a formal position or a quasi-formal position, such as a member of an internal committee.

- Manage the perception of the change effort, particularly as it relates to the motivations of those most highly involved.

- Avoid making a fight without sufficient reason. Avoid making a fight without sufficient resources.

- Keep your discussion related to the beneficial impact of the change. Engage in personal attack only as a necessary part of a planned strategy, and avoid attacking those who have more powerful support than you unless you can isolate them from their support.

- Focus on mutual benefits. Whenever appropriate, endeavor to diminish the fears and discomfort of opponents.

- Maintain an awareness of the message your personal demeanor sends. If you act outraged or outrageous, do so on purpose.

- Remember, you work there. The way you pursue change will leave an impression on the organization, your work community. In your selection of strategies, see if you can select an approach that helps you achieve your goal in a way that humanizes this community and makes it more respectful of its members.

- Use your head to avoid unnecessary risks. Don't give opponents added reasons to discredit you.

Implement and Confirm the Change

- Complete the job. The change agent's work is not done when the organization agrees to accept the change. Agreement signals an expansion or shift in attitude, but in practice the change has not yet occurred. Actually putting the change in place is what the whole business is all about. Those changes that alter the inner workings of the organization also need to be woven into the tapestry of its daily life to ensure their permanence.

- Attend to essential tasks. To make sure that the change becomes fixed within the organization (to the extent that anything is or should be fixed), you need to accomplish two important objectives. First, establish connections with other parts of the organization so these other parts begin to make use of and ultimately rely on the benefits of the change. Next, quickly move to establish clear, predictable, useful procedures. Although there will be an initial period of trial and error, it is important that other people, especially those within the organization, soon learn how to relate to the innovation. Confusion will create frustration and impede the desire of others to make use of the change. If other parts of the system avoid the new design, it will not receive the attention and support it needs to function within the organization. Like a plant, you want the change to quickly take hold and draw nourishment by becoming well-rooted within the organization.

- Acknowledge and perform critical roles. You and the other advocates have some important roles to play during this rooting period. The change needs: *champions,* those who will continue to assert its importance and benefits; *interpreters,* those who help explain what the change is and how it works; and *troubleshooters,* those who are alert to problems in implementation and can identify appropriate action (Brager & Holloway, 1978).

• Make necessary refinements. When your good ideas hit the reality of implementation, you will discover that a number of adjustments must be made. Some of your assumptions will be proven incorrect, and some things you didn't even think of will demand your attention. Expect that you will need to make modifications and be willing to do so. It may be helpful to publicly advance the idea of a "shakedown cruise," a period of time for working the bugs out. You have then created an expectation that alterations are an anticipated and reasonable part of the process.

• Move quickly to secure additional resources. Certain types of changes require specific resources, such as money, staff time, or space. If you are pursuing a change of this sort, you may find out that it requires more institutional support than you had thought. The time to seek additional resources is early in the implementation stage. At that time, there is likely to be an air of enthusiasm and a desire by most people for the project to succeed. If the project stumbles around for a while, people will lose interest and those in authority may be unwilling to commit new resources to an endeavor whose survival is questionable.

• Evaluate the change to see if it is doing what it is supposed to do and not creating new problems.

Some Final Considerations

It is unlikely that the problems plaguing your organization happened all at once. Unless the organization is faced with a major crisis, you will probably not "fix" it all at once. In the overall scheme of things, your efforts may represent only minor changes. However, each one of those changes may have major significance to the people who are immediately affected. Further, these things add up. Taken together, those minor changes you initiated will probably make a major difference.

Improving your organization is an ongoing process. In fact, don't be surprised if one change uncovers a need for other changes. You will discover that many of the changes you brought about will fall short of your hopes. I hope this will not discourage you. Though imperfect, your efforts will lead to advancements, ones that would not have occurred if you remained confined within a narrow definition of what it means to be a professional in the field of human services.

Breakfast at Tommie's

Over the last six weeks, the group of them had been meeting. Perhaps "group" is a bit of an exaggerated description. Today, six people gathered for an early morning breakfast; that's two more than last week and three more than the week before. Today it could be called a group. Amid the clatter of dishes and competition from the conversations of other early morning risers crowded into Tommie's Cafe, plans continued to take shape.

"What do the administrators have to say about this, Beverly?"

"The administrators have a lot of things to worry about, Curtis. I doubt that anyone even cares that you are talking to each other."

"Not yet they don't, Ms. Assistant Director, but they will."

"Oh my, aren't *we* in a friendly mood this morning. Coffee bad, or do you always treat your guests so kindly at this hour?"

Almost two months ago a chance comment after yet another worthless staff meeting set Curtis Greene to thinking. It was his first job out of

school, one he was glad to have, at least most of the time. In the months before graduation, he pictured himself in a nicely decorated office busily helping families get their lives back in order. In the months following graduation, still unemployed, he pictured himself maybe sitting on the other side of the desk. Finally, Darryl had called. Though he was a year behind Darryl in school, they had taken several classes together and become close, only to drift apart once Darryl graduated and started working. The job at Brentwood Community Services, which Darryl had told him about, was now his. Although the office wasn't nicely decorated, it was his, and he could go there every day and sit on the "right" side of the desk.

It was Darryl's remark that started it: "I hope to God that I don't look like all these other people after I've worked here for five years." Curtis hadn't really noticed the look before, tired at 9 A.M. Maybe it was walking into the crowded, shabby waiting room to call your next client. Maybe it was the inane hoops that both the clients and the workers had to jump through to get any services at all. Sure, some of these regulations were imposed by the state, but some were made up by the agency itself, three directors ago. Maybe it was just the inadequacy or the irrelevance of the services themselves. Curtis had really wanted to make a difference. He believed he could. Now, barely half a year on the job, he wasn't as enthusiastic or confident. In five years, five long years, how would he greet 9 A.M.?

So, he talked to Darryl. And he and Darryl talked to Jill. Three weeks later they were still talking to each other, every Friday morning at 7 A.M., feeling pretty sorry for themselves. Then Jill invited Aimee, who asked them how long they intended to whine. Aimee listened to the barrage of excuses intended as a counterattack. Then she repeated her question. Whether it was Jill's look, her barely stifled snicker, or the spontaneous realization of the absurdity of the past three weeks, they laughed so hard that the guy drinking coffee in the next booth jumped, adding a few new designs to his tie. And the "group" was born.

Everything seemed wrong at the agency, but where to start? The demeaning intake procedures, the preposterously high caseload, the indifference to problems in the sur- rounding neighborhoods, the low morale? Where? Maybe the outcome of next week's department directors' meeting would give them a clue. The group had a little surprise for the supervisors that would make them face up to the things that had been ignored too long. In the meantime . . .

"You're right, Bev, that 'Ms. Assistant Director' stuff was unfair, but the 'they'll find out' part you're going to hear about in a minute. I think you need to listen to Randy."

"Beverly, I don't know if Curtis told you, but I'm president of the Darrien Heights Coalition. We're made up of several neighborhood groups. You can probably guess that the people here are pretty fed up with the gangs taking over our neighborhoods, but what you might not know is that they're fed up with you too. We've tried to meet with your director, but he says he's too busy to talk to us. The last guy gave us a lot of promises, and nothing ever happened.

"The governor's office an- nounced last week that they were going to provide some money to groups dealing with gang violence. Maybe Brentwood and the coalition could work together on this, though maybe the coalition would rather picket you folks. Curtis said that he has some ideas about some changes at the agency that would help the situation, and he said that this group here would start drumming up support with some of the other workers. Anyway, I thought I should come here this morning and talk it over with you."

Beverly, who had glanced at Curtis at the mention of "changes at the agency," turned her attention first to Randy, then to the rest of the group. "Before you go making any changes, I think there are a few things *you* need to know first . . . "

Some Questions to Consider

1. If there are no major changes in the way this change effort is being conducted, how is this story likely to end?
2. What information or assumptions led you to this conclusion?
3. Which of the organization's problems would be the focus of your change effort? On what basis would you make your selection?
4. What is Beverly likely to recommend?

What do you think the basis for her recommendations would be? How much would you trust her?

5. If you were Curtis Greene or any other member of the group, what would you have done differently? What would you have done the same?

6. What particular steps would you take at this point to enhance the prospects for success?

CHAPTER 16

Lobbying for Change

Chapter Highlights

- ✥ Social welfare policies are influenced by a variety of forces

- ✥ Understanding the term *lobbying*

- ✥ Getting a good start
  - know regulations governing lobbying
  - know the impact of lobbying on your tax status
  - develop a legislative agenda
  - be clear about what you want to accomplish
  - gain an understanding of the legislative body
  - accept coaching from veterans
  - subscribe to publications
  - explore your state government's web page
  - find allies
  - use a lobbying campaign to build your organization

- ✥ Components of a lobbying effort
  - legislative team
  - alert networks
  - "quality" contacts
  - legislator dossiers
  - testifier banks
  - speakers' bureaus
  - public affairs programs
  - media relations
  - coalitions

- ✥ Outline of the legislative process

- ✥ Important work occurs even when the legislature is not in session

- ✥ Basic lobbying activities

- ✥ Target your actions

- ✥ Work with your team

- ✥ Keep counting votes throughout the process

- ✥ Celebrate victories

- ✥ Be able to argue your opponent's view as well as your own

- ✥ Your credibility is your greatest asset

- ✥ Face-to-face contact

- ✥ Know whom you should lobby

- ✥ Reasons to testify; ways to strengthen testimony

- ✥ Generating effective letters

- ✥ Keeping a bill alive

- ✥ Know your issue and make it stand out

- ✥ Fact sheets

- ✥ Work with other lobbyists

- ✥ Know the opposition

- ✥ Learn how to deal with compromises

- ✥ Monitor your relationships, your messages, and your egos

- ✥ Tactics for killing a bad bill

- ✥ Your confidence and moxie will grow with experience

Developing social welfare policies is hardly a rational process. It is influenced by the divergent values, motivations, and beliefs of all who have a role in defining and refining them. Competing viewpoints from those held by the general public to those of elected and non-elected public officials find their way into laws and regulations that direct and govern our social welfare system. Political conflicts over the nature, causes, and necessary responses to social problems accept momentary resolution in the decisions of public officials (DiNitto, 1995).

This dynamic process is always open to revision and redirection. It is open to influence. Social workers and human services practitioners decide to participate in this process or to refrain from it. Either way, there are consequences for the community and for the people these professionals intend to serve.

Legislative advocacy involves both self-interest and client interest. Practitioners of social work and human services often must respond to attempts to restrict and overregulate their work. In fact, legislators' lack of knowledge about the field is one of the greatest impediments to support for social work (Ewalt, 1994). However, too narrow a focus on self-interest legislation undermines credibility. If practitioners expect support for the profession, we must be seen to be active advocates for the causes we ourselves say we ought to support.

One of the most meaningful ways you as a citizen and as a professional can have an impact on this process is by lobbying public officials. By lobbying I mean purposeful communication with a public official with the intention of influencing a decision that that official may make on a specific matter (Hrebenar & Scott, 1982).

Lobbying may be done on a number of different levels. You may communicate with elected officials, from the local city council to the President of the United States, to influence actions on public issues. A great many national policies started out as local ordinances (Schorf, Fischer, Pollack, Brophy, & Kulman, 1996). You may provide information and insight to a government official who is writing regulations on a public program with the hope of increasing the effectiveness of that program.

Of course, decisions made by Congress affect our lives. Though the professional may certainly lobby his or her congressional delegation, playing a pivotal role in a sustained national lobbying campaign requires a degree of commitment that is normally beyond what most professional practitioners are able to give. Consequently, the focus of this chapter will be on lobbying members of a state legislature to provide a basic example of an approach to lobbying. Many, many decisions that affect the communities you live in and serve are made at this level. Further, it is likely that you can have a significant impact on decisions made by this body.

Decisions by county and other local levels of government also have an impact on issues of vital concern to your community. Though the specific steps in the process of establishing official policy are different for local government, the basic methods for influencing decisions described in this chapter have application to those arenas as well. It is a good idea to start by researching the design and decision-making procedures of the particular government body you hope to influence.

Though lobbying can refer to an individual conversation with a public official, it is the activities related to a more systematic lobbying campaign that will be the subject of this chapter. The prescribed nature of legislative bodies, such as a state legislature, provides for a rather unique community. Your understanding of this community requires an awareness of the way participants in this community operate at both formal and informal levels. Certain rules of etiquette and of process should be recognized and commonly observed. The gamelike character adds yet another dimension to this environment. For all these reasons, I will describe this arena of change with a degree of detail.

The suggestions presented in this chapter were drawn from my own experience as well as from the work of Common Cause (1992), Dear and Patti (1984), Goffin and Lombardi (1988), Haynes and Mickelson (1991), Hrebenar and Scott (1982), Lamiell (1984), League of Women Voters (1976), McLean (1980), Pertschuk (1986), Richan (1992), Smith (1979), and Speeter (1978a).

Getting Started

Your decision to act as a lobbyist should be based on a strong commitment to the issue you are working on. Your belief in your purpose will help you overcome many an obstacle, and your sincere dedication will make those whom you hope to influence more receptive to your message. If your interest is only halfhearted, it is unlikely that you will be very successful.

Know the regulations governing lobbying in your state. Each state has its own set of regulations. You can usually find out how these apply to you by contacting your Secretary of State's office.

Be aware of the impact of your activities on the tax status of the organization you represent. If you are acting on behalf of a tax-exempt organization, check with its accountant or attorney to be sure you are operating within Internal Revenue Service guidelines. Remember, a tax-exempt, nonprofit agency *is* permitted to take part in lobbying activities, maybe more than most agencies realize.

Develop a legislative agenda. Do you intend to support or defeat legislation? Are you going to develop new legislation, influence proposed legislation, or modify legislation in process? Understand that some of the things you do will not have an immediate payoff but will set the stage for later dividends. It is not uncommon for passage of a significant proposal to take several years of effort. As a result, you may want to provide encouragement to your organization by including in your agenda some issues for which you can claim victory in one legislative session.

Be clear about what your legislation is intended to accomplish. Before seeking legislation, make sure that changes in law (as opposed to changes in agency policy) are really the best way to accomplish your purpose. Many legislators are impatient with those who seek legislative change when simpler methods will do.

Gain an understanding of the legislature. Use local sources, particularly public interest groups such as the League of Women Voters and Common Cause, to provide direction. Many advocacy groups have written material that will help you. Check with them to see who publishes political directories. These will be a great aid in helping you understand basic elements of the legislature and identifying its members.

Accept coaching from veterans. As you become more and more involved, you will come to know a number of people who have a great deal of experience and expertise. Many of them will help you learn the ropes.

Subscribe to publications. Special publications that deal with legislative matters are commonly available. Read the sections of the daily newspapers that deal with political and legislative topics. Get on government mailing lists to receive legislative digests (brief summaries of legislation that has been introduced) and other related materials. You may also be able to track legislative information through various computer networks.

Explore your state government's Web page. Most, if not all, states have a Web site. It is likely that you can get committee agendas, committee rosters, biographies on each legislator, and a host of other valuable information. City and county governments also have Web sites that are similarly useful.

Find allies. Successful lobbying employs the energies of many people. Discover who shares your interests and work with them to develop a coordinated approach to the lobbying effort. Throughout the campaign, look for other individuals and groups who can provide assistance. Using the Internet you can contact other activists and advocacy organizations throughout the country. They can help you with background information, including sample legislation.

Lobbying effort can help organize membership. Undertaking lobbying activities is an excellent way to build your organization. Members can play a number of roles, and the process itself is exciting. With its connection to political power, there is a good potential for members to become empowered through their participation in events. Active involvement will increase your group's recognition and establish it as a power to be reckoned with.

Basic Components of an Organized Lobbying Effort

A comprehensive approach to promoting change by influencing political decision making should mobilize and direct community support, create positive community perceptions of your issue, and provide direct contact with elected officials. In addition to some of the general aspects of an organization, the following elements will strengthen your hand as you play the lobbying game.

Legislative team. These people will work directly on the legislation itself. Most of these members will be in direct contact with the legislators, although some will be engaged in research and materials preparation. This team is composed of members of your organization and allied organizations as well as legislators and their staff members. It may also include members of the governor's office. Their duties are further explained in the section describing the legislative process on page 401.

Alert networks. An alert network is designed to mobilize a large number of people in a short period of time. Alert networks can be used to turn people out for rallies and demonstrations, call members to assist in some simple but labor-intensive organizational tasks (like getting out a large mailing on short notice), or to communicate their opinions to selected targets. Your lobbying effort will mainly use the alert network for communication, and it is designed for this purpose. Alert networks are *quantity contact* systems. Their main purpose is to generate as much constituent contact as possible. The more common components of an alert network are a telephone alert system, a mail alert, an E-mail alert, and fax alerts.

A telephone alert system is generally a telephone tree or a variation of a boiler room operation (Figure 16-1). In a simple telephone tree, one person calls two other people, who in turn call two others, who call others, and so on. In addition to calling the other members of the tree, the person receiving the call is to call her or his legislator and communicate a specific message. Each recipient of a phone call is to *write down* the message to be delivered to the next tree member as well as to the legislator to make sure it is delivered accurately. Therefore, keep the message short and to the point.

A tree is usually organized into branches (sometimes according to voting districts), with each branch having its own captain. The captain sees to it that the calls are completed without

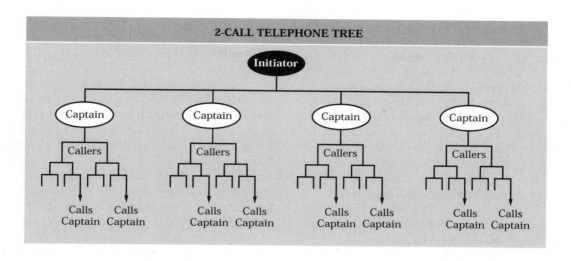

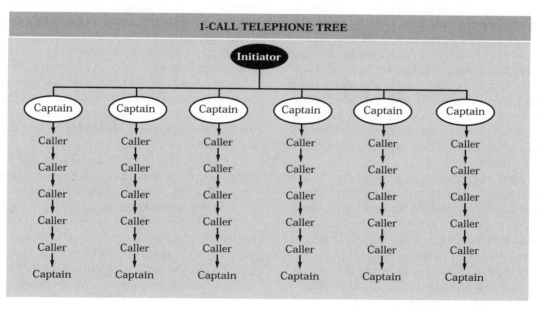

Figure 16-1
A telephone tree gets your message out quickly

the chain being broken. The last person, on the "bottom" of the branch, is to contact the captain. If, after a certain period of time, the captain is not called, she or he will initiate action up from the bottom. (There are many variations to this system. The intent is to make sure that the message doesn't get stopped or changed somewhere along the line.)

A boiler room approach is designed with the intent of increasing accuracy and making sure unanswered phones do not stop delivery of the message. Using this method, a small team of callers, usually six or seven, all call from the same location, perhaps from a social service agency or a real estate office. Each caller has a list of about 40 alert members to call. The members receiving the call only need to call their legislator. In two nights of calling, two different teams can call hundreds of members.

A mail alert is a special request made to the alert members by mail. The letter is sent in a specially designed envelope emphasizing the emergency nature of the request. The letter details the specific request of the member.

E-mail alerts are a simple but effective way to notify your members and other potential supporters of the need for action. Chapter 5 detailed the use of electronic distribution lists and mailing lists. These methods can help you reach a great number of people very quickly.

Fax alerts can be structured in the same way as a telephone tree. A fax alert can increase the clarity and reliability of your message, but there may be problems if you want to keep your communications confidential. Most professionals have access to a fax machine, so this procedure works well with them. However, many other groups don't have routine access to fax machines.

Alert networks require organization and maintenance. Members need to agree *in advance* to perform the actions they are requested to do. They must also receive some orientation and written instructions so they will know how to perform when called to do so. Further, the members need to be kept informed of key issues they may be requested to respond to. This is usually done by means of periodic written updates. Finally, the alert system should be used neither too little nor too frequently. Three times during a six-month period is a good rule of thumb.

Alert networks are worth the effort they require. The ability of your organization to rally a significant number of constituents can make quite an impression as phones begin to ring in legislators' offices. Most legislators now use fax machines and E-mail. These technologies provide members of your group with quick and easy access to lawmakers. Fax numbers and E-mail addresses are commonly printed in legislative guides. They are also available from the legislator's office.

Quality contact development. This is a system for getting specific, particularly influential community members to contact specific lawmakers. Quality contacts are those individuals who have clout in the community or who have a particular relationship with the legislator. Those with a particular relationship would include the legislator's friends, rabbi, physician, business associates, sorority sisters, political allies, and so forth.

Legislator dossier. You should begin collecting as much information on each legislator as possible. Basic information to include would be: key legislative interests; district interests; committee assignments; religious affiliation; professional background; other legislators who are friends, enemies, or who influence; political allies and enemies; educational background; personal interests; social acquaintances; family information; key campaign contributors (this is easily obtainable public information); and quality contacts.

Testifier bank. From time to time you will need to present testimony before a legislative committee. It is helpful to have a team prepared in advance who can present various perspectives on the issue you are addressing. Perhaps a doctor, a single parent, an economist, an attorney, a teenager, or a priest could provide a particularly compelling point of view. These people should be purposefully recruited and prepared for their role. You *don't* want to scramble around at the last minute to find someone who might be able to speak to the issue. Impressions *do* count. Be well prepared so you can make a strong impression.

Speakers' bureau. A handful of well-versed, effective public speakers can help communicate your positions to community groups. Members of your speakers' bureau should be prepared to handle likely questions that may arise, including hostile questions. It is particularly helpful to speak to groups, such as the Rotary or church

Change Agent Tip

These helpful Web sites come from Bill Mann's *Politics on the Net* (1995). This is a very helpful, easy-to-read resource that shows you how to use the Internet to connect with other activists as well as to get information about political parties, people, issues, and more.

The Activist's Oasis *(www.matisse.net/politics/activist/activist.htm)* This is primarily a large collection of links to Net sites of interest to activists.

An Activist's Strategic Guide to the Internet *(www.matisse.net/politics/activist/ actguide.html)* This guide provides a number of questions to help you get your search organized.

Jim Warren's Gopher *(gopher://gopher.path.net.8102)* This site is a collection of electronic newsletters covering political action, government access, cryptography, and privacy. The site provides access to sources that help you use the Net for political action.

Lobbying/Advocacy Techniques *(muon.qrc.com/space/guidelines/lobby_techniquesfaq.html)* Here you can get a guide for lobbying at the real-world level. This guide takes you step by step through the entire lobbying process.

groups, that count targeted legislators among their members.

Public affairs program. You can bring your particular message to targeted community groups through presentation of public affairs programs. These are designed to help community groups examine important community problems and governmental response to them. Such programs are effective in recruiting individual participants or coalition members.

Media relations. An organized strategy for getting your message out through the media should be developed.

External coalitions. It is unlikely that your organization alone can mount a significant legislative campaign (although you *can* have an impact on legislation that has a limited scope). Coordinating your efforts with other organizations will help draw attention to your efforts and provide the resources you need to accomplish the range of tasks that are necessary.

Lobbying campaigns that intend significant changes and that encounter well-organized and well-funded opposition will develop other elements to complement this basic approach.

However, for most situations, the approach I have described here is sufficiently comprehensive. If your lobbying aims are fairly narrow, you may not need to fully develop each of these components. However, the more attention you give to each aspect, the stronger your foundation will be.

A Skeletal Outline of the Legislative Process

Some variation of the elements described here will exist in your state. (Except for Nebraska, all state legislatures have two houses or chambers, commonly the Senate and the House or Assembly. I will refer to the two-house model in this discussion of legislative procedures.)

Legislative session. Find out when the legislature begins its session and how long it is likely to last. Legislative committees may be at work on issues even when the legislative session has concluded. Also, the body may be called into special session from time to time to consider a specific subject.

Be aware of all legislative deadlines, such as dates for introduction of legislation and dates for completing bills in a particular chamber.

Drafting and introduction of legislation. This is the first step in the process, preparing legislation and offering it for consideration. At this time the sponsor of the legislation will work with interested parties to work out the actual language of the bill. The sponsor is the legislator who will introduce the bill and work for its passage. There are circumstances when the sponsor has little or no interest in the legislation. However, since these are not routine, I won't go into them here. (In some states *bill* is a formal term designating a piece of legislation that has proceeded to a certain point in the process. I will use it here as a general term to describe a piece of legislation.) Next, the sponsor may attempt to get other legislators to "sign on" or co-sponsor the bill. Though this indicates support on behalf of the co-sponsors, simply having a large number of co-sponsors does not ensure a bill's passage. The bill is then formally introduced, and usually at this time it is assigned a number. (Some states allow for bills to be filed before the legislative session actually begins, giving the legislation a kind of head start.)

First reading, assignment of bill to committee. Once the bill has been filed, it is formally read into the record and assigned to one or more committees. The committees to which the bill is assigned and the number of committees can make a crucial difference in the life of the bill. Usually the leadership of the particular chamber has some discretion in this matter. (Leadership refers to those legislators who have been elected by their peers to leadership positions; for example, Speaker of the House or Majority Leader. Leadership of the majority party is likely to exert significant control over what occurs in the legislature.) You should influence these decisions if you can.

Committee hearings. The bill is then heard in the committee. At this time, committee members may hear testimony on the bill from interested parties and make changes or amendments to it. If the bill needs substantial work, it may be referred to a subcommittee of members of the full committee. (Even though a bill has been assigned to a committee, it may not be given a hearing. You may need to work to get the bill heard in the first place.)

To continue its journey toward passage, the bill must receive the support of a majority of the subcommittee and full committee. (There are various procedural ways to keep a bill "alive" even if it is not supported by the full committee. I will touch on a few of them later in this chapter.)

Floor action. After passing out of committee, the bill is considered by all the members of the chamber. At this time, members may debate and further amend the bill. Passage from the chamber may require two different votes, with rules for each vote somewhat different. (Again, be careful to check the rules governing floor action in your legislature.)

Action by other chamber. Once the bill has passed the first house, the process is repeated once again in the next chamber.

Concurrence of amendments. Commonly, the bill will receive further amendment in the second chamber. The members of the chamber that first heard the bill must agree to or concur with these changes or the bill will be referred to a conference committee.

Conference committee. If a conference committee is needed, the leadership of each chamber will appoint members to a special committee to resolve the differences. If the members work out an agreement, they send their report to their respective chambers for approval.

Governor's office. Once the legislature passes the bill, it is sent to the governor to sign. If the governor signs the bill, it will officially become law. The new law will probably go into effect within months of its signing. If it has been designated an emergency measure, it may go into effect immediately. (Again, the exact effective date will vary by state.)

The governor may choose to veto the bill. If this occurs, the legislature may have an opportunity to override the veto, which usually requires support of two thirds of each chamber.

MAKING THE ARGUMENT

Be able to argue the other side's point of view as well as your own. This will enable you to:

- Identify weak points in your position you may otherwise (choose to?) ignore
- Better understand the opposing frame of reference so you can communicate to it
- Anticipate arguments so you can preempt or counter them
- Inoculate potential supporters by letting them know what your opposition is likely to tell them

- Emphasize your strengths relative to the weaknesses of the other position
- Demonstrate that your position is based on a strong command of the issue
- Discover possible areas of common ground or common interest

Let the listener know your *position,* your *professional expertise,* and your *experiences.*

Focus on aspects of the issue where the listener's knowledge and values are similar to yours; relate your argument to an outcome you both desire.

Emphasize your areas of agreement with the listener.

Relate the issue to the listener's interests and personal experiences.

Relate the issue to consequences for constituents.

Use real-life examples, humor, and simple logic. Elicit some emotional response (protective response, righteousness, or patriotism). Avoid jargon.

Role-play your discussion. Have a friend play devil's advocate.

Your state may have provisions for the governor to veto a bill without providing the legislature with an opportunity to override. Also, conditions for allowing the bill to become law without the governor's signature may exist.

As you can see, there are many obstacles to passing a piece of legislation. Each step provides its own little drama. That is part of the allure and the frustration of this type of change activity.

Basic Lobbying Activities

If you become involved routinely in legislative action, you will soon discover that it is a year-round endeavor. Periods of intense activity may be followed by periods that are much less hurried. A good portion of the work occurs outside the legislative session. Be sure the elements of your campaign are in place and ready to go when the session begins. Those

groups who wait until the legislature has begun before organizing will usually discover that they got into the game too late. Even if you are going to work on just one piece of legislation, it is important that you get an early start.

The following sequence of activities assumes that you have taken care of some of the initial tasks described earlier, such as registering as a lobbyist, developing your agenda, and gaining an understanding of the legislative process. Now you are ready to put your efforts to work lobbying on behalf of your concerns.

Gather and prepare information. Assemble data, personal stories, legislation from other states, and other information that helps you understand and communicate your issues. Prepare various background pieces and fact sheets. (A few additional tips on issue preparation are provided later in this chapter.)

Develop and prepare a legislative team. Begin developing your team a few months before you need to take action so that roles and expectations are clear. By the time the legislation has been introduced, you will have an internal team composed of key legislators and staff members and an external team composed of members of your and other organizations and perhaps some other lobbyists.

Continue to develop your internal team during the session. A solid internal team would include: legislators who are interested enough in the bill to track it; a legislator who can give you the inside scoop; a legislator to whom other legislators listen; a good legislative debater; and legislators who are in influence positions (for example, leadership or committee chairs).

Not every member of the team will have equal interest. Particularly, some members of your internal team will have limited responsibility. Identify and recruit additional external team members who can help.

Target/rate legislators. To determine the degree of support or opposition you will have, it is very helpful to develop a system for ranking each legislator, particularly those who serve on committees likely to hear your bill. You can choose a simple scale of 1 to 5 to indicate how favorable each legislator is likely to be to your concerns. You can obtain this information by reading various publications, talking to other political activists, or checking voting records with interest groups (for example, Planned Parenthood, Sierra Club, or Chamber of Commerce). You will probably revise this "score card" from time to time during the actual session.

Begin counting possible votes. Through the entire process, *you never stop counting votes.*

Determine your monitoring systems. Figure out how you will keep alert to rumors regarding your bills, hear about proposed action on them, and track their progress.

If you are going to introduce legislation yourself, *recruit a sponsor and co-sponsors of the legislation.* Ideally, these will be individuals who have some influence within the legislature and serve on the committees likely to hear the bill. Further, the sponsor should be committed to the bill and have time to give it attention. Part of your consideration involves which chamber should initiate action on the bill.

Draft legislation. Begin working on the actual language of the bill. The sponsor should have legislative staff help you phrase your ideas in the proper language.

Introduce legislation. The earlier your legislation is introduced, the more time you have to work it through the various hurdles.

Coordinate all steps with team members. Usually your sponsor will serve as the point person in the process. Matters such as assignment to committee, scheduling of hearing dates, and development of amendments should be coordinated for maximum advantage. You should attempt to influence these as much as possible. As feasible, you should work with legislative leadership.

Monitor the process, including rumors. Keep an ear out for amendments.

Use alert networks as appropriate throughout the session.

Use media as appropriate throughout the session.

Keep in contact with the governor's office as needed during the session. Obviously, if the governor's office is hostile to your position, or would simply hope to avoid the issue, your contact would probably only be of a general nature.

Target committee votes. Determine which members of the committee should receive most of your attention.

Lobby the committee directly. Begin to meet with members of the committee. Also, begin to organize constituent contact and other indirect methods of influencing members.

Count votes.

Prepare testimony. Prepare testifiers and shape the message to be presented to the committee. Your message should be geared to specific legislators and to the media. (Additional points on testifying are presented later in the chapter.)

Testify. If you have a strong group of testifiers, you may decide that your personal testimony is not needed.

" MAYBE WE SHOULD LISTEN TO THIS GUY ! "

Lobby the chamber. Once your bill passes committee, direct your attention to other members of the chamber whom you have targeted for lobbying. Indirect methods such as demonstrations and media stories could be used at this time. (You need to determine how much and what type of attention you want to draw to this issue.) Constituent contact should swing into high gear.

Count votes. (Do you get the idea that this is important?)

Organize and conduct floor action. Work with your internal team to identify responsibilities and communication procedures during floor action. Plan floor debate carefully. Determine who your speakers will be and how they will work together to reinforce each other's message. Anticipate and prepare for procedural maneuvers, opponents' arguments, and likely debaters. During the debate, you or other members of your external team will be sitting in the gallery. Arrange for signals so you can communicate with your legislators on the floor. Determine how you can send messages to one another if need be. You all need to pay attention and watch for weak supporters who may be wavering and need some additional attention.

Repeat the process in the second chamber. Essentially you must do the same things to pass your bill in the second chamber as you did in the first. If your internal team is stronger in the first chamber, see how they can assist you in your efforts to get internal support from the other house.

For the last time, *keep counting votes.*

Influence the composition of the conference committee. If a conference committee is needed, try to work with leadership to get members favorable to your position appointed.

Shore up support for the conference committee report. Acceptance of the conference report is normally a routine matter, but you may need to go back to certain legislators to explain the conference agreement and to confirm their support.

Lobby the governor. Members of the lobbying team and their constituents should make contact with the governor or governor's staff to urge that the bill be signed. Indirect methods and direct constituent contact could be employed as well. The type and degree of indirect

FACE-TO-FACE CONTACT

Arrive on time. Dress appropriately. Everything you do should be related to leaving a good impression on the legislator, the secretaries, and other staff. (Phoniness does not leave a good impression.)

Understand the time allotted for the appointment.

Identify yourself, including your professional position. If you are a constituent, say so. Mention any supportive connection to the legislator, particularly business, political, or social connections (for example, "Marian Turner encouraged me to meet with you").

Commend the legislator for current or previous actions you approve of.

Identify the bill you are discussing by name and number. If speaking to a particular point, refer to the page and line.

Provide the legislator with your one-page summary/fact sheet. It is often helpful to have an additional packet of information with a one-page "table of contents" that includes a sentence or two

description of each piece in the packet. If you are suggesting new language, have that prepared to hand to the legislator.

Present your case. (If you believe it is likely that you will be given the time to engage in actual discussion, you can save some of your points to address concerns you anticipate that the legislator will bring up. This conveys the notion that you are responsive.) Listen carefully to the legislator's concerns; don't minimize them. Be clear about your position and just what you want the legislator to do. Remain courteous.

Refer to the support of other legislators who hold *similar* views as the legislator to whom you are now speaking by using their comments. "Senator _____ made a good point about this. She said: _____ ."

On occasion, arrange to meet with the legislator in the local district or on your turf.

Have the legislator meet with a small group of three or

four of you. Provide different "fronts" for the legislator to see (for example, client, educator, business leader, religious leader, or other person with a readily identifiable perspective). The members of the group should be carefully selected. They should clearly understand mutual roles, and each should be well prepared.

Get a commitment if at all possible. The more publicly the commitment is made, the stronger it is likely to be. If you cannot get a commitment at this time, let the legislator know that her or his decision is important to you. Politely say that you will call after she or he has had time to give the matter more thought.

Thank the legislator, regardless of the outcome.

Notify your allies of the outcome.

Send a thank-you letter to the legislator. Provide answers to any questions that were raised and tactfully reiterate one or two essential points.

---

methods will depend on the governor's position on the bill.

Organize an override effort if need be. This usually requires lots of direct lobbying by members of your internal and external teams, mobilization of constituent contact, and use of visible indirect methods.

Celebrate. It is important to have a victory

event involving all key participants soon after the session ends.

Begin to monitor implementation. A new set of activities (outside the scope of this chapter) now needs to take place to influence the development of regulations and other procedures that will enable the new law to fulfill its promise.

Other Things You Should Know or Do to Increase Your Effectiveness

Your credibility is your greatest asset. Your credibility is based on:

- *You as a person.* Build trust. *Never* lie, mislead, threaten, or act in an arrogant or condescending manner. Don't promise what you cannot deliver. Keep confidential information to yourself. Don't back people into a corner. Don't ever say or write anything that you don't want attributed to you. Develop and use a sense of humor. Be courteous. Say thank-you.
- *Your information.* Don't exaggerate the truth or the situation. Double-check the accuracy of your information. Don't fake it if you don't know the answer to a question; instead, promise to get the information. Follow up in a timely way to requests for information.
- *Your base of power.* Be able to mobilize constituents and quality contacts. Demonstrate an ability to use the media. Generate letters in support of your position. Turn people out to legislative hearings. Generate workers for campaigns. If you can, generate dollars for campaigns.

Get known. Once legislators know you (or in some cases know about you), they will pay more attention to your calls, letters, and opinions. Get involved in political campaigns. Attend legislative receptions. Send letters to newly elected officials introducing yourself and information on your issue. Attend and speak out at meetings with legislators. Invite officials to your agency or neighborhood; serve as a tour guide. Arrange to provide a briefing on issues.

Observe the body in action. Attend a few sessions or committee hearings. Keep your eyes open. Listen and learn. This will help you feel familiar with the environment before you begin taking action.

Understand the standard approach in deciding whom to lobby. Lobby supporters first, to alert them, activate them, and inoculate them from opposition arguments. Lobby "undecideds" next, preferably with support from their peers. *Do not lobby strong opponents.* You can use your time for more important things. You won't change their minds, and you may excite them into more vigorous opposition.

Get to know key staff people. Working with staff is not a waste of time. They may be more accessible than the elected official, and they may let you know how the official really sees things. Staff members often shape the lawmaker's perspective.

Acknowledge that there are few permanent friends and few permanent enemies. Don't alienate people, write them off forever, or take them for granted. Legislators are engaged in a number of battles. Past disagreements can be forgotten when building new alliances.

Understand the ways for keeping a bill alive. A bill can be resurrected as an amendment to another bill. A person who voted against the bill can ask to have it reconsidered. (You may use this as a planned tactic.) Understand how to use the initiative and referendum procedures for your state.

Know your strengths and weaknesses. Avoid the tendency to underestimate your strengths and exaggerate your weaknesses. Be accurate in your assessment.

Don't grab personal credit. Allow legislators and when necessary your organization to get the attention.

Recognize that legislators are overwhelmed with information. Don't assume or act as if your issue is the only one that matters. Assert your point while recognizing that the legislator has many other issues to think about. Determine how you will make your issue stand out.

Know your issue. For your own uses, prepare an issue brief, summarizing the history of the issue, noting the key players, organizing key facts and figures, and outlining arguments on *both* sides. This will empower you as you realize that you know far more about the topic than most of the people with whom you will be dealing.

Prepare fact sheets. Provide legislators, media people, and others with a *one-page* summary of your issue. Describe the costs and the impact

TESTIFYING

Your participation in legislative hearings gives legitimacy to your issue and your organization. It gets you on and in the record. It gives you access to a larger audience through media coverage of the hearing. It demonstrates visible action to your members, and it gives them an event in which they can take part. Your ability to turn out a crowd signals broad support for the measure, which will embolden those legislators thinking of supporting your position. Your testimony can provide supportive legislators with a rationale and justification for their actions.

Although testimony and demonstrations of constituent interest at public hearings may help a very few legislators make up their minds, rarely will it be effective in *changing* anyone's mind. Testifying, therefore, is a complement to more essential lobbying activities. It should not be the centerpiece of your efforts.

Coordinate your presentation with other members of your team and with other groups who support your position. Coordinate testimony with the committee chair if you are on friendly terms. Prime supporters on the committee with questions that allow you to emphasize specific points.

Sponsors and some cosponsors should attend and give testimony. Often the sponsor will be the lead testifier. (The lead testifier usually summarizes the bill and its benefits.)

Have a team of testifiers, each emphasizing different aspects of the bill. Each testifier represents a particular community or professional point of view: the taxpayer, the neighborhood leader, the direct beneficiary, the attorney, the economist, or whatever particular views the panel needs to hear.

To the extent possible, coordinate the order in which your testifiers will present.

Consider how you want your argument to build. Understand that initial testifiers can stake out the dimensions of the debate, and they are more likely to get media coverage. Those who testify toward the end of the proceedings can counter arguments, reemphasize key points, and leave the last impressions.

Prepare two papers, one for submission for the committee's written record, and one for your presentation.

Prepare your testimony by role-playing with friends or members of your team. Similar to preparing for an argument, someone should play the devil's advocate. Anticipate questions and prepare responses. Avoid seeking last minute suggestions; they will only confuse you.

Tailor your presentation to the legislators you most want to influence. Make distinct points using a combination of personal experiences and

---

of responding to or ignoring the issue. Provide opposing points of view and counter them. Include your name, your organization's name, and a phone number and address where you can be reached.

Get to know other lobbyists. Particularly get to know like-minded lobbyists. Lobbyists, especially those with common interests, do meet regularly. Become part of such a group. Lobby-

ists help each other out in a variety of ways, not the least of which is with an exchange of information.

Get to know your opposition. Find out who is opposed to you and why. Talk to them. You can better understand their frame of reference and information. You may even discover that their opposition is based on misperception or misunderstanding, a situation you can remedy.

factual information. Things to touch on:

- Your interest in the bill and how you arrived at your conclusions
- Who will benefit
- Who will be hurt by inaction
- Cost efficiency of the measure

Tie your message to dominant themes that are emerging in the legislative session (concern over crime, government waste, or other topics).

It is normal to be nervous. If it is troubling you, Richan (1992) suggests you say "I'm scared" to your mirror. You will find that simple phrase releases a lot of tension. By not having to hide from your apprehension, you can more easily focus on the business at hand.

When making your presentation begin with, "Mister or Madam Chair." Then state your name, title, your agency or organization, and your

position on the bill. Then state your case. Refer to the page number and line number for specific comments. Keep your presentation to 5 or 7 minutes. Don't repeat previous testimony or yourself. When you have completed your presentation, ask for questions. When answering a question, first address the committee chair, then address the member asking the question.

Remain courteous. Convey the notion that committee members are reasonable individuals. Approach them in a way that emphasizes common interest. Don't argue with committee members, and don't attempt to humiliate any particular legislator. If an opponent questions your information, honestly try to answer the question and return to your main points. If your opinion is questioned, restate the question in a manner that allows you to reiterate your basic position. If the questioner persists,

it is proper to restate your basic position and state that you respect the fact that you each have different views of the matter and that you hope "we can agree to disagree."

If you do not know the answer to a question, say: "That's a good question, senator. I don't have that specific information before me. I will look into it and get you the information right away." *Do not fake an answer!* Be prompt in your follow-up.

Speak to the media as well as the committee, using a few catch phrases.

After you have answered all the questions, thank the members of the committee for their interest and their attentiveness to your presentation.

If you are clearly in a no-win situation, consider staying away from the hearing altogether to make a statement or to render the opposition's show a nonevent.

Understand the legislators' screens. Legislators must contend with a huge number of decisions. In determining how to approach an issue, they see how it fits with their own philosophy and values, their constituents' or district's concerns, their party leadership or caucus positions, advocacy groups with which they identify, and fellow legislators' opinions.

When you are working with legislators, see

how they define the situation under discussion. On what aspects do they focus? What do they think they know about it? How does it fit with their value system?

Expect some loss of support. The more controversial your issue, the more likely a few of your supporters will get a little weak in the knees. You will lose a few votes. Be psychologically prepared for this.

Anticipate the likelihood of compromises. Rarely will you get everything you want. You may understand this as you begin the process, but when faced with the need to agree to less than you want, or to make a trade-off, you may feel real disappointment. Be clear about what you have to have—and what you cannot have. Concessions can help you in the long run or limit the possibility of future negotiation. Once the deal has been struck, are you in a better position to move forward or will you remain mired at this point? When faced with a problem, see if you can respond by bringing new ideas to the table rather than by retreating on important concerns. At what point is *not* making a deal a better choice? Remember to identify your BATNA (best alternative to negotiated agreement) before you begin negotiations.

The need to make compromises tests the relationships in an organization. Ideological purists may bang heads against dispassionate pragmatists. Deals will serve some interests better than others. Discuss how you will handle compromises before you are faced with them. Clarify who among you is empowered to make agreements with the opposition.

From a strategic standpoint, try to lock your opponent into an uncompromising extreme position. Your position will look much more attractive to legislators who usually endeavor to claim the high middle ground.

Don't accept a bad bill just to get "something." Other interests may be making deals on the bill at the same time you are. Be aware of the fact that your original piece of legislation may end up with so many amendments that you hardly recognize it. If this occurs, "your" bill may no longer effectively accomplish its intended purpose. Be prepared to withdraw your support from the legislation or even act to prevent its passage in the event that changes are more harmful than helpful.

Create a responsive structure. Your organization will need to respond quickly to legislative events. Develop mechanisms for rapid decision making. Notify allies immediately of any changes, especially changes in the team's position on any point.

Monitor your messages, your relationships, and your egos. Everyone on your team should be communicating identical positions to legislators. Be very careful not to undermine yourselves by sending conflicting messages.

Pay close attention to group maintenance issues. Never let disagreements among yourselves be known to anyone outside the team. Internal bickering that becomes public will seriously weaken your effort. Do not make yourself look good at the expense of any team member. This is a very serious issue. Team members should try to identify in advance how this may occur and how to guard against it.

Learn how to kill bad bills. Killing bills is easier than passing them. By reviewing the legislative process, you can see that the bill must cross many hurdles before it finally reaches the governor's desk. You can trip it up at many different points.

Use delaying tactics so there won't be enough time left in the session to pass it. Get the bill referred to a subcommittee that has difficulty meeting and agreeing. Have your legislators ask for staff to do time-consuming research on the bill. Temporarily remove the bill from the committee agenda. (These and other delaying tactics are more likely to be successful if the bill does not have a sufficient number of strong supporters.) Get the bill referred to a committee chaired by one of your supporters who can use the prerogatives of the chair to bury the bill. Amend the bill to death. Create confusion by raising doubts about its ultimate costs, its questionable legality, its consequences for a particular group of citizens. (Legislators don't want to be seen advancing a questionable proposition, one that just might do more harm than good.) Generate adverse media attention and public displays of constituent opposition. (It is easier to mobilize people against an idea than for one.) Legislators who are in powerful positions can use their influence to make passage of the bill costly to their colleagues supporting it.

LETTER WRITING

The more undecided a legislator is and the less controversial the issue, the greater the impact letters will have. Legislators who are more concerned about reelection are especially sensitive to letters from constituents.

Letters should be timed for the greatest effect; for example, early in the session to build momentum or shortly before a vote on the bill.

Consider having a letter-writing party among members of your organization. Have people bring their own stationery. Supply some yourself. Have several different types available. Use different types of stamps. Letter writers should be instructed on *how* to prepare their letters, but the letters should be written in their own words. Do not use specific phrases.

Do not send form letters.

Use personal letterhead or business stationery if possible. Because envelopes are usually thrown away, put your return address on the letter.

Identify the name and number of the bill and state your reasons for writing; especially relate issues to personal experiences. Show how the bill affects you, your family, your community, your clients, or your livelihood. Clearly identify yourself as a constituent if you are one. Mention the number of people you serve or represent. Open and close your letter with statements that establish rapport, such as: "I know you are concerned about . . . "

Make sure your facts are accurate.

Use your own words. Avoid jargon and slogans.

Be reasonable. Don't ask for something that is outside the legislator's capability to provide.

Don't use threats. Don't impugn the motives of those who oppose you.

Thank the legislator if she or he has voted the "right" way on another issue.

Focus on one issue per letter.

Ask the legislator to *do* something; for example, ask the legislator to vote a certain way.

Ask for a response.

Write a thank-you letter if the legislator does what you requested.

Realize, of course, that all these tactics can be used against your pet bills as well.

Some Final Considerations

Perhaps you can understand the accuracy of public interest lobbyist Mike Pertschuk's (1986) description of members of his profession. "Public interest lobbyists," he says, "perform prodigious feats: as coalition builders—builders of mutual trust, confidence, sustained activity—as social psychologists of victory. They are strategists, parliamentary wizards, rag-pickers of intelligence, networkers of knowledge, accurate head counters, deployers of experts, media mavens, modulators of intemperance. . . . They are the physical embodiment of watchful constituencies. . . . To their younger colleagues they are teachers. And they teach not only the needs and the skills, but the joys of political engagement" (p. 24).

Your confidence and moxie will grow with your awareness of the process, your preparation, and your experience. In fact, it can grow dramatically. You will quickly pick up on the legislative culture, the game, the methods, and the key players. The activity can be pretty heady and contagious. You might get hooked.

The Hearing

Members of the Health Committee have begun drifting into the hearing room. A few committee staff have already arrived. The small, neat stacks of papers they have built indicate that today's agenda will be full, but not frenetic. It is still fairly early in the session—before this year's promise of an expeditious and orderly completion of the legislature's work becomes the butt of yet another session's jokes. Soon they will be joined by Senator Jan Cindrich, the committee chair, and most of the other members of the committee. Today the usual number of reporters will be increased by the attendance of a few scribes from several small, rural papers. A few other rural weeklies have requested the stringers from the Capitol press corps to cover the action on Senate Bill 1142. A photographer from Channel 7 is setting up his camera. A handful of onlookers, some intending to testify on today's items, a class of fifth-graders from a local school, and three well-heeled lobbyists complete the collection.

Over the past few weeks, Roseann Nicoletti has attended hearings to see the Health Committee in action. Those observations have helped her get a better look at how the system works. Today she fidgets in her seat. Today is for real. Looking at Dr. Jane McConnell seated to her left she feels some reassurance. Roseann is pleased that she was able to arrange for a number of people to testify on behalf of Senate Bill 1142, the Rural Prenatal Care bill. She knows that each person is well prepared to testify, and each has a specific viewpoint that the committee should hear. She hopes the work she put into developing this testimony will sway a few votes. She has heard that a number of the senators aren't much in the mood for spending money for prenatal care as the state's health care and education bills continue to mount. They are looking to cut, not add. Though she isn't quite certain who these idiots are, she is certain that if Dr. McConnell's testimony doesn't change their minds, Olivia Arvizu's story will. Olivia, a shy, attractive young woman, will tell the committee of a mother's personal anguish watching her tiny little girl struggle for life in a neonatal intensive care unit. This anguish could have been avoided if Olivia had been able to see a doctor before Raquel was born. She was lucky to have been in the city visiting her cousin when she went into labor. The hospital closest to her hometown would not have been equipped to save Raquel's life.

Roseann catches the eye of Monica Miranda, another member of The Children Need Us Now Alliance, and motions her over. Several Alliance members have provided individuals for the testifying team. Though none of the members of the coalition's steering committee had ever done any lobbying, they knew enough to get an early start. Months before the session was to begin, they met with Senator Cindrich and began working on their plan to establish prenatal care centers in underserved areas. Realizing that the legislature would never fund a full network, they decided to concentrate on non-urban areas. Traditionally conservative legislators from the rural districts would probably support the idea to deliver some services to their constituents. The comprehensive research they have done has clearly demonstrated the need for these services.

"Did you talk to Andy Wooten?" Monica whispers. "You won't believe this, Roseann, but I saw Senator Marulo this morning, and he told me that Andy wants to amend the bill to include two centers in urban areas! Do you think we can figure out just which urban areas he's talking about? Maybe ones where his agency might have an office? What a coincidence! This really burns me. We went through all this two months ago when we decided our strategy, and now Andy goes ahead and makes changes on his own. Don't worry, I told Senator Marulo that we would be satisfied with establishing centers in the rural areas this year. We'll worry about other areas at another time."

Roseann shakes her head. "To tell you the truth, Monica, I'm not all that surprised. I had

a feeling he didn't really agree with this approach. Maybe we should talk to Senator Cindrich about it. We probably should be talking to her pretty soon anyway.

"Let's discuss all that later, OK? Right now I'm too preoccupied. This hearing is the main chance we have to make our point, and I want to make sure everything goes OK. I think I'll go over and talk to Randy Damon. I'm glad the *Messenger* sent him up here to cover the story. I see you got a few papers here too. Good work."

As Roseann walks over to talk to Randy, Monica wonders if she really has anything new to tell him or if she just needs something better to do before the hearing starts. They have given all the papers the same packet of information they sent to the senators. Fifteen pages of well-documented reasons why this bill is needed and what it can accomplish should con-

vince even those who never thought of this problem before.

Monica feels proud of the work they have done. Three months ago she was sitting in an office complaining. Three months ago she didn't even know the name of her state senator. Three months ago she had never written a letter to an elected official. Today she's here at the Capitol. Today she will mail over a hundred letters the Alliance members have generated in support of S.B. 1142. Today she and Roseann will have lunch with April Jefferson and Brad Edgers, two veteran lobbyists who have offered to give the Alliance some tips. Today she is amazed at how much she has learned and the people she has met. Today, not for the first time, she noticed she's enjoying all this.

The sound of the gavel meets Senator Cindrich's voice, bringing the meeting to order. The hearing has begun.

Some Questions to Consider

1. If there are no major changes in the way the change effort is being conducted, how is this story likely to end?
2. What information or assumptions led you to this conclusion?
3. If you were Roseann Nicoletti or Monica Miranda, what would you have done differently? What would you have done the same?
4. What particular steps would you take at this point to enhance the prospects for success?

APPENDIX A

Articles of Incorporation of a Nonprofit Corporation

I. NAME: The name of the Corporation is _____ .

II. PURPOSE: This Corporation does not contemplate pecuniary gain or profit to the members thereof, and the purpose for which it is organized is the transaction of any and all lawful affairs for which nonprofit corporations may be incorporated under the laws of the State of _____, as they may be amended from time to time, and specifically, but not in limitation thereof, the purpose of providing _____. The Corporation may also conduct any and all other activities or affairs of any type whatsoever growing out of, related to, or in any manner whatsoever in connection with any of the items, businesses, relationships, purposes, or powers described in these Articles, but the Corporation is organized exclusively for charitable purposes, including for such purposes, the making of distributions to organizations that qualify as exempt organizations under Section 501(c)(3) of the Internal Revenue Code of 1986, as amended from time to time. No enumeration herein set forth shall in any manner be deemed to be exclusive of object or purpose not enumerated, but on the contrary, such enumerations shall be construed as including all other and further objects and purposes of the same or similar type or character, regardless of how thin, vague, or indefinite the relationship or connection may be. Notwithstanding anything herein to the contrary, the Corporation shall exercise only such powers as are in furtherance of the exempt purposes of organizations described in Section 501(c)(3) or such powers permitted a corporation contributions to which are deductible under Section 170(c)(2) of the Internal Revenue Code of 1986, as amended from time to time.

III. INITIAL CHARACTER OF AFFAIRS: The Corporation initially intends to conduct _____ .

IV. PROHIBITED ACTIVITIES: No substantial part of the activities of the Corporation shall be the carrying on of propaganda or otherwise attempting to influence legislation, and the Corporation shall not participate or intervene in (including the publication or distribution of statements) any political campaign on behalf of any candidate for public office. Notwithstanding any other provision of these Articles, the Corporation shall not carry on any other activities not permitted to be carried on by a corporation exempt from federal income taxation under Section 501(c)(3) of the Internal Revenue Code of 1986, as amended from time to time.

V. STATUTORY AGENT: The name and address of the initial statutory agent of the Corporation is _____ .

VI. KNOWN PLACE OF BUSINESS: The known place of business of the Corporation shall be _____ .

VII. BOARD OF DIRECTORS: The business and affairs of the Corporation shall be managed by the Board of Directors. The number of persons which shall constitute the whole Board of Directors shall not be less than three (3) nor more than twenty-five (25). The specific number of persons on the Board of Directors shall be fixed, from time to time, by the Board of Directors in accordance with these Articles and the Bylaws of the Corporation. Until the first annual election of directors, or until their successors are elected and qualified, the initial Board of Directors shall consist of three (3) directors, and the following persons shall be the initial directors of the Corporation: _____ .

VIII. INCORPORATOR: The Incorporator of the Corporation is as follows: _____ . All powers, duties, and responsibilities of the Incorporator shall cease at the time of delivery of these Articles of Incorporation to _____ for filing.

IX. INDEMNIFICATION OF OFFICERS, DIRECTORS, EMPLOYEES, AND AGENTS: The Corporation shall indemnify any person who incurs expenses by reason of the fact that he or she is or was an officer, director, employee, or agent of the Corporation, in accordance with the procedures more specifically set forth in the Bylaws of the Corporation. This indemnification shall be mandatory under all circumstances in which indemnification is permitted by law.

X. ELIMINATION OF DIRECTOR LIABILITY: The Directors of the Corporation shall have no personal liability to the Corporation for monetary damages for breach of fiduciary duty as a Director, as provided in the _____ . (Note: Check to see if your state has a provision exempting Directors from liability.)

XI. INCOME AND PECUNIARY DISTRIBUTIONS: There shall be no shareholders of the Corporation, and no profits or dividends shall ever be declared by the Corporation. No part of the income of the Corporation shall inure to the benefit of, or be distributable to, any member, director, officer, employee, agent, or other private person, except that the Corporation shall be authorized and empowered to pay reasonable compensation for services rendered and to make payments and distributions in furtherance of the purposes set forth in Article II. No director, officer, employee, agent, or other private person shall be entitled to share in the distribution of any of the Corporation's assets on dissolution of the Corporation.

XII. AMENDMENTS: These Articles may be amended from time to time by the affirmative vote of a majority of the Directors of the Corporation present at a meeting called for such purpose.

XIII. DISSOLUTION: Upon the dissolution of the Corporation, the Board of Directors shall, after paying, or making provision for the payment of, all of the liabilities of the Corporation, dispose of all of its remaining assets exclusively for the purposes of the Corporation in such manner, or to such organization or organizations organized and operated exclusively for such purposes which shall at the time qualify it or them as an exempt organization or organizations under Section 501(c)(3) of the Internal Revenue Code of 1986 (or the corresponding provision of any future United States Internal Revenue Law), as the Board of Directors shall determine. Any such assets not disposed of shall be disposed of by the _____ Court of the State of _____ in the county in which the principal office of the Corporation is located, exclusively for such purposes or to such organization or organizations, as said Court shall determine.

IN WITNESS WHEREOF, the undersigned Incorporator has hereunto set his hand this _____ day of _____ .

ACKNOWLEDGEMENT OF APPOINTMENT AS STATUTORY AGENT: _____ , having been designated to act as statutory agent of _____ , hereby consents to act in that capacity until his removal or resignation is submitted in accordance with the _____ (cite here the official body of state statutes).

APPENDIX B

Bylaws of a Nonprofit Corporation

Article I: Offices and Records

The principal office of the Corporation in the State of _____ shall be located in the City of _____, County of _____, in which place the Corporation shall keep its books, documents, and records. The Corporation may have such other offices either within or without the State of _____ as the Board of Directors may designate or as the business of the Corporation may require from time to time, and in such case, the Corporation may keep its books, documents, and records at such designated offices.

Article II: Members

The Corporation shall have no members.

Article III: Board of Directors

Section 1. Powers, Number, Qualifications, and Election. The affairs of the Corporation shall be managed by the Board of Directors, which shall number no less than three (3) nor more than twenty-five (25), and until changed at an annual or special meeting of the Board of Directors, shall number three (3). The directors need not be residents of the State of _____ and shall be elected at the annual meeting of the Board of Directors to serve until the next annual meeting thereof and until their successors have been elected and qualified.

Section 2. Annual Meeting. The annual meeting of the Board of Directors of the Corporation shall be held at 10:00 A.M. on the second Tuesday of February of each year, if not a legal holiday, and if a legal holiday, on the next succeeding day not a legal holiday. The Board of Directors shall elect the Officers of the Corporation and conduct such other business as it is authorized to transact at the annual meeting. No notice of such meeting need be given.

Section 3. Special Meetings. Special meetings of the Board of Directors may be called by or at the request of the President or any director. The person or persons authorized to call a special meeting of the Board of Directors may fix any place for holding any special meeting of the Board of Directors called by them. Notice of any special meeting shall be given at least five (5) days prior thereto by written notice delivered personally or mailed to each director at his/her business address or by telegram. Neither the business to be transacted at, nor the purpose of, any regular or special meeting of the Board of Directors need be specified in the notice or waiver of notice of such meeting.

Section 4. Quorum. One-third ($\frac{1}{3}$) of the number of directors then serving shall constitute a quorum for the transaction of business, but in no case shall fewer than two (2) directors constitute a quorum. The act of the majority of the directors present at a meeting at which a quorum is present shall be the act of the Board of Directors. If less than a majority of directors is present at a meeting, a majority of the directors then present may adjourn the meeting from time to time without further notice.

Section 5. Resignation of Director. Any director may resign his/her office at any time, such resignation to be made in writing and to take effect from the time of its receipt by the Corporation, unless the time be fixed in the resignation, and in such case it shall take effect from said date. The acceptance of the resignation shall not be required to make it effective.

Section 6. Removal of Director. At a meeting of the Board of Directors called expressly for that purpose, any director may be removed, with or without cause, by a vote of the majority of the directors.

Section 7. Vacancies. Any vacancy occurring in the Board of Directors may be filled by the affirmative vote of a majority of the remaining directors, and any director so chosen shall hold office until the next election of directors when his/her successor is elected and qualified. Any newly created directorship shall be deemed a vacancy. If the Board of Directors accepts the resignation of a director to take effect at a future date, it shall have the power to elect a successor to take office when the resignation becomes effective. In such case, the director so resigning shall not vote regarding the election of such successor director. No reduction in the authorized number of directors shall have the effect of removing a director prior to the expiration of his/her term of office.

Section 8. Compensation. By Resolution of the Board of Directors, the directors may be paid their expenses, if any, of attendance at each meeting of the Board of Directors, but in no case shall the directors receive compensation for attendance at a meeting of the Board of Directors or for any services rendered to the Corporation as directors.

Section 9. Waiver of Notice. Whenever, under the provisions of these Bylaws, any notice is required to be given, a waiver thereof, in writing, signed by the person or persons entitled to such notice, whether before or after the time stated therein, shall be deemed equivalent to the giving of such notice.

Section 10. Informal Action by Directors. Any action required to be taken at a meeting of the directors, or any action which may be taken at a meeting of the directors, may be taken without a meeting if all directors consent thereto in writing, setting forth the actions so taken. Any action so taken shall be deemed taken by Resolution of the Board of Directors by a unanimous vote.

Article IV: Officers

Section 1. Number. The officers of the Corporation shall consist of a President, one or more Vice-Presidents, the number thereof to be determined by resolution of the Board of Directors, a Secretary, and a Treasurer, each of whom shall be elected by the Board of Directors at such time and in such manner as may be prescribed by these Bylaws. Such other officers and assistant officers and agents as may be deemed necessary may be elected or appointed by the Board of Directors or chosen in such other manner as may be prescribed by these Bylaws. Any two or more offices may be held by the same person except the offices of President and Secretary.

Section 2. Election and Term of Office. The officers of the Corporation shall be elected each year at the annual meeting of the Board of Directors. If the election of officers shall not be held at such meeting, such election shall be held as soon thereafter as conveniently may be possible. Each officer shall hold office until his/her successor shall have been duly elected and shall have qualified or until his/her death, resignation, or removal in the manner prescribed in these Bylaws.

Section 3. Removal of Officer. Any officer or agent of the Corporation may be removed by the Board of Directors whenever in its judgment the best interests of the Corporation will be served thereby, but such removal shall be without prejudice to the contract rights, if any, of the person so removed. Election or appointment of an officer or agent shall not of itself create contract rights.

Section 4. Resignation of Officer. Any officer may resign his/her office at any time, such resignation to be made in writing and to take effect from the time of its receipt by the Corporation, unless a time be fixed in the resignation, in which case said resignation shall take effect from that date. The acceptance of the resignation shall not be required to make it effective.

Section 5. Vacancies. A vacancy in any office because of death, resignation, removal, disqualification, or otherwise shall be filled by the Board of Directors for the unexpired portion of the term.

Section 6. President. The President shall preside at all meetings of the Board of Directors of the Corporation. The President may sign and execute all authorized contracts, checks, or other instruments or obligations in the name of the Corporation. Subject to the decision of the Board of Directors, the President shall be in general charge of the property, business, and affairs of the Corporation, and shall perform such additional duties and have such additional powers as may be assigned to him/her by the Board of Directors.

Section 7. Vice-President. Each Vice-President of the Corporation shall have such powers and perform such duties as may be assigned to him/her from time to time by the Board of Directors or as may be delegated to him/her by the President. Each Vice-President shall possess the powers, and may perform the duties, of the President in his/her absence or disability unless

otherwise proscribed by the Board of Directors. In the event there may be more than one (1) Vice-President, each Vice-President in the order of the election thereof shall possess the powers, and may perform the duties, of the President in his/her absence.

Section 8. Secretary. The Secretary shall keep a record in due form of the proceedings of all meetings of the directors and of all committees of the Board of Directors. The Secretary shall give all notices of the Corporation. All books, papers, and correspondence shall be kept in the office of the Corporation and, except as the same may be specifically placed in the custody of the Treasurer, shall be in the Secretary's charge and kept available for inspection by any member of the Board of Directors. The Secretary and/or Assistant Secretary may sign all contracts as shall be authorized by the Board of Directors. The Secretary shall have such other duties and powers as may be assigned to him/her from time to time by the Board of Directors. The Board of Directors may appoint one or more Assistant Secretaries, each of whom shall have such powers and shall perform such duties as shall be assigned by the Board of Directors or the President of the Corporation.

Section 9. Treasurer. The Treasurer shall keep a record of all monies received and paid out and all vouchers and receipts of the Corporation. The Treasurer shall be in general charge of all valuables, checks, and papers belonging to the Corporation except those under the control of the Secretary. The Treasurer shall have such other duties and powers as may be assigned to him/her from time to time by the Board of Directors. The Board of Directors may appoint one or more Assistant Treasurers, each of whom shall have such powers and perform such duties as may be assigned by the Board of Directors or the President of the Corporation.

Section 10. Delegation of Officers' Powers and Duties. In case of the temporary absence of any officer of the Corporation or for any other reason that the Board of Directors may deem sufficient, the Board of Directors may delegate the powers and duties of such officer to any other officer or to any other director for the time specified, provided a majority of the entire Board of Directors concurs therein.

Article V: Fiscal Year

The fiscal year of the Corporation shall be as fixed by the Board of Directors.

Article VI: Contracts, Loans, Checks, and Deposits

Section 1. Contracts. The Board of Directors may authorize any officer or agent of the Corporation to enter into any contract or execute and deliver any instrument in the name of and on behalf of the Corporation, and such authority may be general or confined to specific instances.

Section 2. Loans. No loans shall be contracted on behalf of the Corporation and no evidences of indebtedness shall be issued in its name unless authorized by a resolution of the Board of Directors. Such authority may be general or confined to specific instances.

Section 3. Checks and Drafts. All checks, drafts, or other orders for the payment of money, notes, or other evidences of indebtedness issued in the name of the Corporation shall be signed by such officer or agent of the Corporation and in such manner as shall from time to time be determined by resolution of the Board of Directors.

Section 4. Deposits. All funds of the Corporation not otherwise employed shall be deposited from time to time to the credit of the Corporation in such banks or other financial institutions and depositories as the Board of Directors may select.

Article VII: Providing Housing and Other Projects

The Corporation shall have the authority to provide _____ (name here the main service or activity of the corporation) as determined by the Board of Directors and to engage in other activities in furtherance thereof.

Article VIII: Corporate Seal

The Board of Directors shall provide a corporate seal which shall be circular in form and shall have inscribed thereon the name of the Corporation, the state of incorporation, the words "Corporate Seal," and the year of incorporation.

Article IX: Books and Records

The books, records, and papers of the Corporation shall, at all times during reasonable business hours, be subject to inspection by any director at the principal office of the Corporation.

Article X: Indemnification

Indemnification of any person who incurs expenses by reason of the fact that he/she is or was a director, officer, employee, or agent of the Corporation shall occur in the manner provided for indemnification in the _____ (insert here your state's provision exempting from liability those individuals who work for or serve nonprofit corporations).

Article XI: Amendments

The Board of Directors may make, alter, amend, or repeal these Bylaws by a vote of a majority thereof.

DATED this _____ .

By: _____

ATTEST: _____

References

Ahlbrandt, R. S., Jr., & Cunningham, J. V. (1979). *A new public policy for neighborhood preservation.* New York: Praeger.

Alinsky, S. D. (1972). *Rules for radicals: A pragmatic primer for realistic radicals.* New York: Random House.

Allen, H., & Regional Youth Project. (1981). *The bread game.* San Francisco, CA: Glide Publications.

Allen, S. (1997). Benefit event fundamentals. In J. M. Greenfield (Ed.), *The nonprofit handbook: Fund raising* (2nd ed., pp. 278–298). New York: John Wiley & Sons.

Alliance for Justice. (1997). *Directory of public interest law centers.* Washington, DC: Author.

Amidei, N. (1987). How to be an advocate in bad times. In F. M. Cox, J. L. Erlich, J. Rothman, & J. E. Tropman (Eds.), *Strategies of community organization: Macro practice* (4th ed., pp. 106–114). Itasca, IL: F. E. Peacock.

Arches, J. L. (1997). Burnout and social action. *Journal of Progressive Human Services, 8*(2), 51–62.

Ardman, H., & Ardman, P. (1980). *The woman's day book of fund raising.* New York: St. Martin's.

Arizona Daily Star Editors. (1988). *Media handbook.* Tucson, AZ: Arizona Daily Star.

Baird, J. A. (1997, March). The three Rs of fund raising. *Fund Raising Management,* 14–17.

Bannan, K. J., Boscardian, A., Caster, K., Garris, J., Kwon, R., Love, J. C., Mendelson, E., Sirapyan, N., Lidsky, D., & Munro, J. (1997). Web regional guides. *PC Magazine, 16,* 268–276.

Barker, R. L. (1995). *The social work dictionary* (3rd ed.). Washington, DC: NASW Press.

Barnes, D. (1989). Direct mail trends you need to know about. *National Fund Raiser, 15*(12).

Barnes, S. A. (1988). Understanding the prospect. *National Fund Raiser, 14*(6), 2–3.

Bartlett, H. M. (1958, April). Toward clarification and improvement of social work practice. *Social Work, 3,* 5–8.

Belasco, J. A. (1990). *Teaching the elephant to dance: Empowering change in your organization.* New York: Crown.

Benne, K. D. (1985). The current state of planned changing in persons, groups, communities, and societies. In W. G. Bennis, K. D. Benne, & R. C. Chin (Eds.), *The planning of change* (4th ed., pp. 77–81). New York: Holt, Rinehart & Winston.

Berkowitz, W. R. (1982). *Community impact: Creating grassroots change in hard times.* Cambridge, MA: Schenkman.

Bermant, G., & Warwick, D. P. (1985). The ethics of social intervention: Power, freedom, and accountability. In W. G. Bennis, K. D. Benne, & R. Chin (Eds.), *The planning of change* (4th ed., pp. 449–470). New York: Holt, Rinehart & Winston.

Bernard, J. (1972). Community: Community disorganization. In D. Sills (Ed.), *International encyclopedia of the social sciences* (Vol. 3). New York: Free Press.

Bishop, A. (1994). *Becoming an ally: Breaking the cycle of oppression.* Halifax, Nova Scotia: Fernwood.

Bloom, M. (1990). *Introduction to the drama of social work.* Itasca, IL: F. E. Peacock.

Blumenfeld, E., & Alpern, L. (1986). *The smile connection: How to use humor in dealing with people.* New York: Prentice-Hall.

Bole, W. (1997). Citizens cross racial divide to tackle concrete problems. *Doing Democracy, 4*(2). Brattleboro, VT: Center for Living Democracy.

Booth, H., & Max, S. (1977). *Direct action organizing—strategy planning.* Chicago, IL: Midwest Academy.

Brager, G., & Holloway, S. (1977). A process model for changing organizations from within. *Administration in Social Work, 1*(4), 349–358.

Brager, G., & Holloway, S. (1978). *Changing human service organizations: Politics and practice.* New York: Free Press.

Brakeley, G. A., Jr., (1997). Major gifts from individuals. In J. M. Greenfield (Ed.), *The nonprofit handbook: Fundraising* (2nd ed., pp. 422–441). New York: John Wiley & Sons.

Bratt, R. G. (1987). Dilemmas of community-based housing. *Policy Studies Journal, 16*(2), 324–334.

Breiteneicher J., & Hohler, B. (1993). *Quest for funds revisited: A fund-raising starter kit.* Washington, DC: National Trust for Historic Preservation.

Brentlinger, M. E., & Weiss, J. M. (1987). *The ultimate benefit book.* Cleveland, OH: Octavia Press.

Breton, M. (1994). On the meaning of empowerment and empowerment-oriented social work practice. *Social Work with Groups, 17*(3), 23–37.

Brill, N. (1998). *Working with people: The helping process* (6th ed.). New York: Longman.

Brown, L. N. (1991). *Groups for growth and change.* New York: Longman.

Bryan, W. L. (1980). Preventing burnout in the public interest community. *The Northern Rockies Action Group Papers, 3*(3), 2.

Burghardt, S. (1982). *Organizing for community action.* Newbury Park, CA: Sage.

Burkey, S. (1993). *People first: A guide to self-reliant, participatory rural development.* Atlantic Highlands, NJ: Zed Books.

Burt, M. R., & Pittman, K. J. (1985). *Testing the social safety net.* Washington, DC: The Urban Institute Press.

Case, A. C., & Katz, L. F. (1991). *The company you keep: The effects of family and neighborhood on disadvantaged youths.* Cambridge, MA: National Bureau of Economic Research.

Castaneda, C. J. (1997, July 1). Food fright: 27% going to waste. *USA Today,* p. A3.

Cavanaugh, J. (1980). Program and resource development. In R. L. Clifton & A. M. Dahms (Eds.), *Grassroots administration: A handbook for staff and directors of small community-based social-service organizations* (pp. 13–24). Pacific Grove, CA: Brooks/Cole.

Chaskin, R. J., Joseph, M. L., & Chipeda-Dansokho, S. (1997). Implementing comprehensive community development: Possibilities and limitations. *Social Work, 42*(5), 435–444.

Checkoway, B. (1987). Political strategy for social planning. In F. M. Cox, J. L. Erlich, J. Rothman, & J. E. Tropman (Eds.), *Strategies of community organization: Macro practice* (4th ed., pp. 326–342). Itasca, IL: F. E. Peacock.

Children's Defense Fund. (1997). *State of America's children.* Washington, DC: Author.

Clay, P. L. (1979). *Neighborhood renewal.* Lexington, MA: Lexington Books.

Cohen, B. J., & Austin, M. J. (1994). Organizational learning and change in a public child welfare agency. *Administration in Social Work, 18*(1), 1–19.

Cohen, R. (1979). Neighborhood planning and political capacity. *Urban Affairs Quarterly, 14*(3), 337–362.

Coleman, J. S. (1988). Social capital and schools. *Education Digest, 53*(8), 6–9.

Coleman, J. S. (1993). The rational reconstruction of society. *American Sociological Review, 58*(1), 1–15.

Coley, S. M., & Scheinberg, C. A. (1990). *Proposal writing.* Newbury Park, CA: Sage.

Common Cause. (1992). *Common cause action manual.* Washington, DC: Author.

Conner, A. N., & de la Isla, J. (1984). Information: An effective change tool. In F. Cox, J. L. Erlich, J. Rothman, & J. E. Tropman (Eds.), *Tactics and techniques of community practice* (2nd ed., p. 245n). Itasca, IL: F. E. Peacock.

Corey, M. S., & Corey, G. (1998). *Becoming a helper* (3rd ed.). Pacific Grove, CA: Brooks/Cole.

Coulton, C. J. (1996). Effects of neighborhoods on families and children: Implications for services. In A. J. Kahn, & S. B. Kammerman (Eds.), *Children and their families in big cities: Strategies for service and reform* (pp. 87–120). New York: Columbia University Press.

Cormier, S., & Hackney, H. (1993). *The professional counselor: A process guide to helping* (2nd ed.). Boston: Allyn & Bacon.

Cowan, G., & Egan, M. (1979). *People in systems: A model for development in the human-service professions and education.* Pacific Grove, CA: Brooks/Cole.

Cox, F. M. (1987a). Communities: Alternative conceptions of community: Implications for community organization practice. In F. M. Cox, J. L. Erlich, J. Rothman, & J. E. Tropman (Eds.), *Strategies of community organization: Macro practice* (4th ed., pp. 232–243). Itasca, IL: F. E. Peacock.

Cox, F. M. (1987b). Arenas of community practice: Introduction. In F. M. Cox, J. L. Erlich, J. Rothman, & J. E. Tropman (Eds.), *Strategies of community organization: Macro practice* (4th ed., pp. 187–212). Itasca, IL: F. E. Peacock.

Craver, R. M. (1995, January). Get ready for tomorrow. *Fund Raising Management,* 26–29.

Cross, R. (1992). *Media data.* Tucson, AZ: Tucson Newspapers, Inc.

Crowfoot, J., Chesler, M. A., & Boulet, J. (1983). Organizing for social justice. In E. Seidman (Ed.), *Handbook of social intervention* (pp. 253–255). Newbury Park, CA: Sage.

Dailey, R. C. (1986). Understanding organizational commitment for volunteers: Empirical and managerial implications. *Journal of Voluntary Action Research, 15*(1), 19–31.

Dale, D. (1978). *How to make citizen involvement work: Strategies for developing clout.* Amherst: University of Massachusetts, Citizen Involvement Training Project.

Dale, D., & Mitiguy, N. (1978). *Planning for a change: A citizen's guide to creative planning and program development.* Amherst: University of Massachusetts, Citizen Involvement Training Project.

Daun, D. (1991). Becoming a media resource. In *What's News?* (p. 3). Tucson, AZ: Tucson Newspapers, Inc.

Dear, R. B., & Patti, R. J. (1984). Legislative advocacy: Seven effective tactics. In F. Cox, J. L. Erlich, J. Rothman, & J. E. Tropman (Eds.), *Tactics and techniques of community practice* (2nd ed., pp. 185–197). Itasca, IL: F. E. Peacock.

Decker, V. A., & Decker, L. E. (1978). *The funding process: Grantsmanship and proposal development.* Charlottesville, VA: Community Collaborations.

De Jouvenel, B. (1958). Authority: The efficient imperative. In C. J. Freidrich (Ed.), *Authority, nomos, I.* Cambridge, MA: Harvard University Press.

Devore, W., & Schlesinger, E. (1996). *Ethnic sensitive social work practice* (4th ed.). Boston: Allyn & Bacon.

DiNitto, D. M. (1995). *Social welfare: Politics and public policy* (4th ed.). Boston: Allyn & Bacon.

DiNitto, D. M., & McNeece, C. A. (1989). *Social work.* Englewood Cliffs, NJ: Prentice-Hall.

Dolgoff, R., Feldstein, D., & Skolnik, L. (1997). *Understanding social welfare* (4th ed.). White Plains, NY: Longman.

Dosher, A. (1977a, February 17). *Networks: A key to person-community development.* Paper presented to Office of Youth Development, Department of Health, Education, and Welfare, Denver Hearings.

Dosher, A. (1977b, November 2). *Networking workshop outline.* Paper presented to Pima County Children Youth and Families Community Network, Tucson, AZ.

Dove, T. (1983, July/August). Business in the community: How you can make a difference. *The Journal of Insurance,* 17–22.

Downs, A. (1981). *Neighborhoods and urban development.* Washington, DC: The Brookings Institution.

Doxiadis, C. A. (1968). Foreword. In S. Keller (Ed.), *The urban neighborhood.* New York: Random House.

Dubois, B., & Krogsrud-Miley, K. (1996). *Social work: An empowering profession* (2nd ed.). Boston, MA: Allyn & Bacon.

Dupper, D. R., & Poertner, J. (1997). Public schools and the revitalization of impoverished communities: School linked, family resource centers. *Social Work, 42*(5), 415–422.

Edelwich, J., & Brodsky, A. (1980). *Burn-out: Stages of disillusionment in the helping professions.* New York: Human Sciences Press.

Edwards, E. D., & Edwards, M. E. (1995). Community development with Native Americans. In F. G. Rivera & J. L. Erlich (Eds.), *Community organizing in a diverse society* (2nd ed., pp. 25–42). Boston: Allyn & Bacon.

Egan, J. (1996, April 29). Ready, set, search. *U.S. News & World Report, 120,* 64–68.

Ellsworth, C., Hooyman, N., Ruff, R. A., Stam, S. B., & Tucker, J. H. (1982). Toward a feminist model of planning for and with women. In A. Weicker & S. T. Vandiver (Eds.), *Women, power, and change* (pp. 146–156). Washington, DC: National Association of Social Workers.

Erlich, J. L., & Tropman, J. E. (1974). Overview of strategy. In F. M. Cox, J. L. Erlich, J. Rothman, & J. E. Tropman (Eds.), *Strategies of community organization: A book of readings* (2nd ed., p. 175). Itasca, IL: F. E. Peacock.

Erlich, J. L., & Tropman, J. E. (1987). Introduction. In F. M. Cox, J. L. Erlich, J. Rothman, & J. E. Tropman (Eds.), *Strategies of community organization: Macro practice* (4th ed.). Itasca, IL: F. E. Peacock.

Ewalt, P. L. (1994). Federal legislation and the social work profession. *Social Work, 39*(4), 341–342.

Fabricant, M. (1985). The industrialization of social work. *Social Work, 30*(5), 389–395.

Fallon, D. (1993, January). Collaboration: Effective fundraising in the 90's. *Contemporary Issues in Fundraising,* 20–23.

Fantini, M., & Gittell, M. (1973). *Decentralization: Achieving reform.* New York: Praeger.

Fawcett, S., Seekins, T., Whang, P., Muir, C., & Balcazar, Y. (1982). Involving consumers in decision making. *Social Policy, 2,* 36–41.

Federico, R. C. (1984). *The social welfare institution* (4th ed.). Lexington, MA: D. C. Heath.

Fellin, P. (1995). *The community and the social worker* (2nd ed.). Itasca, IL: F. E. Peacock.

Filley, A., House, R., & Kerr, S. (1976). *Managerial process and organizational behavior* (2nd ed.). Glenview, IL: Scott, Foresman.

Fisch, J. (1989a). Using celebrities to raise funds: A tricky endeavor. *Tax Exempt News, 11*(4), 1–3.

Fisch, J. (1989b). The eight basic truths direct mail fund raisers can't afford to forget. *Tax Exempt News, 11*(4), 5–8.

Fisher, R. (1972). *International conflict and behavioral science.* New York: Basic Books.

Fisher, R. (1984, Summer). Neighborhood organizing: Lessons from the past. *Social Policy,* 9–16.

Fisher, R., & Ury, W. (1991). *Getting to yes: Negotiating without giving in* (2nd ed.). Boston, MA: Houghton Mifflin.

Floro, G. K. (1989). Innocence and satisfactions for a shared-life voluntarism. *Wisconsin Sociologist, 26*(1), 7–14.

Flynn, M. K. (1996, April 29). Taming the Internet. *U.S. News & World Report,* 60–64.

Fong, L. G. W., & Gibbs, J. T. (1995). Facilitating services to multicultural communities in a dominant setting: An organizational perspective. *Administration in Social Work, 19*(2), 1–24.

Freedman, H. A. (1996, December). Is the party over? Charities and special events: Where are the dollars really going? *Fund Raising Management,* 26–30.

Freierman, S. (1997, September 1). Public Internet use grows. *The Arizona,* E3.

Frey, G. A. (1990, March). A framework for promoting organizational change. *Journal of Contemporary Human Services,* 142–147.

Freyd, W., & Carlson, D. M. (1997). Telemarketing. In J. M. Greenfield (Ed.), *The nonprofit handbook: Fund raising* (2nd ed., pp. 317–328). New York: John Wiley & Sons.

Fridena, R. (1983, November). Paper presented to the Social Services Department, Pima Community College, Arizona.

Friere, P. (1973). *Education for critical consciousness.* New York: Seabury.

Garth, T. D. (1997). *1997 metro survey report.* Chicago, IL: Metro Chicago Information Center.

Gates, B. L. (1980). *Social program administration: The implementation of social policy.* Englewood Cliffs, NJ: Prentice-Hall.

Gatewood, E. (1994). *Do it yourself: A simple approach to neighborhood improvement.* Tacoma WA: City of Tacoma.

Geever, J. C., & McNeill, P. (1997). *The Foundation Center's guide to proposal writing* (rev. ed.). New York: The Foundation Center.

Gitman, M. (1998, March 2). Racing to the Internet. *Arizona Daily Star,* ST8–16.

Goffin, S. G., & Lombardi, J. (1988). *Speaking out: Early childhood advocacy.* Washington, DC: National Association for the Education of Young Children.

Goldberg, G. S. (1980, June). New directions for the community service society of New York: A study of organizational change. *Social Service Review,* 184–219.

Golden, S. (1997). The grant-seeking process. In J. M. Greenfield (Ed.), *The nonprofit handbook: Fund raising* (2nd ed., pp. 396–421). New York: John Wiley & Sons.

Goldstein, J. (1993). *Countering recession with innovation.* Princeton, NJ: Davis Information Group.

Gordon, W. E. (1965, July). Knowledge and value: Their distinction and relationship in clarifying social work practice. *Social Work, 10,* 32.

Gottleib, N. (1992). Empowerment, political analyses, and services for women. In Y. Hasenfeld (Ed.), *Human services as complex organizations* (pp. 301–319). Newbury Park, CA: Sage.

Grimes, G. (1996). *The ten minute guide to the Internet and the World Wide Web* (2nd ed.). Indianapolis, IN: Que Corporation.

Gummer, B. (1978, September). A power-politics approach to social welfare organizations. *Social Service Review,* 349–361.

Gutierrez, L. M. (1995). Working with women of color: An empowerment perspective. In J. Rothman, J. L. Erlich, & J. E. Tropman (Eds.), *Strategies of community intervention* (5th ed., pp. 204–212). Itasca, IL: F. E. Peacock.

Gutierrez, L. M., & Lewis, E. A. (1994). Community organizing with women of color: A feminist approach. *Journal of Community Practice, 1*(2), 23–44.

Gutierrez, L. M., & Lewis, E. A. (1995). A feminist perspective on organizing with women of color. In F. G. Rivera & J. L. Erlich (Eds.), *Organizing in a diverse society* (2nd ed., pp. 95–112). Boston: Allyn & Bacon.

Hagebak, B. R. (1982). *Getting local agencies to cooperate.* Baltimore, MD: University Park Press.

Hall, H. (1996). Direct mail: Can it still deliver? *The Chronicle of Philanthropy, 8*(10).

Hallman, H. W. (1984). *Neighborhoods: Their place in urban life.* Newbury Park, CA: Sage.

Haynes, K. S., & Mickelson, J. S. (1991). *Affecting change: Social workers in the political arena* (2nd ed.). New York: Longman.

Heller, S. (1996, March 1). Bowling alone: A Harvard professor examines America's dwindling sense of community. *The Chronicle of Higher Education, 42*(25), A10–12.

Herbert, W. (1996, January 29). The revival of civic life. *U.S. News & World Report,* 63–67.

Hicks, J. (1997). Grass-roots fund raising. In J. M. Greenfield (Ed.), *The nonprofit handbook: Fund raising* (2nd ed., pp. 554–580). New York: John Wiley & Sons.

Hodgkinson, V. A. (1996). *Non-profit almanac: 1996–1997.* San Francisco, CA: Jossey-Bass.

Hodgkinson, V. A., & Weitzman, M. S. (1996b). Giving and volunteering in the United States. Washington, DC: Independent Sector.

Holloway, S. (1987). Staff-initiated organizational change. In National Association of Social Workers, *Encyclopedia of social work* (18th ed., pp. 729–736). Silver Spring, MD: National Association of Social Workers.

Hollyday, J. (1990, June). The costs of social neglect. *Sojourners,* 4–5.

Home, A. L. (1991). Mobilizing women's strengths for social change: The group connection. In A. Vinik & M. Levin (Eds.), *Social action in group work* (pp. 153–173). New York: Haworth.

Horwitz, M. (1954). The recall of interrupted group tasks: An experimental study of individual motivation in relation to social groups. *Human Relations, 7,* 3–38.

Howe, F. (1985, March/April). What you need to know about fundraising. *Harvard Business Review,* 24.

Hoye, D. (1997a, September 1). Getting involved in groups. *Arizona Republic,* E3.

Hoye, D. (1997b, September 1). US West takes on Cox Internet. *Arizona Republic,* E1.

Hrebenar, R. J., & Scott, R. K. (1982). *Interest group politics in America.* Englewood Cliffs, NJ: Prentice-Hall.

Hunt, A. (1986, July/August). Strategic philanthropy. *Across the Board,* 23–30.

Hyde, C. (1992). The ideational system of social movement agencies: An examination of feminist health centers. In Y. Hasenfeld (Ed.), *Human services as complex organizations* (pp. 121–144). Newbury Park, CA: Sage.

Ibanez, A. (1997, October). Sustainable Tucson: A vision for the future. *Tucson Monthly,* 52–61.

Internal Revenue Service. (1997a). *Internal Revenue Service code, exempt organizations, subchapter F.* St. Paul, MN: West Publishing.

Internal Revenue Service. (1997b). *Internal Revenue Service code, public charities, chapter 41.* St. Paul, MN: West Publishing.

Janis, I. L. (1982). *Groupthink: Psychological studies of policy decisions and fiascos* (2nd ed.). Boston, MA: Houghton Mifflin.

Jansson, B. S. (1994). *Social welfare policy: From theory to practice* (2nd ed.). Belmont, CA: Wadsworth.

Jansson, B. S. (1997). *The reluctant welfare state: A history of American social welfare policies* (3rd ed.). Pacific Grove, CA: Brooks/Cole.

Johnson, D. W., & Johnson, F. P. (1997). *Joining together: Group theory and group skills* (6th ed.). Englewood Cliffs, NJ: Prentice-Hall.

Johnson, L. (1998). *Social work practice: A generalist approach* (6th ed.). Boston, MA: Allyn & Bacon.

Johnson, L. C., & Schwartz, C. L. (1997). *Social welfare: A response to human need* (4th ed.). Boston: Allyn & Bacon.

Johnson, R. (1991). *Press plan.* Unpublished manuscript.

Julian, J. (1973). *Social problems.* Englewood Cliffs, NJ: Prentice-Hall.

Kahn, S. (1970). *How people get power: Organizing oppressed communities for action.* New York: McGraw-Hill.

Kahn, S. (1991). *Organizing: A guide for grassroots leaders* (rev. ed.). Silver Spring, MD: National Association of Social Workers.

Kaner, S., Lind, L., Toldi, C., Fisk, S., & Berger, D. (1996). *Facilitator's guide to participatory decision-making.* Gabriola Island, BC: New Society.

Karrass, C. L. (1981). Negotiation strategies. *Business Secrets* (pp. 44–45). New York: Boardroom Reports.

Keller, G. (1983). *Academic strategy: The management revolution in American higher education.* Baltimore, MD: Johns Hopkins.

Keller, S. (1968). *The urban neighborhood.* New York: Random House.

Kennedy, D. M. (1996, August). Neighborhood revitalization: Lessons from Savannah and Baltimore. *National Institute of Justice Journal,* 13–17.

Kettner, P. M., Daley, J. M., & Nichols, A. W. (1985). *Initiating change in organizations and communities: A macro practice model.* Pacific Grove, CA: Brooks/Cole.

Kettner, P. M., Moroney, R. M., & Martin, L. L. (1990). *Designing and managing programs: An effectiveness-based approach.* Newbury Park, CA: Sage.

Kibel, B., & Miner, W. (1996). *The basics of results mapping.* Bethesda MD: Pacific Institute for Research and Evaluation.

Kimble, M. (1991). Newspapers are news. In *What's News?* (pp. 4–5). Tucson, AZ: Tucson Newspapers, Inc.

Kirst-Ashman, K. K., & Hull, G. H. (1997). *Generalist practice with organizations and communities.* Chicago: Nelson-Hall.

Klein, A. F. (1972). *Effective groupwork: An introduction to principle and method.* New York: Association Press.

Klein, K. (1992, December). Budgeting for fundraising. *Grassroots Fundraising Journal,* 3–5.

Konopka, G. (1983). *Social group work: A helping process* (3rd ed.). Englewood Cliffs, NJ: Prentice-Hall.

Kotler, M. (1969). *Neighborhood government: The local foundations of political life.* Indianapolis, IN: Bobbs-Merrill.

Kramer, R., & Specht, H. (1983). *Readings in community organization practice* (3rd ed.). Englewood Cliffs, NJ: Prentice-Hall.

Kretzman, J. P., & McNight, J. L. (1993). *Building communities from the inside out.* Chicago, IL: ACTA Publications.

Krueger, R. A., & King, J. A. (1997). *Involving community members in focus groups* (Focus Group Kit, vol. 5). Thousand Oaks, CA: Sage.

Laird, W., & Hoover, K. (1993). *Evaluation of the neighborhood small grants program.* Tucson, AZ: Tucson Community Foundation.

Lamiell, R. (1984). The people's lobby. In L. Staples (Ed.), *Roots of power: A manual for grassroots organizing* (pp. 188–197). New York: Praeger.

Langton, S. (1982). Networking and community education. In J. M. Brandon & Associates (Eds.), *Networking: A trainers manual* (pp. 212–213). Amherst: University of Massachusetts, Community Education Resource Center, School of Education.

Latting, J. K. (1990). Motivational differences between Black and White volunteers. *Non-Profit and Voluntary Sector Quarterly, 19*(2), 121–136.

Lauffer, A., & Gorodezky, S. (1977). *Volunteers.* Newbury Park, CA: Sage.

Lautman, K. P. (1997). Direct mail. In J. M. Greefield (Ed.), *The nonprofit handbook: Fund raising* (2nd ed., pp. 254–277). New York: John Wiley & Sons.

League of Women Voters. (1976). *Making an issue of it: The campaign handbook.* Publication No. 613.

League of Women Voters Education Fund. (1977). How to plan an environmental conference. In F. Cox, J. L. Erlich, J. Rothman, & J. E. Tropman (Eds.), *Tactics and techniques of community practice* (pp. 111–152). Itasca, IL: F. E. Peacock.

Lefton, J. (1992). Tucson citizen supports local nonprofit organizations. In *Meet the media* (pp. 2–3). Tucson, AZ: Tucson Newspapers, Inc.

Levine, J. R., Baroudi, C., & Young, M. L. (1997). *The Internet for dummies* (4th ed.). Foster City, CA: IDG Books Worldwide.

Levy, C. S. (1973, Winter). The value base of social work. *Journal of Education for Social Work, 9,* 37–38.

Lewin, K. (1951). *Field theory in social science.* New York: Harper.

Lewis, J. (1997). *Welcome to the grants collection.* Tucson, AZ: Tucson-Pima Public Library.

Lewis, J. A., Lewis, M. D., & Souflée, F., Jr. (1991).

Management of human service programs (2nd ed.). Pacific Grove, CA: Brooks/Cole.

Lidsky, D. (1997, August). Think globally surf locally. *PC Magazine, 16,* 265–267.

Lipsky, M. (1984). Bureaucratic disentitlement in social welfare programs. *Social Service Review, 58*(2), 3–27.

Litwak, E., Shiroi, E., Zimmerman, L., & Bernstein, J. (1970). Community participation in bureaucratic organizations: Principles and strategies. *Interchange, 1*(4), 44–60.

Lloyd-Jones, E. (1989). Foreword. In D. Roberts, *Designing campus activities to foster a sense of community.* [New Direction for Student Services, 48.] San Francisco: Jossey-Bass.

Lofquist, W. A. (1993). *The technology of prevention workbook* (expanded ed.). Tucson, AZ: AYD Publications.

Lofquist, W. A. (1996). *The technology of development: A framework for transforming community cultures.* Tucson, AZ: Development Publications.

Long, D. F. (1979). *How to organize and raise funds for small nonprofit organizations.* South Plainfield, NJ: Groupwork Today.

Longres, J. (1995). *Human behavior in the social environment* (2nd ed.). Itasca, IL: F. E. Peacock.

Lotspeich, M. L., & Kleymeyer, J. E. (1976). How to gather data about your neighborhood. *Neighborhood Technical Information Service, 1*(10). Chicago: American Society of Planning Officials.

Luke, T. W. (1989). *Screens of power: Ideology, domination, and resistance in informational society.* Urbana: University of Illinois Press.

Lum, D. (1996). *Social work practice and people of color: A process-stage approach* (3rd ed.). Pacific Grove, CA: Brooks/Cole.

Lumsden, G., & Lumsden, D. (1997). *Communicating in groups and teams: Sharing leadership.* Belmont, CA: Wadsworth.

Lynch, D. J. (1996, September 20). Dying dreams, dead-end streets. *USA Today,* B1–2.

Lynn, K., & Lynn, D. (1992). Common cents fund raising. *New Designs for Youth Development, 10*(2), 34–39.

Male, R. (1993). The politics of thriving as well as surviving. In R. L. Clifton & A. M. Davis (Eds.), *Grassroots administration: A resource book for directors, staff, and volunteers of small community-based nonprofit agencies* (2nd ed., pp. 83–95). Pacific Heights, IL: Waveland Press.

Mancoske, R. J., & Hunzeker, J. M. (1994). Advocating for community services coordination: An empowerment perspective for planning AIDS services. *Journal of Community Practice, 1*(3), 49–58.

Mann, B. (1995). *Politics on the Net.* Indianapolis, IN: Que Corporation.

Marger, M. (1997). *Race and ethnic relations* (4th ed.). Belmont, CA: Wadsworth.

Martí-Costa, S., & Serrano-García, I. (1995). Needs assessment and community development: An ideological perspective. In J. Rothman, J. L. Erlich, & J. E. Tropman (Eds.), *Strategies of community intervention* (5th ed., pp. 257–267). Itasca, IL: F. E. Peacock.

Martin, P. Y. (1980). Multiple constituencies, dominant societal values, and the human service administrator:

Implications for service delivery. *Administration in Social Work, 4*(2), 15–27.

Mason, J. L. (1988). Investing for results: Corporate philanthropic activities. *Vital Speeches of the Day* (Vol. LIV, No. 12, pp. 379–381). New York Press Group.

Mason, R. O., & Mitroff, I. I. (1985). A teleological power-oriented theory of strategy. In W. G. Bennis, K. D. Benne, & R. Chin (Eds.), *The planning of change* (4th ed., pp. 215–223). New York: Holt, Rinehart & Winston.

Max, S. (1980). *Making a first contact with a potential member.* Chicago, IL: Midwest Academy.

Mayer, N. S. (1984). *Neighborhood organizations and community development: Making revitalization work.* Washington, DC: The Urban Institute Press.

Mayer, R. R. (1985). *Program planning: A developmental perspective.* Englewood Cliffs, NJ: Prentice-Hall.

McCreight, M. (1984). Lawsuits for leverage. In L. Staples (Ed.), *Roots to power: A manual for grassroots organizing* (pp. 181–187). New York: Praeger.

McKay, S. (1988, November). The manager: Profile artistic director. *Canadian Business,* 193–196.

McKillip, J. (1987). *Needs analysis: Tools for the human services and education.* Newbury Park, CA: Sage.

McLean, C. (1980). The lobbying process and the community service agency. In R. L. Clifton & A. M. Dahms (Eds.), *Grassroots administration: A handbook for staff and directors of small community-based social service agencies* (pp. 133–140). Pacific Grove, CA: Brooks/Cole.

McNight, J. (1995). *The careless society: Community and its counterfeits.* New York: Basic Books.

Meenaghan, T. M., & Washington, R. O. (1980). *Social policy and social welfare: Structure and applications.* New York: Free Press.

Meyer, A. E. (1945, June 5). *Washington Post.*

Meyerson, D. E. (1994, December). Interpretations of stress in institutions: The cultural production of ambiguity and burnout. *Administrative Science Quarterly, 39,* 628–653.

Mirkin, H. R. (1978). *The complete fundraising guide.* New York: Public Service Materials Center.

Mitiguy, N. (1978). *The rich get richer and the poor write proposals.* Amherst: University of Massachusetts, Citizen Involvement Training Project.

Moerschbaecher, L. S., & Dryburgh, E. D. (1997). Planned giving: Gift vehicles. In J. M. Greenfield (Ed.), *The nonprofit handbook: Fund raising* (2nd ed., pp. 475–508). New York: John Wiley & Sons.

Mondross, J. B., & Berman-Rossi, T. (1992). The relevance of stages of group development theory to community organization practice. In A. Vinik & M. Levin (Eds.), *Social action in group work* (pp. 203–221). New York: Haworth.

Montiel, M., & Ortego Y Gasca, F. (1995). Chicanos, community, and change. In F. G. Rivera & J. L. Erlich (Eds.), *Organizing in a diverse society* (2nd ed., pp. 43–60). Boston: Allyn and Bacon.

Moore, J. (1995). Fundraising by computer: The next frontier? *The Chronicle of Philanthropy, 7*(6).

Morales, A., & Sheafor, B. W. (1986). *Social work: A profession of many faces* (4th ed.). Boston, MA: Allyn & Bacon.

Morgan, G. (1997). *Images of organization* (2nd ed.). Thousand Oaks, CA: Sage.

Moroney, R. (1991). *Social policy and social work: Critical essays on the welfare state.* New York: Aldine de Gruyter.

Morrison, J. D., Howard, J., Johnson, C., Navarro, F. J., Placheta, B., & Bell, T. (1997). Strengthening neighborhoods by developing community networks. *Social Work, 42*(5), 527–534.

Morth, M., & Collins, S. (1996). *The Foundation Center's user-friendly guide: A grantseeker's guide to resources* (rev. ed.). New York: The Foundation Center.

Naparstek, A. J., & Dooley, D. (1997). Countering urban disinvestment through community-building initiatives. *Social Work, 42*(5), 506–514.

Napier, R. W., & Gershenfeld, M. K. (1989). *Groups: Theory and experience* (4th ed.). Boston, MA: Houghton Mifflin.

Napier, R. W., & Gershenfeld, M. K. (1993). *Groups: Theory and experience* (5th ed.). Boston, MA: Houghton Mifflin.

National Association of Social Workers. (1982). Standards for the classification of social work practice. Policy Statement 4. New York: Author.

National Association of Social Workers. (1997). *The National Association of Social Workers code of ethics.* As adopted by the 1979 Delegate Assembly.

National Campus Compact. (1997). *Service matters/service counts.* Providence, RI: The Project for Public and Community Service.

National Commission on Neighborhoods. (1979). *People, building neighborhoods.* Final Report to the President and the Congress of the United States. Washington, DC: U.S. Government Printing Office.

National Network of Grantmakers. (1998). *Grantmakers directory.* San Diego, CA: Author.

National Organization for Human Service Education. (1996). Ethical standards of human service professionals. *Human Service Education 16*(1), 11–17.

Nelson-Jones, R. (1992). *Group leadership: A training approach.* Pacific Grove, CA: Brooks/Cole.

Neuber, K. A., Atkins, W. T., Jacobson, J. A., & Reuterman, N. A. (1980). *Needs assessment: A model for community planning.* Newbury Park, CA: Sage.

Nonprofit Counsel. (1986, March). Planned giving: It's for all: The ten steps for beginning. *Nonprofit Counsel,* 4–9.

Nutt, P. C. (1985). The study of planning process. In W. G. Bennis, K. D. Benne, & R. C. Chin (Eds.), *The planning of change* (4th ed., p. 198). New York: Holt, Rinehart & Winston.

O'Hare, W. P. (1994, September). 3.9 million U.S. children in distressed neighborhoods. *Population Today.*

Olasky, M. (1996). *Renewing American compassion: How compassion for the needy can turn ordinary citizens into heroes.* New York: Free Press.

O'Looney, J. (1993, December). Beyond privatization and service integration: Organizational models for service delivery. *Social Service Review,* 501–534.

O. M. Collective. (1971). *The organizers manual.* New York: Bantam Books.

O'Neal, D. (1996). *Exploring the Internet.* Tucson, AZ: Total Training Solutions.

Palmer, P. (1989, September/October). Community, conflict, and ways of knowing. *Change, 20*–25.

Palmer, P. (1993). *The promise of paradox.* Notre Dame, IN: Ave Maria.

Panas, J. (1989). *Research shows eight reasons why philanthropists make major gifts.* Chicago, IL: Panas, Linzy, & Partners, Inc.

Papworth, J. (1995). *Small is powerful: The future as if people really mattered.* Westport, CN: Praeger.

Parsons, R. J. (1989). Empowerment for role alternatives for low income minority girls: A group work approach. In J. A. B. Lee (Ed.), *Group work with the poor and oppressed* (pp. 27–42). New York: Haworth.

Patti, R. J. (1974). Limitations and prospects of internal advocacy. *Social Casework, 55*(9), 537–545.

Patti, R. J. (1980). Internal advocacy and human services practitioners: An exploratory study. In H. Resnick & R. J. Patti, *Change from within: Humanizing social welfare organizations* (pp. 287–301). Philadelphia, PA: Temple University Press.

Patti, R. J., & Resnick, H. (1975). Changing the agency from within. In R. M. Kramer & H. Specht (Eds.), *Readings in community organization practice* (2nd ed., pp. 65–74). Englewood Cliffs, NJ: Prentice-Hall.

Patton, C. V. (1987). Citizen input and professional responsibility. In F. M. Cox, J. L. Erlich, J. Rothman, & J. E. Tropman (Eds.), *Strategies of community organization: Macro practice* (4th ed., pp. 343–350). Itasca, IL: F. E. Peacock.

Peck, M. (1987). *The different drum: Community making and peace.* New York: Simon & Schuster.

Pendleton, N. (1981). *Fund raising.* Englewood Cliffs, NJ: Prentice-Hall.

Perlman, J. (1979). Grassroot empowerment and government response. *Social Policy, 10*(2), 16–21.

Perlman, R., & Gurin, A. (1972). *Community organization and social planning.* New York: John Wiley & Sons.

Pertschuk, M. (1986). *Giant killers.* New York: W. W. Norton.

Petersen, S. W. (1979). *Successful fundraising.* New York: Caroline House.

Phelan, M. E. (1995). *Nonprofit enterprises: Law and taxation.* Deerfield IL: Clark Boardman Callaghan.

Phelan, M. E. (1997). *Nonprofit enterprises: Law and taxation.* [1997—2 cumulative supplement]. Deerfield, IL: Clark Boardman Callaghan.

Piccard, B. (1988). *Introduction to social work: A primer* (4th ed.). Pacific Grove, CA: Brooks/Cole.

Picker, L. A. (1997). The corporate support marketplace. In J. M. Greenfield (Ed.), *The nonprofit handbook: Fund raising* (2nd ed., pp. 372–395). New York: Wiley.

Pincus, A., & Minahan, A. (1973). *Social work practice: Model and method.* Itasca, IL: F. E. Peacock.

Pollack, D. (1997). *Social work and the courts: A casebook.* New York: Garland.

Pruitt, D. (1981). *Negotiating behavior.* New York: Academic Press.

Pumphrey, M. W. (1959). *The teaching of values and ethics in social work education.* New York: Council on Social Work Education.

Pumphrey, R. (1971). Social welfare: History. In National Association of Social Workers, *Encyclopedia of social work* (16th ed., vol. 2, pp. 1446–1461). Silver Springs, MD: National Association of Social Workers.

Putnam, R. D. (1993). The prosperous community: Social capital and economic growth. *The American Prospect, 35*–42.

Putnam, R. D. (1995, January). Bowling alone: America's declining social capital. *Journal of Democracy, 6*(1), 65–78.

Putnam, R. D. (1996). The strange disappearance of civic America. *The American Prospect, 24,* 34–49.

Randall, N. (1997, August). Saving the Internet from the Web. *PC Magazine, 16,* 303–304.

Rathbun, S. (1986, January 26). *Working with the media.* Presentation to the National Association of Social Workers, Arizona Chapter, District II.

Reeves, R. A., Macolini, R. M., & Martin, R. C. (1987). Legitimizing paltry contributions:. On-the-spot vs. mail-in requests. *Journal of Applied Social Psychology, 17*(8), 731–738.

Regan, D. T. (1971). Effects of a favor on liking and compliance. *Journal of Experimental Social Psychology, 7,* 627–639.

Reid, B. (1997, July 25). Neighbors find unity powerful. *The Arizona Republic,* Community 1–2.

Reinhart, P. C. (1990, July). Forecasting the 1990's: The art of fund raising for the next decade. *Fund Raising Management,* 42–48.

Resnick, H. (1978). Tasks in changing the organization from within (COFW). *Administration in Social Work, 2*(1), 29–44.

Resnick, H., & Menefee, D. (1994). A comparative analysis of organization development and social work, with suggestions for what organization development can do for social work. *Journal of Applied Behavioral Science, 29*(4), 432–445.

Rich, R. C. (1979, Fall). The roles of neighborhood organizations in urban service delivery. *Urban Affairs Papers, 1,* 81–93.

Richan, W. C. (1992). *Lobbying for social change.* New York: Haworth.

Richan, W. C., & Mendelsohn, A. R. (1973). *Social work: The unloved profession.* New York: New Viewpoints.

Rivera, F., & Erlich, J. (1995). *Community organizing in a diverse society* (2nd ed.). Boston, MA: Allyn & Bacon.

Roach, M. J., & O'Brien, D. J. (1982). The impact of different kinds of neighborhood involvement on residents' overall evaluations of their neighborhoods. *Sociological Focus, 15*(4), 379–391.

Robinson, A. (1996). *Grassroots grants: An activists guide to proposal writing.* Berkeley, CA: Chardon Press.

Robinson, B., & Hanna, M. G. (1994). Lessons for academics from grassroots community organizing: A case study—the industrial areas foundation. *Journal of Community Practice, 1*(4), 63–94.

Ronnby, A. (1995). *Mobilizing local communities.* Brookfield, VT: Avebury.

Ronnby, A. (1996). Local development and new cooperatives in Sweden: A grassroots approach. In Bauhaus Dessau Foundation & European Network for Economic Self-Help and Local Development (Eds.), *People's economy, wirtschaft von unten: Approaches toward a new social economy in Europe* (pp. 69–81). Dessau, Germany: Bauhaus Dessau Foundation.

Rothman, J. (1968). Three models of community organization practice. In F. Cox, J. Erlich, J. Rothman, & J. Tropman (Eds.), *Strategies of community organization: A book of readings* (pp. 3–26). Itasca, IL: F. E. Peacock.

Rothman, J., & Tropman, J. (1987). Models of community organization and macro practice perspectives: Their mixing and phasing. In F. M. Cox, J. L. Erlich, J. Rothman, & J. E. Tropman (Eds.), *Strategies of community organization: Macro practice* (4th ed., pp. 3–26). Itasca, IL: F. E. Peacock.

Rubin, H., & Rubin, I. (1986). *Community organizing and development.* Columbus, OH: Merrill.

Ruby, J. F., & O'Brien, M. A. (1978). *United Way-Tucson: Communications kit.* Tucson, AZ: United Way-Tucson.

Russo, J. R. (1993). *Serving and surviving as a human service worker.* Prospect Heights, IL: Waveland Press.

Sachs, J. (1991). Action and reflection in work with a group of homeless people. In A. Vinik & M. Levin (Eds.), *Social action in group work* (pp. 187–202). New York: Haworth.

Sagasti, F. (1990). Interview in *Against the odds* [Videotape]. Visions in video series. (Available from South Carolina Educational Television Network, Columbia, SC.)

Schaller, L. (1972). *The change agent.* Nashville, TN: Abingdon.

Scheie, D., Williams, T., Mayer, S. E., Kroll, B. S., & Dewar, T. (1997a). *Building support for neighborhood action: Lessons from the community foundations and neighborhoods program, 1991–1995.* Minneapolis: Rainbow Research.

Scheie, D., Williams, T., Mayer, S. E., Kroll, B. S., & Dewar, T. (1997b). *Helping neighborhood groups and leaders grow stronger: Lessons from the community foundations and neighborhoods program, 1991–1995.* Minneapolis: Rainbow Research.

Schelling, T. C. (1963). *The strategy of conflict.* Cambridge, MA: Harvard University Press.

Schindler-Rainman, E. (1975). Community development. In K. D. Benne, L. Bradford, J. R. Gibb, & R. Lippit (Eds.), *The laboratory method of changing and learning: Theory and application* (pp. 447–448). Palo Alto, CA: Science & Behavior Books.

Schindler-Rainman, E. (1977). Goals to action. In E. Schindler-Rainman, R. Lippitt, & J. Cole (Eds.), *Taking your meetings out of the doldrums.* La Jolla, CA: University Associates, Inc.

Schmolling, P., Jr., Youkeles, M., & Burger, W. R. (1997). *Human services in contemporary America* (4th ed.). Pacific Grove, CA: Brooks/Cole.

Schorf, J. M., Fischer, D., Pollack, K., Brophy, B., & Kulman, L. (1996, February 19). Speak up! You can be heard! *U.S. News & World Report, 120,* 42–52.

Schumacher, D. (1992). *Get funded: A practical guide for scholars seeking research support from business.* Newbury Park, CA: Sage.

Schwab, W., & Ringel, B. (1991). An evaluation of the utility of five models of neighborhood change: The case of

Cincinnati, Ohio. *Free Inquiry in Creative Sociology, 19*(2), 125–133.

Schwirian, K. P. (1983). Models of neighborhood change. *Annual Review of Sociology, 9,* 83–103.

Senge, P., Kleiner, A., Roberts, C., Ross, R., & Smith, B. (1994). *The fifth discipline fieldbook.* New York: Currency Doubleday.

Shapiro, I., & Greenstein, R. (1997). *Trends in the distribution of after-tax income: An analysis of congressional budget office data.* Washington, DC: Center for Budget and Policy Priorities.

Sharp, G. (1973a). *The politics of nonviolent action: Part one: Power and struggle.* Boston, MA: Porter Sargent.

Sharp, G. (1973b). *The politics of nonviolent action: Part two: The methods of nonviolent action.* Boston, MA: Porter Sargent.

Sharp, G. (1973c). *The politics of nonviolent action: Part three: The dynamics of nonviolent action.* Boston, MA: Porter Sargent.

Shellow, J. R., & Stella, N. C. (1989). *Grant seekers guide* (rev. ed.). Mt. Kisco, NY: Moyer Bell.

Shepard, G. (1991). Backlash in the American dream: Resurgence of racism and the rise of the underclass. In G. Shepard & D. Penna, *Racism and the underclass* (pp. 3–22). New York: Greenwood Press.

Sherif, M. (1936). *The psychology of group norms.* New York: Harper & Row.

Sherman, W. R., & Wenocur, S. (1983, September/October). Empowering the public welfare workers through mutual support. *Social Work,* 375–379.

Shulman, L. (1991). *Interactional social work practice: Toward an empirical theory.* Itasca, IL: F. E. Peacock.

Simmons, J. (1996, January 8). The soul of a new machine. *U.S. News & World Report, 120,* 34–35.

Simpson, D., & Gentile, A. (1986, Spring). Effective neighborhood government. *Social Policy,* 25–30.

Sinnock, B. (1995, August). Fundraising trends move towards more choice, fewer dollars. *The Nonprofit Times,* 27–30.

Sladek, F. E. (1981). *Getting the most of your grant dollar.* New York: Plenum Press.

Smalley, R. E. (1967). *Theory for social work practice.* New York: Columbia University Press.

Smith, D. (1979). *In our own interest: A handbook for the citizen lobbyist in state legislatures.* Seattle, WA: Madrona.

Smith, S. C. (1989). *Reflections on grantseeking.* M. J. Murdock Charitable Trust.

Smucker, R. (1997, August 28). Personal interview with Robert Smucker, Director of Government Relations, Independent Sector.

Speeter, G. (1978a). *Playing their game our way: Using the political process to meet community needs.* Amherst: University of Massachusetts, Citizen Involvement Training Project.

Speeter, G. (1978b). *Power: A repossession manual.* Amherst: University of Massachusetts, Citizen Involvement Training Project.

Splain, M. J. (1984). Negotiations: Using a weapon as a way out. In L. Staples (Ed.), *Roots to power: A manual for grassroots organizing* (pp. 166–170). New York: Praeger.

Staples, L. (1984). *Roots to power: A manual for grassroots organizing.* New York: Praeger.

Steinberg, R. (1997). Bowling together: Fund raising practices and civic engagement. In D. Burlingame (Ed.), *Critical issues in fund raising* (pp. 247–255). New York: Wiley.

Suchman, D. R. (1993). Recreating Vermont Avenue. *Urban Land, 52,* 20–24.

Suchman, D. R. (1994). Revitalizing low-income neighborhoods: Recommendations from ULI advisory series panels. Washington, DC: ULI, The Urban Land Institute.

Suchman, D. R., & Lamb, M. I. (1991). West Dallas poised for change. *Urban Land, 50,* 10–16.

Sussman, V. (1996, February 19). A new precinct: Cyberspace. *U.S. News & World Report,* 58–62.

Thomas, J. C. (1986). *Between citizen and city: Neighborhood organizations and urban politics in Cincinnati.* Lawrence: University of Kansas Press.

Thomas, R. R., Jr. (1990, March/April). From affirmative action to affirming diversity. *Harvard Business Review,* 107–117.

Thomas, S. G. (1997, March 24). Personal tech: Making a fast connection. *U.S. News & World Report, 122,* 67–68.

Three Rivers, A. (1991). *Cultural etiquette: A guide for the well intentioned.* Indian Valley, VA: Market Wimmin.

Tropman, J. E., Johnson, H. R., & Tropman, E. J. (1979). *The essentials of committee management.* Chicago, IL: Nelson-Hall.

Troyer, T. A. (1991, May 18). *What the non-specialist needs to know about the new lobbying rules for charities.* Paper presented to the American Bar Association Tax Section. Washington, DC: Independent Sector.

Tuckman, B. W., & Jensen, M. A. C. (1977). Stages of small group development revisited. *Group and Organizational Studies, 2*(4), 419–427.

Tuller, M. N., & Cantarella, G. M. (1997). *The Foundation Center Directory.* New York: The Foundation Center.

Turner, J. B. (1995). Group work and ethnic diversity. In M. D. Feit, J. H. Ramey, J. S. Wodarski, & A. R. Mann (Eds.), *Capturing the power of diversity* (pp. 7–17). New York: Haworth.

Ulin, S. B. (1997). Benefit event enhancements. In J. M. Greenfield (Ed.), *The nonprofit handbook: Fund raising* (2nd ed., pp. 299–316). New York: John Wiley & Sons.

Von Hoffman, N. (n.d.). Finding and making leaders.

Wagner, A. R. (1995, February 25). *Hope for the American neighborhood: Creating a fourth sector—the community sector.* Paper presented for the Nobel Prize Forum at Augsburg College, Minneapolis, MN.

Walker, A. (1987, Spring). The good that they do. The case for corporate in-kind contributions. *Public Relations Quarterly,* 222–223.

Warheit, G. J., Bell, R. A., & Schwab, J. J. (1984). Selecting the needs assessment approach. In F. Cox, J. L. Erlich, J. Rothman, & J. E. Tropman (Eds.), *Tactics and techniques of community practice* (2nd ed., pp. 41–55). Itasca, IL: F. E. Peacock.

Warren, R. B., & Warren, D. I. (1977). *The neighborhood organizer's handbook.* Notre Dame: University of Notre Dame Press.

Warren, R. B., & Warren, D. I. (1984). How to diagnose a neighborhood. In F. Cox, J. L. Erlich, J. Rothman, & J. E. Tropman (Eds.), *Tactics and techniques of community practice* (2nd ed., pp. 27–40). Itasca, IL: F. E. Peacock.

Warren, R. L. (1975). Types of purposive social change at the community level. In R. M. Kramer & H. Specht (Eds.), *Readings in community organization practice* (2nd ed., pp. 134–149). Englewood Cliffs, NJ: Prentice-Hall.

Wartenberg, T. E. (1990). *The forms of power: From domination to transformation.* Philadelphia, PA: Temple University Press.

Warwick, M. (1994). *Technology and the future of fundraising.* Berkeley, CA: Strathmoor Press.

Webb, C. (1982, May). Communications in fundraising. *Fund Raising Management, 13,* 60.

Weinbach, R. W. (1984, May/June). Implementing change: Insights and strategies for the supervisor. *Social Work,* 282–285.

Weinbach, R. W. (1990). *The social worker as manager: Theory and practice.* New York: Longman.

Wenocur, S. (1992). Should community organization be based on a grassroots strategy? Yes. In E. Gambrill & R. Pruger (Eds.), *Controversial issues in social work* (pp. 289–293). Boston, MA: Allyn & Bacon.

Wernet, S. P. (1994). A case study of adaptation in a nonprofit human service organization. *Journal of Community Practice, 1*(3), 93–111.

Whitehead, P., & Maran, R. (1997). *Internet and World Wide Web simplified* (2nd ed.). Foster City CA: IDG Books Worldwide.

Wichner, D. (1998, March 2). Cable modems give users high-speed Internet access. *Arizona Daily Star,* ST9–12.

Wiener, L. (1996, April 29). ISDN may be the answer to a fast modem that's too slow. *U.S. News & World Report, 120,* 72.

Wilensky, H., & Lebeaux, C. (1965). *Industrial society and social welfare.* New York: Free Press.

Williams, M. R. (1985). *Neighborhood organizations: Seeds of a new life.* Westport, CN: Greenwood Press.

Williams, M. R. (1989). *Neighborhood organizing for urban school reform.* New York: Teachers College Press.

Wilson, M. (1980). Effective volunteer programs. In R. Clifton & A. Dahms (Eds.), *Grassroots administration: A handbook for staff and directors of small community-based social service agencies* (pp. 111–122). Pacific Grove, CA: Brooks/Cole.

Wireman, P. (1984). *Urban neighborhoods, networks, and families: New forms for old values.* Lexington, MA: Lexington Books.

Wolpert, J., Mumphrey, A. J., & Seley, J. E. (1972). *Metropolitan neighborhoods: Participation and conflict over change.* Resource Paper No. 16, Association of American Geographers.

Wrong, D. (1995). *Power: Its forms, bases and uses.* New Brunswick, NJ: Transaction Publishers.

Zack, G. M. (1997). *Tax issues of not-for-profit organizations.* Greenbelt, MD: Nonprofit Resource Center.

Zastrow, C. (1995). *The practice of social work* (5th ed.). Pacific Grove, CA: Brooks/Cole.

Zastrow, C. (1997). *Social work with groups* (4th ed.). Chicago, IL: Nelson-Hall.

Zippay, A. (1992, May). Corporate funding of human service agencies. *Social Work, 37,* 210–214.

Zoom, a quick trip around the world of technology. (1997, August 11). *The Arizona Daily Star,* D2.

Zunz, S. J. (1997). School climate and community norm change. In E. Norman (Ed.), *Drug free youth: A compendium for prevention specialists* (pp. 47–72). New York: Garland.

Credits

This page constitutes an extension of the copyright page. We have made every effort to trace the ownership of all copyrighted material and to secure permission from copyright holders. In the event of any question arising as to the use of any material, we will be pleased to make the necessary corrections in future printings. Thanks are due to the following authors, publishers, and agents for permission to use the material indicated.

Chapter 1: 19: Excerpts from *Cultural Etiquette: A Guide for the Well-Intentioned,* by Amoja Three Rivers. Copyright © 1990 Amoja Three Rivers. Copies are available for $7 from Market Wimmin, Auto Road, Auto, WV 24917. Reprinted by permission.

Chapter 3: 49: Figure 3-1 from *The Technology of Development: A Framework for Transforming Community Cultures,* by W. A. Lofquist, p. 6. Copyright © 1996 Development Publications. Reprinted by permission of the author.

Chapter 9: 191: Figure reprinted by permission of *Harvard Business Review.* An exhibit from "What you need to know about fund raising," by F. Howe, March-April 1985, p. 24. Copyright © 1985 by the President and Fellows of Harvard College; all rights reserved.

Chapter 10: 246: Table from The Grantsmanship Center Training Programs. Copyright © The Grantsmanship Center, 1125 West Sixth Street, Fifth Floor, P. O. Box 17220, Los Angeles, CA 90017. Reprinted by permission.

Chapter 12: 298: Excerpts from *Joining Together: Group Theory and Group Skills,* Sixth Edition, by D. W. Johnson and F. P. Johnson, p. 195. Copyright © 1997 Allyn & Bacon, Inc. Reprinted by permission. **299:** Table 12-1 from *Joining Together: Group Theory and Group Skills,* Sixth Edition, by D. W. Johnson and F. P. Johnson, p. 35. Copyright © 1997 Allyn & Bacon, Inc. Reprinted by permission.

Chapter 13: 338-339: Excerpts from *Getting to Yes: Negotiating Agreement Without Giving In,* Second Edition, by Roger Fisher, William Ury, and edited by Bruce Patton. Copyright © 1981, 1991 by Roger Fisher and William Ury. Reprinted by permission of Houghton Mifflin Co. All rights reserved.

Chapter 14: 362: Table 14-1 from *Neighborhoods: Their Place in Urban Life,* by H. W. Hallman. Copyright © 1984 Sage Publications. Reprinted by permission.

Index

TO THE OWNER OF THIS BOOK:

I hope that you have found *Promoting Community Change: Making It Happen in the Real World*, Second Edition, useful. So that this book can be improved in a future edition, would you take the time to complete this sheet and return it? Thank you.

School: _____

Your instructor's name: _____

1. In what class did you use this book?_____

2. What did you like *most* about *Promoting Community Change*, Second Edition?

_____

_____

3. What did you like *least* about the book? _____

_____

_____

4. How useful were the "Take a Moment to Discover," "Capturing Concepts," and "Change Agent Tip" boxes? Did you use any of them in class?

_____

_____

5. In the space below, or on a separate sheet of paper, please write specific suggestions for improving this book and anything else you'd care to share about your experience in using the book.

_____

_____

_____

_____

_____

_____

_____

_____

Optional:

Your name: _____ Date: _____

May Brooks/Cole quote you, either in promotion for *Promoting Community Change: Making It Happen in the Real World*, Second Edition or in future publishing ventures?

Yes: _____ No: _____

Sincerely,

Mark Homan

FOLD HERE

BUSINESS REPLY MAIL

FIRST CLASS   PERMIT NO. 358   PACIFIC GROVE, CA

POSTAGE WILL BE PAID BY ADDRESSEE

ATT: *Mark Homan* _____

Brooks/Cole Publishing Company
511 Forest Lodge Road
Pacific Grove, California 93950-9968

FOLD HERE

IN-BOOK SURVEY

At Brooks/Cole, we are excited about creating new types of learning materials that are interactive, three-dimensional, and fun to use. To guide us in our publishing/development process, we hope that you'll take just a few moments to fill out the survey below. Your answers can help us make decisions that will allow us to produce a wide variety of videos, CD-ROMs, and Internet-based learning systems to complement standard textbooks. If you're interested in working with us as a student Beta-tester, be sure to fill in your name, telephone number, and address. We look forward to hearing from you!

In addition to books, which of the following learning tools do you currently use in your counseling/human services/social work courses?

_____ **Video** _____ in class _____ school library _____ own VCR

_____ **CD-ROM** _____ in class _____ in lab _____ own computer

_____ **Macintosh disks** _____ in class _____ in lab _____ own computer

_____ **Windows disks** _____ in class _____ in lab _____ own computer

_____ **Internet** _____ in class _____ in lab _____ own computer

How often do you access the Internet? _____

My own home computer is:

_____ Macintosh _____ DOS _____ Windows _____ Windows 95

The computer I use in class for counseling/human services/social work courses is:

_____ Macintosh _____ DOS _____ Windows _____ Windows 95

If you are NOT currently using multimedia materials in your counseling/human services/social work courses, but can see ways that video, CD-ROM, Internet, or other technologies could enhance your learning, please comment below:

_____

_____

_____

Other comments (optional): _____

_____

Name _____ Telephone _____

Address _____

School _____

Professor/Course_____

You can fax this form to us at (408) 375-6414; e:mail to: info@brookscole.com; or detach, fold, secure, and mail.

FOLD HERE

NO POSTAGE
NECESSARY
IF MAILED
IN THE
UNITED STATES

BUSINESS REPLY MAIL
FIRST CLASS   PERMIT NO. 358   PACIFIC GROVE, CA

POSTAGE WILL BE PAID BY ADDRESSEE

ATT: <u>MARKETING</u>

Brooks/Cole Publishing Company
511 Forest Lodge Road
Pacific Grove, California 93950-5098

FOLD HERE